Truth Tree Criteria for Semantic Properties in Propositional Logic

(1) A truth tree *branch* is *closed* if and only if there is an inconsistent fully reduced propositional symbol and its negation of the form $\mathbb{P}$ and ~$\mathbb{P}$ somewhere on it. This is indicated by terminating the branch with an 'X' as soon as the inconsistency appears.

(2) A *truth tree* is *closed* if and only if all its branches are closed.

(3) A wff $\mathbb{P}$ is a *tautology* if and only if ~$\mathbb{P}$ has a closed tree; a wff $\mathbb{P}$ is a *logical inconsistency* if and only if $\mathbb{P}$ itself has a closed tree; a wff $\mathbb{P}$ is a *contingency* if and only if $\mathbb{P}$ is neither a tautology nor an inconsistency (neither the truth tree for $\mathbb{P}$ nor the truth tree for ~$\mathbb{P}$ closes).

(4) A stack of wffs $\mathbb{P}, \mathbb{Q}, \ldots, \mathbb{Z}$ is *logically consistent* if and only if it has an *open tree* (a tree with at least one open branch); the stack is *logically inconsistent* if and only if it has a closed tree.

(5) Wffs $\mathbb{P}$ and $\mathbb{Q}$ are *logically equivalent* if and only if $\mathbb{P} \equiv \mathbb{Q}$ is a tautology (if and only if ~$(\mathbb{P} \equiv \mathbb{Q})$ has a closed tree).

(6) A sequent $\mathbb{P}, \mathbb{Q}, \ldots, \mathbb{Y} \vdash \mathbb{Z}$ is *deductively valid* if and only if the stack $\mathbb{P}, \mathbb{Q}, \ldots, \mathbb{Y}, \sim\mathbb{Z}$ has a closed tree.

Truth Tree Sequent Evaluation Stack

$\mathbb{P}_1$

.

.

.

$\mathbb{P}_m$

~$(\mathbb{Q}_1 \& \ldots \& \mathbb{Q}_n)$

(for sequent $\mathbb{P}_1, \ldots, \mathbb{P}_m \vdash \mathbb{Q}_1, \ldots, \mathbb{Q}_n$ assumptions stacked with negation of conclusion or conjunction of multiple conclusions)

Natural Deduction Rules for Symbolic Propositional Logic

1. *Assumption* (A)

   Any proposition can be introduced at any step in any proof as a given assumption or an auxiliary assumption to begin a subproof. (Foundational rule)

   $\mathbb{P}$ A

2. *Conjunction Introduction* (&I)

   From $\mathbb{P}$ and $\mathbb{Q}$ we can validly deduce $\mathbb{P}$ & $\mathbb{Q}$.
   (Intelim rule)

3. *Conjunction Elimination* (&E)

   From $\mathbb{P}$ & $\mathbb{Q}$ we can validly deduce $\mathbb{P}$ (and/or $\mathbb{Q}$).
   (Intelim rule)

$\mathbb{P}$ & $\mathbb{Q}$		$\mathbb{P}$ & $\mathbb{Q}$	
.		.	
.		.	
.		.	
$\mathbb{P}$	. . . &E	$\mathbb{Q}$	. . . &E

4. *Disjunction Introduction* (∨I)

   From $\mathbb{P}$ (or $\mathbb{Q}$) we can validly deduce $\mathbb{P} \vee \mathbb{Q}$.
   (Intelim rule)

$\mathbb{P}$		$\mathbb{P}$	
.		.	
.		.	
.		.	
$\mathbb{P} \vee \mathbb{Q}$	. . . ∨I	$\mathbb{Q} \vee \mathbb{P}$	. . . ∨I

5. *Disjunction Elimination* (∨E)

   From $\mathbb{P} \vee \mathbb{Q}$, and a proof of R from (auxiliary) assumption $\mathbb{P}$ and a proof of $\mathbb{R}$ from (auxiliary) assumption $\mathbb{Q}$, we can validly deduce $\mathbb{R}$. (The auxiliary assumption numbers for auxiliary assumptions $\mathbb{P}$ and $\mathbb{Q}$ are discharged from the assumption column when the rule is invoked.)
   (Intelim subproof rule)

   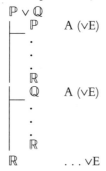

6. *Conditional Introduction* (⊃I)

From a proof of ℚ from (auxiliary) assumption ℙ, we can validly deduce the conditional ℙ ⊃ ℚ. (The auxiliary assumption number for auxiliary assumption ℙ is discharged from the assumption column when the rule is invoked.)
(Intelim subproof rule)

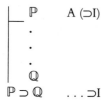

7. *Conditional Elimination* (⊃E)

From ℙ and ℙ ⊃ ℚ we can validly deduce ℚ.
(Intelim rule)

$$
\begin{array}{l}
\mathbb{P} \supset \mathbb{Q} \\
\;\cdot \\
\;\cdot \\
\;\cdot \\
\mathbb{P} \\
\;\cdot \\
\;\cdot \\
\;\cdot \\
\mathbb{Q} \qquad \ldots \supset E
\end{array}
$$

8. *Negation Introduction / Elimination (reductio ad absurdum)* (~IE)

From a proof of the contradiction ℚ, ~ℚ from (auxiliary) assumption ℙ (~ℙ), we can validly deduce ~ℙ (ℙ). (The auxiliary assumption number for auxiliary assumption ℙ (~ℙ) is discharged from the assumption column when the rule is invoked.)
(Intelim subproof rule)

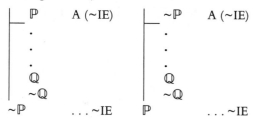

9. *Biconditional Introduction* ($\equiv$I)

From a proof of $\mathbb{Q}$ from (auxiliary) assumption $\mathbb{P}$, and of $\mathbb{P}$ from (auxiliary) assumption $\mathbb{Q}$, we can validly deduce $\mathbb{P} \equiv \mathbb{Q}$. (The auxiliary assumption numbers for auxiliary assumptions $\mathbb{P}$ and $\mathbb{Q}$ are discharged from the assumption column when the rule is invoked.)
(Intelim subproof rule)

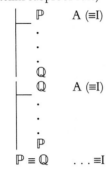

$$\mathbb{P} \equiv \mathbb{Q} \qquad \ldots \equiv\mathrm{I}$$

10. *Biconditional Elimination* ($\equiv$E)

From P ($\mathbb{Q}$) and $\mathbb{P} \equiv \mathbb{Q}$ we can validly deduce $\mathbb{Q}$ ($\mathbb{P}$).
(Intelim rule)

$$\mathbb{P} \equiv \mathbb{Q} \qquad\qquad\qquad \mathbb{P} \equiv \mathbb{Q}$$
$$\cdot \qquad\qquad\qquad\qquad \cdot$$
$$\cdot \qquad\qquad\qquad\qquad \cdot$$
$$\cdot \qquad\qquad\qquad\qquad \cdot$$
$$\mathbb{P} \qquad\qquad\qquad\qquad \mathbb{Q}$$
$$\cdot \qquad\qquad\qquad\qquad \cdot$$
$$\cdot \qquad\qquad\qquad\qquad \cdot$$
$$\cdot \qquad\qquad\qquad\qquad \cdot$$
$$\mathbb{Q} \qquad \ldots \equiv\mathrm{E} \qquad \mathbb{P} \qquad \ldots \equiv\mathrm{E}$$

11. *Reiteration* (R)

Any proposition occurring in a proof or subproof can be repeated in that proof or any more deeply nested subproof it contains (but cannot be repeated in less deeply nested subproofs nor in the main proof).
(Derived rule)

$$\mathbb{P}$$
$$\cdot$$
$$\cdot$$
$$\cdot$$
$$\mathbb{P} \qquad \ldots \mathrm{R}$$

12. *Double Negation* (DN)

From any proposition $\mathbb{P}$ we can validly deduce $\sim\sim\mathbb{P}$, and conversely.
(Derived rule)

$$\sim\sim\mathbb{P}$$
$$\cdot$$
$$\cdot$$
$$\cdot$$
$$\mathbb{P} \qquad \ldots \mathrm{DN}$$
$$\cdot$$
$$\cdot$$
$$\cdot$$
$$\sim\sim\mathbb{P} \qquad \ldots \mathrm{DN}$$

Predicate Logic

Basic Predicate and Quantifier Symbols

Everything is F	$(\forall x)Fx$
Something is F	$(\exists x)Fx$
All F's are G's	$(\forall x)Fx \supset Gx)$
Some F's are G's	$(\exists x)(Fx \,\&\, Gx)$

Quantifier Duality

$(\exists x)\mathbb{P}/x \equiv \sim(\forall x)\sim\mathbb{P}/x$

$(\forall x)\mathbb{P}/x \equiv \sim(\exists x)\sim\mathbb{P}/x$

Predicate Truth Tree Decomposition Rules

$\sim(\forall x)\mathbb{P}/x$ ✓	$\sim(\exists x)\mathbb{P}/x$ ✓	$(\forall x)\mathbb{P}/x$ * α	$(\exists x)\mathbb{P}/x$ ✓
$(\exists x)\sim\mathbb{P}/x$	$(\forall x)\sim\mathbb{P}/x$	$\mathbb{P}/\alpha$	$\mathbb{P}/\alpha$
		unrestricted	*restricted*

in choice and number of substitutions
of object constants for bound
object variables

Natural Deduction Rules for Predicate Logic

1. *Universal Introduction* — $\forall$I

       .
       .
       .

     n. $\ldots \alpha \ldots$ $\ldots$

           $(\forall x)(\ldots x \ldots)$ $\ldots \forall$I

(Restriction: the assumptions on which line n depends must not contain constant α; for uniform substitution of universally quantified variables for object constants)

We can validly infer a universally quantified wff in which all occurrences of a constant in a predicate-constant wff are uniformly replaced by any universal quantifier bound variable, provided that the predicate-constant wff does not rest on any assumptions containing the constant.

(One restriction)

2. *Universal Elimination* — ∀E

.
.
.

$(\forall x)(\ldots x \ldots)$ . . .
$\ldots \alpha \ldots$ . . . ∀E

(unlimited uniform instantiations)

We can validly infer a predicate-constant wff in which all universal quantifier bound variables in a universally quantified wff are uniformly replaced by any constant.

(No restrictions)

3. *Existential Introduction* — ∃I

.
.
.

$\ldots \alpha \ldots$ . . .
$(\exists x)(\ldots x \ldots)$ . . . ∃I

(unlimited selective substitution of existentially bound object variables for object constants)

We can validly infer an existentially quantified wff in which the occurrences of a constant in a predicate-constant wff are selectively replaced by any existentially bound variable.

(No restrictions)

4. *Existential Elimination* — ∃E

.
.
.

$(\exists x)(\ldots x \ldots)$ . . .
│ $\ldots \alpha \ldots$ A (∃E)
│ .
│ .
│ .
│ ℙ   . . .
ℙ   . . . ∃E

(Restriction 1: where constant (α) does not appear in any active proof or subproof step prior to its arbitrary introduction by auxiliary assumption in the ∃E subproof; restriction 2: nor in conclusion ℙ; for selective substitutions of arbitrary object constants to replace existentially bound object variables)

We can validly infer any conclusion wff by making as an auxiliary assumption a predicate-constant wff in which the existentially bound variable is uniformly replaced by an arbitrarily chosen constant that does not occur previously in any active part of the proof, provided that the conclusion wff does not itself contain the constant. When the rule is applied, the auxiliary assumption number is discharged from the assumption column, and the conclusion wff is brought out of the existential elimination subproof into the next less deeply nested proof or subproof.

(Subproof rule; two restrictions)

www.wadsworth.com

wadsworth.com is the World Wide Web site for Wadsworth Publishing Company and is your direct source to dozens of online resources.

At *wadsworth.com* you can find out about supplements, demonstration software, and student resources. You can also send e-mail to many of our authors and preview new publications and exciting new technologies.

wadsworth.com
Changing the way the world learns®

Symbolic Logic

Dale Jacquette

Wadsworth Publishing Company
I(T)P™ An International Thomson Publishing Company

Australia • Canada • Mexico • Singapore • Spain
United Kingdom • United States

Philosophy Editor: Peter Adams
Assistant Editor: Kerri Abdinoor
Editorial Assistant: Mark Andrews
Marketing Manager: Dave Garrison
Print Buyer: Mary Noel
Permissions Editor: Joohee Lee

Production Service: Matrix Productions
Text Designer: Karen Thomas
Copy Editor: Dan Hayes
Cover Designer: Scott K. Templeton
Compositor: G & S Typesetters
Text and Cover Printer: R.R. Donnelley, Crawfordsville

For permission to use material from this text, contact us by
web: http://www.thomsonrights.com
fax: 1-800-730-2215
phone: 1-800-730-2214

Library of Congress Cataloging-in-Publication Data

Jacquette, Dale.
  Symbolic logic / Dale Jacquette.
     p. cm.
  Includes bibliographical references and index.
  ISBN 0-534-53730-8
     1. Logic, Symbolic and mathematical.   I. Title.

BC135.J25 2000
160—dc21   00-028323

For information about our products, contact us:

Thomson Learning Academic Resource Center
1-800-423-0563

Wadsworth / Thomson Learning
10 Davis Drive
Belmont, CA 94002-3098
USA

http://www.wadsworth.com

International Headquarters
Thomson Learning
International Division
290 Harbor Drive, 2nd Floor
Stamford, CT 06902-7477
USA

UK / Europe / Middle East / South Africa
Thomson Learning
Berkshire House
168–173 High Holborn
London WC1V 7AA
United Kingdom

Asia
Thomson Learning
60 Albert Street, #15–01
Albert Complex
Singapore 189969

Canada
Nelson Thomson Learning
1120 Birchmount Road
Toronto, Ontario M1K 5G4
Canada

For my students and my teachers

Logic takes care of itself; all we have to do is to look and see how it does it.

— Ludwig Wittgenstein, *Notebooks 1914–1916* (13.10.14)

Table of Contents

Preface

In learning logic, we sharpen our reasoning skills and explore a formal theory of logical truth and deductively valid inference. The study of symbolic logic is fascinating in its own right, and has unlimitedly many practical applications in understanding the logic of science and everyday thought and language.

This book provides a comprehensive introduction to the central topics of elementary symbolic logic. My purpose is to provide a rigorous streamlined treatment of logical techniques with detailed explanations and a large selection of progressively challenging exercises. This new approach to symbolic logic includes the following innovations:

- All logical concepts are precisely defined and carefully explained in ordinary language with easily understood illustrations.
- The text concentrates on essential topics for students in a first course in elementary symbolic logic. The book omits formal demonstrations of the consistency and completeness and other metatheoretical properties of the logic that cannot usually be covered in a single introductory course while providing a detailed informal explanation of the logic's metatheory.
- Thirty classroom-tested Demonstration Problems break down typical sample exercises into general step-by-step instructions that provide templates for the same kinds of problems students are asked to solve. The Demonstration Problems cover every technical skill students are expected to learn in mastering elementary symbolic logic.

- Many different kinds of exercises at successive levels of difficulty are presented at strategic points within and at the end of each chapter to reinforce understanding of logical methods.

A good symbolic logic text is like a good book of piano lessons. There is no adequate substitute for hands-on practice and experienced guidance in learning to play the piano. And there is similarly no substitute for struggling with and seeing logical problems solved on a chalkboard or projector screen by a talented and enthusiastic instructor. But even piano teachers appreciate a well-designed book of lessons, and it is just as worthwhile for logic students to work with clear explanations of logical methods and an interesting set of problems.

I teach logic by beginning informally with nonsymbolic concepts. I proceed with increasing rigor, developing formal logical symbolisms and decision and proof techniques only when the principles of logic are thoroughly understood. Without a solid grounding in the purpose and theory of logic, students can at best learn to copy patterns of syntax transformation that have no more meaning for them than ancient hieroglyphics. My goal is to leave no attentive student feeling lost or left behind at any turning point. I have accordingly devoted more time than most logic texts to explaining the fundamental ideas of symbolic logic. For the same reason, I have omitted formal proofs of consistency and completeness and other metatheoretical properties of logical systems that are often found in introductory presentations of symbolic logic. I believe that a first course in logic should concentrate on careful explanations of basic concepts, with lavish applications of symbolization techniques, decision methods, and strategies for solving natural deduction proofs. There is little enough time in beginning logic courses for students to conquer these important skills, let alone to grasp complicated metatheoretical demonstrations with the depth and rigor they deserve. The study of logical metatheory in my view is best postponed until a first advanced course and is then most profitably approached from the standpoint of an axiomatic rather than natural deduction proof system. To clarify the limitations of formal decision and proof methods in predicate logic, I explain intuitively without trying to prove the most important concepts and conclusions of logical metatheory.

All the exercises were solved by an undergraduate who assisted me in preparing the instructor's manual and student solutions manual. Students and instructors can therefore be assured that, even though some problems are more difficult than others, all are solvable by persistent beginners with no previous background in symbolic logic. Problems appear from a wide variety of fields, including science, history, religion, art and literature, current events, ordinary reasoning, political theory, and the law, with special emphasis throughout on philosophical sources. There are more exercises than can realistically be worked in any single course. Some problems appear at strategic points within the ongoing commentary as questions "To check your understanding." They help to reinforce basic ideas before proceding to more sophisticated topics. Others are collected as "Exercises" at the end of each chapter to provide a comprehensive review of its contents. By consulting the Demonstration Problems located throughout the text, and listed near the end of the book for handy reference, students have access to relevant models for step-by-step help in solving similar exercises.

A final addendum on advanced topics in symbolic logic offers a preview of the possibilities for continued work in logic, including metatheory, foundations of mathematics, computers, artificial intelligence and machine theory, modal logic, nonstandard logics, philosophical applications, and the history of logic. The glossary-index, in addition to page references, provides brief definitions of all major concepts discussed in the book. The supplements available for this textbook include a student solutions manual with answers to all odd-numbered exercises, an instructor's manual that provides a complete guide to classroom use, and interactive logic lessons for all the exercises on CD-ROM, developed by Nelson Pole. Students using the software can call up text and Demonstration Problems and solve any of the exercises directly on computer. Without giving answers away, the program checks to see whether translations, truth tables, truth trees, and natural deduction proofs are being solved correctly or involve violations of specific rules. The text, solutions manuals, and computer software combine to offer one of the most useful instructional packages currently available for introducing students to the methods of elementary symbolic logic.

I am grateful to my editor, Peter Adams, and his assistant, Kerri Abdinoor, at Wadsworth, for piloting this project to completion and to Clark G. Baxter for getting me airborne. I thank the scores of students in my logic courses at The Pennsylvania State University, who have contributed in many ways to my presentation of formal logical techniques. Andrew R. Martinez was an honors student in one such course who later assisted me in preparing the instructor's and student solutions manuals by solving every exercise in the book, making valuable suggestions for improvement throughout. Nelson Pole, of Cleveland State University, did a superb job of adapting his already successful LogicCoach III instructional software to the needs of my formal system and logical pedagogy. I am indebted to numerous readers whose comments on early drafts helped me to tailor my subject and format to a variety of different classroom needs and teaching styles, including: Joseph Campbell, Washington State University; Sandy Goldberg, University of Kentucky; John Humphrey, Minnesota State University, Mankato; Andrew Mills, Otterbein College; Piers Rawling, University of Missouri, St. Louis; David Shier, Washington State University; Sun-Joo Shin, University of Notre Dame; and Catherine Womack. To the patience and moral support of my wife, Tina, as always, I dedicate the book.

Introduction

What Is Logic?

Logic is the collective name for the principles of correct reasoning. The study of logic investigates these principles and identifies the general rules that distinguish good from bad reasoning.

Logic as a discipline is not a theory that tries to discover how we think in the sense of explaining the causal mechanisms of thought or brain activity—that would be a subject for psychology and cognitive science. Psychology is a *descriptive* empirical study that offers cause-and-effect explanations of how thinking occurs without judging its rightness or wrongness. Logic, in contrast, is a *prescriptive* abstract study like mathematics that seeks to establish rules for correct reasoning and to help thinkers avoid mistaken reasoning.

The purpose of logic is to discover and justify principles that offer the best account of reasoning as it *should ideally* occur. By analogy, mathematics is not the study of how people happen to work with numbers, since in fact we sometimes make mistakes even in simple arithmetic. We would not want to include among the rules of arithmetic whatever we actually do with numbers, because then we would also have to include miscalculations as part of the theory. Mathematics tells us instead how we should work with numbers and the guidelines we should follow if we want to do so correctly. The same is true of logic, although as a more general theory of reasoning.

In beginning geography classes, students are sometimes asked to keep track of all the *maps* they encounter in a single day. It is revealing to discover how many different kinds of maps we use in organizing, recording, and retrieving spatial information. It is similarly useful in understanding the role of logic in our lives to take notice of how frequently we are confronted by *arguments* in reading and discussion, in advertisements, and on the news. How often in an average day are we challenged by the reasoning of others? How often must we criticize arguments and advance reasons of our own in decision making and in explaining and defending our beliefs and choices?

Symbolic logic develops a formal language of abstract symbols to represent logical relations. It is often possible to analyze the same arguments by both informal and symbolic techniques, just as it is possible to do algebra in ordinary English. But symbolic logic as a mathematical notation has distinct advantages over informal logical analysis. Symbolic logic is more precise, more universal, and more extensive in scope. By adopting an exact formal notation, rather like mathematics, symbolic logic is also more effective and efficient in exhibiting logical structures and testing them for logical properties, with fewer opportunities for making mistakes than informal evaluations of reasoning in everyday language.

Why Study Logic?

We already know how to think. We cannot avoid reasoning until we have studied logic, any more than we can stay out of the water until we have learned to swim. We must use our natural reasoning abilities in order to master logic, just as we must first enter the water if we are ever going to learn how to swim. Yet in both cases, good instruction can help us to refine native talents so that we can perform more capably. We study symbolic logic to improve our ability to use certain kinds of reasoning skills. We learn symbolic logic in order to gain special tools by which we can think more logically, according to criteria that have proved useful in expressing and extending our knowledge.

The purpose of this book is to enhance your logical thinking. The lessons it contains are intended to help you to recognize, construct, and critically evaluate your own and others' arguments by means of a formal symbolism. We begin by explaining the concepts of *propositions* and *deductive arguments* and then introduce a symbolic *propositional* and *predicate* system of logic with precise techniques for determining the logical properties of propositions, distinguishing deductively valid from deductively invalid reasoning, and demonstrating logically true propositions and deductively valid arguments.

Logic does not teach us scientific, historical, or religious truths. Rather, logic teaches us logical truths, and it enables us to express our beliefs in logically correct arguments, to avoid many kinds of errors in reasoning, and to increase our knowledge by drawing logically correct inferences. Logic takes its ideal from the structures of good reasoning in every theoretical discipline. However, logic in its generality is not concerned with the specialized content of any particular subject matter. Symbolic logic provides methods for putting thoughts in good logical order and for deriving whatever can be correctly concluded from them. Logic is useful in critically evaluating arguments, avoiding faulty conclusions when they are proposed for our consideration, clarifying our ideas and organizing our thinking, and improving our reading and writing. The importance of having powerful instruments of logical analysis for purposes of systematizing and extending knowledge in the deduction and communication of truths, with all the practical applications these skills make possible, should be obvious. We study symbolic logic because it is an interesting theory of the deductive structures of thought, and because it can help to make us better, more effective thinkers.

Logic has a central role in the humanities and sciences. It features prominently in philosophy, history, law, art and aesthetics, comparative literature and literary criticism, and in mathematics, computer science, and all branches of scientific inquiry as well as in commonsense thinking about the problems of everyday life. We study logic in order to provide ourselves with reliable methods for recognizing logically correct and avoiding logically fallacious reasoning. Studying logic helps us to improve our reading and listening skills by acquainting us with the formal structures of arguments, alerting us to be on the lookout for essential concepts, definitions, propositions, and inferences. These are valuable techniques for every branch of learning. We can better remember the content of information sources as a result of studying logic because logic teaches us to listen and read with a more definite purpose. We are less likely to be taken in by faulty reasoning, and we can apply our logical skills to critically evaluate a wide range of sources from which we can derive useful information by sorting out what is logically correct from what is logically incorrect. We can check and improve our reasoning in drawing the conclusions we wish to support and in structuring our arguments to speak and write more exactly or, in a word, more logically. Symbolic logic as the most abstract development of logical principles has direct applications for all our reasoning, including abstruse questions of theory and policy and the most burning social issues of the day, such as deciding whether to go to the movies or a basketball game.

For these reasons, logic has been an integral part of education since ancient times, beginning with the Greek philosophers. The medieval tradition continued this practice, dividing curricula into the seven liberal arts. These were organized into two main subcategories, the *trivium* (consisting of three basic studies) and the *quadrivium* (consisting of four somewhat more advanced disciplines). The trivium taught logic, rhetoric, and grammar, and the quadrivium taught arithmetic, geometry, astronomy, and music. This is the origin of the commonplace that logical truths are *trivial,* meaning that they were originally part of the trivium or most elementary parts of higher learning. Logic, in one sense, is indeed trivial. We know nothing whatsoever about the weather when we know only the logical truth that either it is raining or it is not raining. Yet, in another and more important sense, logic is anything but trivial. Logic structures all our reasoning. Our thinking can be correct or incorrect, effective or ineffective, and knowledge expanding or stultifying, depending on whether or not we reason logically, whether or not we can offer logically correct formulations of ideas and logically correct inferences, and whether or not we are sufficiently skilled to avoid faulty reasoning. It is partly with these goals in mind that we now join the time-honored practice of perfecting our thinking by studying the principles of logic. We shall see as we proceed that symbolic logic is also interesting for its own sake. The forms of logic are beautiful to contemplate; in their abstract purity, universality, and variety, they are much like the mathematical forms we find repeated in nature, like the spiral in a seashell, or the hexagon in a snowflake or honeycomb. Also, logic can be challenging, exciting, and great intellectual fun.

How Shall We Study Logic?

We study logic by comparing definitions and illustrations of correct reasoning with recognizable types of logical errors. We acquire both types of knowledge in an interplay of exposition and criticism. We learn from our study of logically correct and logically incorrect reasoning how we ought and how we ought not to argue.

To learn logic means to understand its concepts and put pencil to paper to solve logical problems. We must practice the skills we are trying to acquire by working through the Demonstration Problems and exercises within and at the end of each chapter. As you study the lessons in the book and meet each new challenge, you will discover increasing confidence in your understanding of logic and an improvement in your reasoning abilities.

The book is divided into three parts. Part One, *Concepts of Logic,* defines propositions and deductive arguments. Part Two, *Propositional Logic,* introduces a formal symbolism and graphic techniques to symbolize and critically evaluate propositions and deductive arguments, whose logical structures are based on ways of combining propositions by means of the propositional connectives 'not', 'and', 'or', 'if then', and 'if and only if'. Part Three, *Predicate Logic,* builds on propositional logic by adding a formal theory that symbolizes the attribution of properties to individual objects and to quantities of 'all' and 'some' objects.

Every chapter is organized into five main sections: (1) *overview* of the chapter's topics; (2) *main content* of the chapter's subject, interspersed with *Demonstration Problems* and special exercises *To check your understanding;* (3) *summary* of the chapter; (4) *key words* to help you recall the chapter's most important concepts; and (5) *exercises* that range over the subject matter of the entire chapter, concluding with a series of short answer questions for philosophical reflection. These latter questions in each chapter's final exercises are meant to deepen your understanding of logic and to invite you to think about philosophical issues connected with the methods of logic that go beyond testing your purely technical skills. The issues here involve some of the most challenging topics in contemporary philosophy of logic, which logicians and philosophers continue to debate.

Part 1

Concepts of Logic

The materials with which arguments begin are equal in number and identical with the subjects of reasoning. For arguments start with propositions, while the subjects about which reasonings take place are problems.

—Aristotle, *Topics* 101ᵇ14−17

In this introduction to the concepts of logic, we consider the definition of a proposition and an argument. Propositions are true or false sentences, and arguments are sequences of propositions in which assumptions are distinguished from conclusions. Throughout our study of symbolic logic, we will be interested in the logical properties of propositions and the formal structures and deductive validity or invalidity of arguments. We shall therefore need to investigate the underlying definitions and fundamental principles of logic in this first chapter before we begin the systematic development of the elements of symbolic logic.

CHAPTER ONE

Propositions and Arguments

Language is the amber in which a thousand precious and subtle thoughts have been safely embedded and preserved.
—Richard Chevenix Trench, *On the Study of Words* (1858)

IN THIS CHAPTER, we define the concepts of a proposition and argument. A proposition is a true or false sentence that expresses a complete true or false thought. We explain how propositions are different from other kinds of sentences, and we learn how propositions can be combined into arguments. Some of the propositions in an argument are assumptions and others are conclusions. We distinguish between deductively valid and deductively invalid arguments. We develop an informal test of deductive validity, which we apply to several types of arguments. We define sound arguments as deductively valid arguments with only true assumptions.

Propositions

Propositions are true or false sentences.

We do not usually express complete thoughts by means of single words. To say something that is true or false we must put words together into *sentences*. Not every sentence is true or false, and not every sentence expresses a complete thought. The units of language that convey complete true or false thoughts are *propositions*. Propositions are true or false sentences that express complete true or false thoughts.

> **Proposition**
> A *proposition* is a true or false sentence.

Examples of propositions in everyday language include the following:

It is raining.

My dog has fleas.

2 is the absolute value of the square root of 4.

Montréal is the capital of the United States.

Washington DC is the capital of the United States.

Either it is raining or my dog has fleas.

If $2 + 2 = 5$, then Philadelphia is the capital of the United States.

Propositions can be interpreted as concrete or abstract.

Sentences can be understood either as particular physical objects made of ink or sound waves or as more abstract general types. Although logicians are divided about the best way to define the concept of a sentence and a proposition, and some logicians define propositions as the abstract meanings expressed by concrete sentences, we shall avoid these philosophical controversies by construing propositions indifferently as either concrete or abstract true or false sentences.

Propositions often connect subject and predicate terms by a copula.

All propositions are sentences, but not all sentences are propositions.

In English, and in some other but not all natural languages, we grammatically analyze the simplest propositions as connecting a *subject term* to a *predicate term* by means of a *copula*. An easy, but certainly not the only, way to do so is by hooking together a proper noun and adjective by means of some conjugation of the verbs 'to be' or 'to have'. For example, when we say 'Alice is friendly', we grammatically connect the subject term 'Alice' to the predicate term 'friendly' by the copula 'is'. When we put these words together in the most obvious way according to the rules of English grammar, we produce the subject–copula–predicate sentence, 'Alice is friendly'. This is a proposition because it proposes that a certain state of affairs is true—in this case, the state of affairs that Alice is friendly. Such a proposition may or may not be true, depending on the facts of the situation—here, on whether or not it is actually the case that Alice is friendly. The category of propositions according to the definition does not include interrogatives or questions ('Is Alice friendly?'), imperatives or petitions and commands ('Alice, please be friendly!'), or sentences used to express any other ideas that are not complete true or false thoughts.

A copula literally hooks up two vital terms in the expression of a complete thought contained in a proposition. Think of a copula therefore as something like a coupler in plumbing or electrical wiring that connects two pipes or wires together. If we use the symbol '^' to indicate that adjacent terms are to be connected by the conventions of language into a single expression, then the formula for constructing propositions in subject-predicate combinations as expressions of facts can be given as follows:

TYPICAL (BUT NOT UNIVERSAL) GRAMMATICAL
STRUCTURE OF A PROPOSITION

[subject term]ˆ[copula]ˆ[predicate term]
Example: 'Aliceˆisˆfriendly'

Questions and commands or requests are sentences but not propositions.

Although this is the official pattern of subject-predicate propositions, we should recognize that everyday language also has many sorts of colloquial devices by which the same effect is implicitly achieved. If someone asks me, 'Are you leaving today or tomorrow?', I can answer this question by proposing my intention to leave today simply by saying 'Today'. My utterance in this case does not contain a subject term or copula. But it is natural to regard what I have said as shorthand for the more complete and, we might suppose, grammatically more correct expression for the complete thought that 'I am leaving today'. Here, 'I' is the subject term, 'am' (like 'is', 'are', etc.) is the copula, and 'leaving today' is the predicate phrase. The context in which I utter merely 'Today' makes it clear that I intend to communicate an entire proposition conventionally by the use of a single word. In applying symbolic logic to the thought and language of everyday life, we must always be on the lookout for the deeper logical structures concealed beneath alternative colloquial expressions.

Propositions can sometimes be conventionally expressed by means of a single word or phrase rather than an entire sentence.

To Check Your Understanding 1.1 ■

The following sentences have deliberately had their final punctuation removed so as not to reveal too easily their status as propositions, imperatives, or interrogatives. Decide for each sentence to which one (or more) of the three grammatical categories it belongs, briefly explain why, and give an example of how it might be used.

1. Will he close the door
2. When the time comes, you will close the door
3. Sometimes I do and sometimes I do not read before I go to bed
4. You should read every night before you go to bed
5. Should he read before he goes to bed, will you close the door

■

Propositional Symbols

We can abbreviate any proposition we choose by a *propositional symbol*. A propositional symbol is a capital letter of the alphabet that stands for the proposition.

For example, the proposition 'It is raining' can be abbreviated by the propositional symbol 'P' (or 'Q', 'R', etc.). We can choose any propositional symbol we like to abbreviate a proposition, as long as we do so consistently within a single context of analysis.

Propositional symbols abbreviate particular propositions.

It will be convenient in what follows, even before we fully develop the language of symbolic logic, to use propositional symbols as a more concise way of referring to and thinking about propositions. Instead of writing 'It is raining', we can simply write 'P'; instead of writing 'Washington DC is the capital of the United States', we can simply write 'Q'; and so on. This will save space and make it easier visually to consider some of the properties of propositions. By using propositional symbols, we are already reasoning symbolically, and to a limited extent we are already availing ourselves of the advantages of symbolic logic. Although in the next chapter we shall present a more formal definition of the concept, it will also be useful for the time being to speak of the *negation of a proposition,* by which we mean its denial or the assertion that the proposition is false or not true. If 'P' symbolizes a proposition, then 'not-P', which says that it is false or that it is not true or that it is not the case that P, is its negation.

Propositional symbols make it easier to understand complex logical structures.

The negation of a proposition denies that the proposition is true and thereby asserts that the proposition is false.

Arguments

An 'argument' in everyday terminology is an attempt to prove something. An *argument* in symbolic logic is sometimes more precisely described as a series of propositions in which certain conclusions are represented or interpreted as following from certain assumptions. We shall define the concept of an argument in this way:

ARGUMENT

An *argument* is a series of propositions the complete expression of which is divided into assumptions and conclusions by an inference indicator.

An argument is a sequence of propositions divided into assumptions and conclusions.

The following are examples:

If today is Saturday, then tomorrow is Sunday; today is Saturday; therefore, tomorrow is Sunday.

Either the Republicans or the Democrats will win the Senate. But if the Democrats win the Senate, then the Republicans may win the House. The Republicans do not have a chance of winning the Senate. Hence, the Republicans will win the House.

Angle A is identical to angle B. If side C is longer than side D, then angle A is not identical to angle B. Thus, it follows that side C is not longer than side D.

An argument is a special series of propositions, just as a proposition is a special kind of sentence. We define an argument as a series of propositions in which some propositions are assumptions and others are conclusions. We must now explain the difference between assumptions and conclusions and indicate how assumptions are distinguished from conclusions in an argument.

Assumptions and conclusions of arguments are distinguished by inference indicators.

An argument's *assumptions* are the propositions in the argument that are supposed to be true. An argument's *conclusions* by contrast are the propositions that the argument is supposed to prove as following from the assumptions. Informal logic and colloquial language use a variety of devices to signal the separation of assumptions from conclusions in presenting an argument, which are formalized in symbolic logic. Special words or symbols that distinguish an argument's assumptions from its conclusions are known as *inference indicators*. They include such terms as 'therefore', 'hence', 'thus', 'so', 'it follows that', 'now we can see', and 'in conclusion'. To write 'P, therefore Q' is to distinguish P as the assumption and Q as the conclusion in a series of propositions that constitutes an argument. An argument by this definition is any series of propositions divided by an inference indicator.

Not all arguments prove that their conclusions follow from their assumptions, just as not all propositions make true assertions.

An argument is an attempt to prove that certain conclusions follow logically from certain assumptions. However, just as not all propositions succeed in proposing a state of affairs that is actually true, so not all arguments succeed in proving that their conclusions actually follow logically from their assumptions. To qualify as an argument, regardless of its logical merits or defects, a series of propositions must be divided by an inference indicator into at least one proposition that is assumed rather than proved to be true and at least one proposition that is supposed to be proved as a conclusion.

Argument Components (For the Complete Expression of Arguments)
1. *Assumptions* (from which conclusions are supposed to follow) and
2. *Conclusions* (that are supposed to follow from the assumptions) distinguished by
3. *Inference Indicators* ('thus', 'hence', 'therefore', etc.).

Arguments can have multiple assumptions and multiple conclusions, but most arguments have multiple assumptions and only one conclusion.

Most arguments consist of one or more assumptions but exactly one conclusion. Arguments with multiple conclusions are not uncommon in everyday discourse and are accordingly included in the definition. It is always possible to rewrite an argument with multiple conclusions as several arguments with the same assumptions and only one each of the original conclusions.

Consider the argument, 'If today is Saturday, then tomorrow is Sunday; today is Saturday; therefore, tomorrow is Sunday; furthermore, the next day will be Monday'. The argument in this form has two assumptions ('If today is Saturday, then tomorrow is Sunday' and 'Today is Saturday') and two conclusions ('Tomorrow is Sunday' and 'The next day will be Monday'), separated by inference indicators ('therefore' and 'furthermore'). But the argument could be rewritten as two distinct arguments: 'If today is Saturday, then tomorrow is Sunday; today is Saturday; therefore, tomorrow is Sunday' and 'If today is Saturday, then tomorrow is Sunday; today is Saturday; therefore, the next day [after Sunday] will be Monday'. This method divides the original argument with multiple conclusions into two arguments with one conclusion each. However, the awkwardness of reformulating the argument is indicated by the need to bracket information in the second argument that is more naturally conveyed when the inferences are presented together as multiple conclusions from a single set of assumptions. However infrequently we encounter arguments with multiple conclusions, it is worthwhile to recall that they also satisfy the definition of an argument and are possible both in ordinary reasoning and in symbolic logic.

Arguments with multiple conclusions can always be rewritten as multiple arguments with the same assumptions and only one conclusion.

Deductively Valid Arguments

There are different kinds of arguments with different standards of proof. Broadly speaking, there are *deductively valid* and *deductively invalid* arguments. Elementary symbolic logic is concerned exclusively with the deductive validity or deductive invalidity of arguments. We shall define the concept of a deductively valid argument, by contrast with which all other arguments are deductively invalid.

Deductive arguments are supposed to satisfy the stongest standard of proof.

Deductive arguments are expected to satisfy the strongest standard of proof. A deductively valid argument is such that it is *logically necessary* that if its assumptions are true, then its conclusions are true, or such that it is *logically impossible* for its assumptions to be true and its conclusions false. A deductive argument is an argument that is represented or interpreted as being deductively valid. We can also say that a deductive argument is an argument that is either deductively valid or, if deductively invalid, logically defective because it is not deductively valid. To define deductive validity, we first define the concept of a *logical contradiction* in order to define the concepts of logical impossibility and logical necessity.

An argument is deductively valid if and only if it is logically necessary that if its assumptions are true, then its conclusions are true, or such that it is logically impossible for its assumptions to be true and its conclusions false.

> ### Logical Contradiction
> A *logical contradiction* is any proposition that is never true, or that is false under any circumstances, no matter what the world happens to be like, or that is true just in case its negation is true.

As an example of a logical contradiction, we may think of someone who claims that, literally, and without attaching different meanings to the combined propositions, 'Today is Tuesday, and it is not the case that today is Tuesday'. This proposition, as we ordinarily say, is contradictory because it both asserts and denies that a certain state of affairs obtains and so cannot be true no matter what day it is. The concept of logical contradiction can now be used to define the concepts of logical impossibility and logical necessity.

A proposition is logically impossible if and only if it involves a contradiction.

Logical Impossibility and Logical Necessity

The truth of a proposition or the occurrence of a condition is *logically impossible* if and only if the proposition or the adequate description of the state of affairs it proposes involves a logical contradiction. The truth of a proposition or the occurrence of a condition is *logically necessary* if and only if its falsehood or the nonoccurrence of the state of affairs it proposes is logically impossible.

To continue the previous example, the proposition 'Today is Tuesday, and it is not the case that today is Tuesday' is logically impossible. With respect to the conditions described by such a logically contradictory proposition, it is logically impossible for today to be Tuesday and for it not to be the case that today is Tuesday. Similarly, it is logically necessary that it is false that 'Today is Tuesday, and it is not the case that today is Tuesday' and logically necessary that today is not both Tuesday and not Tuesday. We now apply the definition of logical necessity and logical impossibility to the definition of a deductively valid argument.

A proposition is logically necessary if and only if its negation is logically impossible.

Deductively Valid Argument

A *deductively valid argument* is an argument that is such that it is logically necessary that if its assumptions are true, then its conclusions are true, or such that it is logically impossible for its assumptions to be true and its conclusions false.

Nondeductive arguments are deductively invalid.

A nondeductive argument by definition is deductively invalid. But not every argument that aspires to deductive validity succeeds. It is usually pointless, even though perfectly true, to criticize a nondeductive argument as deductively invalid because nondeductive arguments are not supposed to be deductively valid in the first place. We will study several examples of the difference between deductive and nondeductive arguments later. In the meantime, it is worth remarking that in symbolic logic we are concerned with deductive arguments and with the problem of whether or not any given argument is deductively valid or invalid.

If we compare the concept of deductive validity with weaker standards of proof in the empirical sciences, we see that nondeductive proof can sometimes allow the conclusions of a nondeductive argument to be less than logically necessarily true given the truth of the assumptions. According to the definition of deductive validity, a logically correct nondeductive argument can have a false conclusion even when all of its assumptions are true. An example is when I falsely conclude that all swans are white from the true assumption that every swan I have ever seen is white, unaware of the fact that an Australian species is black. This is a nondeductive argument, which is also sometimes classified as an *inductive* argument of *statistical reasoning*. The assumptions may be true, but the conclusion follows only probably rather than with logical necessity. A deductive as opposed to a nondeductive argument truly or falsely asserts that if its premises are true, then it is logically necessary on pain of logical contradiction that its conclusions are also true, or that it is logically impossible in the sense of being logically contradictory for the argument's assumptions to be true and its conclusions false. An example inspired by the nondeductive argument previously discussed is when I argue that if all swans are white, and if the bird in the lake is a swan, then the bird in the lake is white.

Inductive arguments of statistical reasoning are nondeductive.

The distinction between nondeductive and deductively invalid deductive arguments is sometimes difficult to draw. I can offer a deductive argument as an inference that is supposed to be deductively valid but that for one reason or another turns out to be deductively invalid. This is different from offering a nondeductive argument that is not intended to satisfy the strong requirement for deductive validity, even though a nondeductive argument will also be deductively invalid. With respect to our own arguments, we should usually be able to say whether we intend to advance a deductively valid or invalid deductive argument as opposed to a deductively invalid nondeductive argument because usually we know what we are trying to do in offering an argument. In intepreting the arguments of others we are guided by context and background knowledge about the argument, together with whatever information may be available about the argument author's intentions.

Whether an argument is deductive or nondeductive depends on whether it is defective if it fails to be deductively valid.

Demonstration 1:   **Identifying Deductive Arguments**

PROBLEM: To distinguish between deductive and nondeductive arguments.

ARGUMENT: The salmon have always started running before April. It's now the middle of May. So, probably, the salmon have already started running.

STEP 1:   *Identify assumptions and conclusions by inference indicators*
The distinction between assumptions and conclusions is clearly marked by the indicator term 'so, probably'. The assumptions are that the salmon have always started running before April, and that it is now the middle of May. The conclusion is that the salmon have already started running.

STEP 2:   *Reconstruct the argument as an ordered line-numbered sequence*
The argument has the following inferential structure:

1. The salmon have always started running before April.
2. It is now the middle of May.
Therefore, probably,
3. The salmon have already started running.

STEP 3:   *Evaluate the reconstructed argument by applying the definition of a deductively valid argument*
The argument tries to prove that the salmon have already started running from the assumptions that the salmon have always started running before April, and that it is now the middle of May. The argument is nondeductive because it explicitly says that its conclusion is only supposed to hold 'probably' and not with the logical necessity required of a deductively valid argument. This is not to say that all arguments that contain the word 'probably' are inductive. An argument that states 'It is probably raining; therefore, it is probably raining' is evidently deductive because the inference itself is not merely probable. The question is whether the truth of an argument's conclusions, given the truth of its assumptions, as in this case, is supposed to hold with something less than logical necessity. Nor does it seem reasonable to interpret the argument as supposing that if its assumptions are true then its conclusion logically must be true. There is no obvious logically necessary connection between what the salmon have done in the past and what they might be doing this year. There is no logical contradiction in supposing that the argument's assumptions are true and the conclusion false.

Here is another example:

ARGUMENT: Either the salmon have started running or they will start running soon. But the salmon have not started running. Therefore, the salmon will start running soon.

STEP 1:   *Identify assumptions and conclusions by inference indicators*
The distinction between assumptions and conclusion is clearly marked by the indicator term 'therefore'. The assumptions are that either the salmon have started running or they will start running soon, but that the salmon have not started running. The conclusion is that the salmon will start running soon.

STEP 2:   *Reconstruct the argument as an ordered line-numbered sequence*
The argument has the following inferential structure:

1. Either the salmon have started running or they will start running soon.
2. The salmon have not started running.
Therefore,
3. The salmon will start running soon.

STEP 3:   *Evaluate the reconstructed argument by applying the definition of a deductively valid argument*
The argument tries to prove that the salmon will start running soon from the assumptions that either the salmon have started running or the salmon will start running soon, and that the salmon have not started running. The argument is deductive because it does not qualify its conclusion as holding with anything less than logical necessity. It seems reasonable to interpret the argument as supposing that if its assumptions are true then its conclusion logically must be true. If there are just the two possibilities for the salmon to run, as the first assumption states, and if the first possibility is not true, then the second possibility must be true. To hold that the assumptions could be true and the conclusion false is to fall into the logically impossible contradiction that the salmon both will and will not start running soon.

To Check Your Understanding 1.2

Classify and explain your reasons for classifying each of the following arguments as deductive or nondeductive.

1. I know that bee stings can hurt because I was once stung by wasps.
2. If you have ever been stung by a wasp, you know that insects can inflict considerable pain. The pain of a wasp sting is similar to that of a bee sting. If you have ever been stung by a bee, you know that insects can inflict considerable pain.
3. If Simon goes fishing every Sunday, and if today is Saturday, then Simon will go fishing tomorrow.
4. Simon has gone fishing every Sunday now for the past 13 years; so, probably, Simon will go fishing this Sunday too.
5. To cross the glacier, you need special equipment. The only place to get special mountain-climbing equipment for crossing a glacier is at Trader Dirty Jack's Camping and Mining Outfitting Empo-

rium. Therefore, to cross a glacier, you need to visit Trader Dirty Jack's.

6. Whenever I need special outdoor equipment, I can usually find it at Trader Dirty Jack's Camping and Mining Outfitting Emporium. So, if you need special equipment to cross the glacier, the best recommendation I can make is to try Trader Dirty Jack's.

■

Inference Indicators

Many arguments in ordinary language need to be reconstructed in order to understand their logical structures.

The principle of charity requires that whenever possible we try to reconstruct arguments as deductively valid before criticizing their logical form or content.

An argument is a series of assumptions and conclusions, distinguished by inference indicators. The strength of an indicator is often implicit. We do not always say 'P, therefore it follows deductively that Q'. However, in a deductive argument, the inference indicator is supposed to embody the force of logical necessity. If a deductive argument is deductively valid, then if its assumptions are true its conclusions logically must also be true.

The parts of an argument can appear in almost any order. Arguments are not always expressed explicitly by means of the three components. For stylistic and rhetorical reasons, arguments are often presented in an abbreviated fashion. The context of an argument and what we can learn about its author's intent can often help us to piece together a more ideally formulated or, as we shall also say, *reconstructed* argument from its *incomplete expression*. In a reconstructed argument, all ideal argument components are hypothetically attributed to the author, according to the *principle of charity*.

The principle of charity recommends that we critically evaluate only the most deductively complete and correct interpretations of incompletely stated arguments, by which they can reasonably be interpreted. If someone says, 'Today is Saturday, therefore, tomorrow is Sunday', it would be uncharitable to interpret the argument as deductively invalid on the grounds that the truth of the conclusion is not logically necessitated by the truth of the assumption. The reason is that we suppose that most persons who offer such an argument are likely to presuppose the succession of days by which Saturday is always followed by Sunday, and that they are implicitly assuming the proposition that 'If today is Saturday, then tomorrow is Sunday', whereby the inference is made deductively valid. In other cases, it may be more difficult to identify the implicit assumptions or conclusions to complete a partially stated argument, and in still other cases there may be no reasonable reconstructions of an incompletely stated deductively invalid argument as a complete deductively valid argument. The principle of charity does not require us to make up the deficiencies of irredeemably bad inferences. It is difficult as a result to specify generally how every incompletely stated argument should be charitably reconstructed. The difficulty in applying the principle of charity reflects indefinitely many ways in which arguments can be incompletely stated in ordinary language and the vagueness in knowing when it is reasonable and when it is not reasonable to modify the explicit statement of an author's argument. It is partly to avoid the ambiguity of colloquial reasoning that symbolic logic offers a more clearly articulated ideal of the logical structures of completely formulated deductively valid arguments.

There are many different types of inference indicators in ordinary language; there are many different ways of saying 'therefore'.

There are several ways in which we can distinguish between the assumptions and conclusions of an argument in everyday language. Inference indicators usually mark the distinction or point of separation between assumptions and conclusions in expressing an argument. Inference indicators thereby tell us which parts of the sequence of propositions that constitutes an argument are the assumptions and which are the conclusions that are supposed to follow from the assumptions. Inference indicators notably include (but are not limited to) such familiar words and phrases as 'therefore', 'hence', 'thus', 'so', 'it follows that', 'now we can see', and 'in conclusion'. These terms indicate that an argument's assumptions have just been given, and that a conclusion is about to follow. They are often, though not exclusively, used to indicate the deductive inference of conclusions from assumptions. Terms such as 'because', 'for', and 'by reason of' indicate that the argument's conclusions have just been given, and that its assumptions are about to be presented. Assumptions, conclusions, and inference indicators are often, but not always, arranged in the order illustrated by the following example:

Assumptions, conclusions, and inference indicators can appear in any order in ordinary language arguments.

STANDARD ARGUMENT FORM

Assumptions—Inference Indicators—Conclusions

Example: The salmon are running only if the river has melted; but the river has not melted. Therefore, the salmon are not running.

For stylistic reasons, this common pattern is not always followed in presenting arguments. Other combinations are also frequently encountered. In some versions, more than one occurrence of less than all of a complete argument's assumptions, conclusions, and inference indicators appears in different arrangements in the statement especially of complex arguments. The following are all the remaining variations, with examples involving a single occurrence of each of an argument's three basic parts:

VARIANT ARGUMENT FORMS

Conclusions—Inference Indicators—Assumptions

Example: The salmon have not started running. The reason is that the salmon are running only if the river has melted, but the river has not melted.

Inference Indicators—Conclusions—Assumptions

Example: The reason why the salmon are not running is that the salmon are running only if the river has melted, but the river has not melted.

Inference Indicators—Assumptions—Conclusions

Example: As a consequence of the fact that the salmon are running only if the river has melted, but that the river has not melted, the salmon are not running.

Assumptions—Conclusions—Inference Indicators

Example: The salmon are running only if the river has melted, but the river has not melted; the salmon are not running as a consequence.

Conclusions—Assumptions—Inference Indicators

Example: The salmon are not running; the salmon are running only if the river has melted; but the river has not melted; and that's the reason why.

The conventional way of expressing arguments is to begin with the assumptions, followed by an inference indicator, followed by the conclusions.

It is convenient to state arguments in a conventional sequential format in which the assumptions and conclusions are numbered, and assumptions are distinguished from conclusions. The distinction between assumptions and conclusions can now be shown, not by an ordinary English inference indicator but by dividing numbered assumptions and conclusions by a short horizontal line. The horizontal line has the same meaning as if, after stating the argument's assumptions, we were to say 'Therefore', 'Thus', 'Hence', or the like, intending the argument to be understood as a deductive inference, followed by the argument's conclusions. We must be prepared to identify arguments in various different formulations and disguises in different contexts of thought and discourse. We can reconstruct the previous argument according to the standard model as follows:

Arguments reconstructed for logical analysis can include a short horizontal line as a more formal inference indicator.

1. If the salmon are running, then the river has melted.

2. But the river has not melted.

---

3. The salmon are not running.

We now have a good idea of the basic components of arguments. Arguments are series of propositions divided into assumptions and conclusions by inference indicators. Some of the propositions of an argument are its assumptions, which are offered in support of or as the basis for inferring the other propositions that constitute the argument's conclusions. The distinction between assumptions and conclusions is marked by a variety of inference indicators. The three components of an argument—assumptions, conclusions, and inference indicators—can in principle appear in any order, but the order they are given is usually determined by the stylistic or rhetorical choice of indicator term used in distinguishing assumptions from conclusions.

To Check Your Understanding 1.3

In the following deductive arguments, identify the assumptions, conclusions, and inference indicators, and reconstruct the arguments according to the standard model:

1. If theory T is correct, then result R should occur. But result R does not occur. Therefore, theory T is incorrect.
2. Where there is spiritual enlightenment there is wisdom. For where there is spiritual enlightenment there is no despair, and where there is despair there is no wisdom.
3. You will not lose the account. So you will not change lanes now. If you change lanes now you'll miss your exit. If you miss your exit, you won't be able to attend the meeting, and if you're not able to attend the meeting, you'll lose the account.
4. I cannot be in two places at once. If I go to Brazil and attend the chemical weapons disarmament talks in Geneva, then I must be in two places at once. I would rather go to Brazil than attend the chemical weapons disarmament talks in Geneva. Therefore, I will go to Brazil.
5. Do you know why the fire started? Fires begin wherever there is a sufficient supply of oxygen, combustible material, and a sufficient source of heat. And in the attic that day there was plenty of oxygen, plenty of things to burn, and there were frequently sparks from frayed electrical wires falling on the floor.
6. Whenever I so much as play the *Cats* soundtrack at home, my schnauzer becomes violently aggressive. My schnauzer either has a deeply ingrained hatred of all things feline or else is more of a fine arts critic than I had previously imagined. Hence, I will not take my schnauzer to see *Cats*.

Imagination Test for Deductive Validity

It is not enough to know the definitions of deductively valid and deductively invalid arguments. We must also know how to apply the definitions in assessing an argument's deductive validity or invalidity. How can we do this? In particular, how can we tell when a deductive argument has a logical structure such that the truth of its assumptions is sufficient to guarantee the truth of its conclusions? How can we tell when an argument is such that if its assumptions are true, then its conclusions logically must also be true, or such that it is logically impossible for its assumptions to be true and its conclusions false? In other words, how can we tell what is and what is not logically possible?

Intuitively, without presupposing the techniques of symbolic logic, we can approximately determine whether an argument is deductively valid or invalid by testing it in our imaginations to see whether we can conceive of a possible situation or set of circumstances in which the assumptions could be true and the conclusions false. If we can imagine such a situation, then we have good (but not conclusive) informal evidence for supposing that the argument is deductively invalid. If we cannot imagine such a situation, then we have good (but not conclusive) informal evidence for supposing that the argument is deductively valid. This is the *imagination test* for deductive validity.

The imagination test for deductive validity requires that we try to imagine circumstances in which the assumptions of an argument are true and the conclusion false.

IMAGINATION TEST
FOR DEDUCTIVE VALIDITY

Try to imagine a situation or set of circumstances in which the assumptions of an argument are true and the conclusions false. If you can do so, then there is a strong (but not conclusive) reason to believe that the argument is deductively invalid; if you cannot do so, then there is a strong (but again not conclusive) reason to believe that the argument is deductively valid.

The following is a simple application of the imagination test, revealing an argument's deductive invalidity:

1. Grass is green.

2. Snow is purple.

Clearly, we can imagine that the assumption is true and the conclusion false. Indeed, the assumption is true and the conclusion is false, so it is certainly possible for this to be the case. The same is true even if the argument's assumption is true where the conclusion happens to be true, but the truth of the conclusion is not logically guaranteed by the truth of the assumption. An example is the following:

If we can imagine that the assumptions of an argument are true and the conclusions false, then the argument is probably deductively invalid.

1. Grass is green.

---

2. Snow is white.

We can easily imagine possible circumstances in which the assumption is true and the conclusion false. We can imagine grass to be green while imagining that snow could have a color other than white, even though we know that snow is in fact white.

The imagination test can also be applied to prove the validity or invalidity of more sophisticated arguments. Here is a more complicated example in which the imagination test works reasonably well. The argument states:

1. Today is Saturday and tomorrow is Sunday.

---

2. Tomorrow is Sunday.

If we imagine that the assumption is true, then we imagine both that today is Saturday and that tomorrow is Sunday. If in addition we were also to imagine that the conclusion of the argument is false, then we would fall into the logical contradiction of imagining both that it is true that tomorrow is Sunday and false that tomorrow is Sunday. Since we cannot imagine such a contradiction, we conclude by the imagination test that the argument is deductively valid. If the argument's assumption is true, then its conclusion logically must be true; the truth of the conclusion would be logically necessitated by the truth of the assumption, if the assumption were true; and it is logically impossible for the argument's assumption to be true and its conclusion false. Here is another inference:

If we cannot imagine that the assumptions of an argument are true and the conclusions false, then the argument is probably deductively valid.

1. If roses are red, then violets are blue.

2. Roses are red.

---

3. Violets are blue.

Contradictions prevent imagining that the assumptions of a deductively valid argument are true and the conclusions false.

The imagination test requires that we try to imagine a set of circumstances in which the argument's assumptions are true and its conclusion false. If we imagine that the conclusion is false, then we imagine that (all) violets are not (always) blue. In itself, this is not difficult. But we are also supposed to imagine that both assumptions are true. To imagine that if roses are red, then violets are blue, and that roses are red, is in effect to imagine that (all) violets are (always) blue. On pain of logical contradiction, we cannot imagine that the argument's assumptions are true and its conclusion false because we cannot simultaneously imagine both that (all) violets are (always) blue and that (all) violets are not (always) blue.

Now suppose that someone traveling by airplane from New York to Brussels, Belgium, were to offer the following argument in answer to the question how far around the globe he or she has just flown. The traveler argues:

1. The earth rotates once approximately every 24 hours.

2. I have been flying for approximately 8 hours.

3. $8 = 1/3(24)$.

---

4. I have flown approximately one-third the way around the earth.

This is the kind of argument that can sometimes confuse us. It involves arithmetic, which alone, deservedly or not, often lends an air of authority to an inference. It should be intuitively obvious that the argument is deductively invalid. But how can we tell? We decide this by applying the imagination test.

First, we try to imagine a possible situation in which the conclusion is false. Let us suppose that we have not flown approximately one-third the way around the earth, but something significantly less or significantly more. Is that possibility logically compatible with the truth of the assumptions? The answer is yes because the assumptions in steps 1–3 are not only imaginably true but also true as a matter of fact. What kind of situation are we imagining when we imagine that the assumptions of the argument are true and the conclusion false? There are many scenarios that show the argument to be deductively invalid. One example is that in which we fly for 8 hours, as assumption 2 states, and the earth rotates once approximately every 24 hours, but we fly in close circles at such a speed that after 8 hours we land precisely at our takeoff point. We note that the assumptions make no mention whatsoever of the altitude, speed, or direction of the plane's flight relative to the motion of the earth, which can obviously make a difference in how much surface distance the plane covers in its flight.

The argument illustrates the fact that, according to the concept of deductive invalidity and the imagination test for deductive invalidity generally, it is possible for a deductively invalid argument to have only true assumptions and true conclusions. We do not criticize the argument by saying that we definitely did not fly one-third the way around the earth. Perhaps New York City as it turns out is one-third the way around the earth from Brussels. The point is that whether or not the conclusion of the argument happens to be true, the assumptions and the logical structure of the argument are not sufficient by themselves to guarantee the truth of the conclusion. It is possible (given that it is imaginable) for the assumptions of the argument to be true and the conclusion false, whether or not both the assumptions and conclusion happen to be true. This is the mark of a deductively invalid argument. If, as a matter of fact, Brussels is approximately one-third the way around the earth from New York City, then there will have to be a better argument than the one we have been considering to show that this is so. The assumptions of the previous argument are too weak to compel us to accept the conclusion even if the assumptions are true, and even if the conclusion happens to be true.

The imagination test is limited in application, but it can help us to understand the definition of deductive validity.

Let us try the imagination test for deductive validity on another argument. The following is a reconstruction of a thought experiment in Galileo's *Notebooks,* in which he refutes the Aristotelian impetus theory of motion. The impetus theory of motion states that projectiles continue moving in space because they displace the air in front of them, causing currents of air to move back around the projectile and continuously give it a forward push from behind to carry it along with diminishing force until it finally falls. Galileo argues that if the Aristotelian impetus theory of motion were true, then a thread attached to the end of a projectile would be deflected by the displaced air rushing from tip to butt. However, he says that if we perform the experiment, we see that the thread fans out like a streamer behind the projectile, with no sign of being deflected forward by any displacement of air. Hence, Galileo concludes that the Aristotelian impetus theory of motion is false.

This is a typical and highly useful style of argument. The conclusions of a theory are deduced, and then shown not to hold, as a strategy for discrediting the theory as false. Galileo's argument can be reconstructed as follows:

Proving that a theory has false consequences is a useful way of disproving the theory.

1. If the Aristotelian impetus theory of motion is true, then a thread attached to a moving projectile will be deflected forward by a displacement of air rushing backward from the projectile's tip to its butt.

2. But a thread attached to a moving projectile is not deflected forward by any displacement of air rushing from the projectile's tip to its butt; rather, the thread follows directly behind the projectile.

3. The Aristotelian impetus theory of motion is not true.

We can use the imagination test to determine that the argument is deductively valid. The imagination test requires us to try imagining a set of circumstances in which the argument's assumptions are true and its conclusion false.

If the conclusion of Galileo's argument is false, then the Aristotelian impetus theory of motion is true. But we cannot simultaneously imagine the two assumptions of the argument to be true. If we imagine that the Aristotelian impetus theory of motion is true, and that the first assumption is true, then it follows that a thread attached to a moving projectile will be deflected forward by a displacement of air rushing from the projectile's tip to its butt. Therefore, if we imagine that the conclusion of the argument is false and the first assumption is true, then we are in effect imagining that it is true that a thread attached to a moving projectile will be deflected forward. Yet we are also supposed to imagine that the second assumption of the argument is true. The second assumption, however, in stating that the thread is not deflected by a rush of air from behind the projectile, flatly contradicts what we are required to imagine by imagining the falsehood of the argument's conclusion together with the truth of its first assumption.

The imagination test of deductive validity is not always reliable because of limits in individual imaginations and because of the excessive memory requirements of some complex arguments.

The imagination test is not a completely reliable criterion for distinguishing deductive validity from deductive invalidity for two reasons. First, sometimes our imaginations are not as strong or vivid as they need to be to imagine a counterexample to the deductive validity of a deductive argument. We may sometimes for whatever reasons simply be unable to imagine a state of affairs in which the assumptions of an argument are true and the conclusions false, even though such an imaginable state of affairs exists. Second, many arguments contain so many assumptions and conclusions that our memory and imagination would be overtaxed to consider all these propositions at once in order to compare them for contradiction or noncontradiction. We cannot always appeal to psychological conceivability or imaginability as an infallible test of logical possibility because logical possibility and psychological conceivability or imaginability do not always coincide.

The imagination test is nevertheless the best criterion of deductive validity in informal reasoning.

When we are dealing with arguments informally, the imagination test provides the best method for distinguishing deductively valid from invalid inferences. It works to the limited extent it does by offering insight into what is logically possible and what is logically impossible. From this we can judge in a wide range of cases when it is logically possible or impossible for the assumptions of an argument to be true and its conclusions false. An argument can have a deductively invalid logical structure despite having a contingently true conclusion. We should emphasize throughout that criticizing an argument's validity is not the same as criticizing the truth of its conclusions.

■ *Demonstration 2:* **Imagination Test for Deductive Validity** ■

PROBLEM: To critically evaluate an argument for deductive validity or invalidity by the imagination test.

ARGUMENT: "If therefore it were possible for bodies to exist without the mind, yet to hold that they do so must needs be a very precarious opinion, since it is to suppose, without any reason at all, that God has created innumerable beings that are entirely useless and serve to no manner of purpose" (Berkeley, 1710/1957, p. 32).

STEP 1:   *Identify assumptions and conclusions by inference indicators*
The argument concludes that there are no bodies existing independently of (without) the mind. The author's use of the inference indicators 'therefore' and 'since it is to suppose' distinguishes the conclusion from the assumptions in the body of the passage. The assumptions are that if mind-independent objects exist, then they are useless; if there are mind-independent objects, then they are created by God; and there is no reason to believe that God would create anything useless.

STEP 2:   *Reconstruct the argument as an ordered line-numbered sequence*
Here it is easy to reformat the information identified in step 1 to clearly distinguish the assumptions from the conclusion:

1. If mind-independent objects exist, then they are useless.
2. If mind-independent objects exist, then they are created by God.
3. God creates nothing useless (if something is created by God, then it has a use).

---

4. Mind-independent objects do not exist.

STEP 3:   *Evaluate the reconstructed argument by applying the imagination test*
The imagination test of deductive validity requires that we try to imagine a situation in which the assumptions are true and the conclusion false. If we can imagine such a situation, then the argument is probably invalid; if we cannot imagine such a situation, then the argument is probably valid. The best way to proceed is to begin by assuming that the conclusion is false and then try to imagine whether the assumptions could still be true. Here, if the conclusion is false, then mind-independent objects exist. Imagining that mind-independent objects exist while imagining that assumptions 1 and 2 are true entails imagining that mind-independent objects are both useless and created by God. However, we are also supposed to imagine that assumption 3 is true, which states that God creates nothing useless. Trying to imagine that assumptions 1–3 are true and conclusion 4 is false leads us into the contradiction that God both creates and does not create something useless. We cannot imagine that the argument's assumptions are true and its conclusion false. It follows, according to the imagination test of deductive validity, that the argument is deductively valid.

To Check Your Understanding 1.4 ─────────────────────────────────■

Use the imagination test to determine the deductive validity or invalidity of each of these arguments:

(1) 1. The Bible says that God exists.
     2. The Bible is the one and only book the truth of which you can believe absolutely on faith and without further proof.
     3. If God exists, then what the Bible says is true.
     ───────────────────────────────────
     4. God exists and what the Bible says is true.

(2) 1. The government cannot help everyone who needs help.
     2. The federal deficit and military expenditures put an enormous drain on the government's resources.
     3. People are supposed to be responsible for themselves and not turn to the government for help.
     4. Many persons try to defraud the government when they do not really need assistance, and the only way to discourage this practice is to restrict the amount of economic help the government extends to private citizens.
     ───────────────────────────────────
     5. Hence, it stands to reason that no private citizen can or should rely on the government for economic help.

(3) 1. The time to act is now.
     2. If we do not act now, we will be sorry later.
     3. Besides, the only reason we might be sorry later is if we do not act now.
     ───────────────────────────────────
     4. Later, it will simply be too late to act.

(4) 1. If somebody does something soon, there will be rejoicing in the land.
     2. If somebody doesn't do something soon, there will be a terrible price to pay.
     ───────────────────────────────────
     3. If there is no terrible price to pay, there will be rejoicing in the land.

(5) 1. I want to go to law school, but only if I can practice environmental law.
     2. I cannot practice environmental law unless I earn a law degree.
     3. I cannot earn a law degree unless I go to law school.

4. I won't go to law school unless I want to.
_____
5. I want to go to law school.

(6) 1. If God exists, then by definition he is the omnipotent, omniscient, and perfectly benevolent creator of the world.
   2. But there is natural evil (suffering not caused by human decision) in the world.
   3. Either God does not know about the natural evil in the world, or he knows about it but cannot prevent it, or he knows about and could prevent it if he chooses to but chooses not to prevent it.
   4. If God does not know about the natural evil in the world, then he is not omniscient.
   5. If God knows about the natural evil in the world, but cannot prevent it, then he is not omnipotent.
   6. If God knows about the natural evil in the world, and could prevent it if he chose to, but chooses not to prevent it, then he is not perfectly benevolent.
   _____
   7. Either God is not omniscient, or God is not omnipotent, or God is not perfectly benevolent.
   8. God does not exist.

■

_____

Limiting Cases of Deductive Validity

There are two limiting cases of deductive validity.

The definitions of deductive validity and invalidity have some surprising consequences. They unexpectedly qualify certain types of argument as *limiting cases of deductive validity*. Such arguments trivially satisfy the definition of deductive validity but do not fulfill our intuitive expectations of relevance or conceptual connection between assumptions and conclusions. There are two categories of limiting cases of deductively valid arguments: cases in which it is impossible for the assumptions to be true (since then it is impossible both for the assumptions to be true and the conclusions false) and cases in which it is impossible for the conclusions to be false (since then it is also impossible both for the assumptions to be true and the conclusions false).

The following are examples of each:

1. $2 + 2 = 7$
_____
2. Mary Lincoln is president.

Arguments are deduc-
tively valid by default
when their assump-
tions cannot be true,
regardless of the
truth or relevance
of the content of the
conclusions.

Arguments are deduc-
tively valid by default
when their conclu-
sions cannot be false,
regardless of the
truth or relevance
of the content of the
assumptions.

Limiting cases of
deductive validity
are rare in ordinary
reasoning.

1. Abraham Lincoln is president.

2. Either grass is green or it is not the case that grass is green.

LIMITING CASES OF DEDUCTIVE VALIDITY

1. Assumptions cannot be true.
2. Conclusions cannot be false.
In either case, it cannot be both that the assumptions are true and the conclusions false; thus trivially satisfying the definition of a deductively valid argument.

Limiting cases of deductively valid arguments are seldom encountered in everyday contexts. To have a firm grasp of the concept of deductive validity, it is important to understand how some arguments (trivially) satisfy the definition. Try formulating examples of your own in each category, and check them against the definition of deductive validity to make sure you understand the definition and the reasons why such arguments are trivially deductively valid.

To Check Your Understanding 1.5 ■

Use the imagination test in applying the definitions of deductive validity and invalidity to determine the deductive validity or invalidity of the following six arguments. In the case of deductively invalid arguments, indicate the counter-example you imagined in which the assumptions are true and the conclusions false; for deductively valid arguments, indicate whether or not it is a trivial or limiting case.

(1) 1. The storm was over in 15 minutes.
    2. The storm lasted all day, from dawn to dusk.

    3. The storm was over in precisely 10 minutes.

(2) 1. If you stay up all night reading science fiction, then you won't be able to do good work the next day.
    2. You must be able to do good work if you are to pass tomorrow's exam.
    3. You have an exam tomorrow.

    4. You will not stay up all night reading science fiction.

(3) 1. All triangles have three sides and three angles.
   _____
   2. No squares are rectangles.

(4) 1. Ken is a bachelor, whose tenth wedding anniversary is in May.
   _____
   2. Barbie will be asking Ken for a divorce and Skipper will be su-ing Ken for bigamy and alienation of affection from Francie.

(5) 1. The devil knows how to seduce weak sinners with promises of fame, glory, and riches.
   2. If the devil knows how to seduce weak sinners with promises of fame, glory, and riches, then presumably the devil knows how to turn their minds from virtue to vice.
   3. But no one's mind can be turned from virtue to vice unless they have been deprived of knowledge of the greater importance of virtue compared with that of fame, glory, and riches.
   4. Anyone who is unaware of the greater importance of virtue compared with that of fame, glory, and riches is a benighted fool.
   _____
   5. All weak sinners are benighted fools.

(6) 1. All weak sinners are benighted fools.
   _____
   2. The devil can either seduce weak sinners with promises of fame, glory, or riches if they are benighted fools or cannot so seduce them if they are aware of the greater importance of virtue compared with that of fame, glory, or riches.

■

Conditional Arguments

It is not feasible to list exhaustively all of the indefinitely many deductively valid arguments nor to distinguish all deductively valid from deductively invalid forms. The possibilities of combining propositions as assumptions and conclusions with inference indicators are so vast that there is no manageable procedure for cataloging all possible deductively valid and all possible deductively invalid argument types. We shall instead consider some of the most common useful forms.

As we continue to work with arguments, we will become familiar with patterns that frequently occur and learn which are deductively valid and which are not. We can sometimes check the items in either category by the imagination test. The following types of arguments are so frequently encountered in ordinary reasoning that it will be worthwhile to acquaint ourselves with their logical forms as they appear in everyday discourse and to distinguish valid from invalid forms so that it will be easy to recognize them later when they are formalized in symbolic logic.

To illustrate how the imagination test can be used to distinguish deductively valid from deductively invalid inferences, we will consider four frequently encountered types of *conditional arguments*. A conditional argument contains at least one proposition that has an 'if-then' form. That is, a conditional argument contains a conditional proposition, which says that something is true *if*, or conditionally upon, or as a condition of, something else being true. For example, I might say that 'If today is Saturday, then tomorrow is Sunday', where the truth of the proposition that 'Tomorrow is Sunday' is conditional on the truth of the proposition that 'Today is Saturday'. A conditional or 'if-then' proposition has two parts, the 'if' part (here, 'Today is Saturday') and the 'then' part ('Tomorrow is Sunday'). The 'if' part of a conditional is known as the *antecedent,* and the 'then' part is known as the *consequent.* This terminology will be useful in distinguishing two pairs of conditional arguments, two of which are deductively valid and two of which are deductively invalid.

Conditional arguments feature conditional if-then assumptions.

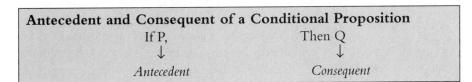

Antecedent and Consequent of a Conditional Proposition

If P,   Then Q

↓   ↓

Antecedent   *Consequent*

Every conditional has an antecedent and a consequent.

The two most common valid conditional arguments are known to medieval logicians as *modus ponendo ponens* and *modus tollendo tollens,* or more simply as *modus ponens* and *modus tollens.* We can think of them as validly inferring the consequent of a conditional by affirming the antecedent and validly inferring the negation of the antecedent by denying the consequent. In *modus ponens,* from the conditional, If P, then Q, and the antecedent of the conditional, P, we can validly deduce the consequent of the conditional, Q (regardless of what 'P' and 'Q' stand for, provided we uniformly substitute the same proposition for symbol 'P' and the same proposition for symbol 'Q', wherever symbols 'P' and 'Q' occur). The form is as follows: If P, then Q; P; therefore, Q. An everyday example is the following:

Two deductively valid forms of conditional argument are modus ponendo ponens (modus ponens) *and* modus tollendo tollens (modus tollens).

1. If yesterday was Saturday, then today is Sunday.

2. Yesterday was Saturday.

3. Today is Sunday.

The argument satisfies the imagination criterion for validity because it is impossible to imagine that the assumptions are true and the conclusion false. Try first to imagine that today is not Sunday (this should be easy even if you happen to be reading this on Sunday). Now, while holding fixed in memory your imagining that today is not Sunday, try at the same time to imagine that yesterday was Saturday, and that if yesterday was Saturday, then today is Sunday. Surely you cannot imagine this. If you try, you do not get very far because you find that your imagination is caught up in the contradiction of trying to imagine both that today is Sunday (in imagining the truth of the assumptions) and that today is not Sunday (in imagining the falsehood of the conclusion). If you cannot imagine that the assumptions are true and the conclusion false, then the imagination test within its limitations indicates that the argument is deductively valid. This is the same basic form of inference as the roses are red, violets are blue argument already tested for deductive validity by the imagination criterion.

Another deductively valid form is *modus tollens*. We see an instance of this type in Galileo's argument. The inference is that from an if-then conditional, If P, then Q, and the negation of Q, it is deductively valid to conclude the negation of P: If P, then Q; not-Q; therefore, not-P. The argument represents a pattern commonly found in testing the truth of a theory by considering the truth or falsehood of its consequences. If a theory implies certain consequences, as does the Aristotelian impetus theory of motion in Galileo's refutation, and if those consequences are false rather than true, then their falsehood reflects back on the falsehood of the theory. This is a further implication of the definition of deductive validity since we do not expect that a true theory could imply false consequences. If we discover even one false consequence of a theory, then we can be sure that the theory is false. The deductively valid inference in this case is appropriately described as denying the consequent (in order to derive the negation of the antecedent). The following is another simplified example from the history of science:

1. If Ptolemaic astronomy is true, then the sun orbits the Earth.
2. But the sun does not orbit the Earth (rather, the Earth orbits the sun).

___

3. Ptolemaic astronomy is not true.

Modus ponens *and* modus tollens *satisfy the imagination test of deductive validity.*

We confirm that this is a deductively valid inference by applying the imagination test. First, try to imagine that conclusion 3 is false. In this case, Ptolemaic astronomy is true. Now, try also to imagine that assumptions 1 and 2 are true. Assumption 1 states that if Ptolemaic astronomy is true, then the sun orbits the Earth. Therefore, in imagining that 3 is false and 1 is true, we are imagining that the sun orbits the Earth. However, we are also supposed to imagine that assumption 2 is true, which states that the sun does not orbit the Earth. This means that in trying to imagine that conclusion 3 is false and assumptions 1 and 2 are true, we must simultaneously imagine that the sun orbits the Earth and that the sun does not orbit the Earth. Of course, we can imagine no such thing. We can only imagine one part of a contradiction or the other as holding true at a time. The inference pattern for *modus tollens* thereby passes the imagination test as a deductively valid argument form.

There are two other conditional arguments that are similar to but still importantly different from *modus ponens* and *modus tollens*. These are deductively invalid conditional inferences, also known as *logical fallacies*. We should learn to recognize a few of the more commonly encountered (and easy-to-commit) deductively invalid conditional forms and to distinguish them from their look-alike valid forms.

Deductively invalid arguments are logical fallacies.

The following argument appears innocent enough and bears a striking resemblance to the previous two. But whereas the previous two arguments are valid inference forms, the following argument is a deductively invalid form of which we must be wary.

1. If this is a rattlesnake, then this is a poisonous reptile.

2. This is a poisonous reptile.

3. This is a rattlesnake.

The argument is deductively invalid. We can easily imagine circumstances in which the assumptions are true but the conclusion is false. It is true, as assumption 1 states, that rattlesnakes are poisonous reptiles. We can imagine, as assumption 2 assumes, that we are confronted by a poisonous reptile. But from the fact that rattlesnakes are poisonous reptiles and that this is a poisonous reptile, it does not follow as conclusion 3 states that therefore this is a rattlesnake. There are poisonous reptiles other than rattlesnakes, and the snake before us, for all we know from the argument's assumptions, might be one of them. Assumptions 1 and 2 could also be true if the poisonous reptile we are pointing out were a gila monster (not a snake at all), a water moccasin (a poisonous snake, but not specifically a rattlesnake), and so on. The general form of this type of deductively invalid inference is If P, then Q; Q; therefore, P. By reason of the terminology for the 'if proposition' (antecedent) and 'then proposition' (consequent) of if-then conditionals, this is known as the *fallacy of affirming the consequent*.

Two deductively invalid forms of conditional argument are the fallacy of affirming the consequent and the fallacy of denying the antecedent.

A companion kind of deductive fallacy that also resembles one of the deductively valid types is known as the *fallacy of denying the antecedent*. It has the complementary form, If P, then Q; not-P; therefore, not-Q. To see why this is deductively invalid, consider the following example:

1. If this is a rattlesnake, then this is a poisonous reptile.

2. This is not a rattlesnake.

---

3. This is not a poisonous reptile.

Good reasoning? Obviously not! Examples of this kind should convince us that whether we argue correctly or not can make more of a difference in our lives and fortunes than purely as matters of abstract theory. There are poisonous reptiles other than rattlesnakes, and from the mere fact that this is not a rattlesnake we would be rash to conclude that therefore this is not a poisonous reptile. It could be a gila monster, a water moccasin, or any number of poisonous reptiles other than a rattlesnake. In evaluating this argument as deductively invalid, we again make use of the imagination test. We try to imagine that the two assumptions are true, but that the conclusion is false. We find that we can easily do so, imagining a counterexample in which the truth of the assumptions does not logically guarantee the truth of the conclusion.

Note again, as with the previous example concerning a deductively invalid attempt to deduce the distance between New York and Brussels from airplane flight time in traveling from one city to the other, that deductively invalid arguments do not necessarily have false conclusions. Perhaps the snake on the path is not after all a poisonous reptile. The point is that the truth of the assumptions that all rattlesnakes are poisonous reptiles and that this is not a rattlesnake by themselves are not sufficient for us to validly conclude that therefore the creature slithering and raising its diamond-patterned hood before us is not a poisonous reptile. It might or might not be, for all that the assumptions have to say. The assumptions, in other words, do not settle the matter, even if we suppose them to be true, as they definitely and incontrovertibly would if they were true and if the argument was deductively valid.

The deductively valid and invalid conditional argument forms we have discussed are presented for comparison in the following table:

Deductively Valid and Invalid Conditional Inferences

DEDUCTIVELY VALID FORMS		DEDUCTIVELY INVALID FORMS	
Modus ponendo ponens	If P, then Q P ——— Q	Affirming the consequent	If P, then Q Q ——— P
Modus tollendo tollens	If P, then Q Not-Q ——— Not-P	Denying the antecedent	If P, then Q Not-P ——— Not-Q

Deductively valid conditional arguments should not be confused with similar deductively invalid conditional arguments.

The contrapositive of a conditional C is a conditional that takes the negation of the consequent of C as its antecedent and the negation of the antecedent of C as its consequent.

A conditional argument in which a conditional proposition is inferred from its contrapositive is deductively valid.

There are many other types of deductively valid and invalid arguments, including other deductively valid and invalid conditional arguments. The diagram shows only two of the most common, useful, deductively valid forms, which it contrasts with the two deductively invalid forms with which the valid forms are easily confused. The following is another frequently encountered conditional argument, in which the *contrapositive* of a conditional is validly inferred. A contrapositive is a conditional proposition in which the antecedent is the negation of the consequent and the consequent is the negation of the antecedent of another conditional. The two conditionals are then said to be contrapositives of one another.

> **Contrapositives**
> If P, then Q   If not-Q, then not-P

Contrapositives are logically equivalent and can be regarded as alternative expressions of the same conditional proposition. We can see informally that it is deductively valid to infer either form of a contrapositive from the other:

1. If P, then Q
———————————
2. If not-Q, then not-P

1. If not-Q, then not-P
———————————
2. If P, then Q

The following are illustrations:

1. If today is Monday, then tomorrow is Tuesday.
————————————————————————
2. If tomorrow is not Tuesday, then today is not Monday.

1. If we can go swimming, then the pool is full.

2. If the pool is not full, then we cannot go swimming.

1. If we can play baseball, then it is not raining.

2. If it is raining, then we cannot play baseball.

To evaluate these inferences informally, use the imagination test to confirm that they are deductively valid. Can you imagine that conclusion 2 is false in the same circumstances in which assumption 1 is true? Looking only at the first argument, if it is true that if today is Monday, then tomorrow is Tuesday, which by the conventions of our calendar is indeed true, can we imagine that it might then be false that if tomorrow is not Tuesday, then today is not Monday? To imagine that if tomorrow is not Tuesday, then today is not Monday, is false is to imagine that it is true that tomorrow is not Tuesday, but today is Monday. If, however, we are imagining that today is Monday and that assumption 1 in the argument is true, then we are in effect imagining that tomorrow is Tuesday because assumption 1 states that if today is Monday, then tomorrow is Tuesday. In other words, if we try to imagine that assumption 1 is true and conclusion 2 is false, we must simultaneously imagine both that tomorrow is Tuesday and that tomorrow is not Tuesday. This would be an outright contradiction that we cannot imagine to be true. Thus, we verify that the first example of a contrapositive conditional argument is deductively valid. Similarly with respect to the other applications, and for the general forms of contrapositive conditional inference.

To emphasize the point that there are other types of conditional arguments that we have not yet considered, we conclude with an example of a deductively valid argument that also features conditional assumptions and a conditional conclusion:

Hypothetical syllogism is another deductively valid form of conditional argument.

Hypothetical Syllogism
1. If P, then Q
2. If Q, then R

3. If P, then R

The following is an illustration:

1. If we win the match, then we win the game.

2. If we win the game, then we win the tournament.

3. If we win the match, then we win the tournament.

This is a deductively valid form of argument, sometimes known as *hypothetical syllogism.* The form is If P, then Q; If Q, then R; therefore, If P, then R. Try evaluating it by the imagination test to confirm that the argument is deductively valid. Can you imagine that conclusion 3 is false in the same circumstances in which assumptions 1 and 2 are true? Now try to devise deductively invalid look-alike forms that are similar in structure but that do not satisfy the imagination test for deductive validity. Use the similarities and differences between the deductively valid and invalid forms in the previous table as a starting place in working out deductively invalid argument types similar to hypothetical syllogism. What counterexamples show that these logically invalid look-alike forms are invalid?

Disjunctive syllogism is a deductively valid form of argument equivalent to modus ponens *and* modus tollens.

Arguments in *modus ponens* and *modus tollens* are equivalent to a common form of argument known as *disjunctive syllogism.* In a disjunctive syllogism, we have the disjunction of two propositions, P or Q, and the negation of one or the other of them, e.g., not-P (otherwise, not-Q). From P or Q and not-P, we can deductively validly deduce Q, and from P or Q and not-Q we can validly deduce P. Applying the imagination test, we see that if P or Q is true, but P is not true (which is to say that not-P is true), then Q is true. If either P or Q is true, but P is not true, then it must be Q that is true. If you know that you will get either an 'A' or a 'B' when you take logic, and if you know that you will not get a 'B', then you can deductively validly infer that you will get an 'A'. This is also the case in deductively validly inferring P from P or Q and not-Q.

Disjunctive syllogism has the following form:

Disjunctive Syllogism	
1. P or Q	1. P or Q
2. Not-P	2. Not-Q
3. Q	3. P

As we shall prove later, these are logically equivalent to *modus ponens* and *modus tollens,* respectively. P or Q is logically equivalent to If not-P, then Q. The disjunctive syllogism on the left is therefore equivalent to If not-P, then Q; Not-P; therefore, Q (which is an instance of the form *modus ponens*). The disjunctive syllogism on the right is similarly equivalent to If not-P, then Q; Not-Q; therefore, P (which is an instance of the form *modus tollens*).

The following is an example:

1. Either the Democrats or the Republicans will win a majority of seats in the House of Representatives.

2. But the Republicans will not win a majority of seats in the House of Representatives.

---

3. The Democrats will win a majority of seats in the House of Representatives.

A similar argument type is *constructive dilemma*. A dilemma is a disjunction in which both disjuncts validly imply the same conclusion. Constructive dilemma has the following form:

Constructive dilemma is a deductively valid form of argument that combines conditional assumptions with a disjunction of their antecedents.

> **Constructive Dilemma**
> 1. P or Q
> 2. If P, then R
> 3. If Q, then R
> ---
> 4. R

The following is an example:

1. Either the Democrats or the Republicans will win a majority of seats in the House of Representatives.

2. If the Democrats win a majority of seats in the House of Representatives, then health care for all citizens and the Social Security program can be funded.

3. If the Republicans win a majority of seats in the House of Representatives, then health care for all citizens and the Social Security program can be funded.

---

4. Health care for all citizens and the Social Security program can be funded.

To Check Your Understanding 1.6

Classify each of the following arguments as valid or invalid deductive argument forms. If the argument is valid, briefly explain how and why it satisfies the imagination test; if it is invalid, give the counterexample by means of which you have determined its invalidity.

(1) 1. If you can do a handstand, I'm a monkey's uncle.
     2. I'm not a monkey's uncle.

---

     3. You can't do a handstand.

(2) 1. If you can do a handstand, I'm a monkey's uncle.
   2. You can't do a handstand.
   _____
   3. I'm a monkey's uncle.

(3) 1. If you can do a handstand, I'm a monkey's uncle.
   2. You can do a handstand.
   _____
   3. I'm a monkey's uncle.

(4) 1. If you can do a handstand, I'm a monkey's uncle.
   2. If I'm a monkey's uncle, then I can do a handstand.
   _____
   3. If you can do a handstand, then I can also do a handstand.

(5) 1. Either you can do a handstand or I'm a monkey's uncle.
   2. If you can do a handstand, then I'm a monkey's uncle.
   _____
   3. I'm a monkey's uncle.

(6) 1. I'm no monkey's uncle.
   2. Either you can't do a handstand or I'm a monkey's uncle.
   _____
   3. You can't do a handstand.

■

Reductio ad Absurdum

Reductio ad absurdum is another useful deductively valid form of argument.

In reductio ad absurdum, the negation of the conclusion is assumed, and a contradiction is validly deduced, in order to validly deduce the conclusion.

Another important category of deductive arguments allows us to reason from an assumption that states the negation of what we are trying to prove, reducing it to an absurdity or explicit logical inconsistency or contradiction, in order to prove that the assumption is false. These are arguments in which false propositions are deliberately chosen as assumptions in order to show that accepting them leads to a contradiction.

Arguments of this kind are instances of *indirect proof* or *reductio ad absurdum*. They prove that we must reject an assumption as false on the grounds that if it were true it would reduce to or validly imply a logical contradiction. A *reductio ad absurdum* reduces a false assumption to an absurdity. The definition of deductive validity forbids the valid deduction of false conclusions from true assumptions, and contradictions are logically necessarily false. It follows that if a contradiction is validly implied by an assumption, then the assumption must be false.

Indirect proofs or *reductio ad absurdum* arguments often offer the best demonstrations of a conclusion. This is particularly so where the conclusion is a necessary truth, the denial of which is self-contradictory, or where the denial of the conclusion can be shown to contradict the argument's other assumptions.

Reductio ad Absurdum (Indirect Proof)

1.	P	[Assumption for *reductio*]
2.	Q	[Other given assumption or assumptions]

3.	R and not-R	[Valid deduction of contradiction from 1 and 2]
4.	Not-P	[Valid deduction of negation of *reductio* assumption]

The use of *reductio* reasoning is seen in the following simple argument:

1. Susan will not run for president.   [Assumption for *reductio*]

2. If Susan will not run for president, then Mark will not run for vice president.

3. Mark will run for vice president.

---

4. Mark will not run for vice   [From 1 and 2; contradicts 3]
president.

5. Susan will run for   [From 3 and 4; negation of assumption 1]
president.

Here, the task is to prove the conclusion in proposition 5, that Susan will run for president. We reason indirectly by assuming that the conclusion is false in assumption 1. Along with assumption 2 that if Susan will not run for president, then Mark will not run for vice president, and the assumption that Mark will run for vice president, we conclude in 4 that Mark will not run for vice president, a proposition that contradicts assumption 3. If we accept the truth of 2 and 3, then we can only suppose that the contradiction results from assumption 1. As a consequence, we reject assumption 1 and deduce that it is false by indirect proof or *reductio ad absurdum* in conclusion 5. The deductive grounds for 5 are that if assumption 1 were true, it would lead to the outright logical contradiction in 3 and 4, and that therefore 1 is not true.

A reductio ad absurdum argument *literally reduces an assumption to an absurdity or contradiction.*

Suppose that I want to prove that there is no greatest even number. I assume the opposite of the conclusion I hope to establish by assuming on the contrary that there is a greatest even number. I will call this supposedly greatest even number 'N'. But if N is an even number, no matter how great, I can always obtain an even number greater than N by adding N + 2. Thus, I have reduced the assumption that there is a greatest even number to an absurdity in the form of an outright logical contradiction. N is the greatest even number (by assumption), and N is not the greatest even number (from the fact that N + 2 is an even number greater than N). The argument can be reconstructed as follows:

1. There is a greatest even number, N.   [Assumption for *reductio*]

2. If N is an even number, then N + 2 is an even number greater than N.

---

3. N + 2 is an even number greater than N.   [1, 2]

4. N is the greatest even number.   [From 1; contradicts 5]

5. N is not the greatest even number.   [From 3; contradicts 4]

6. There is no greatest even number.   [Negation of assumption 1]

A related but trickier example is inspired by the philosopher F. P. Ramsey in his posthumous book, *Foundations of Mathematics and Other Logical Essays* (1931). The argument demonstrates that there are at least two persons living on Earth who have precisely the same number of hairs on their heads from the assumption that there are at least two more persons living on Earth than there are hairs on any one person's head.

The reasoning is by *reductio ad absurdum*. We assume, contrary to the argument's conclusion, that it is not the case that there are two persons living on Earth who have precisely the same number of hairs on their heads, but that every person has a different number of hairs on his or her head compared to those of any other person. The assumption that the conclusion of the argument is false is then reduced to an absurdity. If the hairiest person possesses N hairs, and if, as seems reasonable, there are at least two more persons living on Earth than there are hairs on any one person's head, then there are at least N + 2 persons living on Earth. If the person with the fewest hairs is totally bald, then that person has 0 hairs on his or her head, and the hairiest person by our assumptions can have at most (N + 2) − 1 or N + 1 hairs on his or her head. But if every person has a different number of hairs, as we are supposing in assuming for *reductio* sake that the conclusion of Ramsey's argument is false, then one and only one person living on Earth, the hairiest, has precisely N + 1 hairs. This flatly contradicts the previous assumption that the hairiest person has N hairs. Assuming that the conclusion of Ramsey's argument is false, that no two persons have precisely the same number of hairs on their heads but that every person living on Earth has a different number of hairs, together with the assumption that there are at least two more persons living on Earth than there are hairs on any one person's head, reduces to the absurd conclusion that some person has both precisely N and N + 1 hairs or that some person both has precisely N and does not have precisely N hairs. The argument can be reconstructed as follows for comparison with the previous illustration:

Reductio ad absurdum reasoning is often used in mathematical proofs.

1. The hairiest person living on Earth has N hairs on his or her head.

2. There are at least N + 2 persons living on Earth.

3. It is not the case that at least two persons living on Earth have precisely the same number of hairs on their heads; everyone has a different number of hairs.   [Assumption for *reductio*]

4. If there are at least N + 2 persons living on Earth, and if they all have a different number of hairs on their heads, then, if a totally bald person has 0 hairs, then the hairiest person living on Earth has at least (N + 2) − 1 or N + 1 hairs.

5. The hairiest person living on Earth has precisely N hairs on his or her head and the hairiest person living on Earth does not have precisely N (but at least N + 1) hairs on his or her head.   [Contradiction between 1 and 4]

6. At least two persons living on Earth have precisely the same number of hairs on their heads.   [Negation of assumption 3]

Reductio arguments may at first appear to be logically suspect because they draw inferences from false assumptions and, in fact, from assumptions that the arguments are designed to prove are false. However, *reductio* arguments merely hypothesize propositions that later in the proof are shown to be false when they are proven to imply a contradiction or absurdity. Whereas in non-*reductio* arguments the assumptions are accepted both at the beginning and the end of the inference, in *reductio* arguments at least some assumptions are rejected when they are reduced to a contradiction, and their negations are deduced instead.

False propositions are only provisionally assumed for the sake of argument in reduction ad absurdum reasoning.

To Check Your Understanding 1.7 ━━━━━━━━━━━━━━━━━━━━━━━━━━━━━━■

Give a *reductio ad absurdum* proof for the conclusion of Ramsey's argument in the mathematically simpler case in which it is not assumed that someone could be totally bald in the sense of having 0 hairs, and for which as a result there need be only N + 1 more persons living on Earth than there are hairs on any one person's head. Use the new proof to show again under these conditions that there are at least two precisely equally hairy persons living on Earth with precisely the same number of hairs on their heads.

■

Deductive Validity in Complex Arguments

We usually speak of entire arguments as deductively valid or invalid, with no further complications or distinctions. However, it is possible for a single argument with multiple conclusions to contain both deductively valid and deductively invalid inferences. Consider the following example:

1. If nuclear energy is soon abolished, we may still be able to undo the environmental damage that has already occurred from nuclear wastes.

2. We cannot undo the environmental damage that has already occurred from nuclear wastes.

3. Nuclear energy will not soon be abolished.

4. Some environmental damage is not due to nuclear wastes but rather to more conventional energy sources and pollutants.

Complex arguments can combine both deductively valid and deductively invalid inferences.

Conclusion 3 follows deductively from 1 and 2 by *modus tollens*. But conclusion 4 does not deductively follow from any combination of 1–3. The argument as a whole is partly or in one sense deductively valid and partly or in another sense deductively invalid. The argument contains a deductively valid subargument and another deductively invalid subargument. This type of situation often occurs in arguments as they appear in ordinary discourse. We must be on the lookout not to accept an entire argument as deductively valid just because part of it is deductively valid, and we should always be prepared in principle to pronounce an argument partly deductively valid and partly deductively invalid.

To Check Your Understanding 1.8

For each of the following arguments, use the imagination test to determine whether it is deductively valid, deductively invalid, or partly deductively valid and partly deductively invalid; identify deductively valid and deductively invalid parts where they occur together in the same argument; explain your reasons for evaluating the argument as deductively valid or deductively invalid, and describe the counterexamples you imagined in the case of deductively invalid arguments or parts of arguments.

1. The special theory of relativity entails that space–time is a closed finite topological continuum. Physicists and mathematicians the world over agree that space–time is a closed finite topological continuum. Thus, the special theory of relativity is true, and space–time is a closed finite topological continuum.

2. Cayenne peppers are hotter than quadroto d'oros. Thai fingers are hotter than cayennes. Habañero peppers are hotter than quadroto d'oros. Therefore, Thai fingers are hotter than cayennes and habañeros are hotter than cayennes.

3. Senator Snort has been misappropriating discretionary funds in the budget of the subcommittee he chairs for years. The FBI has been

on to him for a long time and is about to complete its investigation with a surprise sting operation involving some reputed gangland figures connected with racketeering and money laundering. The Senate rules clearly state that whoever is guilty of misappropriating funds deserves the highest censure for a serious breach of professional ethics. Senator Snort should therefore be removed from office at once and made to repay whatever he may have stolen from the public trust.

4. Anthropology and the history of European civilization teach us that only polytheistic religions practice as well as preach nonviolence. Christianity, in its devotion to a jealous God and intolerance of other gods, has in its career condoned the most terrible abuses of violence and bloodshed against the unfaithful and in one Christian splinter group against another. Polytheisms, like Hinduism, in contrast promote greater intercultural social harmony, as the history of civilizations during their time of influence unmistakably shows, because they tolerate more diverse kinds of religious worship. From this it seems reasonable to conclude (1) that Christianity is neither polytheistic nor does it practice what it preaches and (2) that polytheisms are morally superior to monotheisms.

5. Van Gogh cut off a piece of his ear to prove his sincere intentions to a woman of Arles. Anyone intense enough to cut off a piece of any part of his or her body to make a point about their feelings to another person is psychologically unbalanced. The sincerity of anyone who is psychologically unbalanced is not to be trusted in any expression of intention. So, Van Gogh was certainly psychologically unbalanced, as his later institutionalization also testifies. For this reason, furthermore, Van Gogh's cutting off a piece of his ear does not constitute a trustworthy expression of his intentions to the woman of Arles—quite the opposite!

6. My car was recently damaged in a hailstorm. The warranty that applies to all moving parts is valid. I can still drive the car, so I guess all the parts are moving parts. That means I'll be able to have all repairs from the hailstorm paid for under warranty.

∎

Soundness

The definition of deductive logical validity stipulates only that when an argument is deductively valid, then *if* its assumptions are true, *then* its conclusions

Not all deductively valid arguments have true assumptions— or conclusions.

logically must also be true. This leaves it open whether or not the assumptions of any given deductively valid argument are in fact true.

The following is an example of a deductively valid argument with (jointly) false assumptions:

1. Whoever is president is chief executive.

2. Mary Lincoln is president.

_____

3. Mary Lincoln is chief executive.

A good deductive argument is not only deductively valid but also sound.

The first assumption is true, but the second assumption and the conclusion are false. The argument nevertheless is deductively valid because if the premises were true, then the conclusion would have to be true. Applying the imagination test for an argument's deductive validity, we find that we cannot imagine a situation in which assumptions 1 and 2 are true but conclusion 3 is false. If we imagine that Mary Lincoln is not chief executive, then either we are not imagining that she is president or we are not imagining that whoever is president is chief executive. However, only the first assumption is true, whereas the second is false; so that, although the argument is deductively valid, its deductively valid form alone does not logically guarantee that its conclusion is true.

A sound argument is deductively valid and has only true assumptions.

We need a technical term to distinguish arguments that are not only deductively valid but also have only true assumptions. We shall say that a *sound argument* is an argument that is both deductively valid and has only true assumptions. Only sound arguments logically guarantee the truth of their conclusions. From the definitions of a deductively valid and sound deductive argument, it follows that a deductively valid argument need not be sound, but that a sound argument must be deductively valid. Every sound argument is both deductively valid and has only true assumptions, thereby guaranteeing that its conclusions are also true. Nevertheless, not every deductively valid argument is sound, as we have seen in the case of Mary Lincoln as president and as chief executive. Clearly, not all deductively valid arguments have true assumptions or conclusions.

The conclusion of a sound argument must be true.

Sound Argument

A *sound argument* is a deductively valid argument with only true assumptions.

Here is a simple analogy to help explain the difference between deductive validity and *soundness*. I have designed two electrical circuits. One is so well constructed that if I were to connect it to a battery or some other source of power, then electricity would flow from one end to the other, lighting the bulb.

The distinction between deductive validity and soundness can be understood by means of an electrical wiring analogy.

The other circuit has some defect so that even if I were to hook it to power, the circuit would not be completed, and the bulb would not light. By analogy, we can agree that the first circuit whose bulb would light if the juice were turned on is like a deductively valid argument, whereas the second, defective, circuit is like a deductively invalid argument. Whether or not electricity is connected to the second circuit, it will not carry power through the circuit to light the bulb. In the case of the first, correctly made circuit, the bulb also does not light unless I turn on the electricity. If power is not connected to the properly made circuit, it is just like a deductively valid but unsound argument. It has the right structure to carry electricity through the circuit to light the bulb, if only it were connected to power. This is analogous to a deductively valid argument's having a logical structure such that if the assumptions were true, then their truth would carry through to the conclusions. But, the circuit is unactivated by an electrical

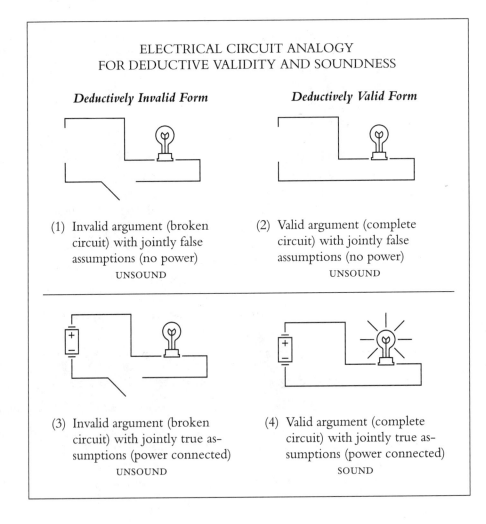

ELECTRICAL CIRCUIT ANALOGY
FOR DEDUCTIVE VALIDITY AND SOUNDNESS

Deductively Invalid Form   **Deductively Valid Form**

(1) Invalid argument (broken circuit) with jointly false assumptions (no power)
UNSOUND

(2) Valid argument (complete circuit) with jointly false assumptions (no power)
UNSOUND

(3) Invalid argument (broken circuit) with jointly true assumptions (power connected)
UNSOUND

(4) Valid argument (complete circuit) with jointly true assumptions (power connected)
SOUND

source, and by analogy the assumptions are not true. The fact that a circuit is correctly made (or an argument deductively valid) does not mean that its bulb lights (that the conclusion of the argument is true); it signifies only that the circuit (argument) is constructed in such a way that if electricity were connected (if the assumptions of the argument were true), then the bulb would light (the conclusion would be true).

Only in case 4 does the lightbulb light (the conclusion of the argument is true) by virtue of having a correct (deductively valid inference) circuit channel for power (truth) from the battery (assumptions) to the lightbulb (conclusion). Note, however, that there can also be unsound arguments with true conclusions but false assumptions, or deductively invalid inferences, which we would have to represent as a complete circuit with a lighted bulb but a broken circuit or no battery attached. We have a new bright idea in deductive reasoning only when the conclusion of a sound deductive argument enlightens us with truth. Yet it is not the business of deductive logic by itself to determine what is or is not true, beyond identifying propositions that because of their logical forms may be logically necessarily true or logically necessarily false. If we want our arguments to guarantee the truth of their conclusions, then we must make sure both that our arguments are structurally correct, which is to say deductively valid, and that our assumptions are true. The search for and verification of true assumptions for use in deductive arguments is largely a matter of scientific and historical inquiry, applying the inductive rules of evidence, and the concept of and criteria for the truth of propositions about the world.

A sound argument is always deductively valid, but not all deductively valid arguments are sound.

The soundness of an argument, as determined by the truth of its assumptions, can not usually be judged by logic alone but by science, history, and other special disciplines concerned with particular matters of fact.

There are distinct categories of evaluation for propositions and arguments.

**CATEGORIES OF EVALUATION
FOR PROPOSITIONS AND ARGUMENTS**

Propositions	*Arguments*
True or false	Deductively valid or invalid
	Sound or unsound

Propositions are true or false; arguments are deductively valid or invalid, sound or unsound.

Finally, we must keep our terminology straight and avoid mistakes in speaking about the properties of arguments and propositions. We say that propositions are true or false, whereas arguments are either deductively valid or invalid, sound or unsound—and never the other way around. It is wrong to say that an entire argument is true or false or that an individual sentence or proposition is deductively valid or invalid or sound or unsound. It is essential that we understand the distinction between deductive validity and soundness and the definitions of deductively valid, invalid, sound, and unsound arguments. Everything to follow in the study of symbolic logic presupposes these fundamental concepts.

┌─■ *Demonstration 3:* **Evaluating Soundness** ■────────┐

PROBLEM: To evaluate an argument for soundness.

ARGUMENT: John Steinbeck lived in California; if John Steinbeck lived in California, then John Steinbeck lived in the United States; hence, John Steinbeck lived in the United States.

STEP 1:   *Identify assumptions and conclusions by inference indicators*
The conclusion is clearly indicated by the inference indicator term 'hence'. The argument asserts a relationship between living in California and living in the United States such that if John Steinbeck lived in California then he lived in the United States, affirms that Steinbeck lived in California, and concludes that therefore Steinbeck lived in the United States.

STEP 2:   *Reconstruct the argument as an ordered line-numbered sequence*
The argument has the following inferential structure:

1. John Steinbeck lived in California.
2. If John Steinbeck lived in California, then John Steinbeck lived in the United States.

---

3. John Steinbeck lived in the United States.

STEP 3:   *Evaluate the reconstructed argument for soundness*
The argument is sound if its logical structure is deductively valid and contains only true assumptions. The inference has the recognizable deductively valid structure of *modus ponens.* So, the question of whether or not the argument is valid depends on whether or not both its assumptions are true. If it is true as we assume that anyone living in California is living in the United States, then if we read a biography of Steinbeck in a reliable source we will discover that Steinbeck did indeed live in Salinas County in California for a part of his life. We can then judge that the argument has a deductively valid logical structure and only true assumptions, which qualifies the argument as sound. If the argument had been deductively invalid, or if any of its assumptions had been false, then the argument would have been unsound.

The following is another example from the history of philosophy, in which the problem of soundness is more complicated:

ARGUMENT: "Every idea is deriv'd from preceding impressions; and we have no impression of self or substance as something simple and individual. We have, therefore, no idea of them in that sense" (Hume, 1739–1740/1978, p. 633).

STEP 1: *Identify assumptions and conclusions by inference indicators*
The conclusion is clearly indicated by the inference indicator term 'therefore'. Hume concludes that we have no idea of the self or substance (as something simple and individual), arguing from the assumptions that every idea originates from sense impressions and that we have no sense impression of the self or substance (as something simple and individual).

STEP 2: *Reconstruct the argument as an ordered line-numbered sequence*
The argument has the following inferential structure:

1. All ideas originate from sense impressions.
2. We have no sense impression of the self or substance (as something simple and individual).

---

3. We have no idea of the self or substance (as something simple and individual).

STEP 3: *Evaluate the reconstructed argument for soundness*
The argument is not obviously unsound. The assumptions are not contradictory, and they have a certain plausibility. We would naturally need to inquire more deeply into the truth of the assumptions in order to definitely conclude that the argument is sound. It is unsettling to realize that we have no idea about something concerning which we have just drawn a very definite conclusion. Do we not have at least enough of an idea about the self or substance to know, according to the argument, that we have no idea of the self or substance? If this is not an outright contradiction, the defense of Hume's position must have something to do with the more technical meaning of 'idea' or the qualification of ideas as originating in simple and individual sense impressions.

To Check Your Understanding 1.9

Answer the following 'yes-or-no' questions; for 'yes' answers, give an example of the kind of argument required to justify your reply:

1. Can a sound argument be deductively invalid?
2. Can a deductively invalid argument be sound?
3. Can a sound argument have a false conclusion?
4. Can an unsound argument be deductively valid?
5. Can an unsound argument have only true assumptions?
6. Can a deductively valid argument have false assumptions?
7. Can a deductively invalid argument have a true conclusion?

To question an argument's soundness by raising doubts concerning the truth of its assumptions is an important element of the critical evaluation of arguments. It is often useful to begin examination of an argument's merits by checking to determine whether it is deductively valid or invalid. If an argument is deductively invalid, then the truth of its conclusions will not be guaranteed by its assumptions, even if they are all true. It is often a more difficult matter to determine whether the content of an argument's assumptions are true or false than it is to decide whether the argument has a valid or invalid deductive form. Deductive validity and invalidity can be informally evaluated by the imagination test and formally, as we shall see, by more mechanical procedures. However, the truth of assumptions often requires us to research facts about the world that can minimally involve a trip to the library and potentially painstaking and time-consuming efforts to confirm or disconfirm their truth by our own laborious historical or scientific detective work that takes us beyond the purely formal resources of symbolic logic.

Summary: Propositions and Arguments

A proposition is a sentence that expresses a complete true or false thought. Propositions propose a true or false assertion about a state of affairs. They must be distinguished from questions or interrogatives and requests, petitions or commands, which are neither true nor false. Arguments are series of propositions that are distinguished as assumptions or conclusions by inference indicators. There are deductive and nondeductive arguments. The logical structure of a deductive argument is such that the truth of its assumptions is supposed to logically necessarily guarantee the truth of its conclusions. A deductively valid argument is such that if its assumptions are true, then its conclusions logically must also be true, or such that it is logically impossible for its assumptions to be true and its conclusions false. We informally evaluate arguments for deductive validity by an imagination test. If we can imagine that the assumptions of an argument are true and the conclusion false, then we have good although imperfect evidence for regarding the argument as deductively invalid and subject to the counterexample we have imagined. If we cannot imagine such a situation, then we have good although imperfect evidence that the argument is deductively valid. There are several commonly encountered types of deductively valid arguments that can be verified by the imagination test and distinguished from similar-appearing deductively invalid types. A sound argument is deductively valid and has only true assumptions. To decide an argument's soundness beyond its deductive validity and logical consistency usually requires a determination of historical or scientific fact.

Key Words

complete thought
sentence
proposition
subject term
predicate term
copula
propositional symbol
negation (of a proposition)
argument
series of propositions
assumption
conclusion
inference indicator term
deductively valid argument
deductively invalid argument
deductive argument
logical contradiction
logically impossible (proposition
  or condition)
logically necessary (proposition
  or condition)
nondeductive argument
inductive argument
statistical reasoning
reconstructed argument

incomplete expression of an
  argument
principle of charity
imagination test for deductive
  validity
conditional argument
antecedent
consequent
modus ponendo ponens
affirming the antecedent
modus tollendo tollens
denying the consequent
logical fallacy
(fallacy of) affirming the consequent
(fallacy of) denying the antecedent
contrapositive
hypothetical syllogism
disjunctive syllogism
constructive dilemma
indirect proof
reductio ad absurdum
limiting cases of validity
sound argument
soundness

Exercises

I: Deductive Argument Concepts   Give a correct concise statement of each of the following concepts; where appropriate give an illustration of each that does not appear in the book.

1. Sentence
2. Proposition
3. Argument
4. Assumption; conclusion
5. Inference indicator
6. Deductively valid argument
7. *Modus ponens; modus tollens;* hypothetical syllogism

8. Disjunctive syllogism; constructive dilemma

9. *Reductio ad absurdum*

10. Sound argument

II: *Propositions, Interrogatives, and Imperatives* For each of the following sentences without punctuation, decide whether the sentence is most naturally interpreted as a proposition, interrogative (question), or imperative (petition or command); in the case of ambiguity, indicate whether and how the sentence might be used in expressing more than one of these.

1. Would you shut the window

2. Would you kindly shut the window

3. Can anyone doubt the sincerity and good intentions of our mayor

4. No one has ever doubted the sincerity and good intentions of our mayor

5. If you go to the store, could you get me some eggs

6. You might pick up some eggs when you go to the store

7. Does anyone know who discovered America

8. When you return from the lake, you will lock up the boathouse

9. Would you help me clean the aquarium

10. Do not forget that the diagonal of a square is always an irrational number

III: *Deductive Validity* Use the imagination test to determine whether each of the following arguments is deductively valid or invalid. In the case of deductively valid arguments, indicate whether or not the argument is a limiting case of deductive validity; in the case of deductively invalid arguments, briefly describe the counterexample you have imagined.

(1) **1.** All whales are cetaceans.

 2. All cetaceans are mammals.

 _____

 3. All whales are mammals.

(2) **1.** If spring is here, summer cannot be far behind.

 2. Summer is not far behind.

 _____

 3. Spring is here.

(3) **1.** Texas is the biggest state in the USA.

 2. Alaska is also the biggest state in the USA.

 _____

 3. Rhode Island is the smallest state in the USA.

(4) **1.** Philip will either go to law school or not go to law school.

    2. Philip will either go to medical school or not go to medical school.

    3. Philip will either go to law school or medical school.

(5) **1.** If physics does not provide the answers to all human problems, then either some discipline other than physics is needed for educated decision making or the methodology of traditional physics must be modified to account for nonphysical phenomena.

    2. There are human problems about the nature of the soul and freedom of the will for which physics does not provide satisfactory answers.

    3. The methodology of traditional physics cannot be modified to account for nonphysical phenomena.

    4. Some discipline other than physics is needed for educated decision making.

(6) **1.** Some business tycoons are excellent athletes.

    2. Some professional basketball players are marketing executives.

    3. Marketing executives cannot both be professional basketball players and not be professional basketball players.

(7) **1.** A candle burns brighter when the oxygen content in a room is increased.

    2. This candle is not burning brighter.

    3. The oxygen content in the room has not been increased.

(8) **1.** The ancient Egyptians practiced mummification rites to ensure the awakening of the soul as a return to the body in an afterlife.

    2. Mummification preserves parts of the body from total decay for long periods of time.

    3. Surviving death and awakening to an afterlife in a return to the body requires that the body be perfectly preserved in its entirety for an unlimited unpredetermined length of time.

    4. Egyptian mummification rites do not ensure the awakening of the soul as a return to the body in an afterlife.

(9) **1.** If you drink either coffee or tea, you can stay alert while solving logic problems.

    2. You cannot drink coffee.

    3. If you are going to stay alert while solving logic problems, you must drink tea.

(10) **1.** The movies create a fantasy world of diversion from everyday difficulties.

    2. When you get involved in the plot, characters, and atmosphere of a good movie, you enter imaginatively into the fantasy world the movie creates.

    3. Sometimes movies pose special difficulties of their own that become our personal difficulties if we become overly concerned about them.

    4. If we see movies every day, and if the movies we happen to see also present difficulties that become our personal difficulties when we become overly concerned about them, then the movies merely present new or additional everyday difficulties.

    5. The movies do not necessarily divert us from all everyday difficulties, except by presenting new or different everyday difficulties.

IV: Validity and Soundness   Critically evaluate the following arguments for validity and soundness.

(1) **1.** If God is good, then there is no suffering in the world.

    2. There is no suffering in the world.

    3. God is good.

(2) **1.** We cannot go to Newport unless we fix the car.

    2. We cannot fix the car unless we buy an air filter.

    3. We cannot buy an air filter unless we go to Newport.

    4. We cannot go to Newport unless we go to Newport.

(3) **1.** One day, all political prisoners will be freed.

    2. Political prisoners are those who are unjustly imprisoned for their political beliefs or activity.

    3. If we work together with international amnesty organizations, we can bring it about that, at some point in the future, no one will be unjustly imprisoned for his or her political beliefs or activity.

    4. At some point in the future, no one will be imprisoned for his or her political beliefs or activity.

(4) **1.** The legal drinking age should be lowered to 18 because young people have proved that they can use alcohol responsibly and, like adults, shouldn't as individuals be punished for the misdeeds of others who hap-

pen to belong to their same age group and who, again like adults, might use alcohol irresponsibly.

2. Eighteen is a reasonable age to set for legal drinking. This is also the age at which young people can vote and can be inducted into the military, possibly to die for their country. Can this be permitted for persons who in their brief brave lives have never had the opportunity legally to taste a beer?

3. The legal drinking age should be lowered to 18.

(5) 1. We should encourage developing nations to improve their economies with ecologically sustainable agriculture and industry.

2. If we want to contribute to a global ecological disaster and make developing nations indefinitely dependent on handouts from wealthier nations, then we should not encourage developing nations to improve their economies with ecologically sustainable agriculture and industry.

3. We shall not contribute to a global ecological disaster and make developing nations indefinitely dependent on handouts from wealthier nations.

(6) 1. An intelligent reader needs to be able to distinguish propaganda from reasonable argument intended as open-minded inquiry.

2. Propaganda often comes disguised in the form of what appears to be a reasonable argument.

3. If you are an intelligent reader, then you must find a way to know the difference between reasonable argument and propaganda (or, for that matter, irony or humor) disguised in the form of apparently reasonable argument.

(7) 1. We need to locate water and firewood to cook dinner.

2. We can locate water to cook dinner if we can find trees to cut firewood.

3. We can find trees to cut firewood if we can locate water to cook dinner.

4. We can find trees to cut firewood if we need to cook dinner.

5. We can locate water if we need to cook dinner.

(8) 1. The corn will suffer if there is too much sun.

2. There will not be too much sun.

3. The corn will not suffer, and there will not be too much sun.

(9) **1.** The mountains always have wildflowers growing on them.

2. Wildflowers are also sometimes in the valley.

---

3. When there are no wildflowers in the valley, we are sure to find them on the mountain.

(10) **1.** You should never judge a book by its cover.

2. Many books are uninterestingly packaged but contain important and fascinating reading matter.

---

3. If you want to find books with important and fascinating reading matter, you should not choose them merely on the basis of their external packaging.

V: Identifying Argument Types   Identify each of the following arguments as *modus ponens, modus tollens,* hypothetical syllogism, disjunctive syllogism, *reductio ad absurdum,* or none of the above. If an argument is none of the types named, indicate whether or not it is an instance of the fallacy of affirming the consequent or denying the antecedent.

(1) **1.** Alex will arrive either on Monday or Tuesday.

2. Alex will not arrive on Tuesday.

---

3. Alex will arrive on Monday.

(2) **1.** Switzerland plans to join the United European Council.

2. If Switzerland plans to join the United European Council, then Switzerland will renounce its constitutional military neutrality.

3. Switzerland will never renounce its constitutional military neutrality.

---

4. Switzerland will renounce its constitutional military neutrality.

5. Switzerland does not plan to join the United European Council.

(3) **1.** If her fingerprints were on the murder weapon, then the defendant was definitely at the scene of the crime.

2. But, according to the prosecution's own expert testimony, the defendant's fingerprints were not on the murder weapon.

---

3. The defendant was not at the scene of the crime.

(4) **1.** If arc A subtends line B, then line B bisects line C.

2. If line B bisects line C, then angle D sweeps arc A.

---

3. If arc A subtends line B, then angle D sweeps arc A.

(5) **1.** If this chemical solution is an acid, it will turn the test reagent pink.

    2. This chemical solution is an acid.

---

    3. This chemical solution will turn the test reagent pink.

(6) **1.** If you had wanted to go scuba diving, you would have brought your tank, mask, belt, and flippers.

    2. You brought your mask and flippers but not your tank and belt.

---

    3. You do not want to go scuba diving.

(7) **1.** If Agent X and the Count d'Lambert were identical, then Count d'Lambert would have had to have been in Austria in April.

    2. But Count d'Lambert was in New York City in April, not in Austria.

---

    3. Agent X and the Count d'Lambert are not identical: not in fact the same person but rather two different men.

(8) **1.** There are no prime numbers evenly divisible by 2.

    2. 2 is a prime number (a number evenly divisible only by 1 and itself).

    3. 2 is evenly divisible by 2.

---

    4. Some prime numbers are evenly divisible by 2.

(9) **1.** If the blue team captures the fort, then the red team will surrender to the yellow team.

    2. Either the blue team or the gray team will capture the fort.

    3. The yellow team has already surrendered to the blue team.

    4. If a team surrenders to any other team, then no team can surrender to it.

---

    5. The gray team will capture the fort.

(10) **1.** If universal doubt were logically possible, then persons could doubt their own existence.

    2. No persons can doubt their own existence.

---

    3. Universal doubt is logically impossible.

VI: Short Answer Questions for Philosophical Reflection

1. Is all meaning propositional? Do questions and commands have nonpropositional meanings, or are they absolutely lacking in meaning? What sort of meaning might they have?

2. Can a valid argument with only true conclusions be unsound? If so, give an example; if not, why not?

3. Can a circular argument, in which the conclusion simply repeats one of the assumptions, be deductively invalid? If so, give an example; if not, why not?

4. Can the truth of an argument's assumptions as well as its validity depend on the argument's form in addition to the content of its assumptions? Can the validity of an argument depend on the content of its assumptions and/or conclusions as well as its form? Why or why not?

5. How can we critically evaluate the soundness of two incompatible arguments when there is a controversy about the truth of the conclusions that each of the conflicting arguments purports to prove?

6. What is the value of a valid deductive argument if deduction merely derives and rearranges the consequences of an argument's assumptions that, in this sense, if we accept the argument, only express what we already believe ourselves to know?

Part 2

Propositional Logic

The utility of Logic is a matter which concerns its bearings upon the student, and the training it may give for other purposes. This logical training consists of the exercise in thinking which the student has to undergo (this science is the thinking of thinking): and in the fact that he stores his head with thoughts, in their native unalloyed character. It is true that Logic, being the absolute form of truth, and another name for abstract truth itself, is something more than merely useful. Yet if what is noblest, most liberal and most independent is also most useful, Logic has some claim to the latter character.

— G.W.F. Hegel, *The Science of Logic* (1812–1816)

We are now ready to begin exploring symbolic logic. Abstract symbols replace entire propositions and logical terms within propositions and arguments in order to emphasize their formal logical structures. We divide symbolic logic into two main systems, propositional and predicate logic. The topic of the next four chapters concerns propositional logic, with predicate logic reserved for Part Three. Predicate logic presupposes and is built on propositional logic. Therefore, the study of propositional logic in this part is fundamental in everything to follow. We first articulate the syntax and semantics, or exact principles of the logical symbolism and its interpretation, of propositional logic. Then we learn two decision methods, truth tables and truth trees, by which we test propositions and arguments for certain logical properties. Finally, we develop a system of rules for rigorously proving all logically true propositions and deductively valid arguments in propositional logic. Along the way, we investigate how logic can be applied to problems of reasoning in ordinary contexts and in philosophy, science, history, and other special disciplines.

CHAPTER TWO

Propositional Syntax and Semantics

All abstract sciences are nothing but the study of relations between signs.
—Denis Diderot, *D'Alembert's Dream* (1830)

THE SYNTAX OF PROPOSITIONAL LOGIC is its formal symbolism for representing propositions and arguments. The semantics of propositional logic explains the meaning of propositions and the deductive validity or invalidity of arguments by assigning precise truth functional interpretations to its syntax.

Propositional Logic

Propositional logic has a distinctive syntax and semantics.

The syntax of logic is its terms and well-formed formulas (wffs).

Propositional logic is a formal theory of propositions and arguments. We distinguish between the logic's *syntax* and *semantics*. Syntax is the alphabet of symbols and *well-formed formulas* (wffs) that are constructed from other symbols according to definite rules. Semantics is the exact formal interpretation by which meaning is assigned to syntax. We symbolize propositions in order to clarify their logical structures and, in later chapters, to make use of formal methods for determining the logical properties of propositions and arguments and to rigorously prove logically true propositions and deductively valid arguments.

Syntax of Propositional Logic

The syntax of logic consists of propositional symbols and propositional connectives.

There are five propositional connectives: negation, conjunction, disjunction, conditional, and biconditional.

The basic syntax of propositional logic can be divided into three categories: *propositional symbols, propositional connectives,* and *parentheses.* These are combined in specific ways to determine what we may alternatively describe as the logic's propositions, or wffs.

Propositions are either *atomic* or *propositionally complex.* Atomic propositions in propositional logic are individual propositional symbols such as 'P', 'Q', and 'R'. Atomic propositions are combined to produce propositionally complex propositions by means of five propositional connectives. The propositional connectives are *negation* (~; not), *conjunction* (&; and), *disjunction* (∨; or), *conditional* (⊃; if then), and *biconditional* (≡; if and only if). Atomic propositions can also be described as those that do not contain any of the propositional connectives and are absolutely simplest in their propositional logical forms, whereas propositionally complex propositions contain at least one of the propositional connectives.

Propositional symbols are single letters of the alphabet that within an application unambiguously abbreviate a single proposition. Instead of writing out the entire sentence, 'Now is the time for all good persons to come to the aid of their country', we simply write 'P'. It is standard, as we have seen, to use letters 'P', 'Q', 'R', etc. as propositional symbols. However, we can also introduce special symbols that have *mnemonic* or memory-aid value by calling to mind a key word in the proposition being abbreviated. If we are to substitute a propositional symbol for the proposition, 'It is raining', we might choose 'R' rather than 'P' to help us to remember that the proposition has something to do with rain. If we are substituting a propositional symbol for the proposition, 'My dog has fleas', we might use 'D' to recall the key word 'dog' in the proposition or 'F' to recall the key word 'fleas'.

Indefinitely many propositional symbols can be defined, including those with mnemonic or memory-aid value.

We may need indefinitely many propositional symbols if there are indefinitely many propositions. We should expect there to be indefinitely many propositions because there are indefinitely many things to say about the world, and especially about large sets of objects such as the numbers that continue the series 1, 2, 3, ... We can equip our propositional logic with as many propositional symbols as needed simply by subscripting any choice of propositional symbols with different numbers, as in P_1, P_2, P_3, . . . , Q_1, Q_2, Q_3, . . . , R_1, R_2, R_3, . . . , etc. In practice, however, we seldom need more than a handful of propositional symbols. By definition, it follows that all propositional symbols are atomic wffs.

Propositional Connectives

The syntax of propositional logic allows us to build up propositionally complex wffs by combining atomic propositions by means of propositional connectives. There are five standard propositional connectives. All are variously expressed in ordinary language, and we can recognize them at once from everyday discourse. We introduce special formal signs to symbolize connectives.

SYMBOLIC PROPOSITIONAL CONNECTIVES

Connective	*Category*	*Construction*	*Symbol*
Not	Negation (~)	Not-P	~P
And	Conjunction (&)	P and Q	P & Q
Or (inclusive)	Disjunction (∨)	P or Q	P ∨ Q
If then	Conditional (⊃)	If P then Q	P ⊃ Q
If and only if	Biconditional (≡)	P if and only if Q	P ≡ Q

We shall explain the meaning and use of these connectives later. Here, we consider only how atomic wffs combine syntactically with propositional connectives to produce propositionally complex wffs.

By combining propositional symbols with propositional connectives, we construct an unlimited number of wffs of any desired length or complexity. However, not any and every combination of symbols is a wff. We must now present rules whereby propositionally complex wffs are constructed out of propositionally simpler, ultimately atomic, wffs. The rules for propositional wffs are stated by means of *propositional variables*. The propositional symbol 'P' abbreviates a particular proposition, such as 'It is raining'. The propositional variable '$\mathbb{P}$' more generally represents any atomic or propositionally complex wff, P, Q, R, ~P, P & Q, P ⊃ Q, etc.

Propositional symbols can be designated generally by propositional variables.

RULES FOR WELL-FORMED FORMULAS (WFFS) OF PROPOSITIONAL LOGIC

1. The propositional symbols P, Q, R, . . . are wffs.
2. $\mathbb{P}$ is a wff if and only if ($\mathbb{P}$) is a wff.
3. If $\mathbb{P}$ is a wff, then ~$\mathbb{P}$ is a wff.
4. If $\mathbb{P}$ and $\mathbb{Q}$ are wffs, then $\mathbb{P}$ & $\mathbb{Q}$ is a wff.

5. If $\mathbb{P}$ and $\mathbb{Q}$ are wffs, then $\mathbb{P} \vee \mathbb{Q}$ is a wff.
6. If $\mathbb{P}$ and $\mathbb{Q}$ are wffs, then $\mathbb{P} \supset \mathbb{Q}$ is a wff.
7. If $\mathbb{P}$ and $\mathbb{Q}$ are wffs, then $\mathbb{P} \equiv \mathbb{Q}$ is a wff.
8. Nothing else is a wff.

The well-formed formulas (wffs) of propositional logic are defined by definite rules.

Negation is a unary propositional connective; conjunction, disjunction, conditional, and the biconditional are binary propositional connectives.

We construct complex propositions in propositional logic by combining propositional symbols with propositional connectives in specific ways. We can negate any proposition, P, thereby denying what it says, by attaching to it the negation sign or tilde '~', to produce ~P. Negation is the only *unary* propositional connective, attaching to a single propositional symbol. We can also connect any two propositions together, regardless of their length or internal complexity, by means of any of the remaining *binary* propositional connectives. Thus, we can form the propositions P & Q, R ∨ S, P ⊃ Q, and R ≡ S. We can continue linking these together by propositional connectives to form even more complex propositions.

We apply the formation rules by uniformly substituting any wff we choose for every occurrence of a propositional variable wherever the variable occurs in a given rule. In principle, there is no limit to the complex sentences we can fashion out of simpler propositions by means of propositional connectives. As we do so, it becomes more important to avoid confusion in understanding how simpler wffs are supposed to be combined together by the connectives in a complex wff. Otherwise, it will not be clear which wffs are supposed to be connected by which propositional connectives. The wffs rules accordingly require a clear method of disambiguating propositional connectives. For this purpose, we first define the concept of the *scope of a propositional connective*. The idea is that a propositional connective combines only certain definite wffs, which are said to fall within its scope. The scope of a propositional connective is the propositionally least complex wff in which the propositional connective occurs. If we consider the wff P ⊃ ~Q, for example, the negation (~) has only wff Q in its scope, whereas the conditional (⊃) has the entire wff P ⊃ ~Q in its scope. The definition states:

The scope of a propositional connective is the least complex wff in which it occurs.

Scope of a Propositional Connective
The *scope* of a propositional connective is the propositionally least complex wff in which the propositional connective occurs.

To avoid ambiguity in the scope of multiple propositional connectives in the same propositionally complex wff, we now add the following parentheses requirement for punctuating the scopes of connectives:

> PARENTHESES REQUIREMENT
> FOR PROPOSITIONAL WFFS RULES
>
> To avoid ambiguity of scope in propositionally complex wffs containing multiple propositional connectives, where a wff to be uniformly substituted for a propositional variable in the application of the wffs rule is itself propositionally complex, we enclose it in parentheses before making the substitution, unless it already contains a negation as its main connective.

The wffs rules for propositional logic are implemented under a parentheses requirement.

The parentheses requirement prevents applications of the wffs rules from producing logically ambiguous sentences such as P ⊃ R & S, P ∨ Q ⊃ R ⊃ S, and P ≡ Q ⊃ R & S ∨ ~P. These constructions are not wffs of logic because they do not assert any definite propositional connection among their component propositional symbols. In the first case, for example, there is no way to know whether P ⊃ (R & S) or (P ⊃ R) & S is being asserted, and this is also true in related cases. By observing the parentheses requirement in following the wffs rules, we can obtain, for example, the following well-formed formulas of propositional logic: P ⊃ Q, R ⊃ S, P ⊃ (R & S), (P ∨ Q) ⊃ (R ⊃ S), and (P ≡ Q) ⊃ (R & (S ∨ ~P)).

The exception by which wffs containing negation as a main connective are not first enclosed in parentheses is made in order to avoid adding parentheses that are not needed to disambiguate the scopes of other connectives. There is no harm done if the exception is not observed. In this case, we would obtain as wffs such formulas as ~(~P), ~(~(~P)), and so on by applying ~P to wffs rule 2, under an exceptionless parentheses requirement, instead of ~~P and ~~~P, or we would obtain P & (~(P & Q)) by applying ~(P & Q) to wffs rule 3, under a similarly exceptionless parentheses requirement, instead of the simpler but equally correct sentence, P & ~(P & Q). The fact that negation is a unary propositional connective prevents ambiguities of scope from arising when negated wffs are substituted for propositional variables in implementing the wffs rules to produce more complex wffs so that the parentheses requirement in such applications is unnecessary.

The parentheses requirement for propositional wffs avoids ambiguities in the scopes of propositional connectives.

When we use propositional connectives, we avoid ambiguity in the resulting expressions by placing parentheses around the complex propositions we wish to stand as units. For the sample propositions discussed previously, we can do this in several ways to construct more complex propositions, including (P ⊃ Q) ∨ (R & S), ((P ⊃ Q) ∨ (R & S)) ∨ (P ⊃ Q), ((P ⊃ Q) ∨ R) & S, and P ⊃ (Q ∨ (R & S)). We can make similar combinations by using conjunction, the conditional, or the biconditional instead of disjunction, and we could make any of these more complicated by negating the entire resulting formula or selected propositional subunits within it, as in ~(~(P ⊃ Q) ∨ ~R) & ~S. Each of these combinations produces a different proposition, with potential differences in their truth or falsehood. Parentheses group propositions together in an obvious way as propositional subunits within a larger, more complex proposition.

The wffs rules forbid nonsensical combinations of symbols.

The formation rules forbid nonsensical syntax combinations. Juxtapositions of propositional symbols such as PQ, Q~, P~Q, &P, P∨, ⊃Q, ≡~Q, and ⊃P)~((⊃ are not wffs because they are not substitution instances of any of the wffs specified by the eight wffs rules under the parentheses requirement. As a result, none of these symbol clusters is true or false, and none symbolizes a proposition as a true or false sentence. All wffs are propositions, but propositions are wffs of symbolic propositional logic only insofar as they are constructed by the rules for wffs under the parentheses requirement. The use of parentheses to punctuate the logical structures of propositional wffs will be discussed in more detail when we discuss the translation of complex propositions into symbolic logic.

There are different notations for representing propositional connectives in alternative systems of propositional logic.

There are variations in the symbolization of propositional connectives in different presentations of standard propositional logic. The negation is sometimes symbolized as a short dash or hyphen, as in '−P', or by the designer negation sign, '¬P'. The conjunction is alternatively symbolized by the caret '∧' or by a dot '·'. The conditional can also be symbolized by an arrow, as in 'P → Q', and the biconditional by the double arrow, 'P ↔ Q'. The symbols we have chosen are widely but not universally used. Although in our system we shall make use exclusively of symbols for propositional connectives indicated in the chart, we should be aware that the previously mentioned alternatives and other, even more unusual, formalisms are also sometimes used by logicians for expressing propositional relations.

■ *Demonstration 4:*   **Identifying Propositional Components** ■

PROBLEM: To find the atomic propositions out of which a more complex proposition is constructed.

PROPOSITION: "The contribution of the protons is positive and that of the electrons negative, and if these objects are never created or destroyed alone then the total charge will be conserved" (Feynman, 1965, p. 61).

STEP 1:   *Identify all propositional connectives*
The sentence contains several propositional connectives—'not', 'and', 'or', and 'if-then'. It is useful to underline or draw circles or boxes around these,

thereby highlighting the remaining propositional components for better identification. This is done by rewriting the sentence as follows:

The contribution of the protons is positive <u>and</u> that of the electrons negative, <u>and if</u> these objects are <u>never</u> created <u>or</u> destroyed alone <u>then</u> the total charge will be conserved.

STEP 2: *List out remaining propositional components*
Taking the propositional components that remain when the propositional connectives have been identified, we get a first approximation to the final list by writing down the fragments of propositions connected together in the sentence. Some of these will be incomplete and not make sense until we have edited them in the final step of reconstructing the argument.

1. The contribution of the protons is positive.
2. That of the electrons negative.
3. These objects are . . . created alone.
4. Destroyed alone.
5. The total charge will be conserved.

STEP 3: *Final edit the propositional components as complete propositions*
Propositions 1 and 5 are already complete. Some fragments connected together by propositional connectives identified in step 2 need only be completed by grammatical rules; others may require deeper insight into the exact meaning of Feynman's complex proposition about microparticle physics. The final list looks as follows:

1. The contribution of the protons is positive.
2. The contribution of the electrons is negative.
3. The protons and electrons are at some time created alone.
4. The protons and electrons are at some time destroyed alone.
5. The total charge will be conserved.

In this identification of propositional components of the sentence, 'never' is treated as the negation of 'ever' or 'at some time'. The intent is to interpret Feynman's term 'never' as equivalent in meaning to 'not ever' or 'not at any time'.

To Check Your Understanding 2.1 ■

Construct six propositionally complex propositions out of the following component propositions using any combination you like of the propositional connectives 'not', 'and', 'or', 'if then', 'if and only if': It is raining; I wish I were in Dixie; Someday scientists will discover extraterrestrial life; My car needs a tune-up; The sidewalks are wet; Space exploration is inadequately funded; I hope I win the trip to Hawaii; My car needs a valve job.

■

Truth Table Semantics

The five propositional connectives are interpreted by truth table definitions.

Propositional connectives are truth functions.

A function converts particular input values to particular output values.

We already have a good working knowledge of the syntax of propositional logic. The syntax consists of propositional symbols and the propositionally complex wffs that can be constructed by means of the propositional connectives and parentheses according to the logic's formation rules. We now explain how propositions and arguments are formally interpreted in the logic's semantics.

A proposition as a true or false sentence has a *truth value* of being true or being false. Symbolic logic defines all five propositional connectives as *truth functions*. To say that a propositional connective is a truth function is to say that the truth or falsehood of a propositionally complex wff is logically determined by the truth values of its constituent propositions, according to the definitions of the propositional connectives by which they are combined. We can think of a function as a kind of machine that converts a certain input to a certain output. Here, the input is the truth values of the wffs that are linked together by the propositional connectives. The propositional connectives are truth functions that accept the truth values of the wffs they combine as input and produce as output the truth values of the propositionally complex wffs in which they occur.

For example, the truth value of the conjunctive wff P & Q is determined by the truth functional definition of the conjunction '&'. The truth function '&' converts the truth values of the component atomic wffs P and Q into the truth value of the propositionally complex wff P & Q. As demonstrated later, conjunction '&' is so defined that P & Q is true if and only if both P is true and Q is true. In other words, the value 'true' (T) is given as output by the truth function, '&', if and only if both P is true (T) and Q is true (T). Otherwise, if the truth value 'false' (F) is given as input to truth function '&' as the value of either P or Q, the function produces the truth value 'false' (F) as its output. Similarly, the truth value of the conditional wff P ⊃ Q is determined by the truth functional definition of the conditional propositional connective '⊃'. This truth function converts the truth values of atomic wffs P and Q into the truth value of the propositionally complex wff P ⊃ Q. The conditional '⊃', in contrast with the conjunction '&', is so defined that P ⊃ Q is true if and only if either P is false or Q is true. That is, the value 'true' (T) is given as output by the truth function '⊃' if and only if the function receives as input either the truth value 'false' (F) for P or the truth value 'true' (T) for Q.

The following diagram illustrates the concept of the propositional connectives as truth functions. It offers a preview of the complete truth functional definitions of all five propositional connectives.

PROPOSITIONAL CONNECTIVES AS TRUTH FUNCTIONS

Input $\longmapsto$	*Propositional Connective*	$\longmapsto$ *Output*
(Truth values of component wffs)	$(\sim, \&, \vee, \supset, \equiv)$	(Truth value of complex wff)

Example:

P is true (T); Q is false (F)		
	$\sim$P	$\sim$P is false (F)
	$\sim$Q	$\sim$Q is true (T)
	P & Q	P & Q is false (F)
	P $\vee$ Q	P $\vee$ Q is true (T)
	P $\supset$ Q	P $\supset$ Q is false (F)
	P $\equiv$ Q	P $\equiv$ Q is false (F)

Propositional connectives as truth functions convert particular input truth values of the propositional symbols in a complex wff to a particular output truth value of the wff as a whole.

We shall next explain the truth functional definitions of all five propositional connectives and then discuss their occurrence in ordinary thought and discourse. Then we will be able to translate propositions and arguments from colloquial expressions into propositional logic as the first step in analyzing logical structures by formal symbolic devices.

Wffs constructed from or translated into atomic propositional symbols by means of propositional connectives and parentheses have the meanings we assign them as abbreviations for propositions in ordinary language. The English interpretation of propositional symbol 'R' could be 'It is raining', 'If it is raining then flowers will bloom', or anything else we decide that it should mean. Similarly, but more specifically, the symbolic propositional connectives $\sim$, &, $\vee$, $\supset$, $\equiv$ mean whatever the connectives mean in ordinary English in the variety of expressions that are symbolized as negation, conjunction, disjunction, conditional, and biconditional ('not', 'and', 'or', 'if then', 'if and only if'). To interpret the meaning of propositional connectives and propositional wffs by

associating them with English words and sentences provides an *informal semantics* for the logic. However, an informal semantics is somewhat unsatisfying because it presupposes that we already know exactly what we mean by the connectives in ordinary English. We give a more precise interpretation of the
propositional connectives as truth functions, and of the wffs and arguments they
are used to construct, in the form of *truth tables*.

A truth table organizes the inputs and outputs of truth values that define
a particular propositional connective as a truth function. Truth table definitions
of the propositional connectives begin with an array of T's and F's for each of

the possible assignments of truth values (true and false) to component wffs. A
propositionally complex wff is then assigned a definite truth value (T or F) for
each combination of truth values of its component wffs. The correlation of possible combinations of truth values of component wffs with the complex wffs
that contain them defines the propositional connectives by which wffs are truth
functionally related. The following is an example of a truth table definition for
any generalized propositional connective, which could be specified for ∼, &, ∨,
⊃, or ≡, represented by '⊗':

$\mathbb{P}$	$\mathbb{Q}$	$\mathbb{P} \otimes \mathbb{Q}$
T	T	T or F
T	F	T or F
F	T	T or F
F	F	T or F

We define every particular propositional connective by choosing whether
its output truth value is to be either T or F for each combination of input truth
values to the component wffs it combines. Thus, if ⊗ is '&', $\mathbb{P} \otimes \mathbb{Q}$ has truth
value 'T' only in the first truth table row, where $\mathbb{P}$ and $\mathbb{Q}$ both have truth value
'T', and in every other truth table row it has truth value 'F'. This combination
of input and output truth values in the truth table for '&', as explained later, is
then the truth table definition for conjunction, &. This is also true for the other
propositional connectives with different specific combinations of input and output truth values. We now introduce truth table definitions for each of the five
propositional connectives and explain their intuitive meaning and the reasons
why they are so defined.

Negation

The definition of negation ('not') can be given in terms of the two possible cases
of truth value assignments to proposition $\mathbb{P}$, which in propositional semantics
could be either true (T) or false (F).

NEGATION

$\mathbb{P}$	$\sim\mathbb{P}$
T	F
F	T

The truth table defines the meaning of the negation symbol '$\sim$' or, as we also say, provides the truth table interpretation or *truth table semantics* of the propositional connective. There are only two cases to consider in this definition since we are supposing that a proposition is either true or false. The negation attaches to a single wff, reversing its truth value from T to F and F to T.

Negation reverses the truth value of a wff.

We negate a proposition such as 'Roses are red' by attaching the connective *not* (or its equivalent). By negating 'Roses are red', we obtain, grammatically, '[It is] not [the case that] roses are red'. The effect of applying negation to a proposition is to make another more complex proposition with the opposite truth value as the proposition we have negated. If it is true that 'Roses are red', then it is false that 'It is not the case that roses are red'. If it is false that roses are red, then it is true that it is not the case that roses are red. We can negate any proposition to produce another proposition as the negation of the first. We can also do this iteratively, repeatedly adding negation to negation, to express the proposition that it is not the case that it is not the case that it is not the case that roses are red, and so on, indefinitely. Try negating and iteratively negating the following propositions: 'The window is closed', 'Picasso is famous', 'Seabiscuit is the fastest racehorse', 'I am leaving today', 'Mark Twain is an American novelist'. What happens to the meaning and the truth value of a proposition when we negate it? What happens when we negate it again?

Conjunction

Conjunction is true only when both conjuncts are true, and it is otherwise false.

Here, we define conjunction ('and'). Whenever we conjoin two propositions, we are claiming that both propositions connected by the truth function are true.

CONJUNCTION

$\mathbb{P}$	$\mathbb{Q}$	$\mathbb{P}$ & $\mathbb{Q}$
T	T	T
T	F	F
F	T	F
F	F	F

The truth table definition of &, like the remaining three connectives ∨, ⊃, and ≡, but unlike negation ~, is a binary rather than unary propositional connective. The definitions of these connectives require a total of four cases of possible truth value inputs to the two component wffs they connect. For any two wffs $\mathbb{P}$ and $\mathbb{Q}$ connected by &, ∨, ⊃, or ≡, it is possible for both $\mathbb{P}$ and $\mathbb{Q}$ to be true (T), for $\mathbb{P}$ to be true (T) and $\mathbb{Q}$ false (F), for $\mathbb{P}$ to be false (F) and $\mathbb{Q}$ true (T), or for both $\mathbb{P}$ and $\mathbb{Q}$ to be false (F). The general formula for calculating the number of possible truth value combinations for any number n of propositional symbols to be considered in any truth table is 2^n (2 to the nth power or 2 multiplied by itself n times). To define the four binary propositional connectives in truth table semantics, as the truth table for & already shows, we need exactly $2^2 = 4$ cases or combinations of input truth values.

Conjunction builds complex wffs out of simpler ones, which are the conjuncts of the resulting conjunction. If I say, 'It is snowing and the sun is shining', however improbable a meteorological event this may be, I am committing myself to the truth of both of the propositions the conjunction contains. I am saying that it is true that it is snowing *and* it is true that the sun is shining. If either one and certainly if both of these propositions should turn out to be false, then the entire conjunction I have uttered is false. A conjunction is true, in other words, if and only if all of its conjuncts are true, whereas if at least one of the conjuncts is false, then the whole conjunction is false.

We can iteratively apply conjunction repeatedly to a proposition, much as we do in constructing iterated negations, to produce more complex conjunctions. Thus, we can combine the previous proposition with others to obtain 'It is snowing and it is snowing' or 'It is snowing and it is snowing and it is snowing'. In combination with our first propositional connective, we can also conjoin negations of propositions and negate conjunctions of propositions.

Disjunction

Disjunction ('or') is logically weaker than conjunction. It is defined by the following truth table:

DISJUNCTION		
$\mathbb{P}$	$\mathbb{Q}$	$\mathbb{P} \vee \mathbb{Q}$
T	T	T
T	F	T
F	T	T
F	F	F

Disjunction is true when any of its disjuncts is true; it is false only when all its disjuncts are false.

Whereas conjunction in propositional logic is true only when all conjuncts are true, disjunction is false if and only if all of its disjuncts are false. If even one is and certainly if both of the disjuncts of a disjunction are true, then the disjunction as a whole is true. That is, a disjunction is true unless all of its disjuncts are false. A single true disjunct is sufficient to make an entire disjunction true, no matter how long or internally complex.

Disjunction generally enables us to express alternative possibilities, such as when we say that 'Picasso is famous or Mark Twain is an American novelist', or 'Picasso is famous or Picasso is not famous'. Whereas a conjunction is true only when all of its conjuncts are true, a disjunction is true provided that at least one of its disjuncts is true. The disjunction, 'Picasso is famous or Mark Twain is not an American novelist' is true by virtue of the fact that the first disjunct, 'Picasso is famous', is true, even though the second disjunct, 'Mark Twain is not an American novelist', is false. A single true disjunct in a disjunctive proposition of any length or complexity is enough by itself to guarantee the truth of the entire disjunction. If the disjunction we have just considered is true, we can obtain a false proposition by negating it, as in 'It is not the case that Picasso is famous or Mark Twain is not an American novelist'. Then, if we wish, we can conjoin or disjoin this proposition with another in more complex combinations, such as 'It is not the case that Picasso is famous or Mark Twain is not an American novelist, and Seabiscuit is the fastest racehorse' or 'It is not the case that Picasso is famous or Mark Twain is not an American novelist, or Seabiscuit is the fastest racehorse'. Iterative disjunctions are also possible, such as 'Picasso is famous or Picasso is famous or Picasso is famous'.

There are inclusive and exclusive kinds of disjunction.

Inclusive disjunctions are true even when both disjuncts are true; exclusive disjunctions are true only when one is but not both disjuncts are true.

Colloquially, there are both *inclusive* and *exclusive* types of disjunction. Inclusive disjunction allows for the possibility that both propositions being disjoined might be true, whereas exclusive disjunction restricts possibility to the truth of only one of the disjuncts. For example, inclusive disjunction seems to be at work in a proposition when we say, 'Either you will find your gloves or I will buy you another pair'. I might buy you another pair of gloves even if you find your gloves, in which case both atomic propositions 'You will find your gloves' and 'I will buy you another pair [of gloves]' could turn out to be true. But if I say, 'The missing glove is either for the right hand or the left hand', then presumably the single glove is either for the right hand or the left hand and not both. In the first case, we allow both possibilities of the disjunction to be included, whereas in the second example we deliberately exclude one or the other. An extreme case of the exclusive sense of disjunction occurs when the propositions disjoined are logically incompatible because both disjuncts logically cannot be true, as in the exclusive disjunction, 'Either you have lost your gloves or it is not the case that you have lost your gloves'. If two simpler propositions are disjoined into an inclusive disjunction, then the resulting proposition asserts only that one or the other is and possibly both propositions are true.

In symbolic logic, as the truth table definition for ∨ indicates, we interpret disjunction as inclusive disjunction, and we express exclusive disjunction when necessary by conjoining an inclusive disjunction with an additional clause to state that not both disjoined propositions are true. In effect, we say, for example, that 'Either today is Monday or today is Tuesday, and it is not the case that today is both Monday and Tuesday'. From now on, whenever we refer to disjunction without qualification, we will mean disjunction in the inclusive sense, referring explicitly when necessary to exclusive disjunction by name. We symbolize disjunction by the propositional connective '∨', which we can use with the other connectives to define the exclusive sense of disjunction. We express the inclusive sense of disjunction by which either proposition P or proposition Q is true by writing P ∨ Q. We express the exclusive sense of disjunction that either disjunct might be true but that not both are true, for example, in the case of a glove that is made either for the right hand or for the left hand but not both:

In symbolic logic, disjunction is understood as inclusive disjunction, and exclusive disjunction is specially defined by inclusive disjunction and the negation of a conjunction of the disjuncts.

$$(R \lor L) \ \& \ \sim(R \ \& \ L)$$

Conditional

Conditional ('if then') propositions link other propositions together in truth dependence relations. We define the conditional in the following truth table:

CONDITIONAL		
P	Q	P ⊃ Q
T	T	T
T	F	F
F	T	T
F	F	T

We can say, for example, 'If Picasso is famous, then Mark Twain is an American novelist' or 'If Mark Twain is an American novelist, then Picasso is famous'. More relevantly, we can use conditional if-then constructions to express logical hypotheses, in which the truth of one proposition is said to depend on that of another. A more useful application is in the compound conditional proposition, 'If Mark Twain is an American novelist, then Samuel Clemens is an American novelist'. An even more worthy illustration involves a combination of propositions thought to express some conditional logical relation, such as 'If a plane geometrical figure is a triangle, then there is at least one plane geometrical figure that has three sides and three angles' or 'If the game is rained out, then it will have to be rescheduled'.

Conditionals are true when their antecedents are false or their consequents true; conditionals are false only when their antecedents are true and their consequents are false.

The truth value of a conditional depends on the truth values of the propositions it combines. The proposition in a conditional to which the 'if' clause attaches, as noted in Chapter 1, is the antecedent, and the proposition to which the 'then' clause attaches is the consequent. We can say that a conditional is true if and only if it is not the case that its antecedent is true and its consequent false. As a result, there need not be any relevant connection between the content of the antecedent and the content of the consequent in order for a conditional to be a true conditional. A true conditional proposes that if its antecedent is true, then its consquent is also true. However, this can occur in many different ways, without the conditional's antecedent and consequent referring to the same things. For example, the conditional, 'If grass is green, then snow is cold', happens to be true if it happens to be true that both grass is green and snow is cold, if it is false that grass is green, or if it is true that snow is cold. If a conditional has a true antecedent and a false consequent, then the conditional is false. Since a conditional proposes only that the truth of the consequent depends or is conditional on the truth of the antecedent, then if the antecedent of a conditional is false or the consequent true, the conditional as a whole is also true. As with the other propositional connectives, there are endless possibilities for combining conditionals iteratively and with other propositions by means of other propositional connectives. An example is the sentence, 'If today is Tuesday, then if today is Tuesday, then today is Tuesday'.

The truth table definition of a conditional can be understood by analogy with promise-making and promise-keeping.

The definition of the conditional is conceptually more difficult than the other truth functions. The fundamental idea of the conditional can best be explained in terms of an analogy with promise-making and promise-keeping. Suppose that I make a conditional promise, 'If you pass logic, then I will pay for your spring vacation in Nassau'. Under what conditions is this proposition true, and under what conditions is it false? By analogy, the conditional proposition is true just in case I keep my promise. So we can ask instead, under what conditions will I have kept my conditional promise to pay for your spring vacation in Nassau *if* you pass logic? Let us think of the possible cases or combinations of truth values of the component atomic propositions connected by the conditional for the propositions 'You pass logic' and 'I pay for your spring vacation in Nassau'.

We encounter the same four combinations as those in our truth table definitions of conjunction and disjunction: It is true that you pass logic and true that I pay for your spring vacation in Nassau, it is true that you pass logic and false that I pay for your spring vacation in Nassau, it is false that you pass logic and true that I pay for your spring vacation in Nassau, or it is false that you pass logic and false that I pay for your spring vacation in Nassau. What are we to say about the truth of the conditional proposition or of my conditional promise in each of these cases? If you pass logic and I pay for your spring vacation in Nassau, then you have met the condition and I did what I said I would do if you passed logic. Here, I should certainly be said to have kept my promise, which we are supposing to be analogous to the conditional proposition's being true. What happens if you pass logic but I do not pay for your spring vacation in Nassau? Then I have broken my word and promised falsely. In this case, you met the condition I set, but I did not keep my promise by doing what I said I would do if the condition were satisfied. The promise and the conditional accordingly should be judged false whenever the antecedent is true but the consequent is false.

A promise is broken only when its terms are satisfied but the promised result is not delivered.

The two remaining cases are trickier. I said cautiously only what I would do *if* you passed logic, but I did not commit myself to either paying or not paying for your spring vacation in Nassau if you do *not* meet the condition by not passing logic. I did not say that I would pay for your spring vacation in Nassau *only if* you pass logic. If it is false that you pass logic, and I either pay or decide not to pay for your spring vacation in Nassau, I cannot reasonably be said to have broken my promise to pay for your vacation *if* you pass logic. Thus, in the last two cases, in which it is false that you pass logic but I either pay or do not pay for your spring vacation in Nassau, I should be regarded as having kept my promise. By analogy, the conditional proposition that expresses my promise should in both of these latter two cases be regarded as true. The only circumstance in which I will have promised falsely is when you meet the condition of the promise by passing logic but I do not do what I promised to do by failing to pay for your spring vacation in Nassau. That is, the only case in which a conditional proposition is false is that in which the antecedent is true and the consequent false. In all other cases, in which the antecedent and consequent are both true, in which the antecedent is false and the consequent true, and in which the antecedent and consequent are both false, the conditional as a whole is true.

Conditionals in propositional logic should not be confused with similar expressions in ordinary language.

Causal connections are not conditionals in the sense of propositional logic.

We must be careful not to confuse the conditional of propositional logic with other conditional-like constructions in ordinary language. The conditional is similar to but cannot be equated with the causal conditional of scientific and empirical reasoning. Ordinarily, when we are considering evidence and cause-and-effect relations in the physical world, we may say, for example, 'If the window is struck, then the glass will shatter.' This superficially has the form of the conditional of propositional logic, but the connection it formulates is causal rather than purely logical. Causal conditionals, unlike the logical conditional of propositional logic, express an instance of a lawlike transaction between two or more events. The reason why this cannot be subsumed as a special case of the conditional in propositional logic is that the logic of causal connection is not adequately captured by the truth conditions of the conditional. A causal connection between events presupposes that if the cause had not occurred, then the effect would also not have occurred. Take away a specific cause, and you take away its specific effects. However, this is not true of the conditional in propositional logic. When the antecedent of a conditional in propositional logic is false, the conditional as a whole is true by default according to the truth table definition, and the consequent of the logical conditional may also be either true or false. In contrast, the causal connection and specific effect expressed by a causal conditional do not obtain when the cause does not obtain or the proposition asserting its occurrence is false. As a result, the conditional propositional connective cannot be used by itself to symbolize causal relations.

Biconditional

A biconditional ('if and only if') proposition links other propositions together in truth interdependent relations. The truth table for the biconditional has the following form:

BICONDITIONAL

P	Q	$P \equiv Q$
T	T	T
T	F	F
F	T	F
F	F	T

A biconditional in effect conjoins two conditionals. To say that P is true if and only if Q is true is to say that if P is true then Q is true, and if Q is true then P is true. The truth table definitions of the conditional and conjunction guarantee that the truth value of $P \equiv Q$ so defined is true provided that it is always the case that either both P and Q are true or both P and Q are false.

Biconditionals are true only when the wffs they connect are both true or both false and are otherwise false where their wffs do not agree in truth value.

The biconditional combines two propositions in such a way that their truth values are always the same. A biconditional holds true just in case the propositions it connects are both true or both false so that they stand or fall together. If the two propositions of a biconditional are true, the biconditional is true; if both propositions are false, the biconditional is also true. Thus, the biconditional proposition that 'P if and only if Q' is true if and only if either both P and Q are true or both P and Q are false. This is the same situation as when both 'If P then Q' and 'If Q then P' are true. The biconditional is false only when one of its component propositions is true and the other false. The force of the biconditional is conveyed in ordinary language by the equivalent expressions, 'if and only if', 'when and only when', 'just in case', and others. The biconditional proposition, 'The game will be rescheduled if and only if the game is rained out', says both that 'If the game is rescheduled, then the game is rained out' and that 'If the game is rained out, then the game is rescheduled'. An example in which both parts of a biconditional are necessarily true, making the biconditional itself true as a whole is seen in the proposition that 'Triangles have three sides if and only if $2 + 2 = 4$'. An example in which both parts of a biconditional are clearly always false, making the biconditional itself true, is the proposition that 'Triangles have four sides if and only if $2 + 2 = 5$'.

Here, for convenience, we summarize all the truth table definitions of the five propositional connectives. The two redundant values for the negation attaching to the same propositional variable are placed in brackets. So much of our work in propositional logic rests on a thorough understanding of and ability to apply the truth table definitions of the propositional connectives that it is worthwhile to memorize them.

It is useful to memorize the truth table definitions of the five propositional connectives.

TRUTH TABLE DEFINITIONS
OF PROPOSITIONAL CONNECTIVES

P	Q	~P	P & Q	P ∨ Q	P ⊃ Q	P ≡ Q
T	T	F	T	T	T	T
T	F	[F]	F	T	F	F
F	T	T	F	T	T	F
F	F	[T]	F	F	T	T

To Check Your Understanding 2.2

Write from memory (as often as necessary until you can correctly recall) the truth table definitions for each of the following truth functional propositional connectives: (1) negation ~, (2) conjunction &, (3) disjunction ∨, (4) conditional ⊃, and (5) biconditional ≡.

Translating Propositions

Translation into symbolic logic is an art that requires understanding the meaning of propositions in ordinary language.

We are now ready to begin translating from English into symbolic logic. We begin with exercises involving single propositional symbols for atomic propositions and work our way up to increasingly complex wffs and finally to entire arguments. As we proceed, we shall comment on the strategies involved in translation and note some of the most useful methods and pitfalls to beware.

The following are some easy sentences to translate. Atomic propositions that contain no propositional connectives are symbolized by atomic propositional symbols or atomic wffs. We could use the standard symbols P, Q, and R, as previously explained, but it is often more interesting to choose mnemonic propositional symbols.

It is raining. — R

Yesterday, all my troubles seemed so far away. — T

Picasso was a flamboyant Spanish artist. — P

These examples are all too simple. — S

We complicate things by considering propositions that require negation for their translations. Note that negation can sometimes be subtly concealed within a proposition so that we do not readily see it in a casual examination of the surface grammar of a sentence we are trying to translate. Here are a few illustrations:

It is not raining. — ~R

Today, my troubles have not yet gone away. — ~A

I haven't a care in the world. — ~C

These examples are no longer so simple. — ~S

Parentheses disambiguate proposition-ally complex wffs in translating from ordinary language to avoid confusion in the scopes of multiple propositional connectives.

As a first step in any translation, we do well to identify the atomic propositions in a conjunctive sentence we are to translate and to assign propositional symbols to these. If necessary, we can accomplish the translation in three separate stages. First, we identify the atomic propositions and uniformly substitute appropriate propositional symbols or atomic wffs for them, leaving the English connectives just as we find them. Second, we substitute the symbolic propositional connectives of our propositional logic for the English connectives. Third, we disambiguate the resulting symbolization by introducing parentheses as needed to ensure that the final resulting expression is a wff with the same logical structure as the colloquial proposition to be translated.

Translation from or-dinary language into symbolic logic can best be achieved by means of a three-stage trans-lation procedure.

THREE-STAGE TRANSLATION PROCEDURE
FOR PROPOSITIONAL LOGIC

1. *Identify* the atomic propositions (that contain no colloquial propositional connectives), and uniformly substitute appropriate propositional symbols for them, leaving the English connectives just as they appear in the proposition to be translated.

2. *Substitute* symbolic propositional connectives ($\sim$, &, $\vee$, $\supset$, $\equiv$) for equivalent English connectives wherever they remain in the partially translated proposition occurring after stage 1.
3. *Punctuate* the partially translated proposition occurring after stage 2, if necessary, by introducing parentheses in order to disambiguate the scopes of whatever multiple propositional connectives may occur in the translation after stage 2 to ensure that the resulting expression is a wff with the same logical structure as the colloquial proposition to be translated.

Here is an example in which we follow the three-stage process in giving a translation. Conjunctions stereotypically involve the English propositional connective 'and', which are translated by substituting the ampersand '&' for 'and' wherever we encounter it in a sentence. The proposition is sufficiently simple to require that we actually implement only the first and second stages of the translation procedure. Consider the sentence:

Hillary and Bill went up the hill.

We identify the atomic propositions. In English, these are 'Hillary went up the hill' and 'Bill went up the hill'. We use 'H' to abbreviate 'Hillary went up the hill' and 'B' to abbreviate 'Bill went up the hill'. Now we write:

H and B   Translation stage 1

As the final step, we substitute the propositional logic symbol for conjunction, the ampersand '&' for 'and', to obtain:

H & B   Translation stage 2

In this instance, even the second stage of the three-stage translation strategy may seem unnecessary. However, we shall soon encounter more complex sentences to symbolize, for which it is good policy to use the three-stage translation procedure whenever we are not absolutely sure of the logical structures to be represented.

We cannot always correctly translate what may appear to be a conjunction in a sentence as a propositional conjunction. Consider the proposition, 'Root beer and vanilla ice cream makes a Brown Cow'. Although the term 'and' appears in the sentence, we would obviously be mistaken to translate the sentence as having the same logical form as that previously discussed (perhaps with different propositional symbols R & V), meaning 'Root beer makes a Brown Cow and vanilla ice cream makes a Brown Cow'. The making of a Brown Cow

Ordinary language is sometimes a misleading guide to propositional logical structure for purposes of translation.

requires that root beer and vanilla ice cream be combined, and the meaning of the word 'and' in such a sentence is that there occurs a mixture of ingredients. It is partly because of these categorical differences between uses of some propositional connectives in ordinary language that translation is more of an art involving the understanding of meaning than of purely mechanical syntax substitutions.

To Check Your Understanding 2.3

In the following propositionally complex propositions, draw a box around the atomic propositions and draw a circle around the propositional connectives:

1. If it doesn't rain, we'll have a picnic.
2. One or another of us must always have the tickets.
3. Either it will hail or snow today, and not both.
4. I can take care of your schnauzer if and only if you can take care of mine.
5. If you can't take care of my schnauzer, you can at least take care of my shitzu.

Colloquial Propositional Equivalents

There are indefinitely many ways of expressing propositional connectives in ordinary language.

The propositional connectives in symbolic logic can represent many different English equivalents. It would be difficult to offer a complete account of such terms because colloquial language is expressively more diverse and less rigidly rule governed than symbolic logic. The most important alternatives are listed and explained here, together with the standard connectives in brackets by which they should be translated. Note that some of these are propositionally identical forms with different English connotations. This is a reflection of the rich resources of ordinary language, the logical structures of which are more narrowly interpreted in symbolic logic.

> SYMBOLIC PROPOSITIONAL EQUIVALENTS
> FOR COLLOQUIAL PROPOSITIONAL CONNECTIVES
>
> **Conjunction**
>
> P *and* Q   P and Q [P & Q]
> P *but* Q   P and Q [P & Q]
> P *also* Q   P and Q [P & Q]

P, Q too	P and Q [P & Q]
Both P *and* Q	P and Q [P & Q]
P *although (despite)* Q	P and Q [P & Q]
P *however* Q	P and Q [P & Q]
P *moreover* Q	P and Q [P & Q]
P *whereas* Q	P and Q [P & Q]
P *nevertheless* Q	P and Q [P & Q]
P *besides* Q	P and Q [P & Q]
P *even though* Q	P and Q [P & Q]
Not only P, *but also* Q	P and Q [P & Q]
Not only P, *but also* Q	P and Q [P & Q]
P *in spite of* the fact that Q	P and Q [P & Q]
P *despite* Q	P and Q [P & Q]
P *plus the fact that* Q	P and Q [P & Q]
P *as well as* Q	P and Q [P & Q]
P *even though* Q	P and Q [P & Q]
P *inasmuch as* Q	P and Q [P & Q]

Disjunction

P *or* Q	P or Q [P ∨ Q]
Either P *or* Q	P or Q [P ∨ Q]
P *or else* Q	P or Q [P ∨ Q]
P *or alternatively* Q	P or Q [P ∨ Q]
P, *otherwise* Q	P or Q [P ∨ Q]
Neither P *nor* Q	Not–(P or Q) [~(P ∨ Q)]
[also equivalent to not-P and not-Q [~P & ~Q]]	

Conditional

If P, *then* Q	If P, then Q [P ⊃ Q]
If P, Q	If P, then Q [P ⊃ Q]
P *if* Q	If Q, then P [Q ⊃ P]
P *when (where)* Q	If Q, then P [Q ⊃ P]
P *whenever (wherever)* Q	If Q, then P [Q ⊃ P]
P *only (just) if* Q	If P, then Q [P ⊃ Q]
[do not confuse 'only if' with 'if and only if']	
P *unless* Q	If not Q then P [~Q ⊃ P]
[weak sense (also equivalent to P ∨ Q or Q ∨ P)]	
P, *given that* Q	If Q, then P [Q ⊃ P]
P *insofar as* Q	If Q, then P [Q ⊃ P]

P *so long as* Q	If Q, then P [Q ⊃ P]
P *is a sufficient condition for* Q	If P, then Q [P ⊃ Q]
P *to the extent that* Q	If Q, then P [Q ⊃ P]
P *provided that* Q	If Q, then P [Q ⊃ P]
P *provided only that* Q	If P, then Q [P ⊃ Q]

Biconditional

P *if and only if* Q	P if and only if Q [P ≡ Q]
P *if but only if* Q	P if and only if Q [P ≡ Q]
P *is equivalent to* Q	P if and only if Q [P ≡ Q]
P *is a necessary and*	P if and only if Q [P ≡ Q]
sufficient condition for Q	
P *unless* Q	P if and only if not-Q [P ≡ ~Q]
[strong sense (also equivalent to ~Q ≡ P)]	
P *just in case* Q	P if and only if Q [P ≡ Q]
P *when and only when* Q	P if and only if Q [P ≡ Q]
P *where and only where* Q	P if and only if Q [P ≡ Q]
P *only (just) insofar as* Q	P if and only if Q [P ≡ Q]
P *only (just) insofar as* Q	P if and only if Q [P ≡ Q]
P *just to the extent that* Q	P if and only if Q [P ≡ Q]

The list contains the most commonly encountered variations, but we should be on the lookout for other possibilities. As we gain confidence in translating from ordinary English to symbolic logic, we improve our understanding of the way propositional connectives function in everyday discourse and our ability to render their meaning more accurately by means of symbolic propositional connectives. To be successful in translation, we must first try to grasp the intent of the propositions and arguments we are trying to translate and then use the symbolic devices at our disposal to formalize their meaning as precisely as we can.

We explain the symbolizations intuitively and by means of examples. To say that something is true *but* (or *although, moreover,* or *as well as*) something else is also true has the propositional form of conjunction. Such a compound proposition is committed to the truth of both propositions it contains. The conjunction in these ordinary language cases also gives a special connotation to the joint assertion of conjoined propositions. To say that P *but* Q is not only to say that *both* P and Q are true (and hence that P but Q has the propositional logical form of conjunction) but also to indicate that the truth of Q may somehow restrict not the truth but the significance or application of P. To say P *despite* Q is to say

Skillful translation requires understanding the meaning of a proposition in ordinary language and then using the propositional symbols, propositional connectives, and parentheses of symbolic logic to represent its logical structure.

that both P and Q are true (and hence that P despite Q has the propositional logical form of conjunction) but that P is true even though Q might otherwise be thought to limit or contradict the truth or likelihood of P. These subtle connotations are not sensitively expressed in the formal symbolic notation of propositional logic. We must recognize that in this and other respects symbolic propositional logic is inadequate to model every aspect of ordinary thought and discourse. Propositional logic claims only to symbolize the truth functional structure of reasoning, which it does very well. Yet, there is more to thought and discourse than purely propositional logical structures.

Any connective in ordinary language that requires that the propositions it connects must be true in order for the entire proposition to be true should be translated as a conjunction.

The sentences '*If* P, Q' and 'Q, *if* P' are conditionals. There is only the question of whether P or Q is the antecedent or consequent. We see on reflection that the antecedent or if-part of the conditional is the proposition to which the 'if' term attaches, and the consequent of the conditional is the remaining proposition or then–part, to which the 'then' term attaches. Thus, in the first sentence, 'If P, Q', P is the antecedent and Q is the consequent. The sentence says that the truth of Q is logically dependent on the truth of P. In the second sentence, 'Q, if P', P is once again the antecedent to which the 'if' term attaches, where the truth of Q is said to be logically dependent on the truth of P or where the truth of P is the condition on which the truth of Q depends. Both of these are then naturally represented as 'If P, then Q' or P ⊃ Q. That there are stylistic variations for expressing the conditional of propositional logic in ordinary language is a tribute to its poetic possibilities. We see this when we compare such equivalent constructions as the canonical 'If you love me still, then think of me nightly' with the more compact 'If you love me still, think of me nightly' and the more lyrical conditional with inverted order of antecedent and consequent, 'Think of me nightly, if you love me still'.

There are various ways of expressing the relation by which the truth of a proposition is conditional on the truth of another.

The sentence 'Q *when* (*where*) P' is also a conditional of the form P ⊃ Q. 'When' and 'where' in ordinary English sometimes express the timeless general conditional sense of 'if' (as in 'You get 3 when you add 2 and 1' and 'The function holds where x is greater than 2'). But often 'when' and 'where' express time-determined or space-determined conditions (as in 'When the door is opened, the alarm sounds' and 'Some animals thrive where human beings barely survive'). When 'when' and 'where' are used to specify conditions for the truth of a proposition as dependent on the truth of another, their propositional logic is symbolized by the conditional '⊃'. This is not to say that 'when' and 'where' always express the conditional of propositional logic. Consider the proposition 'I knew him when he was just a little shaver.' This fixes the occurrence of an event in a span of time by reference to other events but has no obviously propositional structure. It would be implausible to interpret the sentence as meaning something like, 'If [it is true that] he was just a little shaver, then [it is true that] I knew him'. This is also true for the proposition 'I hid the treasure where you'll never find it.' An object or event is located spatially in a certain place by use of the term 'where'. However, it would be a mistake to interpret the propositional logic of the sentence as involving the conditional, 'If [it is true that] you'll never find the treasure, then [it is true that] I hid it'. We cannot apply translation equivalents mechanically, but we must use good judgment to go back and forth between ordinary English and symbolic logic.

'P only if Q' is translated the same as 'If P, then Q'.

'If P, then Q' should not be confused with 'P only if Q'.

The sentence 'P only if Q' is a conditional since it specifies Q as a condition without which P is false. An example to explain the contrast between 'If P, then Q' and 'P only if Q' is the following: I might declare that I will pay my bill *if* I am satisfied with the work, or I might say instead that I will pay my bill *only if* I am satisfied with the work. The first proposition places a condition on my paying, whereby *if* I am satisfied, *then* I will pay. But by this I have not yet said that I will not pay if I am not satisfied. I may have insinuated something like this or intended someone to believe it by my use of the first conditional. However, I have not so far expressed anything the logic of which explicitly announces my refusal to pay if I am not satisfied. To assert my unwillingness to pay if I am not satisfied with the work I must further make a statement equivalent in meaning to the proposition that I will pay my bill *only if* I am satisfied with the work. This says that if the condition of my being satisfied with the work is not met, then I shall not pay, because I have now said that this is the *only* condition under which I will pay.

The 'only if' in 'P only if Q' says something different than that P is true if Q is true. On the contrary, to say that P is true only if Q is true is to say that if Q is not true, then P is not true. We can, if we like, express the 'only if' relation simply as if not-Q, then not-P, or $\sim Q \supset \sim P$, which is the contrapositive of 'If P then Q', or $P \supset Q$. An easy way to remember how to translate 'only if' conditionals in 'P only if Q' is to substitute the symbolic propositional connective '$\supset$' directly for the English phrase 'only if', leaving 'P' and 'Q' in place precisely where they are, with P as antecedent and Q as consequent. Thus, 'P only if Q' directly becomes $P \supset Q$.

The biconditional 'P if and only if Q' contains both an ordinary 'if-then' conditional and an 'only if' conditional in the implicit conjunction, 'P if Q and P only if Q'. The 'P if Q' conjunct is the conditional $Q \supset P$ since Q is the antecedent condition to which the if-part of the proposition attaches, leaving the truth of the consequent P as dependent on the truth of Q. The 'P only if Q' conjunct must then be $P \supset Q$, just as we previously concluded, since we already know and we shall later prove that the biconditional $P \equiv Q$ is logically equivalent to the conjunction $(P \supset Q) \& (Q \supset P)$, meaning that the first is true if and only if the second is true, or that they always share the same truth value, whether true or false.

There are weak and strong forms of 'unless'.

There are *weak and strong forms of the English connective 'unless'*. The proposition 'P *unless* Q' (or '*Unless* Q, P') places a condition on the truth of proposition P and proposition Q. The unless condition in weak and strong senses is a more liberal condition than obtains when P is true only if Q is true. To say 'P unless Q' in the weak sense is to say that P is true, not just or only under one condition but under all conditions with the sole exception of the truth of proposition Q. If I were to say, 'I'll go home before 3:00 pm unless I hear from you', what I have said should probably be understood to mean that if I do not hear from you, then I will go home before 3:00 pm. But it does not mean anything stronger. It does not mean that if I go home before 3:00 pm, then I have not heard from you. There might be conditions under which I go home before 3:00 pm other than simply not hearing from you. Yet sometimes we mean to say something stronger than this. If I say, 'I won't go to the hospital unless my fever exceeds 104°', then I probably mean to say that if my fever does not exceed 104°, then I will not go to the hospital, and that if I do not go to the hospital, then my fever does not exceed 104°. To say 'P unless Q', therefore, can also mean that not only is P true if not-Q is true but also that if P is true, then not-Q is true. That is, 'P unless Q' can also mean that P is true if and only if not-Q is true. This is the strong or biconditional sense of 'unless'. We can formulate the two strengths of this propositional relation in several ways. The most obvious translations for the weak or conditional sense for 'P unless Q' is $\sim Q \supset P$. This is logically equivalent, as we shall later prove, to the contrapositive $\sim P \supset Q$, which in turn are logically equivalent to the disjunctions, $Q \lor P$ and $P \lor Q$. For the strong or biconditional sense of 'unless', we can translate 'P unless Q' as $\sim Q \equiv P$ or $P \equiv \sim Q$. Again, we must use good judgment in understanding the intent of 'unless' as it appears in ordinary language for purposes of symbolization to decide if it is meant to express a conditional or biconditional relation.

Weak and strong forms of 'unless' are sometimes difficult to distinguish.

To say 'P *just in case* Q' is to say that (i) P is true in case Q is true (or that if Q then P) and (ii) P is true just or only in case Q is true (or that P is true only if Q is true or, by equivalence, if P then Q). Together, (i) and (ii) interpret P just in case Q as the biconditional P *if and only if* Q ($P \equiv Q$).

If '*Neither P nor Q*' is true, then both possibilities are ruled out. We can symbolize this proposition in two ways. We exclude the truth of both P and Q by saying that it is not the case that either P or Q is true or equivalently by saying that it is not the case that P is true and it is not the case that Q is true. The propositions $\sim(P \lor Q)$ and $\sim P \,\&\, \sim Q$ are *duals* of one another that obtain by *propositional duality relations*. There is a family of propositional dualities, sometimes known as the *DeMorgan equivalences*. The dualities are named after the 19th-century logician and statistician Augustus DeMorgan, but they were already known to the Stoic logicians of the Hellenistic period (for several centuries after the death of Alexander the Great) in ancient Greece.

PROPOSITIONAL DUALITY
(DEMORGAN EQUIVALENCES)

$$(P \mathbin{\&} Q) \equiv {\sim}({\sim}P \vee {\sim}Q)$$
$$(P \vee Q) \equiv {\sim}({\sim}P \mathbin{\&} {\sim}Q)$$

To Check Your Understanding 2.4

Propositional duality relations express logical equivalences between conjunction and disjunction with negation.

Here are some representative propositions to translate, using our expanded vocabulary list of ordinary language equivalents.

1. I was visiting in New York and Chicago.
2. If you go to San Francisco, you're going to meet some gentle people there.
3. The best way to approach a problem is to consider its origins and consequences, or how it conflicts with other things we believe to be true.
4. Steven will send the package just in case he receives your message.
5. Rebecca is planning to go to law school, although she has yet to apply.
6. Either Iran or Iraq will try to extend its sphere of influence in the Mideast before the end of the century.
7. We make hay when the sun shines.
8. If the patient's blood pressure falls dramatically, then if there are no warning signs of cardiac trouble, we will administer a mild stimulant.
9. She will not approve the loan unless we can prove we have enough collateral not to need the loan.
10. Matt and Mabel will neither drive to Oshkosh nor take the ferry from Manitowoc.

Disambiguating Propositional Relations

Parentheses are sometimes needed to disambiguate the scopes of multiple propositional connectives in translating an ordinary language proposition as a wff of propositional logic.

In translating from ordinary language to the syntax of propositional logic, we often encounter problems of disambiguating the scopes of several propositional connectives. We have already seen that we must sometimes use parentheses to avoid ambiguities of expression in our symbolism. Now we offer more specific guidelines in following the third or punctuation stage of the three-stage translation procedure for propositional logic.

We can appreciate the difficulties of disambiguating syntax involved in translating from ordinary language to propositional logic if we begin with an analogy in elementary arithmetic. What happens when we try to substitute numerals for number words and symbolic arithmetical function symbols $(+, -, =)$ for numerical operation terms such as 'plus', 'minus', and 'equals' in colloquially expressed equations such as '1 plus 2 times $4 = x$'? If we were to translate the equation simply as $1 + 2 \times 4 = x$, in the absence of special conventions on the order of operations we would not know how to calculate value x. Should we first add 1 and 2 and then multiply by 4 to get 12? Or should we multiply 4 times 2 and then add 1 to get 9? It clearly makes a difference how we group together the arithmetical operations the sentence asks us to perform. The standard device for disambiguating expressions of this kind in algebra is to group together operations by parentheses to indicate that they should be performed in a certain order. The first calculation is symbolized by this convention as $(1 + 2) \times 4 = x$, and the second calculation is symbolized as $1 + (2 \times 4) = x$.

The same potential for ambiguity occurs with respect to the scopes of propositional connectives as for algebraic operators in translating from ordinary language into symbolic logic. Consider the following combined conjunctive and disjunctive proposition:

> Mark Twain is not an American novelist and Seabiscuit is the fastest racehorse or Picasso is famous.

The sentence as written could mean one of two things. It might be understood as disjoining the conjunction, 'Mark Twain is not an American novelist' and 'Seabiscuit is the fastest racehorse', with the proposition, 'Picasso is famous', or as conjoining the proposition, 'Mark Twain is not an American novelist', with the disjunction, 'Seabiscuit is the fastest racehorse or Picasso is famous'. We can emphasize the dominant connective in interpreting the sentence in both ways by rewriting the connective in capital letters. The first interpretation then states that 'Mark Twain is not an American novelist and Seabiscuit is the fastest racehorse OR Picasso is famous'. This sentence is predominantly a disjunction that happens to have a conjunction as one of its disjuncts. The second interpretation understands the proposition as predominantly a conjunction that happens to have a disjunction as one of its conjuncts, which by our convention we can transcribe as 'Mark Twain is not an American novelist AND Seabiscuit is the fastest racehorse or Picasso is famous'.

It makes a difference to the truth or falsehood of the resulting translation which of these complex propositions we mean to express. The first interpretation makes the proposition a false conjunction of the false proposition, 'Mark Twain is not an American novelist', with the true disjunction, 'Seabiscuit is the fastest racehorse or Picasso is famous'. The second interpretation makes the proposition a true disjunction of the false conjunction, 'Mark Twain is not an American novelist and Seabiscuit is the fastest racehorse', with the true propo-

Disambiguating wffs by means of parentheses can often make a difference in the truth value of the resulting wffs.

sition, 'Picasso is famous'. The ambiguities in occurrences of propositional connectives in ordinary language can obviously affect the meaning a proposition is judged to express and ultimately whether the proposition is true or false.

In the previous example, the two interpretations are distinguished in ordinary English by setting off the propositions that are to be conjoined or disjoined by means of commas. Thus, the first interpretation of the proposition is more perspicuously written as 'Mark Twain is not an American novelist, and Seabiscuit is the fastest racehorse or Picasso is famous' and the second interpretation as 'Mark Twain is not an American novelist and Seabiscuit is the fastest racehorse, or Picasso is famous'. Use of punctuation outside of symbolic logic is so much a matter of individual style, and so prone to editorial and typesetting error, that we must expect some of the discourse we encounter to be misleading or to pose serious challenges to our efforts to understand and correctly translate a proposition's logical structure. Context can also sometimes help to settle alternative readings of ambiguous expressions. However, in some situations, particularly when we cannot ask the author of a propositionally complex proposition which combination is intended, there may be no conclusion to draw except that the discourse admits of several interpretations, none of which is more reasonable or likely than another. This is one of the limitations of expressing ideas in ordinary language and hence one of the motivations for logicians to develop more precise ways of formulating propositional structures in symbolic logic. We should nevertheless strive to avoid ambiguity in our own thought and writing by using commas and related devices to punctuate complex propositions so that the scopes of whatever colloquial propositional connectives they contain are clearly distinguished.

In propositional logic, we can do this very systematically. We use parentheses to disambiguate complex propositions so that the scope of every propositional connective is clearly indicated. We have already seen how parentheses are introduced when making uniform substitutions for propositional variables in applying the formation rules for propositional wffs. Now we shall consider how to add parentheses to punctuate a wff that appears as the incomplete translation of a proposition in ordinary language in the third stage of our three-stage translation procedure. Consider the following expression:

P & Q ⊃ R ∨ S

The formula is ambiguous. It is not a wff because the scopes of all three of the propositional connectives it contains are unclear. It might be understood to mean any of the following more precisely formulated sentences:

P & (Q ⊃ (R ∨ S))
(P & Q) ⊃ (R ∨ S)

Punctuation by means of commas, colons, and semicolons in ordinary language is sometimes a useful, but not always a reliable, clue to the way in which a proposition should be translated as a wff disambiguated by parentheses.

Alternative placement of parentheses results in logically different wffs with potentially different truth values.

$$(P \mathbin{\&} (Q \supset R)) \lor S$$
$$P \mathbin{\&} ((Q \supset R) \lor S)$$

There is no mechanical procedure for disambiguating wffs by parentheses in translating propositions from ordinary language into symbolic logic.

These propositions have different meanings. The parentheses requirement on the application of propositional wffs rules prevents such truth functionally ambiguous symbol combinations from being constructed as wffs. But when we are translating from English into symbolic logic, we must decide where to place parentheses in the symbolization in order to avoid all such ambiguities.

There is no mechanical procedure to follow in placing parentheses. We must try to understand the meanings of the sentences we wish to translate and experiment with different arrangements of parentheses until we arrive at a propositionally complex wff that best symbolizes the sentence we are trying to translate. If we familiarize ourselves with the potential for ambiguous expression in logical formulas without parentheses, we can begin to develop a reliable sense of how to use parentheses effectively to clarify truth functional relations. Here are some typical examples:

If it rains then either the picnic is canceled or the ball game is called off. (R, P, B)

We might begin to translate the proposition symbolically at first without parentheses as follows:

If R then either P or B.	Translation stage 1
$R \supset P \lor B$	Translation stage 2

The translation as it stands is ambiguous as between $(R \supset P) \lor B$ and $R \supset (P \lor B)$. Which is correct? What do we mean to say with each? The first formula corresponds to the English sentence 'Either if it rains then the picnic is canceled or the ballgame is canceled.' Is that what we are saying in the sentence? No, because the sentence has the sense that if it rains, then one (or possibly both) of two things will happen. The consequent of the conditional 'then' begins with the disjunction 'either', which makes the consequent a disjunction. This is represented by the formula $R \supset (P \lor B)$ and not by $(R \supset P) \lor B$. So, the sentence with parentheses placed around the disjunction rather than the conditional is correct in translation stage 3, as $R \supset (P \lor B)$.

If Enan wins the war, then if Onen loses its oil fields, the Oaquis will raise the price of oil. (W, L, R)

Again, the sentence is written without parentheses in a first approximation as follows:

If W, then if L, then R.   Translation stage 1

W ⊃ L ⊃ R   Translation stage 2

This is similarly ambiguous as between the following two interpretations, clarified by parentheses: W ⊃ (L ⊃ R) and (W ⊃ L) ⊃ R. We must consider their meanings as expressions of the original English sentence and decide which is correct. The example contains nested conditionals, a conditional within a conditional. If the sentence were properly symbolized as the second proposition given previously, then the translation would mean what might be expressed in everyday English as 'If (it is true that) if Enan wins the war, then Onen loses its oil fields, then the Oaquis will raise the price of oil.' This does not seem to be the intent of the sentence. We should therefore conclude in translation stage 3 that W ⊃ (L ⊃ R), rather than (W ⊃ L) ⊃ R, is the correct translation, and that the antecedent or main connecting if-clause of the entire expression is the condition that Enan wins the war. The commas in the original English brought forward into the translation stage 1 in this case make the relationship clear enough.

The first 'then' can only go with the first 'if', which makes W the antecedent of the entire proposition. The first 'then' is also followed immediately by the second 'if', which makes the consequent of the proposition a conditional, whose antecedent L is paired with consequent R. The entire proposition is correctly formulated as a conditional with a conditional consequent rather than as a conditional with a conditional antecedent. Do you see the difference in the two, and do you agree that we have good reasons for preferring the first translation?

Sometimes punctuation in ordinary language, particularly by means of commas but also dashes and parentheses, can indicate the logical groupings of propositional components within a more complex proposition. An easy example is 'Tom and Steve, or Jane are coming', as opposed to 'Tom, and Steve or Jane are coming'. The first, taking a clue from the way some propositional connectives seem to be grouped together and divided from others by commas, might be translated as (T & S) ∨ J, in contrast with the second as T & (S ∨ J). This is often a valuable way to disambiguate ordinary language sentences. How-

ever, punctuation in ordinary language can also be misleading, and we are not always fortunate enough to have sentences punctuated in such a clear fashion, as when someone says in an inherently ambiguous expression: 'Tom and Steve or Jane are coming'. In such cases, we are well advised, even where ordinary language punctuation helps to disambiguate the parts of a propositionally complex sentence, to check our translations against what seems to make the best logical sense of a proposition.

Here is another example:

It is not the case that Tom will not go to the festival or that Lynn will go to the festival, and Steve will not go if Karen does not go. (T, L, S, K)

In this sentence, several potential ambiguities are rolled into one. What, exactly, does the English sentence say? Without parentheses, the sentence is translated:

Not not T or L and not S if not K　　　　　　Translation stage 1

$\sim\sim$T $\vee$ L & $\sim$K $\supset$ $\sim$S　　　　　　Translation stage 2

Try this one yourself. First, what are the possible alternative interpretations of the sentence? How many ways are there to place parentheses around parts of the proposition to express different meanings? There are quite a few; perhaps more than you would first think, especially because of the negation signs. Now look again at the English sentence, and decide which interpretation is correct. The main connective of the sentence seems to be the beginning negation, 'It is not the case that _____'. The sentence tells us that something is not true. What? Does the negation apply to everything that follows in the rest of the sentence or just that 'Tom will not go to the festival or Lynn will go to the festival'? It seems obvious that only the latter is meant to be negated, and that the main connective of the proposition is the conjunction 'and' in 'and Steve will not go if Karen does not go'. Thus, the sentence should consist of a negation outside the parentheses that encloses only the information about Tom and Lynn. The remaining conditional about Steve and Karen stands on its own and does not get included in the scope of the first external negation. Working through the sentence bit by bit, and checking back and forth between the original English and our more precisely formulated symbolic expression as it proceeds, we should arrive at this solution:

$\sim$($\sim$T $\vee$ L) & ($\sim$K $\supset$ $\sim$S)　　　　　　Translation stage 3

Accurate translation from ordinary language into symbolic logic is the foundation of correct logical analysis.

If we had wanted to say something in English to be translated into symbolic notation as $\sim$($\sim$(T $\vee$ L) & ($\sim$K $\supset$ $\sim$S)), then ordinarily we would have used a somewhat different locution, perhaps of the form 'It is not the case *both* that Tom or Lynn will not go to the festival *and* that Steve will not go if Karen does not go.' This adds further emphasis to make it clear that what is being denied is the conjunction of both sets of circumstances. We did not try to translate the first occurrence of negation in the original English sentence by attaching it to the second occurrence of the negation, as in $\sim\sim$(T $\vee$ L) & ($\sim$K $\supset$ $\sim$S)). Do you see why?

■ *Demonstration 5:* **Translating Propositions** ■

PROBLEM: To symbolize a proposition in propositional logic.

PROPOSITION: People are naturally good only if the law is unnecessary, and are naturally evil only if the law is ineffective.

STEP 1: *Identify atomic propositions and truth functional connectives*
We begin by underlining the propositional connectives, to make the atomic propositions appear by contrast, to which we then assign propositional symbols.

People are naturally good <u>only if</u> the law is unnecessary, <u>and</u> are naturally evil <u>only if</u> the law is ineffective.

The atomic propositions are the following:

1. People are naturally good (G).
2. The law is unnecessary (U).
3. People are naturally evil (E).
4. The law is ineffective (I).

STEP 2: *Rewrite the complex proposition by substituting atomic propositional symbols for atomic propositions*

G <u>only if</u> U <u>and</u> E <u>only if</u> I   Translation stage 1

STEP 3: *Rewrite the complex proposition by substituting symbolic propositional connectives for the ordinary language connectives*
Here we simply substitute propositional connectives for the English connectives 'only if' (two occurrences) and 'and' (one occurrence), preserving the order in which they occur in the previous partial translation.

G ⊃ U & E ⊃ I   Translation stage 2

STEP 4: *Punctuate the complex proposition by placing parentheses around the wffs that logically belong together*
The final translation has this form, disambiguating the scopes of the sentence's three propositional connectives:

(G ⊃ U) & (E ⊃ I)   Translation stage 3

The complex English proposition contains two simpler propositions: (i) that people are naturally good only if the law is unnecessary and (ii) that people are naturally evil only if the law is ineffective. The proposition as a whole then is a conjunction. We show that the proposition conjoins two conditional (only if) propositions by enclosing the conditionals in parentheses. This indicates that each conditional proposition is a conjunct in the complete conjunction. The addition of parentheses disambiguates the final symbolization from alternative interpretations, $G \supset (U \ \& \ (E \supset I))$, $(G \supset (U \ \& \ E)) \supset I$, $G \supset ((U \ \& \ E)) \supset I$, and so on.

To Check Your Understanding 2.5 ■

Translate the following English sentences into the notation of symbolic logic following the three-step translation procedure and using parentheses to avoid logical ambiguity.

1. When the clock strikes one, everyone is in bed unless they are still doing their homework. (C, B, H)
2. Triangles have three angles just in case neither squares nor rhomboids do. (T, S, R)
3. I will give you my car if you want me to, but only if you do not use it in another bank robbery. (C, W, B)
4. If the president knew about the diversion of funds to the rebels, then he deliberately violated the law and does not deserve to be president; but if he did not know about the diversion of funds, then he did not have control of his subordinates and does not deserve to be president. (K, V, D, C)
5. Doubts arise when knowledge is not certain, but if knowledge is certain then either it is trivial and not worth doubting, or if not trivial it is at best defectively justifiable. (D, K, T, W, J)

■

Translating Arguments

The next challenge is to translate an entire argument. This is not more difficult than symbolizing a sequence of separate propositions, identifying the indicator term as showing that some of the propositions are the argument's assumptions and that others are conclusions. We will consider several different kinds of examples, from easy to medium difficult to very difficult, to get a sense of the possibilities.

Here is a sample argument to translate. An advertising company takes the following inference as its slogan:

Where there is *Selzfass,* there is real client satisfaction; where there is shoddy amateur advertising, there is no satisfaction; so, remember, where there is *Selzfass* there is no shoddy amateur advertising.

Arguments are translated by translating the propositions that constitute their assumptions and conclusions, representing inference indicators by means of symbolic inference indicators.

How should such an argument be translated? We divide the inference into two assumptions and a conclusion, reading the 'so' as the inference indicator separating the two preceding assumptions from the conclusion that follows. If we avail ourselves of the three-stage translation process, then we first extract the following sentences:

1. Where S, C.
2. Where A, not-C.
_____
3. Where S, not-A.   Translation stage 1

The second stage of the translation is to substitute the appropriate notation for the propositional connectives left over from the first stage. Then, reading 'Where $\mathbb{P}$, $\mathbb{Q}$' as 'If $\mathbb{P}$, then $\mathbb{Q}$', we get

1. $S \supset C$
2. $A \supset {\sim}C$
_____
3. $S \supset {\sim}A$ Translation stage 2

There is no need for a third translation stage in this example, in which assumptions and conclusion in translation stage 2 involve no ambiguity of scope in the propositional connectives they contain. In Chapter 3, we use formal methods to decide whether the argument in this fictitious advertising slogan is deductively valid or invalid.

Demonstration 6: **Translating Arguments**

Translating arguments follows the same three-stage procedure as translating individual propositions.

PROBLEM: To symbolize an argument in propositional logic.

ARGUMENT: People are naturally good only if the law is unnecessary. People are naturally evil only if the law is ineffective. Unless people are naturally good, people are naturally evil. So, either the law is unnecessary or ineffective. (G, U, E, I)

STEP 1:   *Identify atomic propositions and truth functional connectives*
As in a previous demonstration problem, we underline the propositional connectives to make the atomic propositions appear by contrast, to which we then assign propositional symbols.

People are naturally good only if the law is unnecessary. People are naturally evil only if the law is ineffective. Unless people are naturally good, people are naturally evil. So, either the law is unnecessary or ineffective.

The atomic propositions are as follows:

1. People are naturally good (G).
2. The law is unnecessary (U).
3. People are naturally evil (E).
4. The law is ineffective (I).

STEP 2:   *Reconstruct the argument in line-numbered format*

1. People are naturally good <u>only if</u> the law is unnecessary.
2. People are naturally evil <u>only if</u> the law is ineffective.
3. <u>Unless</u> people are naturally good, people are naturally evil (or, People are naturally evil, <u>unless</u> people are naturally good).

---

4. <u>Either</u> the law is unnecessary <u>or</u> the law is ineffective.

STEP 3:   *Replace the atomic propositions with propositional symbols*

The first part of the three-stage translation process gives us the following deductive reconstruction:

1. G <u>only if</u> U.
2. E <u>only if</u> I.
3. <u>Unless</u> G, E (or, E <u>unless</u> G).

---

4. <u>Either</u> U <u>or</u> I.   Translation stage 1

STEP 4:   *Replace the ordinary language connectives with symbolic propositional connectives*

In the second part of the three-stage translation process, we finalize the proof by replacing the ordinary language propositional connectives with their formal symbolic counterparts.

1. $G \supset U$
2. $E \supset I$
3. $\sim G \supset E$

---

4. $U \lor I$ Translation stage 2

Again, because there is no ambiguity of scope among any of the propositional connectives in this problem, there is no need to go beyond translation stage 2 to translation stage 3.

Here is another example. The work of translation is presented in the usual three-stage process, and the preliminaries of identifying and abbreviating atomic propositions by propositional symbols are presupposed:

Tensions in the Mideast will ease only if foreign interests are not threatened. But either foreign interests are threatened and military solutions are attempted, or tensions in the Mideast will ease. Therefore, unless military solutions are attempted, tensions in the Mideast will ease. (T, F, M)

In the first step we obtain:

1. T only if F.

2. Either F and M or T.

3. T unless M.   Translation stage 1

Then, we substitute symbolic propositional connectives for their natural language equivalents:

1. $T \supset F$

2. $F \,\&\, M \lor T$

3. $\sim M \supset T$ Translation stage 2

At last, we punctuate the proposition in assumption 2, the only one that would otherwise contain an ambiguity in the scope of its propositional connectives, by adding parentheses in the obvious way, according to the original English sentence, to obtain:

1. $T \supset F$

2. $(F \,\&\, M) \lor T$

3. $\sim M \supset T$ Translation stage 3

As a final example in this category of medium difficulty, let us try translating the following argument:

When duty and desire conflict, one must do one's duty. But duty and desire conflict when and only when something pleasurable is forbidden. Hence one must do one's duty only when something pleasurable is forbidden. (C, D, P)

The first stage of translation takes us to an argument with a logical structure of the following form:

1. When C, D.

2. C only when P.

3. D only when P.   Translation stage 1

The third stage of translation is not needed when the resulting wffs are not logically complex enough to involve a potential ambiguity of the scopes of multiple propositional connectives.

Next, by substitution of formal syntax for propositional connectives in the ordinary language expression, we obtain an argument in which there is no need to proceed to the third translation stage:

1. C ⊃ D

2. C ⊃ P
___

3. D ⊃ P   Translation stage 2

Now we analyze a choice of more complicated arguments. The following is an inference with additional assumptions and conclusions to translate:

> If the rudder does not break and the fuel holds out, the ship will get safely to port and no one will drown. If the fuel holds out but the rudder breaks, then the ship can be steered by means of its propellers, and if so, then it will get safely to port. If the rudder does not break, the fuel will hold out. Therefore the ship will get safely to port. (R, F, P, D, S)

To begin as before, we uniformly substitute propositional symbols for corresponding propositional symbols but leave the propositional connective contexts in ordinary language intact.

1. If not-R and F, then P and not-D.

2. If F and R, then S, and if S, then P.

3. If not-R, then F.
___

4. P   Translation stage 1

We transform the first version of the formalization to its completed translation by substituting symbolic for ordinary language propositional connectives. Then we obtain, by collapsing the second and third translation stages:

1. (~R & F) ⊃ (P & ~D)

2. ((F & R) ⊃ S) & (S ⊃ P)

3. ~R ⊃ F
___

4. P   Translation stages 2 and 3

Symbolic logic can be used to analyze the validity of arguments in philosophical reasoning.

Finally, we consider a controversial argument from the history of philosophical theology. Many thinkers have tried logically to prove, and perhaps as many to disprove, the existence of God. Lactantius, a third-century B.C.E. writer, in *The Wrath of God,* advances the following trilemma argument against the existence of God.

The argument depends for its conceptual background on a philosophical worry of theologians known as the problem of evil, which the study of theodicy is devoted to trying to solve, avoid, or in any case to better understand. The God of traditional monotheistic religions (Judaism, Christianity, and Islam) is often said by definition to be omniscient or all-knowing, omnipotent or all-powerful, and perfectly benevolent or all-good. Yet there exists natural evil in the world. That is, persons suffer, not apparently as the direct outcome of any exercise of human free will but just because of impersonal facts about the way the world is constituted. If God exists, the argument continues, then there exists an omniscient, omnipotent, and perfectly benevolent being. But if there is natural evil in the world, then either God does not know about the evil, or God knows about but cannot prevent the evil, or God knows about the evil and could prevent it but chooses not to do so. If God does not know about the natural evil in the world, then God is not omniscient. If God cannot prevent the natural evil in the world, then God is not omnipotent. Also, if God chooses not to prevent the natural evil in the world, then God is not perfectly good. Therefore, God does not exist.

We translate the argument into symbolic logic in our three-stage translation procedure by first identifying the atomic propositions and distinguishing them from the propositional connectives. We substitute propositional symbols for the atomic propositions, and transcribe the English propositional connectives in the first translation stage. We can do this graphically by circling the atomic propositions and drawing boxes around the propositional connectives to help distinguish them. Here it appears that eight propositional symbols are required for eight distinct atomic propositions. We use the following abbreviations: God exists (G); There exists an omniscient being (S); There exists an omnipotent being (P); There exists a perfectly benevolent being (B); There exists natural evil in the world (E); God knows about the natural evil in the world (K); God is able to prevent the natural evil in the world (A); God chooses to prevent the natural evil in the world (C).

The translation in its first phase appears as follows:

The deductive validity of complicated arguments in ordinary language can be evaluated if correctly translated into symbolic logic.

1. If G, then S and P and B.
2. E.
3. If E, then either not-K or K and not-A or K and A but not-C.
4. If not-K, then not-S.
5. If not-A, then not-P.
6. If not-C, then not-B.

---

7. Not-G   Translation stage 1

The final step is to substitute propositional connectives for their ordinary language equivalents. Then, again collapsing the second and third translation stages, we have

1. G ⊃ ((S & P) & B)

2. E

3. E ⊃ (~K ∨ ((K & ~A) ∨ ((K & A) & ~C)))

4. ~K ⊃ ~S

5. ~A ⊃ ~P

6. ~C ⊃ ~B

_____

7. ~G   Translation stages 2 and 3

Arguments in symbolic logic can be written as sequents, using the turnstile as a symbolic inference indicator.

We can also write out the assumptions and conclusions of a formalized argument horizontally as a *sequent*.

> **Sequent**
> If $\mathbb{P}_1, \ldots, \mathbb{P}_m$ and $\mathbb{Q}_1, \ldots, \mathbb{Q}_n$ are any wffs, then $\mathbb{P}_1, \ldots, \mathbb{P}_m \vdash \mathbb{Q}_1, \ldots, \mathbb{Q}_n$ is a *sequent* ($m, n \geq 1$).

The turnstile can be interpreted as a 'therefore' sign.

To symbolize arguments in a convenient format, we introduce the *turnstile* symbol or 'therefore' sign, '⊢'. The turnstile is not a truth function or propositional connective but rather a symbolic inference indicator that distinguishes between a sequent's assumptions and conclusions. The turnstile, like an ordinary language inference indicator, represents the claim that the sequent is deductively valid. The turnstile is a symbolic inference indicator with the intuitive force of 'therefore', 'thus', or 'hence'. In the previous example, using this device the argument can also be given as G ⊃ ((S & P) & B), E, E ⊃ (~K ∨ ((K & ~A) ∨ ((K & A) & ~C))), ~K ⊃ ~S, ~A ⊃ ~P, and ~C ⊃ ~B ⊢ ~G.

To Check Your Understanding 2.6

Translate the following arguments as sequents of symbolic propositional logic using the turnstile as a symbolic inference indicator and parentheses to avoid logical ambiguity.

1. It is time for a haircut, or, if it is time for a shave, then if it is time for a haircut, then it is also time for a shave. Therefore, either it is time for a haircut, or either it is not time for a haircut or not time for a shave, or it is time for a shave. (H, S)

2. If the duke dies, the earl must leave the kingdom. If the earl leaves the kingdom, then the king may abdicate, but the queen will continue in his place. Either the king will not abdicate, or the queen

will not continue in his place. Hence, the duke must not die.
(D, E, K, Q)

3. No one denies that the earth is flat. Now, either we eventually sail off the end and are drowned in a pit of demons, or we are taken up by angels just before plunging headlong into the abyss. Then, either there is no end to the earth, or else the earth is not flat, or for other unknown reasons we cannot ever sail off the end. From this, we must conclude that if there is an end to the earth, then we shall be taken up by angels just before plunging headlong into the abyss. (F, S, D, A, E)

4. When the mixture begins to bubble, there will be a delicious aroma of vanilla beans, if the ingredients are unspoiled. As the mixture begins to cool, there will appear either a thin irridescent green film, or a faint red striation across the surface of the liquid. If the irridescent green film appears, then the ingredients are unspoiled. Thus, either the mixture cools or there will be a delicious aroma of vanilla beans. (B, A, S, C, G, R).

5. Either the game will not be played and it will not be broadcast, or it will not be played and not rescheduled. It stands to reason that if there is a public outcry about the cancellation, and enough people write letters of complaint to the managing officials, then the game will be played. So, either there will be no public outcry about the cancellation, or not enough people will write letters of complaint to the managing officials. (P, B, R, O, L)

6. The law does not apply just in case the statute of limitations has run out and either the plaintiff is no longer in residence in the state or there is a jurisdiction dispute. If the complaint is still on file and there has been no injunction against the proceedings, then the law does not apply. Now the complaint is still on file and all parties to the proceedings have been duly notified, but in the meantime there has arisen a jurisdiction dispute. Therefore, the statute of limitations has not run out, but either the plaintiff is no longer in residence in the state or the law applies. (A, S, R, J, F, I, N)

■

Summary: Propositional
Syntax and Semantics

The syntax of symbolic proposition logic consists of its symbols for all possible propositionally well-formed formulas (wffs). The syntax includes propositional symbols that symbolize entire propositions, such as P, Q, R; the five propositional connectives for negation (~), conjunction (&), disjunction (∨), conditional (⊃), and biconditional (≡); parentheses ( ), to avoid logical ambiguity in the groupings of wffs within more complex wffs; and whatever can be constructed out of these components according to the formation rules for propositional wffs. The semantics of propositional logic is provided by truth table definitions of the five propositional connectives. There are alternative terms and phrases for most propositional connectives in ordinary language that are translated by the five propositional connectives. We need to recognize their occurrence in such expressions as 'but', 'although', 'when', 'where', 'only if' 'unless', and 'just in case'. Translation from ordinary language into the symbolic notation of propositional logic is more an art than a mechanical technique. We follow a three-stage translation procedure to transform propositions and arguments from everyday discourse into equivalent expressions that first retain colloquial propositional connectives, which are then replaced with corresponding symbols, the result of which is punctuated if necessary by parentheses in order to produce a wff that avoids all ambiguity in the scopes of any of its multiple propositional connectives. Arguments are translated into the symbolic notation of propositional logic as sequences of propositions, in which inference indicators distinguish assumptions from conclusions.

Key Words

syntax

semantics

well-formed formula (wff)
  (of propositional logic)

propositional symbol

propositional connective

parentheses

atomic

propositionally complex

negation

conjunction

disjunction

conditional

biconditional

mnemonic value (of a propositional
  symbol)

propositional variable

formation rules for wffs

unary propositional connective
  (negation, ~)

binary propositional connective
  (conjunction, &; disjunction, ∨;
  conditional, ⊃; and biconditional, ≡)

scope of a propositional connective

parentheses requirement for wffs
  rules

truth value

truth function

informal semantics

truth table

truth table definition of a
  propositional connective

truth table semantics

disjuncts

inclusive and exclusive disjunction

three-stage translation procedure

weak and strong sense of 'unless'

propositional duality relations

DeMorgan equivalences

sequent

turnstile ('⊢') symbolic inference

   indicator or 'therefore' symbol

Exercises

I: Propositional Syntax and Semantics Concepts   Give a correct concise statement of each of the following concepts; where appropriate give an illustration of each that does not appear in the book:

1. Syntax
2. Semantics
3. Truth function
4. Propositional symbol
5. Propositional variable
6. Atomic proposition
7. Propositionally complex proposition
8. Inclusive disjunction, exclusive disjunction
9. Unary, binary propositional connective
10. Truth functional definition of a propositional connective

II: Atomic Propositions and Propositional Connectives   In each of the following ordinary language expressions, draw a box around the atomic propositions, and draw a circle around the propositional connectives; propose mnemonic propositional symbols for the atomic propositions:

1. I was visiting in New York and Chicago.
2. If you go to San Francisco, you're going to meet some gentle people there.
3. The best way to approach a problem is to consider its origins and consequences, or how it conflicts with other things we believe to be true.
4. Steven will send the package just in case he receives your message.
5. Rebecca is planning to go to law school, although she has yet to apply.
6. Either Iran or Iraq will try to extend its sphere of influence in the Mideast before the end of the century.
7. We make hay when the sun shines.

8. If the patient's blood pressure falls dramatically, then if there are no warning signs of cardiac trouble, we will administer a mild stimulant.

9. She will not approve the loan if we cannot prove that we have enough collateral.

10. Matt and Mabel will neither drive to Oshkosh nor take the ferry from Manitowoc.

11. If today is Monday, and yesterday was Sunday, then either today or tomorrow is a holiday.

12. When danger threatens, the loona-goona bird tries to distract potential predators by feigning injury, unless all nestlings are safely under cover.

13. Elizabeth says that she will be able to attend the kayaking club committee if and only if the rock climbing club is not meeting that day or she does not have an exam to take.

14. Raymond explained that he would be late for dinner only if his car broke down, and he told us in that case not to wait for him unless he calls.

15. If we go to Paris, we'll visit the Louvre and the Museé D'Orsay; but if we go to Amsterdam, we'll either see the Rijksmuseum or the Vincent van Gogh.

16. When these metals react with the reagent, they form two gases and a solid precipitate, and this can only be done in the most extreme cases at atmospheric pressures below sea level.

17. The ancient Chinese invented the wheelbarrow, gunpowder, and moveable type for printing, but it was the Turkish Muslims who perfected the most powerful cannons in the Middle Ages.

18. The problems facing a United Europe are unsolvable except at the cost of a deplorable homogenization of the distinctive indigenous cultures of its member states.

19. Minds are not simply machines if at least some minds can do things no machines can possibly do; moreover, we know full well that there are many things minds can do that no machines can possibly do, if minds can fall in love and machines cannot.

20. Bach and Mozart were classical composers before the time of Chopin and Liszt; yet neither Chopin nor Liszt experimented with electronic music.

III: Transcription from Symbolization to Ordinary Language   For each of these interpretations of atomic propositional symbols, give appropriate transcriptions into ordinary language expressions of the following symbolizations in propositional logic: P, The computer is down; Q, We can locate your account;

R, You are entitled to a rebate; S, We will notify you by mail; T, Tomorrow is another day; U, We will process your application; V, There will be a delay in all business transactions.

1. ~P
2. R ⊃ S
3. (R & Q) ⊃ (U ∨ S)
4. ~(R & Q) ⊃ (U ∨ S)
5. ~(~(R & Q) ⊃ (U ∨ ~S))
6. Q ⊃ ~P
7. S ≡ (V & (P ≡ ~Q))
8. ((~R ⊃ ~S) ∨ (V & Q)) ⊃ S
9. ~(((~R ⊃ ~S) ∨ (V & Q)) ⊃ ~S)
10. (P ⊃ (V & ~Q)) & ((T & U) & (R ⊃ S))

IV: Symbolization of Propositions in Propositional Logic   Translate each of the following propositions from ordinary language into the symbolic notation of propositional logic using the propositional symbols provided; follow the three-stage translation procedure where necessary:

1. If today is Monday, and yesterday was Sunday, then tomorrow is a holiday. (M, S, H)

2. When danger threatens, the loona-goona bird tries to distract potential predators by feigning injury, unless all nestlings are safely under cover. (T, D, S)

3. Elizabeth says that she will be able to attend the kayaking club committee if and only if the rock climbing club is not meeting that day or she does not have an exam to take. (K, R, E)

4. Raymond explained that he would be late for dinner only if his car broke down, and he told us in that case not to wait for him unless he calls. (L, B, W, C)

5. If we go to Paris, we'll visit the Louvre and the Museé D'Orsay; but if we go to Amsterdam, we'll either see the Rijksmuseum or the Vincent van Gogh. (P, L, M, A, R, V)

6. These metals react with the reagent to form gases and a solid precipitate whenever they are heated above crystalization point, and this can only be done in the most extreme cases at atmospheric pressures below sea level. (R, P, H, A)

7. The ancient Chinese invented the wheelbarrow, gunpowder, and moveable type for printing, but it was the Turkish Muslims who perfected the most powerful cannons in the Middle Ages. (W, G, T, C)

8. The problems facing a United Europe are unsolvable unless there occurs a deplorable homogenization of the distinctive indigenous cultures of its member states. (P, H)

9. Minds are not simply machines if at least some minds can do things no machines can possibly do; moreover, we know full well that there are many things minds can do that no machines can possibly do, if minds can fall in love and machines cannot. (M, T, D, L, F)

10. Bach and Mozart were classical composers before the time of Chopin and Liszt; yet neither Chopin nor Liszt experimented with electronic music. (B, L, M, C, E, X)

11. If the Toltecs ruled in Mesoamerica, then if the Aztecs built sun temples for sacrifice before the Maya, then the Maya ruled before the Chaco Canyon peoples. (T, A, M)

12. There is no stopping progress where ideas are freely exchanged and human needs can be satisfied by technological innovation. (S, F, N)

13. It's not the case that if leaders rule then the people follow only if leaders rule, if and only if, when the people do not follow then if the leaders rule then either the people do not follow or the leaders rule. (L, P)

14. When I bend down too quickly, I hear a sound like the roar of the ocean for about 15 seconds; but when I stand up too quickly, I either experience a ringing of the Cologne cathedral bells or a foghorn off the New England coast; although, admittedly, when I sit still for too long, I seem to hear the distant sound of a jackhammer on asphalt. (B, R, Q, C, F, S, J)

15. Plato could not understand his brilliant pupil Aristotle, but Aristotle could understand Plato only if Plato could understand Aristotle and only if Aristotle could not understand Plato. (P, A)

16. If as the universe expands time contracts, then at any moment either the universe does not expand or time contracts. (E, C)

17. Hemingway wrote novels only after he had gained his reputation as a journalist, but despite the wide acclaim earned by the fiction of his early years, most critics regard Hemingway's later prose as stilted and unmusical. (N, J, E, S, M)

18. We will either go to Vermont or New Hampshire this summer just in case we can arrange simultaneous vacation times and find an affordable cottage to rent or are invited to stay with friends. (V, N, S, C, F)

19. Some people are better at math than others, and if some people are better at math than others, then they find it easy to solve math problems; but some people are better at math than others and no one finds it easy to solve math problems, only if it is not the case that some people are better at math than others. (B, E)

20. Unless someone finds a way to the summit, we will not be able to cross the glacier or set up base camp below the mountain until nightfall; and, if we are to observe the precautions we were given, then we must reconnoitre another entrance to the valley pass tomorrow, or else turn back and try again next season. (S, G, C, P, R, T, N)

V: Symbolization of Arguments in Propositional Logic Translate each of the following arguments from ordinary language into the symbolic notation of propositional logic; follow the three-stage translation procedure where necessary.

1. If time is relative, then if the universe is expanding, then eventually it must begin to contract again. But this can only occur if time is not relative. Therefore, time is not relative. (R, E, C)

2. If bananas can be raised, so can apples, but not coconuts. Now, bananas can be raised, if coconuts can be raised wherever apples can. So, we must conclude that we can raise apples if and only if we cannot raise coconuts. (B, A, C)

3. Either the Civil War was a great triumph for liberty, or it was no such thing but the most disastrous episode of senseless bloodshed in American history. If, assuming the Civil War was no great triumph for liberty, but was instead the most disastrous episode of senseless bloodshed in American history, then we can only conclude that ending slavery and maintaining the Union could have been accomplished nonviolently. Hence, ending slavery and maintaining the Union could have been accomplished nonviolently. (T, D, E, M)

4. Either we win or lose on Saturday. If we lose, then if we're lucky in the next game, we can still go on to the state finals. We'll win on Saturday, unless we have to try again next year just in case we're unlucky in the next game. So, even if we cannot go on to the state finals but have to try again next year, we'll still win on Saturday. (W, L, N, S, T)

5. If, if Socrates criticizes Plato then Plato criticizes Aristotle, then disagreement prevails in the ancient Greek Academy. If Theophrastus defends Aristotle, then if Plato does not criticize Aristotle, then Aristotle defends Socrates. Hence, the inescapable and highly paradoxical conclusion, that if

disagreement prevails in the ancient Greek Academy or Aristotle defends Socrates, then, in case Theophrastus defends Aristotle, disagreement prevails in the ancient Greek Academy. (S, P, D, T, A)

6. It's not possible to have both a good time and keep your money. If you don't have a good time and you don't keep your money, then you will have thrown away your fortune and have no positive experiences to show for it. So, you do, as a matter of fact, have positive experiences as a result of spending all your money. (G, K, T, P)

7. Renoir was an Impressionist but Picasso was not, if, that is, either Picasso or Quinault were Impressionists. Either Quinault or Renoir was an Impressionist. But, as everyone knows, Renoir was no Impressionist. Therefore, Picasso was also not an Impressionist. (R, P, Q)

8. If the jury is hung and the accused goes free, then if the law is still in effect, then there'll be a mistrial and a retrial. If the prosecution has its way, there'll be a mistrial and a retrial. The accused goes free only if the prosecution doesn't have its way. Yet it's not the case that the jury is hung only if the law is no longer in effect. Hence, we can clearly conclude that the jury won't be hung. (J, F, L, M, R, P)

9. The dinosaurs are extinct, but not their descendents among certain birds and reptiles. Once the dinosaurs became extinct, there was no dominant life form on Earth, unless you count the newly emerging mammals. If you don't consider the newly emerging mammals as the dominant life form on Earth at the time, then there was no dominant life form just in case either the descendents of dinosaurs among certain reptiles or birds are extinct. Therefore, you must count the newly emerging mammals at the time of the extinction of dinosaurs as the dominant life form on Earth. (D, B, R, L, M)

10. If the body dies but the soul survives, then, if God exists, we may be held accountable before him for our good and bad deeds. If there is a Judgment Day before we die, we may still be held accountable before God for our good and bad deeds. Now, it's by no means true that there will be no Judgment Day if the soul survives the death of the body. Furthermore, it's not the case that if the body dies then God exists. Thus, the soul is immortal. (D, S, E, G, B, J)

11. We should act only if, where we have a chance of succeeding or stalling our opponent, we can win victory and avoid disgrace. If we manage to avoid disgrace or preserve our honor, our labors will have been worth the effort. It follows ineluctably that if we should act, then, if we can at least stall our opponent, our labors will have been worth the effort. (A, C, S, V, D, H, L)

12. If lithography is a fine art, then so is photography. If photography is a fine art, then so is xeroxing. If either xeroxing is not a fine art or woodblock

printing is a fine art, then lithography is not. Hence, if xeroxing is a fine art, then lithography and woodblock printing are fine arts. (L, P, X, W)

13. Had the Austrians and Russians beaten the French before 1812, Napoléon would never have taken Moscow. If the Austrians had beaten the French prior to 1812, then the Russians would have too. If Napoléon did not take Moscow, but the British had thrown in their support for the Austrians, then the course of the war would have been very different. Therefore, if Napoléon had not taken Moscow, then the British would have thrown in their support for the Austrians only if the course of the war had taken a radically different turn. (A, R, N, B, D)

14. Where an ordinary wet match is struck, no flame is produced. But matches cannot be ignited if and only if, if they do not come into contact with water, then they remain perfectly dry. From this, we see plainly, it follows that ordinary matches will not light if and only if they are wet, and, moreover, that they will light provided they do not come into contact with water. (M, W, F, C, I, D, L)

15. Either we are on the Moss–Hanne or the Star Mill Trail. We couldn't be so far off track that we would have wandered out of the park and into the refuge. And I'm quite sure it's not the case that we're still on the Moss–Hanne trail and that we're out of the park. So, I'd say that if we've not wandered out of the park, then we've somehow gotten onto the Star Mill Trail. (M, S, P, R)

16. Let's agree that if stars or stars together with their planets eventually become black holes, but cannot coalesce in deep space, then there's no proof for the theory of a cyclical cosmology. If it's true that black holes cannot coalesce in deep space, then there is after all proof for a cyclical cosmology, then if black holes exert gravitational force on one another, they might be able to change location in deep space. Of course, it's been known for many years that black holes do in fact exert gravitational force on one another across deep reaches of space. Therefore, if stars eventually become black holes, then they can certainly change location in deep space. Moreover, and more important, it follows that there is indeed proof for the existence of a cyclical cosmology. (S, P, C, T, G, L)

17. The price of oil is determined by political events only if there is instability in the oil-producing regions and there is either no international policy in force or revolution is imminent. Either there is no instability in the oil-producing regions or the market finds alternative fuel sources, but either there is an international policy in force or an enormous increase in the costs of petroleum products can be expected, despite the fact that either revolution is by no means imminent or the worldwide demand for oil is significantly diminished. But of course neither an enormous increase in the

costs of petroleum products can be expected nor a significant diminishing of worldwide demand for oil. The price of oil is most definitely determined by political events. Therefore, revolution in the oil-producing regions is imminent. (O, I, P, R, M, E, D)

18. The will is free only if it is causally undetermined or able to choose without compulsion by natural forces and prior events. If the will is causally undetermined, then either it is an immaterial entity or the laws of physics do not strictly apply to it. If the laws of physics do not strictly apply to the will, then free will decisions and actions are causally ungovernable. But, as we know from everyday experience, it is patently not the case that either free will decisions and actions are causally ungovernable or that the will is an immaterial entity. From which we can only conclude that the will is not free. (F, D, C, I, P, G)

19. If Kodiak bears hibernate just in case the photoperiod and temperature are sufficiently reduced, then it should be impossible to prevent them from hibernating in experimental conditions in which these factors are exactly duplicated. Either Kodiaks do not hibernate but remain naturally active all winter, or they migrate to another climate and breed far from their hunting territories. Yet, we have confirmed by yearly observation that these animals in their native habitat either remain active all winter or migrate to another climate and breed far from their hunting territories, only if, where photoperiod and temperature are sufficiently reduced, we can, if we experimentally exactly duplicate these factors, prevent Kodiaks from hibernating. From this, it follows that if Kodiaks do not hibernate, then photoperiod and temperature are insufficiently reduced. (H, P, T, C, D, A, M, B)

20. When a new virus attacks a computer, there is no preventing it from deleting all the files. But if the virus is prevented from attacking, then it is still possible that files will be lost through addressing errors. An operating system crashes only if, where the central processing unit or virtual clock are undamaged, the operating system is made to compensate for assembly language conflicts. We know that our newest machines cannot lose files through addressing errors, and their operating systems are internally prevented from compensating for assembly language conflicts. Therefore, we are absolutely sure that files will not be deleted unless a new virus attacks the computer. (V, D, A, O, P, I, C)

VI: Short Answer Questions for Philosophical Reflection

1. Can there be syntax without semantics?
2. Can there be semantics without formal syntax?

3. Do we recover meaning and express it more accurately when we symbolize sentences from ordinary language in the notation of symbolic propositional logic, or do we inevitably distort and transform it, imposing on it a new meaning of our own?

4. Are all propositions in ordinary language true or false exclusively? Is it possible for some propositions to be neither true nor false, or both true and false? What about a sentence that says of itself, 'I am [this sentence is] false'? Can it be simply true or simply false?

5. Is there any conceptual connection between the conditional truth function of propositional logic and the causal conditional of empirical law and inductive reasoning? If so, what? If not, why not?

6. What is the difference between the logical form of an atomic proposition and a propositionally complex proposition, if any proposition whatsoever can be abbreviated in symbolic propositional logic by means of a single propositional symbol?

CHAPTER THREE

Truth Tables

A proposition is the expression of agreement and disagreement with the
truth-possibilities of the elementary propositions.
— Ludwig Wittgenstein, *Tractatus Logico-Philosophicus* 4.4 (1922)

As A WAY OF TESTING propositions and arguments, we now introduce truth tables. Truth tables are decision methods that give
correct answers to specific questions about the logical properties
of wffs and sequents.

Decision Methods

*A decision method is
an exact procedure for
determining whether
or not a proposition
or argument has
a particular logical
property.*

A *decision method* is an exact step-by-step procedure that determines in a definite
number of steps whether a proposition or argument in symbolic logic has or
does not have a certain logical property.

    We have already seen that testing the validity of arguments by the infor-
mal imagination criterion can be difficult and unreliable. There are inferences
in which it is possible for the assumptions to be true and the conclusions false,
but only in circumstances that we cannot imagine. There are other cases in
which we may convince ourselves that we clearly imagine a possibility that
harbors a hidden inconsistency. We can improve our ability to analyze the logical properties of propositions and arguments by developing a formal decision
method for propositional logic.

*Decision methods
determine whether in-
dividual wffs are tau-
tologies, inconsisten-
cies, or contingencies.*

    We use decision methods in propositional logic to decide (i) whether a
proposition is logically true (a *tautology*), logically false (an *inconsistency*), or neither logically true nor logically false (a *contingency*); (ii) whether or not two or
more propositions are *logically consistent* or *logically inconsistent;* and (iii) whether

108

Decision methods determine whether two or more individual wffs are logically consistent or inconsistent and logically equivalent or nonequivalent.

Decision methods determine whether an argument sequent is deductively valid or invalid.

two or more propositions are or are not *logically equivalent.* We also use decision methods to decide whether an argument is *deductively valid* or *deductively invalid.* These concepts are more rigorously defined and illustrated later by concrete applications. Symbolic propositional logic supports a variety of decision methods. Two of the most important are *truth tables* and *truth trees,* both of which are based on the truth table definitions of propositional connectives. We explain the truth table method for propositional logic primarily as a theoretical foundation for the discussion of the logical properties of propositions and arguments in this chapter, and then in Chapter 4, we discuss truth trees as a more practical, flexible, and universally applicable method.

Truth Tables

A truth table is a display of truth values correlated with wffs according to the truth table definitions of the five propositional connectives. The following is a typical example:

P	Q	(Q	⊃	P)	⊃	P
T	T	T	T	T	|T|	T
T	F	F	T	T	|T|	T
F	T	T	F	F	|T|	F
F	F	F	T	F	|F|	F

Truth table definitions of the five propositional connectives are applied to the main connective in a propositionally complex wff to calculate its truth table analysis.

The truth values of any number of atomic propositional symbols are assigned in every logically possible combination according to *truth table setup rules.* The truth values of any propositionally complex propositions containing the propositional symbols are then truth functionally determined by the truth table definitions of the propositional connectives. The truth value of the complex proposition is displayed in the truth table along with the truth values of all its component propositional symbols.

Truth tables begin with standard truth table setup rules.

In using truth tables as a decision method, we apply the truth table definitions of propositional connectives to a series of wffs. To introduce truth tables as a decision method, we first recall the truth table definitions of the five propositional connectives from Chapter 2.

A tautology is a logically true proposition (necessarily true).

We begin with truth table evaluations of single propositions and then consider their application to arguments. There are three main categories of logical properties by which we classify propositions. We want to know whether a proposition is a logical truth (tautology), a logical falsehood (inconsistency), or neither a logical truth nor a logical falsehood (contingency). A decision method

An inconsistency is a logically false proposition (necessarily false).

TRUTH TABLE DEFINITIONS OF PROPOSITIONAL CONNECTIVES						
$\mathbb{P}$	$\mathbb{Q}$	$\sim\mathbb{P}$	$\mathbb{P} \And \mathbb{Q}$	$\mathbb{P} \lor \mathbb{Q}$	$\mathbb{P} \supset \mathbb{Q}$	$\mathbb{P} \equiv \mathbb{Q}$
T	T	F	T	T	T	T
T	F	[F]	F	T	F	F
F	T	T	F	T	T	F
F	F	[T]	F	F	T	T

A contingency is a proposition that is neither logically true nor logically false (possibly true and possibly false).

should tell us how to classify any wff as a tautology, inconsistency, or contingency. The method should also determine the logical consistency or logical inconsistency, and the logical equivalence or logical nonequivalence, of any choice of wffs. Finally, the method should decide of any argument whether it is deductively valid or invalid. Truth tables, within practical limits, give correct answers to all these questions.

In a truth table, we consider all truth value assignments to the propositional symbols relevant to the truth value of a propositionally complex wff. By defining the propositional connectives in terms of truth value assignments to component propositional symbols, truth table definitions of the propositional connectives determine the truth values of any proposition built up from them by means of the propositional connectives. We work out the truth values of each of the component wffs from the possible combinations assigned to atomic wffs until the truth value of the entire proposition can be calculated from the inputs to each component propositional connective, considered as a truth function. The truth table definitions for the propositional connectives thereby determine the truth table of any propositionally complex wff.

Main Connectives

Every propositionally complex wff has a *main connective*. The main connective of a proposition is the propositional connective by which the entire proposition is classified as a negation, conjunction, disjunction, conditional, or biconditional. We consider a general syntax rule and guidelines for implementing the rule in order to identify main propositional connectives. The rule is based on the definition of the scope of a propositional connective, and the guidelines for implementing the rule are based on the parentheses requirement for propositional wffs.

Truth table analysis requires identifying the main connective in a propositionally complex wff.

We use parentheses to group propositions as truth functional units in different combinations according to the formation rules for propositional wffs.

Main propositional connectives are identified according to a greatest scope rule, together with a fewest parentheses guideline.

The use of parentheses to punctuate a propositionally complex proposition's propositional components creates a nesting of parentheses within parentheses. By the parentheses requirement, a definite propositional connective always links together propositionally complex propositions that are first enclosed within parentheses. The simplest, ultimately atomic, propositions are increasingly more deeply nested within the more encompassing scopes of propositional connectives, as indicated by the number of parentheses in which they are enclosed. There is a progression of internal complexity in a propositionally complex proposition that extends from its atomic wffs to propositionally more complex components, and finally to the entire proposition. If we think of a propositionally complex proposition as being built up in stages by the rules for wffs and the parentheses guidelines, then no matter how propositionally complex a proposition is, it always contains a particular occurrence of a particular propositional connective introduced at the final stage of its construction. This is the proposition's main connective, which has greater scope than any other connective that the proposition may contain and, indeed, has the entire proposition in which it occurs in its scope.

The connective with the greatest scope in a propositionally complex wff is the main propositional connective.

Greatest Scope Rule for Identifying Propositional Main Connectives
The main propositional connective of any propositionally complex wff is the propositional connective that has the greatest scope, or that includes the entire wff in its scope.

The rule tells us in the abstract which is the main propositional connective in a propositionally complex wff. We recall that the scope of a propositional connective is the propositionally least complex wff in which the propositional connective occurs. We can therefore appreciate the fact that the main connective of any propositionally complex wff will always be the propositional connective with the greatest scope. That is, the main propositional connective of any propositionally complex wff is always the one and only propositional connective that includes the entire wff in its scope.

To implement the rule, we need a way of deciding which of several propositional connectives has the greatest scope in a propositionally complex wff, or which connective has the entire wff in its scope. We can do this from a practical standpoint by appealing to guidelines based on the parentheses requirement for wffs. The parentheses requirement stipulates that any wff must be enclosed in parentheses before being uniformly substituted for any of the propositional variables in the formation rules for propositional wffs. Increasingly complex wffs are obtained only by first enclosing simpler wffs in parentheses and then uniformly substituting them for propositional variables in the basic wffs formation rules. The parentheses requirement thereby avoids ambiguity in the scope of propositional connectives, with the result that exactly one propositional connective in any propositionally complex wff will always have the greatest scope, including the entire wff in its scope. By virtue of the parentheses requirement on the formation rules for propositional wffs, this will also be the propositional connective (with one easily explained exception for certain occurrences of negation) that is enclosed by the fewest number of parentheses. Accordingly, we can readily apply the greatest scope rule for identifying main propositional connectives by means of the following guidelines:

Fewest Parentheses Guidelines for Identifying Propositional Main Connectives

The main propositional connective of any propositionally complex wff is identified by the following conditions:

1. If only one propositional connective is enclosed by the fewest number (including zero as a limiting case) of parentheses in the wff, then it is the main connective.
2. If several propositional connectives are enclosed by the same number of parentheses, and all but one are negation signs, then the connective that is not a negation sign is the main connective.
3. If several propositional connectives are enclosed by the same number of parentheses, and all are negation signs, then the leftmost negation sign is the main connective.

The main propositional connective, the connective with the greatest scope in a propositionally complex wff, is identified as the connective surrounded by the fewest number of parentheses, with an exception for negation attaching to propositional symbols and leftmost iterations of negations.

A main propositional connective includes an entire propositional wff in its scope.

The special case for negation is obvious. In a proposition of the form ~P ⊃ Q, even though both the conditional and the negation have precisely the same number of parentheses enclosing them (none), the conditional rather than the negation is the main connective. In a proposition of the form ~(P ⊃ Q), by contrast, it is the negation rather than the conditional that is the main connective. The reason is that according to the wffs formation rules under the parentheses requirement, the wff P must first be negated to become ~P before ~P can be connected to Q by the conditional in ~P ⊃ Q. This means that the negation cannot be the main connective in ~P ⊃ Q because the main connective is always the last one introduced when a complex wff is built up according to the formation rules. The opposite is true when propositional symbols are combined by negation and the conditional in the construction of ~(P ⊃ Q) because here the conditional P ⊃ Q must first be constructed before it can be negated. The main connective in a propositionally complex wff, together with the truth values of the main components, determines the truth value of the wff as a whole. For the same reason, the main connective is always the propositional connective in any complex wff with the greatest scope, which includes the entire wff in its scope.

Demonstration 7: **Identifying Main Connectives**

PROBLEM: To identify the main propositional connective in a propositionally complex wff.

PROPOSITION: P ⊃ (Q ⊃ R)

STEP 1:   *Identify the propositional connectives*
The proposition has two propositional connectives—two occurrences of the
conditional ⊃.

STEP 2:   *Distinguish the main propositional connective by applying the fewest
parentheses guideline*
The main propositional connective is whichever one has the greatest scope
or that includes the entire wff in its scope—that is (with exceptions for certain occurrences of negation that do not apply here), whichever connective
is enclosed by the fewest number of parentheses. The first rather than the
second conditional in the wff is the main connective. It is the operator that
links the primary antecedent of the propositional symbol P with the conditional consequent Q ⊃ R. If we intend the second conditional connective in
the unpunctuated sentence P ⊃ Q ⊃ R to be the main connective, then we
must instead write the proposition with parentheses around the first two
propositional symbols as (P ⊃ Q) ⊃ R. In contrast with the first, this proposition has an antecedent P ⊃ Q that is itself a conditional and proposition R
is the consequent. By considering the definitions of a wff and of the scope of
a propositional connective in a propostionally complex wff, we can also be
assured that the first conditional rather than the second is the main propositional connective because it is the propositional connective with the greatest
scope, which includes the entire wff in its scope.

To Check Your Understanding 3.1 ─────────────────────────────────────

Identify the main propositional connective in each of the following wffs; if the
component wffs are truth functionally complex, continue to identify the main
connective in each component wff.

1. P & (Q ⊃ (R ∨ S))
2. (P & (Q ⊃ (R ∨ ~S))) ⊃ ~R
3. (P & Q) ⊃ ~~(P & (Q ⊃ ~(R ∨ S)))
4. ~(P & Q) ⊃ ~~(P & (Q ⊃ ~(R ∨ S)))

    5. ~((P & Q) ⊃ ~~(P & (Q ⊃ ~(R ∨ S))))
    6. (P & (Q ⊃ (R ∨ ~S))) & ~(P & (Q ⊃ ~(R ∨ S)))

                                                                     ■

Truth Table Setup

A truth table is set up by displaying all the possible combinations of truth values for a choice of propositional symbols. The number of truth table combinations of the two truth values T and F that can be assigned to n propositional symbols is 2^n. In the case of an atomic proposition, in which we have only one propositional symbol, the truth table consists of $2^1 = 2$ rows—one T and one F. This is how truth tables represent the fact that an atomic proposition is always a logical contingency, which may be either true or false, or have either value T or F. If we have two propositional symbols, as in chapter 2's truth table definitions of the binary propositional connectives, then we require exactly $2^2 = 4$ combinations of truth values. If we have three propositional symbols, we need $2^3 = 8$ truth table rows; for four propositional symbols, a truth table must include $2^4 = 16$ combinations of truth value assignments; and so on. It is one of the practical limitations of truth tables that propositions with large numbers of propositional symbols quickly become unwieldy by requiring unmanageably expansive numbers of truth table rows.

Formula for Truth Table Rows
Truth table rows for n propositional symbols = 2^n

Truth tables require 2^n rows to array all possible truth value assignments to n propositional symbols.

    We now present the rules for truth table setup. The rules provide the basic structure of a truth table to be completed in testing the logical properties of propositions or arguments containing a certain number of propositional symbols.

Rules for Truth Table Setup
1. Write down a column consisting of half the number of 2^n ($2^n/2$) T's under the first propositional symbol column in the truth table, followed in the same column by the same number of half of 2^n F's.
2. Move rightward by one column and write down underneath the next propositional symbol a column consisting of half of half of 2^n ($2^n/4$) T's, followed by the same number of F's, followed again by the same number of T's followed by the same number of F's, and so on, decreasing by halves the number of T's followed by the same decreasing number of F's for each successive column beneath each propositional symbol in the same way until reaching the last propositional symbol in the rightmost column of the truth table.

Truth tables should always be set up in the same way for easy comparison and to avoid mistakes in truth table analysis.

It is important to have a systematic method for setting up a truth table by first listing all possible truth value combinations for the relevant number of propositional symbols in the proposition to be analyzed. Each additional propositional symbol doubles the number of rows of alternating T's and F's, where for n rows we always have n/2 T's followed by n/2 F's etc. for each propositional symbol. For a proposition with n propositional symbols, we write down the propositional symbols in the leftmost columns of the truth table. We can do this in any order we please. However, it is standard either to do so alphabetically or in the order from left to right in which the propositional symbols appear in the propositions or arguments to be tested. Then, working left to right, for each of the propositional symbols of the proposition we write down a column of 2^n T's and F's, according to the previous rule.

By setting up every truth table in the same way, we are assured of including the correct number of truth value combinations. If we get into the habit of always setting up truth tables in this same way, then we will not repeat or omit any combinations of truth values, which would invalidate the results, and we will have a uniform method for comparing truth table analyses of different wffs.

Truth table setup requires that we include all combinations of truth values of the component propositional symbols of a proposition or argument to be analyzed, neither excluding nor duplicating any values.

The general formula for each truth table column is to write $2^n/2^m$ T's followed by the same number of F's, where m is the number of each truth table column, working left to right, until $2^n = 2^m$. When the final stage of rule 2 is implemented, we inscribe a total of 2^n alternating truth values in the order T–F–T–F–T–F . . . To set up a truth table with two propositional symbols, we need $2^2 = 4$ truth table rows for, e.g., P, Q, with the sequence under P of T–T–F–F and under Q of T–F–T–F. For three propositional symbols, we need $2^3 = 8$ truth table rows for, e.g., P, Q, R, with the sequence under P of T–T–T–T–F–F–F–F, under Q of T–T–F–F–T–T–F–F, and under R of T–F–T–F–T–F–T–F.

The truth table in general form for the evaluation of any proposition with one propositional symbol P is set up to look as follows:

P
T
F

The truth table in general form for the evaluation of any proposition with two propositional symbols P, Q is set up to look as follows:

P	Q
T	T
T	F
F	T
F	F

The truth table set up for any proposition with three propositional symbols P, Q, R looks as follows:

P	Q	R	
T	T	T	
T	T	F	
T	F	T	
T	F	F	
F	T	T	
F	T	F	
F	F	T	
F	F	F	

Truth tables encounter practical limitations of space for problems involving more than four propositional symbols.

The method of setting up a truth table for analysis works generally for any number of propositional symbols. The difficulty is only having enough paper and time to write down large numbers of combinations for wffs containing many propositional symbols. A sentence with four propositional symbols requires four columns of 16 rows of truth value combinations (8 T's followed by 8 F's, then 4 T's, 4 F's, 4 T's, 4 F's, etc.); a sentence with five propositional symbols requires five columns of 32 rows of truth value combinations, etc. At this rate, things quickly get out of hand. We shall accordingly limit ourselves to truth tables of manageable proportions.

Propositional Semantic Concepts

We now define a series of semantic concepts. The following definitions explain some of the most fundamental logical properties of propositions and arguments. We develop truth tables as a decision method to classify wffs and sequents by the following categories.

Propositional semantic concepts are precisely defined in terms of truth table evaluations of wffs and sequents.

The most important concepts are those that distinguish an individual wff as a tautology, inconsistency, or contingency and that determine whether two or more wffs are logically consistent or inconsistent and logically equivalent or nonequivalent. Finally, we are interested in whether or not an argument sequent is deductively valid or invalid. A tautology is a logical truth that is true in any logically possible circumstances, no matter what facts happen to be true or false in the world. For example, the proposition 'It is raining' is either true or false, depending on the weather. However, the propositions 'Either it is raining or it is not the case that it is raining' and 'If it is raining, then it is raining' are sure to be true by virtue of their logical forms, regardless of whether or not it is actually raining. They cannot fail to be false, and they are accordingly classified as tautologies. In contrast, the proposition 'It is raining and it is not the case that it is raining' is an inconsistency or logical falsehood because its logical form makes it false under any conditions. Neither tautology nor inconsistency are interesting in the sense of conveying definite information about the state of the world. The proposition 'It is raining', on the other hand, proposes more informatively to tell us something that may be true or false, that we could not have known from our understanding of logic and language alone, in a form that we can use in theory and practice. It is a contingent proposition or contingency because its truth is contingent or conditional on the actual state of the world—in this case, on whether or not it is actually raining.

Logical consistency of two or more propositions is just the consistency of their conjunction. To be logically consistent means that the propositions do not contradict one another, or that considered together they are not always false. Logical equivalence is the property of two or more propositions that generally have the same truth value in any logically possible circumstances or that are always either both true or always both false. By truth table definitions it follows that two propositions are logically equivalent if and only if their biconditional is a logical truth or tautology.

Propositional Semantic Concepts

1. If $\mathbb{P}$ is a wff of propositional logic, then $\mathbb{P}$ is a *tautology* if and only if the truth table analysis of $\mathbb{P}$ produces only truth value T in every truth table row in the truth table column for the main propositional connective of $\mathbb{P}$ that evaluates $\mathbb{P}$ as a whole.

2. If $\mathbb{P}$ is a wff of propositional logic, then $\mathbb{P}$ is an *inconsistency* if and only if the truth table analysis of $\mathbb{P}$ produces only truth value F in every truth table row in the truth table column for the main propositional connective of $\mathbb{P}$ that evaluates $\mathbb{P}$ as a whole.

3. If $\mathbb{P}$ is a wff of propositional logic, then $\mathbb{P}$ is a *contingency* if and only if the truth table analysis of $\mathbb{P}$ produces the truth value T in at least one truth table row in the truth table column for the main propositional connective of $\mathbb{P}$ that evaluates $\mathbb{P}$ as a whole, and the truth value F in at least one truth table row in the truth table column for the main propositional connective of $\mathbb{P}$ that evaluates $\mathbb{P}$ as a whole (if and only if $\mathbb{P}$ is neither a tautology nor an inconsistency).

4. If $\mathbb{P}$ and $\mathbb{Q}$ are wffs of propositional logic, then $\mathbb{P}$ and $\mathbb{Q}$ are *logically consistent* if and only if there is a truth table analysis that produces the truth value T in at least one truth table row of the truth table column for the main propositional connective & that evaluates $\mathbb{P}$ & $\mathbb{Q}$ as a whole.

5. If $\mathbb{P}$ and $\mathbb{Q}$ are wffs of propositional logic, then $\mathbb{P}$ and $\mathbb{Q}$ are *logically equivalent* if and only if there is no truth table analysis that produces the truth value T in any truth table row of the truth table column for the

main propositional connective of $\mathbb{P}$ that evaluates $\mathbb{P}$ as a whole and in the same truth table row produces the truth value F in the truth table column for the main propositional connective of $\mathbb{Q}$ that evaluates $\mathbb{Q}$ as a whole, or that produces the truth value F in any truth table row of the truth table column for the main propositional connective of $\mathbb{P}$ that evaluates $\mathbb{P}$ as a whole and in the same truth table row produces the truth value T in the truth table column for the main propositional connective of $\mathbb{Q}$ that evaluates $\mathbb{Q}$ as a whole.

6. If $\mathbb{P}_1, \ldots, \mathbb{P}_n$ and $\mathbb{Q}_1, \ldots, \mathbb{Q}_n$ are wffs of propositional logic, then the sequent $\mathbb{P}_1, \ldots, \mathbb{P}_n \, \mathbb{P} \vdash \mathbb{Q}_1, \ldots, \mathbb{Q}_n$ is *deductively valid* if and only if truth table analysis determines that the corresponding conditional $(\mathbb{P}_1 \, \& \ldots \& \, \mathbb{P}_n) \supset (\mathbb{Q}_1, \ldots, \mathbb{Q}_n)$ is a tautology. (Or, equivalently, if and only if there is no truth table analysis that produces the truth value T in every truth table row of every truth table column that evaluates each of $\mathbb{P}_1, \ldots, \mathbb{P}_n$ and produces the truth value F in any truth table row of any truth table column that evaluates each of $\mathbb{Q}_1, \ldots, \mathbb{Q}_n$.)

Tautology, Inconsistency, and Contingency

Truth tables are used to evaluate individual wffs as tautologies (all T's), inconsistencies (all F's), or contingencies (at least one T and at least one F).

Tautologies as logical truths, and inconsistencies as logical falsehoods, convey no definite information; only contingencies express true or false propositions about actual matters of fact.

The truth value of a complex proposition is a function of the truth values of its component propositions. There are three possible truth value combinations in the truth table analysis of a proposition. A proposition in any logically possible circumstances is (i) always true, (ii) always false, or (iii) sometimes true and sometimes false. These are respectively the truth value signatures of a (i) tautology, (ii) inconsistency, and (iii) contingency.

Tautologies are logically true propositions—propositions that are true in any logically possible circumstances. Inconsistencies are logically false propositions—false in any logically possible circumstances. Contingencies are neither logically true nor logically false but true or false contingently, depending on the facts that happen to prevail. An atomic proposition or propositional symbol considered by itself has no component propositions. An atomic wff or propositional symbol considered by itself is therefore always a logical contingency. The truth value of a propositionally complex wff is a truth function of the truth values of its simpler and ultimately of its atomic wffs, and it can in principle therefore be a tautology, inconsistency, or contingency, depending on its logical structure.

The conditional, 'If snow is white, then snow is white', is a tautology. It does not make any substantive claim about the color of snow but merely asserts that if snow is white, then it is white. This is obviously not saying much. An inconsistency on the contrary is expressed by the sentence, 'Snow is white and it is not the case that snow is white'. Regardless of the color of snow, we here say something that cannot possibly be true but that is logically self-contradictory. Finally, a contingency is formulated by the proposition that 'Snow is white' (a contingent truth, depending on the actual color of snow) or 'Snow is green' (a contingent falsehood, given the actual color of snow). The truth of a tautology and the falsehood of an inconsistency are matters of pure logic. In symbolic propositional logic, the truth of a tautology and falsehood of an inconsistency are determined by the truth table definitions of the propositional connectives. The truth or falsehood of a contingency, as the name suggests, is contingent on circumstances in the world as they happen to obtain or fail to obtain. The negation of any contingency by truth tables is also a contingency because truth table analysis of both a contingency and its negation will contain at least some T's and at least some F's. How we discover or how we may best learn about these contingent truths is not a problem for logic but for science and history and other disciplines that investigate matters of fact.

Classifying Wffs by Truth Tables

Truth tables provide a decision method for classifying individual wffs as tautologies, inconsistencies, or contingencies.

The truth table column for the main propositional connective of a wff being evaluated determines the truth value of the wff as a whole for every combination of truth values to its component propositional symbols and its classification as a tautology, inconsistency, or contingency.

A proposition is shown by truth tables to be a tautology when the truth table column for its main connective contains only T (true) values, it is an inconsistency when the truth table column for its main connective contains only F (false) values, and it is a contingency when the truth table column for its main connective contains at least one T and at least one F (see box on page 120).

We now describe the truth table method for classifying propositions as tautologies, inconsistencies, or contingencies. We set up a truth table with the required number of rows of combinations of truth values for each of the proposition's n distinct atomic propositional symbols using the following formula: Truth table rows for n propositional symbols = 2^n. We identify the main propositional connectives of the wff and each of its component wffs. Then we apply the truth table definitions to work out the truth value for the main propositional connective of each component wff until we have enough information to calculate the truth value for the main propositional connective of the entire wff. We evaluate the completed truth table for the proposition and apply the appropriate definition to classify the proposition as a tautology (if the truth table column for the main connective contains only T's), an inconsistency (if the column contains only F's), or a contingency (if the column contains at least one T and at least one F). All this is rather abstract, so we consider a typical example worked through in detail.

TRUTH TABLE TEST
FOR CLASSIFYING INDIVIDUAL WFFS AS
TAUTOLOGIES, INCONSISTENCIES, OR CONTINGENCIES

Set up the truth table and work out the truth table value for the entire wff. Evaluate the wff according to the truth table column for its main connective.

P	P ∨ ~P	
T	T | T | FT	All T's:
F	F | T | TF	TAUTOLOGY

P	P & ~P	
T	T | F | FT	All F's:
F	F | F | TF	INCONSISTENCY

P	~P ⊃ (P & ~P)	
T	FT | T | T F FT	Some T's; some F's:
F	TF | F | F F TF	CONTINGENCY

■ *Demonstration 8:* **Classifying Wffs by Truth Tables** ■

PROBLEM: To classify a propositionally complex wff by truth tables as a tautology, inconsistency, or contingency.

PROPOSITION: P ⊃ (Q ⊃ R)

STEP 1:   *Set up the truth table*
We follow the rules for truth table setup. There are three propositional symbols, so we need a truth table with eight rows of possible combinations of truth value assignments to P, Q, R. The truth table is set up as shown previously for three propositional symbols, and it is also seen in several stages of completion below.

STEP 2:   *Write the wff to be analyzed above the truth value array and after the propositional symbols*

P	Q	R	P ⊃ (Q ⊃ R)
T	T	T	
T	T	F	
T	F	T	
T	F	F	
F	T	T	
F	T	F	
F	F	T	
F	F	F	

STEP 3: *Identify the main propositional connective in the wff to be analyzed*
We did this for the same wff in Demonstration Problem 7. The main connective is the first or leftmost conditional.

STEP 4: *Work out the wff's truth values for each possible combination of truth values of its component propositional symbols*
In this case, we can complete the analysis in two stages. First, we apply the truth table definition of the conditional to calculate the value of the component propositionally complex wff, Q ⊃ R. We do so by considering each row of truth values for propositional symbols Q and R and applying the truth table definition of the conditional to give the truth value of Q ⊃ R as T in every case except when Q is T and R is F. The next stage of the truth table looks as follows:

P	Q	R	P ⊃ (Q ⊃ R)
T	T	T	T
T	T	F	F
T	F	T	T
T	F	F	T
F	T	T	T
F	T	F	F
F	F	T	T
F	F	F	T

Now we complete the table by working out the truth values for the main connective. We apply the truth table definition of the conditional to the column of truth values for propositional symbol P as the antecedent of the conditional main connective of the entire wff and to the column of truth values for Q ⊃ R as the main conditional's consequent. The truth table is now complete:

P	Q	R	P ⊃ (Q ⊃ R)	
T	T	T	T	T
T	T	F	F	F
T	F	T	T	T
T	F	F	T	T
F	T	T	T	T
F	T	F	T	F
F	F	T	T	T
F	F	F	T	T

CONTINGENCY

STEP 5:   *Classify the fully analyzed wff as a tautology, inconsistency, or contingency by deciding which truth table semantic concept applies*

The truth table column of truth values for the main connective of the wff we have just analyzed does not contain all T's (which is the truth table definition of a tautology), nor all F's (which is the truth table definition of an inconsistency), but it contains at least one T (in rows 1 and 3–8) and at least one F (in row 2) (which satisfies the truth table definition of a contingency). The proposition is therefore neither a tautology nor an inconsistency but rather a contingency.

We illustrate the method in a series of classifications of propositions, from simple to complex. We may need to decide whether the following proposition is a tautology, inconsistency, or contingency:

P ⊃ ~P

The proposition may look like an inconsistency. The conditional states that if P is true, then ~P is true. But is this really a contradiction? We shall not rely on guesswork but evaluate the proposition by truth table analysis. We set up a truth table with only two possible combinations of truth values to consider, representing that P is either T (true) or F (false). Then we apply the truth table definition of the conditional to the main connective. We do so in a series of steps.

Truth table analysis removes the guess-work from evaluating the logical properties of wffs and sequents.

To proceed systematically, we write out the truth values of the propositional symbol under each of its occurrences:

P	P ⊃ ~P	
T	T	T
F	F	F

Then we reverse the truth value for the negation attaching to propositional symbol P in the consequent ~P within the conditional P ⊃ ~P:

P	P ⊃ ~P
T	T FT
F	F TF

Finally, we calculate the truth value of the main connective of the entire proposition, the conditional. We apply the truth table definition of the conditional to the truth values of P as antecedent and to ~P as consequent to fill in the truth table values for the proposition's main connective. To make reading the table easier, but not as a necessary step in the truth table method, we inscribe lines around the evaluation for the main connective. The completed table has the following form:

P	P ⊃ ~P	
T	T |F| FT	CONTINGENCY
F	F |T| TF	

Truth table analysis shows that the proposition is a contingency. The proposition is neither logically necessarily true (all T's) nor logically necessarily false (all F's). The proposition P ⊃ ~P is rather F where P is T and T where P is F. The proposition's truth value is therefore contingent on the truth values of its one and only component propositional symbol P, which can be either T or F.

The truth value of a contingent wff depends or is contingent on actual facts and the circumstances that happen to prevail in the world.

The truth table method can be used to analyze any propositionally complex proposition. We set up the truth table as required, work through the truth values for the propositional symbols of the proposition's propositional components, and then complete the table for the proposition's main connective, interpreting it according to the truth table definitions of tautology, inconsistency, and contingency.

It is important not to confuse the truth table analysis of contingencies and inconsistencies; the truth table for a contingency contains at least one T and at least one F, whereas the truth table for an inconsistency contains only F's in the truth table column for their main propositional connectives.

Often, when we speak of an "inconsistency" in ordinary language, we refer to an assortment of different kinds of things or an uneven mixture. This is what we mean when we say of inconsistent workmanship or inconsistent cake batter that the former is unreliable and the latter lumpy. However, in logic, when we refer to logical inconsistency, we do not mean a truth table evaluation that contains a mixture of T's and F's—which is instead the distinguishing truth table pattern of a logical contingency—but of a truth table evaluation containing only F's. When a proposition is shown by truth table analysis to be logically inconsistent, the table indicates by its column of nothing but F's for the main connective that the proposition cannot possibly be true, but it is a logical falsehood. An inconsistent wff is false under any combination of truth values assigned to its component propositional symbols. To be logically inconsistent, in other words, is to be inconsistent with the truth in any possible circumstances.

To Check Your Understanding 3.2 ───■

> Use truth table analysis to classify each of the following wffs as a tautology,
> inconsistency, or contingency of propositional logic; be sure to identify the
> main propositional connective first and base your evaluation on the final truth
> table evaluation of the wff's main connective.
>
> 1. P ⊃ (Q ⊃ P)
> 2. ~(P ⊃ (Q ⊃ P))
> 3. (P & Q) ≡ (P & (P ∨ Q))
> 4. (P & Q) ≡ ~(P & (P ∨ Q))
> 5. ~((P & Q) ≡ (P & (P ∨ Q)))
> 6. (P ⊃ R) ⊃ ((Q ⊃ R) ⊃ ((P ∨ Q) ⊃ R))

       ■

Applications to Complex Wffs

A truth table interprets the truth functional meanings of wffs. The truth values
for a propositionally complex wff in a truth table are obtained from the truth
values of the propositional symbols and the truth table definitions of the five
propositional connectives.

Wffs of any com-
plexity can be
analyzed by truth
table methods.

    To analyze any propositionally complex wff, we set up the truth table to
display every possible combination of truth values to be assigned to its component wffs and then apply the appropriate truth table definitions for each of the
wff's propositional connectives. The truth value semantics by which the propositional connectives are defined determine the truth values for component
propositions in every truth table row and column. The method of truth table
analysis can now be applied in a series of steps to a more complex proposition.

┌─■ *Demonstration 9:* **Classifying Complex Wffs** ■───────┐
│   **by Truth Tables**   │

PROBLEM: To classify a propositionally complex wff by truth table analysis
as a tautology, inconsistency, or contingency.

PROPOSITION: (P ⊃ (Q ⊃ P)) ≡ (~Q ⊃ (P ⊃ (~Q ∨ P)))

STEP 1: *Set up the truth table*
We follow the rules for truth table setup. There are two propositional symbols, so we need a truth table with four rows of possible combinations of
truth value assignments to P, Q. The truth table is set up as shown previously

for three propositional symbols and is also seen in several stages of completion below.

STEP 2:   *Write the wff to be analyzed above the truth value array and after the propositional symbols*

The truth table prior to evaluating the wff now looks as follows:

P	Q	$(P \supset (Q \supset P)) \equiv (\sim Q \supset ((P \;\&\; \sim P) \supset (\sim Q \lor P)))$
T	T	
T	F	
F	T	
F	F	

STEP 3:   *Identify the main connective*

The main connective of the wff is the biconditional because it is the connective with the greatest scope enclosed by the fewest parentheses. The wff as a whole is a biconditional, with conditional, disjunctive, conjunctive, and negated propositional components.

STEP 4:   *Write down the truth value assignments to all propositional symbols in the wff*

To determine the truth values for the main connective, we first work out the truth values of its component wffs. We do this most completely by writing down the corresponding truth values of P and Q under each and every propositional symbol in the table and then applying the truth table definitions to work out the truth values of each of the wff's component wffs until we have enough information to calculate the column of truth values for the entire wff's main connective.

P	Q	$(P$	$\supset$	$(Q$	$\supset$	$P))$	$\equiv$	$(\sim Q$	$\supset$	$((P$	$\&$	$\sim P)$	$\supset$	$(\sim Q$	$\lor$	$P)))$
T	T	T		T		T		T		T		T		T		T
T	F	T		F		T		F		T		T		F		T
F	T	F		T		F		T		F		F		T		F
F	F	F		F		F		F		F		F		F		F

Now we replace the truth values of negated wffs with the opposite truth values (T for F and F for T) wherever a propositional component is negated:

P	Q	$(P$	$\supset$	$(Q$	$\supset$	$P))$	$\equiv$	$(\sim Q$	$\supset$	$((P$	$\&$	$\sim P)$	$\supset$	$(\sim Q$	$\lor$	$P)))$
T	T	T		T		T		F		T		F		F		T
T	F	T		F		T		T		T		F		T		T
F	T	F		T		F		F		F		T		F		F
F	F	F		F		F		T		F		T		T		F

As we become more adept at using truth tables, we may wish to skip this step, merely recording the opposite truth values for negated atomic wffs at the outset in the first step of truth table evaluation.

STEP 5:   *Apply truth table definitions to component wffs*
We apply the truth table definitions of the propositional connectives to each of the wff's component wffs. To avoid confusion by trying to squeeze too many truth values together in the table, we replace the truth values of the propositional symbols by the truth values of the wffs to which they belong, under each component's main connective. The next step in completing the table then looks as follows:

P	Q	(P ⊃ (Q ⊃ P))	≡	(~Q ⊃ ((P & ~P)	⊃	(~Q ∨ P)))
T	T	T	T	F	F	T
T	F	T	T	T	F	T
F	T	F	F	F	F	F
F	F	F	T	T	F	T

We work out the truth value column for the left-hand side of the biconditional main connective:

P	Q	(P ⊃ (Q ⊃ P))	≡	(~Q ⊃ ((P & ~P) ⊃ (~Q ∨ P)))
T	T	T	F	T
T	F	T	T	T
F	T	T	F	T
F	F	T	T	T

Now we complete the truth value column for the right-hand side of the biconditional main connective:

P	Q	(P ⊃ (Q ⊃ P))	≡	(~Q ⊃ ((P & ~P) ⊃ (~Q ∨ P)))
T	T	T		T
T	F	T		T
F	T	T		T
F	F	T		T

STEP 6:   *Calculate the value of the main connective*
We apply the truth table definition of the biconditional to calculate the value of the main connective in its corresponding truth table column. If we restore all the truth values, the completed truth table looks as follows:

P	Q	(P ⊃ (Q ⊃ P)) ≡ (~Q ⊃ ((P & ~P) ⊃ (~Q ∨ P)))
T	T	T T T T T |T| FT T T F FT T FT T T
T	F	T T F T T |T| TF T T F FT T TF T T
F	T	F T T F F |T| FT T F F TF T FT F F
F	F	F T F T F |T| TF T F F TF T TF T F

STEP 7: *Classify the fully analyzed wff as a tautology, inconsistency, or contingency by deciding which truth table semantic concept applies*

The abbreviated truth table analysis in this example clearly shows that the column of truth values for the main connective of the wff contains only T's. Thus, the wff is a tautology.

P	Q	(P ⊃ (Q ⊃ P)) ≡ (~Q ⊃ ((P & ~P) ⊃ (~Q ∨ P)))	
T	T	T	
T	F	T	
F	T	T	
F	F	T	TAUTOLOGY

The same basic technique, adapted to the peculiarities of each particular proposition, can be followed to identify the proposition's main connective and the main connectives of any of its successively simpler component wffs. From the truth table evaluation of these, it eventually becomes possible to apply the appropriate truth table definition to the main connective of the entire proposition to arrive at its truth table evaluation. Ordinarily, we do not need to rewrite a truth table repeatedly as we work through its stages since we can simply add successive annotations in the appropriate columns of the same table as we follow the step-by-step procedures we have described.

To Check Your Understanding 3.3 ▬

Use truth table analysis to classify each of the following wffs as a tautology, inconsistency, or contingency of propositional logic; be sure to identify the main propositional connective first and base your evaluation on the final truth table analysis of the wff's main connective:

1. (~P ⊃ Q) ⊃ (P ∨ Q)
2. (P & Q) ≡ ~(~P ∨ ~Q)
3. ~(P ⊃ ((P & Q) ∨ (P & ~Q)))
4. (Q ⊃ ~R) ⊃ ((P ⊃ Q) ⊃ (P ⊃ ~R))
5. ~((P & Q) ⊃ ~~(P & (Q ⊃ ~(R ∨ P))))
6. (P & (Q ⊃ (R ∨ ~P))) & ~(P & (Q ⊃ ~(R ∨ P)))

■

Truth Table Shortcuts

As we gain proficiency in setting up and using truth tables, it is possible to take certain shortcuts. We can save time by writing down only the information that is absolutely essential for calculating a proposition's truth value. If, for example, we see that for certain truth value assignments to a proposition's component atomic wffs a conjunction is sure to have at least one false (F) conjunct, then we can proceed immediately to record the truth value of the entire conjunction as F without bothering to record the truth values of all its other individual conjuncts. If a conditional is certain to have a true (T) consequent or false (F) antecedent, then we can record the truth value of the entire conditional as true (T) and otherwise as false (F). This is also true for the disjunction and biconditional, according to their respective truth table definitions. We must be very confident in our ability to take such shortcuts if we are to avoid bookkeeping errors. When in doubt, we should always play it safe by completing the entire table, working through each truth value and truth functional transformation of truth values by the truth table definitions of the propositional connectives in each column and row, and only then as the final step calculate the truth value for the entire wff as determined by its main connective.

By applying the truth table definitions of the five propositional connectives, it is possible to take certain truth table shortcuts to simplify and decrease the amount of time needed for correct truth table analysis.

The following is an example of the shortcuts we can sometimes take in truth table analysis, using an abbreviated truth table to classify the following wff as a tautology, inconsistency, or contingency:

$$(Q \mathbin{\&} R) \supset {\sim}(((P \equiv Q) \supset (P \lor R)) \mathbin{\&} ((Q \supset P) \supset {\sim}(R \lor {\sim}P)))$$

The table for this proposition requires 2^3 or 8 truth value combinations for the atomic propositions, P, Q, R. For simplicity, we omit all but the most informative truth evaluations. We focus only on the connectives we need to evaluate. We also take some obvious truth table shortcuts, such as evaluating an entire conditional as true when its antecedent is false or its consequent is true. The main connective is the first occurrence of the conditional immediately following the leftmost conjunction. This fact allows us to use a shortcut in this particular case by fixing the value of the antecedent as a conjunction of Q and R and applying the truth table definition of the conditional to evaluate the entire proposition as true (T) wherever the antecedent is false (F). Then there are only two undecided cases left to determine—for the first and fifth rows of the truth table, in which the antecedent is true but the consequent might, for all we know thus far, be false. We concentrate our attention on these two remaining cases:

P	Q	R	(Q & R) ⊃ ~(((P ≡ Q) ⊃ (P ∨ R)) & ((Q ⊃ P) ⊃ ~(R ∨ ~P)))
T	T	T	T
T	T	F	F T
T	F	T	F T
T	F	F	F T
F	T	T	T
F	T	F	F T
F	F	T	F T
F	F	F	F T

Truth table shortcuts avoid considering all truth value assignments to component propositional symbols, where the value of an entire wff can be determined more efficiently.

We identify the main connective in the consequent of the wff's main conditional, which is the negation. Within its scope, as indicated by its appearence to the left of the outermost parentheses, the conjunction is the next main connective so that the consequent as a whole is a negated conjunction. Accordingly, we determine whether in these two cases the conjunction is T or F and then reverse its truth value from T to F or F to T to obtain the value of the consequent of the conditional that is the proposition's main connective. If the value of the consequent is F in either case, then the proposition as a whole is F. This means that the proposition is a contingency since the truth table already contains at least some T's. The results are as follows:

P	Q	R	(Q & R) ⊃ ~(((P ≡ Q) ⊃ (P ∨ R)) & ((Q ⊃ P) ⊃ ~(R ∨ ~P)))
T	T	T	T |T|T T T T F T FF T
T	T	F	F |T|
T	F	T	F |T|
T	F	F	F |T|
F	T	T	T |F|F F T T T F TF T
F	T	F	F |T|
F	F	T	F |T|
F	F	F	F |T| CONTINGENCY

A useful truth table shortcut for wffs whose main propositional connective is the conditional is to consider only those cases in which the antecedent of the conditional might be true or in which the consequent might be false.

The wff is a contingency, with all T truth values in the column under the wff's main connective, except for the fifth case, in which the wff is F. If the value of the consequent in another problem were always T, then the wff as a whole would also be T, making the wff a tautology. To ensure that you understand exactly how these tables have been completed, you should work them through yourself, both by completing the required truth values on the page and from scratch, comparing your results with these conclusions. It may also be useful to take a loose piece of paper and try working out the truth table line by line, masking each row to check your understanding of how the table should be completed at each step before proceeding to the next. Then try your hand at the following exercises.

To Check Your Understanding 3.4 ──────────────────────────────── ■

Use truth table analysis to classify each of the following wffs as a tautology, inconsistency, or contingency of propositional logic, taking whatever truth functionally justifiable shortcuts you wish; be sure to identify the main propositional connective first and base your evaluation on the final truth table analysis of the wff's main connective.

1. $P \equiv (Q \& (P \equiv {\sim}Q))$
2. $(({\sim}R \supset {\sim}S) \vee (S \& R)) \supset S$
3. ${\sim}((({\sim}R \supset {\sim}S) \vee (R \& S)) \supset {\sim}S)$
4. $(P \supset (Q \supset R)) \equiv ((P \supset Q) \supset (P \supset R))$
5. $(P \supset (P \& {\sim}Q)) \& ((Q \& P) \& (P \supset Q))$
6. $(P \vee ({\sim}Q \& {\sim}P)) \equiv (P \vee ({\sim}Q \vee ({\sim}P \supset {\sim}(P \& Q))))$
7. ${\sim}((P \supset Q) \& ({\sim}S \supset {\sim}R)) \equiv ((({\sim}P \& {\sim}R) \vee ({\sim}P \& S)) \vee \\ \quad ((Q \& {\sim}R) \vee (S \& Q)))$
8. $(P \supset (Q \supset R)) \equiv ((P \supset Q) \supset {\sim}(P \supset R))$
9. ${\sim}((P \supset (Q \supset R)) \equiv ((P \supset Q) \supset (P \supset R)))$
10. $(P \supset (Q \vee R)) \supset ((Q \vee R) \& ((Q \vee P) \supset (Q \supset R)))$
11. ${\sim}((P \supset (Q \vee R)) \supset {\sim}((Q \vee R) \& ((Q \vee P) \supset {\sim}(Q \supset {\sim}R))))$
12. $((P \& Q) \vee (R \& {\sim}Q)) \supset ((((P \vee R) \& (P \vee {\sim}Q)) \& ((Q \vee R) \& \\ \quad (Q \vee {\sim}Q)))$

■

Truth Tables for Consistency

Truth tables can be used to evaluate two or more wffs for logical consistency or inconsistency.

We can use truth tables to determine whether or not two or more wffs are logically consistent. Wffs are logically consistent if and only if their conjunction is not an inconsistency. That is, two or more wffs are logically consistent if and only if there is at least one truth value assignment to their component wffs (if any) whereby the wffs are all true.

To test several wffs for consistency, we conjoin them by & and set up and complete the truth table for their conjunction. Then we check to determine whether their conjunction is an inconsistency. If it is, we conclude that the wffs are logically inconsistent; if not, we conclude that the wffs are logically consistent.

TRUTH TABLE TEST
FOR LOGICAL CONSISTENCY

Conjoin the wffs to be tested; set up the truth table and work out the truth table value for the entire wff. Evaluate the wff according to the truth table column for the conjunction as its main connective.

P	Q	P & Q
T	T	T
T	F	F
F	T	F
F	F	F

Some T's:
LOGICALLY
CONSISTENT

P	Q	P & ~P
T	T	F
T	F	F
F	T	F
F	F	F

No T's (all F's):
LOGICALLY
INCONSISTENT

▪ *Demonstration 10:* **Truth Tables for Consistency** ▪

PROBLEM: To test two (or more) wffs by truth tables to determine whether they are logically consistent or inconsistent.

PROPOSITIONS: P & Q, ~Q

STEP 1: *Set up the truth table*
The two wffs together have a total of two propositional symbols, P, Q. The truth table to test for their consistency as a result needs to include four rows. We set up the truth table according to the standard form for evaluating wffs with two propositional symbols. It is seen in several stages of completion below.

STEP 2: *Conjoin the wffs to be analyzed, using parentheses to avoid logical ambiguity, and write their conjunction above the truth value array and after the propositional symbols*

P	Q	(P & Q) & ~Q
T	T	
T	F	
F	T	
F	F	

STEP 3:   *Work out the wffs' truth values for each possible combination of truth val-*
ues to their component propositional symbols

The wffs to be evaluated are not very propositionally complex. One is the negation of a propositional symbol in the truth table setup, and the other has only one propositional connective. In more complicated cases, we may need to work out the truth values of the wffs in several steps, as we have in previous examples for truth table evaluations of complex wffs. The next stage of the truth table looks as follows, in which the truth values for the main connectives of the two conjoined wffs are arrayed under the conjunction for P & Q and under the negation for ~Q:

P	Q	(P & Q) & ~Q	
T	T	T	F
T	F	F	T
F	T	F	F
F	F	F	T

We complete the table by working out the truth values for the main connective. We apply the truth table definition of the conjunction to the columns of truth values for the wffs we are testing. The truth table has the following form:

P	Q	(P & Q) & ~Q		
T	T	T	F F	
T	F	F	F T	
F	T	F	F F	LOGICAL
F	F	F	F T	INCONSISTENCY

STEP 4:   *Classify the conjunction of wffs being tested as an inconsistency or not an*
inconsistency; classify the wffs accordingly as logically inconsistent or logi-
cally consistent

The truth table column of truth values for the conjunction contains all F's, indicating that it is an inconsistency. Accordingly, we classify the wffs being tested as logically inconsistent. If the truth table column of truth values for the conjunction had not contained all F's, but even one T—if, that is, the truth table evaluation of the conjunction of wffs to be tested did not reveal their conjunction to be an inconsistency—then the wffs would be classified instead as consistent.

As a further illustration, consider the two wffs ~(P ⊃ (Q & ~Q)), and P & ((Q ∨ ~P) & Q). We conjoin the propositions and complete their truth table so that it appears as follows:

P	Q	(~(P ⊃ (Q & ~Q))) & (P & ((Q ∨ ~P) & Q))							
T	T	T	F	F	T	T	T	T
T	F	T	F	F	F	F	F	F
F	T	F	T	F	F	F	T	T
F	F	F	T	F	F	F	T	F

The two wffs are logically consistent because their conjunction is a contingency. The truth table shows that there are circumstances in which the two propositions are not always both false. Work through the truth value assignments yourself to make sure you understand just how they were calculated.

Suppose that we need to test the following wffs to decide whether they are logically consistent or inconsistent: P ⊃ (Q ⊃ P) and (P ⊃ P) ⊃ ~(Q ∨ ~Q). Again, we complete their truth tables from a single truth table setup and check to see whether or not the two wffs ever have the same truth value in any truth table row.

Logically inconsistent wffs cannot possibly be true; they are evaluated as false, with only F's, under any assignment of truth values to their component propositional symbols.

P	Q	(P ⊃ (Q ⊃ P)) & ((P ⊃ P) ⊃ ~(Q ∨ ~Q))							
T	T	T	T	F	T	F F	T	
T	F	T	T	F	T	F F	T	
F	T	T	F	F	T	F F	T	LOGICAL
F	F	T	T	F	T	F F	T	INCONSISTENCY

The two wffs in this second example are logically inconsistent. Truth tables reveal that one is always T and the other always F so that they never both have either truth value T or truth value F in any truth table row.

To Check Your Understanding 3.5

Use truth tables to evaluate the following pairs of wffs for logical consistency or inconsistency:

1. P; ~(P ⊃ P)
2. P ⊃ (Q ∨ R); (P ⊃ Q) ∨ (Q ⊃ R)
3. ~(P ⊃ (Q ∨ R)); ~(~P ∨ (~Q ⊃ R))
4. ~(P ≡ Q); (P ⊃ (Q ⊃ R)) ≡ ((P ⊃ Q) ⊃ (P ⊃ R))
5. (P ∨ Q) & ((P ⊃ R) & Q); ((P ∨ Q) & ((P ⊃ R) & (Q ⊃ S))) ⊃ ~(R ∨ S)
6. P & (P ⊃ ~P); ~((P ⊃ (Q ∨ R)) ⊃ ~((Q ∨ R) & ((Q ∨ P) ⊃ ~(Q ⊃ ~R))))

Truth Tables for Equivalence

Truth tables can be used to evaluate two or more wffs for logical equivalence or nonequivalence.

Truth tables can also be used to determine the logical equivalence or non-equivalence of two or more wffs. Logical equivalence means that two or more wffs always have the same truth value in any possible circumstances, whether true or false.

The method is to work out the truth table values for the wffs and then to check whether or not the evaluations precisely match case-by-case or line-by-line for the columns indicating the truth values of each of their main connectives. If the truth values for the main connectives of wffs being compared in this way exactly match in every truth table row, then the wffs are logically equivalent; otherwise they are logically nonequivalent. The reason is that truth tables give us the truth functional semantic interpretations of propositional connectives so that if two or more wffs have precisely the same truth tables (for the main connective of each), then by truth table definition they are precisely identical in truth functional meaning.

We accomplish the same purpose by connecting the wffs to be evaluated by the biconditional and testing the resulting biconditional wff by truth table analysis. If the biconditional is a tautology, the wffs are logically equivalent. If the biconditional is not a tautology, the wffs are not logically equivalent but

---

TRUTH TABLE TEST
FOR LOGICAL EQUIVALENCE

Set up the truth table and work out the truth table values for several entire wffs. Evaluate the wffs according to the truth table columns for their main connectives.

P	Q	P ⊃ Q	~P ∨ Q	
T	T	T	T	Columns match
T	F	F	F	perfectly, row for row:
F	T	F	F	LOGICALLY
F	F	F	F	EQUIVALENT

P	Q	P ⊃ Q	P ∨ Q	
T	T	T	T	Columns do NOT
T	F	F	T	match perfectly:
F	T	F	T	LOGICALLY
F	F	F	F	NONEQUIVALENT

logically nonequivalent. However, it is easier and just as accurate to compare truth values for each wff being tested, looking for any discrepancies in their truth values in the same truth table row that would disqualify them as not equivalent, and otherwise judging them as equivalent.

■ *Demonstration 11:* **Truth Tables for Equivalence** ■

PROBLEM: To test two (or more) wffs to determine whether they are logically equivalent or nonequivalent.

PROPOSITIONS: ~(P ⊃ Q); P & ~Q

STEP 1: *Set up the truth table*
The two wffs together have a total of two propositional symbols, P, Q. The truth table to test for their logical consistency as a result needs to include four rows. We set up the truth table according to the standard form for evaluating wffs with two propositional symbols. It is seen in several stages of completion below.

STEP 2: *Work out the wffs' truth values for each possible combination of truth values to their component propositional symbols*
We have now had practice completing truth tables, so we shall not elaborate the method here. The completed truth table in this case is as follows:

P	Q	~(P ⊃ Q)	(P & ~Q)	
T	T	F	F	
T	F	T	T	
F	T	F	F	LOGICALLY
F	F	F	F	EQUIVALENT

STEP 3: *Compare the truth table columns for the main connectives of each wff; classify the wffs accordingly as logically equivalent or logically nonequivalent, depending on whether or not they exactly match in each truth table row.*
The truth table columns for the main connectives of the wffs exactly match. Accordingly, we classify the wffs being tested as logically equivalent. If the truth table columns had been different in any row, then the wffs would be classified instead as logically nonequivalent.

We test several pairs of wffs for logical equivalence. To show by truth tables that contrapositives are equivalent, we work out the truth table evaluations for the main propositional connectives of a conditional, such as P ⊃ Q, and its contrapositive, ~Q ⊃ ~P. We find:

P	Q	P ⊃ Q	~Q ⊃ ~P
T	T	T	T
T	F	F	F
F	T	T	T
F	F	T	T

We made similar claims about the logical equivalence of the conditional (in simplest form) P ⊃ Q, and the disjunction with the negation of the conditional's antecedent as one of its disjuncts, in ~P ∨ Q. This equivalence can also be justified by truth table comparison:

P	Q	P ⊃ Q	~P ∨ Q
T	T	T	T
T	F	F	F
F	T	T	T
F	F	T	T

Logically equivalent wffs always have the same truth value under any assignment of truth values to their component propositional symbols.

To satisfy yourself that the equivalences hold, work out the truth values for each of the main connectives in the wffs being compared. This shows that the wffs have the same truth tables and are therefore logically equivalent.

Wherever we have an exact matching of truth table evaluations for the main connectives of wffs, we also satisfy the truth table definition of the biconditional as holding between any two such equivalent propositions. This means that in the previous two truth tables we have in effect demonstrated the logical equivalences (P ⊃ Q) ≡ (~Q ⊃ ~P) and (P ⊃ Q) ≡ (~P ∨ Q). We can check these claims to see how propositional connectives interrelate by setting up truth tables to prove that these biconditionals are tautologies.

We can now make good on a previous formally unsupported statement that the biconditional in P ≡ Q (in simplest form) is logically equivalent to a conjunction of two conditionals (in correspondingly simple form) as (P ⊃ Q) & (Q ⊃ P); in other words, that (P ≡ Q) ≡ ((P ⊃ Q) & (Q ⊃ P)). The following is an abbreviated truth table analysis that confirms the equivalence:

P	Q	P ≡ Q	(P ⊃ Q) & (Q ⊃ P)	(P ≡ Q) ≡ ((P ⊃ Q) & (Q ⊃ P))	
T	T	T	T	T	
T	F	F	F	T	
F	T	F	F	T	LOGICALLY
F	F	T	T	T	EQUIVALENT

Again, a casual examination of the completed truth table by itself will not be very convincing. You should work through the truth table to determine that it is correct and that it proves what we have claimed. Then you will be in a position to agree that in fact the two wffs in question are logically equivalent.

Wffs are logically equivalent if and only if a biconditional that connects them is a tautology.

By truth table analysis of logical equivalence any two tautologies are logically equivalent, as are any two inconsistencies. The reason is that the truth table evaluations for their main connectives by definition will always be respectively T or F. Not all contingencies are guaranteed to be logically equivalent since the truth table evaluations for their main connectives, though each showing at least one T and at least one F, might have their T's and F's located in different truth table rows. It nonetheless remains true that some contingencies, the contents of which need have nothing to do with one another, can sometimes be logically equivalent.

In contrast, compare the following propositions by truth table analysis to determine that they are not logically equivalent:

P	Q	P ∨ Q	~(P & ~Q)	
T	T	T	T	
T	F	T	F	
F	T	T	T	LOGICALLY
F	F	F	T	NONEQUIVALENT

Logical nonequivalence is indicated in truth table analysis by any discrepancy of truth values (T and F) in any truth table row for the truth table column of the main propositional connectives of the wffs being evaluated.

If you have understood these truth tables and worked through the examples, then you should be ready to test the following pairs of wffs by truth tables to decide whether they are logically equivalent or nonequivalent. Remember that equivalence requires an exact line-by-line matching of truth values in the completed truth table for the main propositional connectives of the wffs being compared, and that even one mismatch in any truth table row implies that the wffs are not logically equivalent but rather nonequivalent.

To Check Your Understanding 3.6

Use truth tables to evaluate the following pairs of wffs for logical equivalence or nonequivalence:

1. P; P ⊃ P
2. P ⊃ (Q ∨ R); ~P ∨ (~Q ⊃ R)
3. P ⊃ (Q ∨ R); ~(~P ∨ (~Q ⊃ R))
4. P ≡ Q; ~(P & ~Q) & (~P ⊃ ~Q)
5. (P ⊃ (Q ⊃ R)) ≡ ((P ⊃ Q) ⊃ (P ⊃ R)); P ⊃ (Q ⊃ P)
6. P & (P ⊃ ~P); ~((P ⊃ (Q ∨ R)) ⊃ ~((Q ∨ R) & ((Q ∨ P) ⊃ ~(Q ⊃ ~R))))

Truth Tables for Sequents

A sequent, recall from its previous definition, is a symbolization of an argument. We now explain how to use truth tables to evaluate the *deductive validity or invalidity* of any sequent.

Truth tables can be used to evaluate argument sequents for deductive validity or invalidity.

To test a sequent for validity by truth tables, we first conjoin all the sequent's assumptions into one complex conjunction (if there is only one assumption, then there is only one conjunct). The conjunction is then made the antecedent of a conditional, which takes a similar conjunction of all the conclusions of the argument (one in the usual limiting case) as the conditional's consequent. As always, parentheses are added according to the parentheses requirement to avoid ambiguity in the scopes of multiple propositional connectives.

Sequents are evaluated by truth table analysis of their corresponding conditionals, taking a conjunction of a sequent's assumptions as the antecedent and a conjunction of the sequent's conclusions as its consequent.

> **Conditional Conversion Rule**
> **for Truth Table Test of Sequent Validity**
> Convert sequent $\mathbb{P}_1, \ldots, \mathbb{P}_m \vdash \mathbb{Q}_1, \ldots, \mathbb{Q}_n$ to the conditional
> $(\mathbb{P}_1 \mathbin{\&} \ldots \mathbin{\&} \mathbb{P}_m) \supset (\mathbb{Q}_1 \mathbin{\&} \ldots \mathbin{\&} \mathbb{Q}_n)$

We then give a truth table analysis of the resulting wff. The main connective for this purpose is always the conditional that separates the conjoined assumptions of the argument from the conjoined conclusions. When the table is complete, we check to see whether the conditional is a tautology. If the conditional is a tautology, with only T's in the truth table column for the conditional main connective, then the corresponding argument is deductively valid. If the conditional is not a tautology, if there is even one F in the truth table column for its main connective, then the corresponding argument from which we constructed the conditional is deductively invalid.

A sequent is deductively valid if and only if truth table analysis identifies its corresponding conditional as a tautology.

A conditional by truth table definition is false if and only if its antecedent is true and its consequent false. If truth table analysis shows that a conditional is a tautology or logically necessary truth, then it is logically impossible for the conditional's antecedent to be true and its consequent false. When we conjoin the assumptions of a sequent as a conditional's antecedent, conjoin the sequent's conclusions as the conditional's consequent, and test the resulting conditional by truth tables to determine whether or not it is a tautology, we are in effect checking to see whether or not it is logically possible for the sequent's assumptions to be true and any of its conclusions false. If the conditional is a tautology, then the corresponding sequent is deductively valid because it is logically impossible for the sequent's assumptions to be true and any of its conclusions false. If the conditional is not a tautology, then the corresponding sequent is deductively invalid because it is logically possible for the sequent's assumptions to be true and at least one of its conclusions false.

To keep our terminology straight, we do not say that a sequent is a tautology or not a tautology but that a sequent is deductively valid or deductively invalid. We do not say that the conditional converted from a sequent by the previously discussed rule is deductively valid or deductively invalid but that the conditional is a tautology or not a tautology. The truth functional correspondence between a deductively valid sequent and a conditional tautology converted from the sequent by the previous rule makes it possible to use truth tables for conditional tautologies as a test for corresponding deductively valid sequents.

TRUTH TABLE TEST
FOR DEDUCTIVE VALIDITY OF SEQUENTS

Convert the sequent to a corresponding conditional; set up the truth table and work out the truth table value for the entire wff. Evaluate the wff according to the truth table columns for the conditional as its main connective.

P	Q	$((P \supset Q) \& P) \supset P$	
T	T	T	All T's:
T	F	T	Sequent is
F	T	T	DEDUCTIVELY
F	F	T	VALID

P	Q	$((P \supset Q) \& P) \supset \sim P$	
T	T	F	NOT all T's:
T	F	T	Sequent is
F	T	T	DEDUCTIVELY
F	F	T	INVALID

■ *Demonstration 12:* **Truth Tables for Sequents** ■

PROBLEM: To test an argument sequent by truth tables to determine whether it is deductively valid or invalid.

SEQUENT: $P \supset Q, P \vdash Q$

STEP 1: *Set up the truth table*
The two wffs together have a total of two propositional symbols, P, Q. The truth table to test for their logical consistency as a result needs to include four

rows. We set up the truth table according to the standard form for evaluating wffs with two propositional symbols. It is seen in several stages of completion below.

STEP 2:   *Apply the conditional construction rule; conjoin the sequent's assumptions as the antecedent, and conjoin the sequent's conclusions as the consequent, of a conditional corresponding to the sequent to be tested using parentheses to avoid logical ambiguity; then write the biconditional above the truth value array and after the propositional symbols*

P	Q	$((P \supset Q)\ \&\ P) \supset Q$
T	T	
T	F	
F	T	
F	F	

STEP 3:   *Work out the conditional's truth values for each possible combination of truth values to their component propositional symbols*

We have now had practice completing truth tables, so we shall not elaborate the method here. The completed truth table is as follows:

P	Q	$((P \supset Q)\ \&\ P) \supset Q$	
T	T	T	
T	F	T	
F	T	T	
F	F	T	VALID

STEP 4:   *Classify the conditional as a tautology or not a tautology; classify the sequent accordingly as deductively valid or deductively invalid*

The truth table column of truth values for the biconditional contains all T's, indicating that it is a tautology. Accordingly, we classify the sequent being tested as deductively valid. If the truth table column of truth values for the conditional had not contained all T's, but had even one F—if, that is, truth table evaluation did not reveal the conditional constructed from the sequent to be tested to be a tautology—then the sequent would be classified instead as deductively invalid.

We illustrate the method by testing some of the arguments that were translated in Chapter 2. First, we present the argument, then test its transformation as a corresponding conditional by truth table analysis, and finally indicate the argument's validity or invalidity as revealed by whether its corresponding conditional is or is not a tautology. The following is an example of an argument and its truth table evaluation for deductive validity:

S ⊃ C, A ⊃ ~C ⊢ S ⊃ ~A

S	C	A	((S ⊃ C) & (A ⊃ ~C)) ⊃ (S ⊃ ~A)					
T	T	T	T	F	F	|T|	F	
T	T	F	T	T	T	|T|	T	
T	F	T	F	F	T	|T|	F	
T	F	F	F	F	T	|T|	T	
F	T	T	T	F	F	|T|	T	
F	T	F	T	T	T	|T|	T	
F	F	T	T	T	T	|T|	T	
F	F	F	T	T	T	|T|	T	VALID

Effective use of truth tables requires an immediate grasp of the truth table definitions of the five propositional connectives.

In this application, the conditional main connective is always true (T). The conditional proposition is therefore a tautology, and the corresponding argument from which we constructed the conditional is deductively valid.

T ⊃ F, (F & M) ∨ T ⊢ ~M ⊃ T

T	F	M	((T ⊃ F) & ((F & M) ∨ T)) ⊃ (~M ⊃ T)					
T	T	T	T	T	T	T	|T|	T
T	T	F	T	T	F	T	|T|	T
T	F	T	F	F	F	T	|T|	T
T	F	F	F	F	F	T	|T|	T
F	T	T	T	T	T	T	|T|	T
F	T	F	T	F	F	F	|T|	F
F	F	T	T	F	F	F	|T|	T
F	F	F	T	F	F	F	|T|	F	VALID

The truth table shows that this argument is also valid. Now consider this inference from Chapter 2:

C ⊃ D, C ⊃ P ⊢ D ⊃ P

C	D	P	((C ⊃ D) & (C ⊃ P)) ⊃ (~D ⊃ P)					
T	T	T	T	T	T	|T|	T	
T	T	F	T	F	F	|T|	T	
T	F	T	F	F	T	|T|	T	
T	F	F	F	F	F	|T|	F	
F	T	T	T	T	T	|T|	T	
F	T	F	T	T	T	|T|	T	
F	F	T	T	T	T	|T|	T	
F	F	F	T	T	T	|F|	F	INVALID

Useful information about counter-examples to a deductively invalid sequent can be found in its truth table.

There are distinct categories of evaluation for the logical properties of wffs and sequents.

An individual wff is true or false and a tautology, inconsistency, or contingency, but it is never deductively valid or invalid; a sequent is deductively valid or invalid, sound or unsound, but never true or false and never a tautology, inconsistency, or contingency—despite the correlation between deductively valid sequents and corresponding conditional tautologies.

The argument appears valid until the final line of truth table evaluation reveals that there is one case in which the conditional is false and hence not a tautology. This means that the corresponding argument from which the conditional is constructed is not deductively valid but deductively invalid.

Truth tables make it possible to determine the validity or invalidity of any correctly translated argument in propositional logic. From a completed truth table, we can read off useful information about the wffs and sequents we have analyzed. In particular, truth tables tell us the exact circumstances in which a given proposition might be false or a corresponding argument invalid. The previous example is a good illustration. The final truth table row makes the conditional under evaluation false in just one circumstance. We see from the table that this is where all three atomic wffs (C, D, and P) are false. Thus, we need only go back to the original statement of the argument which we translated into our symbolism in order to describe a counterexample in which it is logically possible for the assumptions of the argument to be true and the conclusion false. To recall the original statement of the argument, we see that the inference fails to hold only in the circumstances in which it is false that duty and desire conflict, false that one must do one's duty, and false that something pleasurable is forbidden.

As a reminder, we restate the differences between the categories of evaluation for the logical properties of wffs and sequents. Wffs are true or false and may be tautologies, inconsistencies, or contingencies; sequents are deductively valid or invalid, sound or unsound. The logical properties by which wffs are evaluated do not apply to sequents: Sequents are never true or false and are never tautologies, inconsistencies, or contingencies. The logical properties by which sequents are evaluated equally do not apply to wffs: Individual wffs are never deductively valid or invalid nor sound or unsound. The differences are indicated in the following table:

Categories of Evaluation for the Logical Properties of Wffs (Propositions) and Sequents (Arguments)

Wffs (Propositions)	Sequents (Arguments)
True or false	Deductively valid or invalid
Tautology, inconsistency, or contingency	Sound or unsound

To Check Your Understanding 3.7 ────────────────────────────■

Use truth table analysis to determine whether or not the following sequents are deductively valid:

1. ~P & Q, P ∨ R, Q ≡ ~R ⊢ P
2. ~P ∨ (~P & Q), (~P ⊃ Q) ⊃ ~P ⊢ ~P
3. (P ∨ Q) & ((P ⊃ R) & (Q ⊃ S)) ⊢ ~(R ∨ S)

4. (~P & Q) & ~R, (S ∨ Q) ⊃ (~R ≡ Q) ⊢ T ∨ S
5. P & Q, P ⊃ (R ⊃ S), (R ≡ P) ⊃ ~P ⊢ (S & P) ⊃ Q
6. (~P & Q) & ~R, (S ∨ T) ⊃ ~(~R ≡ Q) ⊢ ~(T ∨ S)

∎

Turbo Truth Tables

Turbo truth tables are often more convenient to use than conventional truth tables.

Truth tables are cumbersome to use for problems with more than four propositional symbols. Even truth tables involving three or four propositional symbols can be difficult, time-consuming, and error prone. We must proceed methodically, filling in each truth value assignment to component wffs until the truth table for the entire proposition or sequent emerges. We have already sought ways of streamlining this process by working out only those values minimally needed for truth table determinations and taking shortcuts based on the truth table definitions of certain connectives. With enough paper and patience we can always evaluate the logical properties of propositions and arguments by truth table methods. For complex problems with more than four propositional symbols, truth tables are highly impractical.

Many arguments involve so many propositional symbols that truth table analysis is precluded. These cases reach the working limitations of truth tables. The limit is far surpassed by some of the arguments we have already considered. We see the problem in this progression of previous arguments, beginning with G ⊃ U, E ⊃ I, ~G ⊃ E ⊢ U ∨ I, including (~R & F) ⊃ (P & ~D), ((F & R) ⊃ S) & (S ⊃ P), ~R ⊃ F ⊢ P, and even more dramatically in Lactantius' trilemma disproof of the existence of God: G ⊃ ((S & P) & B), E, E ⊃ (~K ∨ ((K & ~A) ∨ ((K & A) & ~C))), ~K ⊃ ~S, ~A ⊃ ~P, ~C ⊃ ~B ⊢ ~G. The first two arguments have four and five propositional symbols, respectively, and therefore require truth tables with $2^4 = 16$ and $2^5 = 32$ rows of possible truth value combinations. Although 16 truth table rows may be feasible, 32 are unmanageable and are best avoided as a practical paper-and-pencil procedure if another more convenient method is available. The example from Lactantius is worse yet, and it gives a good idea of how the depth of truth tables increases geometrically for problems involving arithmetically increasing numbers of propositional symbols. Here, we have $2^8 = 256$ truth table rows merely to set up the array of possible truth value combinations for the atomic wffs. The corresponding conditional would need to conjoin the six assumptions of the argument into a complex antecedent with the single conclusion as consequent. The truth table for this complex conditional would be tiresome to complete, with many opportunities for bookkeeping errors in misalignments of truth values in truth table columns and rows. We are clearly in need of a more useful general decision method for working with propositions and arguments of greater complexity. For this purpose, we first consider a more expeditious style of applying truth table analysis and then in Chapter 4 we develop a logically related but much easier and more flexible graphic technique.

By understanding how truth tables work, we can modify them to simplify the method. What makes the ordinary truth table method so tedious is that, unless we are taking shortcuts, we must fill in a truth value at each and every space under each and every propositional symbol, and each and every propositional connective in every column and row, until we are in a position to calculate the truth value of the entire proposition by applying the truth table definition of its main connective. This is like doing an exhaustive induction over a large population, checking each swan to make sure it is white in order to confirm the generalization that all swans are white. By analogy, the ordinary truth table method requires that we check each truth table entry in order to completely evaluate a wff or sequent.

We now develop a more compact truth table method based on the truth table definitions of the five propositional connectives. Instead of gathering all relevant truth table information to show that a wff is a tautology, or that a sequent is deductively valid, we try to show the opposite. If we determine that a wff cannot be an inconsistency, or that a sequent cannot be deductively invalid, then we will have shown that the wff is a tautology and that the sequent is deductively valid. Rather than trying to confirm a hypothesis about the logical properties of a wff or sequent by verifying all the truth value data from which the judgment can be made in standard truth table form, we set out instead to try to falsify the wff to determine whether there is any assignment of truth values to its components by which it turns out to be false. To identify a truth value assignment under which a wff is false is comparable to finding a single disconfirming instance falsifying an empirical hypothesis. It is like discovering a single black swan to falsify the generalization that all swans are white instead of checking each white swan to confirm that it is white. If there is such a truth value assignment or, alternatively, if there is not, we can interpret either outcome in terms of standard truth table definitions at a fraction of the time and effort.

We reconsider one of the arguments from a previous section that involves too many propositional symbols for convenient evaluation by standard truth table methods. The argument is converted by the conditional rule to the following proposition:

$$(((G \supset U) \mathbin{\&} (E \supset I)) \mathbin{\&} (\sim G \supset E)) \supset (U \lor I)$$

Instead of working through all the values for all the lesser connectives the proposition contains until we can judge the value of the main connective, we ask a different question: What would it take to make this conditional wff false? The answer by truth table definition is the same for any conditional: The antecedent must be true and the consequent false. How could this happen? It could

Turbo truth tables determine whether there is a truth value assignment that would make a wff false rather than checking each case to determine whether the wff is true or false under each truth value assignment to its component propositional symbols.

Turbo truth tables achieve the same results for many wffs and sequents as complete standard truth tables at a fraction of the time and effort.

only be if the consequent, which in this case is a disjunction, is false by truth table definition, where both disjuncts U and I are false. Therefore, suppose that both of these component wffs are false, and write them underneath wherever U and I occur in the proposition. A number at the left or right of a horizontal row of truth values applies to the single step at which all the additional values in that row are assigned. The number 1 always marks the starting point, and the highest number, enclosed in a circle, shows the point at which the final evaluation of the wff is complete. The numbering is not an essential part of the method but is added here to help you follow the succession of steps.

$$(((G \supset U) \& (E \supset I)) \& (\sim G \supset E)) \supset (U \lor I)$$

$$FFFF1$$

The numbering of steps in a turbo truth table is an optional feature that is used here only to explain the method, and is not necessary when using them to evaluate wffs and sequents.

If the antecedent is to be true, all three conjuncts for the three assumptions of the original argument must also be true. Since U and I are already marked false (F), we know by the truth table definition of the conditional that the wffs G and E cannot be true but must also be false. We add this information to the wff we are annotating (in practice, there is no need to rewrite it every time but merely to add information to a single formula as we proceed). Finally, we note that if G must be false on this assignment, then ~G must be true, and we also add this information:

$$(((G \supset U) \& (E \supset I)) \& (\sim G \supset E)) \supset (U \lor I)$$

$$2FFFFTFFF1$$

This is the end of the line. We see that if ~G is true and E is false, then ~G ⊃ E is false. But, then one of the conjuncts in the antecedent of the conditional cannot be true when the consequent of the conditional is false. This means that if the consequent of the conditional is false, the antecedent must also be false. There is no possible truth value assignment in which the antecedent is true and the consequent false. This means that the wff is a tautology, and the corresponding argument from which the conditional proposition is converted is shown by turbo truth tables to be valid. We indicate the values of the corresponding propositional connectives under the appropriate combinations of truth value assignments:

$$(((G \supset U) \& (E \supset I)) \& (\sim G \supset E)) \supset (U \lor I)$$

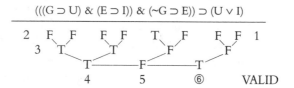

Turbo truth trees offer a quick way to check the deductive validity or invalidity of arguments.

The method also works in evaluating an argument that is deductively invalid. Consider the following variation on the previous example:

$$(((G \supset U) \And (E \supset I)) \And (\sim G \supset \sim E)) \supset (U \lor I)$$

2   F   F   F   F   T   T   F   F   1
   3   T   T   T   F
        T————————T————————F
        4   5   ⑥   INVALID

The *turbo truth table method* can also be used to determine quickly whether or not a wff is a tautology. For this application, we try to assign truth values whereby the wff is false. If we can do so, the wff is not a tautology; if we cannot, then the wff is a tautology. In the first example, we assign truth value T to the antecedent of a conditional to determine whether under such an assignment the consequent can be F. We see at once by the truth table definition of disjunction that the consequent cannot be F if the antecedent is T:

$$P \supset (P \lor (Q \And (S \supset \sim R)))$$

1 T   T
   ② T   TAUTOLOGY

In another wff, it is possible for the antecedent to be true and the consequent false:

$$(Q \supset P) \supset (P \supset Q)$$

1 F   T   T   F
   2 T   F
       ③ F   NOT A TAUTOLOGY

This is a faster and more economical use of truth table definitions of propositional connectives for purposes of evaluating propositions and arguments. In deciding whether arguments are valid or invalid, and testing whether or not an individual proposition is a tautology, the turbo truth table method works very well. Note, however, that if we need to evaluate an individual wff as a tautology, inconsistency, or contingency, the method is not necessarily better than ordinary truth tables. In evaluating argument sequents, we can easily decide whether a corresponding conditional can be made false. If it can, then we know that the conditional is not a tautology, and this is all we need to decide that the corresponding sequent is deductively invalid. But we do not know from this information alone whether the wff is an inconsistency or a contingency. Such further determination requires additional effort so that in many instances turbo tables involve almost as much work as the ordinary truth table method, with greater demands on memory and concentration, and hence greater potential for mistakes.

There are also other limitations of turbo truth tables. The previous example is ideal because there is only one circumstance in which the consequent can be false, where two propositional symbols must also be false. This sets definite constraints on the values of other wffs in the proposition, to be followed up as we indicated in trying to decide whether or not the proposition as a whole can ever be false. In some cases, it is easy to see that there are only limited circumstances in which the antecedent of a conditional can be true or in which it is obvious that the consequent cannot be false or the antecedent cannot be true. However, in other cases there are multiple circumstances in which the consequent of a conditional might be false or the antecedent true. By the time we consider all these possibilities by turbo tables, we might as well have done so in tabular form using a standard truth table. The turbo method works best where, for one reason or another, given the construction of a wff we are trying to evaluate, there is only one or at most two possibilities for the proposition to be false, and where this imposes significant constraints on the values of other occurrences of propositional symbols elsewhere in the wff. As a result, the method favors disjunctions and conditionals. Arguments transformed into single propositions for evaluation always have conditionals as their main connectives, for which turbo tables are therefore advantageous. When we are called on to determine the truth functional properties of other kinds of wffs, particularly conjunctions and biconditionals, it may often be just as well to proceed by standard truth table analysis.

For wffs whose main connectives imply that they can be false in more ways than one, turbo truth tables are not necessarily more efficient than standard truth tables; turbo truth tables work best for conjunctions and conditionals, less so for disjunctions and biconditionals. The facility of turbo truth tables applied to conditionals explains the usefulness of turbo truth tables in evaluating sequents for deductive validity or invalidity.

To Check Your Understanding 3.8

Use turbo truth tables to evalute whether the following sequents are deductively valid or invalid.

1. ~P & Q, P ∨ R, Q ≡ ~R ⊢ P
2. ~P ∨ (~P & Q), (~P ⊃ Q) ⊃ ~P ⊢ ~P
3. (P ∨ Q) & ((P ⊃ R) & (Q ⊃ S)) ⊢ ~(R ∨ S)
4. (~P & Q) & ~R, (S ∨ Q) ⊃ (~R ≡ Q) ⊢ T ∨ S
5. P & Q, P ⊃ (R ⊃ S), (R ≡ P) ⊃ ~P ⊢ (S & P) ⊃ Q
6. (~P & Q) & ~R, (S ∨ T) ⊃ ~(~R ≡ Q) ⊢ ~(T ∨ S)

Reduction of Propositional Connectives

The stroke function ' | ' was discovered by H. M. Sheffer and is sometimes called the Sheffer stroke. It is a function for disjoining negations by combining negation and disjunction in such a way that ℙ | ℚ is logically equivalent to ~ℙ ∨ ~ℚ.

We can use truth tables to prove that all four conventional binary truth functions—&, ∨, ⊃, and ≡—can be reduced to the single | stroke function. A truth functional definition of the four binary propositional connectives in terms of disjoint negation exhibits the equivalences needed to reduce all five truth functional propositional connectives to one. We have already seen that the conjunction ℙ & ℚ is logically equivalent to the negated disjunction ~(~ℙ ∨ ~ℚ), that the conditional ℙ ⊃ ℚ is logically equivalent to the disjunction ~ℙ ∨ ℚ, and that the biconditional ℙ ≡ ℚ is logically equivalent to a conjunction of conditionals in (ℙ ⊃ ℚ) & (ℚ ⊃ ℙ).

All five propositional connectives can be reduced to a single connective that combines the truth functional effect of negation and disjunction or to a single connective that combines negation and conjunction.

To demonstrate the reduction of all five propositional connectives to the Sheffer stroke function, we need only present truth table equivalences for negation and conjunction in terms of the stroke truth function ' | '. The following truth table demonstrates the relevant logical equivalence for a particular choice of propositional symbols:

SHEFFER STROKE EQUIVALENCES
(DISJOINT NEGATION)

ℙ	ℚ	~ℙ	ℙ | ℙ	ℙ & ℚ	(ℙ | ℚ)|(ℙ | ℚ)
T	T	F	F	T	T
T	F	[F]	[F]	F	F
F	T	T	T	F	F
F	F	[T]	[T]	F	F

A similar reduction is possible using the dagger function '↓' discovered by Jean Nicod. The dagger represents joint negation by combining negation and conjunction in such a way that ℙ ↓ ℚ is logically equivalent to ~ℙ & ~ℚ. The truth table for the reduction of disjunction to joint conjunction is identical in form:

NICOD DAGGER EQUIVALENCES
(CONJOINT NEGATION)

ℙ	ℚ	~ℙ	ℙ ↓ ℙ	ℙ ∨ ℚ	(ℙ ↓ ℚ) ↓ (ℙ ↓ ℚ)
T	T	F	F	T	T
T	F	[F]	[F]	T	T
F	T	T	T	T	T
F	F	[T]	[T]	F	F

The possibility of reducing all propositional connectives to a single truth function is interesting for the light it sheds on the underlying logical structures of propositional logic. The reduction demonstrates the essential unity of logical form at the foundations of tautology and deductive validity. Yet the stroke or dagger symbolism involving only a single propositional connective is so difficult to read and impractical to work with that, having understood that the ordinary truth functions can be reduced to just one, we will find it more useful to continue studying propositional logic in terms of all five traditional propositional connectives.

To Check Your Understanding 3.9 ──■

Define the conditional and biconditional in $\mathbb{P} \supset \mathbb{Q}$ and $\mathbb{P} \equiv \mathbb{Q}$ in terms of the stroke function | and in terms of the dagger function ↓ and compare their definitions with stroke and dagger reductions of ~($\mathbb{P}$ & ~$\mathbb{Q}$), ~$\mathbb{P} \vee \mathbb{Q}$, and ($\mathbb{P} \supset \mathbb{Q}$) & ($\mathbb{Q} \supset \mathbb{P}$).

■

Summary: Truth Tables

Truth table definitions of the propositional connectives provide the basis for a truth table decision method. Decision methods are step-by-step procedures that give a definite answer concerning certain logical properties of wffs and sequents. We array all the possible combinations of truth values to the component atomic wffs or propositional symbols of a complex wff to be evaluated in a standard way, and work out the values of each component involving a propositional connective with greater scope, until we are in a position to evaluate the truth value of the entire wff. Truth tables can be used to determine whether an individual wff is a tautology, inconsistency, or contingency and whether two or more wffs are logically consistent or logically inconsistent or logically equivalent or nonequivalent. Truth tables can also be used to determine whether argument sequents are deductively valid or invalid. We can use truth table shortcuts and turbo truth tables to simplify some kinds of truth table analysis.

Key Words

decision method	logically consistent (inconsistent) wffs
tautology	logically equivalent (nonequivalent)
inconsistency	wffs
contingency	truth table

truth tree

main connective (of a propositionally complex wff)

greatest scope rule for identifying main propositional connectives

fewest parentheses guidelines for identifying main propositional connectives

deductively valid (invalid) sequent (argument)

truth table setup rules

deductive validity (invalidity)

conditional conversion rule for truth table test of sequent validity

turbo truth table method

Exercises

I: Truth Table Concepts   Give a correct concise statement of each of the following concepts; where appropriate, give an illustration of each that does not appear in the book:

1. Decision method
2. Truth table
3. Main propositional connective
4. Greatest scope rule for identifying main propositional connectives
5. Fewest parentheses guidelines for identifying main propositional connectives
6. Truth table setup
7. Tautology; inconsistency, contingency
8. Logical consistency; logical equivalence
9. Deductive validity
10. Turbo truth table method

II: Truth Table Evaluation of Wffs   Use truth tables to evaluate the following wffs for classification as tautologies, inconsistencies, or contingencies of propositional logic:

1. R & ((P ⊃ Q) ∨ (~Q ⊃ ~R))
2. ~(((P ⊃ P) ⊃ ~P) ⊃ P) & ~P
3. (P ⊃ (Q & (~R ∨ ~P))) ⊃ ~(~Q ∨ (P ⊃ ~R))
4. ((P & Q) ⊃ (Q ⊃ R)) ∨ (~(Q ⊃ R) ⊃ (~Q ∨ ~P))
5. ((P ∨ Q) & ((P ⊃ R) & (Q ⊃ S))) ⊃ ~(R ∨ ~S)
6. ~(((P ⊃ ~Q) & ~(~(P ∨ R) & (Q ⊃ S))) ⊃ (R ⊃ S))
7. ((P ⊃ (~(Q & R)) ⊃ R)) ⊃ ((R ∨ (P & ~Q)) & (P ⊃ ~(Q & R)))

8. (Q ⊃ S) ≡ (((P ⊃ Q) ≡ (P ∨ S)) & ((Q ⊃ P) ≡ (S ⊃ P)))

9. ~(Q & S) ≡ (((P ⊃ Q) ≡ ~(P ∨ S)) ⊃ ~((Q ⊃ P) ≡ (S ⊃ ~P)))

10. (((R ∨ (P & ~Q)) & (P ⊃ ~(Q & R))) ⊃ R) ∨ (((~P ∨ Q) ⊃ (P & Q)) ≡ P)

III: Truth Table Evaluation of Sequents Use truth tables to evaluate the following sequents as deductively valid or invalid.

1. ~(~A & B), ~(~B ∨ C) ⊢ A

2. S ⊢ (~P ∨ Q) ∨ (Q ⊃ R)

3. P ∨ Q, (P ⊃ R) & (Q ⊃ S) ⊢ R ∨ S

4. ~R, (P ∨ Q) ⊃ (R & ~P), R ∨ Q ⊢ ~P ∨ (R ≡ Q)

5. C ⊃ ((D ⊃ E) ⊃ (D & C)), (C ∨ E) ⊃ D ⊢ C ⊃ (E ⊃ D)

6. G & (A ⊃ B), (B ⊃ G) ⊃ A ⊢ B ≡ ~G

7. U ⊃ ~Q, ~(S ⊃ ~U), (Q & S) ⊃ (S ⊃ ~Q), ~(U ⊃ S) ⊢ ~U

8. ~M ⊃ J, (L & ~M) ⊃ (L ⊃ J), J ⊃ M, ~(L ⊃ ~M) ⊢ ~L

9. P ⊃ (~Q ⊃ R), P & (~Q & ~R), ~Q ⊃ (R ≡ (P ∨ S)) ⊢ Q

10. (P ⊃ Q) & (Q ⊃ P), (R & Q) ∨ (P ∨ ~Q), ~R ⊃ (P & R), (Q ⊃ ~Q) & (~P ⊃ ~Q), R ⊃ (Q ⊃ ~R), (~R ∨ P) & (R ∨ Q) ⊢ ~(R & ~P)

IV: Truth Table Evaluation of Complex Wffs Use truth tables to evaluate the following complex wffs for classification as tautologies, inconsistencies, or contingencies of propositional logic. Then use truth tables to determine whether each of two successive wffs in the list (1 and 2, 2 and 3, 3 and 4, etc.) are logically consistent or inconsistent, and whether they are logically equivalent or nonequivalent:

1. ((R ∨ (P & ~Q)) & (P ⊃ ~(Q & R))) ⊃ R

2. ((P ∨ Q) & ((P ⊃ R) & (Q ⊃ S))) ⊃ ~(R ∨ ~S)

3. ~((((P ⊃ ~Q) & ~(~P ∨ R) & (Q ⊃ S))) ⊃ (R ⊃ S))

4. (Q ⊃ S) ≡ (((P ⊃ Q) ≡ (P ∨ S)) & ((Q ⊃ P) ≡ (S ⊃ P)))

5. ~(Q & S) ≡ (((P ⊃ Q) ≡ ~(P ∨ S)) ⊃ ~((Q ⊃ P) ≡ (S ⊃ ~P)))

6. (((R ∨ (P & ~Q)) & (P ⊃ ~(Q & R))) ⊃ R) ∨ (((~P ∨ Q) ⊃ (P & Q)) ≡ P)

7. (((P ⊃ Q) ⊃ P) ⊃ P) & ((((P ⊃ Q) ⊃ P) ⊃ P) ∨ ~((Q ⊃ P) ≡ (Q ⊃ ~P)))

8. ((P ∨ (Q & ~R)) & (R ⊃ ~Q)) ⊃ (~(P & ~Q) ⊃ ((P & Q) & ~R))

9. ((((P & Q) ⊃ R) & (P ⊃ Q)) & ((P & R) ⊃ S)) ⊃ (P ⊃ (Q ⊃ S))

10. ((((P & Q) ⊃ R) & (P ⊃ Q)) ≡ ((P & ~R) ⊃ S)) ⊃ (P ⊃ ~(Q ⊃ ~S))

V: *Truth Table Evaluation of Complex Sequents*   Use truth tables to evaluate the following complex sequents as deductively valid or invalid.

1. ~(~A & B), ~(~B ∨ C) ⊢ A
2. S ⊢ (~P ∨ Q) ∨ (Q ⊃ R)
3. P ∨ Q, (P ⊃ R) & (Q ⊃ S) ⊢ R ∨ S
4. ~R, (P ∨ Q) ⊃ (R & ~P), R ∨ Q ⊢ ~P ∨ (R ≡ Q)
5. C ⊃ ((D ⊃ E) ⊃ (E & C)), (D ∨ C) ⊃ E ⊢ C ⊃ (E ⊃ D)
6. G & (A ⊃ B), (B ⊃ G) ⊃ A ⊢ B ≡ ~G
7. U ⊃ ~Q, ~(S ⊃ ~U), (T & S) ⊃ (U ⊃ ~Q), ~(T ⊃ Q) ⊢ ~T
8. ~M ⊃ J, (L & ~M) ⊃ (H ⊃ L), J ⊃ M, ~(L ⊃ ~H) ⊢ ~L
9. P ⊃ (~Q ⊃ R), P & (~Q & ~R), ~Q ⊃ (R ≡ (P ∨ R)) ⊢ Q
10. (~A & C) & ~D, (E ∨ D) ⊃ ~(~D ≡ C) ⊢ ~(C ∨ E) & D
11. N ⊃ ((B & ~P) ∨ R), B & ~R, ~N ⊃ P ⊢ ~T ⊃ ~B
12. ~R ⊢ ~(~(P ⊃ Q) & ~(Q ⊃ ~R))
13. (~F ≡ G) ⊃ ~H, (F & I) ∨ (~G & H), (I ∨ G) ⊃ H ⊢ ~G ⊃ ~F
14. P ∨ Q, P ⊃ (T ⊃ R), (T ≡ S) ⊃ ~P ⊢ (~R & S) ⊃ Q
15. P ≡ ~Q, Q ≡ ~R ⊢ P ≡ R
16. B ⊃ C ⊢ ((A ⊃ C) ⊃ ((B ∨ A) ⊃ C)) ≡ (((B ⊃ A) & ~A) ⊃ ~B)
17. (~P ⊃ (Q ⊃ ~P)) ⊃ ~((Q ⊃ R) ⊃ ((P ⊃ Q) ⊃ (P ⊃ R))) ⊢ P ∨ R
18. Q ⊢ ~((Q ≡ ~S) ⊃ (((P ⊃ Q) ≡ (P ⊃ ~S)) & ((Q ⊃ P) ≡ ~(S ⊃ P))))
19. ~M ⊃ (N & (~O ∨ P)), (M & ~N) ⊃ ~M, (O & N) & P ⊢ N & (~O ∨ P)
20. (P ⊃ Q) & (Q ⊃ P), (R & Q) ∨ (P ∨ ~Q), ~R ⊃ (P & Q), (R ⊃ ~Q) & (~Q ⊃ ~P), R ⊃ (Q ⊃ ~P), (~R ∨ P) & (Q ∨ R) ⊢ ~(R & ~P)

VI: *Short Answer Questions for Philosophical Reflection*

1. What is meant by a decision method in symbolic logic?
2. Could all questions about the logical properties of individual propositions and argument sequents in propositional logic be fully decided by decision methods? If decision methods are sometimes called mechanical procedures, is all logical reasoning essentially mechanical?
3. What, if anything, is interesting about tautologies in propositional logic? Since tautologies do not convey definite true or false information, what, if anything, can be learned about logical form from the study of tautologies?

4. What is the relationship between a tautology and an inconsistency as revealed by truth table analysis? If a proposition is a contingency, why is its negation also a contingency?

5. What is entailed about the nature of logic by the fact that the five traditional propositional connectives can all be reduced to a single operator that combines the truth functional effect of negation with any one of the remaining three logical connectives?

6. What is the metaphysical status of negation? What is the status of the other propositional connectives, conjunction, disjunction, conditional, and biconditional? What kinds of things are truth functions? Do they exist? Are they purely imaginary, or are they like abstract mathematical objects?

CHAPTER FOUR

Truth Trees

An intelligent use of symbolism is of utmost importance in the study of structure; one should try from the beginning to develop definite, consistent, and easy habits of expression. . . . Symbolism, then, becomes an organ of discovery rather than mere notation.

—Susanne K. Langer, *An Introduction to Symbolic Logic* (1967)

As ANOTHER MORE GENERAL way of testing wffs and sequents, we now explain the method of truth trees. Truth trees, like truth tables, are decision methods that give correct answers to specific questions about the logical properties of wffs and sequents but are easier and faster to use, especially for problems involving many propositional symbols.

Truth Trees

Truth trees give the same results as truth tables but are a more generally practical decision method.

Truth trees are another decision method for propositional logic. Like truth tables, truth trees are based on the truth table definitions of the propositional connectives. Truth trees can also be used to classify wffs as tautologies, contingencies, or inconsistencies, to compare two or more wffs for consistency and equivalence, and to evaluate argument sequents for deductive validity. Truth trees were developed by Raymond M. Smullyan, as an adaptation of E. W. Beth's method of semantic tableaux, and are sometimes called Smullyan truth trees. The following is a typical example of a completed propositional truth tree:

$$(Q \supset P) \supset ((P \supset Q) \ \& \ (Q \vee P)) \quad \checkmark \ 1$$

$$2 \ \checkmark \quad \sim(Q \supset P) \qquad (P \supset Q) \ \& \ (Q \vee P) \quad \checkmark \ 3$$
$$Q \qquad\qquad\qquad P \supset Q \quad \checkmark \ 4$$
$$\sim P \qquad\qquad\qquad Q \vee P \quad \checkmark \ 5$$

$$\sim P \qquad\quad Q$$

$$Q \qquad P \ \ Q \qquad P$$
$$X$$

It is easy to see why this graphic decision method in logic is known as a *truth tree*. It consists of an array of wffs in branching arrangements like the trunk and branches of an inverted tree. As will soon be shown, a truth tree, like a real tree, grows from a starting place in a series of developmental stages according to a definite set of rules.

Truth trees are easier and faster to use than truth tables. They work effectively for propositions and arguments with large numbers of propositional symbols. Even when truth trees become unwieldy (as all paper-and-pencil methods in logic and mathematics eventually do), for problems involving hundreds of propositional symbols (beyond anything attempted here), they are always significantly more manageable than truth tables. Truth trees provide a test of logical inconsistency in which we reduce wffs to a truth functionally equivalent graphic display. The *truth tree decomposition rules* by which wffs are reduced to an equivalent tree are rooted in the truth table definitions of the propositional connectives and in the fact that any propositional wff is logically equivalent to one of two graphic configurations.

Truth trees, unlike truth tables, are useful for problems containing virtually any number of propositional symbols.

Stacking and Branching

The two basic truth tree configurations are branching (for disjunction) and stacking (for conjunction).

A truth tree begins with a *stack* or vertical array of wffs, which could consist of a single wff as a limiting case. Stacks of wffs include the following examples:

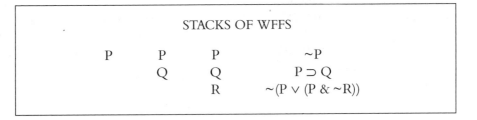

			STACKS OF WFFS
P	P	P	$\sim P$
	Q	Q	$P \supset Q$
		R	$\sim(P \vee (P \ \& \ \sim R))$

Truth trees reduce all the propositionally complex wffs in a stack to a logically equivalent graphic structure consisting of propositional symbols or their negations ('P', '~P', 'Q', '~Q', etc.). A stack of wffs in a completed truth tree in which all propositionally complex wffs other than the negations of atomic wffs or propositional symbols are reduced in this way is said to be *fully decomposed*. Truth trees use two basic pictorial devices for decomposing a stack of wffs into a tree diagram: *stacking* and *branching*.

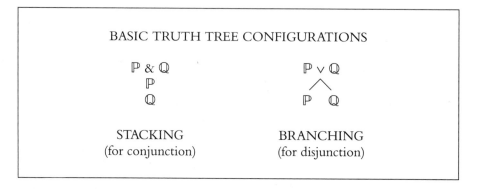

Stacking graphically represents conjunction; branching represents disjunction. Truth tree decomposition rules reduce a stack of wffs to a stacking or branching configuration of wffs, which ultimately consists of atomic wffs or their negations, according to the truth table definitions of the five propositional connectives.

If we are to reduce all propositions to stacking and branching configurations of propositional symbols and their negations, then we already have a way of picturing conjunction and disjunction. A stack of wffs represents their conjunction, whereas a branching of wffs represents their disjunction. To these graphic devices, we add equivalences for reducing negated conjunctions, negated disjunctions, conditionals, negated conditionals, biconditionals, and negated biconditionals to stacking (conjunctive) or branching (disjunctive) configurations. We can reduce any wff in propositional logic to one of these types by beginning with a proposition's main connective and working down to the main connectives of any of its component wffs, arriving at conjunctions or disjunctions of atomic wffs, single propositional symbols, or their negations. When in doubt, we can use truth tables to test the equivalences and ensure we understand why they hold before proceeding.

A stack of wffs is fully decomposed when the application of truth tree decomposition rules has reduced each wff to an equivalent graphic form consisting only of propositional symbols or their negations.

Truth tree decompositions depend on the truth table definitions of the five propositional connectives and on equivalences between wffs containing any propositional main connective or its negation and a conjunction or disjunction.

EQUIVALENCES FOR TRUTH TREE REDUCTIONS
OF PROPOSITIONAL FORMS TO CONJUNCTIONS
OR DISJUNCTIONS

$\sim(\mathbb{P} \,\&\, \mathbb{Q})$	is logically equivalent ($\equiv$) to	$\sim\mathbb{P} \vee \sim\mathbb{Q}$
$\sim(\mathbb{P} \vee \mathbb{Q})$	$\equiv$	$\sim\mathbb{P} \,\&\, \sim\mathbb{Q}$
$\mathbb{P} \supset \mathbb{Q}$	$\equiv$	$\sim\mathbb{P} \vee \mathbb{Q}$
$\sim(\mathbb{P} \supset \mathbb{Q})$	$\equiv$	$\mathbb{P} \,\&\, \sim\mathbb{Q}$
$\mathbb{P} \equiv \mathbb{Q}$	$\equiv$	$(\mathbb{P} \,\&\, \mathbb{Q}) \vee (\sim\mathbb{P} \,\&\, \sim\mathbb{Q})$
$\sim(\mathbb{P} \equiv \mathbb{Q})$	$\equiv$	$(\mathbb{P} \,\&\, \sim\mathbb{Q}) \vee (\sim\mathbb{P} \,\&\, \mathbb{Q})$

To Check Your Understanding 4.1 ■

Use truth tables (or shortcut or turbo truth tables) to verify each of the logical equivalences listed in the box above.

■

Truth Tree Rules

Truth trees require decomposition rules, an application protocol, and interpretation criteria.

Truth trees contain open or closed branches; closed branches have an inconsistent pair of wffs, a propositional symbol and its negation.

We use these equivalences in constructing truth trees. Truth tree decomposition rules are presented. Then a list of definitions and procedures is provided to apply truth trees to propositions and arguments. Finally, examples are given to illustrate how truth tree methods can be used to better advantage in all the same ways as truth tables.

Truth trees are used to demonstrate the inconsistency of a stack of wffs. A truth tree *branch* is a connected vertical array of wffs in a single continuous graphic pathway that extends upward from any wff in the tree through stacking and branching, if any, in the tree back to the original stack. A truth tree branch is thus the path of wffs displayed within the tree from one or another tip of each branching configuration, if any, to its apex in the tree, and from there continuing upward from the connecting tip of the next higher branching configuration, if any, to its apex, and so on, terminating in the original stack as the trunk of the tree. In the limiting case, a truth tree branch consists only of a single stack of wffs, including and possibly limited to the original stack. Here are some examples of trees in which individual branches are outlined for identification:

IDENTIFYING TRUTH TREE BRANCHES

We identify single branches on truth trees.

*Decomposed wffs in
a truth tree stack are
marked with a check
'√'; closed branches
are marked with
an 'X'.*

When a truth tree branch contains a logically inconsistent pair of at least one atomic wff or propositional symbol and its negation ($\mathbb{P}$, $\sim\mathbb{P}$), the branch is said to *close* (*closed branch*). When all the branches in a completed truth tree of fully decomposed wffs are closed, the tree is said to close (*closed tree*). The truth tree method constructs a tree by fully decomposing each proposition in a stack to be tested, marking each with a check mark '√' to ensure that none is overlooked and none duplicated, and stopping whenever an inconsistent pair consisting of an atomic proposition and its negation appear on any branch, marking terminating inconsistent branches with an 'X'. A branch so marked is said to close, and if every branch closes, the entire tree is closed. A closed tree indicates that the stack of propositions being tested is logically inconsistent. An open tree with even one unclosed branch indicates that the stack of propositions being tested is not logically inconsistent but logically consistent. The truth tree representations of a closed branch, open branch, closed tree, and open tree are illustrated as follows:

*A closed truth tree in-
dicates that the stack
being evaluated is
logically inconsistent.*

*We identify open and
closed branches on a
truth tree.*

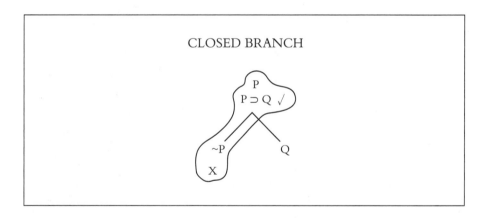

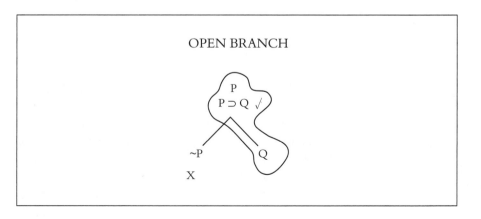

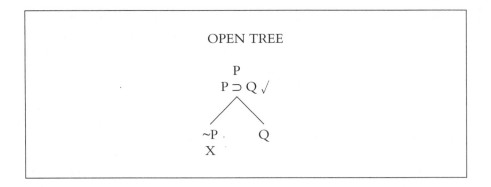

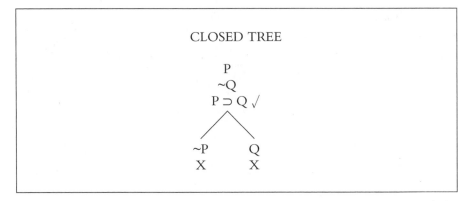

The fact that trees can be used to determine whether or not any set of wffs is logically inconsistent makes it possible to do all the same things we can do with truth tables. We can use truth trees to decide whether or not a proposition is a tautology, inconsistency, or contingency, whether two or more individual propositions are logically consistent or logically inconsistent or whether they are logically equivalent or logically nonequivalent, and whether or not an argument sequent is deductively valid or invalid.

The truth tree decompositions of each of the basic forms in symbolic logic depend on the truth table definitions of the five propositional connectives from the reductions given previously. When we do a truth tree analysis, we break down each proposition in a stack, using check marks to chart our progress, by applying the appropriate decomposition rule to its main connective, stacking or branching the result according to the forms required for its corresponding proposition type. If the components contain additional propositional connectives, we continue successively in the same way with these, identifying the main connective, if any, in each component wff and applying the appropriate decomposition rule to it in a stacking–branching configuration until all the original propositions in the stack are fully decomposed, closing off branches with an 'X' as inconsistencies appear. Then we examine the tree for closure or non-

Logical inconsistency as judged by a closed truth tree can be used to evaluate all the same logical properties of wffs and sequents as in truth tables.

closure, depending on whether or not all its branches close. A fully decomposed tree is finally interpreted according to truth tree definitions for tautology, inconsistency, contingency, logical consistency or inconsistency, logical equivalence or nonequivalence, and deductive validity or invalidity.

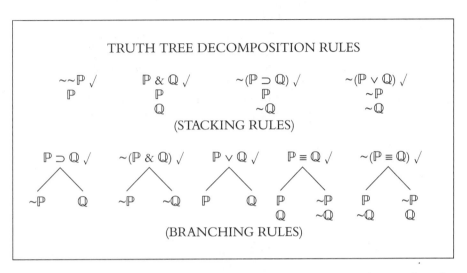

One way to memorize the rules, in addition to rewriting them and working through exercises, is to distinguish them by category as stacking or branching rules. The truth tree decomposition rules for double negation, conjunction, negated conditional, and negated disjunction are stacking rules. The rules for conditional, negated conjunction, and disjunction are branching rules. The rules for the biconditional and negated biconditional combine branching as their primary configuration with the stacking of propositions or their negations at the ends of each branch.

Next, we consider a general set of instructions for applying the truth tree decomposition rules to any stack of wffs:

TRUTH TREE PROTOCOL

1. Begin with a single wff or stack of wffs.
2. Follow the truth tree decomposition rules working successively toward the complete decomposition of the wffs in the stack, applying the appropriate rule to the main connective in each wff and then to the remaining propositional components when they appear as decomposition products in the tree.
3. When there are wffs left to decompose on any part of the tree, decompose them by applying the appropriate decomposition rules to their main connectives at the end of every open branch below their occurrence in the tree.

*Truth tree protocol
describes each step of
truth tree analysis.*

> Never decompose a wff on a branch other than that to which it belongs, and always inscribe the decomposition products below rather than above it in the tree, reading from top to bottom.
> 4. Mark each decomposed wff with a check '√' to avoid omissions or duplications. Mark closed branches with an 'X' when at least one inconsistent pair of any proposition symbol and its negation appears in fully decomposed form on the same branch. Fully decompose every wff unless or until all branches close, and never decompose the same wff more than once.
> 5. Interpret the completed tree as providing information about the logical properties the tree is being used to determine, whether an individual wff is a tautology, inconsistency, or contingency, equivalent to or consistent with another wff, or whether an argument sequent is deductively valid or invalid.

It is essential not to overlook the truth tree decomposition of any wff in a stack being evaluated, and it is equally important not to decompose any wff more than once. The check marks keep track of wffs that have been decomposed and those remaining at any stage of truth tree decomposition. A tree is not finished until the check marks show that all wffs and component wffs or byproducts of decomposition within the tree have been fully decomposed. The check marks ensure that in whatever order we proceed, we do not overlook any wff to be decomposed or decompose any wff more than once.

The order in which wffs in a stack are decomposed does not make any difference in obtaining a correct truth tree evaluation.

The exact order in which we decompose the wffs in a truth tree stack is not important in arriving at a correct truth tree evaluation. We usually produce a simpler tree if we follow the rule of thumb to always first decompose any wff that stacks and then apply branching rules to wffs that branch. The sequence of truth tree decompositions at most affects only the appearance of the tree and not its truth tree evaluation. If we follow the truth tree decomposition rules correctly and correctly interpret the completed tree, we will always get the same results in truth tree evaluations, regardless of the order in which we apply the rules.

Truth trees can be more compactly and efficiently presented by decomposing wffs that stack before wffs that branch.

To make the point, the following is a comparison of two truth trees of the same stack of wffs, P ∨ Q, Q ∨ R, and ~R & (~P & ~Q). In the first, wffs that stack are decomposed before wffs that branch, and in the second wffs that branch are decomposed before wffs that stack. The same evaluation is made by both trees, but the trees look different. The first tree, in which wffs that stack are decomposed before wffs that branch, is less complicated and easier to construct than the second tree, in which wffs that branch are decomposed before wffs that stack. The method prunes excessive branching that may otherwise occur in many truth trees. The check marks are numbered as an optional method of indicating the order in which wffs are decomposed.

STACKING FIRST

```
    P ∨ Q   √ 3
    Q ∨ R
  ~R & (~P & ~Q)   √ 1
    ~R
  ~P & ~Q   √ 2
    ~P
    ~Q
      /\
    P    Q
    X    X
```

INCONSISTENCY
(1 branch; 6 wffs; 3 decompositions)

BRANCHING FIRST

```
         P ∨ Q   √ 1
         Q ∨ R   √ 2
      ~R & (~P & ~Q)   √ 3
          /        \
        P            Q
       / \          / \
      Q    R      Q      R
     ~R   ~R     ~R     ~R
 4 √ ~P & ~Q  X  ~P & ~Q √ 5  X
     ~P          ~P
     ~Q          ~Q
      X           X
```

INCONSISTENCY
(3 branches; 16 wffs; 5 decompositions)

We should be prepared to explain how each stage of truth tree decomposition is justified by truth tree decomposition rules, to name the specific rules applied to each complex wff at each stage, and to justify how the wff is evaluated, depending on whether its truth tree closes or does not close. The check marks from step to step show the order in which the wffs are chosen for decomposition. By writing numbers beside the check marks, much as we did in introducing the turbo truth table method, we indicate the order in which decomposition rules are applied. Note that in the "Stacking First" truth tree, we did not bother to decompose the disjunction Q ∨ R because the tree closed before we could get to it. The rules for truth tree decompositions require that we decompose a propositionally complex wff at the end of every open branch below it in the tree. If all branches close before we have decomposed all the propositionally complex wffs, then we are prohibited by the rules from doing so because in this case there will be no open branches below the remaining wffs in the tree. A tree that closes without decomposing all the wffs in its original stack is inconsistent by virtue of only some of its wffs.

Truth Tree Criteria

Truth tree criteria provide concepts for interpreting truth trees as indicating specific logical properties of wffs and sequents.

To apply truth trees in testing wffs and sequents, we need to understand how closed and unclosed trees are interpreted. The following truth tree concepts enable us to recognize the closure or nonclosure of certain stacks of wffs as having the same logical properties we have already learned to evaluate using truth tables. These criteria guide us in setting up truth trees in required ways to obtain results we can use in deciding whether or not a wff or stack of wffs has a particular logical property.

Truth Tree Criteria for Semantic Properties in Propositional Logic

1. A truth tree *branch* is *closed* if and only if there is an inconsistent fully reduced propositional symbol and its negation of the form ℙ and ~ℙ somewhere on it. This is indicated by terminating the branch with an 'X' as soon as the inconsistency appears.
2. A *truth tree* is *closed* if and only if all its branches are closed.
3. A wff ℙ is a *tautology* if and only if ~ℙ has a closed tree; a wff ℙ is a *logical inconsistency* if and only if ℙ has a closed tree; a wff ℙ is a *contingency* if and only if ℙ is neither a tautology nor an inconsistency (neither the truth tree for ℙ nor the truth tree for ~ℙ closes).
4. A stack of wffs ℙ, ℚ, . . . , ℤ is *logically consistent* if and only if it has an open tree (a tree with at least one open branch); the stack is *logically inconsistent* if and only if it has a closed tree.
5. Wffs ℙ and ℚ are *logically equivalent* if and only if ℙ ≡ ℚ is a tautology [if and only if ~(ℙ ≡ ℚ) has a closed tree].
6. A sequent ℙ, ℚ, . . . , 𝕐 ⊢ ℤ is *deductively valid* if and only if the stack ℙ, ℚ, . . . , 𝕐, ~ℤ has a closed tree.

The first three definitions recapitulate what we have already said about closed trees as showing the logical inconsistency of an individual wff or stack of wffs and the nonclosure of a completed truth tree as indicating the logical consistency of an individual wff or stack of wffs. The following are two examples to illustrate this use of truth trees; both are taken from previous truth table analysis:

$$
\begin{array}{cc}
\text{P \& \sim P} \quad \checkmark & \quad \text{P} \supset \sim\text{P} \quad \checkmark \\
\text{P} & \wedge \\
\sim\text{P} & \sim\text{P} \qquad \sim\text{P} \\
\text{X} & \\
\text{INCONSISTENT} & \quad \text{NOT INCONSISTENT}
\end{array}
$$

In the example on the right, we use the truth tree decomposition rule for a conditional. The rule requires us to decompose a conditional in a branching truth tree configuration, with the negation of the conditional's antecedent at the end of the left side of the branch and the unnegated consequent of the conditional just as it appears at the end of the branch on the right. This is justified by the fact that the conditional P ⊃ Q is logically equivalent by truth tables to the disjunction ~P ∨ Q.

To know that a proposition is not inconsistent is at best a negative result. It excludes one of three categories for the classification of wffs—tautology, inconsistency, and contingency. However, by itself, such a negative result does not positively determine to which of the two remaining categories the proposition belongs. Thus, when we obtain a negative result in truth tree testing whether an individual wff is an inconsistency, and we need to know whether the wff is a tautology or contingency, we must also complete a second truth tree in which we test its negation. As truth tables show, the negation of every tautology is an inconsistency; conversely, the negation of every inconsistency is a tautology. A tautology has a truth table in which only T's occur under the column for its main connective. The truth table for the negation of a tautology must then consist of nothing but F's, which is the truth table of a logical inconsistency. The opposite is true for the negation of an inconsistency. Since a closed truth tree indicates a logically inconsistent wff or set or stack of wffs, and the negation of any tautology is an inconsistency, it follows that a closed truth tree for the negation of a wff indicates that the wff is a tautology. By demonstrating in a truth tree that P & ~P is an inconsistency, we thereby simultaneously show that ~(P & ~P) is a tautology. If the truth trees for neither a wff nor its negation close, then the wff (as well as its negation, again by truth table definition) is a contingency. The truth tree for the negation of the proposition ~(P ⊃ ~P) also fails to close, which means that the original proposition is a contingency, as

An open truth tree is a negative result, indicating that a stack of wffs is not inconsistent.

is its negation. Here, the decomposition rule for a negated conditional comes into play:

$$\sim(P \supset \sim P) \ \checkmark$$
$$P$$
$$\sim\sim P \ \checkmark$$
$$P$$

Double negations are collapsed without explicitly invoking a special rule.

For simplicity and reading ease, from now on we will silently collapse double negations so that instead of writing '$\sim\sim P$' in the second line of the truth table stack in this decomposition, we will simply write 'P'. This saves time and makes our trees neater, speeds up the evaluation process slightly, and allows more information to be gathered from a completed tree at a glance.

Truth trees work because of the fact that any propositional wff can be reduced to truth functionally equivalent stacking or branching forms, according to the truth table definitions of the propositional connectives. A logical inconsistency in a stack of wffs is revealed when the stack is reduced to a closed truth tree by the decomposition rules. The truth tree is a logically equivalent graphic representation of the propositional structures of the wffs in a stack of wffs. If an inconsistency is lurking in the stack, it must eventually come to light in the truth tree reduction as at least one inconsistent pair of fully decomposed wffs consisting of a propositional symbol and its negation appearing somewhere on every branch. A decisive test for logical inconsistency in turn can be used according to the truth tree concepts to test for tautology and contingency, consistency and equivalence of multiple wffs, and deductive validity or invalidity of sequents.

Classifying Wffs by Truth Trees

A closed truth tree for the negation of a wff indicates that the wff is a tautology because the negation of every tautology is an inconsistency and vice versa.

We can use truth trees to classify propositions as tautologies, inconsistencies, or contingencies. It is sometimes necessary to do two truth trees to classify a wff. A negative result in a tree that does not close, as we have seen, requires that we test the negation of the wff to determine whether its tree closes. If the tree for the negation of a wff closes, then the original (unnegated) wff is a tautology (and the negated wff tested is an inconsistency). If the second tree also does not close, then the original (unnegated) wff is a contingency, as is its negation.

TRUTH TREE TEST FOR TAUTOLOGY

$\sim(P \supset P)$ √   (1) Stack NEGATION
P   of wff to test
$\sim$P   (2) Complete truth tree
X

Closed tree indicates TAUTOLOGY

(Open tree would indicate NOT A TAUTOLOGY)

A closed truth tree for a wff indicates that a wff is an inconsistency.

TRUTH TREE TEST FOR INCONSISTENCY

P & $\sim$P   √   (1) Stack wff(s)
P
$\sim$P   (2) Complete truth tree
X

Closed tree indicates INCONSISTENCY

(Open tree would indicate NOT AN INCONSISTENCY)

If the truth tree for a wff does not close, it follows that the wff is not an inconsistency; then it is necessary to also complete a truth tree for the negation of the wff in order to classify the wff more specifically as either a tautology or contingency.

If neither the truth tree for a wff nor the truth tree for the negation of a wff closes, the wff is a contingency.

TRUTH TREE TEST FOR CONTINGENCY

PART 1 $P \supset Q$ √   (1) Stack wff

$\sim$P   Q   (2) Complete truth tree

Open tree indicates NOT AN INCONSISTENCY (negative result)

PART 2 $\sim(P \supset Q)$ (1) Stack NEGATION
P   of wff
$\sim$Q   (2) Complete truth tree

Open tree indicates NOT AN INCONSISTENCY (negative result)

Open tree for both wff and negation of wff indicates CONTINGENCY

One truth tree only is needed to evaluate two or more wffs for logical consistency or inconsistency and for logical equivalence or nonequivalence.

A closed tree for a stack of wffs indicates that they are logically inconsistent; an open tree indicates that they are logically consistent.

A closed tree for the negation of a biconditional connecting two wffs indicates that the biconditional is a tautology, and hence that the wffs are logically equivalent; an open tree indicates that the biconditional is not a tautology, and hence that the wffs are logically nonequivalent.

Truth tree testing of a stack of two or more wffs for logical equivalence or consistency requires only one tree. To determine equivalence, we connect the wffs to be tested by the biconditional, negate the entire biconditional, and decompose the resulting negative biconditional by truth tree rules. If the tree for the negated biconditional closes, it shows that the biconditional is a tautology, which means that the wffs connected thereby are logically equivalent since they always have the same truth values. If the tree does not close, it means that the wffs are not logically equivalent but can sometimes have different truth values. The test for consistency or inconsistency of two or more wffs follows the same procedure as that for the consistency or inconsistency of a single wff. If the completed tree for a stack of two or more wffs does not close, it means that the wffs are logically consistent; if the tree closes, it means that the wffs are logically inconsistent.

Demonstration 13: Classifying Wffs by Truth Trees

PROBLEM: To evaluate the logical status of a complex wff by truth trees. We begin with a problem we have already examined by truth table methods in the previous chapter.

$$(P \supset Q) \supset (\sim P \vee Q)$$

STEP 1:   *Apply the truth tree rule to the main connective*
We begin with a conditional wff (a wff the main propositional connective of which is a conditional) and apply the truth tree decomposition rule for conditionals from the list, breaking it down into a branching configuration as the rule requires with the negation of the entire antecedent at the end of the left end of the branch and the consequent just as it appears in the conditional at the right. We show that we have completed this step by marking the wff with a check.

$$(P \supset Q) \supset (\sim P \vee Q) \quad \surd \; 1$$

$$\sim(P \supset Q) \qquad \sim P \vee Q$$

The decomposition applies to the entire wff being decomposed. We do not need to place the stack or apex of the branch directly beneath the main connective of the wff we are decomposing at any stage of truth tree decomposition. Instead, for convenience we generally center it beneath the stack of wffs to be decomposed, with the understanding that in this way we indicate the decomposition of an entire wff in the stack.

STEP 2:   *Continue truth tree decomposition by applying appropriate rules to the main connectives of each remaining open branch*

We notice that the first step of decomposition leaves us with truth functionally complex wffs involving propositional connectives at both left- and right-hand ends of the main branch. We take the left side first (though we could proceed in the opposite order without making any difference in the final tree). We notice that it is a negated conditional, and we apply the truth tree decomposition rule for negated conditionals to produce a stacking of the negated conditional's antecedent together with the negation of its consequent in the following tree. Again, a check mark indicates that we have completed this step:

$$(P \supset Q) \supset (\sim P \vee Q) \quad \checkmark\,1$$

$$2 \,\checkmark \quad \sim(P \supset Q) \qquad \sim P \vee Q$$
$$P$$
$$\sim Q$$

We similarly decompose the disjunction as the main operator in the wff on the right-hand side of the main branch. This is not a negated disjunction but merely a disjunction with a negated left-hand disjunct. The disjunction branches according to its truth tree decomposition rule. Annotating it with a check mark, the truth tree at this third stage of decomposition looks as follows:

$$(P \supset Q) \supset (\sim P \vee Q) \quad \checkmark\,1 \qquad\qquad \text{TREE 1}$$

$$2 \,\checkmark \quad \sim(P \supset Q) \qquad \sim P \vee Q \quad \checkmark\,3$$
$$P$$
$$\sim Q$$

$$\sim P \qquad Q$$

NOT AN INCONSISTENCY

STEP 3:   *Evaluate the completed truth tree*
The tree is complete at this point. We notice that there are no closed branches, which means that the tree does not close. Applying the appropriate truth tree concept, we conclude that the wff is not an inconsistency. Since this is a negative result, we continue truth tree analysis by doing a truth tree decomposition of the wff's negation. This is done in three successive steps, which are shown below without special commentary.

STEP 4:   *If necessary, give a truth tree analysis of the wff's negation*
Following the same sequence of steps for different main connectives, the truth tree and evaluation of the negation of the wff and the original wff to be tested are presented in the completion of the following:

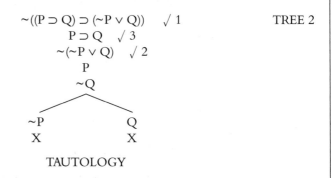

TAUTOLOGY

(ORIGINAL UNNEGATED FORM)

STEP 5:   *Evaluate the completed truth trees*
The truth tree for the original unnegated wff does not close, but the tree for its negation closes. This means that the negated wff is an inconsistency, and the original unnegated wff we are asked to test is a tautology. Truth tree analysis in this way shows that the original wff to be tested is a tautology, confirming our previous truth table analysis.

We use truth tree methods to test the following wffs to classify as tautologies, inconsistencies, or contingencies. The truth trees show the results, which you should study and try to duplicate. Explain each step and then redraw the trees without looking at the diagrams until you are ready to check your answers. Double underlining indicates that a wff is a proposition to be analyzed and not a part of the truth tree by which the wff is analyzed.

$$\underline{\sim P \supset (P \mathbin{\&} \sim P)}$$

TREE 1 $\sim P \supset (P \mathbin{\&} \sim P)$ √ 1 $\sim(\sim P \supset (P \mathbin{\&} \sim P))$ √ 1 TREE 2

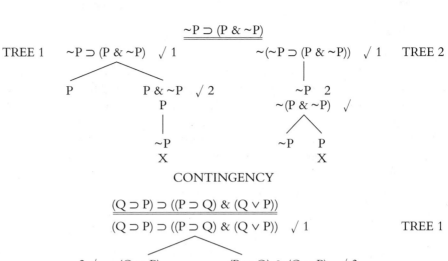

CONTINGENCY

$$\underline{(Q \supset P) \supset ((P \supset Q) \mathbin{\&} (Q \lor P))}$$

$(Q \supset P) \supset ((P \supset Q) \mathbin{\&} (Q \lor P))$ √ 1   TREE 1

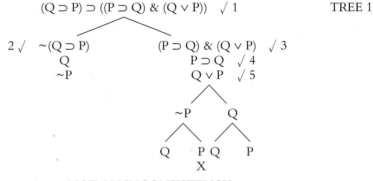

NOT AN INCONSISTENCY

$\sim((Q \supset P) \supset ((P \supset Q) \mathbin{\&} (Q \lor P)))$ √ 1   TREE 2
$Q \supset P$ √ 2
$\sim((P \supset Q) \mathbin{\&} (Q \lor P))$ √ 3

```
                    ~Q                              P
4, 5 √  ~(P ⊃ Q) √   ~(Q ∨ P)    ~(P ⊃ Q)  √   ~(Q ∨ P)  √ 6, 7
           P          ~Q            P           ~Q
          ~Q          ~P           ~Q           ~P
                                                 X
```

CONTINGENCY

$$\underline{(P \supset (Q \supset P)) \equiv (\sim Q \supset (P \supset (\sim Q \lor P)))}$$

$(P \supset (Q \supset P)) \equiv (\sim Q \supset (P \supset (\sim Q \lor P)))$ √ 1   TREE 1

```
        2 √   P ⊃ (Q ⊃ P)                 ~(P ⊃ (Q ⊃ P))
        3 √   ~Q ⊃ (P ⊃ (~Q ∨ P))         ~(~Q ⊃ (P ⊃ (~Q ∨ P)))

              ~P      Q ⊃ P

               Q              NOT AN INCONSISTENCY
```

The numbering of truth tree decomposition steps is an optional way of showing how each tree is made but is not an essential part of the method.

A truth tree need not be completed after it becomes obvious that at least one of its branches cannot close.

It is important to remember that when a truth tree for the negation of wff closes, it is the original unnegated wff that is shown to be a tautology.

In the previous example, we did not bother to complete the tree because we can see that the left-hand branch will never close. The check marks show that all wffs above Q in the branch have already been decomposed, so no further activity can take place on that branch to bring about closure with ~P or Q. If we are using truth trees as a practical test for the logical properties of wffs and sequents, then we will not always want to complete a tree if an incomplete tree already gives us the answer we are seeking. We can think of such truth tree applications as the counterpart of shortcut or turbo truth tables.

$$\sim((P \supset (Q \supset P)) \equiv (\sim Q \supset (P \supset (\sim Q \vee P)))) \quad \checkmark\ 1 \qquad \text{TREE 2}$$

$P \supset (Q \supset P)$	$\sim(P \supset (Q \supset P)) \quad \checkmark\ 5$
$2\ \checkmark\ \ \sim(\sim Q \supset (P \supset (\sim Q \vee P)))$	$\sim Q \supset (P \supset (\sim Q \vee P))$
$\sim Q$	P
$3\ \checkmark\ \ \sim(P \supset (\sim Q \vee P))$	$\sim(Q \supset P) \quad \checkmark\ 6$
P	Q
$4\ \checkmark\ \ \sim(\sim Q \vee P)$	$\sim P$
Q	X
$\sim P$	
X	

TAUTOLOGY

(ORIGINAL UNNEGATED FORM)

$$(Q\ \&\ R) \supset \sim(((P \equiv Q) \supset (P \vee R))\ \&\ ((Q \supset P) \supset \sim(R \vee \sim P)))$$

$$(Q\ \&\ R) \supset \sim(((P \equiv Q) \supset (P \vee R))\ \&\ ((Q \supset P) \supset \sim(R \vee \sim P))) \quad \checkmark\ 1 \quad \text{TREE 1}$$

$$2\ \checkmark\ \ \sim(Q\ \&\ R) \qquad \sim(((P \equiv Q) \supset (P \vee R))\ \&\ ((Q \supset P) \supset \sim(R \vee \sim P)))$$

$$\sim Q \qquad \sim R$$

NOT AN INCONSISTENCY

$\sim((Q \& R) \supset \sim(((P \equiv Q) \supset (P \vee R)) \& ((Q \supset P) \supset \sim(R \vee \sim P)))) \quad \surd \ 1 \qquad$ TREE 2
$Q \& R \quad \surd \ 2$
$((P \equiv Q) \supset (P \vee R)) \& ((Q \supset P) \supset \sim(R \vee \sim P))) \quad \surd \ 3$
Q
R
$(P \equiv Q) \supset (P \vee R) \quad \surd \ 4$
$(Q \supset P) \supset \sim(R \vee \sim P) \quad \surd \ 7$

$5 \ \surd \quad \sim(P \equiv Q) \qquad\qquad\qquad P \vee R \quad \surd \ 6$

$\begin{array}{cc} P & \sim Q \\ \sim Q & P \\ X & X \end{array}$

$\qquad\qquad P \qquad R$

$8, 9 \ \surd \quad \sim(Q \supset P) \qquad \sim(R \vee \sim P) \surd \surd \quad \sim(Q \supset P) \quad \sim(R \vee \sim P) \ \surd \ 10, 11$
$\qquad\qquad\quad Q \qquad\qquad\qquad \sim R \qquad\qquad\qquad Q \qquad\qquad \sim R$
$\qquad\qquad\quad \sim P \qquad\qquad\qquad P \qquad\qquad\qquad \sim P \qquad\qquad P$
$\qquad\qquad\quad X \qquad\qquad\qquad\ X \qquad\qquad\qquad X \qquad\qquad\ X$

CONTINGENCY

Truth trees require specific applications to test for specific logical properties.

A stack of wffs is logically consistent if its truth tree does not close.

Truth trees for classifying wffs work because a closed tree indicates that a wff is logically inconsistent. A tautology is the negation of an inconsistency, and the converse is also true. If the tree for a wff closes, then the wff is an inconsistency, and its negation is a tautology. If neither the tree for a wff nor the tree for its negation close, then the wff is neither an inconsistency nor a tautology and must therefore be a contingency, as is its negation. We test a wff to determine if it is an inconsistency by doing its truth tree and applying the truth tree concept whereby if the tree closes the wff is an inconsistency, and if the tree does not close then the wff is not an inconsistency. We test a wff to determine if it is a tautology by doing the truth tree for its negation and applying the truth tree concept whereby if the tree for the negation of a wff closes then the wff is a tautology, and if the tree does not close then the wff is not a tautology. We test a wff to determine if it is a contingency by completing the truth tree for both the wff and its negation and evaluating the wff as a contingency if and only if neither the tree for the wff nor the tree for the negation of the wff close.

To Check Your Understanding 4.2 ━━━━━━━━━━━━━━━━━━━━━━━━━━━━━━ ■

Use truth trees to determine whether or not the following wffs are tautologies, inconsistencies, or contingencies; note that when a tree does not close, it is necessary to also do the tree for its negation in order to decide to which of the three categories the wff belongs:

1. P ≡ (Q & (P ≡ ~Q))
2. ((~R ⊃ ~S) ∨ (S & R)) ⊃ S
3. ~(((~R ⊃ ~S) ∨ (R & S)) ⊃ ~S)
4. (P ⊃ (P & ~Q)) & ((Q & P) & (P ⊃ Q))
5. (P ∨ (~Q & ~P)) ≡ (P ∨ (~Q ∨ (~P ⊃ ~(P & Q))))
6. ((P ⊃ Q) & (~S ⊃ ~R)) ≡ (((~P & ~R) ∨ (~P & S)) ∨ ((Q & ~R) ∨ (S & Q)))

■

Truth Trees for Consistency

Truth trees, like truth tables, can be used to evaluate wffs to decide whether or not they are logically consistent. A stack of wffs is logically consistent if and only if its completed tree does not close but rather remains open in at least one branch.

TRUTH TREE TEST FOR LOGICAL CONSISTENCY

P　　　　　　　(1) Stack wff(s)
~P　　　　　　(2) Complete truth tree
X

Closed tree indicates LOGICAL INCONSISTENCY

(Open tree would indicate NOT A LOGICAL INCONSISTENCY)

━ *Demonstration 14:*   **Truth Trees for Consistency** ━

PROBLEM: To test two (or more) wffs by truth trees to determine whether they are logically consistent or inconsistent.

PROPOSITIONS: P & Q; ~Q

STEP 1:   *Set up the truth tree*
Since closed truth trees always indicate an inconsistent stack of wffs, we can use trees to test for consistency by simply stacking the wffs to be tested and completing their tree. If the tree closes, then the wffs are logically inconsistent; if the tree does not close, if there is even one open branch, then the wffs are consistent. We stack the wffs as follows:

$$P \& Q$$
$$\sim Q$$

STEP 2:   *Complete the truth tree by applying the rules for truth tree decomposition to the wffs in the stack*
We have now had practice completing truth trees, so we shall not elaborate the method here. The completed truth tree looks as follows:

$$P \& Q \quad \sqrt{}\ 1$$
$$\sim Q$$
$$P$$
$$Q \qquad\qquad \text{LOGICALLY}$$
$$X \qquad\qquad \text{INCONSISTENT}$$

STEP 3:   *Check to see if the tree closes or does not close; classify the wffs being tested accordingly as logically inconsistent or consistent*
The truth tree in this case is so simple that it does not even branch. The tree closes because the stem contains the contradictory pair Q, ~Q. Accordingly, we classify the wffs being tested as logically inconsistent. If the truth tree had not closed, but even one branch remained open, then the wffs would be classified instead as logically consistent. This evaluation confirms the truth table test of the same wffs in Demonstration Problem 10.

Truth trees for consistency work because a closed tree indicates a logically inconsistent stack of wffs. If a tree does not close, its failure to close indicates on the contrary that the stack is logically consistent. Here are some examples in which the propositions to be tested are conjoined and their trees interpreted as indicating logical consistency or inconsistency:

$$\underline{\sim(P \supset (Q \& \sim Q)) \& (P \& ((Q \vee \sim P) \& Q)))}$$

$$\sim(P \supset (Q \& \sim Q)) \& (P \& ((Q \vee \sim P) \& Q))) \quad \checkmark \; 1$$
$$\sim(P \supset (Q \& \sim Q)) \quad \checkmark \; 2$$
$$P \& ((Q \vee \sim P) \& Q) \quad \checkmark \; 3$$
$$P$$
$$\sim(Q \& \sim Q) \quad \checkmark \; 6$$
$$P$$
$$(Q \vee \sim P) \& Q \quad \checkmark \; 4$$
$$Q \vee \sim P \quad \checkmark \; 5$$
$$Q$$

A closed truth tree is the graphic equivalent of a logical inconsistency by virtue of containing an inconsistent pair of wffs, a propositional symbol, and its negation on every branch; this is why a closed truth tree indicates a logically inconsistent wff or stack of wffs.

```
                Q
               / \
              Q   ~P
             / \   X
           ~Q   Q
            X
```

LOGICALLY CONSISTENT

$$\underline{P \supset (Q \supset P)) \& ((P \supset P) \supset \sim(Q \vee \sim Q))}$$

$$(P \supset (Q \supset P)) \& ((P \supset P) \supset \sim(Q \vee \sim Q)) \quad \checkmark \; 1$$
$$P \supset (Q \supset P) \quad \checkmark \; 2$$
$$(P \supset P) \supset \sim(Q \vee \sim Q) \quad \checkmark \; 3$$

```
                    ~P                          Q ⊃ P  √ 6

4, 5 √  ~(P ⊃ P)     ~(Q ∨ ~Q) √  ~Q              ~Q            P
           |              |      / \             / \          / \
           P             ~Q    P  ~Q           P  ~Q        P  ~Q
          ~P              Q   ~P   Q          ~P   Q       ~P   Q
           X              X    X   X           X   X        X   X
```

LOGICALLY INCONSISTENT

To Check Your Understanding 4.3 ─────────────────────────────── ■

Use truth trees to decide whether each of the following pairs of wffs is logically consistent or inconsistent; note that it is necessary at most to complete a single tree for each problem.

1. P; ~(P ⊃ P)
2. P ⊃ (Q ∨ R); (P ⊃ Q) ∨ (Q ⊃ R)
3. ~(P ⊃ (Q ∨ R)); ~(~P ∨ (~Q ⊃ R))
4. ~(P ≡ Q); (P ⊃ (Q ⊃ R)) ≡ ((P ⊃ Q) ⊃ (P ⊃ R))
5. (P ∨ Q) & ((P ⊃ R) & Q); ((P ∨ Q) & ((P ⊃ R) & (Q ⊃ S))) ⊃ ~(R ∨ S)
6. P & (P ⊃ ~P); ~((P ⊃ (Q ∨ R)) ⊃ ~((Q ∨ R) & ((Q ∨ P) ⊃ ~(Q ⊃ ~R))))

■

Truth Trees for Equivalence

Truth trees can be used to test for logical equivalence or nonequivalence.

We now follow the directions for evaluating two or more wffs for logical equivalence, treating the same examples as those previously considered by truth table methods. For this, we must connect the wffs in question into a negated biconditional and test to determine whether the biconditional is a tautology by completing and interpreting the truth tree for its negation.

TRUTH TREE TEST FOR LOGICAL EQUIVALENCE

A closed truth tree for the negation of a biconditional connecting two wffs indicates that the wffs are logically equivalent; an open tree indicates that the wffs are logically nonequivalent.

~(P ≡ ~~P)

P	~P
~P	P
X	X

(1) Stack NEGATION of BICONDITIONAL of wffs

(2) Complete truth tree

Closed tree indicates LOGICAL EQUIVALENCE

(Open tree would indicate LOGICAL NONEQUIVALENCE)

■ *Demonstration 15:* **Truth Trees for Equivalence** ■

PROBLEM: To test two (or more) wffs by truth trees to determine whether they are logically equivalent or nonequivalent.

PROPOSITIONS: $\sim(P \supset Q)$; $P \& \sim Q$

STEP 1:   *Set up the truth tree*
We want to determine whether the biconditional of the wffs to be tested is or is not a tautology. Since closed truth trees always indicate an inconsistent stack of wffs, we can use trees to test whether the biconditional of the wffs is a tautology by completing the tree for the negation of the biconditional of the wffs. If the tree closes, then the negation of the biconditional of the wffs is an inconsistency, and the biconditional is a tautology. This would mean that the wffs are logically equivalent. If the tree does not close, if there is even one open branch, then the negation of the biconditional of the wffs is not an inconsistency, and the biconditional is not a tautology. This would mean that the wffs are not logically equivalent. In this case, the tree would show that the propositions do not always have the same truth value. We construct the negated biconditional of the wffs to be tested for logical equivalence using parentheses to avoid logical ambiguity. This produces the wff, $\sim(P \supset Q) \equiv$ $(P \& \sim Q)$. We enclose the resulting biconditional in parentheses to avoid ambiguity when we attach negation outside the leftmost parenthesis to negate the entire biconditional. We are ready to begin the truth tree with the following setup:

$$\sim(\sim(P \supset Q) \equiv (P \& \sim Q)) \qquad \text{[Negated biconditional of wffs]}$$

STEP 2:   *Complete the truth tree by applying the rules for truth tree decomposition to the wffs in the stack*
We have now had practice completing truth trees, so we shall not elaborate on the method here. The completed truth tree is as follows:

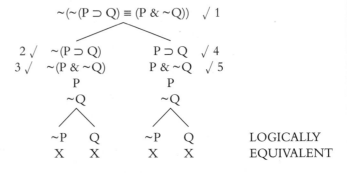

STEP 3:   *Check to determine if the tree closes or does not close; classify the bicon-ditional being tested as a tautology or not a tautology; classify the wffs connected by the biconditional accordingly as logically equivalent or non-equivalent*

The tree closes, indicating that the negation of the biconditional is an in-consistency, and hence that the biconditional is a tautology. This means that the wffs connected by the biconditional are logically equivalent. If the truth tree had not closed, but even one branch remained open, then the negation of the biconditional would not be classified as an inconsistency, the bicondi-tional would not be classified as a tautology, and the wffs connected by the biconditional would be classified instead as logically nonequivalent. This evaluation confirms the truth table test of the same wffs in Demonstration Problem 11.

We now use truth trees to determine whether or not the following two conditional wffs (contrapositives of one another) are logically equivalent: $P \supset Q$ and $\sim Q \supset \sim P$. We set up the negated biconditional of the wffs to be tested and then complete its truth tree:

$$\sim((P \supset Q) \equiv (\sim Q \supset \sim P)) \quad \surd \; 1$$

$$
\begin{array}{ccc}
3 \; \surd \quad P \supset Q & & \sim(P \supset Q) \quad \surd \; 4 \\
2 \; \surd \quad \sim(\sim Q \supset \sim P) & & \sim Q \supset \sim P \quad \surd \; 5 \\
\sim Q & & P \\
P & & \sim Q \\
\end{array}
$$

$$
\begin{array}{cccc}
\sim P & Q & Q & \sim P \\
X & X & X & X \\
\end{array}
$$

LOGICALLY EQUIVALENT

Truth trees for logical equivalence work because they test a biconditional to determine whether it is a tautology. Truth trees determine that a bicondi-tional is a tautology when the truth tree for the negation of the biconditional closes. Study the following decompositions step by step, applying truth tree de-composition rules for the main connective in the proposition and then to each of its propositionally complex decomposition by-products below it in the tree. Do you see why each branch closes? Identify the pair of inconsistent proposi-tional symbols on each branch by virtue of which the entire tree finally closes. The closed tree shows that the equivalence known as contraposition is logically correct. Compare the truth tree method of deciding the equivalence with the truth table method we used earlier.

It is worthwhile to compare truth tree evaluations with truth table evaluations of the same wffs and sequents; the results should always coincide.

$\sim((P \supset Q) \equiv (\sim P \vee Q))$ $\checkmark$ 1

```
                3 √   P ⊃ Q              ~(P ⊃ Q)   √ 4
                2 √  ~(~P ∨ Q)            ~P ∨ Q    √ 5
                       P                     P
                      ~Q                    ~Q
                    ∕    ╲                ∕    ╲
                  ~P      Q             ~P      Q
                   X      X              X      X
```

LOGICALLY EQUIVALENT

Logically equivalent wffs have identical truth conditions and identical truth functional interpretations in propositional logic.

The propositions $P \supset Q$ and $\sim P \vee Q$ are equivalent. The graphic representation of the equivalence is nothing other than the decomposition rule for the conditional. The biconditional $P \equiv Q$ (P if and only if Q) is logically equivalent to the conjunction of conditionals $P \supset Q$ (P if Q) and $Q \supset P$ (P only if Q).

$\sim((P \equiv Q) \equiv ((P \supset Q) \& (Q \supset P))$ $\checkmark$ 1

```
            2 √   (P ≡ Q)                        ~(P ≡ Q)   √ 9
            3 √  ~((P ⊃ Q) & (Q ⊃ P))        (P ⊃ Q) & (Q ⊃ P)  √ 8
               ∕         ╲                            │
              P           ~P                        P ⊃ Q   √ 10
              Q           ~Q                        Q ⊃ P   √ 11
           ∕    ╲       ∕    ╲                       ∕   ╲
  √√√√  ~(P⊃Q) ~(Q⊃P) ~(P⊃Q) ~(Q⊃P)   P        ~P
 4,5,6,7   P     Q      P      Q     ~Q         Q
          ~Q    ~P     ~Q     ~P    ∕  ╲      ∕  ╲
           X     X      X      X  ~P    Q   ~P    Q
                                  X     X ∕  ╲  ∕  ╲
                                        ~Q  P ~Q  P
                                         X  X  X  X
```

LOGICALLY EQUIVALENT

Truth trees for bicon-ditionals and negative biconditionals branch and stack; wffs are stacked at the ends of each branch.

As a final test of the truth tree method for deciding logical equivalence, consider the following truth tree evaluation:

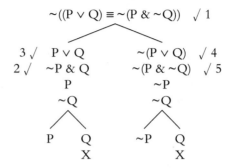

LOGICALLY NONEQUIVALENT

To Check Your Understanding 4.4

Use truth trees to decide whether or not the following biconditionals are tautologies in order to determine whether or not the wffs connected by the biconditional main connectives are logically equivalent; note that for this purpose you will need to do truth tree evaluations of the negations of these biconditionals.

1. $(P \supset Q) \equiv (\sim P \vee Q)$
2. $(P \supset Q) \equiv \sim (P \,\&\, \sim Q)$
3. $(P \equiv Q) \equiv ((P \supset Q) \,\&\, (Q \supset P))$
4. $(P \vee Q) \equiv ((P \supset Q) \supset \sim (Q \supset P))$
5. $(P \vee (Q \,\&\, \sim R)) \equiv \sim ((P \supset Q) \vee \sim (Q \supset \sim P))$
6. $(((P \vee Q) \,\&\, ((P \supset R) \,\&\, (Q \supset S))) \supset \sim (R \vee S)) \equiv ((P \supset Q) \vee (Q \supset R))$

Truth Trees for Sequents

Truth trees can be used to evaluate sequents for deductive validity or invalidity.

To test a sequent for validity or invalidity by truth trees, we stack the sequent's assumptions together with the negation of its conclusion or negation of the conjunction of its multiple conclusions and complete a single tree for the stack. If the tree closes, then the sequent is valid; if the tree does not close, but has even a single open branch, then the sequent is invalid.

A closed tree indicates that the truth of the assumptions is logically in-consistent with the falsehood of the conclusions, or that it is logically impos-sible for the argument's assumptions to be true and its conclusions false. By this criterion, truth trees tell us whether or not an argument satisfies the definition of a valid argument as one in which it is impossible for the assumptions to be true and the conclusions false.

When we set up a truth tree to test an argument with multiple conclusions, we stack the assumptions of the argument together with the negation of the conjunction of the conclusions (or, equivalently, we can also stack the assumptions with the disjunction of the negations of the conclusions). To test a sequent with multiple conclusions of the form $\mathbb{P}_1, \ldots, \mathbb{P}_m \vdash \mathbb{Q}_1, \ldots, \mathbb{Q}_n$ by truth trees, we begin with the following stack:

Truth tree evaluation of a sequent requires stacking the assumptions of the sequent with the negation of its conclusion or the negation of the conjunction of its conclusions.

TRUTH TREE SEQUENT EVALUATION STACK

$$\mathbb{P}_1$$
.
.
.
$$\mathbb{P}_m$$
$$\sim(\mathbb{Q}_1 \,\&\, \ldots \,\&\, \mathbb{Q}_n)$$

(for sequent $\mathbb{P}_1, \ldots, \mathbb{P}_m \vdash \mathbb{Q}_1, \ldots, \mathbb{Q}_n$
assumptions stacked with negation of conclusion
or conjunction of multiple conclusions)

Then the truth tree decomposition and interpretation proceeds normally. If the tree closes, the sequent with its single negated conclusion or negation of conjoined multiple conclusions is deductively valid. If the tree does not close, if even one branch remains open, then the sequent is deductively invalid.

TRUTH TREE TEST FOR DEDUCTIVE VALIDITY OF SEQUENTS

$$P \supset Q \;\checkmark$$
$$P$$
$$\sim Q$$

~P   Q
X   X

(1) Stack assumptions with NEGATION of conclusion
(2) Complete truth tree

Closed tree indicates sequent DEDUCTIVELY VALID

(Open tree would indicate sequent DEDUCTIVELY INVALID)

A sequent is deductively valid if its truth tree closes; it is deductively invalid if its truth tree does not close—always setting up the tree by stacking the sequent's assumptions with the negation of its conclusion or negation of the conjunction of its multiple conclusions.

In testing sequents with multiple conclusions, it will not do to set up the truth tree by stacking the assumptions together with the negation of each conclusion as a separate item. For such a tree to close would indicate not that the sequent with all its multiple conclusions is deductively valid but only that at least one of the conclusions is validly deducible from the assumptions, even if some of the other conclusions are not. When a truth tree set up as described previously closes, it indicates that each of the several conclusions in the sequent follows validly, and that the argument as a whole is deductively valid.

■ *Demonstration 16:*   **Truth Trees for Sequents**   ■

PROBLEM: To test an argument sequent by truth trees to determine whether it is deductively valid or invalid.

SEQUENT: $P \supset Q, P \vdash Q$

STEP 1:   *Set up the truth tree*
To test a sequent by truth trees, we stack the assumptions of the sequent together with the negation of its conclusion or the negation of the conjunction of its multiple conclusions. Since closed truth trees indicate an inconsistent stack of wffs, we can use trees to test whether a stack of wffs consisting of the assumptions and negation of the conclusions of a sequent is inconsistent. If the tree closes, then the stack is inconsistent, indicating that it is inconsistent for the assumptions of the sequent to be true and its conclusions false. Logical inconsistencies are logically impossible, so a closed tree in this case indicates that it is logically impossible for the assumptions of the sequent to be true and its conclusions false, thereby satisfying the definition of a deductively valid argument. A closed tree for a stack of wffs consisting of the assumptions of a sequent and the negation of its conclusion means that the sequent is deductively valid. If the tree does not close, if there is even one open branch, then it is not logically inconsistent for the assumptions of the sequent to be true and its conclusions false, and hence it is not logically impossible for the assumptions of the sequent to be true and its conclusions false. An unclosed tree for a stack of wffs consisting of the assumptions of a sequent and the negation of its conclusion means that the sequent is deductively invalid. We set up a truth tree to test the previously discussed sequent for deductive validity by stacking its two assumptions together with the negation of what in this case is its only conclusion:

$$
\begin{array}{ll}
P \supset Q & \text{[Assumption]} \\
P & \text{[Assumption]} \\
\sim Q & \text{[Negation of conclusion]}
\end{array}
$$

STEP 2: *Complete the truth tree by applying the rules for truth tree decomposition to the wffs in the stack*

We have now had practice completing truth trees, so we shall not elaborate on the method here. The completed truth tree looks as follows:

$$P \supset Q \quad \surd \, 1$$
$$P$$
$$\sim Q$$

$$\sim P \qquad Q$$
$$X \qquad X \qquad\qquad\qquad \text{VALID}$$

STEP 3: *Check to determine if the tree closes or does not close; classify the sequent being tested as deductively valid or invalid*

The tree closes, indicating that the stack of wffs is inconsistent. This means that it is logically inconsistent and hence logically impossible for the assumptions of the sequent to be true and the conclusion of the sequent false. The definition of deductive validity is satisfied in this case, and the tree indicates that the sequent is deductively valid. If the truth tree had not closed, but even one branch had remained open, then the sequent would be classified instead as deductively invalid. This evaluation confirms the truth table test of the same sequent in Demonstration Problem 12.

Sequents require completing only one truth tree to evaluate their deductive validity or invalidity.

Here is the truth tree evaluation of two valid arguments and one invalid argument we previously analyzed by truth table methods. Recall that to test arguments for validity or invalidity by the truth tree method, we must complete just one tree that begins with a stacking of the argument's assumptions together with the negation of its conclusion. We arrive at the following trees for these earlier problems:

$$S \supset C, A \supset \sim C \vdash S \supset \sim A$$
$$S \supset C \quad \surd \, 2$$
$$A \supset \sim C \quad \surd \, 3$$
$$\sim(S \supset \sim A) \quad \surd \, 1$$
$$S$$
$$A$$

$$\sim S \qquad C$$
$$X$$

$$\sim A \qquad \sim C$$
$$X \qquad X$$

VALID

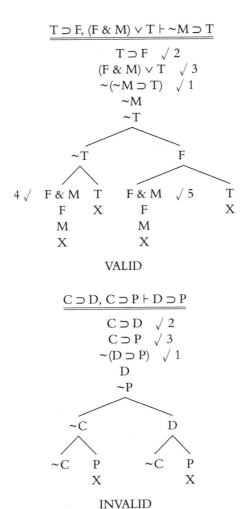

$$T \supset F, (F \& M) \vee T \vdash \sim M \supset T$$

$$T \supset F \quad \checkmark 2$$
$$(F \& M) \vee T \quad \checkmark 3$$
$$\sim(\sim M \supset T) \quad \checkmark 1$$
$$\sim M$$
$$\sim T$$

	~T		F	
4 √	F & M T	F & M √ 5		T
	F X	F		X
	M	M		
	X	X		

VALID

$$C \supset D, C \supset P \vdash D \supset P$$

$$C \supset D \quad \checkmark 2$$
$$C \supset P \quad \checkmark 3$$
$$\sim(D \supset P) \quad \checkmark 1$$
$$D$$
$$\sim P$$

	~C		D
~C	P	~C	P
	X		X

INVALID

We have already considered examples of truth tree evaluations of the validity or invalidity of arguments. Now we turn to three more complex arguments, the first of which we previously tested by turbo truth tables, and the results of which we now verify by truth trees.

$$G \supset U, E \supset I, {\sim}G \supset E \vdash U \vee I$$

$$
\begin{array}{cc}
G \supset U & \surd\,2 \\
E \supset I & \surd\,3 \\
{\sim}G \supset E & \surd\,4 \\
{\sim}(U \vee I) & \surd\,1 \\
{\sim}U & \\
{\sim}I & \\
\end{array}
$$

```
            ~G      U
           /  \     X
         ~E    I
          |    X
         / \
        G   E
        X   X
```

VALID

$$({\sim}R \,\&\, F) \supset (P \,\&\, {\sim}D), ((F \,\&\, R) \supset S) \,\&\, (S \supset P), {\sim}R \supset F \vdash P$$

$$
\begin{array}{cc}
({\sim}R \,\&\, F) \supset (P \,\&\, {\sim}D) & \surd\,5 \\
((F \,\&\, R) \supset S) \,\&\, (S \supset P) & \surd\,1 \\
{\sim}R \supset F & \surd\,4 \\
{\sim}P & \\
(F \,\&\, R) \supset S & \surd\,3 \\
S \supset P & \surd\,2 \\
\end{array}
$$

```
                    ~S        P
                   /  \       X
        6 √   ~(F & R)  S
              /    \    X
            ~F      ~R
           /  \     / \
          R    F   R   F
         / \   X X     / \
  7 √ ~(~R & F) P & ~D √ 8 R   ~F
      / \        |       X    X
     R   F       P
     X           ~D
                 X
```

INVALID

G ⊃ ((S & P) & B), E, E ⊃ (~K ∨ ((K & ~A) ∨ ((K & A) & ~C))), ~K ⊃ ~S,

~A ⊃ ~P, ~C ⊃ ~B ⊢ ~G

G ⊃ ((S & P) & B)   √ 1
E
E ⊃ (~K ∨ ((K & ~A) ∨ ((K & A) & ~C)))   √ 7
~K ⊃ ~S   √ 4
~A ⊃ ~P   √ 5
~C ⊃ ~B   √ 6
G

~G   (S & P) & B   √ 2
X   S & P   √ 3
B
S
P

K   ~S
X

A   ~P
X

C   ~B
X

~E   ~K ∨ ((K & ~A) ∨ ((K & A) & ~C))   √ 8
X

~K   (K & ~A) ∨ ((K & ~A) & ~C)   √ 9
X

10 √ K & ~A   (K & ~A) & ~C   √ 11
K   K & ~A   √ 12
~A   ~C
X   K
~A
X

VALID

By incorporating eight propositional symbols, the last argument is beyond practical check by truth table methods. Truth trees give us the correct result that the argument is deductively valid in a matter of minutes, with little opportunity for bookkeeping errors. The example may therefore serve as an advertisement for the greater practical utility of truth trees compared with truth tables, especially for complex problems involving more than three or four propositional symbols.

Armed with the truth tree decision method, we need fear no wff or sequent. We set up the truth tree stack in the correct way for the particular logical property we wish to check in a proposition or argument and complete the tree by applying the appropriate decomposition rules successively to the main connective in the wffs and to their truth tree decomposition by-products at each stage of decomposition until all are fully decomposed, marking decomposed wffs and closed branches, if any, as we proceed. Finally, we interpret the fully decomposed tree according to the truth tree definitions of logical properties.

Here are examples of truth trees to test the deductive validity of two elementary sequents with multiple conclusions:

Truth trees can be used to evaluate wffs and sequents containing many more propositional symbols than would be practical using truth table methods.

$$P, P \supset Q \vdash Q, Q \vee (P \equiv (S \supset T))$$

P

P ⊃ Q   √ 6

~(Q & (Q ∨ (P ≡ (S ⊃ T))))   √ 1

~Q   ~(Q ∨ (P ≡ (S ⊃ T)))   √ 2
                            ~Q

~P   Q   ~(P ≡ (S ⊃ T))   √ 3
X   X

P   ~P

4 √   ~(S ⊃ T)   S ⊃ T   √ 5
          S   X
         ~T

~P   Q
X   X

VALID

$$P, P \supset Q \vdash Q, R$$

$$
\begin{array}{c}
P \\
P \supset Q \quad \surd 1 \\
\sim(Q \ \& \ R)
\end{array}
$$

```
        /\
      ~P   Q
      X   /\
        ~Q  ~R
        X
```

INVALID

To Check Your Understanding 4.5

Use truth trees to determine whether the following argument sequents are deductively valid or invalid; note that it is necessary at most to complete a single tree for each problem:

1. $P \vdash Q \vee \sim Q$
2. $Q \ \& \sim Q \vdash \sim P$
3. $(Q \vee R) \supset P, \sim P \ \& \ R \vdash Q$
4. $\sim(P \vee \sim Q) \vdash P \supset (\sim Q \ \& \ R)$
5. $\sim P \ \& \ Q, P \vee R, Q \equiv \sim R \vdash P$
6. $P \equiv (Q \vee R), P \equiv \sim Q \vdash \sim(P \equiv R)$
7. $\sim P \vee (\sim P \ \& \ Q), (\sim P \supset Q) \supset \sim P \vdash \sim P$
8. $(P \vee Q) \ \& \ ((P \supset R) \ \& \ (Q \supset S)) \vdash \sim(R \vee S)$
9. $(\sim P \ \& \ Q) \ \& \sim R, (S \vee Q) \supset (\sim R \equiv Q) \vdash T \vee S$
10. $P \ \& \ Q, P \supset (R \supset S), (R \equiv P) \supset \sim P \vdash (S \ \& \ P) \supset Q$
11. $(\sim P \ \& \ Q) \ \& \sim R, (S \vee T) \supset \sim(\sim R \equiv Q) \vdash \sim(T \vee S)$
12. $T \supset \sim S, \sim(P \supset R), (P \ \& \ Q) \supset (R \supset \sim S), \sim(Q \supset \sim T) \vdash \sim P$

Summary: Truth Trees

Truth trees offer a graphic representation of stacking and branching logical structures of wffs that can be used to test wffs and sequents for the same kinds of logical properties as can be tested by truth tables. Truth trees are easier and faster to use than truth tables, especially for problems involving large numbers of propositional symbols. Truth trees apply decomposition rules for the propositional connectives and their negations in order to determine when a stack of wffs is or is not logically inconsistent. The logical consistency or inconsistency of a stack of wffs is interpreted in specific ways as indicating that a wff is a tautology, inconsistency, or contingency; that two wffs are logically consistent or inconsistent; or logically equivalent or nonequivalent; and that a sequent is deductively valid or invalid.

Key Words

truth tree
truth tree decomposition rules
stack (of wffs)
fully decomposed
stacking and branching
   (truth tree configurations)

closure (of truth tree branch
   and of truth tree)
closed (unclosed) branch
closed (unclosed) tree

Exercises

I: Truth Tree Concepts   Give a correct concise statement of each of the following concepts; where appropriate, give an illustration of each that does not appear in the book:

1. Truth tree
2. Stacking; branching
3. Open branch (of a truth tree)
4. Closed branch (of a truth tree)
5. Open tree
6. Closed tree
7. Tautology, inconsistency, contingency (as indicated by truth tree analysis)
8. Logical consistency (as indicated by truth tree analysis)
9. Logical equivalence (as indicated by truth tree analysis)
10. Deductive validity (as indicated by truth tree analysis)

II: Truth Tree Evaluation of Wffs   Use truth trees to evaluate the following wffs for classification as tautologies, inconsistencies, or contingencies of propositional logic. Compare your answers with the truth table evaluations of these same wffs analyzed by truth tables in the exercises from the previous chapter.

1. R & ((P ⊃ Q) ∨ (~Q ⊃ ~R))
2. ~(((P ⊃ P) ⊃ ~P) ⊃ P) & ~P

3. (P ⊃ (Q & (~R ∨ ~P))) ⊃ ~(~Q ∨ (P ⊃ ~R))

4. ((P & Q) ⊃ (Q ⊃ R)) ∨ (~(Q ⊃ R) ⊃ (~Q ∨ ~P))

5. ((P ∨ Q) & ((P ⊃ R) & (Q ⊃ S))) ⊃ ~(R ∨ ~S)

6. ~(((P ⊃ ~Q) & ~(~(P ∨ R) & (Q ⊃ S))) ⊃ (R ⊃ S))

7. (P ⊃ (~(Q & R) ⊃ R)) ⊃ ((R ∨ (P & ~Q)) & (P ⊃ ~(Q & R)))

8. (Q ⊃ S) ≡ (((P ⊃ Q) ≡ (P ∨ S)) & ((Q ⊃ P) ≡ (S ⊃ P)))

9. ~(Q & S) ≡ (((P ⊃ Q) ≡ ~(P ∨ S)) ⊃ ~((Q ⊃ P) ≡ (S ⊃ ~P)))

10. (((R ∨ (P & ~Q)) & (P ⊃ ~(Q & R))) ⊃ R) ∨ (((~P ∨ Q) ⊃ (P & Q)) ≡ P)

III: Truth Tree Evaluation of Sequents   Use truth trees to evaluate the following sequents as deductively valid or invalid. Compare your answers with the truth table evaluations of these same sequents analyzed by truth tables in the exercises from the previous chapter:

1. ~(~A & B), ~(~B ∨ C) ⊢ A

2. S ⊢ (~P ∨ Q) ∨ (Q ⊃ R)

3. P ∨ Q, (P ⊃ R) & (Q ⊃ S) ⊢ R ∨ S

4. ~R, (P ∨ Q) ⊃ (R & ~P), R ∨ Q ⊢ ~P ∨ (R ≡ Q)

5. C ⊃ ((D ⊃ E) ⊃ (D & C)), (C ∨ E) ⊃ D ⊢ C ⊃ (E ⊃ D)

6. G & (A ⊃ B), (B ⊃ G) ⊃ A ⊢ B ≡ ~G

7. U ⊃ ~Q, ~(S ⊃ ~U), (Q & S) ⊃ (S ⊃ ~Q), ~(U ⊃ S) ⊢ ~U

8. ~M ⊃ J, (L & ~M) ⊃ (L ⊃ J), J ⊃ M, ~(L ⊃ ~M) ⊢ ~L

9. P ⊃ (~Q ⊃ R), P & (~Q & ~R), ~Q ⊃ (R ≡ (P ∨ S)) ⊢ Q

10. (P ⊃ Q) & (Q ⊃ P), (R & Q) ∨ (P ∨ ~Q), ~R ⊃ (P & R), (Q ⊃ ~Q) & (~P ⊃ ~Q), R ⊃ (Q ⊃ ~R), (~R ∨ P) & (R ∨ Q) ⊢ ~(R & ~P)

IV: Truth Tree Evaluation of Complex Wffs   Use truth trees to evaluate the following wffs for classification as tautologies, inconsistencies, or contingencies of propositional logic. Then use truth trees to determine whether each of two successive wffs in the list (1 and 2, 2 and 3, 3 and 4, etc.) are logically consistent or inconsistent and whether they are logically equivalent or nonequivalent:

1. ((R ∨ (P & ~Q)) & (P ⊃ ~(Q & R))) ⊃ R

2. ((P ∨ Q) & ((P ⊃ R) & (Q ⊃ S))) ⊃ ~(R ∨ ~S)

3. ~(((P ⊃ ~Q) & ~(~(P ∨ R) & (Q ⊃ S))) ⊃ (R ⊃ S))

4. (Q ⊃ S) ≡ (((P ⊃ Q) ≡ (P ∨ S)) & ((Q ⊃ P) ≡ (S ⊃ P)))

5. ~(Q & S) ≡ (((P ⊃ Q) ≡ ~(P ∨ S)) ⊃ ~((Q ⊃ P) ≡ (S ⊃ ~P)))

6. $(((R \vee (P \& \sim Q)) \& (P \supset \sim (Q \& R))) \supset R) \vee (((\sim P \vee Q) \supset (P \& Q)) \equiv P)$
7. $(((P \supset Q) \supset P) \supset P) \& ((((P \supset Q) \supset P) \supset P) \vee \sim ((Q \supset P) \equiv (Q \supset \sim P)))$
8. $((P \vee (Q \& \sim R)) \& (R \supset \sim Q)) \supset (\sim (P \& \sim Q) \supset ((P \& Q) \& \sim R))$
9. $((((P \& Q) \supset R) \& (P \supset Q)) \& ((S \& R) \supset T)) \supset (P \supset (S \supset T))$
10. $((((P \& Q) \supset R) \& (P \supset Q)) \equiv ((S \& \sim R) \supset T)) \supset (P \supset \sim (S \supset \sim T))$

V: Truth Tree Evaluation of Complex Sequents   Use truth trees to evaluate the following sequents as deductively valid or invalid:

1. $\sim (\sim A \& B), \sim (\sim B \vee C) \vdash A$
2. $S \vdash (\sim P \vee Q) \vee (Q \supset R)$
3. $P \vee Q, (P \supset R) \& (Q \supset S) \vdash R \vee S$
4. $\sim R, (P \vee Q) \supset (R \& \sim P), R \vee Q \vdash \sim P \vee (R \equiv Q)$
5. $C \supset ((D \supset E) \supset (F \& G)), (N \vee T) \supset S \vdash C \supset (E \supset S)$
6. $G \& (A \supset B), (B \supset G) \supset A \vdash B \equiv \sim G$
7. $U \supset \sim Q, \sim (S \supset \sim U), (T \& S) \supset (R \supset \sim Q), \sim (T \supset R) \vdash \sim T$
8. $\sim M \supset J, (L \& \sim M) \supset (H \supset K), J \supset K, \sim (L \supset \sim H) \vdash \sim L$
9. $P \supset (\sim Q \supset R), P \& (\sim S \& \sim T), \sim Q \supset (R \equiv (T \vee S)) \vdash Q$
10. $(\sim A \& C) \& \sim D, (E \vee F) \supset \sim (\sim D \equiv C) \vdash \sim (F \vee E) \& D$
11. $N \supset ((B \& \sim P) \vee R), B \& \sim R, \sim T \supset P \vdash \sim T \supset \sim N$
12. $\sim R \vdash \sim (\sim (P \supset Q) \& \sim (Q \supset \sim R))$
13. $(\sim F \equiv G) \supset \sim H, (F \& I) \vee (\sim G \& J), (I \vee J) \supset H \vdash \sim G \supset \sim F$
14. $P \vee Q, P \supset (T \supset R), (T \equiv S) \supset \sim P \vdash (\sim R \& S) \supset Q$
15. $P \equiv \sim Q, Q \equiv \sim R \vdash P \equiv R$
16. $B \supset C \vdash ((A \supset C) \supset ((B \vee A) \supset C)) \equiv (((B \supset A) \& \sim A) \supset \sim B)$
17. $(\sim P \supset (Q \supset \sim P)) \supset \sim ((Q \supset R) \supset ((P \supset Q) \supset (P \supset R))) \vdash P \vee R$
18. $Q \vdash \sim ((Q \equiv \sim S) \supset (((P \supset Q) \equiv (P \supset \sim S)) \& ((Q \supset P) \equiv \sim (S \supset P))))$
19. $\sim M \supset (N \& (\sim O \vee P)), (Q \& \sim R) \supset \sim M, (Q \& S) \& R \vdash N \& (\sim O \vee P)$
20. $(P \supset Q) \& (Q \supset P), (R \& Q) \vee (P \vee \sim Q), \sim R \supset (S \& T), (U \supset \sim Q) \&$
    $(\sim U \supset \sim V), T \supset (V \supset \sim T), (\sim R \vee P) \& (U \vee W) \vdash \sim (R \& \sim W)$

VI: Short Answer Questions for Philosophical Reflection

1. What is the significance of the fact that there can be multiple correct decision methods in symbolic logic?

2. How should we characterize the correspondences between truth tables and truth trees?

3. Why are truth trees so much more practical to use than truth tables? What do truth trees do, and how exactly do they work in contrast with truth tables?

4. What is the relationship between a tautology and an inconsistency as revealed by truth tree analysis? If a proposition is a contingency, why, according to truth tree method, is its negation also a contingency?

5. Why does truth tree closure prove that a set or stack of propositions is logically inconsistent? How does the fact that a set or stack of propositions that decomposes as a closed truth tree demonstrate that the propositions in the set or stack logically cannot be jointly true?

6. What does the fact that truth tree determinations of logical inconsistency in a stack of wffs make it possible to mechanically decide all the other interesting logical properties of wffs and sequents that can be judged by truth tables reveal about the concepts of logical consistency and logical inconsistency? Why are these properties of wffs so important?

CHAPTER FIVE

Propositional Natural Deduction Proofs

Logic is the art of making truth prevail.

—La Bruyère, *Characters* (1694)

A NATURAL DEDUCTION PROOF can be given for any tautology and any valid sequent in symbolic propositional logic. We explain inference rules and discuss strategies for solving many kinds of natural deduction proofs.

Natural Deduction

We have learned how to use truth tables and truth trees as decision methods for propositional logic. These techniques provide important information about the logical properties of propositions and arguments. But they are not the most useful way of symbolizing the reasoning by which a tautology or deductively valid argument is justified. For this purpose, we now introduce a system of *natural deduction proofs*.

The natural deduction proof of a tautology or valid sequent is a structure of propositions that proceeds according to specified truth-preserving rules. Proofs are deductively valid arguments in which all steps are justified by assumption or deductively valid inferences. To get a better understanding of natural deduction proofs, we now introduce rules for natural deduction proofs in symbolic propositional logic. A simple example of a natural deduction proof looks as follows:

Natural deduction proofs symbolize the reasoning that justifies the deductive validity of a sequent and the logical truth of a tautology.

1	1.	P	A
2	2.	Q	A
1, 2	3.	P & Q	1, 2 &I

We can think of a natural deduction proof as a series of propositions evolving from a starting place consisting of assumptions, through a series of derived propositions obtained by applying deductively valid inference rules to assumptions, and ending in a final conclusion. A proof is built up step by step, beginning with assumptions (marked 'A' in the previous example), and adding one line of proof at a time as we work toward the derivation of the final conclusion. We justify each step of the proof, either as an assumption or as a validly deduced inference from an assumption or assumptions, by the logic's inference rules. We document the particular assumptions on which each proof step depends, and indicate exactly how every inference is related to the assumptions from which it is derived.

Any proposition can be freely assumed; natural deduction proofs accordingly have a foundational assumption rule.

Natural deduction proofs model two aspects of ordinary reasoning. First, natural deduction proofs have a *foundational assumption rule* that permits not only true propositions but also any assumption to enter into a proof. This is an important feature of everyday reasoning. The assumption rule formalizes our ability to draw valid inferences from any assumptions we like, true or false. Second, natural deduction proofs include stylized versions of many of the kinds of deductively valid rules we use in everyday thinking. In natural deduction, we represent some of the most important inference rules by which we deduce conclusions from freely entertained assumptions.

Anatomy of a Natural Deduction Proof

Natural deduction proofs have five components.

We first describe the general features of a natural deduction proof. Proofs in this system consist of five parts. The components are, moving from left to right in the sample diagrammed below, (a) an (optional) *assumption column,* (b) the *proof line number column,* (c) a series of one or more *graphic proof spines,* (d) the *proposition* or *proof step column* (which might be an assumption or conclusion validly derived by natural deduction rules from the assumptions), followed, finally, by (e) the *justification column.*

NATURAL DEDUCTION PROOF STRUCTURE

Given assumption	1	1.	P	A
Given assumption	2	2.	Q	A
Conclusion	1, 2	3.	P & Q	1, 2 &I
a		b c	d	e

(optional)

The proof demonstrates that, from the assumption that proposition P is true and the assumption that proposition Q is true, it follows that proposition P & Q is true. We now describe each of these proof components in detail, beginning with the less difficult concepts of b and d and then explaining the more complex ideas behind a, c, and e.

The proof line number column (b) indicates the sequential ordering of steps in the proof, from beginning to end, numbering each step in turn from top to bottom as 1, 2, 3, etc. for as many steps as the proof contains. The line numbers provide convenient reference points for serially listing and documenting each step of a natural deduction proof.

Natural deduction proofs consist of an (optional) assumption column, proof line number column, series of graphic proof spines, proposition or proof step column (the body of the proof), and a justification column.

The proposition or proof step column (d) contains either assumptions or the intermediate or final conclusions derived from these by means of natural deduction rules. Natural deductive proofs begin with assumptions from which inferred steps and the proof's final conclusions are validly derived by correctly applying specific rules to propositions occurring in previous proof steps. All assumptions and the conclusions derived from them appear in the proposition proof step column (d), which can be thought of as the main body of the proof. The information in other proof columns serves only as a framework and documentation for the use of inference rules by which each step of the proof is justified.

The assumption column (a) lists the assumptions on which each proof step rests. This is the method by which we keep track of the assumptions responsible for each step in the proof. We refer to the assumptions on which a step of the proof depends by citing the line numbers of assumptions used in every inference. There are two kinds of assumptions: *given assumptions* and *auxiliary assumptions*. A given assumption is one that is provided as part of the sequent to be proved. The sequent P,Q ⊢ P & Q, for example, contains two given assumptions, P and Q. In the case of tautologies, no assumptions are given because tautologies, as logical truths, do not depend on the truth of any other propositions but are true in and of themselves by virtue of their logical structures. This is seen in the way we designate a typical tautology, ⊢ P ⊃ P, in which no propositions occur to the left of the turnstile inference indicator, ⊢. An auxiliary assumption is not given but freely assumed by the foundational assumption rule A, which allows us to make any assumption we like. An auxiliary assumption initiates a proof within a proof, also known as a *subproof,* in which conclusions are drawn from additional assumptions that are not part of the sequent or tautology to be proved. Assumptions, given or auxiliary, are identically annotated in the (optional) assumption column of a natural deduction proof. Assumptions of both kinds rest only on themselves and are justified merely by virtue of the fact that they are given or freely assumed. This is shown by repeating the line number of the proof where they are introduced in the corresponding assumption column. In the example, proposition P rests on assumption 1 (on P itself), and proposition Q rests on assumption 2 (Q itself). Therefore, in step 3, when we derive P & Q by applying &I to steps 1 and 2, we annotate the assumption column by indicating that P & Q rests on the assump-

A proof can contain given assumptions and auxiliary assumptions.

tions on which steps 1 and 2 rest, written simply to indicate both assumptions as 1, 2. Other rules require us to introduce and eliminate assumption numbers in more complicated ways, as shown later.

The proof spine (c), together with the assumption column, keeps track of the assumptions on which each step of a proof depends. The spines are vertical lines drawn from top to bottom of the proof between the proof line number column and the proposition proof step column. A short horizontal line, as shown in the previous example, is a graphic inference indicator that distinguishes the assumptions from the conclusions derived from the assumptions. Proof spines tell us at a glance which steps of the proofs are assumptions and which are derived and how logical structures and derivation strategies are related within the proof. We can have proofs within proofs, as we introduce new auxiliary assumptions to begin new subproofs. The inclusion of a proof within another proof is indicated by writing a subordinate proof spine to the right of another superordinate proof spine. A proof spine for a subproof is also known as a subproof spine, and the subproof and the subproof spine are said to be nested within another proof or subproof or proof or subproof spine. The nesting of proof and subproof spines can take many forms. Here are some possibilities, without the body of the proof or any of the documentation for justification, proof step numbers, or assumption columns. We can have proof and subproof spine combinations that look as follows:

Proof spines show graphically the relation between assumptions and conclusions derived from assumptions.

Proof spines can be nested within other proof spines when a proof includes subproofs involving auxiliary assumptions.

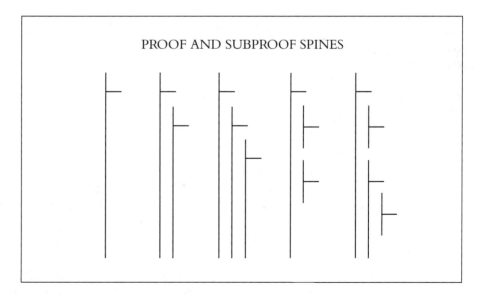

PROOF AND SUBPROOF SPINES

The number of nested subproof spines in a proof demonstrates how deeply we are committed at least temporarily to the truth of auxiliary assumptions. The subproof rules permit us eventually to exit a subproof by applying the appropriate subproof rule. This is indicated in a proof by writing a conclusion to the left below and after the termination of a subproof spine.

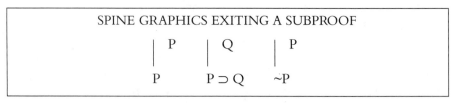

SPINE GRAPHICS EXITING A SUBPROOF

The combined system of assumption column and graphic proof and subproof spine in this system of natural deduction takes advantage of the visually informative display of a proof's logical structure, whereas the assumption numbers listed in the assumption column are more accurate than spines alone in specifying the exact assumptions on which each particular proof step depends. A proof spine by itself shows only that the conclusions attached to the spine rest on some or all of the proof's assumptions. The assumption numbers column indicates more precisely, though not in as graphically informative a way as proof spines, the particular assumptions used to derive each step. The assumption column is included in all proofs illustrated throughout this book, but it is an optional feature of natural deduction proofs, in which proof and subproof spines in a limited fashion serve the same purpose.

Subproof spines show how and when a subproof is exited by a conclusion justified by application of a subproof rule.

The application of rules is indicated in the proof's justification column (e). We cannot make a move within a proof without justifying each step as an assumption or derivation from previous steps by one of the natural deduction rules. Given assumptions are justified simply by the assumption rule, A, with no reference to step numbers, since assumptions stand on their own. Auxiliary assumptions that initiate subproofs are justified by the same rule A, again without reference to step numbers. In the case of auxiliary assumptions, the justification A is followed in parentheses by an abbreviation of the subproof rule for the sake of which the auxiliary assumption is made. If an auxiliary assumption is assumed in order to execute the subproof rule for disjunction elimination, for example (a rule explained below), and abbreviated as ∨E, then the justification column for the step of the subproof that begins with an auxiliary assumption is written as A (∨E). The convention has two purposes: It distinguishes auxiliary assumptions from given assumptions, and it provides strategy reminders that are helpful in complicated proofs, explaining why a subproof with a particular auxiliary assumption is introduced. Many examples of this annotation for auxiliary assumptions in the justification column will be provided when we begin to use subproof rules. In other cases, in which given or auxiliary assumptions are not involved, the justification column refers to the step or steps of the proof to which a rule is applied, along with a standard abbreviation for the name of the rule. An example is seen in the previous proof, in which the conclusion in step 3 is justified by the application of conjunction introduction, abbreviated as

The (optional) subproof column indicates more exactly than proof spines the exact assumptions on which each proof step logically depends.

&I, to proof steps 1 and 2, indicated in the justification column as 1, 2 &I. Some rules require reference to just one proof step, others to two, and still others to a range or several ordered ranges of steps.

Natural Deduction Rules

There are 12 inference rules in our system of natural deduction.

Our system of natural deduction proofs has 12 rules. Each rule is introduced with a brief explanation and an example or two of its applications are given, with strategy suggestions and problems to try. We distinguish two categories of ordinary and subproof rules.

A natural deduction proof is an ordered sequence of propositions, some of which may be given as assumptions, others of which are introduced as auxiliary assumptions from which we derive conclusions, and all others of which are deduced by the rules of inference from given and auxiliary assumptions. We can think of natural deduction rules as rules that permit us to assume wffs and then determine when it is permissible to introduce or eliminate a wff containing a particular propositional connective. The combined rules that permit us to introduce or eliminate a wff containing a certain propositional main connective

Intelim rules combine rules for introducing and eliminating wffs containing each of the propositional connectives as their main connectives.

are known as *intelim rules*. This hybrid term grafts together abbreviations for "introduction" and "elimination" to designate the introduction or elimination of wffs featuring each of the five propositional connectives.

We simplify the explanation of natural deduction rules by first stating their abstract schemata by means of propositional variables $\mathbb{P}$, $\mathbb{Q}$, $\mathbb{R}$, etc. and then illustrating them where appropriate by means of *paradigms* or simple applications using propositional symbols P, Q, R, etc. The forms in which we are interested can be represented even more abstractly than with propositional variables by using pictographic expressions of formal logical relations, such as $\boxtimes$ and $\boxtimes \supset \oplus \vdash \oplus$. Despite their generality, these devices are not as useful as propositional symbols in learning the rules and strategies required for producing natural deduction proofs.

Assumption (A)

$$\text{n.} \quad \mathbb{P} \qquad \text{A}$$

The rule tells us that proposition $\mathbb{P}$ (which could literally be any proposition) can be admitted as an assumption into any line of a proof. We record the fact that this is assumption n by writing the corresponding step number 'n' at which the assumption is made in the far left assumption column. This holds for any line number n of the proof. If we had introduced $\mathbb{P}$ in line 23, we would write '23' in the assumption column, even if, for example, it were only the second of two assumptions. The line number at which an assumption is introduced is the *assumption number.* In the far right justification column, we write 'A', as previously explained, to indicate that our justification for $\mathbb{P}$ is the rule of assumption. If $\mathbb{P}$ is an auxiliary rather than a given assumption, we indicate the subproof rule strategy we are following in introducing the assumption by writing the subproof rule's abbreviation in parentheses after A, as in A ($\vee$E) or A ($\supset$I), again for rules to be explained later.

The rule of assumption (A) justifies the introduction of given assumptions and the use of auxiliary assumptions in a subproof.

In a natural deduction proof, we can draw inferences from any assumption, regardless of whether or not it is true. The first rule we need, therefore, is a rule of assumption (A). The rule permits us to make any assumption anywhere in a proof. This is a very powerful rule since it allows us to add whatever assumptions we like to the formal derivation of a tautology or valid sequent. To avoid trivial proofs, we cannot use the assumption rule to justify assuming whatever conclusion we are supposed to deduce in a proof and let it go at that. Because the rule is so strong, we must pay a price for introducing an assumption. The complete correct proof of a sequent requires that we discharge all auxiliary subproof assumptions, exiting from the subproof when we satisfy its requirements, by writing a conclusion below and to the left of the respective subproof spines. When we do this, we indicate that the final proof of the conclusion of the sequent rests only on its given assumptions. We accordingly distinguish and keep track of a proof's given and auxiliary assumptions so that we always know on which propositions each step of the proof depends. The assumption rule is not an intelim rule because it does not authorize the introduction or elimination of propositions containing any particular propositional connective. It is nevertheless the foundational rule of natural deduction.

Reiteration (R)

It is useful to introduce a rule for reiteration (R). This rule permits us to repeat any proposition appearing anywhere in a proof or subproof below the step at which it is introduced or within a more deeply nested subproof.

Reiteration (R) justifies the repetition of any wff in a proof or within a more deeply nested subproof.

The rule has the following schematic form:

$\mathbb{P}$

.

.

.

$\mathbb{P}$ . . . R

The rule is so obviously valid that it may be unnecessary to explain or try to justify the inferences it permits. If we already have a proposition available for use in a proof, we can repeat it as often as we wish. The only restriction is that we must not try to reiterate a proposition from within a more deeply nested subproof into a less deeply nested subproof or main proof. If reiteration of this sort were permitted, then we could literally prove anything we liked by beginning with a freely assumed subproof auxiliary assumption and reiterating it out into the main body of the proof as a definite conclusion. We shall find the reiteration (R) rule particularly useful in the four subproof rules of disjunctive elimination (∨E), conditional introduction (⊃I), combined negation introduction/elimination (~IE), and biconditional introduction (≡I) subproofs. For convenience, because rule R is so useful and so obviously valid, we have introduced it near the beginning of this enumeration of the natural deduction rules. R is nevertheless a *derived rule* that can be reduced to assumption and the intelim rules. We show how to do this in the section on derived rule reductions.

Double Negation (DN)

The rule of double negation has the following form:

$$\sim\sim\mathbb{P}$$

.

.

.

$$\mathbb{P} \qquad \ldots \text{DN}$$

.

.

.

$$\sim\sim\mathbb{P} \qquad \ldots \text{DN}$$

The validity of DN is guaranteed by the truth table definition of negation. Reversing truth value twice as DN does, from T to F to T or from F to T to F, is obviously truth preserving. Double negation is another derived rule of the natural deduction system that is so useful that we are better off having it available right from the start. DN, like R, is nevertheless a derived rule that can be reduced to assumption and the other intelim rules, as we show in the section on derived rule reductions.

Now we present the logic's nine intelim rules. We shall proceed systematically, explaining each introduction and corresponding elimination rules for each of the five propositional connectives. In principle, the rules might be introduced in any order. For the sake of offering an interesting progression of proofs, we begin with conjunction and then proceed to intelim rules for disjunction, the conditional, negation, and the biconditional.

Conjunction Introduction (&I)

$$\mathbb{P}$$
.
.
.
$$\mathbb{Q}$$
.
.
.
$$\mathbb{P} \,\&\, \mathbb{Q} \qquad \ldots \&I$$

$$\mathbb{P}$$
.
.
.
$$\mathbb{Q}$$
.
.
.
$$\mathbb{Q} \,\&\, \mathbb{P} \qquad \ldots \&I$$

A simple example illustrates the rule in action:

1	1.	P	A
2	2.	Q	A
1, 2	3.	P & Q	1, 2 &I

Conjunction introduction (&I) justifies inferring a conjunction of two wffs from their occurrence in separate lines of a proof.

If P and Q occur in a proof, we can validly infer their conjunction, P & Q. The truth of P & Q in the conclusion depends on whatever assumptions P and Q jointly depend on. These are written in the left-hand assumption column, and the conclusion is justified by application of the rule &I to the propositions in steps 1 and 2, indicated in the right-hand justification column for the conclusion in step 3.

The conjunction of a proposition with another proposition can be written in any order in the paradigm as P & Q or Q & P. The order in which propositions are conjoined is truth functionally irrelevant so that propositions occurring in prior proof lines can be conjoined in any order. Thus, we also have:

1	1.	P	A
2	2.	Q	A
1, 2	3.	Q & P	1, 2 &I

We can also apply &I to a proposition and itself to obtain:

| 1 | 1. | P | A |
| 1 | 2. | P & P | 1, 1 &I |

Conjunction Elimination (&E)

$$\mathbb{P} \,\&\, \mathbb{Q} \qquad\qquad\qquad \mathbb{P} \,\&\, \mathbb{Q}$$

$$
\begin{array}{ll}
\cdot & \qquad\qquad\qquad\qquad \cdot \\
\cdot & \qquad\qquad\qquad\qquad \cdot \\
\cdot & \qquad\qquad\qquad\qquad \cdot \\
\end{array}
$$

$$\mathbb{P} \qquad \ldots \&E \qquad\qquad \mathbb{Q} \qquad\qquad \ldots \&E$$

As an application of the rule, we have in a very simple case:

```
1    1. | P & Q     A
1    2. |  P         1 &E
```

Conjunction elimi-
nation (&E) *justi-
fies inferring either
conjunct from a
conjunction.*

The rule for conjunction elimination enables us to derive conjuncts from a conjunction. Whereas &I is applied to two propositions (or a proposition and itself) as the conjuncts to be conjoined, the rule for &E is applied only to a single proposition, a conjunction broken up by the rule into its component conjuncts. This means, as the assumption column records, that the conclusion P derived from the conjunction P & Q depends only on the assumption or assumptions on which the conjunction itself depends (in this case, assumption 1). We can also validly infer Q instead of P at step 2, and we can continue the derivation to step 3, also deriving Q from step 1 by the rule &E applied to step 1 and resting on assumption 1.

```
1    1. | P & Q     A
1    2. |  Q         1 &E

1    1. | P & Q     A
1    2. |  P         1 &E
1    3. |  Q         1 &E
```

Disjunction Introduction (∨I)

$$\mathbb{P} \qquad\qquad\qquad\qquad \mathbb{P}$$

$$
\begin{array}{ll}
\cdot & \qquad\qquad\qquad\qquad \cdot \\
\cdot & \qquad\qquad\qquad\qquad \cdot \\
\cdot & \qquad\qquad\qquad\qquad \cdot \\
\end{array}
$$

$$\mathbb{P} \vee \mathbb{Q} \qquad \ldots \vee I \qquad\qquad \mathbb{Q} \vee \mathbb{P} \qquad \ldots \vee I$$

A paradigm of the rule is seen in the following example:

```
1    1. | P          A
1    2. |  P ∨ Q      1 ∨I
```

Disjunction intro-
duction (∨I)
*justifies inferring
a disjunction from
either of its disjuncts.*

*Disjunction intro-
duction is also some-
times known as logi-
cal addition.*

If P is true, as step 1 declares, then, as truth tables and trees confirm, disjoining any proposition we like to P validly produces a true disjunction. As the paradigm illustrates, the proposition Q disjoined to a proposition P need not appear anywhere previously in the proof. Disjunction introduction for this reason is also sometimes known as *logical addition*. Like the rule for &E, ∨I is a rule that applies to single propositions.

The following is a simple example of a natural deduction proof that combines the foundational and three intelim rules we have considered so far.

▪ *Demonstration 17:* **Natural Deduction Proof** ▪
Using &I, &E, and ∨I

PROBLEM: To prove a deductively valid sequent by natural deduction rules.

SEQUENT: P & (S & (Q ⊃ R)) ⊢ ((Q ⊃ R) ∨ (S ⊃ T)) & P

The sequent in this case contains one given assumption, which appears to the left of the inference indicator, and one conclusion, which appears to the right. We set up the natural deduction proof by introducing the assumption as the given assumption attaching to a main proof spine. Then we develop a proof strategy for deriving the conclusion of the sequent according to the natural deduction rules.

STEP 1:   *Set up the proof*
We begin by writing the given assumptions. There is only one. We annotate the assumption, line number, proof step, and justification columns:

$$1 \qquad 1. \;\; \big|\!\!- \;\; \text{P \& (S \& (Q} \supset \text{R))} \qquad \text{A}$$

STEP 2:   *Plan a proof strategy*
We notice that the conclusion of the sequent has the conjunction as its main connective. This means that to prove the conclusion we will probably need to use &I. If we are going to use &I, then we need to apply the right rules to assumption 1 to obtain the conjuncts to which we can then apply &I. The conjuncts are (Q ⊃ R) ∨ (S ⊃ T) and P. Therefore, we must somehow derive these propositions from assumption 1. P is easiest to obtain because we can get it directly from assumption 1 by &E. This gives us one of the conjuncts we need. The other conjunct is a disjunction of two conditionals. We can obtain a disjunction by ∨I if either one of the disjuncts appears in the

proof. We can deduce Q ⊃ R from assumption 1 by two applications of &E, whereafter we disjoin it to S ⊃ T. This provides both conjuncts P and (Q ⊃ R) ∨ (S ⊃ T), which we conjoin by applying &I to deduce the sequent's conclusion.

STEP 3: *Apply the appropriate natural deduction rules to begin the proof*
The proof continues when we use &E to extract the conjuncts P and S & (Q ⊃ R). Both depend on assumption 1, as the assumption column now indicates:

1	1.	P & (S & (Q ⊃ R))	A
1	2.	P	1 &E
1	3.	S & (Q ⊃ R)	1 &E

From proof line 3 we require the conditional Q ⊃ R, which we extract by another application to it of &E. We need this proposition to prove the conclusion because the conclusion is a conjunction of P (which we already have) and the disjunction (Q ⊃ R) ∨ (S ⊃ T), which we foresee that we can obtain from Q ⊃ R by ∨I. We do not need the conjunct S in proof line 3 for any further derivations in the proof, so we do not bother to extract it by &E. The proof now looks as follows:

1	1.	P & (S & (Q ⊃ R))	A
1	2.	P	1 &E
1	3.	S & (Q ⊃ R)	1 &E
1	4.	Q ⊃ R	3 &E

Working toward the final conclusion, we now use ∨I to add the disjunct S ⊃ T to the conditional Q ⊃ R, which we obtained in the previous step at proof line 4, to derive the disjunction (Q ⊃ R) ∨ (S ⊃ T). This is one of two conjuncts needed to prove the final conclusion. The proof now has the following form:

1	1.	P & (S & (Q ⊃ R))	A
1	2.	P	1 &E
1	3.	S & (Q ⊃ R)	1 &E
1	4.	Q ⊃ R	3 &E
1	5.	(Q ⊃ R) ∨ (S ⊃ T)	4 ∨I

STEP 4: *Complete the proof*
At this stage we are prepared to draw the final conclusion in the proof by using &I to conjoin the two conjuncts of the conclusion, P, from proof line 2 and the disjunction we have just constructed, (Q ⊃ R) ∨ (S ⊃ T), from proof

line 5. Accordingly, we apply &I to these steps to produce the conclusion. The completed proof looks as follows:

1	1.	P & (S & (Q ⊃ R))	A
1	2.	P	1 &E
1	3.	S & (Q ⊃ R)	1 &E
1	4.	Q ⊃ R	3 &E
1	5.	(Q ⊃ R) ∨ (S ⊃ T)	4 ∨I
1	6.	((Q ⊃ R) ∨ (S ⊃ T)) & P	2, 5 &I

To Check Your Understanding 5.1 ─────────────────────────────────────■

Use truth trees to confirm these sequents' validity; then give natural deduction proofs of each valid sequent using the assumption, derived, and intelim rules A, R, DN, &I, &E, and ∨I:

1. P, Q & R ⊢ P & (Q ∨ S)
2. P & (Q & R) ⊢ (P & Q) & R
3. P, P ∨ Q ⊢ (P & (P ∨ Q)) ∨ R
4. P ⊃ Q, P, Q ⊃ P ⊢ (P ⊃ Q) & (Q ⊃ P)
5. ~(P ⊃ Q) ⊢ (~(P ⊃ Q) & ~(P ⊃ Q)) & ~(P ⊃ Q)
6. ~(P ⊃ Q) ⊢ (~(P ⊃ Q) & ~(P ⊃ Q)) ∨ ((P ⊃ Q) ≡ ~(P ⊃ Q))

■

Disjunction Elimination (∨E)

$$\mathbb{P} \vee \mathbb{Q}$$
$$\quad \mathbb{P} \qquad \text{A } (\vee E)$$
$$\quad \cdot$$
$$\quad \cdot$$
$$\quad \cdot$$
$$\quad \mathbb{R}$$
$$\quad \mathbb{Q} \qquad \text{A } (\vee E)$$
$$\quad \cdot$$
$$\quad \cdot$$
$$\quad \cdot$$
$$\quad \mathbb{R}$$
$$\mathbb{R} \qquad \ldots \vee E$$

Here is a simple application to prove P ∨ Q ⊢ Q ∨ P:

1	1.	P ∨ Q	A
2	2.	P	A (∨E)
2	3.	Q ∨ P	2 ∨I
4	4.	Q	A (∨E)
4	5.	Q ∨ P	4 ∨I
1	6.	Q ∨ P	1, 2–3, 4–5 ∨E

Disjunction elimination (∨E) is a subproof rule that justifies inferring a conclusion that follows from the auxiliary assumption of each of the disjuncts.

The rule for disjunction elimination is our first *subproof rule*. The rule has a more complicated annotation in the assumption column and a more complicated graphic display involving its subproof spine. The justification column as we see for the first time makes reference to three ordered ranges of steps of the proof to which the disjunction elimination intelim rule is applied.

The idea of a subproof rule is to license valid inference from assumptions that are not given but introduced as auxiliary assumptions in a subproof nested within and logically subordinate to the main proof. When a conclusion is reached the truth of which does not depend on the truth of the auxiliary assumption, it can be brought out of the subproof as a conclusion holding independently of the truth of the auxiliary assumption. There can be an unlimited number of subproofs within subproofs, and complicated nestings are sometimes required to solve interesting problems.

The rule for disjunction elimination (∨E) requires a detailed annotation to keep track of the auxiliary assumptions used in two related subproofs. To understand the reasoning behind the rule, consider what we know and do not know when we know only that P ∨ Q. We understand from the truth table definition of disjunction that either P or Q is true (and possibly both) in this case, but we do not know which is true. We cannot conclude definitely that P (is true) since perhaps P is false (in which case Q is true), nor can we conclude definitely that Q (is true) since perhaps on the contrary Q is false (in which case P is true). Therefore, we proceed hypothetically by auxiliary assuming that P is true, to determine what follows from it, and then auxiliary assuming that Q is true, to determine if the same conclusion can be derived from the auxiliary assumption that Q as from the auxiliary assumption that P. If we can deduce the same conclusion (here, Q ∨ P) from the auxiliary assumption of each disjunct, then we know that conclusion holds in either case. Regardless of whether it is P or Q in particular that is true (and certainly if both are true), we know that the conclusion is true on the strength of the disjunction as a whole rather than on the assumption of the truth of either disjunct in particular.

A disjunction elimination subproof divides into two parts, one for the auxiliary assumption of each of two disjuncts.

The subproof divides into two parts. In the first, we consider the possibility that P is true, and in the second we consider the possibility that Q is true. The first part appears in lines 2–3 of the proof and the second in lines 4–5. We begin by auxiliary assuming that P is true. If P is true, then we can conclude by

∨I that Q ∨ P is true. However, since we do not know that P is true, we know only that the conclusion holds if we auxiliary assume P. Next, we auxiliary assume that Q is true and observe that if Q is true, then the same conclusion as before follows by another application of disjunction introduction (∨I), to deduce again the proposition that Q ∨ P. Then it does not matter whether P in particular is true or Q in particular is true because, in either case, if either P is true or Q is true, we can prove that Q ∨ P is true. As a result, in step 6 we are entitled to assert that Q ∨ P holds independently of the auxiliary assumption that P in particular is true and independently of the auxiliary assumption that Q in particular is true. Disjunction elimination (∨E) thus has the form of dilemma. We arrive at the same conclusion from either of two alternatives. In some systems of natural deduction, disjunction elimination is accordingly referred to as *constructive dilemma*.

The justification column in a disjunction elimination subproof makes reference to three ranges of steps in the proof: the disjunction being eliminated and the steps for each of the two parts of the subproof in which each disjunct is auxiliary assumed and the identical conclusion is derived.

The justification column makes reference to three ranges of steps of the proof to which the rule of ∨E is applied. We consult the justification column for information about all the assumptions on which the conclusion depends in annotating the assumption column. The steps are presented in the following order for the ∨E justification column: (i) the step at which the disjunction P ∨ Q to be eliminated occurs (in this case, step 1); (ii) the steps of the first subproof, in which we assume the first disjunct (P) of the disjunction as the first auxiliary assumption of the subproof from which the first statement of the conclusion is deduced (steps 2–3); and (iii) the steps of the second subproof, in which we assume the second disjunct (Q) of the disjunction as the auxiliary assumption of the second subproof from which the second statement of the conclusion (matching exactly the conclusion of the first part) is deduced (steps 4–5). The auxiliary assumptions of each subproof are the disjuncts of the disjunction to be eliminated, just as they appear in the disjunction. The conclusions reached in each of the disjunction elimination subproofs must match exactly. Only when the very same conclusion follows from the assumption of each disjunct are we entitled, as in a dilemma, to conclude after exiting both subproofs that the same proposition holds as the final conclusion of ∨E. The information needed in the justification column for ∨E is summarized as follows:

JUSTIFICATION COLUMN FOR DISJUNCTION ELIMINATION

List in the right-hand proof justification column:

(i)   Proof step number of the disjunction being eliminated
(ii) Range of step numbers of the first subproof, beginning with the auxiliary assumption of the first disjunct of the disjunction to be eliminated,

indicated in (i), and ending with the conclusion exactly matching that of the subproof indicated in (iii)

(iii) Range of step numbers of the second subproof, beginning with the auxiliary assumption of the second disjunct of the disjunction to be eliminated, indicated in (i), and ending with the conclusion exactly matching that of the subproof indicated in (ii)

All these proof steps must be considered in correctly tabulating the assumption column for the final step of an application of the rule when exiting from the ∨E subproof. Collect all the assumption numbers appearing in the justification column for each of the previously mentioned steps and then delete the assumption numbers for the auxiliary assumptions of the two disjuncts in the disjunction to which the rule is applied.

Disjunction elimination is the first rule that eliminates assumption numbers that would otherwise appear in the assumption column. All the other rules we have examined so far require that we enumerate all assumption numbers appearing at each proof line to which a natural deduction rule is applied. In ∨E, however, we do not want to say that the truth of the conclusion rests on the subproof auxiliary assumptions of the disjuncts.

The auxiliary assumptions for a ∨E subproof are introduced only as hypotheses, and we are usually not in a position to know which are true. We auxiliary assume that P is true and arrive at a certain conclusion; then we auxiliary assume that Q is true and arrive at the very same conclusion. Then we know that the conclusion follows whether P or Q is true. However, since the conclusion holds in either case, its truth does not depend on the truth of the assumption that P in particular nor on the assumption that Q in particular. As a result, we do not want the assumption column to state that the truth of the conclusion depends on either of the subproof auxiliary assumptions but rather on whatever assumptions the disjunction as a whole depends. Thus, we discharge the subproof auxiliary assumption line numbers from the assumption column in executing the rule exiting from the ∨E subproof and do not include them in the list of assumptions on which the conclusion depends.

The steps referred to in the justification column for disjunction elimination must be consulted to correctly tabulate the assumption column.

We check each of the steps in the ranges (i)–(iii) referred to in the right-hand justification column and prepare a list of the assumptions on which each of these steps rests. In this application, we must examine steps 1, 2, 3, 4, and 5. Step 1 rests on assumption 1, 2 rests on 2, 3 rests on 2, 4 rests on 4, and 5 rests on 4. As a simple compilation, the list at this stage contains assumptions 1, 2, and 4. But now, we discharge assumption line numbers for auxiliary assumptions because they are not needed to support the conclusion's truth. The auxiliary assumptions 2 and 4 are introduced at steps 2 and 4. In the last step of the proof, we eliminate assumption numbers 2 and 4 from the assumption column of the conclusion and are left with just 1, which is written in the assumption column at line 7 in deducing the final conclusion. The truth of the ∨E conclusion that Q ∨ P rests only on assumption 1 of step 1, which is the given assumption that P ∨ Q.

The same logical relations are depicted graphically by means of the subproof spines. We first inscribe subproof spines for each of the separate ∨E subproofs, one after the other at the same subproof level or depth. The conclusions of each of the auxiliary assumptions that begin the subproofs rest on the auxiliary assumptions and are part of the subproofs in which they are derived. This is shown by writing the matching conclusions of each subproof within the subproof spine. When we have completed both subproofs, and we find that the same conclusion holds in both subproofs, we indicate that the conclusion does not rest on the truth of either of the auxiliary assumed disjuncts in particular but rather on the truth of the disjunction as a whole by exiting from the subproof, rewriting the conclusion outside the ∨E subproof spines, where in this case it attaches to the main proof spine.

Subproof Entrance and Exit

Subproof entry is unrestricted; subproof exit requires definite rules to avoid deductively invalid inference.

We now consider the question of entering and exiting from a subproof in more detail. We can reiterate any wff we like from a prior step in a proof into a more deeply nested subproof. Thus, we can reiterate any prior assumption or conclusion into a ∨E subproof. We can also simply bring down the conclusion by application of any of the proof rules from any less deeply nested proof or subproof into a more deeply nested subproof, without bothering to reiterate the wffs from which the conclusion is derived. The following are examples of valid subproof entrance involving the first part of a ∨E subproof:

1	1.	P ∨ Q	A
2	2.	S	A
3	3.	P	A (∨E)
2, 3	4.	S	2 R

1	1.	P ∨ Q	A
2	2.	P ⊃ Q	A
3	3.	P	A (∨E)
2, 3	4.	P ∨ R	3 ∨I

On pain of invalidity, however, we are not permitted to exit a subproof until we have satisfied certain conditions unique to each subproof rule. In ∨E, we are not permitted to exit from the subproofs for the two disjuncts in the disjunction being eliminated until we obtain an exactly matching conclusion in each of the two subproofs. We exit the ∨E subproofs by rewriting the identical conclusion that follows from the two auxiliary assumptions in the two subproofs below and to the left of the ∨E subproof spine, attaching to the next less deeply nested proof or subproof. We cannot freely exit subproofs by bringing out any and every of the wffs that appear within. If that were possible, then we could prove anything, including contradictions and inconsistencies, simply by reiterating any freely assumed auxiliary assumption from a subproof back out into the main proof. Here is an example in which we invalidly "prove" that God exists (G) from the assumption that either God exists or God does not exist by exiting a ∨E subproof via reiteration rule R:

It is important to study examples involving invalid exiting from subproof to avoid violations of subproof exiting restrictions.

1	1.	G ∨ ~G	A	
2	2.	G	A (∨E)	
2	3.	G	2 R	
2	4.	G	3 R	INVALID! VIOLATION!

The following is another example in which we invalidly try to exit from a subproof with the conclusion of another intelim rule:

1	1.	P ∨ Q	A	
2	2.	P ⊃ S	A	
3	3.	P	A (∨E)	
3	4.	P	3 R	
2, 3	5.	P ∨ R	4 ∨I	INVALID! VIOLATION!

We explain the requirements for exiting each of the subproof rules as they are introduced. In general, we can freely enter, but not freely exit, a subproof. The restrictions governing subproof exit prevent deductively invalid misapplications of the subproof rules. We do not expect to be able to prove that God exists merely from the disjunction that either God exists or God does not exist. The disjunction, after all, asserts that either disjunct could be possible, and here the second disjunct contradicts the first, whereas we do not yet know which to believe. Nor do we expect to be able to prove that the consequent of a conditional is true unless we are given or can prove the conditional's antecedent. The conditional asserts only that the consequent is true if the antecedent is true, which in this case remains to be seen.

Demonstration 18:   **Natural Deduction Proof Using ∨E**

PROBLEM: To prove a deductively valid sequent by natural deduction rules, featuring the disjunction elimination rule ∨E.

SEQUENT: P ∨ Q ⊢ (P ∨ R) ∨ (Q ∨ R)

The sequent in this case contains one given assumption, which appears to the left of the inference indicator, and one conclusion, which appears to the right. We set up the natural deduction proof by introducing the assumption as the given assumption attaching to a main proof spine. Then we develop a proof strategy for deriving the conclusion of the sequent according to the natural deduction rules.

STEP 1:   *Set up the proof*

We begin by writing down the given assumptions. Here there is only one. We fully annotate the assumption, line number, proof step, and justification columns:

$$1 \qquad 1. \; \lfloor \; P \lor Q \qquad A$$

STEP 2:   *Plan a proof strategy*

We notice that the conclusion of the sequent has a disjunction as its main connective. This means that to prove the conclusion we will probably need to use ∨I. If we are going to use ∨I, then we need to have proved either one of the conclusion's disjuncts. The disjuncts are P ∨ R and Q ∨ R. So, somehow we must derive at least one of these propositions from assumption 1. The trouble is that the assumption is itself disjunctive. It says that either P is true or Q is true, but it does not say which one in particular is true or whether both are true. Where we must make use of a disjunctive proposition in a proof, it is usually necessary to use the disjunction elimination rule ∨E. This rule requires us to auxiliary assume each disjunct of the disjunction in turn, trying by means of the other proof rules to deduce precisely the same conclusion, which we then bring out of the two separate ∨E subproofs into the main proof or the next less deeply nested subproof. If we assume P, then we can deduce the entire conclusion of the sequent by two steps of ∨I; if we assume Q, then we can again deduce the entire conclusion of the sequent by two slightly different steps of ∨I. When we have shown that the conclusion holds from the auxiliary assumption of either of the disjuncts, then we can restate the conclusion outside of the ∨E subproofs, indicating that its truth does not depend on the truth of the assumption of either disjunct in particular but depends instead on the truth of the entire disjunction.

STEP 3:   *Apply the appropriate natural deduction rules to begin the proof*

The proof now requires that we set up a disjunction elimination subproof, auxiliary assuming the first disjunct of the disjunction we are trying to eliminate:

```
1    1.  │ P ∨ Q      A
2    2.  │ ┌─ P        A (∨E)
         │ │
```

From proof line 2 we can deduce the disjunction P ∨ R by applying rule ∨I. From this we can deduce the disjunction (P ∨ R) ∨ (Q ∨ R), again by ∨I. The proof then looks as follows:

```
1    1.  │ P ∨ Q                      A
2    2.  │ ┌─ P                        A (∨E)
2    3.  │ │  P ∨ R                    2 ∨I
2    4.  │ │  (P ∨ R) ∨ (Q ∨ R)        3 ∨I
```

This completes the first half of the ∨E subproof strategy. Now we must try to reach the same conclusion from the auxiliary assumption of the second disjunct, Q, in the disjunct P ∨ Q in assumption 1. The proof has the following form:

```
1    1.  │ P ∨ Q                      A
2    2.  │ ┌─ P                        A (∨E)
2    3.  │ │  P ∨ R                    2 ∨I
2    4.  │ │  (P ∨ R) ∨ (Q ∨ R)        3 ∨I
5    5.  │ ┌─ Q                        A (∨E)
5    6.  │ │  Q ∨ R                    5 ∨I
5    7.  │ │  (P ∨ R) ∨ (Q ∨ R)        6 ∨I
```

What we have shown at this point in the proof is that if P is auxiliary assumed, then we can validly deduce the conclusion of the sequent (P ∨ R) ∨ (Q ∨ R), and that if Q is auxiliary assumed, then we can validly deduce the identical conclusion (P ∨ R) ∨ (Q ∨ R). However, we do not know that P in particular is true, nor that Q in particular is true. All we know from assumption 1 is that either P or Q is true, P ∨ Q. Since we have proved that the same conclusion holds regardless of whether P in particular is true or Q in particular is true, we can validly deduce that the conclusion holds from the disjunction P ∨ Q.

STEP 4:   *Complete the proof*

We are now prepared to deduce the final conclusion in the proof by using ∨E to bring the matching conclusions of the two ∨E subproofs back out into the main proof and discharging the assumption numbers for the auxiliary assumptions in the assumption column of the proof's conclusion. This shows that the conclusion does not rest on the truth of the disjunct in either auxiliary assumption of either subproof but rather on the truth of the disjunction containing both disjuncts. We annotate the steps required for the application of ∨E in the justification column as previously explained. We include the disjunction to be eliminated, the range of subproof steps for the auxiliary assumption and its conclusions of the disjunction's first disjunct, and the range of subproof steps and its ultimately matching conclusions for the auxiliary assumption of the disjunction's second disjunct. The completed proof looks as follows:

1	1.	P ∨ Q	A
2	2.	P	A (∨E)
2	3.	P ∨ R	2 ∨I
2	4.	(P ∨ R) ∨ (Q ∨ R)	3 ∨I
5	5.	Q	A (∨E)
5	6.	Q ∨ R	5 ∨I
5	7.	(P ∨ R) ∨ (Q ∨ R)	6 ∨I
1	8.	(P ∨ R) ∨ (Q ∨ R)	1, 2–4, 5–7 ∨E

To Check Your Understanding 5.2

Use truth trees to confirm the following sequents' validity; then give natural deduction proofs of each valid sequent using the assumption, derived, and intelim rules A, R, DN, &I, &E, ∨I, and ∨E:

1. P ∨ (Q ∨ R) ⊢ (P ∨ Q) ∨ R
2. P & (Q ∨ R) ⊢ (P & Q) ∨ (P & R)
3. P, Q ∨ ~Q ⊢ (P & Q) ∨ (~Q ∨ (P & R))
4. (P ∨ Q) & (R ∨ S) ⊢ ((P & R) ∨ (P & S)) ∨ ((Q & R) ∨ (Q & S))
5. (P & Q) ∨ (R & S) ⊢ ((P ∨ R) & (P ∨ S)) & ((Q ∨ R) & (Q ∨ S))
6. ((P ∨ R) & (P ∨ S)) & ((Q ∨ R) & (Q ∨ S)) ⊢ (P & Q) ∨ (R & S)

Conditional Introduction (⊃I)

The next subproof rule permits us to derive a conditional from the auxiliary assumption of its antecedent when we can validly deduce its consequent. The rule of conditional introduction (⊃I) provides a powerful method of proving conditional propositions.

Conditional intro-
duction (⊃I) *is a*
subproof rule that
justifies inferring a
conditional from the
auxiliary assumption
of its antecedent when
the consequent is
validly deduced
within the subproof.

$$\begin{array}{ll}
\quad\vert\!\!\!\!\!\!\!\underline{\quad} \ \ \mathbb{P} & \text{A } (\supset\text{I}) \\
\quad\vert \quad \ . & \\
\quad\vert \quad \ . & \\
\quad\vert \quad \ . & \\
\quad\vert \quad \ \mathbb{Q} & \\
\mathbb{P} \supset \mathbb{Q} & \quad \ldots \supset\text{I}
\end{array}$$

The following is an illustration, to prove the argument sequent Q ⊦ P ⊃
(P & Q):

$$\begin{array}{lll}
1 & 1. \ \underline{\vert \ \ Q} & \text{A} \\
2 & 2. \ \vert \ \underline{\vert \ \ P} & \text{A } (\supset\text{I}) \\
1, 2 & 3. \ \vert \ \vert \ \ P \ \& \ Q & 1, 2 \ \&\text{I} \\
1 & 4. \ \vert \ \ P \supset (P \ \& \ Q) & 2\text{–}3 \supset\text{I}
\end{array}$$

If we assume the antecedent of a conditional we are trying to prove, then,
with this auxiliary assumption and the given assumptions (if any) or other
propositions available in the proof, we can deduce the consequent of the conditional, then we can validly conclude that the conditional holds independently
of the auxiliary assumption of its antecedent.

By assuming the antecedent, and deducing the consequent, we are in effect saying that *if* the antecedent is true, *then* the consequent is also true. This is
just the conditional we are asked to prove. We write out the conditional horizontally, so to speak, after we have proved its stepwise vertical equivalent in the
subproof. We justify the inference in the proof by referring to a range of steps,
beginning with the auxiliary assumption at which the antecedent of the conditional is assumed (in this case, 2) through the step in which the consequent is
proved (here, step 3), and indicate that the rule ⊃I is applied to these steps. In
the assumption column, we write the assumptions on which the deduction rests.
We check both steps 2 and 3, as the justification column requires, to determine
on which assumptions these propositions depend, and discharge the subproof
auxiliary assumption number for the step in which the antecedent is assumed
(assumption 2 in step 2). Discharging assumption 2 in this case leaves only assumption 1, as indicated in the assumption column of line 4, as we exit the subproof. We also show graphically that the truth of the conditional we have
proved does not depend on the truth of the auxiliary assumption of its antecedent by bringing the conditional out of the ⊃I subproof spine into alignment
with the spine of the next less deeply nested proof or subproof. We do this because if the antecedent is true, then the subproof entails that the consequent is
also true. But if the antecedent is false, then by truth tables the conditional is
true by default. Once we have proved the truth of a conditional's consequent
from the auxiliary assumption of its antecedent, the truth of the conditional
as a whole does not depend on the assumption that its antecedent is true. We

indicate this by discharging the antecedent's auxiliary assumption line number from the assumption column.

We can use the rule ⊃I only if the antecedent of the conditional we are trying to derive has been introduced as an auxiliary assumption exactly as it appears in the conditional to be proved. The consequent of the conditional must then be validly deduced as resting on the assumption of its antecedent. The assumption column is consulted to verify that the consequent of the conditional is deduced as dependent on (usually among other assumptions) the auxiliary assumption of the antecedent. In the previous example, the consequent P & Q is deduced in step 3. Checking the assumption column, we see that step 3 rests on assumptions 1 and 2. This satisfies the subproof requirement because P & Q rests in this case on auxiliary assumption P.

Conditional Elimination (⊃E)

$$\mathbb{P} \supset \mathbb{Q}$$

Conditional elimination (⊃E) justifies inferring the consequent of a conditional from the conditional and its antecedent occurring in separate proof steps.

$$\mathbb{P}$$

.
.
.

$$\mathbb{Q} \qquad \ldots \supset E$$

An example of the rule is given in the following simple proof:

1	1.	P ⊃ Q	A
2	2.	P	A
1, 2	3.	Q	1, 2 ⊃E

Conditional elimination is the inference rule of modus ponendo ponens, *or* modus ponens.

Conditional elimination is the inference rule of *modus ponendo ponens*. It permits us validly to deduce (or detach) Q from P, and if P, then Q. Again, ⊃E is not restricted only to assumptions but can also be applied to any propositions that legitimately appear within a proof. It is also valid to use ⊃E to detach the consequent of a conditional proposition if the antecedent and conditional occur in different parts of a proof or subproofs contained within the proof, provided that the consequent does not appear outside the most deeply nested subproof of the conditional or its antecedent. We can use ⊃E within a subproof if the conditional or the antecedent appears in a main proof or less deeply nested subproof. But we cannot, on pain of invalidity, bring the detached consequents deduced by ⊃E back out into a less deeply nested subproof or main proof. The following is an example (at step 3 from steps 1 and 2) in proving the argument sequent, P ⊃ Q ⊢ P ⊃ (Q ∨ R):

1	1.	P ⊃ Q	A	
2	2.	P	A (⊃I)	
1, 2	3.	Q	1, 2 ⊃E	
1, 2	4.	Q ∨ R	3 ∨I	
1	5.	P ⊃ (Q ∨ R)	2–4 ⊃I	VALID

The previous proof illustrates a valid application of ⊃I, in which a conditional is derived in exiting from the subproof at step 5; the antecedent is auxiliary assumed at step 2, and the consequent is deduced at step 4. The following proof is invalid and exemplifies a logically incorrect effort to exit the ⊃I subproof with an intermediate derivation other than a conditional consisting of the auxiliary assumed antecedent and validly derived consequent. Here we see:

1	1.	P ⊃ Q	A	
2	2.	P	A (⊃I)	
1, 2	3.	Q	1, 2 ⊃E	
1, 2	4.	Q	_____	INVALID!
				VIOLATION!

Demonstration 19:   **Natural Deduction Proof Using ⊃I and ⊃E**

PROBLEM: To prove a deductively valid sequent by natural deduction rules, featuring the conditional intelim rules ⊃I and ⊃E.

SEQUENT: P ⊃ Q, P ⊢ S ⊃ Q

STEP 1:   *Set up the proof*
We begin by writing down the given assumptions. We fully annotate the assumption, line number, proof step, and justification columns:

1	1.	P ⊃ Q	A
2	2.	P	A

STEP 2:   *Plan a proof strategy*
We notice that the conclusion is a conditional. This means that to prove the conclusion we will probably need to use ⊃I. If we are going to use ⊃I, then

we must auxiliary assume the conditional's antecedent S in a subproof and try to deduce its consequent, Q. Then we can bring the conditional out of the ⊃I subproof, showing that its truth does not depend on the truth of the auxiliary assumed antecedent. We can obtain proposition Q directly from assumptions 1 and 2 by ⊃E and then reiterate it by rule R into the ⊃I subproof that begins with auxiliary assumption of the antecedent S. We can also begin the ⊃I subproof immediately after step 2 and then deduce Q from steps 1 and 2 by ⊃E and bring Q directly into the ⊃I subproof. Although either strategy would be logically correct, the latter method makes the proof one line shorter, so we shall adopt it.

STEP 3:   *Apply the appropriate natural deduction rules to begin the proof*
We have now shown that if the antecedent S of the conditional we are trying to derive is true, then the consequent Q is also true.

1	1.	P ⊃ Q	A
2	2.	P	A
3	3.	S	A (⊃I)
1, 2	4.	Q	1, 2 ⊃E

To say that from the auxiliary assumption that S it follows that Q validly implies that if S then Q, S ⊃ Q. Accordingly, we exit the subproof and write out the conditional as the final conclusion of the proof.

STEP 4:   *Complete the proof*
The truth of the conditional conclusion now brought out of the ⊃I subproof into the main proof does not depend on the truth of the ⊃I auxiliary assumption of its antecedent. The antecedent is either true or false. If the antecedent is true, then the subproof shows that the consequent is also true so that by truth table definitions the conditional as a whole is true. If the antecedent is false, then the conditional is true by default because, again by the truth table definition of the conditional, a conditional with a false antecedent is true and is only false if its antecedent is true and its consequent false. The independence of the truth of the conditional from the auxiliary assumption of its antecedent is indicated by bringing the conclusion outside the subproof spine and by discharging the assumption number of the subproof auxiliary assumption from the assumption column. We annotate the steps required for the application of ⊃I in the justification column as previously explained in a range of subproof steps beginning with the step at which the auxiliary assumption of the conditional's antecedent is assumed and continuing to the step at which its consequent is deduced. The final proof has the following form:

1	1.	P ⊃ Q	A
2	2.	P	A
3	3.	S	A (⊃I)
1, 2	4.	Q	1, 2 ⊃E
1, 2	5.	S ⊃ Q	3–4 ⊃I

To Check Your Understanding 5.3

Use truth trees to confirm these sequents' validity; then give natural deduction proofs of each valid sequent using the assumption, derived, and intelim rules A, R, DN, &I, &E, ∨I, ∨E, ⊃I, and ⊃E:

1. P ⊢ Q ⊃ (P & Q)
2. P ⊃ Q, Q ⊃ R ⊢ P ⊃ R
3. P ∨ Q, P ⊃ R, Q ⊃ R ⊢ R
4. P ⊃ R ⊢ (Q ⊃ R) ⊃ ((P ∨ Q) ⊃ R)
5. P ⊃ (Q ⊃ R), Q ⊃ (R ∨ R) ⊢ ((P & Q) ∨ Q) ⊃ R
6. Q ⊃ R ⊢ (P ⊃ Q) ⊃ (P ⊃ R)

Negation Introduction/Elimination (~IE)

Negation introduction/elimination (~IE) justifies inferring the negation of an auxiliary assumption, when the assumption leads to a logical inconsistency in the form of a wff and its negation in a subproof.

The following subproof rule combines introduction and elimination inferences for negation. This is the rule for an argument form which was previously introduced as *reductio ad absurdum*. It has the following alternative forms:

ℙ	A (~IE)		~ℙ	A (~IE)
.			.	
.			.	
.			.	
ℚ			ℚ	
~ℚ			~ℚ	
~ℙ	. . . ~IE		ℙ	. . . ~IE

As a paradigm, consider the proof by ~IE of the sequent, Q, P ⊃ ~Q ⊢ ~P:

1	1.	Q	A
2	2.	P ⊃ ~Q	A
3	3.	P	A (~IE)
2, 3	4.	~Q	2, 3 ⊃E
1	5.	Q	1 R
1, 2	6.	~P	3–5 ~IE

*Negation intelim
combines introduction
and elimination rules
for negation; it is
the inference rule
of reductio ad
absurdum.*

The idea of negation introduction/elimination (~IE) is to assume the negation of what we want to prove and then derive a contradiction to prove that the assumption must be false. In this example, we want to prove ~P. We set up a subproof beginning in step 3 with the auxiliary assumption that P. Together with other propositions available to us within the proof (here, given assumptions 1 and 2), we derive the contradiction, Q, ~Q, in steps 4 and 5. By the definition of deductive validity, we know that from true assumptions we can never validly derive a contradiction. Contradictions by truth tables are necessarily false, and it is generally invalid to infer a false from a true proposition. Yet the rules ⊃E and R that we use to get the contradiction are deductively valid. We know as a result that at least one of the assumptions from which we have validly derived a contradiction is false. We conclude that the assumption ~P made for purposes of ~IE is false, given the assumptions that Q and P ⊃ ~Q in steps 1 and 2. Hence, we derive its negation, ~P, in step 6, the negation of auxiliary assumption P in step 3, as the subproof conclusion, exiting from the ~IE subproof.

We notice that the contradiction needed for a ~IE subproof can also involve the ~IE subproof assumption. Here is an example in a proof of the sequent, P ⊃ ~P ⊢ ~P:

1	1.	P ⊃ ~P	A
2	2.	P	A (~IE)
1, 2	3.	~P	1, 2 ⊃E
1	4.	~P	2–3 ~IE

The rule permits us to follow the same subproof strategy in introducing a negation to or eliminating a negation from a proposition after showing that as an auxiliary assumption it leads to a contradiction. The following is an example in which the same basic proof style is used to eliminate rather than introduce a negation to a proposition on the strength of showing that it entails a contradiction for the sequent, ~P ⊃ P ⊢ P:

1	1.	~P ⊃ P	A
2	2.	~P	A (~IE)
1, 2	3.	P	1, 2 ⊃E
1	4.	P	2–3 ~IE

*Negation intelim is
useful in solving
many kinds of proofs;
it is a rule to try in a
proof when other rules
seem ineffective.*

The justification column in both proofs makes reference to a range of steps in the derivation. It begins with the step in which the auxiliary assumption made for purposes of ~IE is introduced (here, step 2) and continues through the step in which the contradiction is derived (in this case, step 3). The rule ~IE is applied to these two steps when we deduce the negation of the proposition we assumed for purposes of ~IE. In the assumption column, we list out the assumptions on which the two steps depend. As with other subproof rules, however, we discharge the assumption line number of the auxiliary assumption. This means that in the example we look at steps 2 and 4 to see that they jointly rest on assumptions 1 and 2. But, we discharge assumption 2 since it is the ~IE auxiliary assumption. The truth of a ~IE conclusion cannot depend on the truth of its auxiliary assumption since they contradict each other and have precisely opposite truth values. Accordingly, as we exit the subproof, we bring the conclusion of ~IE out of the subproof spine to show graphically that its truth does not depend on the truth of the auxiliary assumption, which the conclusion contradicts.

The ~IE rule is useful in many kinds of proofs. A good rule of thumb for natural deduction proof strategy is that when all else fails, but we know by truth tables or truth trees that a sequent is valid or a wff is a tautology, we may do well to try ~IE. There are three basic parts to implementing ~IE.

A three-part protocol is followed for negation intelim: choose an auxiliary assumption, the negation of a wff to be proved; derive a contradiction within the subproof; and exit the subproof with the negation of the auxiliary assumption as the wff to be proved.

NEGATION INTELIM PROTOCOL

1. Choose an auxiliary assumption to set up a ~IE subproof. The assumption, together with the other given and auxiliary assumptions available in the proof, must make it possible to derive a contradiction. (This is not always as straightforward as it may appear, and additional strategy hints are offered later.)
2. Derive a contradiction within the ~IE subproof by means of the system's intelim rules on any two lines of the subproof of the form $\mathbb{P}, \sim\mathbb{P}$.
3. Conclude the subproof by deriving the negation of the auxiliary assumption made for purposes of ~IE, discharging the corresponding auxiliary assumption number from the assumption column, and exiting the subproof by bringing the conclusion out of the ~IE subproof spine into alignment with the next less deeply nested subproof or main proof.

Negation intelim is different from other subproof rules in that the auxiliary assumptions it requires are based only on strategic considerations in obtaining a proof and not on the content of a predetermined wff being introduced or eliminated.

The other subproof intelim rules are fixed in terms of the auxiliary assumptions that must be made in order to enter a proof. When using ∨E, for example, we have no choice but to set up two subproofs in which we auxiliary assume each of the disjuncts of a disjunction we are trying to eliminate, deriving the very same conclusion from each. For ⊃I, we have no choice but to set up a subproof in which we auxiliary assume the antecedent of the conditional we are trying to deduce. But for ~IE, the situation is more open-ended. Here we are free to make any assumption we choose, provided only that it leads to an explicit contradiction in the ~IE subproof, with the understanding that the negation of the auxiliary assumption we deduce will somehow be useful in the proof. Such freedom is part of what makes ~IE so powerful. But it also makes using the rule more demanding of our problem-solving insight and ingenuity.

We offer three kinds of heuristics or strategy hints for using ~IE. These will be put to good use, and we will comment on their effectiveness in helping to solve some difficult proofs in sample problems. If no more obvious proof strategy seems available, then it is usually worthwhile to try ~IE. When we reach this stage of proof discovery, we should keep in mind the following possibilities for making auxiliary assumptions in ~IE subproofs:

STRATEGY HINTS FOR NEGATION INTELIM

1. Try assuming the negation of the entire conclusion to be proved (in the case of conclusions that are already negated, assume their unnegated forms).
2. Try assuming the negation of some useful part of the conclusion to be proved or of some other useful proposition, or part of a proposition, that will help to solve the proof (in the case of negated parts, assume their unnegated forms).
3. Try assuming some combination of 1 and 2, experimenting, if necessary, with different arrangements of combined subproof nestings.

It is important to consider all three categories of auxiliary assumptions for use in negation intelim: We can assume the negation of an entire wff to be proved, the negation of a useful part of the wff, or both in different combinations.

Natural deduction proof discovery requires persistence and a trial-and-error attitude, experimenting with applications of the inference rules to successfully complete a proof.

In using ~IE, we adopt a trial-and-error attitude. We should be prepared to try different possible auxiliary assumptions for ~IE and then retreat to a different strategy if they lead to a dead end. We must not be intimidated by not knowing before we enter into the difficulties of a proof just how it will proceed, but we should allow ourselves to experiment with different possibilities until we discover a successful path that leads from the given assumptions (if any) to the conclusion we are supposed to prove.

The guidelines can help us to do this by focusing our attention on three categories of auxiliary assumptions that are known to work satisfactorily in giving ~IE subproofs. We can overlook an obvious solution to a problem that requires a ~IE subproof if we do not consider all three possibilities. Later, examples of natural deduction proofs in propositional logic that require auxiliary assumptions from category 1, some from 2, and others from 3 will be presented. The choice of an auxiliary assumption is crucial to the success or failure of a ~IE subproof, which makes it important not to overlook any possibility. We should not become discouraged if one or more possibilities from the auxiliary assumption categories do not work out in attempting a particular proof. We must be persistent in trying to discover difficult natural deduction proofs. We can always retrace our steps and try again with another auxiliary assumption or differently nested set of auxiliary assumptions. As we do this, we will at least learn something important about what does *not* work in the proof, and it is hoped that we will be that much closer to identifying a winning strategy. We can learn more about logic from temporary setbacks, by determining what logic cannot be used to do and its limits and boundaries, than from proofs that are too easily solved. The following are more interesting problems involving the intelim rule, ~IE.

■ *Demonstration 20:* **Natural Deduction Proof Using ~IE** ■

PROBLEM: To prove a deductively valid sequent by natural deduction rules, featuring negation intelim rule ~IE.

SEQUENT: $P \supset Q, \sim Q \vdash \sim P$

STEP 1: *Set up the proof*
We begin by writing down the given assumptions. We fully annotate the assumption, line number, proof step, and justification columns:

$$
\begin{array}{llll}
1 & 1. & P \supset Q & A \\
2 & 2. & \sim Q & A
\end{array}
$$

STEP 2: *Plan a proof strategy*
We notice that the conclusion of the sequent is negated. This means that to prove the conclusion we will probably need to use ~IE. If we are going to use ~IE, then we need to auxiliary assume the negation of the conclusion we are trying to obtain and deduce and exhibit a contradiction resulting from the auxiliary assumption. Then we can exit the ~IE subproof with the negation of its auxiliary assumption as a conclusion that does not depend for its truth on the truth of the auxiliary assumption. If we are to prove ~P using ~IE, then we must auxiliary assume P in a ~IE subproof and work toward a contradiction that will justify concluding ~P.

STEP 3: *Apply the appropriate natural deduction rules to begin the proof*
Auxiliary assuming P in the next step of the proof according to the strategy we have developed, the proof now states:

$$
\begin{array}{llll}
1 & 1. & P \supset Q & A \\
2 & 2. & \sim Q & A \\
3 & 3. & P & A \ (\sim IE)
\end{array}
$$

We need to obtain a contradiction in the subproof, and we notice that we can derive a contradiction of the form Q, ~Q from assumptions 1 and 2 together with 3. The first part of the contradiction, Q, follows from steps 1 and 3 by ⊃E, which we bring directly into the ~IE subproof:

```
1       1. | P ⊃ Q    A
2       2. |  ~Q       A
3       3. |   | P     A (~IE)
1, 3    4. |   | Q     1, 3 ⊃E
```

The second part of the contradiction, ~Q, is already available at step 2. According to the subproof rule for ~IE, however, we must bring both parts of the contradiction explicitly into the ~IE subproof. We do this for the second part of the contradiction by applying the reiteration rule R. Then we have:

```
1       1. | P ⊃ Q    A
2       2. |  ~Q       A
3       3. |   | P     A (~IE)
1, 3    4. |   | Q     1, 3 ⊃E
2       5. |   | ~Q    2 R
```

STEP 4: *Complete the proof*

The contradiction required for ~IE is now complete, and we are ready to deduce the sequent's conclusion. We auxiliary assumed P at step 3, and we have now seen that the assumption supports a contradiction of the form Q, ~Q. No contradiction can be validly deduced from only true assumptions. So, the auxiliary assumption that P must be false rather than true. We are assuming 1 and 2 to determine what follows from them, and we accordingly deduce the negation of P, ~P, in the proof's final step (step 6). We annotate the steps required for the application of ~IE in the justification column as previously explained in a range of subproof steps, beginning with the step at which the auxiliary assumption of the negation of the conclusion we are trying to deduce is introduced, and ending at the step at which its negation is deduced. The completed proof looks as follows:

```
1       1. | P ⊃ Q    A
2       2. |  ~Q       A
3       3. |   | P     A (~IE)
1, 3    4. |   | Q     1, 3 ⊃E
2       5. |   | ~Q    2 R
1, 2    6. | ~P        3–5 ~IE
```

Other examples are more complicated and require several nested ~IE subproofs, involving auxiliary assumptions from all three categories of strategy hints for negation intelim in different combinations and in complex interaction with other natural deduction rules.

To Check Your Understanding 5.4 ────────────────────────────── ∎

Use truth trees to confirm these sequents' validity; then give natural deduction proofs of each valid sequent using the assumption, derived, and intelim rules A, R, DN, &I, &E, ∨I, ∨E, ⊃I, ⊃E, and ~IE:

1. ~P ⊃ Q ⊢ P ∨ Q
2. P ⊃ Q, ~Q ⊢ ~P
3. P & Q ⊢ ~(P ⊃ ~Q)
4. ~P ∨ ~Q ⊢ P ⊃ ~Q
5. ~(P ⊃ Q) ⊢ (P & ~Q)
6. P & Q ⊢ ~(~P ∨ ~Q)

∎

The final two rules for biconditional introduction (≡I) and biconditional elimination (≡E) are extensions of counterpart rules for conditional introduction (⊃I) and conditional elimination (⊃E), combined with the effect of conjunction introduction (&I) and conjunction elimination (&E).

───────────────────────────────

Biconditional Introduction (≡I)

```
    ┌─   ℙ        A (≡I)
    │    ·
    │    ·
    │    ·
    │    ℚ
    ├─   ℚ        A (≡I)
    │    ·
    │    ·
    │    ·
    │    ℙ
    ℙ ≡ ℚ          . . . ≡I
```

We begin as before with a particular example for the subproof rule of biconditional introduction (≡I) in proving the sequent, P ⊃ Q, Q ⊃ P ⊢ P ≡ Q:

1	1.	P ⊃ Q	A
2	2.	Q ⊃ P	A
3	3.	P	A (≡I)
1, 2	4.	Q	1, 3 ⊃E
5	5.	Q	A (≡I)
2, 5	6.	P	2, 5 ⊃E
1, 2	7.	P ≡ Q	3–4, 5–6 ≡I

Biconditional introduction (≡I) *is a subproof rule that justifies inferring a biconditional from the combined conditional introduction subproofs of both directions in which the biconditional holds.*

The rule for biconditional elimination combines two conditional introduction subproofs for the two conditionals of which a biconditional is composed. The first subproof in steps 3 and 4 implicitly proves the conditional P ⊃ Q (which, in this case, also appears as assumption 1), whereas the second conditional subproof in steps 4–6 implicitly proves the conditional going in the opposite direction Q ⊃ P (also given as assumption 2). Putting the two together by juxtaposition of the two subproofs yields the biconditional in step 7, P ≡ Q. This is equivalent to proving the two conditionals and then conjoining them to produce the biconditional. Note that the assumption column and subproof spines are treated exactly as they are in conditional introduction (⊃I). The justification column records two ranges of subproof steps for the two subproofs to which the ≡I intelim rule is applied.

Biconditional Elimination (≡E)

This rule is the counterpart of conditional elimination or *modus ponens* (⊃E) for biconditionals.

$$\mathbb{P} \equiv \mathbb{Q} \qquad\qquad \mathbb{P} \equiv \mathbb{Q}$$

$$\begin{array}{ll} \cdot & \cdot \\ \cdot & \cdot \\ \cdot & \cdot \\ \mathbb{P} & \mathbb{Q} \\ \cdot & \cdot \\ \cdot & \cdot \\ \cdot & \cdot \\ \mathbb{Q} \quad \ldots \equiv E & \mathbb{P} \quad \ldots \equiv E \end{array}$$

Biconditional elimination (≡E) *justifies inferring either wff connected by a biconditional from the biconditional and the other wff occurring in separate proof steps.*

From a biconditional of the form P ≡ Q and P (or Q), we can validly deduce Q (or P). It is not a subproof rule but, like conditional elimination, can be used wherever the biconditional and one of its component propositions obtain to validly detach the other component. The following is a simple example to prove the sequent, P ≡ Q, P ⊢ Q:

1	1.	P ≡ Q	A
2	2.	P	A
1, 2	3.	Q	1, 2 ≡E

We can validly detach either biconditional component if we are given or otherwise have available in a proof the other component. Thus, we can just as easily prove the valid sequent, P ≡ Q, Q ⊢ P:

Biconditional elimination is the biconditional version of conditional elimination; it is justified by the fact that a biconditional is logically equivalent to a conjunction of two conditionals holding in both directions, from antecedent to consequent and consequent to antecedent.

1	1.	P ≡ Q	A
2	2.	Q	A
1, 2	3.	P	1, 2 ≡E

We can use ≡E with a subproof if either component or the biconditional appears in a main proof or less deeply nested subproof. But we cannot validly exit the subproof by bringing the detached components deduced by ≡E back out into a less deeply nested subproof or main proof. Here is an example (at step 3 from steps 1 and 2) in proving the argument sequent, P ≡ Q ⊢ P ⊃ (Q ∨ R):

1	1.	P ≡ Q	A	
2	2.	P	A (⊃I)	
1, 2	3.	Q	1, 2 ≡E	
1, 2	4.	Q ∨ R	3 ∨I	
1	5.	P ⊃ (Q ∨ R)	2–4 ⊃I	VALID

The previous proof illustrates a valid application of ⊃I, using ≡E as an intermediate step, in which a conditional is derived in exiting from the subproof at step 5; the antecedent is auxiliary assumed at step 2, and the consequent is deduced at step 4. The following proof, in contrast, is deductively invalid and exemplifies a logically incorrect effort to exit the ⊃I subproof with an intermediate derivation other than a conditional consisting of the auxiliary assumed antecedent and validly derived consequent. The restriction attaches to the rule for ⊃I but directly affects the use of ≡E in a typical subproof context and the conditions under which we can validly exit from the subproof. The example is as follows:

The same restrictions on use of biconditional elimination in exiting subproofs are in force as those for conditional elimination.

1	1.	P ≡ Q	A	
2	2.	P	A (⊃I)	
1, 2	3.	Q	1, 2 ≡E	
1, 2	4.	Q	_____	INVALID! VIOLATION!

Demonstration 21:   Natural Deduction Proof Using ≡I and ≡E

PROBLEM: To prove a deductively valid sequent by natural deduction rules, featuring the conditional intelim rules ≡I and ≡E.

SEQUENT: P ≡ Q ⊢ Q ≡ P

STEP 1:   *Set up the proof*
We begin by writing down the given assumptions. We fully annotate the assumption, line number, proof step, and justification columns:

$$1 \quad 1. \;\vert\!\!-\;\; P \equiv Q \qquad A$$

STEP 2:   *Plan a proof strategy*

We notice that the conclusion is a biconditional. This means that to prove the conclusion we will probably need to use ≡I. If we are going to use ≡I, then we must set up two subproofs, in which we auxiliary assume each part of the biconditional, and show that the other part can be deduced with the subproof. Then we can bring the entire biconditional out of the ≡I subproofs to show that its truth does not depend on the truth of either of its parts. Since the assumption in this problem is also a biconditional, we will undoubtedly need to use ≡E to detach useful wffs within the ≡I subproofs.

STEP 3:   *Apply the appropriate natural deduction rules to begin the proof*

We continue by auxiliary assuming the first part, Q, of the biconditional we are to prove, initiating a ≡I subproof within the main proof:

```
1     1. |   P ≡ Q      A
2     2. |   |   Q       A (≡I)
```

Next, we deduce P from steps 1 and 2 by ≡E:

```
1     1. |   P ≡ Q      A
2     2. |   |   Q       A (≡I)
1, 2  3. |   |   P       1, 2 ≡E
```

This completes the first ≡I subproof. We have proved that if Q is auxiliary assumed, then, together with the given assumption, it is possible to deduce P. Now we begin the second ≡I subproof by assuming P and trying to deduce Q. The structure of the second subproof is the mirror image of the first:

```
1     1. |   P ≡ Q      A
2     2. |   |   Q       A (≡I)
1, 2  3. |   |   P       1, 2 ≡E
4     4. |   |   P       A (≡I)
1, 4  5. |   |   Q       1, 4 ≡E
```

STEP 4:   *Complete the proof*

The truth of the biconditional conclusion is brought out of the ≡I subproofs into the main proof. The assumption numbers of the ≡I subproof auxiliary assumptions are discharged from the assumption column to show that the conclusion does not depend on the truth of either of the ≡I auxiliary assumptions. We annotate the steps required for the application of ≡I in the justification column as previously explained in the ranges of both subproof steps. The final proof has the following form:

1	1.	P ≡ Q	A
2	2.	Q	A (≡I)
1, 2	3.	P	1, 2 ≡E
4	4.	P	A (≡I)
1, 4	5.	Q	1, 4 ≡E
1	6.	Q ≡ P	2–3, 4–5 ≡I

To Check Your Understanding 5.5 ━━━━━━━━━━━━━━━━━━━━━━━━━━━━━━━━━ ∎

Use truth trees to confirm these sequents' validity; then give natural deduction proofs of each valid sequent using the assumption, derived, and intelim rules A, R, DN, &I, &E, ∨I, ∨E, ⊃I, ⊃E, ~IE, ≡I, and ≡E:

1. P ≡ Q ⊢ ~P ≡ ~Q
2. ~P ≡ ~Q ⊢ P ≡ Q
3. P & Q ⊢ P & (P ≡ Q)
4. P ≡ Q, Q ≡ R ⊢ P ≡ R
5. P ≡ ~Q, Q ≡ ~R ⊢ P ≡ R
6. P ≡ ~P ⊢ Q ≡ ~Q

∎

Derived Rule Reductions

We have already presented the derived natural deduction rules reiteration, R, and double negation, DN. It is important to see that both of these rules, although obviously valid and widely useful, do not need to be taken as basic but can be validly derived from foundational assumption rule A and the nine intelim rules.

Reiteration and double negation are derived rules that can be reduced to assumption and the nine intelim rules.

The reiteration R rule is especially useful in subproof derivations. The following is a simple example, involving ∨E, in which one disjunct serves in double capacity as assumption and conclusion for one of the ∨E subproofs in proving the valid argument sequent, P ∨ Q, P ⊃ Q ⊢ Q:

1	1.	P ∨ Q	A
2	2.	P ⊃ Q	A
3	3.	P	A (∨E)
2, 3	4.	Q	2, 3 ⊃E
5	5.	Q	A (∨E)
5	6.	Q	5 R
1, 2	7.	Q	1, 3–4, 5–6 ∨E

Reiteration is also helpful in certain ~IE strategies, where the ~IE rule requires us to exhibit an explicit contradiction of the form $\mathbb{P}$, $\sim\mathbb{P}$ within a subproof, but where one part of the contradiction occurs up until that point only in a less deeply nested proof or subproof and needs to be brought into the ~IE subproof. Several examples of this use of reiteration are provided later in the sample problems.

R seems more basic than rules such as ∨E or ⊃I since it involves nothing more than (validly) reinscribing a wff that is already available within a proof or subproof. However, although R is easily proved by means of the other rules, it is helpless by itself to establish that the other rules are valid. For example, we can obtain the effect of R in the reiterative sequent P ⊢ P by using ⊃I and ⊃E, as in the proof

Although reiteration and double negation can be reduced to the other rules, the opposite is not possible.

1	1.	P	A
2	2.	P	A (⊃I)
3	3.	P ⊃ P	2–2 ⊃I
4	4.	P	1, 3 ⊃E

The reduction shows that we do not strictly need R. On the other hand, how could R alone be used to prove the validity of either ⊃I or ⊃E?

Although R is unnecessary if we have the other intelim rules, it is a useful rule to include because its reduction is cumbersome, the inferences it permits are evidently valid, and we have frequent need for reiteration in proofs that are already complicated in more interesting ways. If the purpose of natural deduction is to reflect our intuitive logic in as systematic a way as possible, then R should be included on the grounds that we often need to remind ourselves of the truth of certain propositions by repeating them in the course of developing an argument. No natural deduction system yet devised does full justice to the actual structures of thought in all their simplicity or complexity. But we come closer to the ideal by adopting rules that include R than by relying on an awkward reduction.

As in the case of R, DN is derived rather than foundational because we can recover its logical force without DN using ~IE. Here is one way to do so:

1	1.	~~P	A
2	2.	~P	A (~IE)
1	3.	~~P	1 R
1	4.	P	2–3 ~IE

1	1.	P	A
2	2.	~P	A (~IE)
1	3.	P	1 R
1	4.	~~P	2–3 ~IE

DN, like R, is so obviously true and potentially useful, and so natural a part of ordinary reasoning, that it is worthwhile simply to add it as a derived rule

The usefulness of re-iteration and double negation in proofs, and the complications that result without them, make it worth-while to include them as inference rules in a special category.

of natural deduction. Note that although an intelim rule such as ~IE can be used to reduce DN, DN by itself cannot reduce ~IE. This makes DN secondary to the primitive intelim rules for the five propositional connectives. In practice, it is often possible to avoid double negations by collapsing them at the translation or symbolization stage, as we do for convenience in truth trees.

If we are asked to prove the sequent, P ⊃ Q, ~~P ⊢ Q, in which the double-negated proposition ~~P appears, then it is easier and more straightforward to prove it in the first rather than the second equally logically correct ways shown:

1	1.	P ⊃ Q	A
2	2.	~~P	A
2	3.	P	2 DN
1, 2	4.	Q	1, 3 ⊃E

1	1.	P ⊃ Q	A
2	2.	~~P	A
3	3.	~P	A (~IE)
2	4.	~~P	2 R
2	5.	P	3–4 ~IE
1, 2	6.	Q	1, 2 ⊃E

Logics sometimes introduce different or additional derived inference rules for natural deduction proofs. These notably include a rule for *modus tollendo tollens,* ℙ ⊃ ℚ, ~ℚ ⊢ ~ℙ; *disjunctive syllogism,* ℙ ∨ ℚ, ~ℙ ⊢ ℚ; and *contraposition,* ℙ ⊃ ℚ ⊢ ~ℚ ⊃ ~ℙ. Some systems permit proofs to make use of uniform substitution instances of any valid sequent or tautology as a derived rule, once it has been validly proved, and we can also do so in any of the problems that follow.

Other derived rules are also permissible in natural deduction proofs, taking uni-form substitution in-stances of any valid sequent once it has been proved.

To illustrate the use of derived inference rules, consider a proof of the sequent P ∨ (Q ⊃ R), ~P ⊢ Q ⊃ R. The argument is deductively valid, as we can see from truth tables or truth trees. If we are to prove the sequent using only the 12 natural deduction rules which we have developed, the proof has the following form:

1	1.	P ∨ (Q ⊃ R)	A
2	2.	~P	A
3	3.	P	A (∨E)
4	4.	~(Q ⊃ R)	A (~IE)
3	5.	P	3 R
2	6.	~P	2 R
2, 3	7.	Q ⊃ R	4–6 ~IE
8	8.	Q ⊃ R	A (∨E)
8	9.	Q ⊃ R	8 R
1, 2	10.	Q ⊃ R	1, 3–7, 8–9 ∨E

The proof is correct but somewhat cumbersome. If we have already proved the general form for disjunctive syllogism, as $P \vee Q$, $\sim P \vdash Q$, then we might simply appeal to it as a derived rule to make it easier in working through natural deduction proofs. The proof in this case would have a much more compact form:

1	1.	$P \vee (Q \supset R)$	A
2	2.	$\sim P$	A
1, 2	3.	$Q \supset R$	1, 2 $\vee$-Syllogism

As another example, we first present a proof of the derived inference rule for contraposition, which states that $P \supset Q \vdash \sim Q \supset \sim P$, and then compare the more complex proof for an instance of the equivalent form:

1	1.	$P \supset Q$	A
2	2.	$\sim Q$	A ($\supset$I)
3	3.	P	A ($\sim$IE)
1, 3	4.	Q	1, 3 $\supset$E
2	5.	$\sim Q$	2 R
1, 2	6.	$\sim P$	3–5 $\sim$IE
1	7.	$\sim Q \supset \sim P$	2–6 $\supset$I

We have just proved contraposition. However, having once proved it, why not use it to make some proofs shorter and less complicated? Consider the proof of the deductively valid sequent, $\sim (P \mathbin{\&} \sim R) \supset (Q \vee S) \vdash \sim (Q \vee S) \supset (P \mathbin{\&} \sim R)$. Relying on our derived inference rule, we can present the proof in only two steps instead of the much longer format we would otherwise require in order to duplicate the reasoning incorporated in the previous proof:

1	1.	$\sim (P \mathbin{\&} \sim R) \supset (Q \vee S)$	A
2	2.	$\sim (Q \vee S) \supset (P \mathbin{\&} \sim R)$	1 Contraposition

It is useful to be able to recognize logical forms in more complex wffs and sequents. A proof system that allows derived inference rules encourages this recognition at the same time that it makes tedious proofs more straightforward.

The disadvantage in using derived rules, as proofs are permitted to move increasingly further away from the foundational assumption, intelim, and derived reiteration and double-negation rules, is that the proofs, although logically valid and more compact, potentially become less intuitively informative the more they are removed from their immediate formal semantic roots in the truth table definitions of the five propositional connectives.

For this reason, and because interesting proofs using only the most primitive rules require more ingenuity and insight into basic logical structure than proofs involving an open-ended set of complex derived rules, we shall not em-

For purposes of illustration, having presented examples of proofs involving such derived rules, all future proofs are done using only the 12 basic inference rules.

phasize or strongly encourage using any derived inference rules other than R and DN in presenting and explaining proofs. We can nevertheless use derived inference rules in solving the problems in the exercises, provided that we have already actually proven the sequents to which we are appealing as derived rules. All the proofs we shall ever need to give can be elegantly presented by means of the 12 rules, and the derivations that result exhibit an inferential structure that is more directly tied to the truth table interpretations of the propositional connectives.

To Check Your Understanding 5.6

Use truth trees to confirm these sequents' validity; then give natural deduction proofs of each valid sequent using the assumption, derived, and intelim rules A, R, DN &I, &E, ∨I, ∨E, ⊃I, ⊃E, ~IE, ≡I, and ≡E. Try solving the problems again using derived natural deduction rules from any of the previous proofs or exercises you have already solved:

1. P ⊢ (P & Q) ∨ (P & ~Q)
2. ~(P ∨ ~Q) ⊢ P ⊃ (~Q & R)
3. P ≡ (Q ∨ R), P ≡ ~Q ⊢ P ≡ R
4. (~P & ~Q) & (P ∨ ~R), Q ≡ ~R ⊢ ~~P
5. (P ∨ Q) ⊃ (R ≡ ~~S) ⊢ ~~Q ⊃ (~S ⊃ ~R)
6. (P ⊃ ~Q) & (Q ⊃ ~R), S ⊃ Q ⊢ S ⊃ (~P & ~R)

For purposes of comparison, the following is a complete list of the 12 natural deduction rules for our system of propositional logic:

**NATURAL DEDUCTION RULES
FOR SYMBOLIC PROPOSITIONAL LOGIC**

1. *Assumption* (A)
   Any proposition can be introduced at any step in any proof as a given assumption or an auxiliary assumption to begin a subproof.
   (Foundational rule)

   ⊢ ℙ   A

2. *Conjunction introduction* (&I)
   From ℙ and ℚ we can validly deduce ℙ & ℚ.
   (Intelim rule)

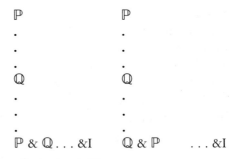

3. *Conjunction elimination* (&E)
   From $\mathbb{P} \,\&\, \mathbb{Q}$ we can validly deduce $\mathbb{P}$ (and/or $\mathbb{Q}$).
   (Intelim rule)

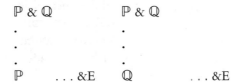

4. *Disjunction introduction* (∨I)
   From $\mathbb{P}$ (or $\mathbb{Q}$) we can validly deduce $\mathbb{P} \vee \mathbb{Q}$.
   (Intelim rule)

5. *Disjunction elimination* (∨E)
   From $\mathbb{P} \vee \mathbb{Q}$, and a proof of $\mathbb{R}$ from (auxiliary) assumption $\mathbb{P}$ and a proof
   of $\mathbb{R}$ from (auxiliary) assumption $\mathbb{Q}$, we can validly deduce $\mathbb{R}$. (The auxiliary assumption numbers for auxiliary assumptions $\mathbb{P}$ and $\mathbb{Q}$ are discharged from the assumption column when the rule is invoked.)
   (Intelim subproof rule)

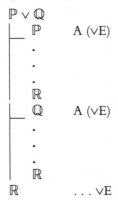

6. *Conditional introduction* (⊃I)
   From a proof of Q from (auxiliary) assumption ℙ, we can validly deduce
   the conditional ℙ ⊃ Q. (The auxiliary assumption number for auxiliary
   assumption ℙ is discharged from the assumption column when the rule
   is invoked.)
   (Intelim subproof rule)

   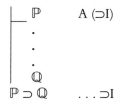

7. *Conditional elimination* (⊃E)
   From ℙ and ℙ ⊃ Q we can validly deduce Q.
   (Intelim rule)

   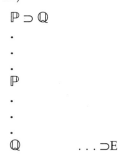

8. *Negation introduction/elimination* (reductio ad absurdum) (~IE)
   From a proof of the contradiction Q, ~Q from (auxiliary) assumption
   ℙ (~ℙ), we can validly deduce ~ℙ (ℙ). [The auxiliary assumption num-
   ber for auxiliary assumption ℙ (~ℙ) is discharged from the assumption
   column when the rule is invoked.]
   (Intelim subproof rule)

   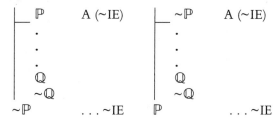

9. *Biconditional introduction* (≡I)
   From a proof of Q from (auxiliary) assumption ℙ, and of ℙ from (auxiliary) assumption Q, we can validly deduce ℙ ≡ Q. (The auxiliary assumption numbers for auxiliary assumptions ℙ and Q are discharged
   from the assumption column when the rule is invoked.)
   (Intelim subproof rule)

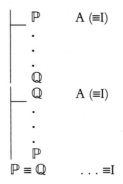

10. *Biconditional elimination* (≡E)
    From ℙ (ℚ) and ℙ ≡ ℚ we can validly deduce ℚ (ℙ).
    (Intelim rule)

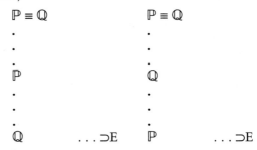

11. *Reiteration* (R)
    Any proposition occurring in a proof or subproof can be repeated in
    that proof or any more deeply nested subproof it contains (but cannot
    be repeated in less deeply nested subproofs nor in the main proof).
    (Derived rule)

    ℙ
    .
    .
    .
    ℙ   . . . R

12. *Double negation* (DN)
    From any proposition ℙ we can validly deduce ~~ℙ and conversely.
    (Derived rule)

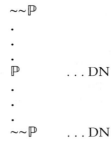

Proving Tautologies

Tautologies and deductively valid sequents can be proved by means of the natural deduction rules.

The proof of a tautology involves no given assumptions but must be undertaken using only auxiliary assumptions in subproofs, all of which must be finally exited and the auxiliary assumptions discharged from the assumption column in the final line of the proof.

Sequents that begin with the turnstile '⊢' and have no propositions written as given assumptions to the left of the turnstile are tautologies or theorems of logic. When these are correctly proved, they rest on no assumptions at all since none are given to use in solving the proof, and therefore they have no assumption numbers in the assumption column of the final step. This means that in their derivations we can use only auxiliary assumptions, which by the end of the proof must all be discharged. The final conclusion of the correct proof of a tautology for the same reason must be brought completely outside of all subproof spines to appear written below and left or outside of the leftmost spine as the original subproof is exited. We consider a typical example in detail.

■ *Demonstration 22:* **Natural Deduction Proof of Tautology** ■

PROBLEM: To prove a tautology by natural deduction rules.

TAUTOLOGY: ⊢ P ⊃ (P ⊃ P)

A tautology has no given assumptions, shown by the absence of wffs to the left of the inference indicator. We cannot set up the proof until we have a preliminary idea of what auxiliary assumptions to make in applying appropriate subproof rules. For this, we must begin with at least a provisional strategy.

STEP 1:   *Plan a proof strategy*

We notice by the fewest parentheses rule that the conclusion of the tautology has the leftmost conditional as its main connective. This means that to prove the conclusion we will probably need to use ⊃I. If we are going to use ⊃I, then we must set up a subproof in which we auxiliary assume the antecedent of the conditional we are trying to prove and then deduce the conditional's consequent. The antecedent is P, and the consequent is a conditional of the form P ⊃ P. The proof will then consist of two nested applications of ⊃I subproofs; after exiting the second, the conclusion will stand outside of both subproof spines and its assumption column will contain no assumption numbers, indicating that the proof of the tautology rests on no given assumptions.

STEP 2:   *Make an appropriate auxiliary assumption to begin a subproof*

We auxiliary assume P to set up a subproof for purposes of ⊃I, with the idea of deducing the consequent of the conditional within the subproof and then bringing the corresponding conditional out of the subproof:

$$1 \quad 1. \quad \lfloor \quad P \qquad A\,(\supset I)$$

STEP 3:   *Apply the appropriate natural deduction rules to continue the proof*
As we turn our attention to the consequent of the conditional tautology, we see that it is a conditional. If we are going to prove it, we must auxiliary assume its antecedent in another more deeply nested subproof:

```
1    1. │  P        A (⊃I)
2    2. │  │  P      A (⊃I)
```

The consequent of the second ⊃I subproof is easily obtained by reiteration from step 2 (or 1):

```
1    1. │  P        A (⊃I)
2    2. │  │  P      A (⊃I)
2    3. │  │  P      2 R
```

The rule for ⊃I now permits the deduction of the conditional that constitutes the consequent of the conditional tautology as a whole. We derive:

```
1    1. │  P        A (⊃I)
2    2. │  │  P      A (⊃I)
2    3. │  │  P      2 R
1    4. │  P ⊃ P     2–3 ⊃I
```

STEP 4:   *Complete the proof*
The proof of the tautology is completed when we deduce the conditional that has P as its antecedent, auxiliary assumed in step 1, and the conditional we have just proved P ⊃ P as its consequent. When we have done this, we will have obtained a conclusion that according to the ⊃I subproof rule does not rest on any given assumptions but appears only below the discontinuation of the outermost subproof spine and with no assumption numbers in its assumption column. The justification column is annotated as previously explained, referring to the range of subproof steps in the first ⊃I subproof:

```
1    1. │  P                A (⊃I)
2    2. │  │  P              A (⊃I)
2    3. │  │  P              2 R
1    4. │  P ⊃ P             2–3 ⊃I
     5. P ⊃ (P ⊃ P)          1–4 ⊃I
```

The proof of a tautology as opposed to a valid argument sequent is easily discernible in a correctly written proof. The first indication is that there are no given assumptions but only auxiliary assumptions, as shown by the parenthetical notations attaching to any and all applications of assumption rule A. The second indication is that when the proof is complete, the final conclusion does not rest on any assumptions but is withdrawn from the main subproof, as the foreshortened spine in the last proof line shows and by the fact that the assumption column for the last line of the proof contains no assumption numbers.

To Check Your Understanding 5.7 ──────────────────────────────────■

Use truth trees to confirm that the following wffs are tautologies; then give natural deduction proofs of each tautology using the assumption, derived, and intelim rules A, R, DN, &I, &E, ∨I, ∨E, ⊃I, ⊃E, ~IE, ≡I, and ≡E:

1. ⊢ (P ⊃ Q) ∨ (Q ⊃ R)
2. ⊢ ((P ⊃ Q) ⊃ P) ⊃ P
3. ⊢ ((P ⊃ ~Q) & Q) ⊃ ~P
4. ⊢ (P & Q) ≡ (P & (P ≡ Q))
5. ⊢ (P ⊃ R) ⊃ ((Q ⊃ R) ⊃ ((P ∨ Q) ⊃ R))
6. ⊢ ~(~P & R) ≡ ((P ∨ ~R) & ((~P ⊃ P) ⊃ P))
7. ⊢ ((((P ⊃ R) & (Q ⊃ R)) & ((~P ⊃ ~R) & (~Q ⊃ ~R))) ⊃ (P ≡ Q)

■

Proof Strategy Hints

It is only possible to prove tautologies and deductively valid sequents.

We can only give proofs of tautologies and valid sequents. It is impossible by correctly following the natural deduction rules to give proofs of propositions other than tautologies or of deductively invalid sequents. If we are successful in obtaining a natural deduction proof for a proposition or argument sequent, then we have shown that the proposition is a tautology and the argument is a valid sequent. But from the fact that we are unable after serious effort to provide a proof of a proposition or argument, it is possible but by no means follows that the proposition is not a tautology, or that the argument is not a valid sequent. It might mean only that we have not tried hard enough or been clever enough to discover the proof. The best method for determining this, before we devote energy to working out a natural deduction proof, is to apply truth tables or trees. We can know, although we shall not try to prove it here, that if a decision method reveals that a proposition is a tautology or an argument is a valid sequent, then we may proceed with confidence that there must exist a valid natural deduction proof by which the logical truth of the tautology or deductive validity of the sequent are formally demonstrated. When in doubt about the provability of a proposition or argument sequent, we should settle the issue first by truth table or truth tree before attempting a natural deduction proof.

Natural deduction proofs are not a mechanical technique like truth tables or truth trees but rather an art like translation from ordinary language into symbolic logic.

Proof discovery in natural deduction systems is an art, like translation, rather than a mechanical procedure, like truth tables or truth trees. We arrive at the proof of a tautology or valid sequent by using the natural deduction rules correctly and with insight, following a practiced repertoire of strategies, with a fearless trial-and-error attitude and sometimes a bit of luck. Proofs are not always easy to derive. If truth tables or trees reveal that a wff is a tautology or a sequent deductively valid, then we can know that there exists a proof, and perhaps several different proofs, which we need only sufficient patience and ingenuity to discover.

Consider the following analogy. Learning how to solve natural deduction proofs is like learning to play chess. It is one thing to be taught how the pieces move on the board—the bishop diagonally, the rook in straight lines, and so on. This is like learning the intelim rules for natural deduction, the kinds of inferences each rule permits, and the restrictions to be observed. However, merely knowing how the chess pieces move is not enough to know how to play winning chess. For this, we must practice, concentrating on the openings and maneuvers that are likely to win, learning from mistakes to avoid certain traps and to recognize opportunities to make successful plays. The same is true of the skills needed to give correct natural deduction proofs. Through practice and experience, logicians begin to develop an eye for promising configurations in finding proofs, and in this way they refine their logical reasoning abilities. We comment at length on some of the more interesting proofs to follow and provide useful strategy hints and suggestions for approaching more difficult proofs. There is no royal road in natural deduction—no adequate substitute for practice and attention to the details of each proof, a desire to learn from mistakes, and a willingness to struggle with challenging proofs until a correct solution is found. The effort put into this aspect of mastering symbolic logic is well repaid by an increase in reasoning effectiveness, because it is in thinking through the strategies necessary to discover such proofs that we learn to engage in high-level deductive inference.

Discovering a correct natural deduction proof requires strategy, like successful game playing.

As a final games analogy, consider the strategy we might adopt in solving a simple box maze. The maze has an entrance and an exit. We go into the maze at one end and we are supposed to come out at the other.

This is similar to the situation we face in solving natural deduction proofs. We have a way to begin the proof—by setting up and considering the implications of given or auxiliary assumptions. The exit from the maze is analogous to attaining the conclusion we are supposed to reach at the end of the proof. We can approach the solution of proofs from both standpoints—from an understanding of where we are to begin and where we are to end. If we are trying to find our way through a maze, we might first go into the entrance and look around to see where we can go from there. We can move to the right for a certain distance, where we are confronted with several options, but we do not

In working out a natural deduction proof, it is useful to consider both the assumptions, given or auxiliary, with which we can work as the beginning point of the proof, and the conclusion, which we are supposed to derive, as the end.

necessarily know immediately where they will lead. We could go to the left or straight ahead, and each of these choices might have special advantages or disadvantages, ultimately leading to a pathway that will take us through twists and turns to the maze exit or leave us stranded at a dead-end, with nothing to do but back out and try again. As an alternative, we might look at the endpoint of the maze, where we are eventually supposed to emerge. Here, we can also trace a path backward into the maze and see what possibilities exist within the maze structure that will eventually lead us from the entrance to the exit. Again, something analogous is true of proof discovery in natural deduction. We know where we are supposed to end up in the proof—at the conclusion we are required to prove. We can therefore apply our knowledge of how the intelim rules work to reflect on the possibilities that might lead to the conclusions we are asked to derive. If we put information from both of these sources together, we can narrow the choices so that we can imagine the missing steps to take us from the most likely starting places to the best pathway through the maze.

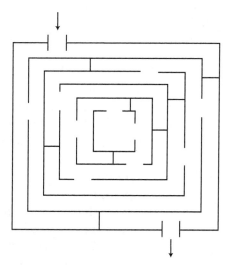

In the examples to follow, this dual approach to problem solving is used to identify a successful proof strategy. It is generally a good idea when setting up a proof to take stock of the information available in the form of given assumptions, if any, and to ask what additional information might be derived by means of the intelim rules. If we are given a conjunction, for example, then we know that we can break its conjuncts apart by the rule &E. If the proposition is a disjunction, it may be necessary to use ∨E by setting up two subproofs with auxiliary assumptions for each of the disjuncts and trying to derive identical conclusions. If we are given a conditional, we know that we can detach the consequent by ⊃E only if we have the antecedent available with which to work, and so on. We should also take note of the conclusion we are asked to prove.

The main connective of the assumptions and conclusions involved in a natural deduction proof often suggests a fruitful strategy.

What strategies does it suggest? If we are asked to prove a proposition, the main connective of which is a conditional, then we might imagine that the best strategy will be to undertake a subproof by auxiliary assuming the antecedent of the conditional and trying to prove the consequent so that we can derive the conditional by ⊃I. If we are supposed to prove a disjunction, we might have the best success by first proving one of the disjuncts and then using ∨I. For negated assumptions or negated conclusions, we cannot use any of our intelim rules to unpack their propositional components because the negation, if it ranges over the entire expression, stands guard, so to speak, over their content. If nothing more likely occurs to us, then we might try a ~IE strategy, assuming the negation of what we need to prove from the three categories of strategy hints discussed previously, working toward a subproof contradiction and deriving the conclusion or some useful part of the proof's conclusion. There are endless possibilities that cannot be fully anticipated here that we learn about through practice simply by doing proofs.

Valid Sequent and Tautology Proofs

The following derivations show proofs in several styles and degrees of difficulty. By studying them, you will see why each assumption is introduced, and how each step in the proof is justified by the inference rules.

For extra practice, do truth trees to test each of the propositions and arguments to make sure they are tautologies or valid sequents before you attempt their natural deduction proofs. To help if you are having trouble working the exercises on your own, try using the following samples as silent tutors. Cover up the entire proof except for the problem statement with a loose sheet of paper, and try to work it through on your own. If you cannot decide how to begin, expose just the first line of the proof as a hint, and try to figure out the remainder for yourself, comparing your answer when you are done. If this is still not enough, or if you get stuck along the way, try exposing the second line, and so on, until you reach a point at which you are sufficiently confident that you can do the proofs entirely by yourself at all levels of difficulty.

The best way to learn how to discover natural deduction proofs is by studying and trying to solve many different kinds of problems.

1. P ⊃ (Q ⊃ R) ⊢ (P & Q) ⊃ R

1	1.	P ⊃ (Q ⊃ R)	A
2	2.	P & Q	A (⊃I)
2	3.	P	2 &E
2	4.	Q	2 &E
1, 2	5.	Q ⊃ R	1, 3 ⊃E
1, 2	6.	R	4, 5 ⊃E
1	7.	(P & Q) ⊃ R	2–6 ⊃I

2. (P & Q) ⊃ R ⊢ P ⊃ (Q ⊃ R)

1	1.	(P & Q) ⊃ R	A
2	2.	P	A (⊃I)
3	3.	Q	A (⊃I)
2, 3	4.	P & Q	2, 3 &I
1, 2, 3	5.	R	1, 4 ⊃E
1, 2	6.	Q ⊃ R	3–5 ⊃I
1	7.	P ⊃ (Q ⊃ R)	2–6 ⊃I

3. Q ⊃ R ⊢ (P ∨ Q) ⊃ (P ∨ R)

Many natural deduction proofs require several nestings of subproofs within subproofs.

1	1.	Q ⊃ R	A
2	2.	P ∨ Q	A (⊃I)
3	3.	P	A (∨E)
3	4.	P ∨ R	3 ∨I
5	5.	Q	A (∨E)
1, 5	6.	R	1, 5 ⊃E
1, 5	7.	P ∨ R	6 ∨I
1, 2	8.	P ∨ R	2, 3–4, 5–7 ∨E
1	9.	(P ∨ Q) ⊃ (P ∨ R)	2–8 ⊃I

4. P ∨ (Q ∨ R) ⊢ Q ∨ (P ∨ R)

1	1.	P ∨ (Q ∨ R)	A
2	2.	P	A (∨E)
2	3.	P ∨ R	2 ∨I
2	4.	Q ∨ (P ∨ R)	3 ∨I
5	5.	Q ∨ R	A (∨E)
6	6.	Q	A (∨E)
6	7.	Q ∨ (P ∨ R)	6 ∨I
8	8.	R	A (∨E)
8	9.	P ∨ R	8 ∨I
8	10.	Q ∨ (P ∨ R)	9 ∨I
5	11.	Q ∨ (P ∨ R)	5, 6–7, 8–10 ∨E
1	12.	Q ∨ (P ∨ R)	1, 2–4, 5–11 ∨E

5. (P & Q) ≡ P ⊢ P ⊃ Q

1	1.	(P & Q) ≡ P	A
2	2.	P	A (⊃I)
1, 2	3.	P & Q	1, 2 ≡E
1, 2	4.	Q	3 &E
1	5.	P ⊃ Q	2–4 ⊃I

6. P ⊃ Q ⊢ ~(P & ~Q)

1	1.	P ⊃ Q	A
2	2.	P & ~Q	A (~IE)
2	3.	P	2 &E
2	4.	~Q	2 &E
1, 2	5.	Q	1, 3 ⊃E
1	6.	~(P & ~Q)	2–5 ~IE

7. ~(P & ~Q) ⊢ P ⊃ Q

1	1.	~(P & ~Q)	A
2	2.	P	A (⊃I)
3	3.	~Q	A (~IE)
2, 3	4.	P & ~Q	2, 3 &I
1, 2, 3	5.	~(P & ~Q)	1 R
1, 2	6.	Q	3–5 ~IE
1	7.	P ⊃ Q	2–6 ⊃I

Now we prove the valid sequents we tested by truth tree method in Chapter 4. Seeing how the same problems can be solved by different techniques in symbolic logic demonstrates how related formal methods converge on the same set of results. We confine our remarks only to proofs that seem especially tricky or instructive.

Any sequent or wff that is confirmed by truth tables or truth trees to be deductively valid or a tautology can be proved by natural deduction in propositional logic.

8. S ⊃ C, A ⊃ ~C ⊢ S ⊃ ~A

1	1.	S ⊃ C	A
2	2.	A ⊃ ~C	A
3	3.	S	A (⊃I)
4	4.	A	A (~IE)
1, 3	5.	C	1, 3 ⊃E
2, 4	6.	~C	2, 4 ⊃E
1, 2, 3	7.	~A	4–6 ~IE
1, 2	8.	S ⊃ ~A	3–7 ⊃I

A common useful strategy in proving conditionals is to auxiliary assume the antecedent in a subproof for conditional introduction and to assume the negation of the consequent in a subproof for negation intelim.

This and the previous problem involve a fairly common strategy in natural deduction. When we are required to prove a conditional, it is an obvious move to auxiliary assume the antecedent and try to derive the consequent. Where no other more likely method obtains for deriving the consequent, it is often useful to auxiliary assume the negation of the consequent, working toward a contradiction, and then deriving the consequent to which the antecedent can be attached in a final application of ⊃I. The important point is that, having made an auxiliary assumption of the antecedent of a conditional for purposes of ⊃I, the consequent remaining to be proved can be treated in effect as a new problem, and we can approach it with the same set of strategies using more deeply nested subproofs.

9. T ⊃ F, (F & M) ∨ T ⊢ ~M ⊃ T

1	1.	T ⊃ F	A
2	2.	(F & M) ∨ T	A
3	3.	~M	A (⊃I)
4	4.	F & M	A (∨E)
5	5.	~T	A (~IE)
4	6.	M	4 &E
3	7.	~M	3 R
3, 4	8.	T	5–7 ~IE
9	9.	T	A (∨E)
9	10.	T	9 R
2, 3	11.	T	2, 4–8, 9–10 ∨E
2	12.	~M ⊃ T	3–11 ⊃I

Reiteration can be used to repeat the same wff in the conclusion as in the auxiliary assumption of a disjunction elimination subproof, if the conclusion happens to occur as one of the disjuncts in the disjunction.

This proof is interesting not only because of its use of reiteration rule R but also because, as can be seen from the assumption column for step 11, assumption 1 is not needed for the conclusion but is redundant. If for some reason we want to include the assumption in the derivation of the conclusion, we can do so easily by conjoining the assumption in step 1 with the conclusion in step 11 using &I and then extracting the conclusion once again by &E so that the same proposition rests on all three assumptions 1, 2, and 3.

10. G ⊃ U, E ⊃ I, ~G ⊃ E ⊢ U ∨ I

1	1.	G ⊃ U	A
2	2.	E ⊃ I	A
3	3.	~G ⊃ E	A
4	4.	~(U ∨ I)	A (~IE)
5	5.	G	A (~IE)
1	6.	U	1, 5 ⊃E
1	7.	U ∨ I	6 ∨I
4	8.	~(U ∨ I)	4 R
1, 4	9.	~G	5–8 ~IE
1, 3, 4	10.	E	3, 9 ⊃E
1, 2, 3, 4	11.	I	2, 10 ⊃E
1, 2, 3, 4	12.	U ∨ I	11 ∨I
1, 2, 3	13.	U ∨ I	4–12 ~IE

This proof illustrates the occasional need to rely on the third guideline for introducing auxiliary assumptions for ~IE. Here, it is expedient not only to assume the negation of the entire conclusion we are trying to prove, but also that of a useful part of another proposition. There are several different ways to prove this sequent. Can you see another strategy that will also work?

Negation intelim sometimes requires several auxiliary assumptions in several nested applications.

Proofs can become much longer and more complicated than these. The best way to develop a proof strategy is to break the problem down into subtasks and work through each in turn. As we solve more problems in logic, we acquire skills and insight into logical structures that help make proofs increasingly easier. The following is an example from the most complicated argument sequent that we tested for validity by the truth tree method in Chapter 4. It is the formal proof of the validity of Lactantius' trilemma or problem of evil argument against the existence of God:

11. G ⊃ ((S & P) & B), E, E ⊃ (~K ∨ ((K & ~A) ∨ ((K & A) & ~C))),
    ~K ⊃ ~S, ~A ⊃ ~P, ~C ⊃ ~B ⊢ ~G

1	1.	G ⊃ ((S & P) & B)	A
2	2.	E	A
3	3.	E ⊃ (~K ∨ ((K & ~A) ∨ ((K & A) & ~C)))	A
4	4.	~K ⊃ ~S	A
5	5.	~A ⊃ ~P	A
6	6.	~C ⊃ ~B	A
2, 3	7.	~K ∨ ((K & ~A) ∨ ((K & A) & ~C))	2, 3 ⊃E
8	8.	G	A (~IE)
1, 8	9.	(S & P) & B	1, 8 ⊃E
10	10.	~K	A (∨E)
4, 10	11.	~S	4, 10 ⊃E
1, 8	12.	S & P	9 &E
1, 8	13.	S	12 &E
14	14.	G	A (~IE)
1, 8	15.	S	13 R
4, 10	16.	~S	11 R
1, 4, 8, 10	17.	~G	14–16 ~IE
18	18.	(K & ~A) ∨ ((K & A) & ~C)	A (∨E)
19	19.	K & ~A	A (∨E)
19	20.	~A	19 &E
5, 19	21.	~P	5, 20 ⊃E
1, 8	22.	S & P	9 &E
1, 8	23.	P	22 &E
24	24.	G	A (~IE)
1, 8	25.	P	23 R
5, 19	26.	~P	21 R
1, 5, 8, 19	27.	~G	24–26 ~IE

Natural deduction proofs of complicated sequents or tautologies can extend over many steps, with many layers of internested subproofs.

28	28.	(K & A) & ~C	A (∨E)
28	29.	~C	28 &E
6, 28	30.	~B	6, 28 ⊃E
1, 8	31.	B	9 &E
32	32.	G	A (~IE)
1, 8	33.	B	31 R
6, 28	34.	~B	30 R
1, 6, 8, 28	35.	~G	32–34 ~IE
1, 5, 6, 8, 18	36.	~G	18, 19–27, 28–35 ∨E
1, 2, 3, 4, 5, 6, 8	37.	~G	7, 10–17, 18–36 ∨E
1, 2, 3, 4, 5, 6	38.	~G	8–37 ~IE

An interesting aspect of this proof is its use of several nested applications of ~IE. It is relatively easy to derive a contradiction from the wealth of given assumptions in the proof, together with the auxiliary assumption G made for purposes of ~IE. The question is what use to make of the contradictions. There are several possibilities, dictated in the main by the fact that the contradictions appear within the context of several nested applications of ∨E. For this rule, it is necessary to derive precisely matching conclusions in each of the subproofs. Since contradictions are rife within the disjunction elimination subproofs, it seems natural to take advantage of them by reasserting auxiliary assumption G for ~IE and then reiterating the contradictory propositions deduced in each part in order to obtain ~G in identical ∨E subproof conclusions. The proof might be shortened by using &E to bring the conjuncts required for contradiction directly into the ~IE subproofs rather than exhibiting them first in the ∨E subproofs and then reiterating them.

Natural deduction proofs of tautologies are further illustrated by proving a series of tautologies that we have already confirmed by truth tables and truth trees. We continue numbering the examples from where we left off with the previous proof.

12. ⊢ (P ⊃ Q) ⊃ (~P ∨ Q)

1	1.	P ⊃ Q	A (⊃I)
2	2.	~(~P ∨ Q)	A (~IE)
3	3.	P	A (~IE)
1, 3	4.	Q	1, 3 ⊃E
1, 3	5.	~P ∨ Q	4 ∨I
2	6.	~(~P ∨ Q)	2 R
1, 2	7.	~P	3–6 ~IE
1, 2	8.	~P ∨ Q	7 ∨I
1	9.	~P ∨ Q	2–8 ~IE
	10.	(P ⊃ Q) ⊃ (~P ∨ Q)	1–9 ⊃I

Proofs of tautologies have no given assumptions with which to begin and, when complete, must be shown to depend on no assumptions whatsoever.

13. ⊢ (P ⊃ Q) ≡ (~Q ⊃ ~P)

1	1.	P ⊃ Q	A (≡I)
2	2.	~Q	A (⊃I)
3	3.	P	A (~IE)
1, 3	4.	Q	1, 3 ⊃E
2	5.	~Q	2 R
1, 2	6.	~P	3–5 ~IE
1	7.	~Q ⊃ ~P	2–6 ⊃I
8	8.	~Q ⊃ ~P	A (≡I)
9	9.	P	A (⊃I)
10	10.	~Q	A (~IE)
8, 10	11.	~P	8, 10 ⊃E
9	12.	P	9 R
8, 9	13.	Q	10–12 ~IE
8	14.	P ⊃ Q	9–13 ⊃I
	15.	(P ⊃ Q) ≡ (~Q ⊃ ~P)	1–7, 8–14 ≡I

Assumption columns and exiting from all subproof spines with no main proof spine show that a tautology proof is complete.

14. ⊢ (P ⊃ (Q ⊃ P)) ≡ (~Q ⊃ (P ⊃ (~Q ∨ P)))

1	1.	P ⊃ (Q ⊃ P)	A (≡I)
2	2.	~Q	A (⊃I)
3	3.	P	A (⊃I)
3	4.	~Q ∨ P	3 ∨I
	5.	P ⊃ (~Q ∨ P)	3–4 ⊃I
	6.	~Q ⊃ (P ⊃ (~Q ∨ P))	2–5 ⊃I
7	7.	~Q ⊃ (P ⊃ (~Q ∨ P))	A (≡I)
8	8.	P	A (⊃I)
9	9.	Q	A (⊃I)
8	10.	P	8 R
8	11.	Q ⊃ P	9–10 ⊃I
	12.	P ⊃ (Q ⊃ P)	8–11 ⊃I
	13.	(P ⊃ (Q ⊃ P)) ≡ (~Q ⊃ (P ⊃ (~Q ∨ P)))	1–6, 7–12 ≡I

The remaining tautology demonstrated by truth trees in Chapter 4 is the equivalence (P ⊃ Q) ≡ (~P ∨ Q). However, since the first half of this has already been proved in problem 12, and since we have already discussed several examples of ≡I, we shall simply prove the converse conditional.

15. ⊢ (~P ∨ Q) ⊃ (P ⊃ Q)

1	1.	~P ∨ Q	A (⊃I)
2	2.	P	A (⊃I)
3	3.	~P	A (∨E)
4	4.	~Q	A (~IE)
2	5.	P	2 R
3	6.	~P	3 R
2, 3	7.	Q	4–6 ~IE
8	8.	Q	A (∨E)
8	9.	Q	9 R
1, 2	10.	Q	1, 2–7, 8–9 ∨E
1	11.	P ⊃ Q	2–10 ⊃I
	12.	(~P ∨ Q) ⊃ (P ⊃ Q)	1–11 ⊃I

Tautologies, as logical truths, do not depend on the truth of any other wff.

To Check Your Understanding 5.8

Use truth trees to confirm that these sequents are deductively valid and wffs are tautologies; then give natural deduction proofs of each valid sequent using the assumption, derived, and intelim rules A, R, DN, &I, &E, ∨I, ∨E, ~IE, ⊃I, ⊃E, ≡I, and ≡E:

1. P ∨ (~P & Q), (~P ⊃ Q) ⊃ R ⊢ R
2. (P ∨ Q) ⊃ (R & ~P), Q ∨ R, ~R ⊢ ~P
3. ~P ⊃ ((R ∨ Q) ⊃ (S & T)), (T ∨ U) ⊃ ~V ⊢ ~P ⊃ (Q ⊃ ~V)
4. (P & ~Q) ⊃ R, P ⊃ ~Q, (~S & ~~R) ⊃ ~T ⊢ P ⊃ (~S ⊃ ~T)
5. ~(~P & ~Q) ∨ ~(~R & ~S), ~Q & ~S, ~T ⊃ (~S ⊃ (~R & ~P)) ⊢ T
6. P ⊃ (~Q & (~R ∨ ~S)), T ∨ U, ~V, (Q ∨ T) & ((R ∨ U) & (~S ∨ V)), P ⊢ ~S
7. ⊢ P ⊃ ((Q & ~P) ⊃ R)
8. ⊢ (P ∨ Q) ∨ ~(~Q ⊃ P)
9. ⊢ P ≡ (((P & Q) ∨ (P & ~Q)) ∨ ~(P ⊃ Q))

Summary: Propositional Natural Deduction Proofs

We can prove any truth functional tautology or valid sequent in propositional logic by using our 12 natural deduction rules. The rules include a foundational assumption rule, 9 intelim or introduction and elimination rules for each of the five truth functional propositional connectives (with negation introduction and elimination combined in a single rule), and 2 derived rules for reiteration and double negation. Proofs require several kinds of documentation to keep track of the given and auxiliary assumptions and inference rules on which each proposition in a proof depends. Proof discovery is not a purely mechanical technique. We approach derivations in natural deduction as requiring a winning game-playing strategy, in which we master the basic rules and practice working problems to acquire proof discovery skills. Proofs of valid sequents are not complete until all auxiliary assumptions, if any, have been discharged and the conclusion is shown to depend only on given assumptions; proofs of tautologies involve no given assumptions and are not complete until all auxiliary assumptions are discharged.

Key Words:

natural deduction proof
foundational assumption rule
assumption column
proof line number column
graphic proof and subproof spine
proposition (proof step) column
justification column
given assumption
auxiliary assumption
subproof
intelim rule
paradigms
assumption number
derived rule
assumption (A)
reiteration (R)
double negation (DN)
conjunction introduction (&I)

conjunction elimination (&E)
disjunction introduction (∨I)
logical addition
disjunction elimination (∨E)
subproof rule
constructive dilemma
conditional introduction (⊃I)
conditional elimination (⊃E)
modus ponendo ponens
negation introduction/elimination
  (~IE)
reductio ad absurdum
biconditional introduction
biconditional elimination
modus tollendo tollens
disjunctive syllogism
contraposition

Exercises

I: Propositional Proof Concepts   Give a correct concise statement of each of the following concepts; where appropriate, give an illustration of each that does not appear in the book:

1. Natural deduction proof
2. Foundational rule

3. Given assumption
4. Auxiliary assumption
5. Introduction rule; elimination rule; intelim rule
6. Valid sequent proof; tautology proof
7. Subproof
8. Entering, exiting a subproof
9. Derived rule
10. Reiteration; double negation

II: Proofs of Deductively Valid Sequents   Give natural deduction proofs of the following valid argument sequents in propositional logic; for extra practice, verify by truth tree method that each sequent is valid before proceeding to its proof:

1. ~P ⊃ (Q & ~R), R ⊢ P
2. A ⊃ (B ⊃ C), ~D ⊃ (A ∨ C), A ⊃ B ⊢ C ∨ D
3. F ⊃ G, H ⊃ F, ~H ⊃ (I ∨ J) ⊢ ~G ⊃ (I ∨ J)
4. (P ⊃ (Q ∨ R)) ⊃ (S ⊃ P), ~P ⊢ ~S
5. ~M ⊃ ~(N ∨ O), ~(N & ~P) ⊢ ~N ∨ (P & M)
6. ~C ∨ D, E ⊃ ~F ⊢ (E ∨ C) ⊃ (~F ∨ D)
7. (~P ∨ Q) ⊃ (S & R), (S ∨ T) ⊃ U ⊢ ~P ⊃ U
8. (F ∨ G) ⊃ ((H ∨ I) ⊃ J), ~K ⊃ (~L & ~J) ⊢ F ⊃ (H ⊃ K)
9. (A ∨ B) ∨ ~C, ~(D & ~B) ⊃ ~(A ∨ B), C ⊢ A & C
10. P ⊃ ~Q, R ⊃ (P & ~Q), Q ⊢ ~R
11. M & ~N, O ⊃ ~(P ∨ Q), ~R ⊃ ~(~P ∨ ~Q), R ⊃ (T & U), Q ⊃ V, ~V ⊢ T
12. (P ≡ Q) & (P ≡ R) ⊢ P ≡ (Q ∨ R)
13. S ⊃ (T ≡ ~R), ~Q, (Q ∨ ~R) ⊃ ~T, (T ≡ ~R) ⊃ (Q & (T ∨ S)), R ⊃ Q ⊢ S ⊃ (~T & ~R)
14. A ⊃ ~B, (A ∨ C) & ~D, (C ∨ E) ≡ ~B ⊢ ~B
15. P ⊃ Q, Q ⊃ R, R ⊃ P ⊢ ((Q ≡ R) & (R ≡ P)) & (P ≡ Q)
16. (F ⊃ G) & H, I ∨ (~G ⊃ ~F) ⊢ (G ∨ ~F) ∨ (H & I)
17. ~N ⊃ ~M, O, P ⊃ (~N ∨ ~O) ⊢ ~M ∨ ~P
18. C & ~D, E ∨ (F ∨ G), (G ⊃ H) & ~H, ~(C ⊃ D) ⊃ ~E ⊢ F
19. A ∨ ~B, B ≡ C, (A ∨ D) ⊃ ~(E & C) ⊢ (B ∨ C) ⊃ ~E
20. ((~(P & Q) ⊃ R) & (~P ∨ R)) ⊃ (R ⊃ ~(T ∨ S)) ⊢ (~T ⊃ S) ⊃ ~R

III: *Proofs of Tautologies*   Give natural deduction proofs of the following tautologies in propositional logic; for extra practice, verify by truth tree method that each proposition is a tautology before proceeding to its proof

1. $\vdash P \lor \sim P$
2. $\vdash (P \;\&\; \sim P) \supset Q$
3. $\vdash Q \supset (P \supset Q)$
4. $\vdash \sim P \supset (P \supset Q)$
5. $\vdash (P \supset (Q \;\&\; \sim Q)) \supset \sim P$
6. $\vdash (P \supset Q) \equiv \sim (P \;\&\; \sim Q)$
7. $\vdash \sim (P \supset Q) \equiv (P \;\&\; \sim Q)$
8. $\vdash (P \supset Q) \equiv (\sim P \lor Q)$
9. $\vdash \sim (P \supset Q) \equiv \sim (\sim P \lor Q)$
10. $\vdash (P \supset Q) \equiv (\sim Q \supset \sim P)$
11. $\vdash \sim (P \supset Q) \equiv \sim (\sim Q \supset \sim P)$
12. $\vdash (P \;\&\; Q) \equiv \sim (P \supset \sim Q)$
13. $\vdash \sim (P \;\&\; Q) \equiv (P \supset \sim Q)$
14. $\vdash (P \;\&\; Q) \equiv \sim (\sim P \lor \sim Q)$
15. $\vdash \sim (P \;\&\; Q) \equiv (\sim P \lor \sim Q)$
16. $\vdash (P \lor Q) \equiv \sim (\sim P \;\&\; \sim Q)$
17. $\vdash \sim (P \lor Q) \equiv (\sim P \;\&\; \sim Q)$
18. $\vdash (P \lor Q) \equiv (\sim P \supset Q)$
19. $\vdash \sim (P \lor Q) \equiv \sim (\sim P \supset Q)$
20. $\vdash (P \equiv Q) \equiv (\sim P \equiv \sim Q)$
21. $\vdash \sim (P \equiv Q) \equiv \sim (\sim P \equiv \sim Q)$
22. $\vdash (P \equiv Q) \equiv ((P \supset Q) \;\&\; (Q \supset P))$
23. $\vdash \sim (P \equiv Q) \equiv \sim ((P \supset Q) \;\&\; (Q \supset P))$
24. $\vdash (P \equiv Q) \equiv ((\sim P \lor Q) \;\&\; (Q \supset P))$
25. $\vdash \sim (P \equiv Q) \equiv \sim ((\sim P \lor Q) \;\&\; (Q \supset P))$
26. $\vdash (P \equiv Q) \equiv ((P \supset Q) \;\&\; (\sim Q \lor P))$
27. $\vdash \sim (P \equiv Q) \equiv \sim ((P \supset Q) \;\&\; (\sim Q \lor P))$
28. $\vdash \sim (P \equiv Q) \equiv \sim ((\sim P \lor Q) \;\&\; (\sim Q \lor P))$
29. $\vdash (P \equiv Q) \equiv (\sim (P \;\&\; \sim Q) \;\&\; (\sim Q \lor P))$
30. $\vdash \sim (P \equiv Q) \equiv \sim (\sim (P \;\&\; \sim Q) \;\&\; (\sim Q \lor P))$
31. $\vdash (P \equiv Q) \equiv ((\sim P \lor Q) \;\&\; \sim (Q \;\&\; \sim P))$

32. ⊢ ~(P ≡ Q) ≡ ~((~P ∨ Q) & ~(Q & ~P))

33. ⊢ (P ≡ Q) ≡ (~(P & ~Q) & ~(Q & ~P))

34. ⊢ ~(P ≡ Q) ≡ ~(~(P & ~Q) & ~(Q & ~P))

35. ⊢ (P ≡ Q) ≡ ((P ⊃ Q) & (~P ⊃ ~Q))

36. ⊢ ~(P ≡ Q) ≡ ~((P ⊃ Q) & (~P ⊃ ~Q))

37. ⊢ (P ≡ Q) ≡ ((P ⊃ Q) & ~(Q & ~P))

38. ⊢ ~(P ≡ Q) ≡ ~((P ⊃ Q) & ~(Q & ~P))

39. ⊢ (P ≡ Q) ≡ (~(P & ~Q) & (Q ⊃ P))

40. ⊢ ~(P ≡ Q) ≡ ~(~(P & ~Q) & (Q ⊃ P))

41. ⊢ (P ≡ Q) ≡ ((~Q ⊃ ~P) & (Q ⊃ P))

42. ⊢ ~(P ≡ Q) ≡ ~((~Q ⊃ ~P) & (Q ⊃ P))

43. ⊢ (P ≡ Q) ≡ (~(P & ~Q) & (Q ⊃ P))

44. ⊢ (P ≡ Q) ≡ ~(~(~P ∨ Q) ∨ ~(~Q ∨ P))

45. ⊢ ~(P ≡ Q) ≡ (~(~P ∨ Q) ∨ ~(~Q ∨ P))

46. ⊢ (P ≡ Q) ≡ ~((P & ~Q) ∨ ~(~Q ∨ P))

47. ⊢ ~(P ≡ Q) ≡ ((P & ~Q) ∨ ~(~Q ∨ P))

48. ⊢ (P ≡ Q) ≡ ~(~(~P ∨ Q) ∨ (Q & ~P))

49. ⊢ ~(P ≡ Q) ≡ (~(~P ∨ Q) ∨ (Q & ~P))

50. ⊢ (P ≡ Q) ≡ ~((P & ~Q) ∨ (Q & ~P))

51. ⊢ ~(P ≡ Q) ≡ ((P & ~Q) ∨ (Q & ~P))

52. ⊢ (P ≡ Q) ≡ ((~Q ⊃ ~P) & (~P ⊃ ~Q))

53. ⊢ ~(P ≡ Q) ≡ ~((~Q ⊃ ~P) & (~P ⊃ ~Q))

54. ⊢ (P ≡ Q) ≡ ~(~(~Q ⊃ ~P) ∨ ~(~P ⊃ ~Q))

55. ⊢ ~(P ≡ Q) ≡ (~(~Q ⊃ ~P) ∨ ~(~P ⊃ ~Q))

IV: Proofs of Deductively Valid Arguments from Ordinary Language Symbolize each of the following valid arguments in propositional logic, verify by truth tree method the validity of your translation (adjusting if necessary to make the symbolization valid), and then give a natural deduction proof of the sequent:

1. If ignorance is bliss, then most people must be ecstatic. From this we must conclude that either most people are (secretly) ecstatic, or ignorance is anything but bliss. (I, E)

2. There is no time to see the Painted Desert, or we will never make it to the Grand Canyon. Either we make it to the Grand Canyon, or we visit Crater National Monument. Obviously, we'll not visit Crater National Monument. So, I'm afraid there's no time to see the Painted Desert. (P, G, C)

3. I will gladly go with you to New York, unless, that is, you take me to see *Cats*. Thus, you'll take me to see *Cats* if you take me to see *Cats* when I gladly go with you to New York. (G, C)

4. If love or money makes the world go around, then beauty keeps the stars in the sky and happiness rules the fish in the sea. Now no one can seriously suppose that happiness rules the fish in the sea. It follows at once that money does not make the world go around. (L, M, B, H)

5. The moon isn't made of green cheese, or I'm a monkey's uncle. If 9 and 9 are 99, then pork comes from a porcupine (Edward Lear). So, if the moon is made of green cheese or 9 and 9 are 99, then either I'm a monkey's uncle or pork comes from a porcupine. (G, M, N, P)

6. When the buzzer goes off, you should take the muffins out of the oven. When you're ready to take the muffins out of the oven, you should not begin to ice them until they've cooled. You should begin to ice the muffins. Therefore, when the buzzer goes off, the muffins should be cooled. (B, M, I, C)

7. The killer did the crime and made his getaway just in case the window was broken from the inside. Now, it's neither the case that the window was broken from the inside nor that the killer failed to commit the crime. I think we can safely conclude, then, Watson, that the killer, hiding somewhere in this very room, has not yet made his getaway. (K, G, B)

8. If either Dr. Jekyll or Mr. Hyde calls for an appointment, please tell him I'm unavailable for professional consultation for the next 3 months. Of course, just between you and me, I will in fact of course be available for professional consultation at least some time during the next 3 months. As a result, it follows that Dr. Jekyll won't call for an appointment. (J, H, A)

9. Luciano takes aspirin only when he has a headache. When Luciano is at the opera, he never has a headache. So, Luciano takes aspirin only when he is not at the opera. (A, H, O)

10. Now look, buddy, the sign says, "Parking for Affengeil customers only." That means you can park here in the lot only if you're doing business at Affengeil's. You obviously aren't doing business at Affengeil's. So, you can't park here and that's that. (P, A)

11. The iceman discovered buried frozen in a glacier in the Alps is more than 5000 years old. Late Stone Age humans in central Europe had an advanced metal technology if, where, if the iceman was found with a copper ax, then he must have obtained it from skilled Stone Age central European metalworkers, but only if the iceman is more than 5000 years old. Therefore, there is no doubt but that late Stone Age humans in central Europe had an advanced metal technology. (I, M, A, S)

12. Either modern science has all the answers or religious mysticism should be our path. If modern science has all the answers, then it will eventually solve all our problems and we do not have to go to church. Now, religious mysticism should not rationally be chosen. Modern science does not have all the answers or mystical experience is visited on us as a gift of grace, only if we have to go to church. Thus, mystical experience is visited on us as a gift of grace and we don't have to go to church. (S, R, C, V, G)

13. Wherever evil lurks, there is also good. For, either there is no evil or there is some good, or there is no good whatsoever. If evil is wronging the good, then there is no good. Yet it's always the case that evil triumphs without a struggle. But we can agree that evil never struggles without there being some good, and, more important, that evil triumphs without a struggle only if evil is wronging the good. Finally, there is no evil. That's why I say that wherever evil lurks, there is also good. (E, G, W, T, S)

14. It's not fair to make me work overtime without extra pay. If the job is important enough to the company to make me work late, it's important enough for them to offer reasonable compensation. If the job isn't important enough to the company to offer reasonable compensation only if the job just plain isn't important enough to make me work late, then I am not being exploited by my employer only if it's fair to make me work overtime without extra pay. That makes it clear as rain that I'm being exploited by my employer. (F, P, L, R, E)

15. Apes can use language only if they are capable of higher thought processes. If apes are capable of higher thought processes, then there must be an ape logic, even if it is just the same as ours. But, of course, if there is an ape logic, then apes can use language. Furthermore, there is no ape logic unless apes cannot use language. From this we infer two vital facts—that apes cannot use language and that there most definitely is no ape logic. (A, T, L)

16. When the truth is found, we shall be happy and free at last. Therefore, if the truth is found we shall be happy at last, and if the truth is found, we shall either be free at last or end our days as rash and foolish skeptics, cursing the darkness we have only created ourselves. (T, H, F, S)

17. It is time to go only when Philip starts dropping hints about his pictures from Italy. But if Margo wants to show home movies of Denmark, we shall change our names and stealthily move out of town. Either it's time to go, or Margo wants to show home movies of Denmark and demonstrate her Bali sword dance. So, either Philip starts dropping hints about his pictures from Italy, or we shall stealthily move out of town. (T, P, D, C, M, S)

18. If the ancient Greeks had defeated the Persians at Marathon, then the credit for victory goes to their genius, esprit de corps, valor, good luck, and the

favor of the gods, where the Greek and Persian armies were evenly matched. Thus, where the ancient Greek and Persian armies were evenly matched, the credit for victory would go to the Greek's having the favor of the gods, at least if they defeated the Persians. (D, G, E, V, L, F, M)

19. Submarine warfare has become obsolete only if air power has superior capability over all naval forces and sonar technology can reveal the exact location of any submerged submarine at sea. If either air power has superior capability over all naval forces or sonar technology can reveal the exact location of any submerged submarine at sea, then it has already become a practical military necessity to dismantle the Navy's nuclear submarine fleet. Ladies and gentlemen, we can only conclude that if submarine warfare is obsolete, then it is a practical military necessity to dismantle the Navy's nuclear submarine fleet. (S, A, R, D)

20. We should always try to help those less fortunate than ourselves. After all, we are not unemployed or not suffering from ill health. Now, if we are not both prevented by circumstances and unable by lack of means, then certainly we should always try to help those less fortunate than ourselves. And, although we are prevented by circumstances only if we are unemployed, we are not unable by lack of means unless we are suffering from ill health. (H, U, S, P, L)

V: Proofs of Valid Argument Sequents and Tautologies from Previous Exercises
Give natural deduction proofs of all the propositions and argument sequents from Chapter 4's Exercises that were determined by truth tree method to be tautologies or logically valid inferences in propositional logic.

VI: Short Answer Questions for Philosophical Reflection

1. What is a proof?
2. Can everything be proved, or must some things be accepted without proof?
3. Why can we not give a correct proof of an invalid argument sequent or of an argument that is not deductively valid?
4. What do we learn from proofs of tautologies and valid sequents that we cannot learn from truth tables or truth trees?
5. What is the relation between the proof of a valid sequent, P, . . . , Q ⊢ R, and a corresponding conditional tautology, ⊢ (P & . . . & Q) ⊃ R?
6. What can we learn about the nature of reasoning from the natural deduction model's foundational free assumption rule? What does the possibility of natural deduction proofs reveal about the freedom of thought in its ability to entertain and draw conclusions from whatever true or false assumptions it chooses?

Part 3

Predicate Logic

If controversies were to arise, there would be no more need of disputation between two philosophers than between two accountants. For it would suffice to take their pencils in their hands, to sit down to their slates, and to say to each other (with a friend as witness, if they liked): Let us calculate.

—Gottfried W. Leibniz, *Die philosophische Schriften,* VII (1875–90)

The logic presented so far concerns only propositional relations, based on truth table definitions of the five propositional connectives, and the concept of a deductively valid argument. We now go beyond propositional logic, using it as a foundation on which to build a system of predicate logic. A predicate logic symbolizes the attribution of properties to objects and quantities of objects, to which propositional logic, limited only to propositional symbols and connectives, is syntactically insensitive. Predicate logic is needed because there are logically true wffs that should count as tautologies and sequents that satisfy the general definition and informal criteria for a deductively valid inference that are not recognized as tautologies or deductively valid sequents in propositional logic. We expand propositional logic to predicate logic by introducing new syntax and semantics, extending the truth tree decision method to predicate logic, and adding natural deduction rules for proving tautologies and deductively valid sequents in predicate logic. Finally, we apply predicate logic to analyze reasoning about logical paradoxes and word problems, the formal theory of relations, the concept of identity, specifically numbered quantities of things, and descriptions featuring the definite article 'the'.

CHAPTER SIX

Predicate Syntax and Semantics

There are two fundamental methods of proving general propositions, one for universal propositions, the other for such as assert existence.
— A. N. Whitehead and Bertrand Russell, *Principia Mathematica* (1910)

AN EXPRESSIVELY MORE COMPLEX predicate logic is defined within the framework of propositional logic. The syntax and semantics of predicate logic make it possible to symbolize logically true wffs that are not tautologies of propositional logic, and deductively valid sequents that are not deductively valid in propositional logic.

Predicate Syntax

Propositional logic is not adequate for all tautologies and deductively valid sequents.

Propositional logic provides the framework and foundation for an expressively more complete predicate logic.

The propositional logic we have developed, with its decision methods and natural deduction proofs, provides a powerful but expressively incomplete symbolic logic. Propositional logic, as the logic of the five propositional connectives, symbolizes only truth functional properties of wffs and sequents.

Propositional logic can identify and prove every tautology and every valid sequence the logic symbolizes. But, there are propositions and arguments whose logical properties cannot be understood in purely truth functional terms and as a result cannot be adequately symbolized in propositional logic. There are tautologies, logically true propositions, that are not tautologies of symbolic propositional logic, and there are arguments that satisfy the intuitive definition of validity but are not deductively valid by virtue of the truth functional properties of their component propositions. We complete our system of elementary symbolic logic by introducing the syntax and semantics, decision methods, and natural deduction rules for an expanded set of wffs and sequents that go beyond the expressive limitations of propositional logic.

We begin by considering an argument that is deductively but not propositionally valid. The example is one that has enjoyed a certain fame in the history of logic:

1. All men are mortal.

2. Socrates is a man.

------

3. Socrates is mortal.

The inference appears valid in the technical but informal sense that if assumptions 1 and 2 are true, then the conclusion in 3 cannot possibly be false. It is logically impossible for all men to be mortal and for Socrates to be a man, but for Socrates not to be mortal. But although the argument, known in classical logic as illustrating one type of *syllogism,* is intuitively valid, it is not propositionally valid by virtue of the truth functional properties of its assumptions and conclusion. If we translate the argument into the notation of propositional logic, then, since the three propositions are each different and contain no propositional connectives, the inference must be symbolized as follows:

There are wffs that satisfy the definition of a tautology but are not recognized as such in propositional logic; there are sequents that satisfy the definition of deductive validity but are not recognized as such in propositional logic.

1. P

2. Q

------

3. R

The argument, formulated as such, is propositionally invalid, as we would see from its truth table or truth tree. This means that the argument, though valid, cannot be identified as deductively valid when symbolized in and using the methods of propositional logic. If we want to represent the formal properties of the argument in such a way that it turns out to be not only intuitively but also formally valid in symbolic logic, then we must add something more to the purely truth functional relations symbolized in propositional logic. We must expand propositional logic into a more powerful system that recognizes the deductive validity of intuitively valid arguments such as the Socrates syllogism.

Predicate logic symbolizes property– object relations, in which properties are predicated of objects.

The validity of the Socrates syllogism involves *properties,* such as being human and being mortal, that are attributed to *objects,* such as Socrates, and the members of a *set of objects,* such as the set of all human beings. The property of being human is predicated of Socrates. The property of being mortal is predicated of all things that have the property of being human. Finally, the conclusion states that the property of being mortal must therefore be truly predicated of Socrates. There are two features of these facts that can be exploited to develop a more expressive symbolism. We can exhibit the internal structure of individual *subject–predicate propositions* if, instead of merely representing them by means of a propositional symbol such as P, Q, R, we adopt a symbolism that explicitly exhibits their *property−object relation* in which a property is attributed to an object or set of objects. In predicate logic, we express property−object relations by attaching a property term or *predicate* to an object term or *constant*. Property−object relations in the simplest cases in predicate logic are thus represented symbolically by *predicate−constant expressions*. Additionally, we require a set of symbolic devices for representing *quantities* of objects that are said to have a certain property. If we can symbolize the property−object relation in the proposition that Socrates has the property of being mortal, then we should also be able (truly or falsely) to say that *something* is mortal, that *everything* is mortal, that *not all things* are mortal, that *nothing* is mortal, and the like.

Predicate logic also symbolizes the attribution of properties to quantities of objects, to all or some, not all or none.

In developing predicate logic, we do not replace but rather add to our original system of propositional logic. Propositional logic offers the truth functional foundation on which we shall now build a more complete predicate system. We continue to use propositional connectives. But we add new terms and operators, new decision procedures, and new natural deduction proof rules for dealing with property−object and quantificational relations in symbolic logic.

Predicating Properties of Objects

The objects to which properties are predicated in predicate logic constitute a semantic domain.

We now add two new kinds of terms to the syntax of propositional logic. Constants function in predicate logic like proper names in ordinary English ('John' and 'Mary') by designating particular objects (John, Mary). The objects we refer to by constants are said to belong to a *semantic domain*. We can think of the semantic domain as containing everything to which we can refer. The semantic domain may include quarks, electrons, raindrops, DNA molecules, chairs, persons, cars, trees, houses, stars, galaxies, numbers, sets, God, and all the other objects we can name or otherwise designate in thought and language.

The constants added to the syntax of predicate logic are lowercase letters taken from the beginning of the alphabet (a, b, c, . . .) or others with mnemonic significance ('j' for John, 'm' for Mary). There may be indefinitely many objects, so we may need indefinitely many constants. In practice, a relatively short list will usually do, but in the abstract we can consider an indefinite supply of constants to be available by adding numerical sub- or superscripts 1, 2, 3, . . . to the constants a, b, c, . . . , just as we can imagine ourselves outfitted by the same method with an indefinite number of propositional symbols. This device provides a limitless supply of constants: a_1, a_2, a_3, . . . ; b_1, b_2, b_3, . . . ; c_1, c_2, c_3, . . . , ... Since there are indefinitely many natural numbers, we are assured by this method of an unlimited number of constants so that every object in the semantic domain can be named by a constant.

Objects are designated by object constants, and properties are represented by predicates, in the syntax of predicate logic.

We use predicates to represent an object's properties. Predicates can be thought of as naming properties in somewhat the same way that constants name objects. We refer in ordinary language to an object's having such properties as being red, round, Greek, human, mortal, and others. In predicate logic, we symbolize properties by capital letters from the middle of the alphabet (F, G, H, . . .) or choose others with mnemonic significance ('R' for red, 'M' for mortal). Again, if we need more, we can always provide an indefinite number of predicates by sub- or superscripting numerals. Then we have an endless supply of predicates: $F_1, F_2, F_3, \ldots ; G_1, G_2, G_3, \ldots ; H_1, H_2, H_3, \ldots , \ldots$.

To represent property–object relations, we combine constants with predicates by juxtaposing predicate symbols to the left of constants. The spatial proximity of predicates and constants serves the same purpose as the *copula* (conjugations of the verbs 'to be' and 'to have') in ordinary language. The copula is implicit in every predicate–constant combination in predicate logic. The following are examples:

Alice is a woman — Wa

Lincoln is president — Pl

Mary is First Lady — Lm

Socrates is a man (human) — Hs

There are two kinds of properties: qualities and relations.

Qualities are represented by predicates with one object term place; relations are represented by relational predicates with more than one object term place.

Predicates that take only one constant represent *qualities*. Such predicates have only one *object term place* because they only have room to attach one constant term. There are also more complex kinds of predicates involving more than one constant, and in principle some predicates might require indefinitely many constants. These are said to represent *relations*. Examples of relations include being to the left of (a two-place relation), being the sister of (two-place), and being older than someone but younger than someone else (three-place). Thus, we can have:

Mary is the wife of Abraham — Wma

Abraham is the husband of Mary — Ham

Abraham was president of the United States — Pau

Mary was older than Abraham but younger than Sara — Yams

A relation holding between n objects is an n-adic relation and is represented by an n-ary relational predicate.

A relation holding between *n* objects is said to be an *n-adic relation* and to be represented by an *n-ary relational predicate* with *n* object term places. If we allow n to begin with 0, then we can regard propositional symbols as 0-ary relational predicates and quality predicates as 1-ary or unary relational predicates, in the limiting case. However, we shall preserve intuitive distinctions between propositions, qualities, and relations and between propositional symbols, and quality and relational predications, by defining a relation as an n-adic relation represented by an n-ary relational predicate, for n beginning with or greater than or equal to 2 ($n \geq 2$).

To avoid confusion, we adopt a convention about the order in which object terms are to occur in the expression of a relation. When we write 'Wma' for 'Mary is the wife of Abraham', we typically, though not inevitably, mean to say that the object designated by the object term in the first object term place after the relational predicate is the 'W' (wife) of the object designated by the object term in the second object term place. To state 'Wma' is in effect to say that 'W' is a two–place predicate. By the usual convention, the object designated in the object term place immediately next to the 'W' is the wife of the object designated in the next rightmost object term place. This means, in the current context (reading from left to right), that the first designated object is the wife of the second designated object. This order of terms reflects a stipulation about how to symbolize the relation. We stipulate the order simply by deciding which kinds of terms representing which kinds of objects related by the predicate are to appear in each object term place. We could just as easily reverse their order when attaching them to the relational predicate, as long as we do so consistently. Then we might interpret the relation with equal justification to mean that the first object designated in the object term place immediately next to the 'W' *is* not the wife of but rather *has* as wife the object (a particular person) designated in the next rightmost object term place. If the alternative convention were adopted, we would then need to formulate the relation by which Mary is the wife of Abraham as 'Wam'.

The order of constants or of object term places for constants in a relational predicate is conventional; any order is acceptable, provided that it is consistently observed in the same context of analysis.

There are no hard and fast rules about the order of terms to be specified in the use of a relational predicate to express a relation among objects. We just have to decide how we wish the term to be understood and then follow the convention consistently to avoid ambiguity. It is standard, but not necessary, where an object is said in ordinary language to be related in a certain way to another object to write the terms in the same order in symbolic logic. The relational predicate is written first, followed immediately by the object term for the first-mentioned object said to be related to the next-mentioned object and so on for as many objects as are said to be related. To formulate the complex three-term relation, 'Susan is standing between George and Elizabeth', we might do so according to this convention by writing the proposition Bsge; for the sentence, 'George is standing between Susan and Elizabeth', we might write Bgse, and so on. By adopting a single consistent convention for writing relational predications, we minimize the risk of ambiguity in translating relations in predicate logic.

To Check Your Understanding 6.1 ────────────────────────────── ■

In each of the following propositions, identify and symbolize all quality and relational predications, using the constants and predicate symbols provided, and explaining the argument-place conventions for relational predications you have adopted.

1. Julius is Caesar. (C, j)
2. Cicero is an orator and lawyer, but Seneca is a philosopher. (O, L, P, c, s)
3. Vasco de Gama is an explorer if Columbus is, but Columbus is no explorer unless Magellan is both explorer and trail-blazer. (E, T, v, c, m)
4. The Earth orbits the Sun between Mars and Venus (O, e, s, m, v)
5. Einstein is a better physicist than Galileo, Descartes, or Newton, but only if Galileo is a better physicist than Descartes, and Newton is a lesser physicist than Descartes or Galileo. (P, e, g, d, n)
6. Rufus is a prize-winning schnauzer, whose ancestors include Diderot and Maximilian on his father's side, and Hector and Olympus on his mother's. (P, S, A, F, M, r, d, m, h, o)

■

Quantifying Over Sets of Objects

Quantifying over a set of objects requires quantifiers and object variables in the syntax of predicate logic.

The next addition to our syntax permits us to predicate properties to quantities or sets of objects. The objects in the semantic domain can be considered collectively according to their properties. When we speak of *all* or *some* red objects, we are *quantifying over a set of objects* and saying something about their properties by general reference to whatever objects are red, rather than predicating the property of being red to a particular object individually named by a constant. If we say, as in the Socrates syllogism, that 'All men are mortal', then we are quantifying over the set of all objects that have the property of being human and attributing to each of those objects the further property of being mortal.

Quantifications make it possible to attribute properties to all or some objects in a set of objects.

To symbolize quantifications, we add *quantifiers* and *object variables* to the syntax of propositional symbols, propositional connectives, inference indicators, object constants, and predicates. Object variables function in logic much like pronouns in ordinary language. We want to be able to speak generally of something's having a certain property and to assert that something, everything, nothing, not everything, at least one thing, and so on, has a property or some combination of properties. If we are going to symbolize quantifications, we must adopt a special symbolism to represent the quantifiers '*All* things . . .' and '*Some* things . . .' in propositions such as 'All men are mortal' and 'Some men are mortal'. To these symbolic quantifiers, we must further add a special symbolism to represent the general reference to objects in the domain 'All *things . . .*' and 'Some *things . . .*' in fully explicated propositions such as 'All [things that are] men are [things that are] mortal' and 'Some [things that are] men are [things that are] mortal'. 'All men are mortal' predicates the property of mortality to the objects in a *quantity* or set of men (human beings)—to *all* of them, to *everything* that has the property of being human.

Quantifiers bind variables in quantified predicate wffs.

The terms that make general reference indifferently to any objects in the semantic domain are object variables. We use lowercase letters (x, y, z) from the end of the alphabet to serve as object variables. If we need more, we usually work backwards to include w, v, u, and so on. In case of greater need, we can ensure we do not run out by affixing numerals to them, as already suggested for propositional symbols, object constants, and predicates. This gives us x_1, x_2, x_3, . . . ; y_1, y_2, y_3, . . . ; z_1, z_2, z_3, ... Object variables do not refer to particular objects but to any objects in the semantic domain, all or some of which may then be described as having certain properties. As a result, object variables, unlike object constants and predicates, never have mnemonic significance because object variables by definition stand for any object whatsoever.

There are two kinds of quantifiers: universal and existential.

A *quantification* involves the replacement of constants in a property–object proposition with *quantifier bound variables*. The quantifiers that bind variables are symbols that represent quantities of objects, all objects or some objects. There are two kinds of quantifiers, *universal* and *existential*. The universal quantifier is symbolized by '∀' (an upsidedown letter 'A', meaning 'for *all* objects in the domain'). The existential quantifier is symbolized by '∃' (a backwards letter 'E', meaning 'there *exists* an object in the domain'). A quantifier binds an object variable by the juxtaposition of their symbols. If we combine quantifier symbol '∀' with object variable 'x', then we can express the universal quantification, 'For all x . . .' as '∀x'. For ease of reading, but not as an essential part of syntax, the quantifier with its bound variable is standardly enclosed in parentheses as '(∀x)'. If we combine quantifier symbol '∃' with object variable 'x', then we can express the existential quantification, 'For some x . . .' as '(∃x)'. The choice of variable is not determined, and we could as easily have chosen 'y', 'z', etc. However, we standardly begin with 'x' and do not proceed to introduce other variables unless we need to in order to avoid confusion with quantifications that already contain 'x'.

Predicate Wffs

We restate the requirements for quantifications in predicate logic by supplementing our previous wffs rules and parentheses requirement for propositional logic with the following rules. We introduce a *predicate variable, ℱ*, to represent any predicate, in the way that the propositional variable $\mathbb{P}$ represents any wff. We introduce Greek *object constant variables,* $\alpha_1, \ldots, \alpha_n$ to represent any object constants 'a', 'b', 'c', and italicized *metavariables,* $x_1, \ldots, x_n$ to represent any object variables 'x', 'y', 'z'.

RULES FOR WELL-FORMED FORMULAS (WFFS)
OF PREDICATE LOGIC

1. If $\mathbb{P}$ is a propositional wff, then $\mathbb{P}$ is a predicate wff.
2. If $\mathbb{P}$ and $\mathbb{Q}$ are wffs, then $\sim \mathbb{P}$, $\mathbb{P} \ \& \ \mathbb{Q}$, $\mathbb{P} \vee \mathbb{Q}$, $\mathbb{P} \supset \mathbb{Q}$, and $\mathbb{P} \equiv \mathbb{Q}$ are wffs.
3. If $\mathbb{P}$ is a wff containing no quantifier bound variable x, then $(\forall x)\mathbb{P}$ is a wff and $(\exists x)\mathbb{P}$ is a wff.
4. If $\mathcal{F}$ is a predicate and $\alpha_1, \ldots, \alpha_n$ are constants, then $\mathcal{F}\alpha_1 \ldots \alpha_n$ is a wff ($n \geq 1$).
5. If $\mathbb{P}$ is a wff of the form $\mathcal{F}\alpha_1 \ldots \alpha_n$, then $(\forall x_i)(\mathcal{F}\alpha_1 \ldots x_i \ldots \alpha_n)$ is a wff and $(\exists x_i)(\mathcal{F}\alpha_1 \ldots x_i \ldots \alpha_n)$ is a wff, in which every occurrence of α_i is replaced by x_i ($i \geq 0$, $n \geq 1$).
6. Nothing else is a wff.

The rules comprehend all and only the wffs of predicate logic. We obtain a quantified relation of the form $(\forall x)(\forall y)Fxy$, for example, by beginning with a wff of the form Fab under rule 4. Then we apply rule 5 to Fab to obtain $(\forall y)Fay$, and again to $(\forall y)Fay$ to obtain $(\forall x)(\forall y)Fxy$. The same is true in symbolizing all complex wffs of predicate logic. Note that an expression of the form $(\forall x)Fa$ is a wff of predicate logic not because of wffs rule 5 but by rule 3. Rule 4 qualifies Fa as a wff, which by rule 3 introduces the *vacuously* quantified predicate wff $(\forall x)Fa$.

The general form for predicate–constant expressions, $\mathcal{F}\alpha_1 \ldots \alpha_n$, allows as wffs any quality or predicate relations involving any number of constant terms attached to any n-ary predicate. In the limiting case, where $n = 1$, we obtain the quality predication Fa, and where $n > 1$, we successively obtain such relational wffs as Gab, Gaa, Habc, Haab, Haaa, Iabcd, Iaccd, Iaaaa, Jabcde, Jabbdd, and Jeeeee. The ellipses ($\ldots$) in $(\forall x_i)(\mathcal{F}\alpha_1 \ldots x_i \ldots \alpha_n)$ and $(\exists x_i)(\mathcal{F}\alpha_1 \ldots x_i \ldots \alpha_n)$ permit quantification by selective replacement of a constant by a quantifier bound variable in a predicate–constant wff, leaving any choice of other constants intact. In the simplest case, if we have Fa as a wff by rule 4, then by rule 5 we can obtain $(\forall x)Fx$ or $(\exists x)Fx$. If by rule 4 we have Fab, then by rule 5 we can first obtain partial quantifications, $(\forall x)Fxb$, $(\forall x)Fax$, $(\exists x)Fxb$, and $(\exists x)Fax$ (or $(\forall y)Fyb$, etc.). Then, by further applications of rule 5, we obtain $(\forall x)(\forall y)$ Fxy, $(\forall y)(\forall x)Fyx$, $(\exists y)(\forall x)Fax$, $(\exists x)(\exists y)Fyx$, etc. We can also use rule 4 to produce predicate expressions such as Fa, Gab, Habc, to which we then apply rule 2 and the parentheses requirement to obtain wffs of the form Fa, Gab ∨ Habc. To these constructions we apply rule 5 repeatedly in several steps to obtain (∀z) (Gab ∨ Habz) and (∃y)(∀z)(Gay ∨ Hayz). Then, using rule 2, we connect Fa to the previous wff by the conditional first to obtain the wff Fa ⊃ (∃y)(∀z)(Gay ∨ Hayz), which we can then further quantify by rule 5 to obtain (∀x)(Fx ⊃(∃y) (∀z)(Gxy ∨ Hxyz)). The predicate wffs rules incorporate all the wffs of propositional logic, to which are added all the predicate–constant, quantificational, and propositional connections of predicate–constant and quantificational wffs.

To express complete wffs in predicate logic, we symbolize properties as predicates and designate sets of objects collectively referred to by quantifier bound object variables. Thus, we can symbolize the predicate expression in ordinary language, 'All things are good', in two stages as 'For all x, x is good' and as (∀x)Gx (or, for that matter, as (∀y)Gy, (∀z)Gz, and so on). We can symbolize 'Some things are good' as (∃x)Gx (or as (∃y)Gy, (∃z)Gz, etc.). Wherever a variable appears in an expression, it is said that the variable *occurs* or has an *occurrence*. In the expressions just considered, 'x' occurs twice in (∀x)Gx, and 'y' occurs three times in (∃y)(Gy & Hy). We number the occurrences from left to right and speak of the first occurrence of variable 'x' in (∀x)Gx as the one that attaches directly to the quantifier symbol and of the second occurrence of the variable as the one that attaches directly to predicate G. An occurrence of an object variable is either *bound* or *unbound* (*free*). An occurrence of a variable is bound just in case it falls within an attached quantifier's *scope*. We define the scope of a quantifier in much the same way as the scope of a propositional connective:

Variables have a definite number of occurrences in a predicate wff.

Scope of a Quantifier
The *scope* of a quantifier is the least complex wff in which the quantifier occurs.

The scope of a quantifier is defined in a similar way as the scope of a propositional connective— as the least complex wff in which the quantifier occurs.

The scope of a quantifier is punctuated by parentheses if there is any possibility of ambiguity. In the proposition (∀x)Gx, for example, both occurrences of object variable 'x' are bound by the universal quantifier, and there is no free variable. In a construction of the form (∀x)Gx & Fy, in contrast, only the two occurrences of 'x' are bound, and the occurrence of 'y' is free and unbound by any quantifier. Open or free variable sentences are not wffs of predicate logic because they do not express complete thoughts. We do not know in such an expression what, if anything, is supposed to be true or false about the objects that have property F. For the same reason, we do not include as a wff any ambiguous constructions such as (∀x)Gx & Fx, in which it is unclear whether the third occurrence of the 'x' is bound by the quantifier. There are no predicate wffs containing free variables, and all object variables are unambiguously bound by exactly one quantifier. We would need to rewrite the previous sentence as $(\forall x)(Gx \ \& \ Fx)$ in order to make it a proposition and in order for it to qualify as a wff.

There are also wffs of predicate logic in which quantifiers bind an object variable to a propositional symbol. Thus, if P is a propositional symbol, we can quantify it by writing $(\forall x)P$ or $(\exists y)P$. The first proposition might be interpreted as saying that 'All things are such that P [is true]' and the second as 'Some things are such that P [is true]'. Since bound variables occur only directly attached to the quantifier symbol in these propositions, they do not express more than the propositional symbols themselves. To say that all things are such that P is true is just to say that P is true, and to say that some things are such that P is true is just to say that P is true. Although these kinds of quantifications are permitted to count as wffs in predicate logic, for obvious reasons they are described as vacuous quantifications.

Vacuous quantifications appear in wffs whose quantifiers bind no variables.

Finally, the rules comprehend wffs containing *monadic* and *polyadic,* including *mixed multiple quantifications.* Monadic quantifications involve only a single quantifier, as in $(\forall x)Fx$, $(\exists x)Fx$, $(\forall x)(Fx \supset Gx)$, and $(\exists x)(Fx \ \& \ Gx)$. Polyadic and mixed multiple quantifications involve more than one quantifier, often with overlapping scopes. They include, among many other more complicated possibilities, wffs such as $(\forall x)(\forall y)(Fx \supset Gy)$ and $(\exists x)(Fx \ \& \ (\forall y)Gxy)$. We follow standard practice by introducing simpler monadic quantifications first, before advancing to syntactically more complex polyadic and mixed multiple quantifications.

There are monadic and polyadic, including mixed multiple, quantifications.

■ *Demonstration 23:*   **Identifying Predicate Wffs**   ■

PROBLEM: To apply the wffs rules for predicate logic to distinguish wffs from non-wffs.

SYMBOL COMBINATIONS: $(\exists x)P$; $\forall \sim \supset a$; $(\forall x)(\exists y)Gab$; $(\forall x)(\exists y)Gxb$; $(\forall x)Fx$ $\& \ Gyb$

STEP 1:   *Check to determine whether any symbol combinations can be eliminated as obvious violations of wffs rules*
In the four examples, $\forall \sim \supset a$ is an obvious example that can be eliminated immediately as a non-wff.

STEP 2:   *Check to determine whether any of the symbol combinations contains a free variable that would disqualify it as a wff*
In the four examples, $(\exists x)P$ contains no free or bound variables, $(\forall x)(\exists y)Gab$ and $(\forall x)(\exists y)Gxb$ contain no free variables, but $(\forall x)Fx \ \& \ Gyb$ contains a free occurrence of variable y in a truth function of the quantification of a predi-

cate expression and another relational predicate expression. ($\forall$x)Fx & Gyb can therefore be eliminated as a non-wff.

STEP 3:   *Describe a sequence of applications of the wffs rules by which remaining symbol combinations could be constructed*

($\exists$x)P is the (vacuous) existential quantification of a propositional symbol P, which qualifies as a wff by construction from wffs rule 1; ($\forall$x)($\exists$y)Gab is the (vacuous) universal and (vacuous) existential quantification of a predicate expression Gab, which qualifies as a wff by construction from wffs rules 4 and 1; and ($\forall$x)($\exists$y)Gxb is the universal and (vacuous) existential quantification of a predicate expression Gab, which qualifies as a wff by construction from wffs rules 4, 2, and 5.

STEP 4:   *Summarize and reconsider the results of evaluation*

Wffs: ($\exists$x)P; ($\forall$x)($\exists$y)Gab; ($\forall$x)($\exists$y)Gxb
Non-wffs: $\forall\sim\supset$a; ($\forall$x)Fx & Gyb

To Check Your Understanding 6.2 ■

In the following syntax combinations, decide which are wffs and which are not wffs; explain how each wff satisfies the wffs rules for predicate logic; rewrite non-wffs as wffs that satisfy the predicate wffs rules; and distinguish any vacuous quantifications:

1. ($\exists$x)P
2. ($\forall$x)$\sim$Q
3. ($\forall$x)$\sim\sim$Fx
4. ($\exists$x)P & Fy
5. ($\exists$x)P & Gaa
6. ($\forall$x)$\sim$($\exists$y)Gxy
7. ($\forall$x)($\forall$y)Fa
8. ($\forall$x)($\forall$x)Fx
9. ($\forall$x)($\forall$y)Fx
10. ($\forall$x)($\exists$x)Gab
11. ($\forall$x)($\exists$y)Gxx
12. ($\forall$x)($\exists$y)Gyx

■

Quantifier Duality

A *quantifier duality* relation holds between universal and existential quantifications. The duality implies that we could eliminate either one of the quantifiers as less basic than the other and define it as a derived symbol in terms of the other with negation, just as we could eliminate all propositional operators except for negation and conjunction, defining disjunction, the conditional, and biconditional in terms of negation and conjunction (or disjoint negation in the stroke ' | ' function or joint negation in the dagger '$\downarrow$' function). We follow the standard practice of adopting the universal quantifier as fundamental in our rules for wffs, and we define the existential quantifier in terms of the universal quantifier and negation. However, we could just as correctly adopt the existential quantifier as fundamental and define the universal quantifier in terms of the existential quantifier and negation.

If $\mathbb{P}$ is a truth function of predicate–constant wffs, then $\mathbb{P}/x$ is the (free variable) expression (not a wff) that results by selectively replacing any object constant α wherever it occurs in $\mathbb{P}$ by any object variable x. Then we can interdefine universal and existential quantifications as follows:

QUANTIFIER DUALITY

$$(\exists x)\mathbb{P}/x \equiv \sim(\forall x)\sim\mathbb{P}/x$$
$$(\forall x)\mathbb{P}/x \equiv \sim(\exists x)\sim\mathbb{P}/x$$

As an application, we present the simplest case of quantifier duality for wffs involving a single quality predicate F, where Fx is uniformly substituted for $\mathbb{P}/x$:

$$(\exists x)Fx \equiv \sim(\forall x)\sim Fx$$

$$(\forall x)Fx \equiv \sim(\exists x)\sim Fx$$

These are intuitively correct because, in the first equivalence, to say that something has property F is to say that not everything does not have or fails to have property F. In the second equivalence, to say that everything has property F is to say that there is nothing that does not have or fails to have property F.

Dualities offer a choice between several expressions for the same ordinary language equivalents in predicate notation. Just as we can formulate the proposition 'Neither P nor Q' in at least two ways in propositional logic as a result of the DeMorgan duality equivalence $\sim(P \vee Q) \equiv (\sim P \,\&\, \sim Q)$, so in predicate logic we can express, for example, the sentence, 'Nothing is free' alternatively and, as we shall soon be able to prove, logically equivalently to 'Everything is not free' either as $\sim(\exists x)Fx$ or as $(\forall x)\sim Fx$. Many variations of these equivalences are also implied by quantifier duality.

To Check Your Understanding 6.3 ———————————————————————■

Which of the following pairs of propositions are duality related in predicate logic?

1. $\sim(\forall x)Fx$; $(\exists x)\sim Fx$
2. $\sim(\forall x)\sim Fx$; $\sim(\exists x)Fx$
3. $(\exists x)\sim Fx$; $\sim(\forall x)\sim Fx$

4. $\sim(\exists x)Fx$; $(\forall x)\sim Fx$
5. $(\forall x)(Fx \supset Gx)$; $(\forall x)\sim Gx \supset (\forall x)\sim Fx$
6. $\sim(\forall x)(Fx \supset Gx)$; $(\exists x)\sim Gx$ & $(\exists x)\sim Fx$

■

Propositional Connectives in Predicate Logic

Propositional connectives enter into predicate wffs in many complex ways.

When we want to express complex relations among an object's properties, we quantify truth functions of predicate wffs. We use the conditional in universal quantifications to express the proposition that all F's are G's and the conjunction to express the existential proposition that some F's are G's, or that at least one F is a G. The universal proposition that all F's are G's is symbolized in predicate logic as $(\forall x)(Fx \supset Gx)$, and the existential proposition that some F's are G's is symbolized as $(\exists x)(Fx$ & $Gx)$.

The conditional in the symbolization of the universal proposition that all F's are G's, $(\forall x)(Fx \supset Gx)$, represents a relation between the objects with property F and the objects with property G. The relation states that if something has property F then it has property G. The conditional is uniquely suited to represent the inclusion of all objects with property F in that part of the semantic domain containing all objects with property G. If the universal statement that all F's are G's is true, then if any particular object has property F, it also has property G. The truth conditions for the conditional in Fa $\supset$ Ga leave it open whether or not object a has property F. The wff says only that a is such that *if* a has property F *then* a has property G. The same applies to the universal quantification of this conditional predicate wff as $(\forall x)(Fx \supset Gx)$, which leaves it open whether or not any object in the semantic domain has property F but says only that everything in the semantic domain is such that *if* it has property F, *then* it has property G. If we use the quantified conditional to symbolize the universal proposition that all frogs are green, then we are saying in effect that everything is such that if it is a frog, then it is green, and, equivalently, that there are no frogs that are not green. This is not yet to say that there are any frogs or any green things.

To symbolize the universal 'All F's are G's' requires the conditional; to symbolize the existential 'Some F's are G's' requires conjunction.

To correctly symbolize the existential proposition that some F's are G's, we use conjunction rather than the conditional. To say that some F's are G's is to say that there is at least one object that has both property F and property G. If we used the conditional to formalize an existential quantification in $(\exists x)(Fx \supset Gx)$, it would say only that there is at least one object in the logic's semantic domain which is such that, conditionally, if it has property F, then it has property G. Suppose that no F's are G's but that something is G. Then from

(∃x)Gx, as we shall later see, we can validly deduce (∃x)(Fx ⊃ Gx). However, we cannot interpret this as saying that some F's are G's because we assumed that although something is G, no F's are G's. Similar reasons explain why we cannot correctly symbolize 'All F's are G's' by the universal conjunction (∀x)(Fx & Gx) since this more strongly says that everything is both F and G. If we are to symbolize the proposition that some F's are G's, it will not do merely to assert conditionally that there is at least one object which is such that if it has property F, then it has property G. We must rather say that there is at least one object that categorically has both property F and G in the existential conjunction, (∃x)(Fx & Gx).

In one sense, existential propositions are stronger than universal propositions. An existential expresses commitment to the existence of an object that has both properties F and G, whereas the universal says only that everything in the domain is conditionally such that if it has property F, then it has property G. In another sense, however, universal propositions are logically stronger than existential propositions because they quantify over all and not just some objects in the domain, and because a universal (∀x)ℙ logically implies the existential (∃x)ℙ, but not conversely. If everything is F, then something is F, but it does not follow that if something is F, then everything is F. We can, and sometimes must, combine conjunctions with the universal quantifier and conditionals with the existential quantifier. However, to do so is not to symbolize the quantifications 'All F's are G's' and 'Some F's are G's'. We will instead have said by (∀x)(Fx & Gx) that 'Everything is both F and G' and by (∃y)(Fy ⊃ Gy) that 'At least one thing is such that if it is F, then it is also G.'

Here are some predicate wffs involving universal and existential quantification with their ordinary language interpretations:

Universal wffs imply existential wffs, but not the converse.

PROPOSITIONAL CONNECTIVES IN PREDICATE WFFS

Any propositional connectives can occur within the scope of either quantifier in any combination permitted by the wffs rules for predicate logic.

(∀x)Fx	Everything is or has property F.
(∃x)Fx	Something has F.
(∀y)(Fy ⊃ Gy)	All F's are G's.
(∃x)(Fx & Gx)	Some F's are G's.
~(∃x)(Fx & Gx)	No F's are G's.
~(∀y)(Fy ⊃ Gy)	Not all F's are G's.
(∃x)(Fx & ~Gx)	Some F's are not G's.
(∃x)~(Fx & Gx)	Something is not both F and G.
(∀y)(Fy ⊃ ~Gy)	No F's are G's.

$(\forall y)\sim(Fy \supset Gy)$ Everything is F but not G.
$(\forall x)(Fx \ \& \ Gx)$ Everything is both F and G.
$(\exists y)(Fy \supset Gy)$ Something is such that if it is F, then it is also G.

Translating Monadic Quantifications

We now consider translations of English sentences into predicate symbolism in greater detail. This is a useful point at which to remind ourselves that translation from ordinary language into symbolic logic is not a mechanical procedure like truth tables or truth trees but an art that requires judgment and interpretive skill.

Translation demands sensitivity to the nuances of meaning in ordinary language and an effort to grasp the thought intended by a sentence or argument to be translated. We then try to express the same thought in symbolic logic using the devices of its specialized notation to represent the logical structures in which we are interested, going back and forth as often as necessary in order to check that the same ideas are expressed in the logical symbolism as in colloquial language. If translation into symbolic logic is an art rather than a mechanical technique, it is nevertheless an important part of logical analysis. Without it, or with only an imperfect mastery of translation techniques, we cannot make good use of decision methods such as truth tables or truth trees to evaluate the logical properties of propositions and arguments or natural deduction proofs. The use we may try to make of decision methods and natural deduction proofs in that case will only be as informative as the translations from ordinary thought and language with which we begin.

Translation from ordinary language into predicate logic follows much the same general pattern as that for propositional logic.

We learn to translate propositions and arguments into predicate logic by working step by step through some typical examples. To begin, we may consider a translation exercise that combines some of the basic quantificational relations we have already described with propositional connectives in everyday discourse. We have already seen how to translate predicate–object and quantified sentences containing only one predicate, and even how to translate a sentence containing two or more predicates representing the properties of a single object and related by simple propositional connectives. However, there are many more complicated combinations, which we should investigate systematically.

Predicate translations require understanding the attribution of properties to individual objects or quantities of objects.

When we translate a sentence containing several predicates, we are ascribing properties, qualities or relations, to objects or sets of objects. The predicates distinguish a set of objects that have the property represented by the predicate, which can be logically related to other objects or sets of objects. These objects are distinguished as having potentially different properties represented by other predicates. For example, if we want to translate the English sentence, 'All fish are vertebrates', using the predicate symbols 'F' for 'fish' (the property of being a fish) and 'V' for 'vertebrate' (the property of being a vertebrate), then we single out the set of fish (in this case, all of them) and attribute to any object in that set the further property (in this case, of being a vertebrate) of being included in the set of objects that have the property of being a vertebrate. It is instructive to work through the process of this simple translation one step at a time, commenting on the interpretation of the translation as we build it up symbol by symbol. Then we will be in a better position to consider the complications that can occur in doing more sophisticated translations.

We use the universal quantifier '∀' with an attached variable 'x' (although we could equally correctly choose 'y', 'z', etc.) to translate the first part of the sentence, which says that 'All . . .'. We interpret this in predicate logic as meaning 'All x are . . .' or 'For all x, . . .'. This states simply:

$$(\forall x)$$

Predicate wffs express relations between sets of objects, represented by quantifiers, object constants and variables, and propositional connectives.

Next, we specify a set of objects by attaching a predicate term. This makes it explicit, as the sentence requires, that we are not speaking generally of any and all existent objects in the semantic domain but more specifically of all objects with a certain property. Then we can say something definite, in this case, about all fish, or about all objects that have the property of being a fish. The addition does not yet complete the translation but takes us another step further. We say formally in predicate logic that 'All fish are . . .', when we write:

$$(\forall x)(Fx \ldots$$

The sentence we are translating states that all fish are vertebrates. So, we must connect what we have thus far said in designating the set of all fish by adding that the objects so designated also have the property of being vertebrates, or of being included in the set of all vertebrates. To do this, we express a logical relation between the set of all fish and the set of all vertebrates. We do not want to maintain that all fish are all vertebrates but rather that everything that is a fish is also a vertebrate. We need to express the logical relation between the set of all fish and the set of all vertebrates by which every object that belongs to the set of all fish also belongs to the set of all vertebrates. For the sentence we are translating, the logical relation between members of the two sets is a conditional. We want to be able to say conditionally of every object in the logic's semantic domain that *if* that object is a fish, *then* that object is a vertebrate.

The conditional propositional connection holding between predications involving objects from the set of all fish and the set of all vertebrates is expressed by completing the predicate wff to read:

$(\forall x)(Fx \supset Vx)$

The function of the three occurrences of the variable 'x' in the formula is worth emphasizing. The first occurrence is attached to the quantifier, in this case, the universal $\forall$ in $(\forall x)$. Here, it serves the purpose of expressing the quantity of objects in the semantic domain whose properties are to be considered. The fragment $(\forall x)$ says 'For all x, . . .' or 'Every object x is such that . . .'. The other two occurrences of variable 'x' attached to predicate symbols 'F' and 'V' in the completed translation have the same effect in predicate logical symbolism as a pronoun, such as 'he', 'she', or 'it', in ordinary English. By writing out more perspicuously the intent of the symbolization, we could read the entire expression as saying that:

For all objects x, if x is a fish, then x is a vertebrate.

Equivalently, in order to make the pronoun status of the bound variables explicit, we can also say:

Every object x is such that, if *it* is a fish, then *it* is a vertebrate.

Constants in predicate logic function like proper names; quantifier bound variables function like pronouns.

The idea is that whereas constants in predicate logic function more or less like names (John, Mary) in ordinary language, bound variables attached to predicates, as opposed to those attached directly to quantifiers, function as singular pronouns (he, she, it).

To Check Your Understanding 6.4 ——————————————————————————————■

Explain in each case why it would be incorrect to translate the sentence, 'All fish are vertebrates', as any of the following:

1. $(\forall x)Fx \supset Vx$
2. $(\forall x)Fx \supset Vy$
3. $(\forall x)Fx \supset (\forall x)Vx$
4. $(\forall x)Fx \supset (\forall y)Vy$
5. $(\forall x)(Fx \supset (\forall x)Vx)$
6. $(\forall x)(Fx \supset (\forall y)Vy)$

■

Similar considerations apply in translating existentially quantified sentences, in which the logical connection required is usually conjunction rather

In giving translations from ordinary language into predicate logic, it is often useful to consider alternative similar formulations in order to choose the most appropriate interpretation.

than the conditional. We translate 'Some vertebrates are fish', for example, as $(\exists x)(Vx \ \& \ Fx)$, which can be expanded into a more precise English statement as:

Some (or, For some) objects x, x is a vertebrate and x is a fish.

Equivalently, again, in order to make the pronoun status of the bound variables explicit, we can also say:

Some (or, at least one) object x is such that *it* is a vertebrate and *it* is a fish.

We can now apply these skills to symbolize the Socrates syllogism. We adopt the mnemonic predicate 'H' to represent the property of being a man (human), 'M' for being mortal, and constant 's' to refer to Socrates. Then we have:

1. $(\forall x)(Hx \supset Mx)$

2. Hs
_____

3. Ms

This way of symbolizing the argument is more informative than the previous purely propositional version, $P, Q \vdash R$. Later we shall see how this type of translation can be used in conjunction with more powerful decision methods and natural deduction techniques to prove that the argument is deductively valid.

We translate property–object propositions in predicate logic by juxtaposing predicate and constant terms. A choice of any single constant term is needed for translating quality predications, whereas multiple constant terms are required for translating relational predications. We can choose constant and predicate symbols that serve to remind us of the ordinary language terms they abbreviate. To translate 'Fido is a dog', for example, we might naturally symbolize the proposition as Df. To translate propositions in which objects with properties are related by the ordinary language quantifiers 'All', 'Some (at least one)', 'None', and the like, we replace object constants with the appropriate quantifier bound variables, using truth functional propositional connectives as necessary to express the relations between classes of objects with the properties represented by the predicates. We translate the proposition 'All schnauzers are dogs' as $(\forall x)(Sx \supset Dx)$, 'Some schnauzers are dogs' as $(\exists x)(Sx \ \& \ Dx)$, 'No schnauzers are nondogs' as $\sim(\exists x)(Sx \ \& \sim Dx)$, and so on.

We can also combine property–object expressions involving constants with quantified components. This is necessary, for example, in translating the

Object constants and predicates, like propositional symbols, can be chosen for mnemonic or memory-aid value.

sentence, 'Some dogs are not schnauzers, but Fido is a dog' as $(\exists x)(Dx \ \& \sim Sx)$ & Df. When in doubt, we should make sure that our translation produces a wff according to the formation rules for predicate wffs. We can similarly combine predicate expressions with propositional variables, where the latter do not lend themselves to further translation into propositional or predicate formulations. For example, if we are to translate the sentence, 'Some schnauzers are cuddly and $2 + 2 = 4$', we might naturally do so by the proposition $(\exists x)(Sx \ \& \ Cx)$ & P.

Demonstration 24: **Predicate Translation**

PROBLEM: To symbolize a complex proposition in predicate logic.

PROPOSITIONS: All dolphins are cetaceans; some cetaceans are either whales or dolphins.

STEP 1: *Identify quantifiers and propositional connectives*
We supplement a previous convention by double underlining propositional connectives and highlighting quantifiers by single underlining. We do this not only for explicit quantifiers but also for constructions in which quantification is implied. This makes the atomic propositions stand out more clearly for symbolization.

All dolphins are cetaceans.

Some cetaceans are either whales or dolphins.

STEP 2: *Assign predicate symbols to abbreviate ordinary language predicates*
We assign predicate symbols to the relevant ordinary language predicate expressions. The predicates in the proposition are as follows:

1. Dolphins (D) are cetaceans (C).
2. Cetaceans (C) are whales (W).
3. Cetaceans (C) are dolphins (D).

D is the property of being a dolphin, C is the property of being a cetacean; W is the property of being a whale.

STEP 3: *Use quantifiers in combination with propositional connectives to symbolize the relations among predications of properties to objects expressed in the proposition*
The first part of the proposition says that *all* dolphins are cetaceans. This requires a universal quantification that all D's are C's. The universal quantifier binds variables attaching to conditionally related predications. The proposition states that if anything is a D then it is a C. This is also true for the second

proposition in which it is asserted that all cetaceans are either whales or dolphins. The two propositions are accordingly symbolized:

$(\forall x)(Dx \supset Cx)$
$(\exists x)(Cx \& (Wx \lor Dx))$

STEP 4:   *Check the meaning*

As a final step, we consider whether the proposition as symbolized expresses the same meaning as the original ordinary language sentence. The translation of the first proposition seems correct. However, in the second translation there is a minor problem. The consequent of the universal conditional in the second conjunct is a disjunction. We know that disjunction in truth functional propositional logic is inclusive. We probably do not want the proposition to be translated in such a way that it permits a cetacean to be both a whale and a dolphin, so we may wish to make adjustments to capture the exclusive rather than inclusive sense of 'or'. It is possible that someone might want to express the inclusive disjunction here, but from our knowledge of the relevant concepts it seems more charitable to symbolize the proposition by means of exclusive disjunction. We make the following correction to redo this part of the translation of the second proposition:

$(\exists x)(Cx \& ((Wx \lor Dx) \& \sim(Wx \& Dx)))$

To Check Your Understanding 6.5 ────────────────────────────────────■

Using the predicate symbols provided, symbolize the following propositions as wffs of predicate logic.

1. All fish are aquatic. (F, A)
2. Some mammals are aquatic. (M, A)
3. Some aquatic mammals are whales. (A, M, W)
4. All whales are aquatic mammals if and only if they are cetaceans. (W, A, M, C)
5. No fish are cetaceans. (F, C)
6. Not all mammals are cetaceans. (M, C)

■

'Only' Quantifications and Exceptions

There are other tricky quantifications. One is the 'only' relation, which we find, for example, in sentences such as 'Only schnauzers can be entered in the dog show'. Another is the stipulation of exceptions to a generalization, as when we say, 'All dogs except schnauzers can be entered in the dog show'.

Predicate logic can be used to translate 'only' quantifications and exceptions to generalizations.

The 'only' construction qualifies a universal quantification in predicate logic in much the same way as does the 'only if' conditional in propositional logic. In propositional logic, we translate 'P only if Q' as the conditional P ⊃ Q. This symbolizes the relation between these propositions as being such that Q is a necessary condition for proposition P to hold true so that if Q is false, then so is P. When we say, 'Only objects with property F have property G', as in, 'Only [objects with the property of being] schnauzers [have the property of being such that they] can be entered in the dog show', we are saying in effect the converse of the universal statement that 'All schnauzers can be entered in the dog show' ('All [objects with the property of being] schnauzers [have the property of being such that they] can be entered in the dog show'). The translation for 'All schnauzers can be entered in the dog show' is simply (∀x)(Sx ⊃ Ex). To say, on the contrary, that, 'Only schnauzers can be entered in the dog show', is to say that there is only one condition under which something can be entered in the dog show, and that is if it is a schnauzer. If something is not a schnauzer, it cannot be entered in the show. By parallel formulation with the 'only if' of propositional logic, we accordingly translate this kind of sentence as (∀x)(Ex ⊃ Sx). Finally, just as we translate the biconditional 'P if and only if Q' in propositional logic as P ≡ Q, equivalent to the conjunction of P ⊃ Q and Q ⊃ P, so too in predicate logic we translate 'All and only F's are G's' as the universally quantified biconditional, (∀x)(Fx ≡ Gx). This formula is logically equivalent to the universally quantified conjunction, (∀x)((Fx ⊃ Gx) & (Gx ⊃ Fx)), and indeed, as we shall later be able to prove, to the conjunction of universally quantified formulas, (∀x)(Fx ⊃ Gx) & (∀x)(Gx ⊃ Fx).

To express an exception to a universal generalization, we attach appropriate clauses to the antecedent of the universally quantified conditional. Thus, to translate the sentence, 'All dogs except schnauzers can be entered in the dog show', we conjoin a qualification to this effect to the universal quantification's antecedent. The qualification indicates that any object that, conditionally, has the property of being a dog, but does not have the property of being a schnauzer, has the property of being such that it can be entered in the dog show, and that any object that, conditionally, has the property of being a schnauzer cannot be entered in the dog show. We write the exception for this example as follows: (∀x)((Dx & ~Sx) ⊃ Ex) & ((∀x)(Dx & Sx) ⊃ ~Ex)).

Translation is an art, not a mechanical technique.

Other qualifications, involving more complicated applications of conditionals, conjunctions, disjunctions, and the like, are also possible. We may need to use various combinations of propositional connectives, propositional variables, object constants, object variables, and quantifiers to symbolize the predicate meaning conveyed by ordinary language equivalents.

To Check Your Understanding 6.6 —————————————————————————————— ∎

Using the predicate symbols provided, symbolize the following propositions in predicate logic.

1. Only whales and dolphins are cetaceans. (W, D, C)
2. All and only cetaceans are aquatic mammals. (C, A, M)
3. All cetaceans are whales, unless they are dolphins. (C, W, D)
4. Some cetaceans are dolphins, but only whales and dolphins are cetaceans. (C, D, W)
5. Killer whales are cetaceans but are dolphins rather than true whales. (K, C, D, W)

∎

Translation skills in predicate logic require complex symbolizations of relations.

Translating n–adic relations as n-ary relational predications is similar to translating 1–ary quality predications. There are subtleties in some of the relations holding between objects that can be expressed by different combinations of universal and existential quantifications. Consider the differences between the following sentences and their translations into predicate symbolism. For some translations, it is useful to introduce the special identity relational predicate 'I', where, in Iab, objects a and b are said to be identical. We write 'Sab' to indicate that a is b's schnauzer.

RELATIONAL PREDICATE WFFS

John loves Mary.	Ljm
Mary loves John.	Lmj
John loves himself.	Ljj
John loves everything.	(∀x)Ljx
John loves something.	(∃x)Ljx
Something loves John.	(∃x)Lxj
John loves nothing.	~(∃x)Ljx
Nothing loves John.	~(∃x)Lxj
John loves only Mary.	Ljm & ~(∃x)(~Ixm & Ljx)
John loves everything except Mary.	(∀x)(~Ixm ⊃ Ljx) & ~Ljm
John is loved by everything.	(∀x)Lxj
John is loved by everything except Mary.	(∀x)(~Ixm ⊃ Lxj) & ~Lmj
Only John loves Mary.	(∀x)(Lxm ⊃ Ixj)
Only Mary loves John.	(∀x)(Lxj ⊃ Ixm)
John loves all things that love him.	(∀x)(Lxj ⊃ Ljx)

John loves all things that love Mary.	$(\forall x)(Lxm \supset Ljx)$
John loves something that loves Mary.	$(\exists x)(Lxm \ \& \ Ljx)$
John loves only things that love Mary.	$(\forall x)(Ljx \supset Lxm)$
John loves only things that love him.	$(\forall x)(Ljx \supset Lxj)$
John loves all and only things that love him.	$(\forall x)(Ljx \equiv Lxj)$
All things that love John love Mary.	$(\forall x)(Lxj \supset Lxm)$
All things that love Mary love John.	$(\forall x)(Lxm \supset Lxj)$
Nothing that loves Mary loves John.	$\sim(\exists x)(Lxm \ \& \ Lxj)$
Nothing that loves John loves Mary.	$\sim(\exists x)(Lxj \ \& \ Lxm)$
Only John's schnauzer loves Mary.	$(\forall x)(Lxm \supset Sxj)$
Only John's schnauzer loves John.	$(\forall x)(Lxj \supset Sxj)$
Everything loves John.	$(\forall x)Lxj$
Everything loves John and Mary.	$(\forall x)(Lxj \ \& \ Lxm)$
Something is such that if it loves Mary, then it loves John.	$(\exists x)(Lxm \supset Lxj)$
Not everything loves Mary.	$\sim(\forall x)Lxm$

Translating Polyadic and Mixed Multiple Quantifications

Polyadic and mixed multiple quantifications involve several quantifiers falling within the scopes of propositional connectives.

The same basic principles apply when we turn from monadic quantifications to translate polyadic and mixed multiple quantifications involving wffs with more than one quantifier. When universal and existential quantifiers are combined, they make it possible to express relations among different quantities of objects. We can distinguish between these two categories of polyadic mixed multiple quantifications, where 'D' in 'Dab' is the relational property of devouring, 'a devours b':

$(\exists x)(\forall y)Dxy$

$(\forall y)(\exists x)Dxy$

Although these wffs superficially look very similar, they say very different things. The first wff, $(\exists x)(\forall y)Dxy$, formalizes the relation whereby everything is devoured by something, literally an omnivore. The second wff, $(\forall y)(\exists x)Dxy$, states that everything, or each object in the logic's semantic domain, devours something. The difference between their meanings should be obvious. The first wff is true just in case there exists something that devours everything, including, presumably, itself. The second wff in contrast is true just in case everything, or each thing considered individually, devours something, which is to say at least one thing that is not necessarily the same thing that each thing devours, where it might be that just one and the same thing is devoured by each thing and where, unlike the first wff's commitment to the existence of an omnivore, it does not imply that the devourer devour itself.

Quantifiers are combined with propositional connectives in comlex ways in polyadic and mixed multiple quantificational predicate wffs.

A slightly more complicated example is the following English sentence expressing a relation between the members of two sets of objects, fish and vertebrates, to be translated into predicate logic:

Some fish devour some vertebrates.

This sentence is interesting because it involves the two-place relation of devouring. To devour or eat something whole is a two-place relation because it involves something that devours or does the devouring and something that is devoured. Ordinarily, these are different things; no eater eats itself whole, although there is no strictly logical necessity to prevent this from happening. If we are trying to capture the sense in which devouring occurs in the natural world, we shall need to keep the two categories of objects, devourer and the devoured, in logically separate categories in the resulting translation.

Different bound variables, 'x' and 'y', can be used to distinguish reference to sets of objects that have the property of being a fish or of being a vertebrate so that we can separate the objects from one set that are said to devour members of the other set in formalizing the two-place relation of devouring. It is worth pointing out more explicitly why we cannot use the same bound variable in translating the sentence. Let 'F' represent the quality of being a fish, 'V' the property of being a vertebrate, and 'Dab' the relation in which a devours b. If we tried to render the English in this way, we would not do justice to the implied meaning whereby the devouring fish is not expected to be identical to the devoured vertebrates. We should not, therefore, try to translate the sentence as having this logical form:

$$(\exists x)((Fx \ \& \ Vx) \ \& \ Dxx)$$

This says that some fish is a vertebrate and devours itself. If we wanted to say more simply that something devours itself, we could just write $(\exists x)Dxx$. However, this is not what we typically mean when we think of the relation of devouring. For now, we shall assume as a matter of common sense in understanding the ordinary language sentence to be translated that nothing devours itself.

We also cannot use the same bound variable in wffs where two or more quantifiers are required for translation. If we want to translate the sentence, 'Someone loves everyone', it will clearly not do to symbolize the relation by means of a single bound variable as (∃x)(∀x)Lxx. To write (∃x)(∀x)Lxx is non-sense and does not satisfy the formation rules for wffs in predicate logic. There is no determining from the syntax whether the existential or universal quantifier has jurisdiction over the bound variable 'x' in Lxx. If we are to express this proposition correctly, we must accordingly introduce another object variable in the formula (∃x)(∀y)Lxy. Since the universal quantifier ranges over all the objects in the logic's semantic domain, it is implied by this formalization that someone loves him- or herself. The fact that we have used distinct bound object variables in order to avoid ambiguity in the expression does not preclude the possibility of different quantifiers ranging over, and predications included in the wff thereby having appilcation to, at least some of the same objects.

Translating proposi-tions and arguments involving polyadic and mixed multiple quantifications re-quires careful atten-tion to the scopes of quantifiers and propo-sitional connectives and to which particu-lar variables are bound by which par-ticular quantifiers.

What we need instead is a formalization in which the thing that devours (the fish) is at least not necessarily the same thing that is devoured (the verte-brate). We need to be able to express the relation whereby some object in the logic's semantic domain is a fish and some object in the logic's semantic domain is a vertebrate and that the first mentioned thing, identified as an entity having the property of being a fish, devours the second mentioned thing, identified as an entity having the property of being a vertebrate. We arrive, in this way, at the following translation of the sentence:

$$(\exists x)(\exists y)((Fx \,\&\, Vy) \,\&\, Dxy)$$

This statement does not exclude the possibility that the fish and vertebrate, x and y, are identical. However, it has the virtue, by comparison with the pre-vious symbolization, of not requiring that they be the same. To state that the objects referred to in the sentence are not identical involves adding a clause to stipulate that $x \neq y$, which we will learn to use later. For now, note that the translation conveys the idea that some fish devours some vertebrate, and that the two are not necessarily the same. A precise rendering of the translation back into logically more regimented English can help us to understand the process of translation from colloquial language into symbolic predicate notation and can be given in the following statement:

We must distinguish between similar for-mulations of polyadic and mixed multiple quantifications.

> Some (or, For some) objects x, and some (for some) objects y, x is a fish and y is a vertebrate, and x devours y.

Equivalently, in order to make the pronoun status of the bound variables more explicit, we can also say:

> Some (or, At least one) object x is such that *it* is a fish, and some (at least one) object y is such that *it* is a vertebrate, and the *first mentioned object* devours the *second mentioned object.*

The same reasoning applies when we need to translate sentences of comparable structural complexity involving different quantifiers. The following are the remaining variations of the translations we have just described:

Some fish devour all vertebrates.

$$(\exists x)(\forall y)(Fx \ \& \ (Vy \supset Dxy))$$

All fish devour some vertebrates.

$$(\forall x)(\exists y)(Fx \supset (Vy \ \& \ Dxy))$$

All fish devour all vertebrates.

$$(\forall x)(\forall y)((Fx \ \& \ Vy) \supset Dxy)$$

It should be clear why there exist just these four possible variations involving just these four different combinations of the existential and universal quantifiers. The universal quantifications in the last two translations, unlike the preceding two examples, evidently require a conditional instead of the conjunction in order to express the appropriate logical connection between sets of objects distinguished as fish, vertebrates, and the relation whereby all fish devour some or all vertebrates. The reason, as previously explained, is the same as that by which we explain why simpler universal quantifications of the form 'All F's are G's' require a conditional rather than a conjunction, to be translated as $(\forall x)(Fx \supset Gx)$ instead of $(\forall x)(Fx \ \& \ Gx)$. We do not want the translation to say that everything in the universe is a fish and a vertebrate, and that all the fish devour all the vertebrates, but only that anything in the semantic domain is such that, if it is a fish, then it devours anything that is a vertebrate.

Practicing reverse translation, from symbolic wffs in predicate logic to ordinary language expressions, is a useful way to improve translation skills.

The translation technique we have elaborated can be expanded to include more than two quantifier bound variables. We might need such symbolizations in order to translate logical relations expressed in complex ordinary language sentences. These kinds of situations can occur in several different ways. We can have multiple complex relations necessitating symbolic relation terms with more than two object term places in order to express the relation of more than two quantities of entities distinguished by different predicate attributions. For example, consider the following sentence:

All fish prefer some vertebrates to some mollusks.

We should translate the three-term preference relation in the following way, where Pabc means that a prefers b to c. Then we have

$$(\forall x)(\exists y)(\exists z)(Fx \supset ((Vy \ \& \ Mz) \ \& \ Pxyz))$$

It is easy to imagine alternative combinations of quantified relations suggested by this translation. As an exercise in reverse translation, read back the colloquial and more rigorously regimented English sentences for which each of the following mixed multiple quantifications is the predicate logic symbolization. Some of these may be useful in certain translation contexts, whereas others may have no obvious practical application:

$(\forall x)(\forall y)(\forall z)(Fx \supset ((Vy \& Mz) \& Pxyz))$

$(\exists x)(\exists y)(\exists z)(Fx \supset ((Vy \& Mz) \& Pxyz))$

$(\exists x)(\forall y)(\exists z)(Fx \supset ((Vy \& Mz) \& Pxyz))$

$(\exists x)(\exists y)(\forall z)(Fx \supset ((Vy \& Mz) \& Pxyz))$

$(\exists x)(\forall y)(\forall z)(Fx \supset ((Vy \& Mz) \& Pxyz))$

$(\forall x)(\exists y)(\forall z)(Fx \supset ((Vy \& Mz) \& Pxyz))$

$(\forall x)(\forall y)(\exists z)(Fx \supset ((Vy \& Mz) \& Pxyz))$

Whereas before we considered the possible variations of exactly two quantifiers so that we had four combinations, here, with three mixed multiple quantifiers, we have eight combinations. The general formula for the total number of possible combinations, the same as that used in computing the number of truth table rows for n propositional symbols, where n is now the number of quantifiers, is 2^n, assuming that the English sentence to be translated involves only the conditional and conjunction occurring with the same internal propositional structure. We obtain another list of possibilities as we consider variations in the propositional connectives within each of the predicate wffs. Now we have:

$(\forall x)(\forall y)(\forall z)(Fx \& ((Vy \& Mz) \& Pxyz))$

$(\exists x)(\exists y)(\exists z)(Fx \& ((Vy \& Mz) \& Pxyz))$

$(\exists x)(\forall y)(\exists z)(Fx \& ((Vy \& Mz) \& Pxyz))$

$(\exists x)(\exists y)(\forall z)(Fx \& ((Vy \& Mz) \& Pxyz))$

$(\exists x)(\forall y)(\forall z)(Fx \& ((Vy \& Mz) \& Pxyz))$

$(\forall x)(\exists y)(\forall z)(Fx \& ((Vy \& Mz) \& Pxyz))$

$(\forall x)(\forall y)(\exists z)(Fx \& ((Vy \& Mz) \& Pxyz))$

$(\forall x)(\forall y)(\forall z)(Fx \& ((Vy \& Mz) \supset Pxyz))$

$(\exists x)(\exists y)(\exists z)(Fx \& ((Vy \& Mz) \supset Pxyz))$

$(\exists x)(\forall y)(\exists z)(Fx \& ((Vy \& Mz) \supset Pxyz))$

$(\exists x)(\exists y)(\forall z)(Fx \& ((Vy \& Mz) \supset Pxyz))$

$(\exists x)(\forall y)(\forall z)(Fx \& ((Vy \& Mz) \supset Pxyz))$

$$(\forall x)(\exists y)(\forall z)(Fx \ \& \ ((Vy \ \& \ Mz) \supset Pxyz))$$
$$(\forall x)(\forall y)(\exists z)(Fx \ \& \ ((Vy \ \& \ Mz) \supset Pxyz))$$

And so on.

The general formula for considering all the possible combinations for mixed multiple quantifications, again where n is the number of quantifiers and m is the number of propositional connectives in any internal arrangement, is 2^{nm}.

We have simplified things considerably by specifying at the outset the sets of objects to which different quantities of x, y, and z, as fish, vertebrates, and mollusks, respectively, are to belong. The only question is whether the three-term preference relation P is to be logically related to this conjunction of predications to universally or existentially quantified sets of objects by conjunction or the conditional, depending on whether the formula is existential, with an existential quantifier as the leftmost operator, or universal, with a universal quantifier as the leftmost operator. If the formula is an existential, as previously explained, we use conjunction. If the formula is a universal, we use the conditional. The three-term preference relation then expresses the quantity of first-mentioned objects that prefer the relevant quantity of second-mentioned objects to the relevant quantity of third-mentioned objects. We thereby symbolize as mixed multiple quantifications the propositions that all fish prefer all vertebrates to some mollusks; some fish prefer some vertebrates to some mollusks, some fish prefer all vertebrates to all mollusks, and so on.

There are useful general guidelines for translating propositions and arguments as polyadic and mixed multiple predicate wffs and sequents in predicate logic.

POLYADIC AND MIXED MULTIPLE PREDICATE WFFS

Everything loves something.	$(\forall x)(\exists y)Lxy$
All fish have gills.	$(\forall x)(Fx \supset (\exists y)Gxy)$
No zebras eat any alligators.	$\sim(\exists x)(\exists y)((Zx \ \& \ Ay) \ \& \ Exy)$
Everything that turns around anything comes around something else.	$(\forall x)(\forall y)(Txy \supset (\exists z)(\sim Izy \ \& \ Cxz))$
If all men are mortal, then some dogs are not loved by all men.	$(\forall x)(Hx \supset Mx) \supset (\exists y)(Dy \ \& \ \sim(\forall z)(Hz \supset Lyz))$
Only John loves his schnauzer.	$(\forall x)(Sxj \supset (\forall y)(Lyx \supset Iyj))$
Only John's schnauzer loves John's schnauzer.	$(\forall x)(\forall y)((Sxj \ \& \ Lyx) \supset Syj)$ or: $(\forall x)(Sxj \supset (\forall y)(Lyx \supset Iyx))$

L, loves (two-place relational predicate); F, fish; G, is the gill of (two-place relational predicate); Z, zebra; A, alligator; E, eats (two-place relational predicate);

T, turns around (two-place relational predicate); I, is identical to (two-place relational predicate); C, comes around (two-place relational predicate); H, human; M, mortal; D, dog; S, being the schnauzer of some dog owner (two-place relational predicate); j, John (constant)

■ *Demonstration 25:* **Mixed Multiple Quantification** ■

PROBLEM: To symbolize a complex proposition involving mixed multiple quantification in predicate logic.

PROPOSITION: Something is sticky, and whatever grasps it is also grasped by it.

STEP 1: *Identify quantifiers and propositional connectives*
We follow a previous convention by double underlining propositional connectives and highlighting quantifiers by single underlining. We do this not only for explicit quantifiers but also for constructions in which quantification is implied. This makes the atomic propositions stand out more clearly for symbolization.

Something is sticky, and whatever grasps it is also grasped by it.

Here the first quantifier appears to be an existential ('something') and the second a universal ('whatever'). The proposition that something is sticky is related to a universal assertion that whatever grasps something sticky is in turn grasped by that sticky thing.

STEP 2: *Specify predicate symbols to abbreviate ordinary language predicates*
We assign predicate symbols to the relevant ordinary language predicate expressions. The predicates in the proposition are

   sticky (S); grasps (G)

'Sticky' is a one-place quality predicate (something has the quality of being sticky), whereas grasping is a two-place relational predicate (something grasps something else; there is a grasper and a graspee). We shall stipulate that in Gab, a grasps b (or that b is grasped by a), rather than the other way around.

STEP 3: *Use quantifiers in combination with propositional connectives to symbolize the relations among predications of properties to objects expressed in the proposition*
The first part of the proposition claims that *something* is sticky. We begin the symbolization by writing the existential quantifier with bound variables in

the object place of predicate 'S' to symbolize the proposition that something is sticky as (∃x)Sx. The proposition also says that something is sticky *and whatever* it grasps is grasped by it. The translation requires the use of conjunction and universal quantification. We first add parentheses to the existential wff so that we can enclose all of the following content and still have the existential quantifier bind later occurrences of the variable x ('x' will symbolize the 'it' in the proposition, the *it* that is such that when anything grasps it, it grasps back). Now we write (∃x)(Sx & (∀y)(Gyx ⊃ Gxy)). This wff says that there is at least one thing that is sticky, and everything is such that if it grasps that sticky thing it is grasped by the sticky thing.

STEP 4:   *Check the meaning*
As a final step, we consider whether the proposition as symbolized expresses the same meaning as the original ordinary language sentence. The translation seems correct, and so we accept the wff as an accurate symbolization of the proposition.

To Check Your Understanding 6.7   ▬

Using the predicate symbols provided, symbolize the following propositions in predicate logic:

1. All novels are not equally appealing to every reader. (N, E, R)
2. Some days, everything goes wrong until something unexpected goes right. (D, W, U, R)
3. When someone tells someone a secret, that person might tell someone else, until at last everyone knows. (P, T, S, K)
4. Every person loves, and is loved by, somebody; but nobody loves, or is loved by, everybody. (P, L)
5. Not everyone shares their ideas with others, but some persons positively go out of their way to share their ideas with others. (P, S, I)
6. Some dogs are too temperamental to be entered in some dog shows; although no dogs have such a bad attitude that they cannot be entered in any dog show. (D, T, E, B)

Internal Propositional Complexities

Another way in which predicate wffs can be complicated is by incorporating more internally complex propositional logical structures. We get a sense of the full range of possibilities by considering a few examples, building on the kinds

Predicate wffs can contain internally complex propositional logical structures involving multiple propositional connectives with overlapping scopes.

of translations we have already developed. Suppose that we need to translate an English sentence that states:

> If all fish devour some vertebrates, then the fish are not devoured by the vertebrates.

We should recognize the conditional as a further internal feature of the logical structure of this sentence, in addition to whatever propositional connective, conjunction or conditional, may be needed in order to express existential or universal quantifications within the sentence. We can then translate the sentence in the following way, to reflect its conditional logical form:

$$(\forall x)(\exists y)((Fx \supset (Vy \,\&\, Dxy)) \supset \sim Dyx)$$

Translation into polyadic and mixed multiple quantificational wffs combines all the skills needed for translation in propositional and predicate logic.

The possibilities of even more internally complex logical relations within quantified predicate wffs literally explode when we consider the combinations that might be used to translate logically complicated sentences from colloquial language into the symbolic notation of predicate logic. Here are just a few of the unlimitedly many kinds of constructions that we might encounter and that we should be prepared to translate:

> No fish devour any vertebrates, unless the vertebrates devour the fish.
> $$\sim(\exists x)(\forall y)((Fx \,\&\, Vy) \supset (\sim Dyx \supset Dxy))$$

We apply the translation rule for (weak) 'unless' connectives from propositional logic in order to express the logical structure of this relatively simple predicate wff. We say that the vertebrates do not devour the fish by writing that it is not the case that the objects distinguished by predicate attribution as vertebrates (the y's) devour the objects distinguished by predicate attribution as fish (the x's). The vertebrates not devouring the fish is in turn the condition on which it is said that no fish devour any vertebrates, expressed by the negative existential. The translation exemplifies the standard translation practice in predicate logic of first singling out a set or sets of objects in the semantic domain by predicate attribution (the F's and the V's) and then making some further statement about their properties, in which each stands to the members of another distinguished set of objects. Here, we capture the sense of the propositional 'unless' clause in the sentence to be translated by saying that no fish devour any vertebrates if the vertebrates do not devour the fish.

As another example, consider the English sentence:

> Either, if all fish devour all vertebrates, then the vertebrates do not devour the fish, or the vertebrates devour the fish and the fish devour the vertebrates.

The translation can be given as follows:

$$(\forall x)(\forall y)((((Fx \& Vy) \supset Dxy) \supset {\sim}Dyx) \vee (Dyx \& Dxy))$$

As a final illustration:

When some fish devour no vertebrates, then the vertebrates devour the fish, the fish do not devour the vertebrates, and, if the fish devour the fish, then the vertebrates devour the fish or the vertebrates devour the vertebrates.

Here is a direct translation:

$$(\exists x){\sim}(\exists y)(((Fx \& Vy) \& Dxy) \supset ((Dyx \& {\sim}Dxy) \& (Dxx \supset (Dyx \vee Dyy))))$$

We can continue, adding more internal propositional complexities. We can combine these with more specified sets of quantified objects involving more qualities and more relations, including relations with more object term places for three or more objects, indefinitely. Such is the logical complexity of ordinary thought and language that we can multiply the complications made possible by the syntax combinations in predicate logic which we have considered in virtually unlimited ways. If ordinary language has the capacity for making logically complex statements of this order, then we must also be ready to formalize them by translating their logical structures into predicate symbolism.

Overlapping Quantifier Scopes

Predicate wffs can contain multiple quantifiers with complexly overlapping scopes.

There are additional ways in which mixed multiple quantifiers can occur in predicate translations. We proceed systematically by distinguishing several categories of complications involving quantifier scope. There are three main sources of complexity, which can combine with one another to ramify the resulting complications in a predicate wff. The categories include those in which there are two or more mixed multiple quantifiers, in which the scopes of the respective quantifiers overlap, and in which their scopes do not overlap. Within the category of wffs in which the scopes of quantifiers overlap, there are two additional possibilities. One of the quantifiers can overlap with that of another either by being embedded within the propositional logical structure of a predicate wff or by not being so embedded. Where the scopes of quantifiers do not overlap, there is no further subdivision of categories, which is why there are three rather than four basic types of complication among predicate wffs. The possibilities, with typical but highly simplified examples, are presented in the following diagram.

BASIC TYPES OF SYNTACTICAL COMPLICATIONS IN PREDICATE WFFS		
	Quantifier scopes overlap	Quantifier scopes do not overlap
Quantifier not propositionally embedded in scope of another quantifier	$(\forall x)(\exists y)(Fx \supset Gxy)$ I	$(\forall x)Fx \supset (\exists x)Hx$ II
Quantifier propositionally embedded in scope of another quantifier	$(\forall x)(Fx \supset (\exists y)Gxy)$ III	

The types of syntactical complications in predicate wffs can be divided into three basic categories.

We have already considered several types of syntactical complications in category I, involving quantifiers that overlap in scope but are not propositionally embedded in the scope of another quantifier. We must now examine categories II and III. Any of the three types of complications can occur, and we must understand and be prepared to recognize the differences between them in order to be able to give correct translations. There is no category IV because where quantifier scopes do not overlap in the first place, there is no opportunity for them to do so in different ways by having one such quantifier propositionally embedded or not propositionally embedded in the scope of another quantifier.

The second (category II) way in which mixed multiple quantifiers can occur in predicate wffs is when quantified wffs are taken as propositions to be related by propositional connectives in complex formulas that have an overall propositional structure but that happen to involve quantified expressions to which some combination of the negation, conjunction, disjunction, or the conditional or biconditional is applied. The following are representative instances, along with their symbolizations in predicate logic:

If all fish are vertebrates, then either some vertebrates are not fish, or all vertebrates are fish.

$$(\forall x)(Fx \supset Vx) \supset ((\exists x)(Vx \ \& \sim Fx) \lor (\forall x)(Vx \supset Fx))$$

In translating this sentence, we could have but would not need to have chosen a different variable than 'x' for the existential quantifier and the second or even for the first universally quantified wff. The reason why we do not need to use a different variable in this case is that the scopes of the three quantifiers, as we have defined the concept of quantifier scope, do not overlap. Each of the three quantifiers has a logically distinct scope so that there is no possibility of confusing the sets of objects distinguished by predicate attributions and further statements of qualities or relations within each quantified subformula of the entire wff. The same logical relations could equally well be expressed by the formulas and by other logically equivalent sentences that do not begin with a universal quantification as the antecedent of the main conditional connective involving variable 'x':

$$(\forall x)(Fx \supset Vx) \supset ((\exists y)(Vy \,\&\, {\sim}Fy) \lor (\forall x)(Vx \supset Fx))$$
$$(\forall x)(Fx \supset Vx) \supset ((\exists x)(Vx \,\&\, {\sim}Fx) \lor (\forall y)(Vy \supset Fy))$$
$$(\forall x)(Fx \supset Vx) \supset ((\exists y)(Vy \,\&\, {\sim}Fy) \lor (\forall y)(Vy \supset Fy))$$
$$(\forall x)(Fx \supset Vx) \supset ((\exists y)(Vy \,\&\, {\sim}Fy) \lor (\forall z)(Vz \supset Fz))$$

.

.

.

etc.

There is no need to use any other variables than 'x' in the three distinctly quantified subformulas. A good rule of thumb to prevent logically irrelevant syntactical complications in predicate logic translations, as already mentioned, is not to use different bound variables unless we absolutely need to in order to avoid logical confusions in the symbolization of a predicate wff. One argument in support of the principle is that if we choose to use different variables where we do not really need to do so, then there is no single preferred way to write the sentence, as the previous proliferation of different translations indicates. The more uniformity we achieve in our translations, provided they are otherwise logically correct, the more informative they will be when we actually apply them in analyzing reasoning. However, we emphasize again that there is nothing logically mistaken about any of the previous translations and no reason from a strictly logical point of view, as opposed to considerations of practical convenience, to prefer any of these translations over any of the others.

It is preferable to use the same bound variable in a polyadic or mixed multiple predicate wff when the quantifiers do not overlap in scope.

As another example of a wff with an overall propositional logical structure that connects together quantified predicate wffs, consider two final translations in this category:

Some fish are vertebrates if and only if no vertebrates are mollusks or arthropods.

$$(\exists x)(Fx\ \&\ Vx) \equiv\ \sim(\exists x)(Vx\ \&\ (Mx \lor Ax))$$

The translation is relatively uncomplicated. The biconditional is evidently the main connective, relating an existential predicate wff with a negative existential. The negative existential in turn involves a conjunction as its main propositional connective and disjunction as a subordinate propositional connective in the second conjunct. Now compare the following sentence and its translation:

Neither all vertebrates are fish nor some mollusks are arthropods, unless no arthropods are fish.

$$(\exists x)(Ax\ \&\ Fx) \supset\ \sim((\forall x)(Vx \supset Fx) \lor (\exists x)(Mx\ \&\ Ax))$$

Relying on our understanding of symbolization in propositional and predicate logic, we translate the (weak) 'unless' clause in the second sentence as we would ordinarily do in a purely propositional logical context, rendering P unless Q as $\sim Q \supset P$. Here, the Q (weak) 'unless' clause is already negated, as the negative existential wff translating the English 'No arthropods are fish' in $\sim(\exists x)(Ax\ \&\ Fx)$. The consequent of the conditional that provides the overall propositional logical structure of the wff is just the negation of a disjunction to express the 'neither–nor' connective. Again, we could but do not need to do so, and in this sense perhaps we should prefer not to choose different bound object variables for the three quantified predicate wffs in the resulting translation.

Accurate translation is the foundation of correct logical analysis in predicate as in propositional logic.

The possibilities for constructing even more complicated arrangements of syntax in predicate wffs from the basic combinations we have already considered in categories I and II are virtually endless. Although much of ordinary language embodies logically less complex relations, it is always conceivable that the propositions and arguments in which we are interested might embody any permissible degree of logical complexity, combining both propositional and predicate logical structures, in which there is no overlap of quantifier scope.

We now consider category III of complicated wffs. Some sentences to be translated into predicate symbolism require that quantifiers be embedded more deeply within the scope of another quantifier, in the internal propositional structure of the resulting wff. It is usually sufficiently clear from the colloquial statement of a proposition or argument to be translated whether or not a quantifier needs to be propositionally embedded within the scope of another quantifier. When such a situation occurs, we must choose different variables to be bound by the quantifiers in order to avoid logical confusions and, indeed, to obey the formation rules for predicate logic wffs. We try to understand the logical relations expressed in ordinary language and then convey the same content with the same logical structure in the formal syntax of predicate logic using all its devices for clarifying meaning and disambiguating logical form in achieving a precise logical formulation.

The third category of complex translations in predicate logic occurs whenever we need to translate a proposition in which a quantity of objects distinguished by a predicate attribution is described as having some additional property by virtue of entering into a relation with another quantity of objects. The best way to understand the need for quantifiers to be propositionally embedded in the scope of other quantifiers is to compare wffs in which the embedded quantifier is exported to the left of the remainder of the wff and to reflect on the difference such a change in the location of the quantifier makes to the wff's meaning. Consider two imaginable translations of a sentence that says:

> Some things are such that if they are fish, then it is not the case that they devour everything.

We might imagine trying to translate the sentence in either of the following two ways:

$$(\exists x)(Fx \supset \sim(\forall y)Dxy)$$
$$(\exists x)\sim(\forall y)(Fx \supset Dxy)$$

Only the first is a correct translation of the English sentence. There is an important difference in their meanings. It may be difficult at first to appreciate the distinction, but one way of characterizing their interpretations is to notice that the first sentence is false only if everything that exists is a fish, and everything is devoured by that fish. The second sentence, in contrast, is false only if all fish devour all things. The two sentences are evidently not logically equivalent, as we will later be able to show by the predicate truth tree method we develop in Chapter 7.

Although there are some translations like the previous one in which there are subtle logical differences in the meaning of wffs with propositionally embedded versus exported quantifiers, in most translations the deep propositional embedding or exportation of quantifiers within the scope of other quantifiers makes no difference in meaning. The equivalence can be seen in a comparison of alternative translations of the following sentence:

The exact order of quantifiers is not always essential to correct translation of a mixed multiple predicate wff.

> If there exists a mollusk, then there exists a fish that devours that mollusk.

We correctly translate this proposition as:

$$(\exists x)(Mx \supset (\exists y)(Fy \ \& \ Dyx))$$

This formalization clearly indicates that the existence of a mollusk-devouring fish is conditional on the existence of a mollusk. The sentence makes good sense in this translation because we do not suppose that there could exist a mollusk-devouring fish if there were no mollusks. More important, in what sense would it be a mollusk-devouring fish if there were no mollusks for it to devour? However, it is equally correct to export the second existential quantifier so that it stands in juxtaposition either to the right or the left of the other quantifier, expressing logically indistinguishable meanings, as:

$$(\exists x)(\exists y)(Mx \supset (Fy \, \& \, Dyx))$$
$$(\exists y)(\exists x)(Mx \supset (Fy \, \& \, Dyx))$$

There are many other examples in which the correct translation of a sentence from colloquial language into predicate logic can be alternatively equivalently expressed either by propositionally embedding a quantifier or by exporting it from the internal propositional structure of a wff within the overlapping scope of another quantifier. For example, consider the proposition that:

If all fish devour some vertebrates, then they also devour some mollusks.

The sentence can be translated as follows:

$$(\forall x)(\exists y)((Fx \, \& \, Vy) \supset Dxy) \supset (\exists z)(Mz \, \& \, Dxz))$$

It is not absolutely essential to translate the sentence by propositionally embedding the second existential quantifier within the scope of the other quantifiers. We may appear to express a different sentence when we export the second existential quantifier to take the entire remainder of the expression in its scope. The wff in that case states:

$$(\forall x)(\exists y)(\exists z)(((Fx \, \& \, Vy) \supset Dxy) \supset (Mz \, \& \, Dxz))$$

The existence of mollusks devoured by fish is conditional in both translations on the circumstance of all fish devouring some vertebrates; otherwise, the sentence to be translated does not commit itself in one way or another to the existence or nonexistence of some mollusks to be devoured by all fish. The conditional existence of such mollusks is adequately expressed by either the first or second translation, which can be shown to be logically equivalent.

There is no easily stated principle by which the difference between translations that most naturally involve propositionally embedded quantifiers and those for which simply exporting the same quantifier provides an equally logically correct translation. We can only proceed intuitively, trying to make the

There is no easily stated principle for determining when quantifiers can or cannot be exported from within the scope of a propositional connective, or when multiple exported quantifiers can be rearranged, in logically equivalent predicate wffs.

translation agree with our understanding of what the colloquial expression conveys about the properties of objects belonging to specified sets. We can also formally check the logical equivalence or nonequivalence of embedded and exported variants of a translation once we have a decision method available in the form of predicate truth trees.

It may be comforting to know that in many cases translating propositions either by propositionally embedding or by exporting quantifiers within the scopes of overlapping quantifiers frequently yields logically equivalent wffs. The nonequivalences generally occur, as in the previous example, when negated quantifiers are exported from deep propositional embeddings. Thus, the following wffs are also logically nonequivalent: $(\forall x)(Fx \supset {\sim}(\forall y)Dxy)$, $(\forall x){\sim}(\forall y)(Fx \supset Dxy)$, $(\forall x)(Fx \supset {\sim}(\exists y)Dxy)$, and $(\forall x){\sim}(\exists y)(Fx \supset Dxy)$. In questionable cases, we must rely on decision methods evaluating the logical equivalence or nonequivalence of predicate wffs as alternative translations of the same colloquial proposition.

Prenex Normal Form

Any predicate wff can be written in prenex normal form.

One guide to the exporting of quantifiers in mixed multiple quantifications is provided by the rules for *prenex normal form*. We define prenex normal form as follows:

> **Prenex Normal Form**
> A predicate wff $\mathbb{P}$ is in *prenex normal form* if and only if $\mathbb{P}$ contains no quantifiers, or $\mathbb{P}$ consists of a number of quantifiers (with 1 as a limiting case), followed by or attaching to a string of predicate symbols containing no quantifiers.

Prenex normal form means that a predicate wff contains no quantifiers or consists of several quantifiers followed by a string of predicate symbols containing no quantifiers.

By the definition, wffs such as P, ${\sim}$P, and P $\supset$ Q are in prenex normal form. Similarly, $(\forall x)Fx$, $(\exists x)Fx$, $(\forall x)(Fx \supset Gx)$, and $(\exists x)(Fx \ \& \ Gx)$ are in prenex normal form, as are $(\exists x)(\forall y)Fxy$, $(\forall x)(\exists y)(Fx \supset Gy)$, and $(\forall x)(\forall y)((Fx \ \& \ Gy) \supset Hxy)$. In contrast, $(\forall x)Fx \supset (\forall x)Gx$ is not in prenex normal form because, to speak intuitively, it does not have all of its quantifiers lined up together on the left, as the definition requires. Other wffs that are not in prenex normal form include mixed multiple quantifications in which some quantifiers are embedded within the scope of a propositional connective or within the scope of any other quantifier, such as $(\exists x)Fx \supset (\forall y)Gy$ and $(\exists x)(Fx \supset (\forall y)Gy)$.

We shall now claim, but not try to rigorously prove, that for every predicate wff $\mathbb{P}$ there is a logically equivalent wff $\mathbb{P}^*$ in prenex normal form. Predicate wffs that are not already in prenex normal form can be transformed into prenex normal form through a series of logically equivalent reformulations by the following four syntax rules:

Prenex Normal Form Rules

For every predicate wff $\mathbb{P}$ that is not already in prenex normal form, there is a logically equivalent wff $\mathbb{P}^*$ in prenex normal form, obtained by implementing these transformation rules:

For convenience, we shall speak of any component syntax combinations within a wff $\mathbb{P}$, even if they are not themselves wffs, and generalize over such structures by substituting lowercase Greek letters for the relevant combinations. If $\mathbb{P}$ is $(\forall x)(Fx \supset Gx)$, for example, we refer to a part of its internal syntactical structure as $Fx \supset Gx$, even though this is not a wff, and generalize reference to this kind of structure as $\varphi \supset \psi$.

1. Replace all occurrences of the conditional '$\supset$' in $\varphi \supset \psi$ within $\mathbb{P}$ by the logically equivalent expression $\sim\varphi \vee \psi$; replace all occurrences of the biconditional '$\equiv$' in $\varphi \equiv \psi$ within $\mathbb{P}$ by the logically equivalent expression $(\varphi \& \psi) \vee (\sim\varphi \& \sim\psi)$, according to truth table definitions.
2. Drive all negation signs inward from their occurrences outside or to the left of any quantifiers in the wff as it appears after application of step 1 so that all such negations attach directly only to predicates or propositional symbols, reversing the sign of the quantifier from $\forall$ to $\exists$, and from $\exists$ to $\forall$, and collapsing double negations whenever they appear into none, to produce logically equivalent reformulations according to quantifier duality, whereby $\sim(\forall x)\varphi$ becomes $(\exists x)\sim\varphi$ and $\sim(\exists x)\varphi$ becomes $(\forall x)\sim\varphi$.
3. Rewrite all quantifier bound variables in the wff as it appears after application of step 2 so that no two quantifiers bind the same variable term, but no variable is unbound by any quantifier.
4. Rewrite the entire wff by moving all the quantifiers to the left of the remaining wff in the same left-to-right order in which they appear after application of step 3, punctuating as necessary with parentheses so that no variable is unbound.

To illustrate the transformation rules, we proceed through all four steps, as applicable, to convert each of the following predicate wffs into prenex normal form:

First example: $(\exists x)Fx \supset (\forall y)Gy$

Step 1: $\sim(\exists x)Fx \vee (\forall y)Gy$
Step 2: $(\forall x)\sim Fx \vee (\forall y)Gy$

Step 3: $(\forall x)\sim Fx \lor (\forall y)Gy$ (no change required)
Step 4: $(\forall x)(\forall y)(\sim Fx \lor Gy)$ PRENEX NORMAL FORM

Second example: $\sim(\exists x)Fx \ \& \ (\forall x)\sim Gx$

Step 1: $\sim(\exists x)Fx \ \& \ (\forall x)\sim Gx$ (no change required)
Step 2: $(\forall x)\sim Fx \ \& \ (\forall x)\sim Gx$
Step 3: $(\forall x)\sim Fx \ \& \ (\forall y)\sim Gy$
Step 4: $(\forall x)(\forall y)(\sim Fx \ \& \ \sim Gy)$ PRENEX NORMAL FORM

Third example: $(\exists x)(Fx \supset (\forall y)Gy)$

Step 1: $(\exists x)(\sim Fx \lor (\forall y)Gy)$ (compare with first example)
Step 2: $(\exists x)(\sim Fx \lor (\forall y)Gy)$ (no change required)
Step 3: $(\exists x)(\sim Fx \lor (\forall y)Gy)$ (no change required)
Step 4: $(\exists x)(\forall y)(\sim Fx \lor Gy)$ PRENEX NORMAL FORM

Fourth example: $(\forall x)(Fx \equiv (\exists y)Gy)$

Step 1: $(\forall x)((Fx \ \& \ (\exists y)Gy) \lor (\sim Fx \ \& \ \sim(\exists y)Gy))$
Step 2: $(\forall x)((Fx \ \& \ (\exists y)Gy) \lor (\sim Fx \ \& \ (\forall y)\sim Gy))$
Step 3: $(\forall x)((Fx \ \& \ (\exists y)Gy) \lor (\sim Fx \ \& \ (\forall z)\sim Gz))$
Step 4: $(\forall x)(\exists y)(\forall z)((Fx \ \& \ Gy) \lor (\sim Fx \ \& \ \sim Gz))$
                                  PRENEX NORMAL FORM

Not all predicate wffs in prenex normal form are the result of an application of the prenex rules, but any predicate wff, even if already in prenex normal form, can be transformed by the rules into a logically equivalent wff in prenex normal form.

We have not yet proven that the wffs resulting from the prenex transformation rules are logically equivalent to the wffs with which we began. However, in Chapters 7 and 8, we will have the necessary tools to demonstrate their equivalence in any chosen example, and we will see how to do so. By following the four rules, we can always convert a predicate wff that is not already in prenex normal form into a logically equivalent reformation in prenex normal form.

The rules produce only predicate wffs in prenex normal form and promise to do so beginning with any predicate wff that is not already in prenex normal form. The rules do not provide a method for producing all wffs in prenex normal form. Although $(\forall x)(Fx \supset Gx)$ is already in prenex normal form, it is not expressed in a prenex normal form that can be obtained by application of the four prenex normal form transformation rules to any wff since no wff transformed by the rules to prenex normal form will preserve the conditional, $\supset$ (or biconditional, $\equiv$). The prenex rules at most guarantee that we can convert any wff into prenex normal form, but it does not follow that all wffs in prenex normal form are necessarily a product of the rules. In the case of $(\forall x)(Fx \supset Gx)$, which is already in prenex normal form, we can easily transform it by the prenex rules into a logically equivalent expression that is also in prenex normal form but does not contain a conditional, applying only rule 1, to obtain $(\forall x)(\sim Fx \vee Gx)$. We can do the same for any other predicate wff, whether or not it is already in prenex normal form.

Prenex normal form answers some questions about the logical equivalence of predicate wffs involving quantifiers exported from within the scope of another quantifier or propositional connective.

The rules enable us to determine at a syntactical level whether certain wffs with some quantifiers embedded within the scope of certain propositional connectives or other quantifiers are logically equivalent to some other wffs in which the quantifiers are exported. However, the transformation rules do not help in reaching equivalence judgments for every case. The method, for obvious reasons, does not tell us, for example, whether $(\forall x)(\exists y)(\forall z)Fxyz$ is or is not logically equivalent to $(\exists y)(\forall x)(\forall z)Fxyz$. The prenex rules, in limited ways, determine in other cases that wffs with quantifiers embedded within the scope of a propositional connective or another quantifier are logically equivalent to wffs in which all quantifiers are exported. Therefore, for example, $(\forall x)(Fx \supset {\sim}(\forall y)Dxy)$ and $(\forall x){\sim}(\forall y)(Fx \supset Dxy)$ are logically nonequivalent, as are $(\forall x)(Fx \supset {\sim}(\exists y)Dxy)$ and $(\forall x){\sim}(\exists y)(Fx \supset Dxy)$. The prenex rules show that the wffs in each of the following sets are logically equivalent:

$(\forall x)(Fx \supset {\sim}(\forall y)Dxy)$

$(\forall x)({\sim}Fx \vee {\sim}(\forall y)Dxy)$

$(\forall x)({\sim}Fx \vee (\exists y){\sim}Dxy)$

$(\forall x)(\exists y)({\sim}Fx \vee {\sim}Dxy)$ (and also $(\forall x)(\exists y)(Fx \supset {\sim}Dxy)$)

$(\forall x)(Fx \supset {\sim}(\exists y)Dxy)$

$(\forall x)({\sim}Fx \vee {\sim}(\exists y)Dxy)$

$(\forall x)({\sim}Fx \vee (\forall y){\sim}Dxy)$

$(\forall x)(\forall y)({\sim}Fx \vee {\sim}Dxy)$ (and also $(\forall x)(\forall y)(Fx \supset {\sim}Dxy)$)

To check your understanding of the definition of prenex normal form and the transformation rules, identify all the wffs mentioned in this chapter that are already in prenex normal form and those that are not in prenex normal form. Then use the four rules to transform into prenex normal form any wffs that are not already in prenex normal form.

To Check Your Understanding 6.8 ———————————————————————■

Use the prenex transformaton rules to convert the following wffs into prenex normal form:

1. $P \supset (\forall x)Fx$
2. $(\forall x)Fx \supset (\exists x)Fx$
3. $(\forall x)(Fx \supset (\exists y)Fy)$

4. $Q \supset ((\forall x)Fx \supset (\exists y)Gy)$
5. $(\forall x)Fx \equiv (\exists x)Gx$

■

Ambiguous Quantifiers

Quantifiers in ordinary language are sometimes logically ambiguous.

There is an ambiguity in the indefinite article as an ordinary language quantifier 'a'. Sometimes when we say 'a', as in 'A woman was elected senator', we mean a particular woman, Senator Harris from California. Sometimes, when we say 'A woman deserves equal pay for equal work', we mean any woman, or women in general.

Symbolizing the first sentence requires an existential quantification in predicate logic since we do not suppose that every woman was elected. In the second case, the intent is to assert that every woman, and not just some particular woman, deserves equal pay for equal work. This requires a universal quantification. If 'W' is the property of being a woman and 'S' the property of being elected senator, then, for the first sentence, we have $(\exists x)(Wx \,\&\, Sx)$. If 'D' represents the quality of deserving equal pay for equal work, then we symbolize the second sentence as $(\forall x)(Wx \supset Dx)$. Universal quantifications are sometimes expressed in ordinary language without explicit quantifier terms. Sentences such as 'Whales are mammals' are intended to state in abbreviated form the universal generalization that 'All whales are mammals' or, equivalently, 'Every whale is a mammal'. However, if we say 'Roses are red', the intent may be only to declare that 'Some roses [perhaps the author's favorite kind] are red'. Context alone informs us whether a quantificationally ambiguous proposition in everyday discourse should be symbolized by means of universal or existential generalization in order to capture its meaning more precisely. It is an important advantage of predicate logic that it enables us to disambiguate these kinds of quantifications as they appear in ordinary language, and thereby contribute greater clarity and rigor to their expression.

Universal quantifications are sometimes expressed in ordinary language without explicit quantifiers.

■ *Demonstration 26:*   **Translation of Ambiguous** ■
                          Quantifiers

PROBLEM: To symbolize a quantificationally ambiguous proposition in predicate logic.

PROPOSITION: A kayaker shoots the rapids.

STEP 1:   *Identify quantifiers and propositional connectives*

We follow a previous convention by double underlining propositional connectives and highlighting quantifiers by single underlining. We do this not only for explicit quantifiers but also for constructions in which quantification is implied. This makes the atomic propositions stand out more clearly for symbolization.

A kayaker shoots the rapids.

STEP 2:   *Specify predicate symbols to abbreviate ordinary language predicates*

We assign predicate symbols to the relevant ordinary language predicate expressions. The predicates in the proposition are as follows:

kayaker (K); shoots (S); rapids (R)

Note that being a K (kayaker) is a one-place quality predicate, that S (shooting) is a two-place relational predicate that relates something that does the shooting to something that is shot, and that being a R (rapids) is another one-place quality predicate.

STEP 3:   *Use quantifiers in combination with propositional connectives to symbolize the relations among predications of properties to objects expressed in the proposition*

The English proposition is ambiguous, so without more information we cannot be absolutely certain whether the ordinary language quantifier 'a' is supposed to predicate a property to all kayakers or some particular kayaker. We shall symbolize both quantifications, but we observe that context and background convention suggests that the universal quantification is probably intended. We try to sound out each part of the wff as it should be translated into predicate logic. The sentence says that if anything is a kayaker, then that thing shoots the rapids. Does this mean that every (or some) kayaker shoots every rapids? Is it more likely to mean that every (or some) kayaker shoots some or at least one rapids? Again, we shall symbolize both interpretations while recognizing that in this case it is more likely that the second existential quantification is intended.

STEP 4:   *Consider alternative possible translations*

Here we shall consider four possible translations of the quantificationally ambiguous ordinary language proposition.

1. The first translation is universal both in quantifying over things that are kayakers and in quantifying over things that are rapids. This states that every kayaker shoots every rapids. More literally, it says that for any x, if x is a kayaker, then for any y, if y is a rapids, then x shoots y.

If we think that the original proposition is supposed to be true, then this would not be a plausible translation, given our background knowledge that there are too many rapids for every kayaker to shoot:

$$(\forall x)(Kx \supset (\forall y)(Ry \supset Sxy))$$

2. The second translation is universal in quantifying over things that are kayakers but existential in quantifying over things that are rapids. It says in effect that every kayaker shoots some rapids. More literally, again, it says that for any x, if x is a kayaker, then there is some y such that y is a rapids and x shoots y:

$$(\forall x)(Kx \supset (\exists y)(Ry \ \& \ Sxy))$$

3. The third translation is existential in quantifying over things that are kayakers but universal in quantifying over things that are rapids. This proposition says that some kayaker shoots every rapids. In pidgin English, it says that there is at least one x such that x is a kayaker, and, for any y, if y is a rapids, then x shoots y:

$$(\exists x)(Kx \ \& \ (\forall y)(Ry \supset Sxy))$$

4. The fourth translation is existential both in quantifying over things that are kayakers and in quantifying over things that are rapids. It says that some kayaker shoots some rapids, or that there is at least one x such that x is a kayaker and there is at least one y such that y is a rapids, and x shoots y:

$$(\exists x)(Kx \ \& \ (\exists y)(Ry \ \& \ Sxy))$$

STEP 4:   *Choose a translation from among the available alternatives as the most likely or plausible*

Although some translations might seem better than others, any of the four in the right circumstances could be correct. Without more information, it is difficult to know which of the translations to prefer. Translation 1 is the strongest, 4 is the weakest. Indeed, translation 1 is arguably too strong if we think it unlikely that anyone would propose that every kayaker shoots every rapids. Although this could be the sense intended, it is implausible and uncharitable to attribute it to a speaker without special cause. Translation 4, on the other hand, may be too weak. Why would anyone bother to state the obvious fact that some kayakers shoot some rapids? The sentence nevertheless might be used with this meaning when whitewater kayaking as a sport is first beginning. We can think of possible applications of such a proposition, but it does not seem very promising as an interpretation of what an ordinary well-informed speaker is likely to mean by expressing the sentence. Translation 3 is also a bit too strong because it requires that some kayaker shoots every rapids. This might be the intent of the proposition, if it were used to call attention to the accomplishments of an especially ambitious kayaker. Perhaps there is a (at least one) kayaker who has gone to the trouble of traveling all around the world and shooting every rapids. On intuitive grounds, however, translation 2 seems to be the most reasonable. It says that all kayakers shoot at least one rapids. This does not seem too demanding of those who profess to be kayakers. One might say that according to the proposition anyone who considers himself or herself to be a kayaker will shoot at least one rapids. If forced to choose, therefore, translation 2 might appear to be the most appropriate version.

To Check Your Understanding 6.9 ━━━━━━━━━━━━━━━━━━━━━━━━━━ ▪

Using the predicate symbols provided, symbolize the following propositions in predicate logic:

1. All little children got the blues. (L, C, G, B)
2. No one who has been to Graceland is ever quite the same. (G, S)
3. Every butterfly in this collection comes from the Amazon delta. (B, C, A)
4. Sometimes a schnauzer is a poodle's best friend. (T, S, P, B, F)
5. Some patients want the doctor to tell them the truth, and some patients want the doctor to shield them from the truth whenever it is unpleasant. (P, D, W, T, S, U)
6. You (any person) can fool some of the people some of the time, and you can fool all of the people some of the time, but you can't fool all of the people all of the time. (P, F, T)

▪

Translating Predicate Arguments

Translating predicate arguments requires translating predicate propositions as assumptions and conclusions.

Arguments are series of propositions divided into assumptions and conclusions by inference indicators. If we know how to translate individual propositions in predicate logic, then we can combine them in translating predicate inferences. We adapt the model of argument translation in propositional logic to the syntax of predicate logic, where arguments pose no special problem. We translate predicate assumptions and conclusions into predicate logic as we would any other predicate propositions, separating them by the turnstile (⊢) as an inference indicator, just as we do in propositional logic. An example we have already considered is the Socrates syllogism: $(\forall x)(Hx \supset Mx)$, $Hs \vdash Ms$. We practice translating predicate arguments in exercises at the end of the chapter.

Predicate Semantics

Semantics for predicate logic involves the extensions of predicates consisting of objects with the properties represented by the predicates.

A wff in predicate logic is interpreted by a *model*. We can formulate complex mathematical expressions for models in set theory, and we can picture the set theory relations an interpretation requires by a diagramming method. We shall describe models for predicate semantics in a precise but nonmathematical vocabulary and then outline a method for graphically representing models in the *interpretation* of predicate wffs.

An interpretation assigns objects in the domain to constants and quantifier bound variables in predicate wffs and assigns sets of objects in the domain to predicates as extensions of predicates. In somewhat the same way as truth values T and F are assigned to wffs in propositional logic, interpretations in predicate logic determine that a predicate wff is a tautology if and only if it is true on every interpretation, an inconsistency if and only if it is false on every interpretation, and a contingency if and only if it is true on at least one interpretation and false on at least one interpretation. If we specify a semantic domain consisting of the set of all books in the library, then if we interpret the wff $(\exists x)Nx$ by assigning to constant 'a' the object *Moby Dick,* as a book in the library, and to predicate 'N' the extension consisting of all objects that have the property of being a novel, then $(\exists x)Nx$ on this interpretation is true since *Moby Dick* is indeed a novel. If the library contains no fiction, but only, for example, science textbooks, then no assignment of books to the constants of the logic designating books in the library will interpret $(\exists x)Nx$ as a true wff but only as a contingent falsehood.

The truth conditions for predicate wffs are interpreted by means of relational predicate transforms.

According to the wffs rules for predicate logic, there are just five categories of wffs. We begin by explaining some of the concepts for interpretations in predicate logic. A *relational predicate transform* is a predicate obtained by transforming an n-place relational predication into a 1-place quality predicate. We do this by taking any predicate wff of the form $\mathscr{F}\alpha_1 \ldots \alpha_n$ and hyphenating all its object constants except for the last, which we simply delete. The relational predicate transform of $\mathscr{F}\alpha_1 \ldots \alpha_n$ is thus $\mathscr{F}\text{-}\alpha_1\text{-} \ldots \text{-}\alpha_{n-1}$. In ordinary language, we can take the relational predication, 'Steven is stronger than Carl', and convert it into the relational predicate transform 'Stronger-than-Carl'. If the predication is true, then being Stronger-than-Carl is a 1-place quality of Steven's. If it is true that $Sa_1 \ldots a_n$, then it is true that $S\text{-}a_1\text{-} \ldots \text{-}a_{n-1}a_n$. Finally, we speak of the *extension of a predicate* as the set of all objects in the logic's domain that have the property symbolized by the predicate. The model by which all wffs of predicate logic are interpreted is given by the following conditions:

Semantic Interpretation of Predicate Wffs

1. If $\mathbb{P}$ is a propositional wff, then $\mathbb{P}$ is true if and only if $\mathbb{P}$ is true as interpreted truth functionally according to the truth table semantics for propositional logic.
2. If $\mathbb{P}$ is a wff of the form $(\forall x)\mathbb{Q}$ or of the form $(\exists x)\mathbb{Q}$, then $\mathbb{P}$ is true if and only if $\mathbb{Q}$ is true (i.e., universal and existential quantifications in this category of wffs are vacuous).
3. If $\mathbb{P}$ is a wff of the form $\mathscr{F}\alpha_1 \ldots \alpha_n$ ($n \geq 1$), then $\mathbb{P}$ is true if and only if α_n is an object in the extension of relational predicate transform $\mathscr{F}\text{-}\alpha_1\text{-}\ldots\text{-}\alpha_{n-1}$ in the predicate semantic domain.
4. If $\mathbb{P}$ is a wff of the form $(\forall x_i)(\mathscr{F}\alpha_1 \ldots x_i \ldots \alpha_n)$ ($i, n \geq 0$), then $\mathbb{P}$ is true if and only if *every* object (other than objects $\alpha_1, \ldots, \alpha_{i-1}$, $\alpha_{i+1}, \ldots \alpha_n$) is an object in the extension of relational predicate transform $\mathscr{F}\text{-}\alpha_1\text{-}\ldots\text{-}\alpha_{n-1}$. If $\mathbb{P}$ is a wff of the form $(\exists x_i)(\mathscr{F}\alpha_1 \ldots x_i \ldots \alpha_n)$, then $\mathbb{P}$ is true if and only if *at least one* object (other than objects $\alpha_1, \ldots, \alpha_{i-1}, \alpha_{i+1}, \ldots, \alpha_n$) is an object in the extension of relational predicate transform $\mathscr{F}\text{-}\alpha_1\text{-}\ldots\text{-}\alpha_{n-1}$.
5. If $\mathbb{P}$ is a wff of the form $\sim\mathbb{Q}$, $\mathbb{Q} \& \mathbb{R}$, $\mathbb{Q} \vee \mathbb{R}$, $\mathbb{Q} \supset \mathbb{R}$, or $\mathbb{P} \equiv \mathbb{Q}$, then $\mathbb{P}$ is true if and only if $\mathbb{P}$ is true when interpreted truth functionally according to the truth table definitions of the propositional connectives, given the truth values of $\mathbb{Q}$ and $\mathbb{R}$, as determined by interpretation requirements 1–4.

In effect, the model interprets predicate wffs in such a way that, in the simplest case, Fa ('Alice is friendly') is true if and only if object a (Alice) belongs to the set of all objects in the extension of predicate 'F'; that is, the set of all objects that have property F (all the things that are or have the property of being friendly).

The negation of the proposition ~Fa is true just in case a is not included in the extension of predicate 'F'. If Alice is not friendly, then she will obviously not be included in the set of all objects that possess the property of being friendly. Since ~Fa is the negation of Fa, we can also say, once we have explained how to interpret Fa, that ~Fa is true if and only if Fa is false. In this way, we understand the meaning of predicate wffs that attribute 1-place predicates or qualities to individual objects in the logic's semantic domain.

The proposition $Fa_1 \ldots a_n$ is true according to the interpretation of predicate wffs just in case object a_n is included in the extension of the relational predicate transform $F\text{-}a_1\text{-}\ldots\text{-}a_{n-1}$. The principle is somewhat abstract, and the idea of a relational predicate transform might seem strange. We can see how the interpretation is supposed to work by considering a relatively simple example. Let F be the relational property of being the friend of. This is clearly a relation rather than a quality because for the property to be instantiated there must be someone who is the friend and someone whom she or he befriends. If I am a friend, I am a friend of somebody, and in that case I am related to the person by the relational property of friendship. I may be the friend of John, Mary, Steve, or Susan. In the simplest case, we might write Fab to indicate that object a is the friend of object b. When will such a wff be true? Informally, of course, the proposition will be true when it is actually the case that a is the friend of b, and otherwise the proposition will be false. According to the logic's formal semantics, the wff is true if and only if object b is included in the extension of the relational predicate transform F-a. This is not merely the set of all objects that have the property of being a friend to anyone at all, but more specifically the set of all objects that are friends of object a. We can therefore read the relational predicate transform F-a as friends of-a (or a's friends). Then Fab will be true if and only if b is in the extension of all objects that have the property of being a friend-of-a (or one of a's friends).

The same principle holds for complicated relational predicates involving more than two object term places. The wff Babc, which might be informally interpreted as object c is situated between objects a and b, is true according to the semantics if and only if object c is in the extension of relational predicate transform B-a-b. We can read this as referring to the relational property of being-between-a-and-b, which may or may not be true of object c. This is also true for any relational predicate. The negation of such an n-place relational predication, $\sim Fa_1 \ldots a_n$, is true by the propositional component of predicate semantics if and only if $Fa_1 \ldots a_n$ is false. More specifically, $\sim Fa_1 \ldots a_n$ is true if and only if object a_n is not included in or is excluded from the extension of relational predicate transform $F\text{-}a_1\text{-}\ldots\text{-}a_{n-1}$. In the previous examples, this would mean that ~Fab is true just in case object b is not included in the extension of F-a, where b is not a friend-of-a or does not have the relational property of being a friend-of-a (or one of or among a's friends), and that ~Fabc is true just in case object c is not included in the extension of F-a-b, where c is not situated between a and b, or does not have the relational property of being between-a-and-b, and is excluded from the extension of relational predicate transform F-a-b.

The universally quantified wff $(\forall x)Fx$ says that everything is F or has property F. According to predicate semantics, the wff is true if and only if every object in the logic's semantic domain is included in the extension of predicate 'F'. Its negation, $\sim(\forall x)Fx$, is true just in case $(\forall x)Fx$ is false; that is, just in case

Predicate semantics gives a formal interpretation for every predicate wff.

A universal quantification is true if it holds for every object in the logic's semantic domain.

An existential quantification is true if it holds for at least one object in the logic's semantic domain.

there is at least one object in the logic's semantic domain that is not included in the extension of predicate 'F'. Similar considerations apply in the case of n–place relational properties as for 1–place qualities, again invoking the device of relational predicate transforms for quantifications of the form $(\forall x)Fa_1 \ldots a_n x$. Here, we say that everything in the semantic domain is F-related to objects $a_1 \ldots a_n$ if and only if every object in the domain is included in the extension of the relational predicate transform $F\text{-}a_1\text{-} \ldots \text{-}a_n$. For example, everything is the friend of object a in $(\forall x)Fax$ just in case every object in the logic's semantic domain is included in the extension of the relational predicate transform F-a; everything is between objects a and b in $(\forall x)Babx$ just in case every object in the logic's semantic domain is included in the extension of the relational predicate transform B-a-b. If any object is excluded from the extensions, then the negations of the wffs, $\sim(\forall x)Fa_1 \ldots a_n x$, or $\sim(\forall x)Fax$ and $\sim(\forall x)Babx$, are true instead. From these basic forms, all multiple universal quantifications, such as $(\forall x_1) \ldots (\forall x_n)Fx_1 \ldots x_n$, and their negations are also interpreted, systematically replacing each constant by corresponding universal quantifier bound variables and applying the same predicate semantic principles for each resulting wff. This is also the case for the existential quantification $(\exists x)Fx$, where the wff is true if and only if at least one object in the logic's domain is included in the extension of predicate 'F', with corresponding adjustments for $(\exists x)Fa_1 \ldots a_n x$, $(\exists x_1) \ldots (\exists x_n)Fx_1 \ldots x_n$, and their negations.

The universal quantification relating objects with different properties, $(\forall x)(Fx \supset Gx)$, is interpreted as a universalization of the conditional sentence $Fa \supset Ga$ for any object a. In particular, $(\forall x)(Fx \supset Gx)$ is true if and only if every object in the logic's semantic domain is such that if it has property F, then it has property G. The semantics requires that in this case, any object in the domain that is included in the extension of all objects with property F is also included in the extension of all objects with property G. The existential quantification $(\exists x)(Fx \& Gx)$ is similarly interpreted by the semantics as true if and only if there is at least one object in the semantic domain that is such that it has both property F and property G; that is, if and only if there is at least one object that belongs to the extension of predicate 'F', consisting of all objects with property F, and to the extension of predicate 'G', consisting of all objects with property G. The negations of these quantifications are interpreted correspondingly. With obvious modifications, the semantics also interpret wffs of the form $(\forall x)(Fx \& Gx)$, $(\exists x)(Fx \supset Gx)$, and their negations. More complicated n–place relational predicates, such as Ssc ('Steven is stronger than Carl'), are interpreted by the model as true if and only if object a_n (Steven) belongs to the set of all objects in the extension of the relational predicate transform $S\text{-}a_{n-1}$ ('Stronger-than-Carl'). This is also the case for n–place predications that take any number of object terms n.

Relational predicate transforms interpret n-ary relational predicate wffs for any number n object term places.

Predicate Semantic Concepts

Predicate semantic concepts are defined for tautologies, inconsistencies, and contingencies, logical consistency and inconsistency, logical equivalence and non-equivalence, and deductive validity and invalidity.

We now define several important semantic concepts for predicate logic. The following definitions parallel those already provided for propositional logic to explain the concepts of tautology, inconsistency, contingency, logical consistency, and logical equivalence of individual or pairs of wffs and the deductive validity of sequents:

Predicate Semantic Concepts

1. If $\mathbb{P}$ is a wff of predicate logic, then $\mathbb{P}$ is a *tautology* if and only if $\mathbb{P}$ is true on every predicate interpretation.
2. If $\mathbb{P}$ is a wff of predicate logic, then $\mathbb{P}$ is an *inconsistency* if and only if $\mathbb{P}$ is false on every predicate interpretation.
3. If $\mathbb{P}$ is a wff of predicate logic, then $\mathbb{P}$ is a *contingency* if and only if $\mathbb{P}$ is true on at least one predicate interpretation and $\mathbb{P}$ is false on at least one predicate interpretation (if and only if $\mathbb{P}$ is neither a tautology nor an inconsistency).
4. If $\mathbb{P}$ and $\mathbb{Q}$ are wffs of predicate logic, then $\mathbb{P}$ and $\mathbb{Q}$ are *logically consistent* if and only if there is at least one predicate interpretation on which $\mathbb{P}$ is true and $\mathbb{Q}$ is true.
5. If $\mathbb{P}$ and $\mathbb{Q}$ are wffs of predicate logic, then $\mathbb{P}$ and $\mathbb{Q}$ are *logically equivalent* if and only if there is no predicate interpretation on which $\mathbb{P}$ is true and $\mathbb{Q}$ is false or $\mathbb{P}$ is false and $\mathbb{Q}$ is true.
6. If $\mathbb{P}_1, \ldots, \mathbb{P}_n$ and $\mathbb{Q}_1, \ldots, \mathbb{Q}_n$ are wffs of predicate logic, then the sequent $\mathbb{P}_1, \ldots, \mathbb{P}_n \vdash \mathbb{Q}_1, \ldots, \mathbb{Q}_n$ is *deductively valid* if and only if there is no predicate interpretation on which all $\mathbb{P}_1, \ldots, \mathbb{P}_n$ are true and any $\mathbb{Q}_1, \ldots, \mathbb{Q}_n$ are false.

Alternative Semantic Principles

Predicate wffs can also be interpreted by means of n-tuples rather than relational predicate transforms.

There is an equivalent alternative formal semantics for predicate logic. Instead of considering the inclusion of a single object in or its exclusion from the extension of a relational predicate transform, we can redefine the extension of any n-place predicate to accommodate ordered sets of objects, known as *n-tuples*.

An n-tuple is an ordered set of n objects in the logic's semantic domain, $<a_1, \ldots, a_n>$. The idea of an ordered set, indicated by angle brackets, is that each item has a definite place in a definite sequence and cannot be freely rearranged from the exact order in which each is specified. The first listed object occurs in first place, the second object occurs in the second place, and so on.

The extension of an n–place relation R is the set of n-tuples of objects such that the first object in each n-tuple bears relation R to the other objects in the n-tuple. The semantics of the logic assigns a set of n-tuples of the objects in the logic's domain to each n-place predicate. This makes it possible to determine the truth or falsehood of every n-place predicate–constant expression, by means of which universally and existentially quantified expressions are interpreted as generalizations of 1-place predicate–constant expressions. The predicate wff Sab is true on this interpretation, for example, just in case the n-tuple <a, b> is in the extension of relational predicate 'S'. Thus, if 'S' represents the relation of being stronger than, then the sentence Sab is true just in case the n-tuple <a, b> is included in the set of all n-tuples such that the first ordered item in the n-tuple is an object that is stronger than the second ordered item in the n-tuple.

Although n-tuples offer an equivalent formal semantics for predicate logic, relational predicate transforms may be preferable because in some ways they are simpler and more intuitive.

We can adopt either relational predicate transform semantics or n-tuple semantics to formally interpret the meaning of predicate wffs. The method of relational predicate transforms is chosen as an adequate and, in some ways, more intuitive application of the idea of including a single object in, or excluding it from, the extension of a 1-place quality predicate to the analysis of indefinitely many n-place relational predicates. The advantage of a semantics involving relational predicate transforms is that, by means of a simple syntactical transformation, it interprets the meaning of every predicate wff by the general principle of the inclusion of a single object or single set of objects in, or its exclusion from, another set of objects. The disadvantage of n-tuple semantics, despite its formal adequacy, is that it unnecessarily complicates the interpretation of predicate wffs. It does so by introducing n-tuples as ordered sets of objects for each of the endlessly different ways in which objects may be ordered. The ordering of objects in n-tuples, moreover, must be understood as expressing the relations that are supposed to be interpreted by the n-tuples. An n-tuples semantics invokes the existence of ordered sets of objects over and above the individual objects that belong to the logic's semantic domain and the ordinary unordered sets of objects in or from which they are included or excluded.

Circle Diagrams

The semantics of predicate logic can be explained by means of circle diagrams.

We can further explain the semantics of predicate wffs by drawing *circle diagrams* to indicate the domain of objects over which quantifications range. When we say that all objects have a certain property, we mean that each and every object belonging to the logic's domain has the property. When we say that some objects have a property, we mean that the domain contains at least one object with the property.

Circle diagrams can be used to map every basic quantification in predicate logic. We picture inclusions in and exclusions of objects from semantic subdomains of objects with particular properties by labeling circles within circles with corresponding predicate symbols. The set of all objects that have the property symbolized by a predicate is the extension of the predicate. The set of all objects that do not have the property symbolized by a predicate is the *extension complement* of the predicate. The outermost circle in a circle diagram always represents the entire semantic domain and is labeled 'O' for 'objects'. The 'x' inside the circle indicates that the domain is not empty but rather contains at least one object. The same device is used to indicate occupation by objects of subdomains represented by inner circles. The method of circles is an adaptation of diagramming techniques first developed by Leonhard Euler and John Venn.

Circle diagrams picture all basic semantic relations expressed by predicate wffs.

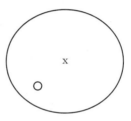

**Semantic Domain
of All Objects**

We diagram the proposition that Fa or that object a has property F by drawing a smaller circle representing the set of all objects with property F within the circle representing the semantic domain of all objects. Then we inscribe the constant a within the circle representing the set of all objects with property F to show that object a is included among the set of all objects with property F.

Circle diagrams represent the inclusion in or exclusion from one object or set of objects from another.

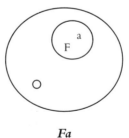

Fa

The negation of Fa or ~Fa is shown by a diagram in which constant 'a' is written outside the circle representing the set of all objects with property F to show that object a is excluded from the set of all objects with property F.

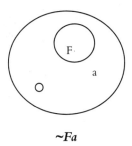

~Fa

We use a variation of the same graphic principle to diagram the formal semantic interpretation of any n-place predication $Fa_1 \ldots a_n$ or its negation $\sim Fa_1 \ldots a_n$, following the method of relational predicate transforms.

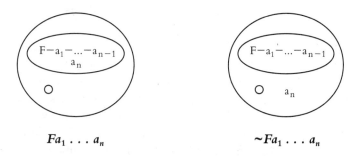

$Fa_1 \ldots a_n$ $\sim Fa_1 \ldots a_n$

Circle diagrams are the graphic equivalent of the interpretation of predicate wffs by means of relational predicate transforms.

To represent the meaning of the predicate expression, 'Everything is F', we draw a circle labeled 'F'. The F circle represents all the objects in the domain with property F. We shade in every part of domain circle O outside of circle F to indicate that there are no objects in the domain that are not in the subdomain of objects with property F. Finally, we mark an 'x' in circle F to show that there is at least one object with property F. The completed diagram looks as follows:

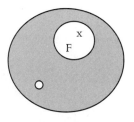

'Everything is F'

$(\forall x)Fx$

$\sim(\exists x)\sim Fx$

Now we present a circle diagram for the existentially quantified proposition that 'Something is F' or 'At least one thing is F':

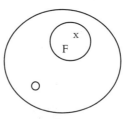

'Something is F'

$(\exists x)Fx$

$\sim(\forall x)\sim Fx$

The 'x' in the inner circle in the diagram indicates that the extension of predicate F is not empty but contains at least one object. The absence of an 'x' within circle O but outside circle F leaves it open whether or not there are any non-F objects in the set of all objects that do not have the property represented by the predicate in the predicate extension complement. Since 'Everything is F' implies that 'Something is F', we do not want circle diagrams to prejudge the question whether when something is F, something is also non-F. It could be true that something is F because everything is F, to the exclusion of any non-F's.

We can also represent the assertion that nothing has property F, or that everything lacks or fails to have property F. We shade in the circle representing the extension of predicate F, to picture the fact that it contains no objects.

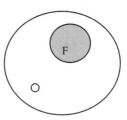

'Nothing is F'

$\sim(\exists x)Fx$

$(\forall x)\sim Fx$

We similarly represent the proposition that not everything is F or that something is non–F by marking the extension complement of F in circle O outside circle F with an 'x' to show that it contains an object. The diagram also properly leaves open whether or not there is an F or some object that has property F.

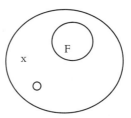

'Not everything is F'

$\sim(\forall x)Fx$

$(\exists x)\sim Fx$

To represent the meaning of the proposition that 'All F's are G's', $(\forall x)(Fx \supset Gx)$, we draw a circle within a circle. The outer circle is labeled 'G' to stand for the extension of predicate G. The inner circle is labeled 'F' to stand for the extension of predicate 'F'. The outer circle represents collectively all the objects of the logic's semantic domain that have property G. The inner circle represents collectively all the objects of the logic's semantic domain that have property F. By enclosing the F circle within the G circle, we graphically represent the proposition that everything in the logic's semantic domain is such that if it has property F, then it has property G. The diagram shows this by virtue of the fact that it pictures the set of all the objects with property F included or enclosed within the set of all the objects with property G. If anything has property F, it has property G because all the F's are included among the G's.

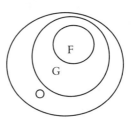

'All F's are G's'

$(\forall x)(Fx \supset Gx)$

$\sim(\exists x)(Fx \ \& \sim Gx)$

To represent the existentially quantified expression that some objects have or at least one object has property F, we draw overlapping circles for the

Intersections of circles represent properties shared by some but not all objects.

extensions of predicates 'F' and 'G', indicating by an 'x' that there is at least one object in the intersection of their extensions that has both property F and property G.

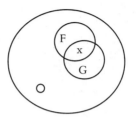

'Some F's are G's'

(∃x)(Fx & Gx)

~(∀x)(Fx ⊃ ~Gx)

The intersection of the extensions of predicates 'F' and 'G' is completely shaded-in to represent the proposition that 'No F's are G's'.

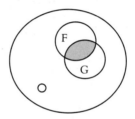

'No F's are G's'

~(∃x)(Fx & Gx)

(∀x)(Fx ⊃ ~Gx)

The negation of the universal quantification that all F's are G's has the following diagram:

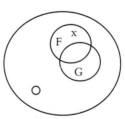

'Not all F's are G's'

~(∀x)(Fx ⊃ Gx)

(∃x)~(Fx ⊃ Gx)

(∃x)(Fx & ~Gx)

*Circle diagrams depict
set theoretical rela-
tions in the semantics
of predicate logic.*

As a final indication of how the semantics of the most basic predicate relations can be diagrammed, consider the circle diagram interpretations of universal conjunctions and existential conditionals and their negations.

To diagram the proposition that everything is F and G, we draw inter-
secting circles F and G, place an 'x' in their intersection, and shade in all areas
of the diagram outside the intersection of circles F and G. This shows that there
is nothing in the semantic domain that does not have both properties F and G.

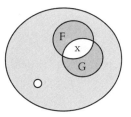

'Everything is F and G'

$(\forall x)(Fx \ \& \ Gx)$

$\sim(\exists x)(Fx \supset Gx)$

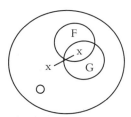

'Something is such that if it is F then it is G'

$(\exists x)(Fx \supset Gx)$

$\sim(\forall x)(Fx \ \& \sim Gx)$

The existential condition says in effect that there is something that is either G or not F. This disjunctive possibility is represented by marking an 'x' as
extending alternatively across two possible different locations in the diagram, as
belonging to the extension of objects with property G, or as belonging to the
extension of objects that do not have property F.

In the following diagram, because there are several ways in which objects
can fail to be both F and G, we indicate a range of possible locations for the objects that would make the proposition true by connecting three different 'x' to-
kens with line segments. The proposition is true just in case there is an object
in any of these three locations in the domain.

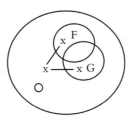

'Not everything is F and G'

$\sim(\forall x)(Fx \ \& \ Gx)$

$(\exists x)\sim(Fx \ \& \ Gx)$

$(\exists x)(Fx \supset \sim Gx)$

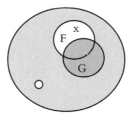

'Nothing is such that if it is F then it is G'

$\sim(\exists x)(Fx \supset Gx)$

$(\forall x)\sim(Fx \supset Gx)$

$(\forall x)(Fx \ \& \sim Gx)$

Circle diagrams can be used as a decision method for predicate logic.

    It is possible to use circle diagrams as a limited kind of decision method in predicate logic. The method is to diagram the assumptions of the argument and then check to determine whether in diagramming the assumptions we have thereby also diagrammed the conclusion. We apply the technique here to the Socrates syllogism. The first assumption says that 'All men are mortal' or $(\forall x)(Hx \supset Mx)$, which we diagram as follows:

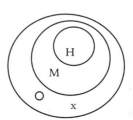

The second assumption states that 'Socrates is a man (human being)' or Hs, which we picture by adding constant 's' to the diagram in the circle representing the extension of predicate 'H', among the set of all objects that are human beings. Then the diagram looks as follows:

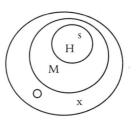

VALID

We check to see whether by diagramming the argument's two assumptions we have also diagrammed the conclusion. The conclusion of the argument is that 'Socrates is mortal'. We see that by placing constant 's' in circle H, we have also placed constant 's' in circle M because circle H is contained within circle M. The diagram satisfies the requirements for representing a deductively valid argument, and we conclude as the imagination test also confirms that the Socrates syllogism is deductively valid.

We can describe semantic models for predicate logic in more formalized ways. For this, we apply the principles of mathematical set theory to characterize the inclusions of objects in and exclusions of objects from certain object subdomains. The point of introducing circle diagrams is to give a pictorial representation of the same set theoretical relations by which predicate wffs and sequents are interpreted. The diagrams help us to understand the meaning of basic expressions in predicate logic by visualizing a domain of objects and subdomains of objects within the domain as extensions of predicates representing the objects' properties. This is analogous to the way truth tables define the truth functional meaning of wffs in propositional logic. However, just as truth tables fail to provide a fully general practical method for determining the logical properties of individual propositions and arguments in propositional logic, so too in predicate logic circle diagrams fail to provide a fully general practical method of determining the logical properties of individual predicate wffs and sequents. The limitations of circle diagramming, like the limitations of truth tables in propositional logic, provide an incentive to develop predicate truth trees as a more useful decision method.

Like truth tables, circle diagrams have practical limitations that restrict their usefulness to relatively uncomplicated wffs and sequents involving few predicates.

To Check Your Understanding 6.10 ————————————————————————————————————— ▪

Interpret the truth conditions for each of the following wffs, according to the semantic principles for predicate logic. Use circle diagrams to represent each of the following predicate expressions for properties F, G, H. Explain what your diagrams picture and how each diagram relates to the symbolization of the sentences as wffs of predicate logic.

1. All frogs are green.
2. Some horned frogs are green.
3. Some frogs are such that if they are green then they are horned.
4. Some horned frogs are nongreen.
5. Every green frog is horned, and only horned frogs are green.
6. Green frogs are always horned, whereas some horned frogs are nongreen.

▪

Summary: Predicate Syntax and Semantics

Propositional logic provides the foundation for predicate logic. Object constants designating objects in the logic's semantic domain are attached to predicates designating properties to represent property–object relations. Universal and existential quantifiers bind object variables to express quantified propositions that all or some objects have a certain property. The universal quantifier with the conditional symbolizes universal generalizations of the form 'All F's are G's'. The existential quantifier with conjunction symbolizes existential generalizations of the form 'Some F's are G's'. Universal quantifications imply existential quantifications, but not conversely. Translation from ordinary language into predicate symbolism requires disambiguation of colloquial quantifiers and use of propositional connectives and quantified predicate expressions to symbolize only clauses and exceptions to generalizations. Mixed multiple quantifications involve object variables bound by different quantifiers in different combinations. A semantic model interprets the wffs and sequents of predicate logic, in which conditions for their interpretation are defined in terms of the inclusion of an object or set of objects in, or its exclusion from, another set of objects as the extension of a predicate. Circle diagrams picture interrelations among subsets of the extensions of predicates, providing a graphic representation of the semantics of predicate logic.

Key Words

predicate logic
syllogism
subject–predicate proposition
property–object relation
property
object
set of objects
(property) predicate
(object) constant
predicate—constant expression
quantity
semantic domain
copula
quality
object term place
relation
n-adic relation
n-ary relational predicate
all
some
quantifying over set of objects
quantifier
(object) variable
quantity
quantification
quantifier bound variable

universal quantifier
existential quantifier
predicate variable
object constant variable
metavariable
occurrence of an object variable
bound variable
unbound (free) variable
quantifier scope
vacuous quantification
monadic quantification
polyadic quantification
mixed multiple quantification
quantifier duality
only quantifications
exceptions to generalizations
prenex normal form
semantic model
interpretation
relational predicate transform
extension of a predicate
n-tuple
circle diagram
extension complement (of a
   predicate)

Exercises

I: Predicate Syntax and Semantics Concepts   Give a correct concise statement of each of the following concepts; where appropriate, give an illustration of each that does not appear in the book:

1. Subject; predicate
2. Object constant; object variable
3. Property; quality; relation
4. Universal quantifier; existential quantifier
5. Free variable; bound variable

6. Scope of quantifier
7. Prenex normal form
8. Semantic domain
9. Extension of a predicate; extension complement
10. Circle diagram of predicate relations

II: *Subject and Predicate* Identify subjects and predicates in each of the following propositions; specify whether each predicate represents a quality or relation:

1. All roads lead to Rome.
2. Every good boy deserves favor.
3. Beth realizes that she cannot be all things to all people.
4. Any friend of Marcus is a friend of Tully, but some friends of Gaius are friends only of friends of Lucretius.
5. Alan knows all and only whatever Betty knows, who doubts the teachings of Zarathustra.
6. Some new days bring special challenges and unexpected opportunities, but some days generate more problems than some people can handle.
7. Randy likes a good western, but Sandy likes only romantic comedies, and Candy likes some mysteries but no thrillers, unless they happen to be set in Victorian England.
8. All bananas are tropical fruit, and all tropical fruit are delicious and healthful, though some are less nourishing than temperate zone fruits.
9. If the Toltecs influenced the Aztecs, and the Aztecs influenced the Maya, then if the Maya influenced the Chaco Canyon tribes, then the Toltecs influenced the Chaco Canyon tribes.
10. Bach and Mozart were classical composers; yet neither Mozart nor Bach were as accomplished performers by modern standards as Chopin or Liszt.

III: *Transcription from Symbolization to Ordinary Language* For each of the following symbolizations and interpretations predicates, give transcriptions into ordinary language expressions. Explain how each of the wffs can be constructed in a series of applications of the wffs rules for predicate logic. F, famous; G, generous; H, honest; I, is identical to.

1. $(\forall x)(\forall y)(Ixy \equiv Iyx)$
2. $(\forall x)(((Fx \ \& \ Gx) \supset Hx) \supset Gx)$

3. $(\exists x)(\forall y)(((Fx \And Gx) \supset Hx) \equiv Ixy)$

4. $(\forall x)(\forall y)(Ixy \supset ((Fx \equiv Fy) \And (Gx \equiv Gy)))$

5. $(\forall x)(\exists y)(Ixy \And ((Fx \And Hx) \And \sim Gy))$

6. $(\forall x)(\forall y)(((Fx \And Gy) \And (Hx \lor Hy)) \supset \sim Ixy)$

7. $(\exists x)(\exists y)(Ixy \supset \sim (Fx \And \sim Fy))$

8. $(\exists x)(\exists y)(\exists z)((Ixy \And Iyz) \supset Ixz)$

9. $\sim(\exists x)(\exists y)(\forall z)(((Fx \And Gy) \And Hz) \supset \sim (Ixy \lor Ixz))$

10. $(\forall x)(\forall y)((Fx \lor Gy) \supset (\exists z)(((Hz \And Hy) \supset Hx) \And (Izy \And \sim Iyx)))$

IV: Symbolization of Propositions in Predicate Logic Translate each of the following propositions from ordinary language into predicate logic; follow the two-stage symbolization process where necessary:

1. All roads lead to Rome. (R, L, r)

2. Every good boy deserves favor. (G, B, D, F)

3. Beth cannot be all things to all people. (B, P, b)

4. Any friend of Marcus is a friend of Tully, but some friends of Gaius are friends only of friends of Lucretius. (F, m, t, g, l)

5. Alan knows all and only whatever Betty knows, who doubts the teachings of Zarathustra. (K, D, T, a, b, z)

6. Some new days bring special challenges and unexpected opportunities, but some days generate more problems than some people can handle. (N, D, B, S, C, U, O, G, H, P)

7. Randy likes a good western, but Sandy likes only romantic comedies, and Candy likes some mysteries but no thrillers, unless they happen to be set in Victorian England. (L, G, W, R, C, M, T, S, r, s, c, v)

8. All bananas are tropical fruit, and all tropical fruit are delicious and healthful, though some are less nourishing than temperate zone fruits. (B, T, F, D, H, L, Z)

9. If the Toltecs influenced the Aztecs, and the Aztecs influenced the Maya, then if the Maya influenced the Chaco Canyon tribes, then the Toltecs influenced the Chaco Canyon tribes. (T, I, A, M, C)

10. Bach and Mozart were classical composers; yet neither Mozart nor Bach were as accomplished performers by modern standards as Chopin or Liszt. (C, A, b, m, c, l)

11. Any qualified chemist can test any soil sample for mineral content, but only a licensed oxides specialist can determine exact amounts of trace metals in some volcanic earths. (Q, C, T, S, L, O, D, A, M, V, E)

12. Plato could not understand his brilliant pupil Aristotle, nor could Aristotle understand his brilliant pupil Theophrastus, but Aristotle could understand Plato and Plato could understand Theophrastus. (U, B, P, p, a, t)

13. Some schnauzers are loyal companions to anyone who feeds them, whereas some obey only those who walk them every day. (S, L, C, P, F, O, W, D)

14. Mozart was a better keyboardist than Bach, and Bach was certainly a better keyboardist than either Chopin or Liszt; yet neither Chopin nor Liszt was as skilled an orchestrator as Bach nor as accomplished a composer as Mozart. (K, O, C, m, b, c, l)

15. Every dog has his hour in the sun. (D, H, S)

16. No responsible individual writes letters to any newspaper editorial column. (R, I, W, L, N, E, C)

17. Some day, everyone will own a 3-D holographic viewphone, over which they can broadcast and receive any 3-D image to or from anyone. (D, P, O, T, H, V, B, R, I)

18. No logicians are philanderers, but some statisticians are incontinent only if all category theorists are degenerate fundamentalists. (L, P, S, I, C, D, F)

19. Adam and Eve lived in a beautiful garden, where Adam named all the wild but friendly animals, and they could eat of every ordinary tree, but they could not eat of the Tree of the Knowledge of Good and Evil. (L, B, G, N, W, F, A, E, O, T, a, e, t)

20. If any Hatfield feuds with any McCoy, then some McCoy feuds with some Hatfield, but not of course with every one; though Caleb feuds with Zeke and Zeke feuds with Abner. (H, F, M, c, z, a)

V: Symbolization of Arguments in Predicate Logic   Translate each of the following arguments from ordinary language into predicate logic; follow the two-stage symbolization process where necessary:

1. At least one evangelist is fraudulent. All charlatans are fraudulent. So, all charlatans are evangelists. (E, F, C)

2. Every pain is a distraction. Some pains are unbearable. Therefore, some distractions are unbearable. (P, D, B)

3. Some primates are not gorillas. But all primates are mammals. Thus, some mammals are not gorillas. (P, G, M)

4. All artists are creative. No creative person is motivated by greed. So, no persons motivated by greed are artists. (A, C, P, G)

5. No politicians are likely to vote for salary rollbacks. Only cynical politicians would not vote for salary rollbacks. Hence, salary rollbacks will be voted for only by politicians who are not cynical. (P, V, S, C)

6. Some dogs are schnauzers. All dogs are canines. Therefore, some canines are schnauzers. (D, S, C)

7. To be a lawyer is to assume a sincere responsibility to the truth. Only those who worship the truth assume responsibility to it. Thus, lawyers always worship the truth. (L, A, S, R, T, W)

8. Show me a Frenchman, and I'll show you a gourmand. But all gourmands are nonascetics. It follows that all ascetics are non-Frenchmen. (F, G, A)

9. No person hates himself or herself. Anyone who does not love someone who loves everyone hates them. Thus, there is someone who is not loved by someone only if he or she does not love that person. (P, H, L)

10. Albert can fix anything and Bertrand can fix something. So, if anything is broken, Cecil can have it repaired only if it is broken. (F, B, R, a, b, c)

11. Whenever Tina remembers her bicycle trip, she thinks of Holland. Tina plans no bicycle trip unless she can go to Holland. As a result, when Tina goes to Holland, she remembers her bicycle trip. (R, B, T, P, G, t, h)

12. A schnauzer likes anyone who pets it. Victor is a schnauzer and Rose pets it. So, Victor likes Rose. (S, L, P, v, r)

13. If all pyromaniacs are fiends, then someone is a sociopath. Every sociopath is a fiend. Therefore, either Wolfgang is not a pyromaniac or Wolfgang is a fiend. (P, F, S, w)

14. Someone here knows how to navigate by the stars. So, obviously, someone knows how to navigate by the stars or can find their way by dead reckoning. (N, R)

15. Nancy is a nurse, and Linda's supervisor. Someone is both a nurse and Nancy's supervisor. Anyone who supervises everyone who supervises anyone supervises everyone else. Therefore, someone is a nurse and supervises both Nancy and Linda. (N, S, n, l)

16. At least one scoundrel repents. All those who wronged Sebastian are neither among the holy elect nor in pursuit of greater enlightenment. Someone converses with the devout and is among the holy elect. Hence, not everyone wronged Sebastian. (S, R, W, H, E, P, G, C, D, s)

17. If there are tickets left, then Cindy will be notified. At least one performance outdoes itself but although some tickets are left, they are not for Wednesday's show. Therefore, Cindy will be notified. (T, N, P, O, W, S, c)

18. All published books or journal articles are well written and interesting. Not everything is both interesting and well written. From this it follows logically that at least something is not a journal article. (P, B, J, W, I)

19. No information processing mechanism experiences sensation or conscious thought. But all minds experience conscious thought. Thus, any mind or

information processing mechanism experiences conscious thought. (I, E, S, C, T, M)

20. There are unsolved mysteries if and only if all unsolved mysteries or puzzling occurrences are supernatural. There are supernatural occurrences. Not all mysteries are solved. Therefore, there are unsolved mysteries that are supernatural occurrences. (U, M, P, O, S)

VI: *Short Answer Questions for Philosophical Reflection*

1. What is the difference between an object and a property?

2. What are the requirements of reference and true predication? How do names designate objects? What is it for an object to have a property? How are properties truly predicated of objects?

3. How or by what principle are objects included in the semantic domain of predicate logic?

4. What is the significance of the fact that predicate dualities make it possible with negation to reduce either quantifier to the other?

5. Is it possible to refer to and truly predicate properties of nonexistent objects? Could a nonexistent object at least have the property of being nonexistent, and of being an object, of not being the Eiffel Tower or the Pyramid of Giza?

6. Can a nonexistent object have both a property and its complement? Are there any properties or kinds of properties that an object cannot freely be assumed to have? Are there any properties or kinds of properties such that an object cannot have both the property and its complement?

CHAPTER SEVEN

Predicate Truth Trees

Logic, like any science, has as its business the pursuit of truth. What are true are certain statements; and the pursuit of truth is the endeavor to sort out the true statements from the others, which are false.

—W. V. O. Quine, *Methods of Logic* (1950)

As a DECISION METHOD for predicate logic, we now develop additional rules for predicate truth trees. Within limits that do not apply to propositional logic, predicate truth trees provide definite answers to the same kinds of questions about the logical properties of predicate wffs and sequents as propositional truth trees do for propositional wffs and sequents.

Predicate Trees

Truth trees are adapted from propositional logic as a decision method for predicate logic.

All the truth tree rules, protocol, and methods of testing wffs and sequents in propositional logic also apply to truth trees in predicate logic.

We can extend the truth tree method from propositional to predicate logic. There are sophisticated formal limitations that prevent *predicate truth trees* from being as generally effective as propositional truth trees. For most practical applications we are likely to encounter, however, predicate truth trees are perfectly adequate. We shall proceed without regard for the exceptions by introducing truth trees as the most useful decision method for predicate logic, and later explain the method's limitations.

The guidelines for propositional truth trees also apply to predicate trees. We follow the same basic procedures as discussed previously, to which we add new rules for testing predicate wffs and sequents. Recall that in using propositional truth trees we apply decomposition rules to the wffs in a stack, checking for closure of branches and of the entire tree wherever pairs of atomic wffs and

Predicate truth trees can be used to evaluate predicate wffs and sequents for all the same kinds of logical properties as propositional truth trees applied to propositional wffs and sequents.

their negations appear on the same branch. We rely on the same definitions of semantic concepts for propositional logic when applying predicate truth trees as a test of syntactical inconsistency; in determining whether a wff is a tautology, inconsistency, or contingency; in checking the logical consistency or inconsistency, and logical equivalence or nonequivalence, of two or more wffs; and when verifying the deductive validity or invalidity of argument sequents.

We identify a predicate tautology, for example, in the same general way as we identify a propositional tautology when the truth tree for its negation closes. We verify a deductively valid sequent in predicate logic, as in propositional logic, by a closed truth tree in which we decompose a stack of wffs consisting of the sequent's assumptions and the negation of its conclusion or the negation of the conjunction of its multiple conclusions. The only difference here is that the wffs that enter into a truth tree stack include predicate and propositional wffs. We must accordingly have special decomposition rules for predicate wffs.

Identifying Main Operators

Predicate truth trees require identifying predicate main operators, quantifiers, or propositional main connectives.

We first need to be able to recognize the *main operator* of a predicate wff. We can designate a quantifier or propositional connective indifferently as an operator in a predicate wff and state that the predicate wff must have either a particular quantifier or propositional connective as its main operator. As in locating the main connective in a propositional wff, we identify the main operator of a predicate wff by applying a greatest scope rule, facilitated in practice by a set of fewest parentheses guidelines. According to the wffs rules for predicate logic, the main operator of a predicate wff is determined by the following principle:

A greatest scope rule applied generally to quantifiers and propositional connectives determines the predicate main operator in a predicate wff.

> **Greatest Scope Rule for Identifying Predicate Main Operators**
> The main operator in any predicate wff is the operator, whether a propositional connective or quantifier, with the greatest scope.

The main operator of a predicate wff is whatever operator, whether propositional connective or quantifier, has the greatest scope. The scope of a propositional connective or quantifier is the least complex wff in which the connective or quantifier occurs. However, in order to implement the *greatest scope rule* for identifying predicate main operators, we need a way of determining which operator in a predicate wff has the greatest scope. For this purpose, as in identifying propositional main connectives, we introduce practical guidelines based on the use of parentheses in applying the formation rules for predicate wffs.

Fewest parentheses guidelines are useful in implementing the greatest scope rule for identifying predicate main operators.

Fewest Parentheses Guidelines for Identifying Predicate Main Operators

The main operator in any predicate wff is (1) the propositional connective, other than negation, if there is one, that (i) does not fall within the scope of any quantifier as indicated by parentheses and (ii) satisfies the least parentheses rule for propositional main connectives; otherwise, it is (2) the leftmost quantifier, if there is one, or (3) the leftmost iterated negation (including one as a limiting case) attached to the leftmost quantifier.

The following are examples to illustrate how the rule works. Notice that propositional symbols by themselves have no main operator under the main operator rule. Apply the main operator rule and *fewest parentheses guidelines* to each of these wffs to determine if your evaluations are in agreement.

Predicate main operators can be discerned in a large selection of typical examples.

MAIN OPERATORS IN PREDICATE WFFS

Wff	*Main operator*
P	None
~P	Negation ~
P ⊃ Q	Conditional ⊃
(∀x)Fx	Universal quantifier (∀x)
(∀x)~Fx	Universal quantifier (∀x)
(∃x)~~Fx	Existential quantifier (∃x)
~(∀x)Fx	Negation ~
~(∀x)~Fx	Negation ~ (leftmost)
(∀x)(P ⊃ Q)	Universal quantifier (∀x)
(∀x)(Fx ⊃ Gx)	Universal quantifier (∀x)
(∃x)(Fx & Gx)	Existential quantifier (∃x)
(∀x)~(Fx ⊃ Gx)	Universal quantifier (∀x)
(∃x)~(Fx & Gx)	Existential quantifier (∃x)
(∀x)Fx ⊃ (∀x)Gx	Conditional ⊃
(∃x)Fx & (∃x)Gx	Conjunction &
~(∀x)(Fx ⊃ Gx)	Negation ~
~(∃x)(Fx & Gx)	Negation ~
~(∀x)Fx ⊃ (∀x)Gx	Conditional ⊃
~(∃x)Fx & (∃x)Gx	Conjunction &
~((∀x)Fx ⊃ (∀x)Gx)	Negation ~

(∀x)(∀y)(Fx ⊃ Gy)	Universal quantifier (∀x) (leftmost)
(∀x)(∃y)(Fx ⊃ Gy)	Universal quantifier (∀x)
(∃x)(∃y)(Fx & Gy)	Existential quantifier (∃x) (leftmost)
(∃x)(∀y)(Fx & Gy)	Existential quantifier (∃x)
(∀x)(∃y)((Fxy & Gyx) ⊃ Fyy)	Universal quantifier (∀x)
(∀x)Fx ⊃ (∃y)(∀z)(Gya & Hyz)	Conditional ⊃
(∀x)(Fx ⊃ (∃y)(∀z)(Gya & Hyz))	Universal quantifier (x) (leftmost)
∼(∀x)Fx ⊃ (∃y)(∀z)(Gya & Hyz)	Conditional ⊃
∼(∀x)(Fx ⊃ (∃y)(∀z)(Gya & Hyz))	Negation ∼ (negative universal)
∼((∀x)Fx ⊃ (∃y)(∀z)(Gya & Hyz))	Negation ∼ (negative conditional)

As in identifying propositional main connectives in accord with the wffs rules in propositional logic, predicate main operators are identified in accord with the predicate wffs rules.

If a propositional connective satisfies the greatest scope rule for propositional main connectives and does not contain part of any wff that falls within a quantifier's scope, then the connective is the wff's main operator. If there is no such propositional connective, then the leftmost quantifier is the wff's main operator. The reason has to do with the wffs rules and parentheses requirement for propositional and predicate wffs. We can think of the main operator as the one that would be added last if we were building the wff from the ground up, using the simplest possible wffs and applying the wffs rules. A wff that has a quantifier as its main operator is one to which the predicate wffs rule 5 is applied in the final step of its construction. A wff that has a propositional connective as its main operator is one to which one of the propositional wffs rules 2−6 is applied in the final step of its construction.

The following is a more complete description of how the greatest scope rule and parentheses guidelines for identifying predicate main operators are applied in representative cases from the previous examples. The first wff, P, has no main operator since it contains no operators whatsoever, and hence none with the greatest scope. Wffs such as ∼P and P ⊃ Q are similarly easy to judge because they contain no quantifiers and only one propositional connective, which by default must be the predicate main operator. This is also the case with respect to wffs containing only one quantifier in the leftmost position that includes the entire wff in its scope, such as (∀x)Fx and (∀x)∼Fx. In the case of (∀x)∼Fx and (∃x)∼∼Fx, note that the quantifiers include the entire wffs within their scopes, including the negations embedded within them. Where negation is attached to a quantifier that would otherwise be the main operator—that is, if the negation were not present, in wffs such as ∼(∀x)Fx and ∼(∀x)∼Fx—the negation is the predicate main operator, and the wffs in these cases are classified as negative or negated universals. This is also the case for negative or negated existentials, ∼(∃x)Fx and ∼(∃x)∼Fx (not included in the list).

A single quantifier with an entire wff in its scope embedding a binary propositional connective, such as the conditional in $(\forall x)(Fx \supset Gx)$ or the conjunction in $(\exists x)(Fx \ \& \ Gx)$ (or disjunction or biconditional, with internal negations that have the whole or any part of the expression under the scope of the quantifier in their scope, as in $(\forall x)\sim(Fx \supset Gx)$ or $(\exists x)(Fx \ \& \sim Gx))$, is always the predicate main operator. The fewest parentheses guidelines, in contrast, indicates in the case of wffs such as $(\forall x)Fx \supset (\forall x)Gx$ that the propositional connective is the predicate main operator. The conditional here includes the entire wff in its scope, whereas parentheses show that the first universal quantifier has only the wff $(\forall x)Fx$ in its scope and that the second universal quantifier has only the wff $(\forall x)Gx$ in its scope. As a result, neither quantifier has greater scope than the conditional. By virtue of being the operator with greatest scope, the conditional in $(\forall x)Fx \supset (\forall x)Gx$ is the predicate main operator, with a universally quantified antecedent and a universally quantified consequent. There is an important difference in the scope of the negations of the following wffs: $\sim(\forall x)Fx \supset (\forall x)Gx$, $\sim((\forall x)Fx \supset (\forall x)Gx)$. In the first, the main operator is still the conditional because it is the operator with the greatest scope, including the entire wff in its scope, with a negative universal as antecedent. The second wff, as parentheses indicate, is a negative conditional in which the negation is the operator with the greatest scope, including the entire wff in its scope. The conditional, by comparison, has only the lesser wff enclosed within the outermost parentheses in its scope. The two universal quantifiers, as the fewest parentheses guidelines indicate, have even lesser scopes, consisting only of the quantified component wffs $(\forall x)Fx$ and $(\forall x)Gx$, precisely as in the original unnegated wff $(\forall x)Fx \supset (\forall x)Gx$.

For wffs in prenex normal form, such as $(\forall x)(\exists y)(Fx \supset Gy)$, $(\exists x)(\exists y)$ $(Fx \ \& \ Gy)$, and $(\forall x)(\exists y)((Fxy \ \& \ Gyx) \supset Fyy)$ from the list, the predicate main operator is always the leftmost quantifier. Regardless of the length or internal logical complexity of the wff, the same rules apply in determining the predicate main operator for wffs not in prenex normal form. The following is an example: $(\forall x)Fx \supset (\exists y)(\forall z)(Gya \ \& \ Hyz)$. Here, the conditional is evidently the operator with the greatest scope, including the entire wff, whereas the quantifiers at most have only the antecedent or consequent of the conditional in their respective scopes. If parentheses indicate that an entire expression of this sort falls within the scope of negation, as in $\sim((\forall x)Fx \supset (\exists y)(\forall z)(Gya \ \& \ Hyz))$, then, by the greatest scope rule, the predicate main operator is the negation and the wff must be classified as a negative conditional with a universally quantified antecedent and a mixed multiple quantified consequent.

To Check Your Understanding 7.1 ———■

In each of the following symbolizations identify the main operator and indicate whether the wff is propositional or predicate; do the same for each of the main operators of every propositional or predicate component (if any) of the wffs:

1. $(\forall x)\sim Gx$
2. $(\exists x)Fx \,\&\, Ga$
3. $(\exists x)\sim(Fx \,\&\, Ga)$
4. $(\forall x)\sim Gx \supset (\forall x)\sim Fx$
5. $\sim(\forall x)\sim Gx \supset (\forall x)\sim Fx$
6. $\sim((\forall x)\sim Gx \supset (\forall x)\sim Fx)$
7. $(\forall x)(\exists y)(Fxy \supset Gyx)$
8. $(\forall x)(Fx \supset (\exists y)Gxy)$
9. $(\forall x)Fx \supset (\exists y)Gy$

■

Predicate Truth Tree Rules

Predicate truth trees require four new rules, in addition to the rules for propositional truth trees, for predicate wffs whose predicate main operators are universal or existential quantifications and their negations.

To apply truth tree decomposition rules in predicate logic, we first identify the main operator. If the main operator is a propositional connective other than a negation attached to a quantifier, we proceed just as we would for a propositional truth tree. If the main operator is a conjunction, we stack its conjuncts; if it is a disjunction, we branch its disjuncts, and so on. If the main operator is a quantifier or a negated quantifier, then we proceed according to the following rules.

We add four predicate truth tree rules for wffs whose main operator is a universal, existential, negated universal, or negated existential quantifier to the propositional truth tree decomposition rules previously discussed. We use predicate and constant variables and object metavariables in the following statement of truth tree rules. The propositional variable with a slash mark and metavariable $\mathbb{P}/x$ stands for any truth function of predicate wffs in which variable 'x' is

Predicate wffs whose predicate main operator is a propositional connective are decomposed according to the appropriate propositional truth tree decomposition rule.

PREDICATE TRUTH TREE DECOMPOSITION RULES

$\sim(\forall x)\mathbb{P}/x$ $\quad\sqrt{}$	$\sim(\exists x)\mathbb{P}/x$ $\quad\sqrt{}$	$(\forall x)\mathbb{P}/x$ $\quad *\,\alpha$	$(\exists x)\mathbb{P}/x$ $\quad\sqrt{}$
$(\exists x)\sim\mathbb{P}/x$	$(\forall x)\sim\mathbb{P}/x$	$\mathbb{P}/\alpha$	$\mathbb{P}/\alpha$
		unrestricted	*restricted*

in choice and number of substitutions of object constants for bound object variables

---

selectively replaced by any constant 'α'. The propositional variable with a slash mark and constant variable $\mathbb{P}/\alpha$ stands for any unquantified predicate wff with any constant 'α' uniformly replaced by any quantifier bound variable 'x' in $(\forall x)\mathbb{P}/x$ or $(\exists x)\mathbb{P}/x$.

Classifying Wffs by Predicate Trees

Check marks are used as in propositional truth trees.

To illustrate all four of the rules, we begin with a wff whose main operator is a propositional connective, but whose component wffs are both quantified. Suppose that we are required to do a truth tree decomposition of the proposition $(\forall x)Fx \supset (\forall x)Gx$. We recognize by the main operator rule and parentheses guidelines that the conditional is the predicate main operator. We begin the truth tree by decomposing the wff as an ordinary conditional, according to the propositional truth tree rule, writing the negation of the antecedent below the left-hand branch and the consequent at the end of the right-hand branch:

$$(\forall x)Fx \supset (\forall x)Gx \quad \checkmark \quad 1$$
$$\sim(\forall x)Fx \qquad (\forall x)Gx$$

Predicate wffs whose predicate main operator is a negated quantifier are decomposed by driving negation inward and changing the sign of the quantifier from universal to existential or existential to universal.

To decompose the negated quantifiers in the left branch, we invoke a rule based on quantifier duality. We reduce negated universal wffs to existential negated wffs and negated existential wffs to universal negated wffs. In such cases, we say that negation has been *driven inward* to the immediate right of the quantifier, which at the same time is reversed in sign from universal to existential or from existential to universal. The rule for decomposing negated universals converts $\sim(\forall x)Fx$ to $(\exists x)\sim Fx$, and the rule for decomposing negated existentials converts $\sim(\exists x)Fx$ to $(\forall x)\sim Fx$. In a negated universal wff, such as $\sim(\forall x)Fx$, we drive negation inward and reverse the quantifier sign from universal to existential to produce $(\exists x)\sim Fx$. In a negated existential wff, such as $\sim(\exists x)Fx$, we drive negation inward and reverse the quantifier sign from existential to universal to produce $(\forall x)\sim Fx$.

In the most elementary applications, predicate truth tree rules for decomposing negated quantified wffs have the following forms. A check mark, as in propositional truth trees, indicates that the wff has been decomposed:

Check marks are used as in propositional truth trees.

$$\sim(\forall x)Fx \quad \checkmark \qquad \sim(\exists x)Fx \quad \checkmark$$
$$(\exists x)\sim Fx \qquad\qquad (\forall x)\sim Fx$$

To continue with the same tree, we apply the rule for negative universals to the wff on the left-hand branch to get the following decomposition:

$$(\forall x)Fx \supset (\forall x)Gx \quad \checkmark \ 1$$

2 $\checkmark$ $\sim(\forall x)Fx$ $(\forall x)Gx$
        $(\exists x)\sim Fx$

Universally quanti-
fied wffs are decom-
posed by eliminating
the quantifier and
substituting any con-
stants that may help
to achieve closure
in the tree for all
variables bound by
the same universal
quantifier.

This leaves only universally and existentially quantified expressions to be decomposed. Recall that a universally quantified proposition of the form $(\forall x)Fx$ states that everything has property F. If $(\forall x)Fx$ is true, then it is true that any particular individual we care to name has property F. Thus, if $(\forall x)Fx$ is true, then so is Fa, Fb, Fc, and so on for all the individual objects named by 'a', 'b', 'c', etc. The truth tree rule for universals decomposes a wff of the form $(\forall x)Fx$ when we write below it Fa (and/or Fb, Fc, etc. without restriction, choosing instantiations to maximize the possibilities of obtaining closure in the tree). The rule has the following form in its simplest application:

$$(\forall x)Fx \ *a$$
$$Fa \qquad\qquad\qquad \text{UNRESTRICTED}$$

Universally quanti-
fied wffs can be re-
peatedly decomposed,
substituting an un-
limited number of
different constants
for universally bound
variables.

It would be misleading to put a check mark beside a universal wff when we apply its decomposition rule. We can continue to decompose a universally quantified wff as often as we like, using as many different object constants 'a', 'b', 'c', etc. as necessary, until we believe we have exhausted the possibilities of closing the branch on which it appears. We should not generally regard a tree as complete when we have applied the truth tree decomposition rule to a universally quantified wff if we can see that further substitutions of other constants may help to close an otherwise unclosed branch. It is good practice to indicate by some kind of notation other than a check mark that we have applied a decomposition rule to a universally quantified wff in a tree. The notation should also make it possible to determine when we have considered all the possibilities that might lead to closure in a tree, by replacing its universally bound variables by every constant that appears anywhere on the same branch. If the branch or entire tree does not close, then we can be sure that no further substitutions of constants for universally bound object variables could possibly achieve closure, and we can consider our work with the universal wff complete.

Instead of using a check mark, we mark a universally quantified wff with an asterisk (*) and write beside it the constant we used to replace the universally bound variables in the formula each time we apply the universal decomposition rule to the wff. We optionally number each application of a truth tree

Universally quantified wffs are not marked with a check mark when the predicate truth tree decomposition rule is applied to them because they can be repeatedly instantiated since they are never entirely fully decomposed.

rule for easy reconstruction of truth tree decomposition steps. The following are examples.

ANNOTATING PREDICATE TRUTH TREE DECOMPOSITIONS
OF UNIVERSALLY QUANTIFIED WFFS

$(\forall x)Fx$ *a 1 *b 2 *c 3 . . . $(\forall x)Fx$ *a 1 *a 2 *b 3 *a 4
  Fa   Fa
  Fb   Fa
  Fc   Fb
  .   Fa
  .
  .

Universally quantified wffs are marked with an asterisk, and the particular constant is substituted for their universally bound variables, each time the rule is applied.

The asterisk-constant method has the advantage of check marks otherwise used in truth trees. It provides a convenient way of keeping track of whether or not a universally quantified wff has been decomposed. It also avoids the misleading impression that when we have once applied the *predicate truth tree decomposition rule* for universally quantified wffs, substituting one constant for its universally bound variables, we have fully decomposed the wff or finished with it altogether in the tree and need not consider it again.

A universally quantified wff is inexhaustible with respect to the number of times we can apply its decomposition rule. We can replace its universally bound variables with as many constants as we choose. But since our only purpose is to check for closure or nonclosure in a predicate truth tree, we usually reach a point relatively soon after which further replacement of variables by additional constants in a universally quantified wff offers no further opportunities for closure. There is no reason to continue decomposing a universally quantified wff in a tree when all the constants appearing in a tree through the decomposition of other wffs have already been substituted for its universally bound variables. If the branch or the tree does not close then, it is never going to close. The asterisk-constant notation also indicates when we have reached this point because we can cross-check the constants written alongside the asterisks to make sure that no constant appearing anywhere in a still open branch has been overlooked in decomposing any universally quantified wff.

To continue the previous example, we need go no further than a single substitution of a constant for the universally bound variable in $(\forall x)Gx$ to take the truth tree to the next stage:

$(\forall x)Fx \supset (\forall x)Gx$ $\checkmark$ 1

2 $\checkmark$ ~$(\forall x)Fx$ $(\forall x)Gx$ *a 3
        $(\exists x)$~Fx   Ga

In practice, it is never worthwhile to continue to decompose a universally quantified wff by substituting constants that do not appear anywhere in the same branch of a predicate truth tree, since to go beyond these cannot help to achieve closure.

We will never get closure in the right-hand branch (nor in the left-hand branch). If we had reason to expect closure with another constant we could in principle continue to decompose the universal formula indefinitely as follows:

$$(\forall x)Fx \supset (\forall x)Gx \quad \checkmark \quad 1$$

$$2 \quad \checkmark \quad \begin{array}{c} \sim(\forall x)Fx \\ (\exists x)\sim Fx \end{array} \qquad \begin{array}{c} (\forall x)Gx \quad *a \; 3 \; *b \; 4 \; *c \; 5 \ldots \\ Ga \\ Gb \\ Gc \\ \cdot \\ \cdot \\ \cdot \end{array}$$

Existentially quantified wffs are decomposed by eliminating the quantifier and substituting an arbitrarily chosen constant that does not appear anywhere on the same branch of the tree for all variables bound by the same existential quantifier.

The only remaining predicate truth tree rule is for existentially quantified propositions. It is superficially similar in formal appearance to the decomposition rule for universally quantified propositions. It carries an important restriction on the choice of object constants that we are permitted to substitute for existentially bound object variables. The following is the simplest application of the rule:

$$(\exists x)Fx \quad \checkmark$$
$$Fa \qquad\qquad\qquad\qquad \text{RESTRICTED}$$

The restriction is that the object constant 'a' (or 'b', 'c', etc.) chosen to replace all the existentially quantified variables in the wff must be *arbitrary* in the sense that the constant cannot have appeared anywhere previously on the same branch of the tree. We examine correct uses of the decomposition rule for existentials, and then consider violations of the rule, in order to get a sense of how things can go wrong if we do not observe the restriction.

Predicate truth trees, in closing or remaining open, are interpreted in all the same ways as propositional truth trees.

First, we return to the conditional proposition we have been analyzing. Although constant 'a' appears on the right-hand branch in the decomposition of the universal $(\forall x)Gx$, no constant appears in the left-hand branch where we are now to decompose the existential $(\exists x)\sim Fx$. Thus, we are free to substitute any, although at most one, arbitrarily chosen constant for the existentially bound variable. It is customary to choose the first previously unused letter of the alphabet on any given branch of a tree. Here, no other constants have yet appeared, so we are free to choose 'a'. The final step of truth tree decomposition in the example looks as follows:

$$(\forall x)Fx \supset (\forall x)Gx \quad \surd \; 1$$

$$\begin{array}{ll} 2 \; \surd \quad \sim(\forall x)Fx & (\forall x)Gx \quad *a \; 3 \\ 4 \; \surd \quad (\exists x)\sim Fx & Ga \\ \quad\quad \sim Fa \end{array}$$

NOT AN INCONSISTENCY

This completes the tree. As can be seen, the tree does not close. Nor does the tree for the negation of the wff. We show by predicate truth trees that the formula in this example is neither a tautology nor an inconsistency, but that both the original formula and its negation are contingencies:

$$\sim((\forall x)Fx \supset (\forall x)Gx) \quad \surd \; 1$$
$$(\forall x)Fx \quad *a \; 4$$
$$\sim(\forall x)Gx \quad \surd \; 2$$
$$(\exists x)\sim Gx \quad \surd \; 3$$
$$\sim Ga$$
$$Fa$$

CONTINGENCY

Predicate truth trees, within limitations, can be used to classify individual wffs as tautologies, inconsistencies, or contingencies of predicate logic.

The example illustrates another important implication of the restriction on the truth decomposition rule for existentials. Here, we have a single branch, where both $(\forall x)Fx$ and $(\exists x)\sim Gx$ are ready to be decomposed. We do not need to reduce $(\forall x)Fx$ before $(\exists x)\sim Gx$ just because one appears above the other in the stack. As a general principle, it is better on the same truth tree branch to decompose all existentials before decomposing any universals. Universal decomposition is unrestricted, so we can substitute any constant for universally bound variables to maximize the possibility of obtaining closure. Existential decomposition, in contrast, is restricted to the arbitrary choice of a constant that has not appeared previously on the same branch. The best way to maximize closure with fully reduced propositions containing constants in place of quantifier bound variables that contradict one another (Fa, ~Fa; Gb, ~Gb, etc.) when we have both universals and existentials on the same branch is therefore to decompose all existentials, observing the rule's restriction, before unrestrictedly decomposing any universals.

Predicate Trees for Consistency, Equivalence, and Validity

We adapt our previous use of propositional truth trees to test for logical consistency and equivalence to predicate wffs. The tests are set up in the same way. The only difference is that we now apply the four new truth tree decomposition rules for predicate logic to wffs that appear in the trees.

Predicate truth trees can be used to determine whether two or more wffs are logically consistent or inconsistent and whether they are logically equivalent or nonequivalent.

To test for logical consistency of two or more predicate wffs, we stack the wffs and check to determine whether their tree closes. If the tree closes, then the wffs in the stack are logically inconsistent. If the tree does not close, if there remains at least one open branch, then the wffs in the stack are logically consistent. To test for logical equivalence of two or more predicate wffs, we connect the wffs by the biconditional and check to determine whether the biconditional is a tautology by completing the predicate truth tree for its negation. If the tree for the negation of the biconditional of the wffs closes, then the wffs are logically equivalent; if the tree for the negation of the biconditional of the wffs does not close, if there remains at least one open branch, then the wffs are logically nonequivalent.

Arguments are series of propositions divided into assumptions and conclusions by inference indicators. If we know how to do truth trees for sequents in propositional logic, and if we know how to decompose any individual wff in predicate logic, then we can combine these skills in using predicate truth trees to test sequents involving predicate wffs. We extend the truth tree method for sequents in propositional logic to predicate logic, for which sequents pose no special problem. We test stacks of assumptions and negations of conclusions by predicate truth trees as we would any other predicate propositions and judge the results by the same standards of closed trees for deductively valid sequents and open trees for deductively invalid sequents.

Predicate truth trees, within limitations, can be used to determine whether a sequent is deductively valid or invalid.

■ *Demonstration 27:* **Predicate Truth Trees** ■

PROBLEM: To evaluate the deductive validity or invalidity of a predicate argument by predicate truth trees.

ARGUMENT: Consider the classical syllogism about Socrates, humanity, and mortality. We have already translated the argument into predicate logic in the following way:

1. $(\forall x)(Hx \supset Mx)$
2. Hs

---

3. Ms

   ('Socrates')

STEP 1:   *Set up the truth tree*
To set up the truth tree to evaluate the argument's validity, we begin as we do for propositional truth trees. We stack the assumptions of the argument together with the negation of its conclusion. This gives us:

$$(\forall x)(Hx \supset Mx)$$
$$Hs$$
$$\sim Ms$$

STEP 2: *Apply the predicate truth tree rule to the main operator*

The main operator in the first proposition is the universal quantifier, so we apply the decomposition rule for universally quantified expressions which we have just introduced. We choose object constant 's' to substitute for the universally bound object variable 'x' in the proposition. Given that 's' already appears in the stacked statements of the second assumption and the negation of the conclusion, this substitution offers the best possibility of obtaining closure in the tree.

$$(\forall x)(Hx \supset Mx) \quad *s \ 1$$
$$Hs$$
$$\sim Ms$$
$$Hs \supset Ms$$

STEP 3: *Continue predicate truth tree decomposition*

The proposition that appears as a result of the first application of truth tree rules is Hs ⊃ Ms. Its main operator is the conditional, a propositional connective. We next present its truth tree decomposition by applying the propositional truth tree decomposition rule for the conditional. This yields:

$$(\forall x)(Hx \supset Mx) \quad *s \ 1$$
$$Hs$$
$$\sim Ms$$
$$Hs \supset Ms \qquad \checkmark \ 2$$

```
            /\
        ~Hs    Ms
         X      X            VALID
```

STEP 4: *Evaluate the completed predicate truth tree*

We obtain the expected result, confirming both our intuitive and circle diagram evaluations, that the argument is logically valid.

Truth Tree Protocol for Predicate Logic

The restrictions on truth tree decomposition of existentially quantified wffs impose a priority ordering on the application of propositional and predicate truth tree rules. We introduce the following truth tree protocol to explain how these

There is a definite protocol that determines the order in which different types of wffs must be decomposed in predicate truth trees; this is one respect in which predicate truth trees are different from propositional truth trees.

priorities should be observed to maximize the possibilities of closure in a predicate truth tree:

TRUTH TREE PROTOCOL
FOR PREDICATE LOGIC

P1. Apply the appropriate propositional truth tree decomposition rule to decompose a wff, the main operator of which is a truth functional *propositional connective*, whenever a wff with a propositional connective as its main operator appears in the tree.

P2. When a negation ~ is the main operator attached to a quantifier, in a *negated quantifier*, apply the predicate truth tree decomposition rules to convert negative universals into existential negations and negative existentials into universal negations; the rules drive negation inward by quantifier duality and reverse quantifier signs from universal to existential and from existential to universal: $\sim(\forall x)\mathbb{P}/x$ becomes $(\exists x)\sim\mathbb{P}/x$; $\sim(\exists x)\mathbb{P}/x$ becomes $(\forall x)\sim\mathbb{P}/x$.
(For truth tree annotation, see ‡.)

P3. When an existentially quantified wff appears, eliminate the quantifier and uniformly substitute an (alphabetically first) arbitrary constant α_1, ..., α_n (that does not appear anywhere previously on the same branch of the tree) for every occurrence of the existentially bound variable in the wff.
(For truth tree annotation, see ‡.)
(If there is more than one existentially quantified wff, then different constants must be uniformly substituted for respective existentially bound variables.)

P4. When a universally quantified wff appears, eliminate the quantifier and uniformly substitute for every universally bound variable as many constants α_1, ..., α_n as may maximize the possibility of branch and tree closure.
(For truth tree annotation, see ‡.)
(If there is more than one universally quantified wff, there is no restriction on uniformly substituting the same or different constants for universally bound variables.)

‡   As in propositional truth trees, each decomposed wff is marked with a check '$\sqrt{}$' or '*a', '*b', '*c', etc., in the case of universally quantified wffs, to avoid omissions or duplications. Closed branches are marked with an 'X', when at least one inconsistent pair of any proposition symbol and its negation appears in fully decomposed form on the same branch.

Truth trees in predicate logic can involve cyclical patterns of rule applications reflecting such priority sequences as P1 → P4 → P2, P1 → P2 → P3 → P1, P2 → P1 → P4 → P2. These and other patterns occur because of changing circumstances in the tree as rules are applied to break down previous wffs and new wffs appear. There can also be iterative patterns of rule applications, such as P1 → P1 → P2 → P2. We do not need to, and in many cases cannot, proceed sequentially through P1 → P2 → P3 → P4 before completing the tree or returning to any of P1–P3.

Predicate truth trees can involve different orderings of applications of the separate phases of the predicate truth tree protocol, including cyclical patterns.

We can appreciate the importance of the truth tree protocol if we ask what happens when we do not observe the restrictions on the truth tree rule for existentially quantified wffs. The best way to illustrate the difficulty is to compare following the rule with deliberately violating it in testing an argument that we know to be deductively invalid. Suppose we must evaluate the validity of the argument, 'Some flowers are red; Something is a flower; Therefore, everything is red'. The inference is obviously invalid. We are not entitled to conclude from the assumption that some flowers are red and that some flowers exist, that therefore everything that exists is red. The assumptions leave open whether or not everything is red, or whether or not there are not also nonred things. The argument might be symbolized as $(\exists x)(Fx \,\&\, Rx)$, $(\exists x)Fx \vdash (\forall x)Rx$. The correct truth tree for this inference has the following form, after we stack the assumptions with the negation of the conclusion and perform the first step of reducing the negative universal to its existential counterpart with negation driven inward:

$$(\exists x)(Fx \,\&\, Rx)$$
$$(\exists x)Fx$$
$$\sim(\forall x)Rx \quad \checkmark \; 1$$
$$(\exists x)\sim Rx$$

The check mark shows that the three propositions remaining to be decomposed are all existentials. We demonstrate the correct use of the truth tree decomposition rule for existentials. The restriction on existential decomposition is satisfied by uniformly substituting for existentially bound variables only arbitrary constants that have not appeared anywhere previously on the same branch of the tree. The first substitution is unproblematic; because no constants have yet appeared, we can choose 'a'. The second and third substitutions require us to uniformly substitute constants that have not yet occurred, namely, 'b' and 'c'. If we follow the existential decomposition rule correctly by observing its restriction on arbitrary choice of constants, then the argument is shown by predicate truth trees to be deductively invalid. The order in which we decompose the three existential wffs is immaterial.

$$
\begin{array}{ll}
(\exists x)(Fx\ \&\ Rx) & \checkmark\ 2 \\
(\exists x)Fx & \checkmark\ 4 \\
\sim(\forall x)Rx & \checkmark\ 1 \\
(\exists x)\sim Rx & \checkmark\ 5 \\
Fa\ \&\ Ra & \checkmark\ 3 \\
Fa & \\
Ra & \\
Fb & \\
\sim Rc & \quad\quad\quad\quad\quad\quad\quad\quad\quad \text{INVALID}
\end{array}
$$

[CORRECT USE OF ∃ DECOMPOSITION RULE;
ARGUMENT RIGHTLY SHOWN TO BE INVALID]

The restriction on existential truth tree decomposition must be observed in order to avoid incorrect evaluations.

The tree does not close, indicating that the argument is invalid. If we had violated the restriction on the truth tree decomposition rule for existentially quantified propositions, then the argument would wrongly appear by truth tree method to be logically valid. If we disregard the restriction, then we have:

$$
\begin{array}{ll}
(\exists x)(Fx\ \&\ Rx) & \checkmark\ 2 \\
(\exists x)Fx & \checkmark\ 4 \\
\sim(\forall x)Rx & \checkmark\ 1 \\
(\exists x)\sim Rx & \checkmark\ 5 \\
Fa\ \&\ Ra & \checkmark\ 3 \\
Fa & \\
Ra & \\
Fa & \quad\quad\quad\quad\quad [\text{VIOLATION!}] \\
\sim Ra & \quad\quad\quad\quad\quad [\text{VIOLATION!}] \\
\\
X & \quad\quad\quad\quad\quad [\text{WRONG EVALUATION!}]
\end{array}
$$

We now consider a variation of the Socrates syllogism to further illustrate the protocol for predicate truth tree rules. The argument states 'All men are mortal; someone is a man; therefore someone is mortal'. The argument is symbolized, and its truth tree is set up by stacking the assumptions together with the negation of the conclusion:

1. $(\forall x)(Hx \supset Mx)$

2. $(\exists x)Hx$
_____

3. $(\exists x)Mx$

$$
\begin{array}{l}
(\forall x)(Hx \supset Mx) \\
(\exists x)Hx \\
\sim(\exists x)Mx
\end{array}
$$

As in the previous problem, it would be unwise to begin with the universal quantifier decomposition rule because if we substitute, for example, constant 'a' for the universally bound variable 'x' in (∀x)(Hx ⊃ Mx), then we will already have a constant in the tree and, according to the restriction on the existential quantifier decomposition rule, we will not be able to use that same constant in decomposing the existential formula (∃x)Hx. This will make it more difficult and time-consuming to check for closure in the tree. Since the predicate truth tree decomposition of existentials is restricted, and the decomposition rule for universals is unrestricted, we prefer whenever possible to do existential decompositions first and reserve universal decompositions until last. Then we can match constants to be substituted for universally bound object variables to the object constants that have already appeared in the tree from existential decompositions in order to maximize the possibilities of obtaining closure.

The restriction on existential truth tree decomposition requires that the predicate truth tree protocol be followed in order to maximize the possibilities of obtaining closure in the most efficient way.

The previous stack contains no propositional connectives as main operators. We proceed to the next step of the protocol. There is a negative existential to decompose, for which we drive negation inward and reverse the quantifier sign from existential to universal. This leads to the next stage of the tree:

$$(\forall x)(Hx \supset Mx)$$
$$(\exists x)Hx$$
$$\sim(\exists x)Mx \quad \surd\ 1$$
$$(\forall x)\sim Mx$$

The protocol requires that we next take care of the existential wff (∃x)Hx. By virtue of the content of the argument, and because of our decision not to use the universal decomposition rule before the existential, the tree at this point contains no object constants. Thus, we are free to substitute whatever object constant we like for the existentially bound variable 'x' in (∃x)Hx. It is standard to begin at the beginning of the alphabet, so we replace (∃x)Hx with Ha in the tree, which now looks as follows:

$$(\forall x)(Hx \supset Mx)$$
$$(\exists x)Hx \quad \surd\ 2$$
$$\sim(\exists x)Mx \quad \surd\ 1$$
$$(\forall x)\sim Mx$$
$$Ha$$

We are only permitted to make one uniform replacement of an arbitrarily chosen object constant (one that does not appear anywhere previously above its projected location in the same branch of the tree) for the existentially bound variables in the existentially quantified formula we are decomposing. We place a check mark immediately on application of the rule to the existential wff to show that it has been decomposed.

The check marks indicate that there are two propositions left to decompose, both of which are universally quantified formulas. We are free to make whatever and as many substitutions of object constants for the universally bound variables in these universally quantified formulas as are likely to increase our chances of obtaining closure in the tree. Notice that object constant 'a' already occurs in the tree as a result of our previous application of the truth tree decomposition rule to the existentially quantified proposition. So, it seems reasonable to suppose that if closure is to occur in the tree it will be by virtue of also substituting object constant 'a' for the universally bound variable 'x' in the two universally quantified propositions that remain to be reduced. Working through the tree as before, applying the rule for decomposing the unquantified conditional Ha ⊃ Ma and then the universally quantified proposition (∀x)~Mx, freely substituting constant 'a' for universally bound variable 'x', we complete the tree as follows:

Existentially quantified wffs should always be decomposed before universally quantified wffs in order to satisfy the restriction on decomposing existentials since the decomposition rule for universals is unrestricted.

$$
\begin{array}{c}
(\forall x)(Hx \supset Mx) \quad *a\ 3 \\
(\exists x)Hx \quad \sqrt{}\ 2 \\
\sim(\exists x)Mx \quad \sqrt{}\ 1 \\
(\forall x)\sim Mx \quad \sqrt{}\ 5 \\
Ha \\
Ha \supset Ma \quad \sqrt{}\ 4 \\
\diagup\!\diagdown \\
\sim Ha \qquad Ma \\
X \qquad \sim Ma \\
X
\end{array}
$$

VALID

Predicate truth tree rules are best assimilated by studying examples and working exercises to solve problems.

By adding four new rules to propositional truth trees, and observing the protocol on applications of the rules, we can test wffs and sequents for the same kinds of logical properties in predicate logic as in propositional logic. We have worked through several examples, and more challenging applications are given later. As in learning to use propositional truth tables, truth trees, and natural deduction proofs, it is important to study illustrations and practice your ability to apply the rules by working through many kinds of problems.

To Check Your Understanding 7.2

Use truth trees to test the following predicate wffs to determine whether they are tautologies, inconsistencies, or contingencies and the following sequents to determine whether they are deductively valid or invalid:

1. $(\forall y)((\forall x)Fx \supset Fy)$
2. $(\forall x)(Fx \supset Gx) \supset ((\exists x)Fx \supset (\exists x)Gx)$
3. $(\forall x)\sim(Fx \supset Fx) \supset ((\exists x)Gx \supset (\forall x)Gx)$
4. $(\forall x)(Fx \supset \sim Gx) \supset ((\forall x)Fx \supset (\forall x)Gx)$
5. $\sim((\forall x)(Fx \supset Gx) \supset ((\forall x)Fx \supset (\forall x)Gx))$
6. $(\forall x)(\exists y)(\forall z)Fxyz \vdash (\forall x)(\forall z)(\exists y)Fxyz$
7. $(\forall x)(Fx \supset Gx) \vdash (\forall x)\sim Gx \supset (\forall x)\sim Fx$
8. $(\forall x)(Fx \supset \sim Gx) \vdash (\forall x)\sim Gx \supset (\forall x)\sim Fx$
9. $(\exists x)(Fx \& (\forall y)(Gy \supset Hxy)), (\forall x)(Fx \supset (\forall y)(By \supset \sim Hxy))$
   $\vdash (\forall x)(Gx \supset \sim Bx)$

■

Applications to Complex Wffs and Sequents

The following are more interesting cases. We begin with efforts to determine whether a predicate wff is a tautology, inconsistency, or contingency and proceed to sequents with mixed multiple quantifications. Study each example to make sure you understand how the decomposition is done, following each step in the truth tree from setup to closure or nonclosure.

The first complex wff tree illustrates two important lessons. It reminds us that the placement of parentheses in predicate logic can make an enormous difference in whether the wff is a tautology or not a tautology, and it reinforces the fact that in some trees we must not consider the tree to be complete until we have exhausted all possible decompositions of universally quantified wffs in the stack. For the sake of comparison, we shall evaluate the wff $(\exists x)(Fx \supset (\forall y)Fy)$ and compare it with the superficially similar but logically nonequivalent wff $(\exists x)Fx \supset (\forall y)Fy$. Here is the tree for the first proposition. We confirm that the wff is not an inconsistency, and then show that it is a tautology:

The exact placement of parentheses in a predicate wff can be very significant in its interpretation and truth conditions.

NOT AN INCONSISTENCY

$$\sim(\exists x)(Fx \supset (\forall y)Fy) \quad \sqrt{\ } \ 1$$
$$(\forall x)\sim(Fx \supset (\forall y)Fy) \quad *a\ 2 \quad *b\ 6$$
$$\sim(Fa \supset (\forall y)Fy) \quad \sqrt{\ } \ 3$$
$$Fa$$
$$\sim(\forall y)Fy \quad \sqrt{\ } \ 4$$
$$(\exists y)\sim Fy \quad \sqrt{\ } \ 5$$
$$\sim Fb$$
$$\sim(Fb \supset (\forall y)Fy) \quad \sqrt{\ } \ 7$$
$$Fb$$
$$\sim(\forall y)Fy$$
$$X$$

TAUTOLOGY

(ORIGINAL UNNEGATED FORM)

Universally quantified wffs must sometimes be repeatedly decomposed using different constants in order to exhaust all possibilities of closure in a predicate truth tree.

In this tree, it would have been tempting to quit after step 5, where it appears that no closure can obtain between Fa and ~Fb. We see by the asterisk marking of the universal wff at step 2 that so far we have decomposed it only by replacing the universally bound variable 'x' by constant 'a'. Since constant 'b' also occurs in the tree after step 5, we recognize that it may be worthwhile to also try replacing the universally bound variable 'x' by constant 'b', which we do in step 6, thereby closing the tree. Indeed, the tree closes at this stage without the need to further decompose ~(∀y)Fy, first as (∃y)~Fy and ultimately as ~Fc.

Now we see that the lookalike conditional wff, (∃x)Fx ⊃ (∀y)Fy, is not a tautology. We first verify that it is not an inconsistency:

$$\underline{(\exists x)Fx \supset (\forall y)Fy} \quad \sqrt{\ } \ 1$$

$$2\ \sqrt{\ } \quad \sim(\exists x)Fx \qquad\qquad (\forall y)Fy \quad *a\ 4$$
$$3\ *a \quad (\forall x)\sim Fx \qquad\qquad\quad Fa$$
$$\sim Fa$$

NOT AN INCONSISTENCY

We obtain an inconsistent pair, Fa and ~Fa, but not on the same branch. The fact that the tree does not close indicates that the wff is not an inconsistency. Next, we determine that the wff is also not a tautology by testing its negation. For this, we enclose the entire wff in parentheses, negate it, and then complete its tree:

$$\sim((\exists x)Fx \supset (\forall y)Fy) \quad \checkmark \; 1$$
$$(\exists x)Fx \quad \checkmark \; 2$$
$$\sim(\forall y)Fy \quad \checkmark \; 3$$
$$Fa$$
$$(\exists y)\sim Fy \quad \checkmark \; 4$$
$$\sim Fb$$

NOT A TAUTOLOGY (CONTINGENCY)

Completed predicate truth trees are interpreted in the same ways as are propositional truth trees.

Here, we must observe the restriction on truth tree decomposition for existentials, substituting a different choice of constant for the second existential wff once it appears in the stack. The pair Fa and ~Fb are not logically inconsistent, so the tree will never close. The original unnegated wff is therefore not a tautology but a contingency.

The placement of parentheses is crucial in determining whether very similar predicate wffs are or are not tautologies, and whether sequents are or are not deductively valid. The difference parentheses can make underscores the importance of exact logical punctuation in translating propositions and arguments from ordinary language into symbolic logic before testing their logical properties by predicate truth trees. Thus, if we are translating the English sentence, 'If something is friendly, then everything is friendly', we should choose the second formulation given previously, whereby we symbolize it as $(\exists x)Fx \supset (\forall y)Fy$, which is neither a tautology nor an inconsistency but a contingency of predicate logic. The counterexamples that disprove this wff as a tautology are plentiful. For example, it might well be true that something is friendly but contingently true or false that everything is friendly, which makes the conditional respectively true or false and hence a contingency rather than a tautology or inconsistency. On the other hand, if we are translating the sentence, 'There is something which is such that if it is friendly, then everything is friendly', then we must place parentheses as in the first formulation, as $(\exists x)(Fx \supset (\forall y)Fy)$, whereby the resulting wff is a tautology.

The proposition may not immediately seem to be a tautology, but we can see that it is a logical truth by reflecting that either everything is F or it is not the case that everything is F. If everything is F, then Fa is true and $(\forall y)Fy$ is true so that $Fa \supset (\forall y)Fy$, a conditional with a true antecedent and a true consequent, is true. Then it follows that something is such that if it is F, then everything is F, $(\exists x)(Fx \supset (\forall y)Fy)$. If, on the contrary, it is not the case that everything is F, then something, call it 'a', is not F. In this case, the conditional $Fa \supset (\forall y)Fy$ is true by virtue of being a conditional with a false antecedent. Again, it follows immediately that something is such that if it is F (which by hypothesis it is not), then everything is F. The differences between these forms in ordinary language can often be very subtle, but the stakes are high in achieving a correct translation leading to a correct logical evaluation.

The predicate truth tree method is further illustrated in the following evaluations of predicate wffs and sequents:

$$\underline{((\forall x)(Gx \supset Hx)\ \&\ (\exists x)(Fx\ \&\ Gx)) \supset (\exists x)(Fx\ \&\ Hx)} \quad \checkmark\ 1$$

2 √　~(∀x)(Gx ⊃ Hx) & (∃x)(Fx & Gx)　　　　　(∃x)(Fx & Hx)　√ 8
3 √　~(∀x)(Gx ⊃ Hx)　　　　　　　　　　　　　　　Fa
4 √　(∃x)(Fx & Gx)　　　　　　　　　　　　　　　Ha
6 √　(∃x)~(Gx ⊃ Hx)
　　5 √　Fa & Ga
　　　　Fa
　　　　Ga
7 √　~(Gb ⊃ Hb)
　　　Gb
　　　~Hb

NOT AN INCONSISTENCY

The tree does not close, so the proposition is not an inconsistency. Turning from this negative result, we do a truth tree of the negation of the proposition to determine whether the proposition is a tautology or contingency:

$$\sim(((\forall x)(Gx \supset Hx)\ \&\ (\exists x)(Fx\ \&\ Gx)) \supset (\exists x)(Fx\ \&\ Hx)) \quad \checkmark\ 1$$

　　　　　(∀x)(Gx ⊃ Hx) & (∃x)(Fx & Gx)　√ 2
　　　　　~(∃x)(Fx & Hx)　√ 3
　　　　　(∀x)(Gx ⊃ Hx)　*a 8
　　　　　(∃x)(Fx & Gx)　√ 4
　　　　　(∀x)~(Fx & Hx)　*a 6
　　　　　Fa & Ga　√ 5
　　　　　Fa
　　　　　Ga
　　　　　~(Fa & Ha)　√ 7

　~Fa　　　　　　~Ha
　　X　　　　　　Ga ⊃ Ha　√ 9

　　　　　　　　~Ga　　Ha
　　　　　　　　X　　　X

TAUTOLOGY

(ORIGINAL UNNEGATED FORM)

Predicate truth tree
rules eliminate
quantifiers from wffs
in a stack until the
resulting wffs are de-
composable according
to propositional truth
tree rules.

$$\underline{(\exists x)(Fx \mathbin{\&} Gx),\ (\exists x)(Fx \mathbin{\&} (\forall y)(Gy \supset {\sim}Hxy)) \vdash (\exists x)(Fx \mathbin{\&} {\sim}(\forall y)(Fy \supset Hyx))}$$

$(\exists x)(Fx \mathbin{\&} Gx)$ √ 2
$(\exists x)(Fx \mathbin{\&} (\forall y)(Gy \supset {\sim}Hxy))$ √ 4
${\sim}(\exists x)(Fx \mathbin{\&} {\sim}(\forall y)(Fy \supset Hyx))$ √ 1
$(\forall x){\sim}(Fx \mathbin{\&} {\sim}(\forall y)(Fy \supset Hyx))$ *a 6
Fa & Ga   √ 3
Fa
Ga
Fb & $(\forall y)(Gy \supset {\sim}Hby)$ √ 5
Fb
$(\forall y)(Gy \supset {\sim}Hby)$ *a 10
${\sim}(Fa \mathbin{\&} {\sim}(\forall y)(Fy \supset Hya))$ √ 7

~Fa $(\forall y)(Fy \supset Hya))$ *b 8
X   Fb ⊃ Hba   √ 9

~Fb   Hba
X   Ga ⊃ ~Hba   √ 11

~Ga   ~Hba
X   X

VALID

$$\underline{(\exists x)(Fx \mathbin{\&} (\forall y)(Gy \supset Hxy)),\ (\forall x)(Fx \supset (\forall y)(By \supset {\sim}Hxy)) \vdash {\sim}(\forall x)(Gx \supset {\sim}Bx)}$$

$(\exists x)(Fx \mathbin{\&} (\forall y)(Gy \supset Hxy))$ √ 1
$(\forall x)(Fx \supset (\forall y)(By \supset {\sim}Hxy))$ *a 3
$(\forall x)(Gx \supset {\sim}Bx)$ √ 5
Fa & $(\forall y)(Gy \supset Hay)$ √ 2
Fa
$(\forall y)(Gy \supset Hay)$ *a 10
Fa ⊃ $(\forall y)(By \supset {\sim}Hay)$ √ 4

~Fa $(\forall y)(By \supset {\sim}Hay)$ *a 7
X   Ga ⊃ ~Ba   √ 6

Ga   ~Ba
8 √ Ba ⊃ ~Haa   Ba ⊃ ~Haa   √ 9

~Ba   ~Haa   ~Ba   ~Haa
11, 12 √ √ Ga ⊃ Haa   Ga ⊃ Haa   Ga ⊃ Haa   Ga ⊃ Haa √ √ 13, 14

~Ga   Haa   ~Ga   Haa   ~Ga   Haa   ~Ga   Haa
X   X   X   X

INVALID

To Check Your Understanding 7.3 ───────────────────────────────── ∎

> Use truth trees to test the following predicate wffs to determine whether they are tautologies, inconsistencies, or contingencies and the following sequents to determine whether they are deductively valid or invalid:

1. (∃x)(~Gx & Fa) ≡ (Fa & (∃x)~Gx)
2. ~(∀x)(Fx ⊃ ~Gx) ≡ ~(∃x)(Fx & Gx)
3. ~(((∃x)~Gx ⊃ (∃x)Fx) ⊃ (∃x)(~Gx ⊃ Fx))
4. ((∀x)Fax & ~(∃x)Fxb) ⊃ ((∀x)Gx ⊃ (∀x)(Hxc ⊃ ~Gx))
5. (∃x)Fx ⊃ ~(∀x)Fx ⊢ ~((∃x)Fx & ~(∃x)~Fx)
6. (∀x)(∀y)(Sxy ≡ (∀z)(Txz ≡ Tyz)) ⊢ (∀x)(∀y)(Sxy ⊃ Syx)
7. (∀x)(Hx ⊃ Ax) ⊢ (∀x)((∃y)(Hy & Txy) ⊃ (∃y)(Ay & Txy))
8. ~(∃x)Pxx, (∀x)(∀y)(∃z)((Lzy & ~Lxz) ⊃ Pxy) ⊢ (∃x)~(∃y) (~Lyx ⊃ ~Lxy)
9. (∀x)(Hx ⊃ Ax) ⊢ ~(∀x)((∃y)(Hy & Txy) ⊃ (∃y)(Ay & ~Txy))

∎

Truth Tree Evaluation of Prenex Equivalents

Predicate truth trees can be used to verify prenex normal form equivalents.

We continue by examining truth trees for more complicated wffs and sequents. We consider first the wffs that were reformulated by the four prenex normal form transformation rules to confirm that the transformations are logically equivalent. For each of the examples, we take the original wff and connect it by the biconditional to its prenex transform and check to determine that the biconditional is a tautology by completing the predicate truth tree for its negation. The following are the results for the first three examples; the fourth is left as an exercise:

First example:

$$\sim(((\exists x)Fx \supset (\forall y)Gy) \equiv (\forall x)(\forall y)(\sim Fx \lor Gy)) \quad \checkmark\ 1$$

To verify the logical equivalence of predicate wffs transformed into prenex normal forms, the wffs and their transforms are connected by a bicon- ditional and tested to determine if the bi- conditional is a tau- tology by completing the predicate truth tree for the negation of the biconditional.

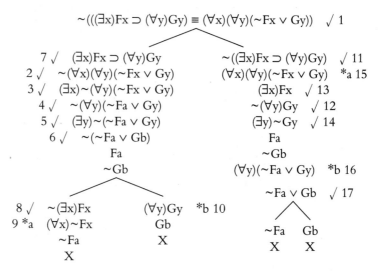

LOGICALLY EQUIVALENT

Second example:

$$\sim((\sim(\exists x)Fx \& (\forall x(\sim Gx) \equiv (\forall x)(\forall y)(\sim Fx \& \sim Gy)) \quad \checkmark\ 1$$

$\begin{array}{ll} 2\ \checkmark & \sim(\exists x)Fx\ \&\ (\forall x)\sim Gx \\ 4\ \checkmark & \sim(\forall x)(\forall y)(\sim Fx\ \&\ \sim Gy) \\ 3\ \checkmark & \sim(\exists x)Fx \\ 11\ *b & (\forall x)\sim Gx \\ 10\ *a & (\forall x)\sim Fx \\ 5\ \checkmark & (\exists x)\sim(\forall y)(\sim Fx\ \&\ \sim Gy) \\ 6\ \checkmark & \sim(\forall y)(\sim Fa\ \&\ \sim Gy) \\ 7\ \checkmark & (\exists y)\sim(\sim Fa\ \&\ \sim Gy) \\ 8\ \checkmark & \sim(\sim Fa\ \&\ \sim Gb) \end{array}$

$\begin{array}{ll} \sim(\sim(\exists x)Fx\ \&\ (\forall x)\sim Gx) & \checkmark\ 12 \\ (\forall x)(\forall y)(\sim Fx\ \&\ \sim Gy) & *a\ 16 \end{array}$

$\begin{array}{ll} 14\ \checkmark\ (\exists x)Fx & \sim(\forall x)\sim Gx \quad \checkmark\ 13 \\ Fa & (\exists x)Gx \quad \checkmark\ 15 \\ 17\ *a\ (\forall y)(\sim Fa\ \&\ \sim Gy) & Ga \\ 18\ \checkmark\ \sim Fa\ \&\ \sim Ga & (\forall y)(\sim Fa\ \&\ \sim Gy)\ *a\ 19 \\ \sim Fa & \sim Fa\ \&\ \sim Ga \quad \checkmark\ 20 \\ \sim Ga & \sim Fa \\ X & \sim Ga \\ & X \end{array}$

Fa   Gb
~Fa   ~Gb
X   X

LOGICALLY EQUIVALENT

Third example:

$$\sim((\exists x)(Fx \supset (\forall y)Gy) \equiv (\exists x)(\forall y)(\sim Fx \vee Gy)) \quad \checkmark\ 1$$

3 $\checkmark$ $(\exists x)(Fx \supset (\forall y)Gy)$ $\sim(\exists x)(Fx \supset (\forall y)Gy)$ $\checkmark$ 13
2 $\checkmark$ $\sim(\exists x)(\forall y)(\sim Fx \vee Gy)$ $(\exists x)(\forall y)(\sim Fx \vee Gy)$ $\checkmark$ 14
5 *a $(\forall x)\sim(\forall y)(\sim Fx \vee Gy)$ $(\forall x)\sim(Fx \supset (\forall y)Gy)$ *a 15
4 $\checkmark$ $Fa \supset (\forall y)Gy$ $(\forall y)(\sim Fa \vee Gy)$ *b 19
                                                        $\sim(Fa \supset (\forall y)Gy)$ $\checkmark$ 16

               $\sim Fa$ $(\forall y)Gy$ $\checkmark$ 12   Fa
7 $\checkmark$ 6 $\checkmark$ $\sim(\forall y)(\sim Fa \vee Gy)$ $\sim(\forall y)(\sim Fa \vee Gy)$ $\sim(\forall y)Gy$ $\checkmark$ 17
9 $\checkmark$ 8 $\checkmark$ $(\exists y)\sim(\sim Fa \vee Gy)$ $(\exists y)\sim(\sim Fa \vee Gy)$ $(\exists y)\sim Gy$ $\checkmark$ 18
11 $\checkmark$ 10 $\checkmark$ $\sim(\sim Fa \vee Gb)$ $\sim(\sim Fa \vee Gb)$ $\sim Gb$
               Fa   Fa $\sim Fa \vee Gb$ $\checkmark$ 20
               $\sim Gb$ $\sim Gb$
                X   Gb $\sim Fa$ Gb
                                    X   X   X

LOGICALLY EQUIVALENT

Fourth example:

$$\sim((\forall x)(Fx \equiv (\exists y)Gy) \equiv (\forall x)(\exists y)(\forall z)((Fx \& Gy) \vee (\sim Fx \& \sim Gz)))$$

Try the predicate truth tree for this example to check your understanding. Next, we work through a series of trees for some of the nonequivalent wffs involving exported quantifiers, as well as the trees for their prenex normal form equivalences, obtained by the prenex rules in Chapter 6.

$$\sim((\forall x)(Fx \supset \sim(\forall y)Dxy) \equiv (\forall x)\sim(\forall y)(Fx \supset Dxy)) \quad \checkmark\ 1$$

4 *a $(\forall x)(Fx \supset \sim(\forall y)Dxy)$ $\sim(\forall x)(Fx \supset \sim(\forall y)Dxy)$
2 $\checkmark$ $\sim(\forall x)\sim(\forall y)(Fx \supset Dxy)$ $(\forall x)\sim(\forall y)(Fx \supset Dxy)$
3 $\checkmark$ $(\exists x)(\forall y)(Fx \supset Dxy)$
8 *b $(\forall y)(Fa \supset Day)$
5 $\checkmark$ $Fa \supset \sim(\forall y)Day$

               $\sim Fa$ $\sim(\forall y)Day$ $\checkmark$ 6
9 $\checkmark$ $Fa \supset Dab$ $(\exists y)\sim Day$ $\checkmark$ 7
                                    $\sim Dab$
         $\sim Fa$ $Fa \supset Dab$

LOGICALLY NONEQUIVALENT

For this problem, we need go no further than step 9, in which it becomes clear that no further decomposition of wffs within the tree will possibly produce closure in the far left branch, and that therefore the entire tree remains open. The wffs in question are thus shown to be logically nonequivalent. In contrast, the following wffs related by the prenex normal form transformation rules are logically equivalent:

$$\sim((\forall x)(Fx \supset \sim(\forall y)Dxy) \equiv (\forall x)(\exists y)(\sim Fx \lor \sim Dxy)) \quad \checkmark 1$$

5 *a	$(\forall x)(Fx \supset \sim(\forall y)Dxy)$		$\sim(\forall x)(Fx \supset \sim(\forall y)Dxy)$	$\checkmark 12$

5 *a $(\forall x)(Fx \supset \sim(\forall y)Dxy)$ $\sim(\forall x)(Fx \supset \sim(\forall y)Dxy)$ $\checkmark 12$
2 $\checkmark$ $\sim(\forall x)(\exists y)(\sim Fx \lor \sim Dxy)$ $(\forall x)(\exists y)(\sim Fx \lor \sim Dxy)$ *a 15
3 $\checkmark$ $(\exists x)\sim(\exists y)(\sim Fx \lor \sim Dxy)$ $(\exists x)\sim(Fx \supset \sim(\forall y)Dxy)$ $\checkmark 13$
4 $\checkmark$ $\sim(\exists y)(\sim Fa \lor \sim Day)$ $\sim(Fa \supset \sim(\forall y)Day)$ $\checkmark 14$
9 *b $(\forall y)\sim(\sim Fa \lor \sim Day)$ Fa
6 $\checkmark$ $Fa \supset \sim(\forall y)Day$ $(\forall y)Day$ *b 18
          $(\exists y)(\sim Fa \lor \sim Day)$ $\checkmark 16$

~Fa $\sim(\forall y)Day$ $\checkmark 7$ $\sim Fa \lor \sim Dab$ $\checkmark 17$
10 $\checkmark$ $\sim(\sim Fa \lor \sim Dab)$ $(\exists y)\sim Day$ $\checkmark 8$
Fa $\sim Dab$ ~Fa   ~Dab
Dab $\sim(\sim Fa \lor \sim Dab)$ $\checkmark 11$ X   Dab
X   Fa   X
           Dab
           X

LOGICALLY EQUIVALENT

In Chapter 6, we similarly claimed, but did not formally demonstrate, that $(\forall x)(Fx \supset \sim(\exists y)Dxy)$ and $(\forall x)\sim(\exists y)(Fx \supset Dxy)$ are logically nonequivalent, but that $(\forall x)(Fx \supset \sim(\exists y)Dxy)$ and its prenex transform, $(\forall x)(\forall y)(\sim Fx \lor \sim Dxy)$, are logically equivalent. We are now in a position to show this by predicate truth trees:

$$\sim((\forall x)(Fx \supset \sim(\exists y)Dxy) \equiv (\forall x(\sim(\exists y)(Fx \supset Dxy)) \quad \checkmark 1$$

6 *a $(\forall x)(Fx \supset \sim(\exists y)Dxy)$ $\sim(\forall x)(Fx \supset \sim(\exists y)Dxy)$
2 $\checkmark$ $\sim(\forall x)\sim(\exists y)(Fx \supset Dxy)$ $(\forall x)\sim(\exists y)(Fx \supset Dxy)$
3 $\checkmark$ $(\exists x)(\exists y)(Fx \supset Dxy)$
4 $\checkmark$ $(\exists y)(Fa \supset Day)$
5 $\checkmark$ $Fa \supset Dab$

~Fa   Dab
7 $\checkmark$ $Fa \supset \sim(\exists y)Day$ $Fa \supset \sim(\exists y)Day$

~Fa $\sim(\exists y)Day$

LOGICALLY NONEQUIVALENT

*Prenex rules provide
an unlimited number
of problems to test
logical equivalence by
predicate truth trees.*

As before, we need go no further to see that the tree will never close. We have decomposed the universal wff at step 6 by substituting constant 'a' for the universally bound variable 'x'. No other choice of constants will produce closure with the wff ~Fa, where ~Fa and ~Fa obviously are not inconsistent. This indicates, as previously claimed, that the wffs in question are logically non-equivalent. The equivalence of the first wff and its prenex transform in contrast is seen in the following tree:

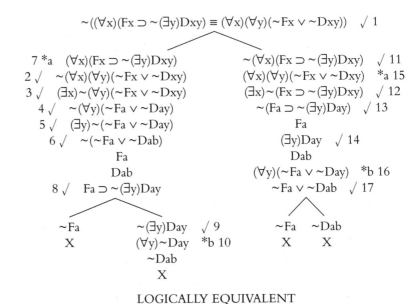

LOGICALLY EQUIVALENT

These trees provide a partial but by no means general rigorous demonstration of the correctness of the prenex normal form transformation rules.

To Check Your Understanding 7.4

Use predicate truth trees to confirm that the wffs converted to prenex normal form in *To Check Your Understanding 6.8* problems in Chapter 6 are in fact logically equivalent. If any trees fail to verify the expected equivalences, first recheck the trees, and then go back and recheck your use of the prenex transformation rules to make sure you have applied them correctly. Then redo the trees if any of your transformations need to be changed to make sure that the original problem wffs and their corrected prenex normal forms are logically equivalent.

Square of Opposition

The square of opposition displays several important relations among wffs in predicate logic.

It is possible to present several noteworthy predicate relations in a *square of opposition*. The square of opposition was originally devised by the ancient Greek philosopher Aristotle as a way of representing the logical relations holding among four basic types of quantificational propositions. By comparing the traditional square of opposition with the symbolization of its relations in our symbolism, we can derive an important presupposition about the existence of all quantified objects in modern predicate logic.

Aristotle distinguishes between universal and particular and between affirmative and negative propositions. This division makes possible four combinations of judgments at the four corners of the square of opposition, abbreviated as A, E, I, and O propositions. They are propositions of the following kinds:

Square of opposition relations involve categorical AEIO wffs.

A: Universal affirmative (All F's are G's)

E: Universal negative (No F's are G's)

I: Particular affirmative (Some F's are G's)

O: Particular negative (Some F's are not G's)

The traditional square of opposition presents the logical relations among these basic propositions in a graphic display:

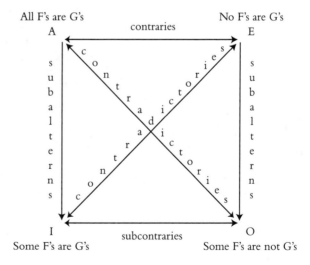

The square shows the logical relations among some quantified wffs. A wff $\mathbb{Q}$ is a *subaltern* of a wff $\mathbb{P}$ if and only if $\mathbb{Q}$ is validly deducible from $\mathbb{P}$ but $\mathbb{P}$ is not validly deducible from $\mathbb{Q}$. Wffs $\mathbb{P}$ and $\mathbb{Q}$ are *contraries* if and only if $\mathbb{P}$ and $\mathbb{Q}$ cannot both be true, although both might be false. Wffs $\mathbb{P}$ and $\mathbb{Q}$ are *subcontraries* if and only if both $\mathbb{P}$ and $\mathbb{Q}$ can be true, but both cannot be false. Wffs $\mathbb{P}$ and $\mathbb{Q}$ are *contradictories* if and only if $\mathbb{P}$ and $\mathbb{Q}$ cannot both be true or be false.

By consulting the square of opposition as a convenient summary and memory device for recalling the logical relations among AEIO propositions, it is possible to quickly confirm or disconfirm many predicate inferences that fit or fail to fit the prescribed patterns for valid inference, contradiction, contrary opposition, or subalternation. However, the predicate relations involving the four types of propositions in the traditional square of opposition hold logically only if it is presupposed that an object to which the properties in question are universally or particularly and affirmatively or negatively predicated actually exist. Suppose that we translate the AEIO propositions as indicated below, as we would ordinarily expect to do in our predicate symbolism. They have the following forms:

AEIO TRANSLATIONS WITHOUT EXPLICIT EXISTENCE CONDITIONS

A: $(\forall x)(Fx \supset Gx)$
E: $(\forall x)(Fx \supset \sim Gx)$
I: $(\exists x)(Fx \& Gx)$
O: $(\exists x)(Fx \& \sim Gx)$

Then the logical relations detailed in the traditional square of opposition cannot all be verified in modern symbolic logic. Contradictory relations are no problem, but the contrary and subaltern relations do not obtain. This is easy to determine by predicate truth trees. The corresponding square of opposition for predicate logic with the previous AEIO translations has the following imperfect form:

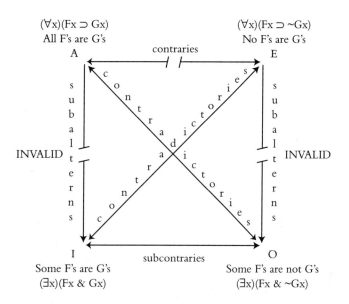

Contraries and sub-alterns in the traditional square of opposition are deductively invalid when symbolized without explicit existence conditions in standard predicate logic.

A tree to show how the A–I subaltern relation fails on this interpretation is seen in what follows. The tree to demonstrate the invalidity of the E–O subaltern relation has virtually the same structure.

$$(\forall x)(Fx \supset Gx) \quad *a\ 4$$
$$\sim(\exists x)(Fx\ \&\ Gx) \quad \sqrt{}\ 1$$
$$(\forall x)\sim(Fx\ \&\ Gx) \quad *a\ 2$$
$$\sim(Fa\ \&\ Ga) \quad \sqrt{}\ 3$$

```
                    ~Fa                ~Ga
          6 √   Fa ⊃ Ga           Fa ⊃ Ga   √ 5
               /    \             /     \
             ~Fa    Ga         ~Fa      Ga
                                         X              INVALID
```

Predicate AEIO wffs can be reformulated with explicit existence conditions.

To restore the complete traditional square of opposition relations without sacrificing the relations that already obtain according to the translations proposed previously in the square, we must make explicit the presupposition of Aristotelian logic that an object with a property to which another property is universally affirmed, universally negated, particularly affirmed, or particularly negated actually exists. The necessary conversions of the AEIO propositions as understood in Aristotelian logic into predicate logic are given as follows:

AEIO TRANSLATIONS WITH EXPLICIT EXISTENCE CONDITIONS

A: $(\exists x)Fx \mathbin{\&} (\forall x)(Fx \supset Gx)$
E: $(\exists x)Fx \mathbin{\&} (\forall x)(Fx \supset {\sim}Gx)$
I: $(\exists x)Fx \supset (\exists x)(Fx \mathbin{\&} Gx)$
O: $(\exists x)Fx \supset (\exists x)(Fx \mathbin{\&} {\sim}Gx)$

The logical relations in the traditional square of opposition can then be correctly transcribed into modern predicate logic in the following amended diagram:

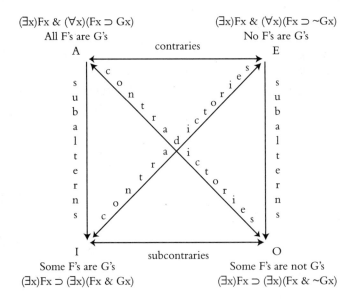

$(\exists x)Fx \mathbin{\&} (\forall x)(Fx \supset Gx)$
All F's are G's
A

contraries

$(\exists x)Fx \mathbin{\&} (\forall x)(Fx \supset {\sim}Gx)$
No F's are G's
E

subalterns   contradictories   subalterns

I
Some F's are G's
$(\exists x)Fx \supset (\exists x)(Fx \mathbin{\&} Gx)$

subcontraries

O
Some F's are not G's
$(\exists x)Fx \supset (\exists x)(Fx \mathbin{\&} {\sim}Gx)$

All the inference relations exhibited in the traditional square of opposition are deductively valid when predicate AEIO wffs are reformulated with explicit existence conditions.

We can use predicate truth trees to verify all the logical relations required in the traditional square of opposition for the AEIO propositions as correctly translated into modern symbolic predicate logic.

■ *Demonstration 28:*   **Square of Opposition Relations**   ■

PROBLEM: To evaluate logical relations in the square of opposition by predicate truth trees.

RELATION: Consider the relation of subalterns in the square of opposition:

$$(\exists x)Fx \;\&\; (\forall x)(Fx \supset {\sim}Gx) \vdash (\exists x)Fx \supset (\exists x)(Fx \;\&\; {\sim}Gx)$$

STEP 1:   *Set up the truth tree*
To set up the truth tree to evaluate the relation, we begin as we do in propositional truth trees. We stack the assumptions of the argument together with the negation of its conclusion. This gives us:

$$(\exists x)Fx \;\&\; (\forall x)(Fx \supset {\sim}Gx)$$
$${\sim}((\exists x)Fx \supset (\exists x)(Fx \;\&\; {\sim}Gx))$$

STEP 2:   *Apply the predicate truth tree rules*
We have now had practice completing truth trees, so we shall not elaborate on the method here. The completed truth tree in this case is:

$$(\exists x)Fx \;\&\; (\forall x)(Fx \supset {\sim}Gx) \quad \sqrt{}\ 1$$
$${\sim}((\exists x)Fx \supset (\exists x)(Fx \;\&\; {\sim}Gx)) \quad \sqrt{}\ 2$$
$$(\exists x)Fx \quad \sqrt{}\ 6$$
$$(\forall x)(Fx \supset {\sim}Gx) \quad {*}a\ 4$$
$$(\exists x)Fx$$
$${\sim}(\exists x)(Fx \;\&\; {\sim}Gx) \quad \sqrt{}\ 5$$
$$(\forall x){\sim}(Fx \;\&\; {\sim}Gx) \quad {*}a\ 8$$
$$Fa$$
$$Fa \supset {\sim}Ga \quad \sqrt{}\ 7$$

```
                    ~Fa                  ~Ga
                     X          ~(Fa & ~Ga)   √ 9

                                  ~Fa    Ga
                                   X      X              VALID
```

Notice that it is unnecessary in this tree to decompose the second occurrence of the existential wff $(\exists x)Fx$ that appears at the fifth line of the tree as part of the decomposition of the negated conditional conclusion of the inference ${\sim}((\exists x)Fx \supset (\exists x)(Fx \;\&\; {\sim}Gx))$. The reason is that although the subaltern relation depends on the condition that something with property F exists, the condition is already satisfied by the decomposition of $(\exists x)Fx$ in the third line at step 6. It would be just as deductively valid to infer that $(\exists x)Fx$ & $(\forall x)$ $(Fx \supset \sim Gx) \vdash (\exists x)(Fx$ & $\sim Gx)$, which can also be verified by a predicate truth tree. The same is true for the second part of the subaltern relation proven below. The existence condition is also essential for some of the other square of opposition relations.

STEP 3:   *Check to determine if the relation holds in one direction only*
The subaltern relation is supposed to hold only in one direction. To complete our evaluation of this square of opposition relation, we verify that the relation does not hold in the opposite way.

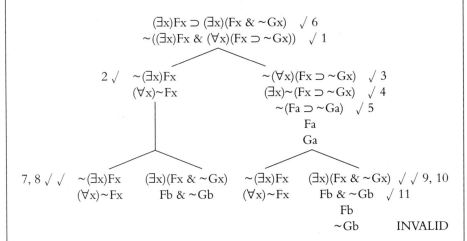

The tree is not yet complete. But enough has been done to see the far right branch and hence the tree as a whole cannot close. The branch remains open because of the restriction on predicate truth tree decompositions by which existential wffs on the same branch must be reduced to predicate-constant wffs containing arbitrary constants that have not appeared anywhere previously on the same branch of the tree.

STEP 4:   *Evaluate the entire logical relation*
The two truth trees confirm the square of opposition depiction of the logical relation of predicate subalterns. The closure of the first tree shows that the relation holds from $(\exists x)Fx$ & $(\forall x)(Fx \supset \sim Gx)$ to $(\exists x)Fx \supset (\exists x)(Fx$ & $\sim Gx)$, whereas the fact that the second tree remains open and does not close shows that the relation does not hold in the opposite direction from $(\exists x)Fx \supset (\exists x)(Fx$ & $\sim Gx)$ to $(\exists x)Fx$ & $(\forall x)(Fx \supset \sim Gx)$. This agrees with the arrow for subalternation in the square of opposition which points only in the direction now confirmed by truth tree analysis.

To Check Your Understanding 7.5 ──────────────────────────────────■

> Use predicate truth trees to prove all the remaining subaltern, contrary, sub-contrary, and contradictory relations diagrammed in the predicate square of opposition; note that some involve biconditional predicate relations, whereas others are only conditional. In which of these is the existential condition in the symbolization of predicate contraries necessary and in which is it unnecessary?

■

Limitations of Predicate Trees

Predicate truth trees are limited in ways that propositional truth trees are not.

Predicate truth trees are a decision method, but not a fully effective decision method, for predicate logic; because of specially constructible wffs in predicate logic that deny their own provability or identifiability by decision method, predicate truth trees do not determine for every arbitrary wff whether or not it is a tautology, nor for every arbitrary sequent whether or not it is deductively valid.

The limitations of predicate truth trees have negligible impact on their practical use for logical analysis and evaluation of wffs and sequents in predicate logic.

We have seen predicate truth trees involving universally quantified wffs that can be endlessly decomposed by substituting increasingly more constants for universally bound variables. When we have exhausted all the possibilities for closure in the tree, then we say that the tree is open, even though we could in principle continue to replace universally quantified variables in wffs within the tree's stack by additional constants.

This is an important distinction between predicate and propositional truth trees. Propositional truth trees, in contrast, always terminate after a finite number of steps in a definite evaluation of a stack of wffs. There is another even more logically interesting difference. Predicate truth trees, unlike propositional trees, are not an effective decision method that determines for every arbitrary wff whether or not it is a tautology and for every arbitrary sequent whether or not it is deductively valid. There are sentences and arguments that can be specially constructed in predicate logic, but not in propositional logic, that state of themselves that they are not identifiable by any decision method or are not provable. If true, such sentences cannot be identified by truth trees, nor are they provable in any system of natural deduction.

Predicate truth trees, as a consequence, are a useful and possibly the best imaginable decision method for predicate logic. However, they are not a fully effective decision method that will always give correct results in testing every wff and sequent of predicate logic. The rigorous proof of these results is a subject for continuing study in the *metatheory* of logic. An informal discussion of the limitations of decision methods and natural deduction proofs in predicate logic is recommended for interested readers in the addendum on "Advanced Topics in Symbolic Logic" following Chapter 8, under the heading Metatheory. The limitations of predicate truth trees circumscribe a gray area of wffs and sequents for which there is no effective decision method. The formal limitations of predicate logic concern only a fraction of logically peculiar sentences that we are unlikely to encounter in practice and that do not affect the usefulness of predicate truth trees in analyzing the logical structures of ordinary reasoning.

Summary: Predicate Truth Trees

By adding four new rules and a protocol for applying the rules, the truth tree decision method for propositional logic is extended to predicate logic. Two of the rules convert negative universals into existential negations and negative existentials into universal negations, as an application of quantifier duality. The remaining two rules decompose universal propositions and existential propositions by giving conditions under which object constants can be substituted for quantifier bound object variables. Universals are unrestrictedly decomposed by uniformly substituting as many of any object constants as may maximize closure in a branch. Existentials are restrictedly decomposed by selectively substituting an arbitrarily chosen constant for an existentially bound variable, for which the constant must not appear anywhere previously on the same branch. With these differences, predicate truth trees function exactly like the propositional truth trees on which they are based, all the rules of which predicate trees also include. Predicate truth trees are set up in the same way to test wffs for classification as tautologies, inconsistencies, or contingencies; to test stacks of wffs for logical consistency or inconsistency and for logical equivalence or nonequivalence; and to test sequents for deductive validity or invalidity. There is no generally effective decision method for all logically consistent wffs and sequents with logically consistent assumptions and conclusions, and, in particular, predicate truth trees are not a generally effective decision method. The method fails, however, only for specialized constructions that as a practical matter are not encountered in ordinary applications of predicate logic.

Key Words

predicate truth tree
main operator
greatest scope rule (for identifying
    predicate main operators)
fewest parentheses guidelines (for
    identifying predicate main
    operators)
driving negation inward (by
    quantifier duality)
predicate truth tree decomposition
    rules

arbitrary (choice of object constant
    for predicate truth tree
    decomposition of existentially
    quantified proposition)
truth tree protocol for predicate
    logic
square of opposition
subaltern (predicate relations)
contrary
subcontrary
contradictory

Exercises

I: Predicate Decision Method Concepts Give a correct concise statement for each of the following concepts; where appropriate, give an illustration of each that does not appear in the book:

1. Main operator
2. Predicate truth tree
3. Driving negation inward
4. Quantifier duality relations
5. Arbitrary object constant
6. Restriction on truth tree rule for existentials
7. Square of opposition
8. Contradictory predicate relations
9. Contrary, subcontrary predicate relations
10. Subaltern predicate relations

II: Truth Tree Evaluation of Wffs Use predicate truth trees to evaluate the following wffs for classification as tautologies, inconsistencies, or contingencies of predicate logic:

1. $(\forall x)\sim Fx \ \& \sim(\exists x)Fx$
2. $\sim(\exists x)Fx \lor \sim(\forall x)\sim Fx$
3. $\sim((\exists x)\sim Fx \supset \sim(\forall x)Fx)$
4. $\sim(\forall x)Fx \equiv (\exists x)\sim Fx$
5. $P \supset ((\forall x)Fx \supset (\forall x)(P \supset Fx))$
6. $(\forall x)(P \supset Fx) \lor \sim(P \supset (\forall x)Fx)$
7. $(\forall x)(Fx \supset Gx) \supset ((\forall x)\sim Gx \supset (\forall x)\sim Fx)$
8. $(\forall x)(Fx \supset Gx) \supset ((\exists x)\sim Gx \lor \sim(\exists x)\sim Fx)$
9. $(\forall x)(\exists y)(\forall z)Fxyz \lor (\forall x)\sim(\forall z)(\exists y)Fxyz$
10. $(\exists x)(Fx \ \& \ (\forall y)(\sim Gy \supset Hxy)) \ \& \ (\sim(\forall x)(Fx \supset (\forall y)(By \supset \sim Hxy)) \equiv (\forall x)(Gx \supset \sim Bx))$

III: Truth Tree Evaluation for Consistency and Equivalence   Use predicate truth trees to evaluate the following pairs of wffs for consistency or inconsistency and for equivalence or nonequivalence:

1. (∃x)Fx; (∃x)~Fx
2. (∃x)Fx; ~(∃x)Fx
3. (∀x)Fx; (∃x)~Fx
4. (∃x)Fx; ~(∃x)~Fx
5. (∀x)(Fx ⊃ Gx); (∀x)Fx & (∀x)Gx
6. (∃x)(Fx ∨ Gx); (∃x)Fx ∨ (∃x)Gx
7. (∃x)(Gx & Fx); (∃x)(~Gx & Fx)
8. ~(∃x)(Fx ⊃ (P & ~P)); (∃x)(Fx ⊃ (P & ~P))
9. (∀x)(Fx ⊃ ~Gx) & ~(∃x)(~Gx & Hx); ~(∀x)~(Gx & Hx)
10. (~(∃x)Fx ≡ ~(∀x)Gx) & (∃x)(Fx & ~Hx); ~(∃x)Hx ∨ (∃x)~Gx

IV: Truth Tree Evaluation of Sequents   Use predicate truth trees to evaluate the following sequents as deductively valid or invalid; explain what each result implies about validity relations in predicate logic:

1. (∃x)Fx ⊢ Fa
2. Fa ⊢ (∀x)Fx
3. (∃x)Fx ⊢ (∀x)Fx
4. (∀x)Fx ⊢ (∃x)Fx
5. (∀x)(Fx ⊃ Gx) ⊢ (∀x)(Fa ⊃ Gx)
6. (∀x)(Fx ⊃ Gx) ⊢ (∀x)(Fx ⊃ Ga)
7. (∀x)(Fx ⊃ Gx) ⊢ Fa ⊃ Gb
8. (∀x)(Fx ⊃ Gx) ⊢ Fa ⊃ Ga
9. ~Fa ⊢ (∀x)(Fx ⊃ Gx)
10. ~Fa ⊢ (∃x)(Fx & Gx)
11. Fa, Gb ⊢ (∃x)(Fx & Gx)
12. Fa, Ga ⊢ (∃x)(Fx & Gx)
13. ~(∃x)Fx ⊢ (∀x)(Fx ⊃ Gx)
14. (∀x)(Fx ⊃ Gx), (∃x)Fx ⊢ (∃x)Gx
15. (∀x)(Fx ⊃ Gx), (∃x)Fx ⊢ (∀x)Gx
16. (∀x)(Fx ⊃ Gx), (∀x)Fx ⊢ (∀x)Gx
17. (∀x)(Fx ⊃ Gx), (∀x)Fx ⊢ (∃x)Gx

18. (∃x)(Fx ⊃ Gx), (∀x)Fx ⊦ (∀x)Gx
19. (∃x)(Fx ⊃ Gx), (∃x)Fx ⊦ (∀x)Gx
20. (∃x)(Fx ⊃ Gx), (∀x)Fx ⊦ (∃x)Gx
21. (∃x)(Fx ⊃ Gx), (∃x)Fx ⊦ (∃x)Gx
22. (∀x)(Fx ⊃ ~Gx), (∃x)Gx ⊦ (∃x)(Fx ⊃ Gx)
23. (∀x)(Fx ⊃ ~Gx), (∃x)Gx ⊦ (∀x)(Fx ⊃ Gx)

V: Truth Tree Evaluations of Wffs and Sequents from Previous Exercises   Give predicate truth tree evaluations of all the wffs and sequents from Chapter 6's final symbolization exercises to determine in the case of wffs whether they are tautologies, inconsistencies, or contingencies and in the case of sequents whether they are deductively valid or invalid.

VI: Short Answer Questions for Philosophical Reflection

1. Is it possible to refer to an object without thinking of it?
2. Can we refer collectively to objects or sets of objects without having any particular objects in mind?
3. What is the justification for requiring arbitrary constants as substitutes for existentially bound variables in predicate truth tree decompositions of existential propositions?
4. What is the relation between the propositional substructure and predicate superstructure of predicate logic?
5. Is logic necessarily an instrument of the truth? Can logic be used in the service of falsehood? Can logic lead us more easily into error than illogic?
6. Could there be a predicate wff or sequent whose truth tree involved infinitely unsatisfied and inexhaustible possibilities for closure? What are the theoretical and practical implications of the fact that a universally quantified wff in predicate logic can never be fully decomposed?

CHAPTER EIGHT

Predicate Natural Deduction Proofs

> The task of formalizing first order logic (or setting up the predicate calculus) is to find a formal system (or a schema of formal systems) such that all and only the valid sentences are theorems.
>
> —Hao Wang, *Popular Lectures on Mathematical Logic* (1981)

WE NOW ADD FOUR new rules to extend our system of natural deduction proofs from propositional to predicate logic. Strategies are discussed as we consider practical and theoretical applications of predicate natural deductive proofs.

Natural Deduction Rules for Predicate Logic

All rules of propositional natural deduction proofs are preserved, and four new intelim rules for introducing and eliminating universally and existentially quantified wffs are added.

Predicate logic is built on propositional logic. The underlying structure of predicate logic is truth functional, involving the five propositional connectives. All 12 of the natural deduction rules of propositional logic are also natural deduction rules of predicate logic. Adding to the 12 natural deductive rules for propositional logic, we introduce four intelim rules for the universal and existential quantifiers. We begin with the easiest rules—universal elimination, $\forall E$, and existential introduction, $\exists I$—and then explain universal introduction, $\forall I$, and the subproof rule for existential elimination, $\exists E$. We present an abstract schema for each rule and then illustrate its use with paradigms and applications, as we did in advancing the rules for natural deduction proofs in propositional logic.

Universal Elimination (∀E)

.
.
.

$(\forall x)(. . . x . . .)$ . . .
$. . . \alpha . . .$ . . . ∀E

(Unlimited uniform instantiations)

Universal elimination (∀E) justifies instantiating any universally quantified wff by eliminating its quantifier, and uniformly substituting any constant for every variable universally bound by the quantifier.

If a universal proposition says that all objects have a certain property, then any particular object must also have the property. If everything is F, then a in particular is F (Fa), b in particular is F (Fb), c in particular is F (Fc), and so on. If everything is self-identical, then Anna is self-identical, Beatrice is self-identical, Carlos is self-identical, etc. The rule of universal elimination (∀E) permits us to validly derive from any universal proposition a particular proposition in which the universal quantifier is eliminated, and all occurrences of the variable bound by the quantifier are uniformly replaced by any chosen constant. The following is an application of the rule:

| 1 | 1. | (∀x)Fx | A |
| 1 | 2. | Fa | 1∀E |

Universal elimination is unrestricted.

We could also validly conclude in step 2 that Fb, Fc, or whatever we liked, replacing the universally bound variable 'x' by any constant. We could continue within the proof to derive in successive steps 3, 4, and so on Fa, Fb, Fc, and Fd, citing in each case the rule ∀E applied to step 1. For simplicity, we introduce step 1 as a given assumption, as we did in introducing the intelim rules of propositional logic. However, the rule can be used to eliminate any universal proposition occurring within a proof, whether or not it is an assumption.

The requirement that universally bound variables be uniformly replaced by constants according to rule ∀E is demonstrated in the following truth trees, in which the invalidity of trying to derive $(\forall x)(Fa \supset Gx)$ or $(\forall x)(Fx \supset Ga)$ from $(\forall x)(Fx \supset Gx)$ can be seen:

$$(\forall x)(Fx \supset Gx) \quad {}^*a\ 4 \quad {}^*b\ 6$$
$$\sim(\forall x)(Fa \supset Gx) \quad \checkmark\ 1$$
$$(\exists x)\sim(Fa \supset Gx) \quad \checkmark\ 2$$
$$\sim(Fa \supset Gb) \quad \checkmark\ 3$$
$$Fa$$
$$\sim Gb$$
$$Fa \supset Ga \quad \checkmark\ 5$$

```
              ┌──────────┴──────────┐
            ~Fa                     Ga
             X                    Fb ⊃ Gb   √ 7
                                   ┌──┴──┐
                                 ~Fb     Gb
                                          X
```

INVALID

$$(\forall x)(Fx \supset Gx) \quad {}^*a\ 4 \quad {}^*b\ 6$$
$$\sim(\forall x)(Fx \supset Ga) \quad \checkmark\ 1$$
$$(\exists x)\sim(Fx \supset Ga) \quad \checkmark\ 2$$
$$\sim(Fb \supset Ga) \quad \checkmark\ 3$$
$$Fb$$
$$\sim Ga$$
$$Fa \supset Ga \quad \checkmark\ 5$$

```
                 ┌──────────┴──────────┐
               ~Fa                     Ga
     7 √    Fb ⊃ Gb                     X
            ┌──┴──┐
          ~Fb     Gb
           X
```

INVALID

Universal elimination follows the usual subproof entry and exiting requirements.

The unrestricted uniform substitution of any constant for any universally bound variable by ∀E parallels the unlimited possibilities of uniform instantiations of universal formulas in predicate truth trees.

The ∀E rule can be used anywhere within a proof or subproof. We can instantiate a universally quantified formula by ∀E within a subproof by bringing any of its instantiations directly into a more deeply nested subproof without reiterating the universal. On the other hand, it is deductively invalid to instantiate a universally quantified formula in the opposite direction by bringing an instantiation out of a subproof that contains the universal, exiting into a less deeply nested proof or subproof. We are not permitted to use ∀E in this way because the inference P ⊢ Fa is deductively invalid:

```
1    1. │   P              A
2    2. │  ┌─  (∀x)Fx      A (~IE)
2    3. │  │    Fa          2 ∀E
2    4. │   Fa            _____
```
                                            [VIOLATION!]
                                            [INVALID!]

To Check Your Understanding 8.1

Use the predicate intelim rule ∀E, together with propositional rules, to give natural deduction proofs of the following sequents:

1. (∀x)Fx ⊢ Fd
2. (∀x)(Fx ⊃ Gx), ~Ga ⊢ ~Fa
3. (∀x)(Fx ⊃ Gx), (∀x)(Gx ⊃ Hx) ⊢ Fa ⊃ Ha
4. (∀x)(Fx ∨ Gx), (∀x)(Fx ⊃ Hx), Gb ⊃ Hb ⊢ Hb ∨ Gb
5. (∀x)Fx, (∀x)(Fx ⊃ Gx), ~Gb ⊢ (∀x)Hx
6. (∀x)(Fx ⊃ Gx), (∀x)(~Hx ⊃ ~Gx), Fc ⊢ Ga ∨ Hc

Existential Introduction (∃I)

.
.
.

```
. . . α . . .              . . .
(∃x)(. . . x . . .)        . . . ∃I
```

(Unlimited selective substitution of existentially bound object variables for object constants)

If, in a proof, we have a proposition that says that object a (or b, c, etc.) in particular has property F, then we can validly deduce that something has property F. If Alice is friendly, then something is friendly. There exists in our semantic domain in this case at least one object that has the property of being friendly. Accordingly, we are justified in inferring from the proposition that Fa, the existentially quantified proposition that something has property F, (∃x)Fx.

Existential introduction (∃I) justifies existentially quantifying any predicate-constant wff, selectively replacing any constant with an existentially bound variable.

```
1    1. │  Fa            A
1    2. │   (∃x)Fx       1∃I
```

The example makes Fa an assumption. However, it could also be derived from other propositions within a proof. The existentially bound variable 'x' is chosen without restriction. We could just as easily have derived from Fa an existential formula stating that there exists or is at least one object y such that Fy or w, z, and so on in (∃y)Fy, (∃w)Fw, and (∃z)Fz. Nor are we obligated to replace every occurrence of a constant with the existential quantifier according to the rule. It is logically valid selectively to existentialize a proposition of the form Fa & Ga as (∃x)(Fx & Ga), or (∃x)(Fa & Gx), and then, for example, as (∃x)(∃y) (Fx & Gy) or the like. If it is true that Alice is friendly and it is true that Alice is generous, then it is certainly true that something is such that it is friendly and Alice is generous; it is also true that something is such that Alice is friendly and that the aforementioned something is generous. We can also validly deduce vacuous existential quantifications of the form (∃x)Fa or (∃x)P, in which the quantifier does no work.

Existential introduction is unrestricted.

To verify that these inferences are deductively valid, complete their predicate truth trees before attempting the following proofs.

To Check Your Understanding 8.2

Use the predicate intelim rules ∀E and ∃I, together with propositional rules, to give natural deduction proofs of the following sequents; for extra practice, show that each is valid by predicate truth tree:

1. (∀x)Fx ⊢ (∃x)Fx
2. ~(∃x)Fx ⊢ ~(∀x)Fx
3. (∀x)(Fx ⊃ Gx), Fa ⊢ (∃y)Gy
4. (∀x)(~Fx ∨ Gx), Fb ⊢ (∃z)Gz
5. Fa & Ga ⊢ (∃x)(Fa & Gx) ∨ (∃x)(Fx & Ga)
6. Fa & Ga ⊢ ((∃x)(Fx & Gx) ∨ (∃y)(Fy & Gy)) ∨ (∃x)(∃y)(Fx & Gy)

The rules ∀E and ∃I apply without restriction in predicate proofs. They are similar in this respect to the unrestricted propositional logic rules for conjunction elimination, &E, and disjunction introduction, ∨I. There is a semantic analogy between these two propositional logic rules and the two predicate rules just introduced.

Universal and existential quantifications in predicate logic are similar but ultimately reducible, respectively, to conjunctions and disjunctions in propositional logic.

If we suppose the logic's semantic domain to be finite rather than infinite in extent, however humanly unthinkably large it might be, then we can simply interpret (∀x)Fx as the enormous conjunction Fa & Fb & . . . & Fn, for n finitely many objects, and (∃x)Fx as the enormous disjunction Fa ∨ Fb ∨ . . . ∨ Fn, for n finitely many objects. If we assume that there are infinitely many objects such as numbers and sets, then we cannot achieve a full reduction of predicate logic to propositional logic. The reason is that whenever we try to read (∀x)Fx as the conjunction Fa & Fb & . . . & Fn, we must also say that the conjunction with final conjunct Fn has at last included *all* the objects in the logic's domain. This reintroduces the universal quantifier, which the reduction to a propositional conjunction is supposed to eliminate. This is also the case for efforts to reduce the existential to a propositional disjunction.

Universal Introduction (∀I)

> .
> .
> .
>
> . . . α . . .   . . .
> $(\forall x)(. . . x . . .)$ . . . ∀I
>
> (Restriction: the assumptions on which line n depends must not contain constant α; for uniform substitution of universally quantified variables for object constants)

Universal introduction (∀I) *justifies inferring a universally quantified wff from a predicate-constant wff when the wff does not depend on the truth of any assumption containing the same constant.*

The rule for *universal introduction*, ∀I, deduces a universally quantified proposition from an object constant predication, provided that the constant expression does not rest on any assumptions containing the constant. It is deductively invalid to infer that everything has a property merely from the fact that a particular thing—a, b, or c— has the property. We can validly universalize Fa as $(\forall x)Fx$, according to the ∀I rule for universal introduction, only if proposition Fa does not rest on any assumptions that contain constant 'a'. The ∀I rule, like some intelim rules in propositional logic, requires us to consult the assumption column of a derivation in progress in order to decide whether or not we can proceed. The rule in a simple application looks as follows:

$$(\forall x)(Fx \supset Gx), (\forall x)Fx \vdash (\forall x)Gx$$

1	1.	$(\forall x)(Fx \supset Gx)$	A
2	2.	$(\forall x)Fx$	A
1	3.	$Fa \supset Ga$	1 ∀E
2	4.	Fa	2 ∀E
1, 2	5.	Ga	3, 4 ⊃ E
1, 2	6.	$(\forall x)Gx$	5 ∀I

The sequent is valid. If everything is such that if it has property F, then it has property G, and if everything has property F, then everything must also have property G. The crucial inference is from step 5 to step 6. Step 5 says that object a *in particular* has property G. What then justifies us in inferring that *everything* has property G in step 6? We are permitted to draw the inference because the assumption column and proof spine show that the proposition Ga does not

Universal introduction has an important restriction, which must be observed in order to avoid deductively invalid inferences in predicate natural deduction.

The restriction on universal introduction prohibits universalization of any constant-predicate wff if the truth of the wff depends on the truth of any assumption containing the same constant, as indicated by proof spines and the assumption column.

rest on any assumptions that contain constant 'a'. If Ga were to rest on any assumption containing constant 'a', then we would be invalidly inferring a universal proposition that everything has a property merely on the strength of an assumption that a particular object has the property. Step 5, according to the assumption column, rests on assumptions 1 and 2. Neither assumption 1 nor assumption 2 contains constant 'a'. We are therefore free to universalize proposition Ga and conclude in step 6 that everything has property G. The conclusion is valid because the truth of the generalization, as the assumption column shows, does not depend on assumptions about particular objects but about all objects.

The restriction on ∀I can be appreciated when we see that without it we could make deductively invalid inferences. The simplest example is the invalid inference of (∀x)Fx from Fa. We know that the inference is invalid because it does not follow logically from the fact that Alice is friendly that therefore everything is friendly. Were it not for the restriction that ∀I can only be applied to universalize a proposition that does not rest on any assumptions containing the constant to be replaced by a universally bound variable, we could deduce the following deductively invalid sequent:

1	1.	Fa	A
2	2.	(∀x)Fx	1 ∀I [VIOLATION!] [INVALID!]

Many other more complicated invalid universalizations are also blocked by the restriction on ∀I. The tree demonstrates the invalidity of the inference Fa ⊢ (∀x)Fx:

$$Fa$$
$$\sim(\forall x)Fx \quad \surd\ 1$$
$$(\exists x)\sim Fx \quad \surd\ 2$$
$$\sim Fb \qquad\qquad\qquad \text{INVALID}$$

The uniform substitution of universally quantified variables for constants is required for valid application of ∀I. The open truth trees for the invalid inference of either (∀x)(Fa ⊃ Gx) or (∀x)(Fx ⊃ Ga) from (∀x)(Fx ⊃ Gx) show this clearly in previous examples to illustrate the uniform substitution requirements on rule ∀E. On the other hand, it is deductively valid to deduce the vacuous universal quantifications (∀x)Fa and (∀x)P. The restriction on ∀I does not apply in these situations because constant 'a' is not replaced by a universally quantified bound variable.

What happens if we do not observe the restriction on ∀I? What if we try to universally quantify a proposition that rests on assumptions containing the constant in question? If the restriction is not observed, then deductively invalid

Failure to observe the restriction on universal introduction can result in deductively invalid inferences, as in trying to infer that everything has a property from the assumption that a given particular object has the property.

inferences can occur. The restriction on ∀I prevents these kinds of mistakes. Consider the example below concerning Socrates' mortality. The assumptions in steps 1 and 2 are true. But what if we tried to conclude after step 4 that therefore everything that exists is mortal? That would evidently be a deductively invalid inference, since not everything that exists is capable of dying. The ∀I restriction blocks deductively invalid universalizations when the assumption column shows that the proposition we are trying to universalize rests on an assumption containing the constant we are proposing to replace with a universally bound variable. Were it not for this restriction, we could equally "prove" the false conclusion that everything in the semantic domain is friendly from the true assumption that Alice in particular is friendly.

The quantifier intelim rules enable us to reduce quantified expressions to unquantified predicate-constant expressions. We can work with these using more basic propositional rules, such as A and ⊃E (as well as any of the others: &I, &E, ∨I, ∨E, ⊃I, ~IE, ≡I, ≡E, R, and DN), to derive useful intermediate conclusions. Where appropriate restrictions are satisfied, we can then apply quantifier introduction rules to obtain quantifications of these intermediate conclusions to complete the proof.

Demonstration 29: **Predicate Proofs**

PROBLEM: To prove a deductively valid sequent by predicate natural deduction rules ∀E, ∃I, and ∀I.

SEQUENT: We apply the rules we have developed so far to provide a formal justification for the syllogism about Socrates' mortality. The assumptions are that 'All men are mortal' and 'Socrates is a man', and the conclusion is that therefore 'Socrates is mortal'. If we symbolize 'Socrates' as before by constant 's' and the properties of being a man by 'H' and being mortal by 'M', we can prove the following sequent by predicate natural deduction rules:

$(\forall x)(Hx \supset Mx), Hs \vdash Ms$
('Socrates')

STEP 1: *Set up the proof*
The sequent contains two given assumptions, which we write down along with natural deduction documentation in assumption and justification columns in the usual format as follows:

1	1.	$(\forall x)(Hx \supset Mx)$	A
2	2.	Hs	A

STEP 2: *Eliminate the universal quantification*
The first assumption is universally quantified. If we are to work with the information it contains, we must eliminate the universal quantifier by ∀E. Because ∀E is unrestricted, we can uniformly substitute any object constants for the object variable 'x' bound by the universal quantifier. Since constant 's' already appears in the second assumption, it is strategically useful to instantiate the universal by constant 's' rather than by 'a', 'b', 'c', etc. When we apply ∀E, the proof looks as follows:

1	1.	(∀x)(Hx ⊃ Mx)	A
2	2.	Hs	A
1	3.	Hs ⊃ Ms	1∀E

STEP 3: *Use propositional natural deduction rules to obtain the conclusion*
The propositions in proof lines 2 and 3 are now subject–predicate expressions without quantifiers, to which we can therefore apply propositional natural deduction rules to obtain further conclusions. In this case, the proof continues easily by means of ⊃E used to detach the proposition Ms that Socrates is mortal, at which the proof aims. The completed proof has the form:

1	1.	(∀x)(Hx ⊃ Mx)	A
2	2.	Hs	A
1	3.	Hs ⊃ Ms	1∀E
1, 2	4.	Ms	2, 3 ⊃E

To Check Your Understanding 8.3

Use the predicate intelim rules ∀E, ∃I, and ∀I, together with propositional rules, to give natural deduction proofs of the following sequents; for extra practice, show that each is valid by predicate truth trees:

1. (∀x)(Fx & Gx) ⊢ (∀x)Fx
2. (∀x)(Fx ⊃ Gx), (∀x)Fx ⊢ (∀x)Gx
3. (∀x)(Fx ⊃ Gx), (∀x)~Gx ⊢ (∀x)~Fx ∨ Gb
4. (∀x)(Fx ⊃ Gx), (∀x)(Hx & ~Gx) ⊢ (∀x)Hx
5. (∀x)(Fx ∨ Gx), (∀x)(Fx ⊃ Hx), (∀x)(Gx ⊃ Hx) ⊢ (∀x)Hx
6. (∀x)(Fx ∨ ~Fx), (∀x)(Fx ⊃ Gx), (∀x)(~Fx ⊃ Gx) ⊢ (∀x)Gx

Existential Elimination (∃E)

Existential elimination (∃E) *is a sub-proof rule (the only subproof rule in predicate natural deduction) that justifies inferring a wff that does not contain an arbitrarily chosen constant uniformly substituted for existentially quantified variables in a subproof auxiliary assumption.*

Existential elimination has two restrictions, which must be observed in order to avoid deductively invalid inferences in predicate natural deduction.

The first restriction on existential elimination is that the constant uniformly substituted for an existentially bound variable in the subproof auxiliary assumption made in implementing the rule must be arbitrary in that it cannot have occurred anywhere previously in an active part of the proof.

$$
\begin{array}{ll}
\vdots & \\
(\exists x)(\dots x \dots) & \dots \\
\quad \underline{\dots \alpha \dots} & \text{A } (\exists E) \\
\quad \vdots & \\
\quad \mathbb{P} & \dots \\
\mathbb{P} & \dots \exists E
\end{array}
$$

(Restriction 1: where constant (α) does not appear in any active proof or subproof step prior to its arbitrary introduction by auxiliary assumption in the ∃E subproof; restriction 2: nor in conclusion $\mathbb{P}$; for selective substitutions of arbitrary object constants to replace existentially bound object variables)

An existential wff is similar to a disjunction. When we know that the disjunction P ∨ Q is true, we know that either P or Q is (or possibly both are) true, but we do not know which is true. We apply disjunction elimination ∨E to a disjunction by auxiliary assuming each disjunct in two subproofs to check both possibilities, to determine if we can reach the same conclusion from the auxiliary assumption of either disjunct. Similarly, when we know that the existential proposition (∃x)Fx is true, we know that something somewhere in the logic's domain has property F, but we do not know which particular object has the property.

We proceed with ∃E in a similar way to that for ∨E. We set up an ∃E subproof with the auxiliary assumption that a certain object has the property. We choose an arbitrary constant that has not occurred previously in any preceding step of the proof. Since we know that something has property F, we refer to the thing, whatever it is, as 'a', provided that we do not already know anything about a. There are two restrictions to observe in applying ∃E: (i) The constant substituted for existentially bound variables in the existential proposition to be eliminated must be arbitrary in the sense that the constant occurs nowhere previously in the proof or in an active subproof that has not yet been exited and (ii) the conclusion to be repeated in the final step of ∃E and withdrawn in exiting from the ∃E subproof into the next less deeply nested proof or subproof must not contain the arbitrarily chosen constant of the ∃E subproof auxiliary assumption.

The second restriction on existential elimination is that the conclusion derived in exiting from the subproof must not contain the arbitrarily chosen constant introduced in the subproof auxiliary assumption.

We ensure that the constant chosen for the ∃E auxiliary assumption is arbitrary by requiring that it does not already occur in any still *active part of the proof.* An active part of a proof is any part in which the given or auxiliary assumptions are still in force, as indicated by the proof and subproof spines, where a subproof has not yet been exited. The following are the basic forms of active and inactive parts of proofs, in which a previous occurrence of constant '*α*' affects whether or not the substitution of constant '*α*' for an existentially bound variable is permitted in an ∃E subproof:

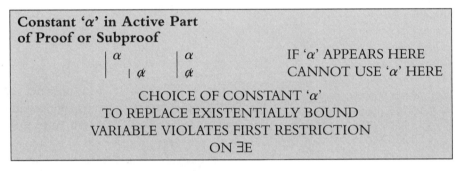

Constant '*α*' in Active Part of Proof or Subproof

| *α* | *α* | IF '*α*' APPEARS HERE
| *α̸* | *α̸* | CANNOT USE '*α*' HERE

CHOICE OF CONSTANT '*α*'
TO REPLACE EXISTENTIALLY BOUND
VARIABLE VIOLATES FIRST RESTRICTION
ON ∃E

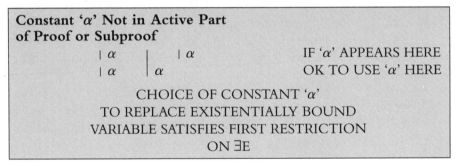

Constant '*α*' Not in Active Part of Proof or Subproof

| *α* | *α* | IF '*α*' APPEARS HERE
| *α* | *α* | OK TO USE '*α*' HERE

CHOICE OF CONSTANT '*α*'
TO REPLACE EXISTENTIALLY BOUND
VARIABLE SATISFIES FIRST RESTRICTION
ON ∃E

The first restriction on existential elimination is similar to the restriction on the predicate truth tree decomposition rule for existentials.

The first restriction on ∃E is similar to the parallel requirement for arbitrarily chosen constants in the truth tree decomposition rule for existentials. We use the instantiated wff in the proof until we eventually reach a useful conclusion in the proof that does not contain the arbitrarily chosen constant. This satisfies the second restriction on ∃E. Then we repeat the conclusion in the next step of the proof, exiting ∃E subproof, and bringing the conclusion into the main proof or next less deeply nested subproof. To document use of the rule in a proof, the justification column requires reference to the step number of the existentially quantified wff being eliminated and then the range of intermediate ∃E subproof steps. The assumption number of the auxiliary assumption is discharged from the assumption column, which retains the line numbers of all other assumptions used in reaching the conclusion. As an illustration, suppose we are given that everything is such that if it is F, then it is G, and that there is something that is F. It should then follow that something is G.

$$(\forall x)(Fx \supset Gx), (\exists x)Fx \vdash (\exists x)Gx$$

1	1.	$(\forall x)(Fx \supset Gx)$	A
2	2.	$(\exists x)Fx$	A
3	3.	Fa	A ($\exists$E)
1	4.	Fa $\supset$ Ga	1$\forall$E
1, 3	5.	Ga	3, 4 $\supset$E
1, 3	6.	$(\exists x)Gx$	5 $\exists$I
1, 2	7.	$(\exists x)Gx$	2, 3–6 $\exists$E

The justification column refers to three steps in applying rule $\exists$E: (i) step 2 containing the existentially quantified wff to be eliminated; (ii) step 3 in which the auxiliary assumption is made for purposes of existential elimination, in which an arbitrarily chosen constant that appears nowhere previously in a still active part of the proof is substituted for the existentially bound variable in the existentially quantified wff to be eliminated; and (iii) the wff step 6 that follows as a conclusion from the auxiliary assumption, in which the arbitrarily chosen constant of the subproof auxiliary assumption does not occur. As in proofs requiring auxiliary assumptions in propositional logic, we refer to these steps in order to keep track of the assumptions used in each step of the derivation to determine the assumptions on which they depend. Then we discharge from the assumption column any auxiliary assumptions made in applying the rule. We look in this case at steps 2, 3, and 6, for which we notice that step 2 depends on assumption 2, step 3 rests on $\exists$E auxiliary assumption 3, and step 6 depends on assumptions 1 and 3. Auxiliary assumption 3 is discharged, but assumptions 1 and 2 are retained so that step 7 depends, as it should, only on given assumptions 1 and 2.

What if the two restrictions on the rule for existential elimination were not observed? Then, as in violations of the restriction on universal introduction, $\forall$I, it is possible to make deductively invalid inferences. The restrictions are necessary to preserve deductive validity in predicate logic. To show that this is true, we consider what happens if the restrictions are violated. Suppose, with respect to the first $\exists$E restriction, that we were not required to choose an arbitrary constant for purposes of existential elimination, but that we could repeat one that appears previously in an active part of the proof. Here is an example:

1	1.	$(\exists x)(Fx \supset Gx)$	A	
2	2.	$(\exists x)Fx$	A	
3	3.	Fa $\supset$ Ga	A ($\exists$E)	
4	4.	Fa	A ($\exists$E)	[VIOLATION!]
3, 4	5.	Ga	3, 4 $\supset$E	
3, 4	6.	$(\exists x)Gx$	5 $\exists$I	
2, 3	7.	$(\exists x)Gx$	2, 3–6 $\exists$E	[INVALID!]
1, 2	8.	$(\exists x)Gx$	1, 2–7 $\exists$E	[INVALID!]

The sequent is deductively invalid because it does not follow merely from the fact that something is such that, if it has property F, then it has property G, and from the fact that something has property F, that therefore something has property G. Whatever has property F, and whatever is such that, if it has property F, then it has property G could be different things altogether. For example, suppose that someone (George) is such that, conditionally, if he were president, then he would be the first Buddhist American president, and suppose that someone (Ronald) is or has the property of being president. Does it follow that there is or exists someone who is the first Buddhist American president? Even if the assumptions are true, they are not powerful enough to guarantee the truth of the conclusion. To ensure that the conclusion cannot be invalidly derived, we require that any introduction of a constant made in an ∃E auxiliary assumption must be arbitrary in the sense that it does not occur in any still active part of the proof. The violation of this restriction occurs at step 4, which is where the trouble begins. The choice of constant 'a' in step 4 is not arbitrary because constant 'a' also occurred previously in step 3. We could have observed the restriction by using a different constant (e.g., 'b') in an alternative step 4′, from which the conclusion Ga (or Gb, etc.) cannot validly be derived. The invalid inference is thereby blocked by the first restriction on ∃E.

Failure to observe the first restriction on existential elimination can result in deductively invalid inferences, as in trying to infer that the same object has a property from the assumption that some or at least one object has a property and that some or at least one object has a logically related property.

What about the second restriction? Suppose we were not required to limit the formal application of ∃E to situations in which the proposition to be repeated in the final step of ∃E, the step to which the justification by means of ∃E is to apply, does not contain the constant introduced in the auxiliary assumption for purposes of ∃E. What if we could complete an ∃E subproof by withdrawing a proposition containing the constant from the ∃E subproof? Here is a simple case:

1	1.	(∃x)Fx	A	
2	2.	Fa	A (∃E)	
2	3.	Fa	2 R	
1	4.	Fa	1, 2–3 ∃E	[VIOLATION!] [INVALID!]

Failure to observe the second restriction on existential elimination can result in deductively invalid inferences, as in trying to infer that a particular individually named object has a property from the assumption that some or at least one object has the property.

From the fact that something has property F, it does not follow that object a in particular has property F. We do not even know what particular object object a is since we are required to choose constant 'a' arbitrarily as a dummy constant or placeholder to represent whatever object has property F. The constant cannot be the name of an object we already know something about or about which we already have some information in the proof. We are not entitled from the existential assumption to infer anything definite about object a in particular, as in the illicit conclusion in step 3, that object a in particular has property F. To do so would invalidly deduce more specific information in the conclusion than the nonspecific assumption contains. The second restriction on the use of existential elimination ∃E prevents us from making this kind of deductively invalid inference.

To Check Your Understanding 8.4 ———————————————■

Use the predicate intelim rules ∀E, ∃I, ∀I, and ∃E, together with propositional rules, to give natural deduction proofs of the following sequents:

1. ~(∀x)~Fx ⊢ (∃x)Fx
2. (∃x)(Fx & Gx) ⊢ (∃x)Fx
3. (∀x)(Fx ⊃ Gx), (∃x)Fx ⊢ (∃x)Gx
4. (∃x)(Fx & Gx) ⊢ (∃x)Fx & (∃x)Gx
5. (∃x)~(∀y)(Fxy ⊃ Fyx) ⊢ (∃x)(∃y)(Fxy & ~Fyx)
6. (∀x)~(Fx & Gx), (∃x)(Fx & Hx) ⊢ (∃x)(Hx & Fx)

■

The following is a convenient summary of the four new natural deduction rules for predicate logic, including a brief statement of how each of the rules works and of the restrictions that apply to ∀I and ∃E. We add the following four predicate intelim rules to the 12 rules already available for natural deduction proofs in propositional logic.

NATURAL DEDUCTION RULES FOR PREDICATE LOGIC

1. *Universal introduction* — ∀I

.
.
.

n.   . . . α . . .   . . .
      (∀x)(. . . x . . .)   . . . ∀I

(Restriction: the assumptions on which line n depends must not contain constant 'α'; for uniform substitution of universally quantified variables for object constants)

We can validly infer a universally quantified wff in which all occurrences of a constant in a predicate-constant wff are uniformly replaced by any universal quantifier bound variable, provided that the predicate-constant wff does not rest on any assumptions containing the constant.
(One restriction)

2. *Universal elimination* — ∀E

    .

    .

    .

$(\forall x)(\ldots x \ldots)$ . . .

$\ldots \alpha \ldots$ . . . ∀E

(Unlimited uniform instantiations)

We can validly infer a predicate-constant wff in which all universal quantifier bound variables in a universally quantified wff are uniformly replaced by any constant.
(No restrictions)

3. *Existential introduction* — ∃I

    .

    .

    .

$\ldots \alpha \ldots$ . . .

$(\exists x)(\ldots x \ldots)$ . . . ∃I

(Unlimited selective substitution of existentially
bound object variables for object constants)

We can validly infer an existentially quantified wff in which the occurrences of a constant in a predicate-constant wff are selectively replaced by any existentially bound variable.
(No restrictions)

4. *Existential elimination* — ∃E

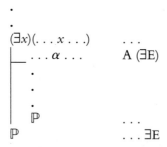

(Restriction 1: where constant 'α' does not appear in any active proof or subproof step prior to its arbitrary introduction by auxiliary assumption in the ∃E subproof; restriction 2: nor in conclusion $\mathbb{P}$; for selective substitutions of arbitrary object constants to replace existentially bound object variables)

We can validly infer any conclusion wff by making as an auxiliary assumption a predicate-constant wff in which the existentially bound variable is

uniformly replaced by an arbitrarily chosen constant that does not occur previously in any active part of the proof, provided that the conclusion wff does not itself contain the constant. When the rule is applied, the auxiliary assumption number is discharged from the assumption column, and the conclusion wff is brought out of the existential elimination subproof into the next less deeply nested proof or subproof.
(Subproof rule; two restrictions)

Strategy Hints

The best advice in working out predicate natural deduction proofs, in addition to the suggestions made in connection with derivations for propositional logic, is to read the conclusion of a valid sequent or tautology to determine whether its main operator is a quantifier or propositional connective. If the main operator is a propositional connective, then we begin as we would in propositional logic. We apply propositional intelim rules, and follow the strategies we would consider if we were doing a proof in that system, until it becomes necessary to apply quantifier intelim rules. If, on the other hand, the main operator of the conclusion is a quantifier, then we try to think of how the wff would appear without the quantifier, with constants in place of universally or existentially bound variables. We try to derive the unquantified version of the wff and then, provided we satisfy whatever restrictions may be relevant, we apply the appropriate quantifier introduction rules ∀I or ∃I to complete the proof. This is the *fundamental heuristic* for proof discovery in predicate logic.

Predicate natural deduction strategy is based on a fundamental heuristic.

FUNDAMENTAL HEURISTIC FOR PREDICATE NATURAL DEDUCTION PROOFS

1. Determine the main operator of the conclusion in a predicate natural deduction proof of a valid sequent or tautology.
2. If the main operator is a propositional connective, then begin by implementing an overall strategy in which you try to derive the conclusion as you would in the corresponding type of propositional natural deduction proof, using quantifier introduction and elimination rules where necessary.
3. If the main operator is a quantifier or quantifiers, consider how the conclusion would appear without its quantifiers, with constants in place of

quantifier bound variables, as an expression in which a propositional connective is the main operator, and try to deduce the resulting predicate-constant expression with the proof before applying the appropriate quantifier introduction rules to obtain the final conclusion.

The fundamental heuristic for predicate natural deduction is to determine whether the main operator of the conclusion in a proof is a propositional connective or quantifier.

Here is an example of the strategy to be followed in proving a valid predicate sequent where the main operator of the conclusion is a propositional connective rather than a quantifier. Suppose we are asked to prove the elementary tautology, $\vdash (\forall x)Fx \supset (\exists x)Fx$. The main operator is the propositional connective '$\supset$', so we set about solving the proof by beginning with a conditional introduction $\supset$I strategy. We auxiliary assume the entire antecedent of the conditional, quantifier and all, and initiate a $\supset$I subproof in which we try to derive the consequent. The proof is propositional in its overall structure, but it involves the use of predicate intelim rules. It has the following form:

1	1.	$(\forall x)Fx$	A ($\supset$I)
1	2.	Fa	1 $\forall$E
1	3.	$(\exists x)Fx$	2 $\exists$I
	4.	$(\forall x)Fx \supset (\exists x)Fx$	1–3 $\supset$I

If the main operator in the conclusion of a predicate natural deduction proof is a propositional connective, we proceed with a propositional proof strategy.

If the main operator is a quantifier, we consider the conclusion as it would appear without the quantifier but with constants substituted for quantifier bound variables and aim at the wff in this form as a penultimate conclusion, applying the appropriate quantifier introduction rule when the penultimate conclusion has been deduced.

The following is a more interesting case, proving the tautology positively tested by predicate truth trees in Chapter 7: $\vdash ((\forall x)(Gx \supset Hx) \ \& \ (\exists x)(Fx \ \& \ Gx)) \supset (\exists x)(Fx \ \& \ Hx)$. The main operator is also a propositional connective—the second conditional, '$\supset$'. As before, we proceed by auxiliary assuming the antecedent in a conditional introduction $\supset$I subproof and then derive the consequent. After assuming the antecedent, we notice that the consequent we must now deduce within the $\supset$I subproof has the existential quantifier as its main operator. We imagine the conclusion bereft of its quantifier to reveal the underly-

1	1.	$(\forall x)(Gx \supset Hx) \ \& \ (\exists x)(Fx \ \& \ Gx)$	A ($\supset$I)
1	2.	$(\forall x)(Gx \supset Hx)$	1 &E
1	3.	$(\exists x)(Fx \ \& \ Gx)$	1 &E
4	4.	$Fa \ \& \ Ga$	A ($\exists$E)
1	5.	$Ga \supset Ha$	2 $\forall$E
4	6.	Ga	4 &E
1, 4	7.	Ha	5, 6 $\supset$E
4	8.	Fa	4 &E
1, 4	9.	$Fa \ \& \ Ha$	7, 8 &I
1, 4	10.	$(\exists x)(Fx \ \& \ Hx)$	9 $\exists$I
1	11.	$(\exists x)(Fx \ \& \ Hx)$	3, 4–10 $\exists$E
	12.	$((\forall x)(Gx \supset Hx) \ \& \ (\exists x)(Fx \ \& \ Gx)) \supset$ $(\exists x)(Fx \ \& \ Hx)$	1–11 $\supset$I

ing propositional form, Fa & Ha. We work toward this preliminary conclusion in the subproof before applying ∃I to deduce the existential generalization by which we exit from the ∃E subproof and then use ⊃I to conclude with the conditional tautology.

Of the two conjuncts contained in the auxiliary ⊃I assumption, one is universally quantified and the other existentially quantified. To avoid conflicts with the restriction on existential elimination, we begin with an ∃E subproof. This gives us maximum flexibility in choosing arbitrary constants to replace the existentially bound variables for purposes of existential elimination. The proof of Fa & Ha, the conclusion stripped of its existential quantifier, appears in step 9, prior to existentialization in step 10. The unquantified formula cannot be brought out of the ∃E subproof. The second restriction on ∃E is that we must deduce a wff that does not contain the arbitrary constant of the subproof's auxiliary assumption. We satisfy the second restriction on ∃E, in this case, by existentially quantifying the wff before exiting the subproof in step 11, deducing the consequent of the conditional tautology needed for the final conclusion in step 12.

We gain skill in discovering predicate natural deduction proofs by studying and solving many different kinds of examples.

Here is a slightly more complicated example. The proof requires an application of ~IE to prove a valid sequent. The main operator of the conclusion is negation, whose scope extends over the entire universally quantified wff in the sequent (∃x)(Fx & Gx) ⊢ ~(∀x)(Fx ⊃ ~Gx):

1	1.	(∃x)(Fx & Gx)	A
2	2.	Fa & Ga	A (∃E)
3	3.	(∀x)(Fx ⊃ ~Gx)	A (~IE)
3	4.	Fa ⊃ ~Ga	3 ∀E
2	5.	Fa	2 &E
2	6.	Ga	2 &E
2, 3	7.	~Ga	5, 6 ⊃E
2	8.	~(∀x)(Fx ⊃ ~Gx)	3–7 ~IE
1	9.	~(∀x)(Fx ⊃ ~Gx)	1, 2–8 ∃E

Again, the order of subproofs is important. If we had reversed the order of proof steps 2 and 3, nesting the ∃E subproof within the ~IE subproof, rather than the other way around, then the restrictions on the ∃E subproof could not have been satisfied.

In contrast, proofs of conclusions that have quantifiers as main operators require a predicate strategy in which propositional intelim rules play a role only after the quantifiers are eliminated. We begin by imagining the conclusion as it would appear without quantifiers but with constants uniformly replacing bound variables. We work toward this conclusion by means of propositional intelim rules, and then, where appropriate, we apply quantifier introduction rules. For

Truth trees are often useful indicators of the constants that might be substituted for quantifier bound variables in complex predicate natural deduction proofs.

example, consider a proof of the argument sequent shown to be deductively valid by predicate truth trees in Chapter 7: (∃x)(Fx & Gx), (∃x)(Fx & (∀y)(Gy ⊃ ~Hxy)) ⊢ (∃x)(Fx & ~(∀y)(Fy ⊃ Hyx)). The conclusion, stripped of its main operator, the existential quantifier, looks as follows: Fb & ~(∀y)(Fy ⊃ Hyb). This is a conjunction, which we can try to derive by proving each of its conjuncts. The first conjunct is Fa; the second is a negative universal formula, ~(∀y)(Fy ⊃ Hya). For this sequent, we may need to resort to the propositional intelim rule, ~IE. We auxiliary assume (∀y)(Fy ⊃ Hya), as the negation of the wff we hope to prove, and work toward a contradiction with this and whatever additional information is provided in the proof. To decide what constants ('a', 'b', 'c', etc.) may need to be substituted for particular bound variables, we consult the truth tree by which the sequent is judged valid. Truth trees often provide a valuable source of hints about how to proceed in predicate natural deduction proofs, especially in solving proofs involving mixed multiple quantifications. An advance plan for the proof, in which we think through as many steps as possible before writing down any propositions, helps to avoid mistakes and dead-ends.

1	1.	(∃x)(Fx & Gx)	A
2	2.	(∃x)(Fx & (∀y)(Gy ⊃ ~Hxy))	A
3	3.	Fa & Ga	A (∃E)
4	4.	Fb & (∀y)(Gy ⊃ ~Hby)	A (∃E)
4	5.	Fb	4 &E
4	6.	(∀y)(Gy ⊃ ~Hby)	4 &E
4	7.	Ga ⊃ ~Hba	6 ∀E
3	8.	Ga	3 &E
3, 4	9.	~Hba	7, 8 ⊃E
10	10.	(∀y)(Fy ⊃ Hya)	A (~IE)
10	11.	Fb ⊃ Hba	10 ∀E
4, 10	12.	Hba	5, 11 ⊃E
3, 4	13.	~Hba	9 R
3, 4	14.	~(∀y)(Fy ⊃ Hya)	10–13 ~IE
3	15.	Fa	3 &E
3, 4	16.	Fa & ~(∀y)(Fy ⊃ Hya)	14, 15 &I
3, 4	17.	(∃x)(Fx & ~(∀y)(Fy ⊃ Hyx))	16 ∃I
2, 3	18.	(∃x)(Fx & ~(∀y)(Fy ⊃ Hyx))	2, 4–17 ∃E
1, 2	19.	(∃x)(Fx & ~(∀y)(Fy ⊃ Hyx))	1, 3–18 ∃E

The first restriction on existential elimination must be observed especially where two or more wffs in a proof are existentially quantified, requiring different constants in their respective subproof auxiliary assumptions.

The proof begins with two existentially quantified given assumptions. In order to make use of these propositions, we set up two ∃E subproofs in which we auxiliary assume counterpart formulas containing arbitrarily chosen constants to replace the existentially bound variables. Since there are two such propositions, we cannot choose the same constants for the auxiliary assumptions of each ∃E subproof but must substitute different ones and work within the subproof restrictions toward the mixed multiple existentially quantified conclusion. The proof is accomplished in a few steps, observing the restrictions on ∃E.

To Check Your Understanding 8.5 ─────────────────────────────────── ∎

Use the predicate intelim rules ∀E, ∃I, ∀I, and ∃E, together with propositional rules, to give natural deduction proofs of the following sequents:

1. (∀x)~Fx ⊢ ~(∃x)Fx
2. ~(∃x)Fx ⊢ (∀x)~Fx
3. (∃x)~Fx ⊢ ~(∀x)Fx
4. ~(∀x)Fx ⊢ (∃x)~Fx
5. (∀x)(P ⊃ Fx) ⊢ P ⊃ (∀x)Fx
6. ~P ⊃ (∀x)Fx ⊢ (∀x)(~P ⊃ Fx)
7. (∀x)(Fx ⊃ Gx) ⊢ (∃x)~Gx ⊃ (∃x)~Fx
8. (∀x)(Fx ⊃ Gx) ⊢ (∀x)~Gx ⊃ (∀x)~Fx
9. (∃x)(Fx & (∀y)(Gy ⊃ Hxy)), (∀x)(Fx ⊃ (∀y)(By ⊃ ~Hxy)) ⊢ (∀x)(Gx ⊃ ~Bx)

∎

Proving Valid Sequents in Predicate Logic

Deductively valid sequents can be proven in predicate natural deduction.

The following proofs of deductively valid sequents further illustrate predicate natural deduction methods. Check to make sure that each step is justified by the inference rules and that the restrictions that apply to rules ∀I and ∃E are observed.

1. (∀x)(Gx ⊃ Hx), (∃x)(Fx & Gx) ⊢ (∃x)(Fx & Hx)

1	1.	(∀x)(Gx ⊃ Hx)	A
2	2.	(∃x)(Fx & Gx)	A
3	3.	Fa & Ga	A (∃E)
1	4.	Ga ⊃ Ha	1 ∀E
3	5.	Ga	3 &E
1, 3	6.	Ha	4, 5 ⊃E
3	7.	Fa	3 &E
1, 3	8.	Fa & Ha	6, 7 &I
1, 3	9.	(∃x)(Fx & Hx)	8 ∃I
1, 2	10.	(∃x)(Fx & Hx)	2, 3–9 ∃E

This is a relatively straightforward proof. Importantly, the auxiliary assumption that inaugurates the ∃E subproof in step 3 is undertaken prior to application of ∀E in step 4, even though the existential proposition in the second assumption at step 2 comes after the universal assumption in step 1. This ensures that the choice of constant 'a' as a replacement for the existentially bound variable in the proposition is arbitrary and poses no conflict with constants that might otherwise already be instantiated. The final application of ∃E in step 10 comes only after a wff is deduced that does not contain the arbitrarily chosen constant a to replace the existentially bound variable in the auxiliary assumption that begins the ∃E subproof, in observance of the second restriction on ∃E.

2. (∀x)Fx ∨ (∀x)Gx ⊢ (∀x)(Fx ∨ Gx)

1	1.	(∀x)Fx ∨ (∀x)Gx	A
2	2.	(∀x)Fx	A (∨E)
2	3.	Fa	2 ∀E
2	4.	Fa ∨ Ga	3 ∨I
2	5.	(∀x)(Fx ∨ Gx)	4 ∀I
6	6.	(∀x)Gx	A (∨E)
6	7.	Ga	6 ∀E
6	8.	Fa ∨ Ga	7 ∨I
6	9.	(∀x)(Fx ∨ Gx)	8 ∀I
1	10.	(∀x)(Fx ∨ Gx)	1, 2–5, 6–9 ∨E

Some valid sequents involve the distribution of quantifiers over the scopes of propositional connectives.

Here is an example of a problem in which the main operator of a given assumption is also a main propositional connective, the disjunction in step 1. The strategy of the proof is accordingly ∨E, in which quantifier rules are invoked to work with the auxiliary assumptions of the universally quantified disjuncts in arriving at the universally quantified conclusion in step 10. The rule ∀I is correctly applied at steps 5 and 9 in obtaining exactly matching ∨E sub-

3. (∀x)(Fx ⊃ Gx) ⊢ ~(∃x)(Fx & ~Gx)

1	1.	(∀x)(Fx ⊃ Gx)	A
2	2.	(∃x)(Fx & ~Gx)	A (~IE)
3	3.	Fa & ~Ga	A (∃E)
4	4.	(∃x)(Fx & ~Gx)	A (~IE)
1	5.	Fa ⊃ Ga	1 ∀E
3	6.	Fa	3 &E
1, 3	7.	Ga	5,6 ⊃I
3	8.	~Ga	3 &E
3	9.	~(∃x)(Fx & ~Gx)	4–8 ~IE
2	10.	~(∃x)(Fx & ~Gx)	2, 3–9 ∃E
1	11.	~(∃x)(Fx & ~Gx)	2–10 ~IE

proof conclusions. The assumption column and proof spines reveal that the wffs to be universalized in both derivations do not rest on any assumptions containing constant 'a'. Rather, they depend, in the first case, on the universally quantified auxiliary assumption 2 and, in the second case, on the universally quantified auxiliary assumption 6.

Some valid sequents involve quantifier dualities with internal complications resulting from logically equivalent propositional logical structures.

The conclusion is negated, which suggests the underlying main propositional proof strategy of ~IE. Auxiliary assuming the negation of the conclusion introduces an existentially quantified wff into the subproof beginning at step 2. This in turn requires an ∃E subproof beginning at step 3. The proof is facilitated by nesting another subproof for ~IE within the ∃E subproof at step 4. The auxiliary assumption for this subproof is the same wff as in step 2. The nesting of subproofs makes it possible to take advantage of a contradiction forthcoming from available wffs within the ∃E subproof in such a way so as to satisfy the second restriction on ∃E. We first deduce a wff that does not contain the arbitrarily chosen constant of the ∃E subproof auxiliary assumption and then bring it out of the ∃E subproof, where it is used in a final application of ~IE.

4. ~(∃x)(Fx & ~Gx) ⊢ (∀x)(Fx ⊃ Gx)

1	1.	~(∃x)(Fx & ~Gx)	A
2	2.	Fa	A (⊃I)
4	3.	~Ga	A (~IE)
3, 4	4.	Fa & ~Ga	2, 3 &I
3, 4	5.	(∃x)(Fx & ~Gx)	4 ∃I
1	6.	~(∃x)(Fx & ~Gx)	1 R
1, 3	7.	Ga	3–6 ~IE
1	8.	Fa ⊃ Ga	2–7 ⊃I
1	9.	(∀x)(Fx ⊃ Gx)	8 ∀I

The proof has a negated existentially quantified given assumption. There is no immediate way to make use of the information that this wff contains within the scope of the negation. The negation stands guard over the content of the wff. As in similar problems in propositional proofs, the best strategy is to work toward the derivation of something that contradicts the wff in step 1. This is done in steps 2–5. The choice of the ⊃I subproof auxiliary assumption in step 2 is guided by the consideration that the conclusion of the proof has a quantifier as its main operator. According to the fundamental heuristic for predicate proofs, we try to imagine the conclusion as it would appear without the quantifier. This is the unquantified conditional predicate formula, Fa ⊃ Ga. Since the expression has a conditional as its main connective, we move toward its proof by propositional rules. We auxiliary assume the antecedent of the conditional, Fa, in step 2 and then the negation of its consequent, ~Ga, in a ~IE subproof beginning at step 3. Then we derive a contradiction with the negative

Negated quantifiers as predicate main operators in assumptions or conclusions of a sequent to be proved usually signal the need for a negation intelim strategy.

existential in assumption 1 in step 1. The application of ∀I in step 9 observes the restriction of allowing a predicate formula to be universalized only if it does not depend on any assumption containing the constant to be uniformly replaced by a universally bound variable. The assumption column and proof spine show that the conclusion rests only on assumption 1, which does not contain constant 'a'.

5. (∀x)(Fx ⊃ P) ⊢ (∃x)Fx ⊃ P

1	1.	(∀x)(Fx ⊃ P)	A
2	2.	(∃x)Fx	A (⊃I)
3	3.	Fa	A (∃E)
1	4.	Fa ⊃ P	1 ∀E
1, 3	5.	P	3–4 ⊃I
1, 2	6.	P	2, 3–5 ∃E
1	7.	(∃x)Fx ⊃ P	2, 6 ⊃I

The proof is guided by the fact that the conclusion has a propositional connective as its main operator. The proof requires a ⊃I subproof, the antecedent of the conditional for which is auxiliary assumed in step 2. This in turn is an existentially quantified wff that requires another nested ∃E subproof for purposes of eliminating the existential. The consequent of the conditional is a propositional symbol P. Since this does not contain the constant of the ∃E auxiliary assumption, there is no obstacle to repeating the conclusion as it first appears in step 5 again in step 6, exiting the ∃E subproof by implementing the ∃E rule. The final step completes the proof by applying the ⊃I propositional intelim rule, linking together the auxiliary assumed antecedent and the derived consequent of the conditional.

Predicate natural deduction proofs can also involve propositional symbols within the scope of a quantifier or propositional connective.

6. (∃x)Fx ⊃ P ⊢ (∀x)(Fx ⊃ P)

1	1.	(∃x)Fx ⊃ P	A
2	2.	Fa	A (⊃I)
2	3.	(∃x)Fx	2 ∃I
1, 2	4.	P	1, 3 ⊃E
1	5.	Fa ⊃ P	2, 4 ⊃I
1	6.	(∀x)(Fx ⊃ P)	5 ∀I

This sequent proves the converse of the previous problem. Since the conclusion of the proof has a universal quantifier as its main operator, it is appropriate to imagine how the wff would appear without its quantifier but with constants in place of the universally bound variable. This is the formula Fa ⊃ P, toward which the proof first aims. The conditional is derived by means of a ⊃I subproof, beginning with the auxiliary assumption of the antecedent in step 2 and working to deduce the consequent in step 4. The conditional is deduced in step 5 from the auxiliary assumed antecedent Fa and consequent P detached from the given assumption and existentially quantified antecedent (∃x)Fx in step 4. It rests only on assumption 1, as the assumption column and subproof spine show, which does not contain constant 'a'. The restriction on ∀I is thereby satisfied so that there is no obstacle to universalizing the conditional in concluding step 6.

7. (∃x)Fx ⊢ ~(∀x)~Fx

1	1.	(∃x)Fx	A
2	2.	Fa	A (∃E)
3	3.	(∀x)~Fx	A (~IE)
3	4.	~Fa	3 ∀E
2	5.	Fa	2 R
2	6.	~(∀x)~Fx	3–5 ~IE
1	7.	~(∀x)~Fx	1, 2–6 ∃E

Here, the conclusion has negation as its main operator. The proof accordingly follows a propositional strategy. The given assumption is an existentially quantified expression, and an ∃E subproof is accordingly introduced, with an auxiliary assumption in which the existentially bound variable in the wff is replaced by an arbitrarily chosen constant. Another auxiliary assumption begins a ~IE subproof, and a contradiction is derived in support of the final conclusion. The wff is first derived within an ∃E subproof and then brought out into the main proof, exiting from the ∃E subproof, by executing ∃E in step 7. The second ∃E restriction is satisfied because the proposition in step 6 does not contain the arbitrarily chosen constant in the ∃E subproof auxiliary assumption.

When using universal introduction or existential elimination, one should always double check to make sure the restrictions on these rules have been satisfied.

8. ~(∀x)~Fx ⊢ (∃x)Fx

1	1.	~(∀x)~Fx	A
2	2.	~(∃x)Fx	A (~IE)
3	3.	Fa	A (~IE)
3	4.	(∃x)Fx	3 ∃I
2	5.	~(∃x)Fx	2 R
2	6.	~Fa	3, 5 ~IE
2	7.	(∀x)~Fx	6 ∀I
1, 2	8.	~(∀x)~Fx	1 R
1	9.	(∃x)Fx	2–8 ~IE

The proof involves a double-nested ~IE subproof. The approach is recommended by the fact that the assumption is a negated universal quantification. There is no other more direct way to unlock the information contained within it, so we are more or less obligated to proceed by indirect proof to obtain a contradiction. The choice of auxiliary assumptions is indicated by the possibility of obtaining a contradiction with the given assumption and the negation of the proof's conclusion. The sequent demonstrates one of the quantifier duality relations.

9. $\sim(\exists x)\sim Jx \vdash (\forall x)(Jx \vee Kx)$

1	1.	$\sim(\exists x)\sim Jx$	A
2	2.	$\sim Ja$	A ($\sim$IE)
2	3.	$(\exists x)\sim Jx$	2 $\exists$I
1	4.	$\sim(\exists x)\sim Jx$	1 R
1	5.	Ja	2–4 $\sim$IE
1	6.	$Ja \vee Ka$	5 $\vee$I
1	7.	$(\forall x)(Jx \vee Kx)$	6 $\forall$I

In this proof, we satisfy the restriction on $\forall$I in step 7, because the unquantified wff we must universalize does not depend on any assumptions containing constant 'a'. The assumption column and proof spine show us that it rests only on assumption 1, which on inspection does not contain the constant.

10. $(\forall x)(\forall y)(Nxy \supset \sim Nyx) \vdash (\forall x)\sim Nxx$

1	1.	$(\forall x)(\forall y)(Nxy \supset \sim Nyx)$	A
2	2.	Naa	A ($\sim$IE)
1	3.	$(\forall y)(Nay \supset \sim Nya)$	1 $\forall$E
1	4.	$Naa \supset \sim Naa$	3 $\forall$E
1, 2	5.	$\sim Naa$	2, 4 $\supset$E
1	6.	$\sim Naa$	2–5 $\sim$IE
1	7.	$(\forall x)\sim Nxx$	6 $\forall$I

The assumption column is the best guide as to whether the truth of a conclusion within a proof depends on an assumption containing a given constant, as in satisfying the restriction on universal introduction.

Here, we are free to universalize the wff in step 6 because the restriction on $\forall$I is satisfied. The assumption column and proof spine show that the wff does not rest on any assumptions containing the constant 'a', to be replaced by the universally bound variable. The choice of constant 'a' to replace both universally bound variables 'x' and 'y' in steps 3 and 4 is dictated by the need to derive the conclusion, in which the same variable appears in both argument places of the relational predicate. We can also see the need for this substitution by doing the predicate truth tree for the problem and observing the constants required to replace universally bound variables in order to obtain closure. The tree has the following structure:

$$(\forall x)(\forall y)(Nxy \supset \sim Nyx) \quad *a \; 3$$
$$\sim(\forall x)\sim Nxx \quad \surd \; 1$$
$$(\exists x)Nxx \quad \surd \; 2$$
$$Naa$$
$$(\forall y)(Nay \supset \sim Nya) \quad *a \; 4$$
$$Naa \supset \sim Naa \quad \surd \; 5$$

```
              /\
             /  \
        ~Naa    ~Naa
          X       X
```

VALID

11. $(\exists x)(\sim Rx \;\&\; Wa) \vdash Wa \;\&\; (\exists x)\sim Rx$

1	1.	$(\exists x)(\sim Rx \;\&\; Wa)$	A
2	2.	$\sim Rb \;\&\; Wa$	A ($\exists$E)
2	3.	Wa	2 &E
2	4.	$\sim Rb$	2 &E
2	5.	$(\exists x)\sim Rx$	4 $\exists$I
2	6.	$Wa \;\&\; (\exists x)\sim Rx$	4, 5 &I
1	7.	$Wa \;\&\; (\exists x)\sim Rx$	1,2–7 $\exists$E

The restriction on universal introduction and the second restriction on existential elimination are very specific; the restriction is not violated if a constant other than the restricted occurs in an assumption or conclusion within the proof.

To observe the restriction on $\exists$E, we choose a constant other than 'a' to replace the existentially bound variable since 'a' already appears in the given assumption. When we apply $\exists$E in step 7, we can do so correctly despite the fact that the proposition in step 6 contains constant 'a'. This is because 'a' is not the arbitrarily chosen constant which we substituted for the existentially bound variable 'x' in assumption 1, when we auxiliary assumed the wff for the $\exists$E subproof at step 2. Constant 'b' was introduced instead at this step, in keeping with the first restriction on $\exists$E. If, on the other hand, step 6 had contained constant 'b', then we would not have been able to apply the rule.

12. $(\exists x)Qxb \supset (\forall x)Lx, (\forall x)Qax \vdash (\forall x)(Zxc \supset Lx)$

1	1.	$(\exists x)Qxb \supset (\forall x)Lx$	A
2	2.	$(\forall x)Qax$	A
3	3.	Zdc	A ($\supset$I)
2	4.	Qab	2 $\forall$E
2	5.	$(\exists x)Qxb$	4 $\exists$I
1, 2	6.	$(\forall x)Lx$	1, 5 $\supset$E
1, 2	7.	Ld	6 $\forall$E
1, 2	8.	$Zdc \supset Ld$	3–7 $\supset$I
1, 2	9.	$(\forall x)(Zxc \supset Lx)$	8 $\forall$I

The choice of constant 'd' in the ⊃I auxiliary assumption at step 3 might appear surprising. The truth tree for this problem provides clues about which constants to use. The fundamental heuristic in solving predicate natural deduction proofs recommends the auxiliary assumption at step 3. We consider the conclusion we are required to derive and ask whether the main operator is a propositional connective or quantifier. Here, the main operator is clearly the quantifier. We imagine the conclusion as it would appear without the quantifier, with constants substituted for bound variables. Since constants 'a', 'b', and 'c' already appear in the given assumptions, it seems advisable to introduce a new constant, as we do in auxiliary assuming Zdc.

13. (∀x)(Tx ⊃ Sx) ⊢ (∀x)((∃y)(Ty & Cxy) ⊃ (∃y)(Sy & Cxy))

1	1.	(∀x)(Tx ⊃ Sx)	A
2	2.	(∃y)(Ty & Cay)	A (⊃I)
3	3.	Tb & Cab	A (∃E)
1	4.	Tb ⊃ Sb	1 ∀E
3	5.	Tb	3 &E
1, 3	6.	Sb	4, 5 ⊃E
3	7.	Cab	3 &E
1, 3	8.	Sb & Cab	6, 7 &I
1, 3	9.	(∃y)(Sy & Cay)	8 ∃I
1, 2	10.	(∃y)(Sy & Cay)	2, 3–9 ∃E
1	11.	(∃y)(Ty & Cay) ⊃ (∃y)(Sy & Cay)	2–10 ⊃I
1	12.	(∀x)((∃y)(Ty & Cxy) ⊃ (∃y)(Sy & Cxy))	11 ∀I

The fundamental heuristic for predicate natural deduction determines a proof's overall strategy.

This proof is instructive in several ways. Notice that without the universal quantifier, the main operator of the conclusion to be proved is a conditional. This suggests proceeding by a nested application of ⊃I. The choice of auxiliary assumption for the ⊃I subproof beginning in step 2 is made on the basis of the fundamental heuristic, imagining how the conclusion of the sequent would appear without the main quantifier. The truth tree also confirms a set of constants to substitute for bound variables in making auxiliary assumptions for predicate subproof rules in the proof. As in some previous examples, the proposition in step 11 to which ∀I is applied obeys the rule's restriction, as the assumption column and proof spine show, because it does not rest on any assumption that contains constant 'a' to be replaced by the universally bound variable 'x' in step 12.

14. (∀x)(Dx ⊃ Mx), (∀x)(~Fx ⊃ ~Dx), (∀x)((Mx & Fx) ⊃ ~Ex)
⊢ Dp ⊃ ~Ep

1	1.	(∀x)(Dx ⊃ Mx)	A
2	2.	(∀x)(~Fx ⊃ ~Dx)	A
3	3.	(∀x)((Mx & Fx) ⊃ ~Ex)	A
1	4.	Dp ⊃ Mp	1 ∀E
2	5.	~Fp ⊃ ~Dp	2 ∀E
3	6.	(Mp & Fp) ⊃ ~Ep	3 ∀E
7	7.	Dp	A (⊃I)
1, 7	8.	Mp	4, 7 ⊃E
9	9.	~Fp	A (~IE)
2, 9	10.	~Dp	5, 9 ⊃E
7	11.	Dp	7 R
2, 7	12.	Fp	9–11 ~IE
1, 2, 7	13.	Mp & Fp	8, 12 &I
1, 2, 3, 7	14.	~Ep	6, 13 ⊃E
1, 2, 3	15.	Dp ⊃ ~Ep	7–14 ⊃I

Some valid sequents involve constants as well as quantifier bound variables.

The given assumptions are all universal quantifications, for which instantiation to a predetermined constant 'p' is unrestricted. The body of the proof involves standard applications of the propositional rules.

15. ~(∃x)Axx, (∀x)(∀y)(∃z)((Bzy & ~Bxz) ⊃ Axy) ⊢
(∃x)(∃y)(~Byx ⊃ ~Bxy)

1	1.	~(∃x)Axx	A
2	2.	(∀x)(∀y)(∃z)((Bzy & ~Bxz) ⊃ Axy)	A
2	3.	(∀y)(∃z)((Bzy & ~Baz) ⊃ Aay)	2 ∀E
2	4.	(∃z)((Bza & ~Baz) ⊃ Aaa)	3 ∀E
5	5.	(Bba & ~Bab) ⊃ Aaa	A (∃E)
6	6.	~Bab	A (⊃I)
7	7.	Bba	A (~IE)
6, 7	8.	Bba & ~Bab	6, 7 &I
5, 6, 7	9.	Aaa	5, 8 ⊃E
5, 6, 7	10.	(∃x)Axx	9 ∃I
1	11.	~(∃x)Axx	1 R
1, 5, 6	12.	~Bba	7–11 ~IE
1, 5	13.	~Bab ⊃ ~Bba	6–12 ⊃I
1, 5	14.	(∃y)(~Byb ⊃ ~Bby)	13 ∃I
1, 5	15.	(∃x)(∃y)(~Byx ⊃ ~Bxy)	14 ∃I
1, 2	16.	(∃x)(∃y)(~Byx ⊃ ~Bxy)	4, 5–15 ∃E

Proofs involving wffs with polyadic or mixed multiple quantifications require careful attention to the choice of constants in using predicate intelim rules.

The proof requires foresight to see what substitutions of constants for bound variables will best serve the derivation of nested ⊃I and ~IE subproofs. When a proposition contains mixed multiple quantifiers, we must generally work from the outermost or leftmost quantifier inward, using one quantifier elimination rule at a time until we have reduced the proposition to a counter-part form containing only truth functionally propositional connections of un-quantified predications. In this case, we go from left to right in steps 3 and 4 until we have revealed the existential quantifier. We eliminate the existential by initiating an ∃E subproof, beginning with an auxiliary assumption, in which an arbitrarily chosen constant replaces occurrences of the existentially bound variable. The choice of the same constant 'a' to replace universally bound variables 'x' and 'y' unrestrictedly in steps 3 and 4 is determined by the usefulness of having such a wff in a proof for ~IE purposes, given assumption 1. The substitution is also suggested by truth tree analysis of the sequent. The tree confirms the previous replacement of bound variables by constants:

$$\sim(\exists x)Axx \quad \surd \; 1$$
$$(\forall x)(\forall y)(\exists z)((Bzy \;\&\; \sim Bxz) \supset Axy) \quad *a \; 3$$
$$\sim(\exists x)(\exists y)(\sim Byx \supset \sim Bxy) \quad \surd \; 2$$
$$(\forall x)\sim Axx \quad \surd \; 12$$
$$(\forall x)\sim(\exists y)(\sim Byx \supset \sim Bxy) \quad *b \; 6$$
$$(\forall y)(\exists z)((Bzy \;\&\; \sim Baz) \supset Aay) \quad *a \; 4$$
$$(\exists z)((Bza \;\&\; \sim Baz) \supset Aaa) \quad \surd \; 5$$
$$(Bba \;\&\; \sim Bab) \supset Aaa \quad \surd \; 10$$
$$\sim(\exists y)(\sim Byb \supset \sim Bby) \quad \surd \; 7$$
$$(\forall y)\sim(\sim Byb \supset \sim Bby) \quad *a \; 8$$
$$\sim(\sim Bab \supset \sim Bba) \quad \surd \; 9$$
$$Bba$$
$$\sim Bab$$

11 $\surd$ ~(Bba & ~Bab)   Aaa
                                    ~Aaa
                                    X

     ~Bba   Bab
      X   X

VALID

Predicate truth trees can sometimes help in choosing constants for predicate natural deduction proofs.

The application of ∃E is delayed until step 16, in accord with the rule's second restriction. The restriction prohibits the conclusion of an ∃E subproof from containing the arbitrarily chosen constant ('b'), substituted for the exis-tentially bound variable in the auxiliary assumption, by which the ∃E subproof is introduced.

The following is a proof that appears as though it would be easy to solve but that involves complicated internestings of propositional and predicate subproofs to satisfy the ∃E restrictions. The tree shows that the sequent is deductively valid:

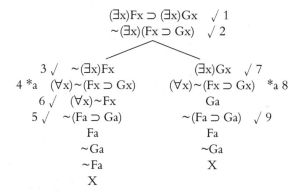

A natural deduction proof of the sequent has the following form:

16. (∃x)Fx ⊃ (∃x)Gx ⊢ (∃x)(Fx ⊃ Gx)

1	1.	(∃x)Fx ⊃ (∃x)Gx	A
2	2.	~(∃x)(Fx ⊃ Gx)	A (~IE)
3	3.	Fa	A (⊃I)
3	4.	(∃x)Fx	3 ∃I
1, 3	5.	(∃x)Gx	1, 4 ⊃E
6	6.	Gb	A (∃E)
7	7.	~(Fb ⊃ Gb)	A (~IE)
8	8.	Fb	A (⊃I)
6	9.	Gb	6 R
6	10.	Fb ⊃ Gb	8–9 ⊃I
6	11.	Fb ⊃ Gb	7–10 ~IE
6	12.	(∃x)(Fx ⊃ Gx)	12 ∃I
1, 3	13.	(∃x)(Fx ⊃ Gx)	5, 6–12 ∃E
14	14.	~Ga	A (~IE)
1, 3	15.	(∃x)(Fx ⊃ Gx)	13 R
2	16.	~(∃x)(Fx ⊃ Gx)	2 R
1, 2, 3	17.	Ga	14–16 ~IE
1, 2	18.	Fa ⊃ Ga	3–17 ⊃I
1, 2	19.	(∃x)(Fx ⊃ Gx)	18 ∃I
1	20.	(∃x)(Fx ⊃ Gx)	2–19 ~IE

Predicate Proofs of Prenex Equivalents

Proofs of some of the prenex normal form equivalences produced and confirmed by predicate truth trees in previous chapters are now presented. We could prove the equivalences by demonstrating that the biconditionals linking them as in the trees are tautologies. For simplicity, we instead prove them as inferences holding in both directions, from original wff to its prenex normal transform and from prenex normal transform to original wff. The proofs are as follows:

17. $(\exists x)Fx \supset (\forall y)Gy \vdash (\forall x)(\forall y)(\sim Fx \lor Gy)$

1	1.	$(\exists x)Fx \supset (\forall y)Gy$	A
2	2.	$\sim(\forall x)(\forall y)(\sim Fx \lor Gy)$	A ($\sim$IE)
3	3.	Fa	A ($\sim$IE)
3	4.	$(\exists x)Fx$	3 $\exists$I
1, 3	5.	$(\forall y)Gy$	1, 4 $\supset$E
1, 3	6.	Gb	5 $\forall$E
1, 3	7.	$\sim Fc \lor Gb$	6 $\lor$I
1, 3	8.	$(\forall y)(\sim Fc \lor Gy)$	7 $\forall$I
1, 3	9.	$(\forall x)(\forall y)(\sim Fx \lor Gy)$	8 $\forall$I
2	10.	$\sim(\forall x)(\forall y)(\sim Fx \lor Gy)$	2 R
1, 2	11.	$\sim$Fa	3–10 $\sim$IE
1, 2	12.	$\sim$Fa $\lor$ Gb	11 $\lor$I
1, 2	13.	$(\forall y)(\sim Fa \lor Gy)$	12 $\forall$I
1, 2	14.	$(\forall x)(\forall y)(\sim Fx \lor Gy)$	13 $\forall$I
1	15.	$(\forall x)(\forall y)(\sim Fx \lor Gy)$	2–14 $\sim$IE

Predicate natural deduction proofs confirm prenex form equivalences obtained by prenex transformation rules and verified by predicate truth trees.

An interesting feature of the previous proof is the use of $\lor$I to add a disjunct containing constant 'c' at step 7, which does not appear in any of the previous assumptions, so that $\forall$I can be used without violating its restriction in steps 8 and 9. This proof establishes the validity of the prenex normal form of the assumption in the conclusion. The opposite derivation is now proven:

18. $(\forall x)(\forall y)(\sim Fx \lor Gy) \vdash (\exists x)Fx \supset (\forall y)Gy$

1	1.	$(\forall x)(\forall y)(\sim Fx \lor Gy)$	A
2	2.	$(\exists x)Fx$	A ($\supset$I)
3	3.	Fa	A ($\exists$E)
1	4.	$(\forall y)(\sim Fa \lor Gy)$	1 $\forall$E
1	5.	$\sim Fa \lor Gb$	4 $\forall$E
6	6.	$\sim Fa$	A ($\lor$E)
7	7.	$\sim Gb$	A ($\sim$IE)
3	8.	Fa	3 R
7	9.	$\sim Fa$	6 R
3, 6	10.	Gb	7–9 $\sim$IE
11	11.	Gb	A ($\lor$E)
11	12.	Gb	11 R
1, 3	13.	Gb	6, 6–10, 11–12 $\lor$E
1, 3	14.	$(\forall y)Gy$	13 $\forall$I
1, 2	15.	$(\forall y)Gy$	2, 3–14 $\exists$E
1	16.	$(\exists x)Fx \supset (\forall y)Gy$	2–14 $\supset$I

The following proof is interesting because of the assumption for ~IE made at step 2. The proof is obviously valid. But why choose Fa to begin the sub-proof? There are two ways to think about the choice. First, its negation would be a useful fragment of the conclusion as it would appear without the universal quantifiers. If we observe the fundamental heuristic for predicate natural deduction proofs, then we are to imagine the conclusion prior to universalization by ∀I. The conclusion could look like ~Fa & ~Gb, which is the penultimate conclusion derived in step 8. In order to prove it, we must prove each of its conjuncts, beginning with ~Fa, which we can obtain by assuming its negation and working toward a contradiction. The other reason for assuming Fa at step 2 is that we can see that by ∃I we easily obtain (∃x)Fx, which contradicts the first conjunct of the given assumption and thereby provides the contradiction to complete the proof of ~Fa by ~IE in step 5. From the second conjunct of the given assumption, it is then possible to derive the second conjunct of the conclusion as it would appear without its quantifiers, deducing ~Gb at step 7. The two wffs are conjoined and then universally quantified in two steps at 9 and 10; note that the restriction on ∀I is satisfied because steps 8 and 9 rest only on assumption 1, which does not contain either of the constants 'a' or 'b', to be replaced successively by universally quantifier bound variables.

19. ~($\exists$x)Fx & ($\forall$x)~Gx $\vdash$ ($\forall$x)($\forall$y)(~Fx & ~Gy)

1	1.	~($\exists$x)Fx & ($\forall$x)~Gx	A
2	2.	Fa	A (~IE)
2	3.	($\exists$x)Fx	2 $\exists$I
1	4.	~($\exists$x)Fx	1 &E
1	5.	~Fa	2–4 ~IE
1	6.	($\forall$x)~Gx	1 &E
1	7.	~Gb	6 $\forall$E
1	8.	~Fa & ~Gb	5, 7 &I
1	9.	($\forall$y)(~Fa & ~Gy)	8 $\forall$I
1	10.	($\forall$x)($\forall$y)(~Fx & ~Gy)	9 $\forall$I

The next proof involves an interesting use of nested ~IE subproofs. They are needed to overcome the problem we have elsewhere encountered of dealing with the restriction on exiting from an $\exists$E subproof with a conclusion that does not contain the arbitrary constant of the $\exists$E assumption. Notice that at step 13, it was not important to substitute constant 'a' for the universally bound variable 'y' in ($\forall$y)(~Fa & ~Gy). We could have just as strategically substituted another constant, such as 'b' or 'c', and the part of the proof leading to the intermediate conclusion that ($\forall$x)~Gx in step 15, and the final conclusion in step 16, would have worked just as well.

20. ($\forall$x)($\forall$y)(~Fx & ~Gy) $\vdash$ ~($\exists$x)Fx & ($\forall$x)~Gx

1	1.	($\forall$x)($\forall$y)(~Fx & ~Gy)	A
2	2.	($\exists$x)Fx	A (~IE)
3	3.	Fa	A ($\exists$E)
1	4.	($\forall$y)(~Fa & ~Gy)	1 $\forall$E
1	5.	~Fa & ~Gb	4 $\forall$E
6	6.	($\exists$x)Fx	A (~IE)
3	7.	Fa	3 R
1	8.	~Fa	5 &E
1, 3	9.	~($\exists$x)Fx	6–8 ~IE
1, 2	10.	~($\exists$x)Fx	2, 3–9 $\exists$E
1	11.	~($\exists$x)Fx	2–10 ~IE
1	12.	($\forall$y)(~Fa & ~Gy)	1 $\forall$E
1	13.	~Fa & ~Ga	12 $\forall$E
1	14.	~Ga	13 &E
1	15.	($\forall$x)~Gx	14 $\forall$I
1	16.	~($\exists$x)Fx & ($\forall$x)~Gx	11, 15 &I

It is sometimes neces-
sary to duplicate an
auxiliary assumption
for negation intelim
within an existential
elimination subproof
in order to derive a
conclusion that satis-
fies the second restric-
tion on existential
elimination so that
the subproof can be
validly exited.

The next proof is similar but does not encounter the problem of having to deal with the complications resulting from internestings of ∃E and ~IE subproofs. Of interest is the fact that the derivation involves the assumption for ~IE of the entire conclusion in the overarching ~IE subproof, beginning at step 3, and again of assumption Fa in step 4, with a similar justification as before. The remaining steps of the proof are familiar from previous examples.

21. (∃x)(Fx ⊃ (∀y)Gy) ⊢ (∃x)(∀y)(~Fx ∨ Gy)

1	1.	(∃x)(Fx ⊃ (∀y)Gy)	A
2	2.	Fa ⊃ (∀y)Gy	A (∃E)
3	3.	~(∃x)(∀y)(~Fx ∨ Gy)	A (~IE)
4	4.	Fa	A (~IE)
2, 4	5.	(∀y)Gy	2, 4 ⊃E
2, 4	6.	Gb	5 ∀E
2, 4	7.	~Fa ∨ Gb	6 ∨I
2, 4	8.	(∀y)(~Fa ∨ Gy)	7 ∀I
2, 4	9.	(∃x)(∀y)(~Fx ∨ Gy)	8 ∃I
3	10.	~(∃x)(∀y)(~Fx ∨ Gy)	3 R
2, 3	11.	~Fa	4–10 ~IE
2, 3	12.	~Fa ∨ Gb	11 ∨I
2, 3	13.	(∀y)(~Fa ∨ Gy)	12 ∀I
2, 3	14.	(∃x)(∀y)(~Fx ∨ Gy)	13 ∃I
2	15.	(∃x)(∀y)(~Fx ∨ Gy)	3–14 ~IE
1	16.	(∃x)(∀y)(~Fx ∨ Gy)	1, 2–15 ∃E

The following proof is similar to the last problem in that its given assumption is an existentially quantified wff requiring a subproof and auxiliary assumption for ∃E, beginning at step 2, that is not discharged until the final step of the proof at step 16. The conclusion also has an existential quantifier as its main operator, which invites us to imagine the conclusion as it would appear without the quantifier. It has the penultimate form Fa ⊃ (∀y)Gy, which is proven in step 14, prior to existentialization in step 15, before exiting from the ∃E subproof by repeating the same conclusion in the final step.

22. (∃x)(∀y)(~Fx ∨ Gy) ⊢ (∃x)(Fx ⊃ (∀y)Gy)

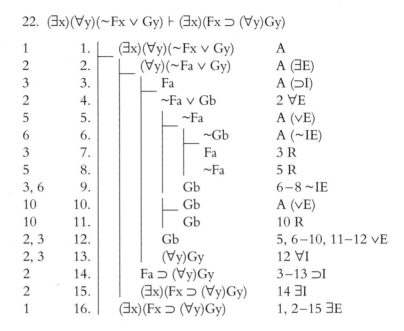

1	1.	(∃x)(∀y)(~Fx ∨ Gy)	A
2	2.	(∀y)(~Fa ∨ Gy)	A (∃E)
3	3.	Fa	A (⊃I)
2	4.	~Fa ∨ Gb	2 ∀E
5	5.	~Fa	A (∨E)
6	6.	~Gb	A (~IE)
3	7.	Fa	3 R
5	8.	~Fa	5 R
3, 6	9.	Gb	6–8 ~IE
10	10.	Gb	A (∨E)
10	11.	Gb	10 R
2, 3	12.	Gb	5, 6–10, 11–12 ∨E
2, 3	13.	(∀y)Gy	12 ∀I
2	14.	Fa ⊃ (∀y)Gy	3–13 ⊃I
2	15.	(∃x)(Fx ⊃ (∀y)Gy)	14 ∃I
1	16.	(∃x)(Fx ⊃ (∀y)Gy)	1, 2–15 ∃E

The next proof is comparatively complicated. It contains two nested applications of ~IE, along with ∃E, and several steps involving ∨I, in which wffs are added that contain constants with no prior history in the proof, to satisfy the restriction on ∀I at step 9 and again at step 20.

Prenex equivalences require complicated strategy choices in predicate natural deduction.

The choice of ~(∃y)(∀z)((Fa & Gy) ∨ (~Fa & ~Gz)) as the auxiliary assumption for the overarching ~IE subproof, beginning at step 3, deserves comment. Why not assume the negation of the entire conclusion, ~(∀x)(∃y)(∀z) ((Fx & Gy) ∨ (~Fx & ~Gz)), or the completely unquantified wff, (Fa & Gb) ∨ (~Fa & ~Gc)? The former would not be a good choice because in order to use it as part of a contradiction in the predominant ~IE subproof, we would need to derive all (∀x)(∃y)(∀z)((Fx & Gy) ∨ (~Fx & ~Gz)). Unfortunately, this wff is unavailable to us because of the restriction on ∀I. The restriction prevents universalizing any wff that rests on an assumption containing the constant we propose to replace with a universally bound variable.

All the intermediate conclusions throughout this portion of the proof depend on assumption 4, as the assumption column indicates, which contains constant 'a'. As a result, we are not free to universalize (∃y)(∀z)((Fa & Gy) ∨ (~Fx & ~Gz)) to obtain (∀x)(∃y)(∀z)((Fx & Gy) ∨ (~Fx & ~Gz)) in any of the ~IE subproofs. We cannot do so until we have discharged assumption 4. We do this by exiting from the ∃E subproof, beginning at step 6, which we cannot do until step 11. However, by this point, the relevant applications of ~IE must already be complete. This eliminates the first assumption. The second assumption is equally unacceptable because it contains the arbitrary constant 'b' of the ∃E subproof, beginning at step 6, which also prohibits us from exiting the ∃E subproof.

23. (∀x)(Fx ≡ (∃y)Gy) ⊢ (∀x)(∃y)(∀z)((Fx & Gy) ∨ (~Fx & ~Gz))

1	1.	(∀x)(Fx ≡ (∃y)Gy)	A
1	2.	Fa ≡ (∃y)Gy	1 ∀E
3	3.	~(∃y)(∀z)((Fa & Gy) ∨ (~Fa & ~Gz))	A (~IE)
4	4.	Fa	A (~IE)
1, 4	5.	(∃y)Gy	2, 4 ≡E
6	6.	Gb	A (∃E)
4, 6	7.	Fa & Gb	4, 6 &I
4, 6	8.	(Fa & Gb) ∨ (~Fa & ~Gc)	7 ∨I
4, 6	9.	(∀z)((Fa & Gb) ∨ (~Fa & ~Gz))	8 ∀I
4, 6	10.	(∃y)(∀z)((Fa & Gy) ∨ (~Fa & ~Gz))	9 ∃I
1, 4	11.	(∃y)(∀z)((Fa & Gy) ∨ (~Fa & ~Gz))	5,6–10 ∃E
3	12.	~(∃y)(∀z)((Fa & Gy) ∨ (~Fa & ~Gz))	3 R
1, 3	13.	~Fa	4–11 ~IE
14	14.	Gb	A (~IE)
14	15.	(∃y)Gy	14 ∃I
1, 14	16.	Fa	2, 15 ≡E
1, 3	17.	~Fa	13 R
1, 3	18.	~Gb	14–17 ~IE
1, 3	19.	~Fa & ~Gb	13, 18 &I
1, 3	20.	(Fa & Gb) ∨ (~Fa & ~Gc)	19 ∨I
1, 3	21.	(∀z)((Fa & Gb) ∨ (~Fa & ~Gz))	20 ∀I
1, 3	22.	(∃y)(∀z)((Fa & Gy) ∨ (~Fa & ~Gz))	21 ∃I
1	23.	(∃y)(∀z)((Fa & Gy) ∨ (~Fa & ~Gz))	3–22 ~IE
1	24.	(∀x)(∃y)(∀z)((Fx & Gy) ∨ (~Fx & ~Gz))	23 ∀I

The underlying logical structure of predicate natural deduction proofs is usually propositional.

Here is an even longer and more complicated proof. The complexity is due in part to the fact that we must prove a biconditional conclusion, incorporating the equivalent of two lengthy conditional subproofs. The proof also exhibits an interesting double nesting of ∃E subproofs and a structure of multiple ∨E and ~IE subproofs. Proofs of this kind test our ability to follow several strategies at once, keeping an eye on the end result without losing sight of details needed to arrive at each intermediate conclusion.

24. $(\forall x)(\exists y)(\forall z)((Fx \ \& \ Gy) \lor (\sim Fx \ \& \ \sim Gz)) \vdash (\forall x)(Fx \equiv (\exists y)Gy)$

1	1.	$(\forall x)(\exists y)(\forall z)((Fx \ \& \ Gy) \lor$ $(\sim Fx \ \& \ \sim Gz))$	A
2	2.	Fa	A ($\equiv$I)
1	3.	$(\exists y)(\forall z)((Fa \ \& \ Gy) \lor$ $(\sim Fa \ \& \ \sim Gz))$	1 $\forall$E
4	4.	$(\forall z)((Fa \ \& \ Gb) \lor$ $(\sim Fa \ \& \ \sim Gz))$	A ($\exists$E)
4	5.	$(Fa \ \& \ Gb) \lor (\sim Fa \ \& \ \sim Gc)$	4 $\forall$E
6	6.	Fa & Gb	A ($\lor$E)
6	7.	Gb	6 &E
8	8.	$\sim$Fa & $\sim$Gc	A ($\lor$E)
9	9.	$\sim$Gb	A ($\sim$IE)
2	10.	Fa	2 R
8	11.	$\sim$Fa	8 &E
2, 8	12.	Gb	9–11 $\sim$IE
2, 4	13.	Gb	5, 6–7, 8–12 $\lor$E
2, 4	14.	$(\exists y)Gy$	13 $\exists$I
1, 2	15.	$(\exists y)Gy$	3, 4–14 $\exists$E
16	16.	$(\exists y)Gy$	A ($\equiv$I)
17	17.	Gd	A ($\exists$E)
1	18.	$(\exists y)(\forall z)((Fa \ \& \ Gy) \lor$ $(\sim Fa \ \& \ \sim Gz))$	1 $\forall$E
19	19.	$(\forall z)((Fa \ \& \ Ge) \lor$ $(\sim Fa \ \& \ \sim Gz))$	A ($\exists$E)
19	20.	$(Fa \ \& \ Ge) \lor$ $(\sim Fa \ \& \ \sim Gd)$	19 $\forall$E
21	21.	Fa & Ge	A ($\lor$E)
21	22.	Fa	21 &E
23	23.	$\sim$Fa & $\sim$Gd	A ($\lor$E)
24	24.	$\sim$Fa	A ($\sim$IE)
17	25.	Gd	17 R
23	26.	$\sim$Gd	23 &E
17, 23	27.	Fa	24–26 $\sim$IE
17, 19	28.	Fa	20, 21–22, 23–27 $\lor$E
1, 17	29.	Fa	18, 19–28 $\exists$E
1, 16	30.	Fa	16, 17–29 $\exists$E
1	31.	$Fa \equiv (\exists y)Gy$	2–15, 16–30 I$\equiv$
1	32.	$(\forall x)(Fx \equiv (\exists y)Gy)$	31 $\forall$I

The same reasoning justifies the choice of the auxiliary assumption $\sim(\exists y)(\sim Fa \vee \sim Day)$ at step 2 rather than the negation of the entire conclusion, $\sim(\forall x)(\exists y)(\sim Fx \vee \sim Dxy)$, as in proof 23. We need an assumption to contradict an intermediate conclusion that we can validly deduce without violating the restriction on $\forall I$. The difficulty here, as before, is that we cannot universalize $(\exists y)(\sim Fa \vee \sim Day)$ to obtain $(\forall x)(\exists y)(\sim Fx \vee \sim Dxy)$ as long as the wff rests on an assumption containing constant 'a'. The offending assumption is not discharged until after we have exited the $\sim IE$ subproof at step 16. Only when we have exited the $\sim IE$ subproof are we free to universalize the wff that contradicts the main $\sim IE$ auxiliary assumption to conclude finally that $(\forall x)(\exists y)(\sim Fx \vee \sim Dxy)$.

25. $(\forall x)(Fx \supset \sim(\forall y)Dxy) \vdash (\forall x)(\exists y)(\sim Fx \vee \sim Dxy)$

1	1.	$(\forall x)(Fx \supset \sim(\forall y)Dxy)$	A
2	2.	$\sim(\exists y)(\sim Fa \vee \sim Day)$	A ($\sim$IE)
3	3.	Fa	A ($\sim$IE)
1	4.	$Fa \supset \sim(\forall y)Day$	1 $\forall$E
5	5.	$\sim Dab$	A ($\sim$IE)
1, 3	6.	$\sim(\forall y)Day$	3, 4 $\supset$E
5	7.	$\sim Fa \vee \sim Dab$	5 $\vee$I
5	8.	$(\exists y)(\sim Fa \vee \sim Day)$	7 $\exists$I
2	9.	$\sim(\exists y)(\sim Fa \vee \sim Day)$	2 R
1, 2, 3	10.	Dab	5–9 $\sim$IE
1, 2, 3	11.	$(\forall y)Day$	10 $\forall$I
1, 3	12.	$\sim(\forall y)Day$	3, 4 $\supset$E
1, 2	13.	$\sim Fa$	3–12 $\sim$IE
1, 2	14.	$\sim Fa \vee \sim Day$	13 $\vee$I
1, 2	15.	$(\exists y)(\sim Fa \vee \sim Day)$	14 $\exists$I
1	16.	$(\exists y)(\sim Fa \vee \sim Day)$	2–15 $\sim$IE
1	17.	$(\forall x)(\exists y)(\sim Fx \vee \sim Dxy)$	16 $\forall$I

The next proof illustrates the same kind of tactics needed to satisfy the restrictions on quantifier introduction and elimination. Here, the underlying strategy is the classic decision to auxiliary assume the antecedent of the conditional conclusion, Fa, in step 2, as it would appear without its predicate main operator, together with the auxiliary assumption of the negation of the consequent of the conditional. The restriction on $\forall I$ is satisfied upon exiting from the $\supset I$ subproof at step 20, permitting universalization of the conclusion in step 21.

26. $(\forall x)(\exists y)(\sim Fx \lor \sim Dxy) \vdash (\forall x)(Fx \supset \sim(\forall y)Dxy)$

1	1.	$(\forall x)(\exists y)(\sim Fx \lor \sim Dxy)$	A
2	2.	Fa	A ($\supset$I)
3	3.	$(\forall y)Day$	A ($\sim$IE)
1	4.	$(\exists y)(\sim Fa \lor \sim Day)$	1 $\forall$E
5	5.	$\sim Fa \lor \sim Dab$	A ($\exists$E)
6	6.	$\sim Fa$	A ($\lor$E)
7	7.	Dab	A ($\sim$IE)
2	8.	Fa	2 R
6	9.	$\sim Fa$	6 R
2, 6	10.	$\sim Dab$	7–9 $\sim$IE
11	11.	$\sim Dab$	A ($\lor$E)
11	12.	$\sim Dab$	11 R
2, 5	13.	$\sim Dab$	5, 6–10, 11–12 $\lor$E
14	14.	$(\forall y)Day$	A ($\sim$IE)
3	15.	Dab	3 $\forall$E
2, 5	16.	$\sim Dab$	13 R
2, 5	17.	$\sim(\forall y)Day$	14–16 $\sim$IE
1, 2, 3	18.	$\sim(\forall y)Day$	4, 5–17 $\exists$E
1, 2	19.	$\sim(\forall y)Day$	3–18 $\sim$IE
1	20.	$Fa \supset \sim(\forall y)Day$	2–19 $\supset$I
1	21.	$(\forall x)(Fx \supset \sim(\forall y)Dxy)$	20 $\forall$I

Satisfying the restrictions especially on existential elimination sometimes requires delaying applications of certain rules and paying attention to the order in which subproofs are nested within other subproofs.

A simpler proof is possible in this case. Again, it is useful to auxiliary assume not the negation of the entire conclusion but the negation of the conclusion as it would appear without its leftmost universal predicate main operator. The final conclusion is universalized only in the last proof step, when all auxiliary assumptions needed to work the intermediate $\sim$IE subproofs containing constant 'a' are discharged, and all $\sim$IE subproofs have been validly exited.

27. $(\forall x)(Fx \supset \sim(\exists y)Dxy) \supset (\forall x)(\forall y)(\sim Fx \lor \sim Dxy)$

1	1.	$(\forall x)(Fx \supset \sim(\exists y)Dxy)$	A
2	2.	$\sim(\forall y)(\sim Fa \lor \sim Day)$	A ($\sim$IE)
3	3.	Fa	A ($\sim$IE)
1	4.	$Fa \supset \sim(\exists y)Day$	1 $\forall$E
5	5.	Dab	A ($\sim$IE)
5	6.	$(\exists y)Day$	5 $\exists$I
1, 3	7.	$\sim(\exists y)Day$	3, 4 $\supset$E
1, 3	8.	$\sim$Dab	5–7 $\sim$IE
1, 3	9.	$\sim Fa \lor \sim Dab$	8 $\lor$I
1, 3	10.	$(\forall y)(\sim Fa \lor \sim Day)$	9 $\forall$I
2	11.	$\sim(\forall y)(\sim Fa \lor \sim Day)$	2 R
1, 2	12.	$\sim Fa$	3–11 $\sim$IE
1, 2	13.	$\sim Fa \lor \sim Day$	12 $\lor$I
1, 2	14.	$(\forall y)(\sim Fa \lor \sim Day)$	13 $\forall$I
1	15.	$(\forall y)(\sim Fa \lor \sim Day)$	2–14 $\sim$IE
1	16.	$(\forall x)(\forall y)(\sim Fx \lor \sim Dxy)$	15 $\forall$I

The final derivation in this series illustrates many of the vital lessons we have learned in presenting predicate natural deduction proofs. Again, following the fundamental heuristic for predicate proofs, we observe that the predicate main operator in the conclusion is the universal quantifier, and we accordingly work toward a penultimate conclusion, $Fa \supset \sim(\exists y)Day$, that does not contain the quantifier. We apply a standard strategy of auxiliary assuming the antecedent Fa for $\supset$I at step 2 and auxiliary assuming the negation of the consequent $(\exists y)Day$ at step 3. Satisfying the restriction on $\forall$I at step 21, we complete the proof by universalizing the wff in step 22 to obtain $(\forall x)(Fx \supset \sim(\exists y)Dxy)$.

28. $(\forall x)(\forall y)(\sim Fx \lor \sim Dxy) \vdash (\forall x)(Fx \supset \sim(\exists y)Dxy)$

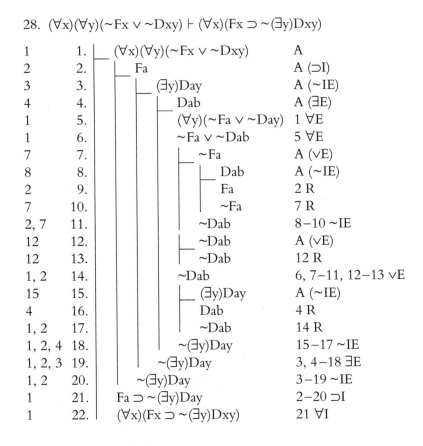

1	1.	$(\forall x)(\forall y)(\sim Fx \lor \sim Dxy)$	A
2	2.	Fa	A ($\supset$I)
3	3.	$(\exists y)Day$	A ($\sim$IE)
4	4.	Dab	A ($\exists$E)
1	5.	$(\forall y)(\sim Fa \lor \sim Day)$	1 $\forall$E
1	6.	$\sim Fa \lor \sim Dab$	5 $\forall$E
7	7.	$\sim Fa$	A ($\lor$E)
8	8.	Dab	A ($\sim$IE)
2	9.	Fa	2 R
7	10.	$\sim Fa$	7 R
2, 7	11.	$\sim Dab$	8–10 $\sim$IE
12	12.	$\sim Dab$	A ($\lor$E)
12	13.	$\sim Dab$	12 R
1, 2	14.	$\sim Dab$	6, 7–11, 12–13 $\lor$E
15	15.	$(\exists y)Day$	A ($\sim$IE)
4	16.	Dab	4 R
1, 2	17.	$\sim Dab$	14 R
1, 2, 4	18.	$\sim(\exists y)Day$	15–17 $\sim$IE
1, 2, 3	19.	$\sim(\exists y)Day$	3, 4–18 $\exists$E
1, 2	20.	$\sim(\exists y)Day$	3–19 $\sim$IE
1	21.	$Fa \supset \sim(\exists y)Day$	2–20 $\supset$I
1	22.	$(\forall x)(Fx \supset \sim(\exists y)Dxy)$	21 $\forall$I

To Check Your Understanding 8.6

Use the predicate intelim rules $\forall$E, $\exists$I, $\forall$I, and $\exists$E, together with propositional rules, to give natural deduction proofs to confirm the logical equivalences produced by the prenex normal form transformation rules to the wffs in previous chapters, *To Check Your Understanding 6.7*, as verified by predicate truth trees in *To Check Your Understanding 7.3*.

Proving Tautologies in Predicate Logic

The strategies used for natural deduction proofs are the same in proving predicate tautologies as in proving valid sequents. Predicate tautologies are introduced by means of the turnstile '$\vdash$' and have no propositions written as given assumptions to the left of the turnstile. When a predicate tautology is correctly proved, it rests on no given assumptions since none are needed or provided in solving the proof, and therefore it has no assumption numbers in the assump-

Tautologies can be proved in predicate logic by following the same basic format but using all predicate natural deduction rules, as those in propositional logic.

tion column of the final step. This means that in proving predicate tautologies we can use only auxiliary assumptions, which by the end of the proof must all be discharged. The conclusion of the correct proof of a tautology for the same reason must be brought completely outside of all subproof spines to appear written below and to the left or outside of the leftmost spine as the original subproof is exited. In all other respects, tautology proofs in predicate logic are exactly like deductively valid sequent proofs.

To Check Your Understanding 8.7 ■

Use the predicate intelim rules ∀E, ∃I, ∀I, and ∃E, together with propositional rules, to give natural deduction proofs of the following sequents and tautologies:

1. ⊢ (∀y)(Fy ⊃ (∃x)Fx)
2. ⊢ (∀x)Fx ⊃ (∀x)(Gx ⊃ Fx)
3. (∀x)Fx, (∃x)Gx ⊢ (∃x)(Fx & Gx)
4. (∃x)Fx ⊃ (∃x)Gx ⊢ (∃x)(Fx ⊃ Gx)
5. (∃x)Fx ⊃ (∀x)Gx ⊢ (∀x)(Fx ⊃ Gx)
6. (∀x)(Fx ∨ Gx) ⊢ (∀x)Fx ∨ (∃x)Gx
7. ⊢ (∀x)(Fx ⊃ Gx) ⊃ ((∃x)Fx ⊃ (∃x)Gx)
8. ⊢ (∀x)(Fx ⊃ Gx) ⊃ ((∀x)Fx ⊃ (∀x)Gx)
9. (∀x)(∃y)(∀z)~Fxyz ⊢ (∀x)(∀z)(∃y)~Fxyz

■

The Barber Paradox

An example of a predicate natural deduction proof of a tautology is the barber paradox.

A famous paradox is proved as a predicate tautology. The surprising conclusion is that there cannot exist a barber who shaves all and only those persons who do not shave themselves. The reason why there can be no such barber is apparent when we ask who would shave the barber. The barber either shaves or does not shave himself. This is a tautology of predicate logic, sometimes known as *excluded middle*—the facts are logically limited to one possibility or the other, with no third choice or middle ground. If the barber shaves himself, then, since the barber is supposed to shave only those persons who do not shave themselves, he does not shave himself. If, on the other hand, the barber does not shave himself, then, since he is supposed to shave all persons who do not shave themselves, he shaves himself. Thus, it follows paradoxically that the barber shaves himself if and only if he does not shave himself. This is a contradiction, from which it follows that there exists no barber who shaves all and only those persons who do not shave themselves.

We formulate the conclusion of the paradox as a tautology of predicate logic:

$$\vdash \sim(\exists x)(\forall y)(Sxy \equiv \sim Syy)$$

The interpretation is obvious if we allow the relational predicate 'S' to represent 'shaves'. Then the theorem states that there exists no x such that for any y, x shaves y if and only if y does not shave y. We verify that the proposition is a tautology of predicate logic by completing the truth tree for its negation:

$$
\begin{array}{c}
(\exists x)(\forall y)(Sxy \equiv \sim Syy) \quad \checkmark \; 1 \\
(\forall y)(Say \equiv \sim Syy) \quad {}^{*}a \; 2 \\
Saa \equiv \sim Saa \quad \checkmark \; 3 \\
\end{array}
$$

$$
\begin{array}{cc}
Saa & \sim Saa \\
\sim Saa & Saa \\
X & X
\end{array}
$$

TAUTOLOGY
(ORIGINAL UNNEGATED FORM)

The choice of constant 'a' to replace the universally bound variable 'y' in giving the truth tree decomposition of $(\forall y)(Say \equiv \sim Syy)$ is imposed as the only way of achieving closure. The instantiation is also justified by the informal explanation of the paradox. We produce an unexpected contradiction when we ask, 'Who shaves a barber who shaves all and only those persons who do not shave themselves?' To conclude that the barber shaves himself if and only if he does not shave himself is symbolized as $Saa \equiv \sim Saa$, where the same object, a (the barber), is both shaver and shaved if and only if he is not both shaver and shaved.

Knowing that the proposition is a tautology of predicate logic, we should be prepared to prove it by natural deduction. There are no given assumptions, but we can avail ourselves of an auxiliary assumption with an introductory sub-proof for purposes of ~IE. The same contradiction as previously discussed is then deduced from the assumption that the barber shaves himself. The proof has the following form:

Predicate truth trees verify that the barber paradox statement is a tautology.

1	1.	$(\exists x)(\forall y)(Sxy \equiv \sim Syy)$	A ($\sim$IE)
2	2.	$(\forall y)(Say \equiv \sim Syy)$	A ($\exists$E)
2	3.	$Saa \equiv \sim Saa$	2 $\forall$E
4	4.	Saa	A ($\sim$IE)
2, 4	5.	$\sim Saa$	3, 4 $\equiv$E
6	6.	$(\exists x)(\forall y)(Sxy \equiv \sim Syy)$	A ($\sim$IE)
4	7.	Saa	4 R
2, 4	8.	$\sim Saa$	5 R
2, 4	9.	$\sim(\exists x)(\forall y)(Sxy \equiv \sim Syy)$	6–8 $\sim$IE
1	10.	$(\exists x)(\forall y)(Sxy \equiv \sim Syy)$	1 R
1, 2	11.	$\sim Saa$	4–10 $\sim$IE
1, 2	12.	Saa	3, 11 $\equiv$E
13	13.	$(\exists x)(\forall y)(Sxy \equiv \sim Syy)$	A ($\sim$IE)
1, 2	14.	Saa	12 R
1, 2	15.	$\sim Saa$	11 R
1, 2	16.	$\sim(\exists x)(\forall y)(Sxy \equiv \sim Syy)$	13–15 $\sim$IE
1	17.	$\sim(\exists x)(\forall y)(Sxy \equiv \sim Syy)$	1, 2–16 $\exists$E
	18.	$\sim(\exists x)(\forall y)(Sxy \equiv \sim Syy)$	1–17 $\sim$IE

The proof contains several internested applications of $\sim$IE. They help to exhibit a contradiction derived from the biconditional $Saa \equiv \sim Saa$ and to validly derive a result that does not contain constant 'a' so that we can exit the $\exists$E subproof. The previous formulation solves these difficulties in an economical way, proving that there exists no barber who shaves all and only those persons who do not shave themselves.

To Check Your Understanding 8.8 ━━━━━━━━━━━━━━━━━━━━━━━■

Use the symbolization, truth trees, and natural deduction proof techniques of predicate logic to prove a veterinarian version of the barber paradox, according to which there can be no veterinarian who shaves the schnauzers of all and only those veterinarians who do not shave their own schnauzers.

■

Word Problems

Word problems challenge all symbolic logic skills.

Word problems, like the barber paradox, are important because they apply methods of symbolic logic to everyday reasoning. Word problems provide a cumulative test of all the skills we have acquired, including symbolizing of propositions and arguments, evaluating wffs and sequents by the truth tree decision method, and delivering natural deduction proofs of tautologies and deductively valid sequents. If we know how to use symbolic logic in understanding simple word problems, then we may be ready to apply the techniques we have learned to more interesting inferences.

We begin with a relatively simple word problem and then consider a more complicated example as a demonstration. In Plato's dialogue, the *Meno,* Meno asks:

Can you tell me, Socrates, can virtue be taught? (70a1)

The importance of the question is practical as well as theoretical. There may be implications in the correct answer to Meno's query for how children are raised and whether criminals can be rehabilitated by being taught to be virtuous. After an extended discussion, in which Socrates admits that he does not even know what virtue is, let alone whether it can be taught, and also convinces Meno of the difficulties in precisely defining the concept of virtue, Socrates proposes to address the question by what he calls the "geometer's method." He proceeds hypothetically by offering a conditional that may be accepted as true even by those who do not fully understand the nature of virtue. Socrates continues:

So let us speak about virtue also, since we do not know either what it is or what qualities it possesses, and let us investigate whether it is teachable or not by means of a hypothesis, and say this: Among the things existing in the soul, of what sort is virtue, that it should be teachable or not? (87b2−6)

The hypothesis Socrates and Meno consider is given in several different forms. The primary version occurs when Socrates maintains that:

Tell me this: if not only virtue but anything whatever can be taught, should not there be of necessity people who teach it and people who learn it? (89d5−7)

To Socrates' rhetorical question, Meno assents: "I think so" (89d7). Socrates proceeds by reformulating the assumption in contrapositive form when he states:

Then again, if on the contrary there are no teachers or learners of something, we should be right to assume that the subject cannot be taught? (89e1−2)

All reasoning in ordinary language has an underlying logical structure that can be symbolized.

Socrates, however, maintains that in fact there are no teachers, and hence no learners, of virtue. We need not be concerned about the details of his reasoning. Socrates seems to conclude inductively, on the basis of past experience and the hearsay testimony and his examination of others, that genuine teachers of virtue do not exist. Socrates is particularly impressed by the fact that rich and noble persons who want the very best education for their children, who spared no expense in hiring tutors in other arts to train them, have not been successful in identifying teachers adept in training pupils to be virtuous. The inference depends to a large extent on the definition of what it means to be the teacher of an art or *techné* in Greek. By this term, Socrates and Meno understand a skill that can be broken down into a series of steps and communicated to a student for imitation and assimilation. In this sense, although there definitely are teachers of music, gymnastics, mathematics, and the like, it is not clear that there are teachers of virtue who can transmit its practice as a skill. In defense of Socrates' position, it might be observed that whereas it is easy to find guitar teachers, karate teachers, and algebra teachers, it is by no means as obvious where or how to find persons who are qualified and effective in teaching others to be virtuous. Whether or not we agree with Socrates' claim that there are no teachers of virtue, we can consider the proposition as the second assumption of his argument.

The conclusion, then, from these two assumptions is that virtue cannot be taught. Meno and Socrates have the following exchange:

> If there are no teachers, neither are there pupils? — As you say.
> And we agreed that a subject that has neither teachers nor pupils is not teachable? — We have so agreed.
> Now there seem to be no teachers of virtue anywhere? — That is so.
> If there are no teachers, there are no learners? — That seems so.
> Then virtue cannot be taught?
> Apparently not, if we have investigated this correctly. (96c1–d1)

(Plato, *Plato's Meno,* translated by G. M. A. Grube. Hackett, Indianapolis, IN, 1976)

An accurate translation is essential to correct logical analysis of a word problem argument.

We can use predicate logic to analyze the structure of Socrates' argument that virtue cannot be taught. The first assumption is that if anything is capable of being taught, then there are teachers and pupils or learners of it. The second assumption is that there are no teachers of virtue. If we adopt predicate 'C' for the property of being teachable or capable of being taught, 'T' for the relational property of being a teacher of a subject, 'P' for the relational property of being a pupil or learner of a subject, and 'V' for the property of being a virtue, then we can symbolize the argument as follows:

1. $(\forall x)(Cx \supset ((\exists y)Tyx \ \& \ (\exists y)Pyx))$

2. $(\forall x)(Vx \supset \sim(\exists y)Tyx)$

---

3. $\sim(\exists x)(Vx \ \& \ Cx)$

Assumption 1 says that whatever is capable of being taught has teachers and pupils, or that if anything is capable of being taught, then there are teachers and pupils of it. Assumption 2 says that there are no teachers of any virtue. Conclusion 3 is that there are no virtues that are capable of being taught.

We can now use predicate truth trees to test the argument for deductive validity or invalidity. The tree looks as follows when we stack the assumptions with the negation of the conclusion:

Truth tree analysis is important to determine that an argument translated as a sequent of symbolic logic is deductively valid before trying to prove it by natural deduction.

$$(\forall x)(Cx \supset ((\exists y)Tyx \ \& \ (\exists y)Pyx)) \quad *a \ 3$$
$$(\forall x)(Vx \supset \sim(\exists y)Tyx) \quad *a \ 8$$
$$(\exists x)(Vx \ \& \ Cx) \quad \checkmark \ 1$$
$$Va \ \& \ Ca \quad \checkmark \ 2$$
$$Va$$
$$Ca$$
$$Ca \supset ((\exists y)Tya \ \& \ (\exists y)Pya) \quad \checkmark \ 4$$

$\sim Ca$　　　$(\exists y)Tya \ \& \ (\exists y)Pya \quad \checkmark \ 5$
X　　　　　　$(\exists y)Tya \quad \checkmark \ 6$
　　　　　　　$(\exists y)Pya) \quad \checkmark \ 7$
　　　　　　　Tba
　　　　　　　Pca
　　　　　$Va \supset \sim(\exists y)Tya \quad \checkmark \ 9$

$\sim Va$　　　　$\sim(\exists y)Tya \quad \checkmark \ 10$
X　　　　　　$(\forall y)\sim Tya \quad *b \ 11$
　　　　　　　$\sim Tba$
　　　　　　　X　　　　　　　　VALID

Since the argument is deductively valid, we can prove the inference by means of predicate natural deduction rules. The simplest proof might be presented as follows:

Proving a sequent in a natural deduction system explains why the sequent is deductively valid and justifies each step in the inferences that can be used in its logical derivation.

1	1.	$(\forall x)(Cx \supset ((\exists y)Tyx \& (\exists y)Pyx))$	A
2	2.	$(\forall x)(Vx \supset \sim(\exists y)Tyx)$	A
3	3.	$(\exists x)(Vx \& Cx)$	A ($\sim$IE)
4	4.	$Va \& Ca$	A ($\exists$E)
1	5.	$Ca \supset ((\exists y)Tya \& (\exists y)Pya)$	1 $\forall$E
4	6.	Ca	4 &E
1, 4	7.	$(\exists y)Tya \& (\exists y)Pya$	5, 6 $\supset$E
2	8.	$Va \supset \sim(\exists y)Tya$	2 $\forall$E
4	9.	Va	4 &E
10	10.	$(\exists x)(Vx \& Cx)$	A ($\sim$IE)
1, 4	11.	$(\exists y)Tya$	7 &E
2, 4	12.	$\sim(\exists y)Tya$	8, 9 $\supset$E
1, 2, 4	13.	$\sim(\exists x)(Vx \& Cx)$	10–12 $\sim$IE
1, 2, 3	14.	$\sim(\exists x)(Vx \& Cx)$	3, 4–13 $\exists$E
1, 2	15.	$\sim(\exists x)(Vx \& Cx)$	3–14 $\sim$IE

The proof has several formally interesting features. It depends on Socrates' hypothetical generalization in the first assumption that whatever is teachable or is capable of being taught has both teachers and pupils. If constant 'a' is an arbitrarily chosen virtue, such as patience or courage, in steps 4–12, then Socrates is saying that if patience or courage are capable of being taught, then there are teachers and pupils of patience or courage. If Socrates is also correct in assuming that there are no teachers of any virtues, then we are brought into contradiction with the auxiliary assumption that there exists at least one virtue capable of being taught.

Although the argument as we have reconstructed it is deductively valid, the truth or plausibility of Socrates' two assumptions might be disputed on philosophical grounds. It might be said, for example, that there are subjects, especially in Socrates' time, such as computer repair that can be taught but for which there may not happen to exist any teachers or pupils. A critic might object that it would still be true that computer repair is capable (in principle) of being taught, even if no one ever chooses to become a teacher or student of that *technê*. But could someone who was truly virtuous and capable of teaching others to be virtuous choose *not* to do so? By symbolizing the argument, and charitably interpreting it as deductively valid, we understand the inference more clearly, which facilitates critical analysis of its merits and defects.

Now we apply the same methods of predicate logic to a more challenging series of arguments in another word problem from the history of philosophy. We break down the steps we have followed in analyzing the previous word problem for more careful study.

▪ *Demonstration 30:* **Word Problems** ▪

PROBLEM: To symbolize, test by truth trees, and prove tautologies or valid sequents in a predicate word problem expressed in ordinary language.

ARGUMENT: Maximus Tyrius' proof that there is no injustice.
The example comes from Arthur Schopenhauer, the 19th century German idealist philosopher. Schopenhauer, in his monumental treatise, *The World as Will and Representation* (1819, Vol. 2, p. 86), writes:

A real gem of philosophical . . . argumentation, passing into decided sophistication, is the following reasoning of the Platonist Maximus Tyrius, which I will quote, as it is short. "Every injustice is the taking away of a good thing; there is no good thing other than virtue. Virtue, however, cannot be taken away, therefore it is not possible for the virtuous to suffer injustice from the wicked. It remains either that no injustice at all can be suffered, or that the wicked endures it from the wicked. But the wicked person possesses no good at all, for only virtue is such a good; therefore no good can be taken from him. Thus he also cannot suffer any injustice; hence injustice is an impossible thing."

STEP 1:   *Give a preliminary informal analysis of the problem*
The argument is interesting in its own right, and it exhibits a wide range of predicate deductive structures. We divide the argument into component sequents, evaluating each in turn, and then advance an overall assessment of the argument's logic. The argument makes a provocative claim since we know that injustice in the world abounds. At the very least, the argument involves a strained technical sense of the word "injustice" by which only injustice as stipulated, and not in the ordinary meaning of the term, does not exist. The proof turns on the conception of injustice as the taking away of a good and the assumptions that virtue is the only good and that virtue cannot be taken away. The inference also presupposes a suspicious division of all persons into either-or categories of the righteous and the wicked. The distinction implausibly allows that the righteous need possess only one virtue, whereas the wicked are entirely lacking in any virtue. We learn more about the argument's validity or invalidity through formalization and application of logical methods, by which the exact source of difficulty can be located.

STEP 2:   *Translate subarguments into predicate logic*
Fully explicated, Maximus' argument contains a surprising wealth of predicate deductive inferences. Let 'R' represent the property of being virtuous or

righteous, 'W' represent wicked, 'I' represent injustice, 'Sabc' represent that a suffers b from c, 'G' represent being a good thing, 'Tabc' represent that a takes b away from c, 'V' represent a virtue, and 'Pab' represent that a possesses b. Then Maximus' argument can be symbolized as a dilemma in several stages. The proposition that injustice is suffered only through infliction of wrong by the wicked is an implicit premise. It is proven in the following sequence:

Subargument 1

$$(\forall x)(Rx \vee Wx)$$
$$(\forall x)(Ix \supset \sim(\exists y)(\exists z)(Ry \;\&\; Szxy))$$
$$\overline{}$$
$$(\forall x)(Ix \supset (\forall y)(\forall z)(Szxy \supset Wy))$$

The previous conclusion, together with the righteous–wicked dichotomy, provides the disjunctive basis of the main dilemma. It states that injustice is suffered only either by the righteous from the wicked or by and from the wicked. This in the author's statement is the proof's more explicit starting place:

Subargument 2

$$(\forall x)(Rx \vee Wx)$$
$$(\forall x)(Ix \supset (\forall y)(\forall z)(Szxy \supset Wy))$$
$$\overline{}$$
$$(\forall x)(Ix \supset (\forall y)(\forall z)(Syxz \supset ((Ry \;\&\; Wz) \vee (Wy \;\&\; Wz))))$$

Maximus' dilemma now appears in two parts. It is assumed that injustice is the taking away of a good, that virtue is the only good, and that virtue cannot be taken away. These assumptions support Maximus' conclusion that no injustice is suffered by the righteous from the wicked in the dilemma's first horn.

Subargument 3

$$(\forall x)(Ix \supset (\forall y)(\forall z)(Syxz \supset (\exists w)(Gw \;\&\; Tzwy)))$$
$$(\forall x)(Gx \supset Vx)$$
$$(\forall x)(Vx \supset (\forall y)\sim(\exists z)Tyxz)$$
$$\overline{}$$
$$\sim(\exists x)(\exists y)(\exists z)(Ix \;\&\; Ry \;\&\; Wz \;\&\; Syxz)$$

Here and after in formulating the conclusion, we have taken the liberty of removing internal parentheses from the conjunction. This makes the complex formula somewhat easier to read and involves no risk of ambiguity of scope of the propositional connectives. The proposition that

~(∃x)(∃y)(∃z)(Ix & Ry & Wz & Syxz), as you can verify by truth trees, is logically equivalent to ~(∃x)(∃y)(∃z)(((Ix & Ry) & Wz) & Syxz). If we wanted to restore the internal parentheses, we could do so in this way or, equivalently, as ~(∃x)(∃y)(∃z)((Ix & Ry) & (Wz & Syxz)) or ~(∃x)(∃y)(∃z)(Ix & (Ry & (Wz & Syxz))).

The second horn of Maximus' dilemma has a similar structure. Now it is maintained that since the wicked do not possess virtues to be taken from them, the wicked also do not suffer injustice from the wicked.

Subargument 4

$$(\forall x)(Ix \supset (\forall y)(\forall z)(Syxz \supset (\exists w)(Gw \ \& \ Tzwy)))$$
$$(\forall x)(Gx \supset Vx)$$
$$(\forall x)(Wx \supset \ {\sim}(\exists y)(Gy \ \& \ Pxy))$$
$$(\forall x)(\forall y)({\sim}Pxy \supset \ {\sim}(\exists z)(Tzyx))$$

$$\overline{ {\sim}(\exists x)(\exists y)(\exists z)(Ix \ \& \ Wy \ \& \ Wz \ \& \ Syxz) }$$

The argument is complete when the conclusion that an injustice is inflicted only by the wicked and suffered only by the righteous or the wicked is put together with the two dilemma horns. These propositions then prove that injustice is not suffered by the righteous from the wicked nor by the wicked from the wicked. The final conclusion is that injustice is not suffered by or from anyone—that is, there is no injustice:

Subargument 5

$$(\forall x)(Ix \supset (\forall y)(\forall z)(Syxz \supset ((Ry \ \& \ Wz) \lor (Wy \ \& \ Wz))))$$
$${\sim}(\exists x)(\exists y)(\exists z)(Ix \ \& \ Ry \ \& \ Wz \ \& \ Syxz)$$
$${\sim}(\exists x)(\exists y)(\exists z)(Ix \ \& \ Wy \ \& \ Wz \ \& \ Syxz)$$

$$\overline{ {\sim}(\exists x)(\exists y)(\exists z)(Ix \ \& \ Syxz) }$$

STEP 3:   *Test the subarguments by predicate truth trees for deductive validity or invalidity*

The subarguments are justified by predicate truth trees. The check marks and decomposition sequence numbers have been eliminated, but they can be penciled in to evaluate each tree for accuracy, in following the sequence of decompositions by which each tree is constructed. Here are the results:

Truth tree 1

$(\forall x)(Rx \lor Wx)$
$(\forall x)(Ix \supset \sim(\exists y)(\exists z)(Ry \ \& \ Szxy))$
$\sim(\forall x)(Ix \supset (\forall y)(\forall z)(Szxy \supset Wy))$
$(\exists x)\sim(Ix \supset (\forall y)(\forall z)(Szxy \supset Wy))$
$\sim(Ia \supset (\forall y)(\forall z)(Szay \supset Wy))$
Ia
$\sim(\forall y)(\forall z)(Szay \supset Wy))$
$(\exists y)\sim(\forall z)(Szay \supset Wy))$
$\sim(\forall z)(Szab \supset Wb))$
$(\exists z)\sim(Szab \supset Wb))$
$\sim(Scab \supset Wb))$
$Scab$
$\sim Wb$
$Ia \supset \sim(\exists y)(\exists z)(Ry \ \& \ Szay)$

```
              ┌──────────────┴──────────────┐
            ~Ia                  ~(∃y)(∃z)(Ry & Szay)
             X                   (∀y)~(∃z)(Ry & Szay)
                                  ~(∃z)(Rb & Szab)
                                  (∀z)~(Rb & Szab)
                                   ~(Rb & Scab)
                              ┌────────┴────────┐
                             Rb               Scab
                            Rb ∨ Wb             X
                          ┌───┴───┐
                         Rb      Wb
                          X       X                      VALID
```

Truth tree 2

$$(\forall x)(Rx \lor Wx)$$
$$(\forall x)(Ix \supset (\forall y)(\forall z)(Szxy \supset Wy))$$
$$\sim(\forall x)(Ix \supset (\forall y)(\forall z)(Syxz \supset ((Ry \& Wz) \lor (Wy \& Wz))))$$
$$(\exists x)\sim(Ix \supset (\forall y)(\forall z)(Syxz \supset ((Ry \& Wz) \lor (Wy \& Wz))))$$
$$\sim(Ia \supset (\forall y)(\forall z)(Syxz \supset ((Ry \& Wz) \lor (Wy \& Wz))))$$
$$Ia$$
$$\sim(\forall y)(\forall z)(Syaz \supset ((Ry \& Wz) \lor (Wy \& Wz)))$$
$$(\exists y)\sim(\forall z)(Syaz \supset ((Ry \& Wz) \lor (Wy \& Wz)))$$
$$\sim(\forall z)(Sbaz \supset ((Rb \& Wz) \lor (Wb \& Wz)))$$
$$(\exists z)\sim(Sbaz \supset ((Rb \& Wz) \lor (Wb \& Wz)))$$
$$\sim(Sbac \supset ((Rb \& Wc) \lor (Wb \& Wc)))$$
$$Sbac$$
$$\sim((Rb \& Wc) \lor (Wb \& Wc))$$
$$\sim(Rb \& Wc)$$
$$\sim(Wb \& Wc)$$
$$Ia \supset (\forall y)(\forall z)(Szay \supset Wy)$$

```
                    ┌──────────┴──────────┐
                  ~Ia          (∀y)(∀z)(Szay ⊃ Wy)
                   X             (∀z)(Szac ⊃ Wc)
                                  Sbac ⊃ Wc
                                ┌────┴────┐
                              ~Sbac      Wc
                                X         │
                                     ┌────┴────┐
                                    ~Rb       ~Wb
                                  ┌──┴──┐       X
                                ~Wb    ~Wc
                              Rb ∨ Wb   X
                              ┌──┴──┐
                             Rb    Wb
                              X     X              VALID
```

The three remaining subargument truth trees are left as an exercise to check your understanding.

Step 4:   *Use predicate natural deduction rules to prove each valid subargument*
We derive the valid subarguments by predicate natural deduction. The interpretation makes use of an interesting application of ~IE in the main subproof and is then repeated later, in the most complicated case, in a nested structure seven assumption levels deep. The technique copes in an instruc-

tive way with the subproof exiting restrictions on existential elimination. It offers a conclusion within an existential elimination subproof that does not contain the constants chosen to replace existentially bound variables in existential elimination auxiliary assumptions. The method is used with variations in the first two proofs. The remaining three subargument proofs are left as an exercise to check your understanding.

Proof of Subargument 1

1	1.	$(\forall x)(Rx \lor Wx)$	A
2	2.	$(\forall x)(Ix \supset \sim(\exists y)(\exists z)(Ry \& Szxy))$	A
3	3.	Ia	A ($\supset$I)
2	4.	Ia $\supset \sim(\exists y)(\exists z)(Ry \& Szay)$	2 $\forall$E
2, 3	5.	$\sim(\exists y)(\exists z)(Ry \& Szay)$	3, 4 $\supset$E
1	6.	Rb $\lor$ Wb	1 $\forall$E
7	7.	Rb	A ($\lor$E)
8	8.	Scab	A ($\supset$I)
9	9.	$\sim$Wb	A ($\sim$IE)
7, 8	10.	Rb & Scab	7, 8 &I
7, 8	11.	$(\exists z)(Rb \& Szab)$	10 $\exists$I
7, 8	12.	$(\exists y)(\exists z)(Ry \& Szay)$	11 $\exists$I
2, 3	13.	$\sim(\exists y)(\exists z)(Ry \& Szay)$	5 R
2, 3, 7, 8	14.	Wb	9–13 $\sim$IE
2, 3, 7	15.	Scab $\supset$ Wb	8–14 $\supset$I
16	16.	Wb	A ($\lor$E)
17	17.	Scab	A ($\supset$I)
16	18.	Wb	16 R
16	19.	Scab $\supset$ Wb	17–18 $\supset$I
1, 2, 3	20.	Scab $\supset$ Wb	6, 7–15, 16–19 $\lor$E
1, 2, 3	21.	$(\forall z)(Szab \supset Wb)$	20 $\forall$I
1, 2, 3	22.	$(\forall y)(\forall z)(Szay \supset Wy)$	21 $\forall$I
1, 2	23.	Ia $\supset (\forall y)(\forall z)(Szay \supset Wy)$	3–22 $\supset$I
1, 2	24.	$(\forall x)(Ix \supset (\forall y)(\forall z)(Szxy \supset Wy))$	23 $\forall$I

Proof of Subargument 2

1	1.	$(\forall x)(Rx \lor Wx)$	A
2	2.	$(\forall x)(Ix \supset (\forall y)(\forall z)(Szay \supset Wy)$	A
3	3.	Ia	A $(\supset I)$
4	4.	$Sbac$	A $(\supset I)$
2	5.	$Ia \supset (\forall y)(\forall z)(Szay \supset Wy)$	2 $\forall$E
2, 3	6.	$(\forall y)(\forall z)(Szay \supset Wy)$	3, 5 $\supset$E
2, 3	7.	$(\forall z)(Szac \supset Wc)$	6 $\forall$E
2, 3	8.	$Sbac \supset Wc$	7 $\forall$E
2, 3, 4	9.	Wc	4, 8 $\supset$E
1	10.	$Rb \lor Wb$	1 $\forall$E
11	11.	Rb	A $(\lor$E$)$
1, 11	12.	$Rb \ \& \ Wc$	9, 11 &I
1, 11	13.	$(Rb \ \& \ Wc) \lor (Wb \ \& \ Wc)$	12 $\lor$I
14	14.	Wb	A $(\lor$E$)$
2, 3, 4, 14	15.	$Wb \ \& \ Wc$	9, 14 &I
2, 3, 4, 14	16.	$(Rb \ \& \ Wc) \lor (Wb \ \& \ Wc)$	15 $\lor$I
1, 2, 3, 4	17.	$(Rb \ \& \ Wc) \lor (Wb \ \& \ Wc)$	10, 11–13, 14–16 $\lor$E
1, 2, 3	18.	$Sbac \supset ((Rb \ \& \ Wc) \lor (Wb \ \& \ Wc))$	4–17 $\supset$I
1, 2, 3	19.	$(\forall z)(Sbaz \supset ((Rb \ \& \ Wz) \lor (Wb \ \& \ Wz)))$	18 $\forall$I
1, 2, 3	20.	$(\forall y)(\forall z)(Syaz \supset ((Ry \ \& \ Wz) \lor (Wy \ \& \ Wz)))$	19 $\forall$I
1, 2	21.	$Ia \supset (\forall y)(\forall z)(Syaz \supset ((Ry \ \& \ Wz) \lor (Wy \ \& \ Wz)))$	3–20 $\supset$I
1, 2	22.	$(\forall x)(Ix \supset (\forall y)(\forall z)(Syxz \supset ((Ry \ \& \ Wz) \lor (Wy \ \& \ Wz))))$	21 $\forall$I

STEP 5: *Give a final evaluation of the argument's strengths and weaknesses*
Schopenhauer's sarcasm makes it clear that he rejects Maximus' proof. Since a philosopher's derision by itself is no refutation, however, and the logical structure of the proof on this reconstruction is deductively valid, it remains to decide exactly where if anywhere the problem occurs. Symbolization displays the logical form of Maximus' inferences. It shows that if there is an error lurking in the argument, it is not logical in nature but has to do with the definitions of terms or with the truth or falsehood of substantive claims expressed in the assumptions. The mechanical methods of logic leave no room for doubt that there is at least nothing logically fishy about the proof.

An obvious proposition to question is the assumption of subarguments 1 and 2 (implicit in all five subarguments and their trees) that all persons are righteous or wicked, $(\forall x)(Rx \lor Wx)$. We know from experience that most if not all persons are not totally righteous or totally wicked but generally have a mixture of good and evil. This possibility is left open by the symbolization's use of inclusive disjunction. Maximus' argument is correct if wickedness implies that the wicked are lacking any virtue and hence, where virtue is the only good, that the wicked are devoid of any good. The righteous, by implication, are those who have at least some virtue, even if only a little. This entails that most if not all persons are righteous by Maximus' definition, and no one is genuinely wicked. The dilemma horn that considers injustice as suffered by the wicked from the wicked is then included only for the sake of logical completeness, and the real work of the argument is done by the first dilemma horn.

The first horn of Maximus' dilemma considers the injustice done to the righteous, in however diluted a sense, by the wicked. If this is deemed impossible by the argument or by Maximus' definitions of the terms "righteous" and "wicked," then the conclusion is trivialized since in this case no one is truly wicked. It follows automatically, then, with considerably less deductive ado, that the righteous do not suffer injustice from the wicked simply because there are no wicked persons to commit acts of injustice. The effect is to shift attention to the opening background assumption of the dilemma formalized in subargument 1, in which the terms of the argument are set as directed only toward the impossibility of the wicked inflicting injustice on the righteous or the wicked. Without this framework, it might be thought possible for the righteous or the wicked to suffer injustice from the righteous. In the current interpretation, the wicked are totally wicked, but the righteous are not totally righteous and so might commit all kinds of wrongdoing. Maximus' proof equally forestalls this objection. It shows that neither the righteous nor the wicked can suffer injustice from the righteous. To suffer injustice is supposed to mean to have a good taken away, where virtue as the only good cannot be taken away from the righteous and where the wicked have no virtue, and hence no good, of which to be deprived. This suggests that the proof may not need to distinguish between the righteous and the wicked. However, it is difficult to see how the basic structure of Maximus' dilemma could be preserved if the distinction were eliminated since it divides the argument into its two main parts, according to whether injustice is assumed to be suffered by the righteous or the wicked.

If there is any sleight of hand in Maximus' inference, it must result from his narrow conception of injustice as the taking away of a good, in the assumption that virtue is the only good, or in the assumption that virtue cannot be taken away. To accept Maximus' argument, we must agree that persons lacking all virtue have no good whatsoever and cannot suffer injustice understood as the taking away of a good. These premises may be difficult to believe. They involve philosophical issues that go beyond the purely formal structure of the proof and beyond what can be investigated by formal logical methods. There is ample material in what Schopenhauer calls Maximus' "real gem of philosophical . . . argumentation" for reflecting on the uses of predicate logic in symbolizing propositions and truth tree testing predicate wffs and sequents.

To Check Your Understanding 8.9 ━━━━━━━━━━━━━━━━━━━━━━━━━━━━━━━━━━━━━━■

Use the truth tree and natural deduction proof techniques of predicate logic to verify and prove the deductive validity of subarguments 3–5 of Maximus Tyrius' argument that there is no injustice.

■

Logic of Relations

Predicate logic can be used to formalize an abstract theory of relations.

Predicate logic can be used to formulate and prove important theorems about the logic of relations. Many of the wffs and sequents we have already proven concern particular relations. We now symbolize some general categories of relations and determine how they are deductively interrelated. There are other kinds of relations that shall not be discussed, but we can draw many worthwhile conclusions about the theory of relations generally by distinguishing formally between *reflexive, symmetric,* and *transitive* relations and their complements and contraries.

Basic types of relations include reflexive, symmetric, and transitive.

The following statements define some of the most basic types of relations:

Relation R is *reflexive* $=_{df} (\forall x)Rxx$

Relation R is *symmetric* $=_{df} (\forall x)(\forall y)(Rxy \supset Ryx)$

Relation R is *transitive* $=_{df} (\forall x)(\forall y)(\forall z)((Rxy \ \& \ Ryz) \supset Rxz)$

A reflexive relation is one that every object has toward itself. An example is the relation of self-identity, in which everything is identical to itself. A symmetric relation is one that mirrors its relata. Thus, R is a symmetric relation just in case, for any objects, if the first object is R related to the second, then the second is also R related to the first. An example is the relation of sitting next to, where if anything sits next to anything else, then that thing also sits next to the first. Another example is siblinghood (being the brother or sister of), where if anything is the sibling of something else, that thing is the sibling of the first. A transitive relation is one in which, for any three objects, if the first object bears the relation to the second, and the second bears it to the third, then the first object bears the relation to the third object. An example involves the relation of being older than, where if Jean is older than Marilyn, and Marilyn is older than Ray, then Jean is older than Ray. Another example is equality, as in elementary arithmetic, where, if A = B and B = C, then A = C.

The complements of these relations are also defined:

Relation R is *nonreflexive* $=_{df}$ ~$(\forall x)Rxx$

Relation R is *nonsymmetric* $=_{df}$ ~$(\forall x)(\forall y)(Rxy \supset Ryx)$

Relation R is *nontransitive* $=_{df}$ ~$(\forall x)(\forall y)(\forall z)((Rxy \mathbin{\&} Ryz) \supset Rxz)$

Relations can also be nonreflexive, nonsymmetric, and nontransitive.

These forms codify, first, the idea that R is nonreflexive. A relation is nonreflexive if it is not the case that everything bears relation R toward itself. An example is being honest, if we suppose that not all persons are honest with themselves. For R to be nonsymmetric is for it not to be the case that everything is such that if it bears R to something else, then that thing bears R to it. The honesty example works here as well, where, unfortunately, it is not the case that everyone who is honest with another person is treated honestly by that person. Another example is being friendly to, where obviously it is not true that everyone who is friendly to another person has their friendliness returned. A relation R is nontransitive if it is not the case that of any three objects, if the first bears R to the second, and the second to the third, then the first also bears R to the third. An example is admiring, where from the fact that someone admires another person, and that person admires a third, it does not logically follow that the first person admires the third.

The contraries of the three basic relation types are:

Relation R is *irreflexive* $=_{df}$ $(\forall x)$~Rxx

Relation R is *asymmetric* $=_{df}$ $(\forall x)(\forall y)(Rxy \supset$ ~$Ryx)$

Relation R is *intransitive* $=_{df}$ $(\forall x)(\forall y)(\forall z)((Rxy \mathbin{\&} Ryz) \supset$ ~$Rxz)$

Relations can also be irreflexive, asymmetric, and intransitive.

Contrary relations are those in which objects more definitely are such that if they satisfy certain conditions, then the relation does not hold. An example is the irreflexive relation of being older than, since nothing is older than itself. A relation is asymmetric if it is such that for any two objects, if the relation holds between the first and second, then the relation definitely does not hold (not that it merely does not follow that it holds) between the second and the first. An example is the relation of being taller than, where if anything is taller than another thing, that thing is definitely not taller than the first. A relation is intransitive if, for any three objects, if the first bears the relation to the second, and the second bears the relation to the third, the first object definitely does not bear the relation to the third. An example is the relation of being the mother of, where, of any three objects, if the first is the mother of the second, and the second is the mother of the third, the first most definitely is not the mother (but is rather the grandmother) of the third. Another example is the relation of being immediately to the left (or right) of, where, of any three objects, if the first is immediately to the left (or right) of the second, and the second is immediately to the left (or right) of the third, then the first is definitely not immediately to the left (or right) of the third because the second thing by hypothesis is always between the first and third.

There are interesting logical relationships among different categories of relations.

The theory of relations we have sketched can be used to demonstrate some interesting logical interrelations among the 12 categories of relations. The definitions make it possible to prove the following theorems of relation theory. The truth trees have been omitted, but they can be completed for extra practice to confirm that each of the following wffs about relations is a tautology of predicate logic:

R1   ⊢ $(\forall x)(\exists y)Rxy \supset (\exists y)(\exists x)Rxy$

1	1.	$(\forall x)(\exists y)Rxy$	A ($\supset$I)
1	2.	$(\exists y)Ray$	1 $\forall$E
3	3.	Rab	A ($\exists$E)
3	4.	$(\exists x)Rxb$	3 $\exists$I
3	5.	$(\exists y)(\exists x)Rxy$	4 $\exists$I
1	6.	$(\exists y)(\exists x)Rxy$	2, 3–5 $\exists$E
	7.	$(\forall x)(\exists y)Rxy \supset (\exists y)(\exists x)Rxy$	1–6 $\supset$I

This proof establishes a basic quantifier implication and distribution consequence for relations. Next, we prove that if R is asymmetric, then R is irreflexive:

R2   ⊢ $(\forall x)(\forall y)(Rxy \supset {\sim}Ryx) \supset (\forall x){\sim}Rxx$

1	1.	$(\forall x)(\forall y)(Rxy \supset {\sim}Ryx)$	A ($\supset$I)
2	2.	Raa	A (${\sim}$IE)
1	3.	$(\forall y)(Ray \supset {\sim}Rya)$	1 $\forall$E
1	4.	Raa $\supset$ ${\sim}$Raa	3 $\forall$E
1, 2	5.	${\sim}$Raa	2, 4 $\supset$E
1	6.	${\sim}$Raa	2–5 ${\sim}$IE
1	7.	$(\forall x){\sim}Rxx$	6 $\forall$I
	8.	$(\forall x)(\forall y)(Rxy \supset {\sim}Ryx) \supset (\forall x){\sim}Rxx$	1–7 $\supset$I

Here, we demonstrate that if R is intransitive, then it is irreflexive:

R3 ⊢ $(\forall x)(\forall y)(\forall z)((Rxy \& Ryx) \supset \sim Rxz) \supset (\forall x)\sim Rxx$

1	1.	$(\forall x)(\forall y)(\forall z)((Rxy \& Ryx) \supset \sim Rxz)$	A ($\supset$I)
2	2.	Raa	A ($\sim$IE)
1	3.	$(\forall y)(\forall z)((Ray \& Rya) \supset \sim Raz)$	1 $\forall$E
1	4.	$(\forall z)((Raa \& Raa) \supset \sim Raz)$	3 $\forall$E
1	5.	$(Raa \& Raa) \supset \sim Raa$	4 $\forall$E
2	6.	Raa & Raa	2, 2 &I
1, 2	7.	$\sim$Raa	5, 6 $\supset$E
1	8.	$\sim$Raa	2–7 $\sim$IE
1	9.	$(\forall x)\sim Rxx$	8 $\forall$I
	10.	$(\forall x)(\forall y)(\forall z)((Rxy \& Ryx) \supset \sim Rxz) \supset$ $(\forall x)\sim Rxx$	1–9 $\supset$I

Now we prove that if R is any reflexive relation, then it is not the case that R is intransitive:

R4 ⊢ $(\forall x)Rxx \supset \sim(\forall x)(\forall y)(\forall z)((Rxy \& Ryz) \supset \sim Rxy)$

1	1.	$(\forall x)Rxx$	A ($\supset$I)
2	2.	$(\forall x)(\forall y)(\forall z)((Rxy \& Ryz) \supset$ $\sim Rxy)$	A ($\sim$IE)
1	3.	Raa	1 $\forall$E
1	4.	Raa & Raa	3, 3 &I
2	5.	$(\forall y)(\forall z)((Ray \& Ryz) \supset \sim Ray)$	2 $\forall$E
2	6.	$(\forall z)((Raa \& Raz) \supset \sim Raa)$	5 $\forall$E
2	7.	$(Raa \& Raa) \supset \sim Raa$	6 $\forall$E
1, 2	8.	$\sim$Raa	4, 7 &E
1	9.	$\sim(\forall x)(\forall y)(\forall z)((Rxy \& Ryz) \supset$ $\sim Rxy)$	2–8 $\sim$IE
	10.	$(\forall x)Rxx \supset \sim(\forall x)(\forall y)(\forall z)((Rxy \&$ $Ryz) \supset \sim Rxy)$	1–9 $\supset$I

The formal theory of relations is an example of applied predicate logic.

We conclude with a more complicated proof of the theorem that relation R does not hold between any two objects if and only if R is both symmetric and asymmetric:

R5   ⊢ (∀x)(∀y)~Rxy ≡ ((∀x)(∀y)(Rxy ⊃ Ryx) & (∀x)(∀y)(Rxy ⊃ ~Ryx))

1	1.	(∀x)(∀y)~Rxy	A (≡I)
2	2.	Rab	A (⊃I)
3	3.	~Rba	A (~IE)
1	4.	(∀y)~Ray	1 ∀E
1	5.	~Rab	4 ∀E
2	6.	Rab	2 R
1	7.	Rba	3–6 ~IE
1	8.	Rab ⊃ Rba	2–8 ⊃I
1	9.	(∀y)(Ray ⊃ Rya)	8 ∀I
1	10.	(∀x)(∀y)(Rxy ⊃ Ryx)	9 ∀I
11	11.	Rab	A (⊃I)
12	12.	Rba	A (~IE)
11	13.	Rab	11 R
1	14.	(∀y)~Ray	1 ∀E
1	15.	~Rab	1 ∀E
1, 11	16.	~Rba	12–15 ~IE
1	17.	Rab ⊃ ~Rba	11–16 ⊃I
1	18.	(∀y)(Ray ⊃ ~Rya)	17 ∀I
1	19.	(∀x)(∀y)(Rxy ⊃ ~Ryx)	18 ∀I
1	20.	(∀x)(∀y)(Rxy ⊃ Ryx) & (∀x)(∀y)(Rxy ⊃ ~Ryx)	10, 19 &I
21	21.	(∀x)(∀y)(Rxy ⊃ Ryx) & (∀x)(∀y)(Rxy ⊃ ~Ryx)	A (≡I)
22	22.	Rab	A (~IE)
21	23.	(∀x)(∀y)(Rxy ⊃ Ryx)	21 &E
21	24.	(∀y)(Ray ⊃ Rya)	23 ∀E
21	25.	Rab ⊃ Rba	24 ∀E
21, 22	26.	Rba	22, 25 ⊃E
21	27.	(∀x)(∀y)(Rxy ⊃ ~Ryx)	21 &E
21	28.	(∀y)(Ray ⊃ ~Rya)	27 ∀E
21	29.	Rab ⊃ ~Rba	28 ∀E
21, 22	30.	~Rba	22, 29 ⊃E
21	31.	~Rab	22–30 ~IE
21	32.	(∀y)~Ray	31 ∀I
21	33.	(∀x)(∀y)~Rxy	32 ∀I
	34.	(∀x)(∀y)~Rxy ≡ ((∀x)(∀y)(Rxy ⊃ Ryx) & (∀x)(∀y)(Rxy ⊃ ~Ryx))	1–20, 21–33 ≡I

To Check Your Understanding 8.10 ━━━━━━━━━━━━━━━━━━━━━━━━━━━━━━━━━━━ ∎

Use the predicate intelim rules ∀E, ∃I, ∀I, and ∃E, together with propositional rules, to give natural deduction proofs of the following logical consequences of the theory of relations presented previously, any proposition of which can be added as a given assumption in proofs of the following propositions and argument sequents; do the truth tree for each first for extra practice, and explain what each theorem states in ordinary English:

1. ⊢ (∀x)(∀y)~Rxy ⊃ (∃x)~Rxx
2. ⊢ ~(∃x)Rxx ∨ ~(∀x)(∀y)(Rxy ⊃ ~Ryx)
3. ⊢ (∀x)Rxx ⊃ (∀x)(∀y)(∀z)((Rxy & Ryz) ⊃ Rxy)
4. ⊢ (∀x)(∀y)(∀z)((Rxy & Ryz) ⊃ Rxz) ⊃ ((∃x)~Rxx ∨ ~(∀x)(∀y)(Rxy ⊃ ~Ryx))
5. ⊢ ((∀x)(∀y)(∀z)((Rxy & Ryz) ⊃ Rxz) & (∀x)(∀y)(∀z)((Rxy & Ryz) ⊃ ~Rxz)) ⊃ (∀x)(∀y)(Rxy ⊃ ~Ryx)
6. ⊢ (∀x)(∀y)(∀z)~(Rxy & Ryz) ≡ ((∀x)(∀y)(∀z)((Rxy & Ryz) ⊃ Rxz) & (∀x)(∀y)(∀z)((Rxy & Ryz) ⊃ ~Rxz))

━━━ ∎

Identity

Identity is a particular kind of relation that can be defined in predicate logic.

Using predicate logic, we can apply definitions of the basic types of relations to characterize interesting relations. Here, we use predicate logic to advance a formal theory of *identity*. The theory might be developed to make many assertions about identity, including—what on reflection seems intuitively correct—that the identity relation is reflexive, symmetric, and transitive. The logic of relations permits the following statement as an extralogical foundation of a formal theory of identity:

$$(\forall x)(\forall y)(\forall z)((Ixx \ \& \ (Ixy \supset Iyx)) \ \& \ ((Ixy \ \& \ Iyz) \supset Ixz))$$

We can also write this formula in terms of the more familiar identity predicate:

$$(\forall x)(\forall y)(\forall z)((x = x \ \& \ (x = y \supset y = x) \ \& \ ((x = y \ \& \ y = z) \supset x = z))$$

To understand the relational structure of identity has applications in many problems involving identity. We need a definition to explain the conditions by

*Identity relations
are important in
mathematics and
philosophy.*

which any objects x and y are identical. Let predicates 'F^1', . . . , 'F^n' include any one of infinitely many complete and consistent sets of all the unary properties or their complements (or more narrowly selected subsets thereof) available for predication to any objects. Then the identity relation is symbolized as a version of *Leibniz's law (of the identity of indiscernibles and indiscernibility of identicals)*, using predicate logic, in the following biconditional:

$$(\forall x)(\forall y)(x = y \equiv ((F^1x \ \& \ F^2x \ \& \ . . . \ \& \ F^nx) \equiv (F^1y \ \& \ F^2y \ \& \ . . . \ \& \ F^ny)))$$

The proposition states that x and y are identical if and only if they share all their properties in common. An object is rightly judged identical if there are no differences in the properties truly predicated of it, whereas different objects are rightly judged nonidentical if even one property of one object is not a property of the other.

If reference to the set of propositions F^{1}a & F^{2}b & . . . & F^{n}c seems too imprecise, we may wish to quantify over properties, just as we now quantify over ordinary objects, by writing $(\forall \varphi)(. . . \varphi . . .)$ when we need to speak of *all* properties and $(\exists \varphi)(. . . \varphi . . .)$ when we need to speak of *some* properties or at least one property. We can see from previous arguments about the irreducibility of $(\forall x)Fx$ to Fa & Fb & . . . & Fn and of $(\exists x)Fx$ to Fa ∨ Fb ∨ . . . ∨ Fn that the previous symbolization will not be appropriate if there are infinitely many objects or if we need to add that a, b, . . . , n are all the objects. If these

*A first-order logic per-
mits the predication of
properties only to ob-
jects; a second-order
or higher order logic
permits the predica-
tion of properties to
other properties.*

conditions apply, then we must make the move from the predicate logic we have developed so far as a *first-order logic*—a predicate logic in which properties can be predicated of objects, but properties cannot be predicated of other properties—to a *second-order* or *higher order logic,* in which properties can be predicated of objects and properties.

The ascent to a higher order logic, in which objects and properties can be quantified over, permits the following more compact formalization of Leibniz's principle of the identity of indiscernibles and indiscernibility of identicals:

$$(\forall x)(\forall y)(x = y \equiv (\forall \varphi)(\varphi x \equiv \varphi y))$$

*The predicate logic
we have developed is
a first-order logic.*

We shall not try to explain all the rules that might be needed in order to work with wffs in higher order logic. For present purposes, it will suffice to permit the introduction and elimination of higher order quantifications over properties by intelim rules that exactly parallel the rules for first-order quantifications over objects. Thus, we shall say, without trying to develop a new logical system for the inference, that from $(\forall \varphi)\varphi a$ we can validly infer Fa, Ga, Ha, and the like, and from Fa we can validly infer $(\exists \varphi)\varphi a$, and so on.

To Check Your Understanding 8.11 ──────────────────────────────────■

Use the predicate intelim rules $\forall E$, $\exists I$, $\forall I$, and $\exists E$, together with propositional rules and Leibniz's law, to give natural deduction proofs of the following logical consequences of the identity theory presented previously, any proposition of which can be added as a given assumption in proofs of the following propositions and argument sequents:

1. $(\forall x)(x = x)$
2. $(\forall x)(\exists y)(x = y)$
3. $(\forall x)(\forall y)(x = y \supset y = x)$
4. $(\forall x)(\forall y)(x = y \equiv y = x)$
5. $(\forall x)(\forall y)((x = y \ \& \ Fx) \supset Fy)$
6. $(\forall x)(\forall y)(x = y \supset (Fx \equiv Fy))$
7. $(\forall x)(\forall y)((x = y \ \& \sim Fx) \supset \sim Fy)$
8. $(\forall x)(\forall y)((x = y \ \& \ y = z) \supset x = z)$
9. $(\forall x)(\forall y)(x = y \equiv (\forall \varphi)(\varphi x \equiv \varphi y)) \supset (\forall x)(\forall y)(\forall \varphi)(x = y \supset (\varphi x \equiv \varphi y))$

■

Specific Numbers of Objects

Identity can be used in predicate logic to symbolize predications to specific numbers of objects.

We can use identity relations to symbolize predications to specific numbers of objects. If we want to express the proposition that exactly one object has property F, we can do so by using predicate logic with identity to state that something or at least one thing x has property F, and that anything else y has property F if and only if it is identical to x. Anything that might also be thought to have property F is thereby said to be identical with only one object. The predication of property F to exactly one object can then be formulated as follows:

Exactly one F:
$(\exists x)(Fx \ \& \ (\forall y)(Fy \equiv x = y))$

To say that no more than two objects have property F, we similarly write:

No more than two F's:
$(\exists x)(\exists y)((Fx \ \& \ Fy) \ \& \ (\forall z)(Fz \equiv (x = z \lor y = z)))$

Here, because we are speaking of two objects, we must say that there is at least one thing, x, that has property F, and there is at least one thing, y, that has property F, and that anything else, z, has property F if and only if it is identical either to x or to y. Anything that might be thought to have property F is thereby said to be identical to either one of the existentially quantified objects already said to have property F. The formula, however, does not yet express the proposition that exactly two objects have property F. For all it says about there being at least one object, x, that has property F and at least one object, y, that has property F, it might be the case that x is the same object as y. To rule out this possibility, and thereby express the proposition that exactly two objects or that no less than two and no more than two objects have property F, we must add a clause to the previous formula that states that existentially quantified objects x and y are not identical. For convenience, we can write $a \neq b$ instead of $\sim Iab$ on the strength of the equivalence that $(\forall x)(\forall y)(x \neq y \equiv \sim Ixy)$.

Exactly two F's:
$(\exists x)(\exists y)(((Fx \ \& \ Fy) \ \& \ x \neq y) \ \& \ (\forall z)(Fz \equiv (x = z \lor y = z)))$

Exactly n objects, and no more than n objects, can be said to have a certain property, for any number n.

The method is easily generalized to predicate a property to no more than, and to exactly, any chosen number of objects. To represent the predication of F to no more than three objects, we need an expression, like the previous one, for no more than two objects with property F but that contains three predication conjuncts and three identity disjuncts. To represent the predication of F to exactly three objects, we need an expression, like the previous one, for exactly two objects with property F but with three predication conjuncts, three nonidentity conjuncts, and three identity disjuncts. Then we have:

No more than three F's:
$(\exists w)(\exists x)(\exists y)(((Fx \ \& \ Fx) \ \& \ Fy) \ \& \ (\forall z)(Fz \equiv ((w = x \lor x = z) \lor y = z)))$

Exactly three F's:
$(\exists w)(\exists x)(\exists y)((((Fx \ \& \ Fx) \ \& \ Fy) \ \& \ ((w \neq x \ \& \ w \neq y) \ \& \ x \neq y)) \ \& \ (\forall z)(Fz \equiv ((w = x \lor x = z) \lor y = z)))$

To see how the method can be fully generalized for any predications of a property F to no more than and to exactly any specific number of objects n, we can formulate predicate expressions involving an extended range of quantifiers, conjunctions, and disjunctions with the identity relation as follows:

No more than n F's:
$(\exists x_1) \ldots (\exists x_n)((Fx_1 \ \& \ldots \ \& \ Fx_n) \ \&$
$(\forall x_{n+1})(Fx_{n+1} \equiv (x_1 = x_{n+1} \lor \ldots \lor x_n = x_{n+1})))$

Exactly n F's:

$(\exists x_1) \ldots (\exists x_n)(((Fx_1 \& \ldots \& Fx_n) \& (x_1 \neq x_2 \& \ldots \& x_{n-1} \neq x_n)) \&$
$(\forall x_{n+1})(Fx_{n+1} \equiv (x_1 = x_{n+1} \lor \ldots \lor x_n = x_{n+1})))$

Definite Description

Predicate logic can be used to symbolize a formal theory of definite description.

Predicate logic has a philosophically interesting application to the analysis of *definite descriptions* in ordinary language. A definite description is a proposition in which an object is singled out as uniquely satisfying a description of its properties.

In English, definite descriptions are most commonly expressed by means of the definite article 'the'. The presence of the article by itself does not necessarily indicate a definite description. Definite description is more a matter of a specific use of the definite article than a general feature. 'The time has come to act', 'The Yankees won the pennant', and 'The king of France is bald' all attribute properties to definitely described objects. We represent definite descriptions in predicate logic by combining the identity relation with quantifiers to express the uniqueness of definitely described objects.

Bertrand Russell, in his 1905 essay "On Denoting," provides a powerful analysis of definite descriptions. Russell applies predicate logic to symbolize definite descriptions in ordinary language, which he formalizes by means of predication, negation, and identity. To symbolize the unanalyzed *definite description operator* or *descriptor,* Russell introduces the inverted Greek letter iota, 'ι'. This is a special quantifier, which Russell defines in predicate logic. To symbolize 'The king of France is bald', Russell offers the following statement:

$B(\iota x)Kxf$

Identity expressions for exactly one object having a certain property symbolize the uniqueness implied by a definite description.

Russell proposes a three-part analysis of the expression. The three conditions are an *existence* requirement, a *uniqueness* requirement, and the *predication* of a property to the actually existent unique entity identified in the first two conditions. *The* object satisfying a certain description by this account is the *one and only object* that satisfies the description. Definite descriptions can be analyzed by the method described previously as the predication of a property to a specific number of objects, and in particular to exactly one definitely described object. To represent the analysis with all three conditions, Russell offers a statement that we might formulate in our development of predicate logic as follows:

$B(\iota x)Kxf \equiv (\exists x)(Kxf \& (\forall y)((Kyf \equiv x = y) \& Bx))$

According to Russell's analysis, B(ꓕx)Kxf is false because there exists no king of France. This addresses one of several philosophical problems for which Russell advanced his theory of definite descriptions. To say that B(ꓕx)Kxf is true implies that there is a king of France, and that he is bald. To deny that B(ꓕx)Kxf is true suggests, if it does not actually imply, that there is a king of France, and he is not bald. Russell further exploits an ambiguity in the scope of the negation in these predicate wffs to distinguish between falsely saying that the king of France is bald and falsely saying that the king of France is not bald and truly saying, on the grounds that the king of France does not exist, that it is not the case (or it is false) that the king of France is bald. We do not want to symbolize 'The king of France is not bald' in such a way that the proposition turns out to be a true predication of the property of being bald to a real existent and currently reigning king of France, nor in such a way that the proposition cannot be understood as contradicting the proposition that 'The king of France is bald'. The difference in placement of the negation, and therefore in the scope of the negation operator, in Russell's solution appears in two different ways of symbolizing 'The king of France is not bald':

$$\sim(\exists x)(Kxf \,\&\, (\forall y)((Kyf \equiv x = y) \,\&\, Bx)) \quad \boxed{\text{TRUE}}$$
$$(\exists x)(Kxf \,\&\, (\forall y)((Kyf \equiv x = y) \,\&\, \sim Bx)) \quad \boxed{\text{FALSE}}$$

To Check Your Understanding 8.12 —————————————————————————————————————■

Use Russell's theory of definite descriptions in predicate logic to symbolize and evaluate the truth or falsehood of the following propositions, formally distinguishing ambiguities in the scope of negation as necessary:

1. The winged horse flies.
2. The winged horse does not fly.
3. The winged horse is mythological.
4. The winged horse is not mythological.
5. The mythological winged horse exists.
6. The mythological winged horse does not exist.

                                                                                    ■

Deductive Incompleteness

In Chapter 7, we remarked that there is no effective decision method for predicate logic by which any arbitrary wff can be shown to be a tautology or not a tautology nor any arbitrary sequent can be shown to be deductively valid or invalid.

The deductive incompleteness of predicate logic, like the limitations of predicate truth trees, is more a matter of theoretical interest than a practical restriction on the use of predicate natural deduction in actual applications; any tautology and any deductively valid sequent of predicate logic can be identified by predicate truth trees and proved by predicate natural deduction rules.

The same limitations that apply to decision methods for predicate logic also apply to predicate natural deduction proofs. The undecidable wffs of predicate logic are deductively unprovable, and they enter into sequents that cannot be proven or disproven in any logically consistent predicate deductive proof system. Yet any wff or sequent that is shown to be a tautology or a deductively valid inference of predicate logic can be proven by predicate natural deduction proofs. As noted at the end of Chapter 7, the undecidable wffs and sequents of predicate logic are highly specialized constructions, and we can proceed with the courage that, despite the logic's theoretical limitations, any predicate tautology or deductively valid predicate sequent is decidable by predicate truth trees and provable by predicate natural deduction rules. The gray area that prevents predicate logic from being decidable and deductively complete is not a practical limitation on ordinary uses of the rules for trees and proofs in analyzing the logic of predicate wffs and sequents.

Summary: Predicate Natural Deduction Proofs

In this chapter, we learned to give natural deduction proofs for tautologies and valid sequents in predicate logic. The 12 proof rules of propositional logic are supplemented by 4 new intelim rules for predicate logic. There are introduction and elimination rules for universal and existential quantifiers. Some of the rules have restrictions in working with quantifiers and constants that must be observed in order to avoid invalid inferences. Predicate proofs can be used to study problems of philosophical interest, including the barber paradox, Plato's recounting of Socrates' argument that virtue cannot be taught, Maximus Tyrius' argument that there can be no injustice, and the formal theory of relations, identity, and definite description. The undecidability of predicate logic, and its lack of effective decision methods, is also reflected in the logic's deductive incompleteness as a limitation on predicate natural deduction proofs. As with the limitations on predicate truth trees, the deductive incompleteness of predicate logic is of more abstract theoretical interest than a practical obstacle to working through ordinary proofs.

Key Words

predicate natural deduction proof
predicate intelim rules
universal elimination ($\forall$E)
existential introduction ($\exists$I)
universal introduction ($\forall$I)
existential elimination ($\exists$E)
restriction on a predicate intelim
   rule (for $\forall$I and $\exists$E)
unrestricted predicate intelim rule
   ($\forall$E and $\exists$I)
active part of a proof or subproof
uniform replacement of quantifier
   bound object variables by an
   object constant
selective replacement of quantifier
   bound object variables by an
   object constant
fundamental heuristic
excluded middle
relation
reflexive relation
symmetric relation

transitive relation
nonreflexive relation
nonsymmetric relation
nontransitive relation
complementary relation
irreflexive relation
asymmetric relation
intransitive relation
contrary relation
identity
Leibniz's law
identity of indiscernibles
indiscernibility of identicals
first-order logic
second-order logic
higher order logic
definite description
definite description operator
   (descriptor) ($\imath$x).
existence condition
uniqueness condition
predication

Exercises

I: Predicate Proof Concepts   Give a correct concise statement of each of the following concepts; where appropriate, give an illustration of each that does not appear in the book:

1. Natural deduction proof in predicate logic

2. Predicate intelim rules

3. Selective substitution of a constant for an existentially bound variable

4. Reflexive (nonreflexive, irreflexive) relation

5. Symmetric (nonsymmetric, asymmetric) relation

6. Transitive (nontransitive, intransitive) relation

7. Leibniz's law of the identity of indiscernibles and indiscernibility of identicals

8. Definite description theory

9. Uniqueness of definitely described object

10. Deductive incompleteness of predicate logic

II: *Proofs of Valid Sequents*   Give natural deduction proofs for the following valid argument sequents in predicate logic; for extra practice, verify by truth tree method that each sequent is valid before proceeding to its proof:

1. $(\forall x)(Fx \equiv Gx) \vdash (\exists x)Fx \equiv (\exists x)Gx$

2. $(\forall x)(Fx \equiv Gx) \vdash (\forall x)Fx \equiv (\forall x)Gx$

3. $(\forall x)(Fx \vee {\sim}Gx) \vdash {\sim}(\exists x)({\sim}Fx \mathbin{\&} Gx)$

4. $(\exists x)(Fx \mathbin{\&} {\sim}Gx), (\forall x)(Fx \supset Hx) \vdash (\exists x)({\sim}Gx \mathbin{\&} Hx)$

5. $(\forall x)(\forall y)(Hxy \supset Fx), (\exists x)(\exists y)Hxy \vdash (\exists x)Fx$

6. $(\forall x)(Fx \supset Gx), Fa, (\exists x)Gx \supset (\forall x)(Fx \supset {\sim}Hx) \vdash (\exists x){\sim}Hx$

7. $(\forall x)({\sim}(\forall y)Hxy \supset (\forall y)((\forall z)Hyz \mathbin{\&} Hxy)) \vdash (\exists x)(\forall y)Hxy$

8. $(\forall x)(\forall y)(Hxy \supset Fx), (\forall x)(\forall y)(Fx \supset Gxy) \vdash (\forall x)Hxa \supset (\exists x)Gbx$

9. ${\sim}(\exists x)Hxa, (\forall x)({\sim}Txb \supset Hbx) \vdash (\exists x)Txb$

10. $(\forall x)(Fx \supset (Gx \mathbin{\&} {\sim}Hx)), (\forall x)(Kx \supset Fx) \vdash (\forall x)Kx \supset (\exists x)(Fx \mathbin{\&} Gx)$

11. $(\forall x)({\sim}(\exists y)({\sim}Fx \mathbin{\&} Hyx) \mathbin{\&} {\sim}(\exists y)Hxy), (\forall x)(\forall y)(Hxy \vee Hyx) \vdash (\exists x)Fx$

12. $(\exists x)Fx, (\exists x)(Gx \vee Kx), (\exists x)Gx \supset (\forall y)(Fy \supset Ky) \vdash (\exists z)Kz$

13. ${\sim}(\exists x)Fx \supset (\exists x){\sim}Gx \vdash (\forall x)Gx \supset ((\exists x)Fx \mathbin{\&} (\forall x)Gx)$

14. $(\forall x)(Fx \supset Gx), (\exists x)Gx \supset (\forall y)(Fy \supset Ky) \vdash (\forall z)Fz \supset (\forall z)Kz$

15. ${\sim}(\exists x)Fx, (\forall x)Gx \vdash (\forall y){\sim}({\sim}Gy \equiv {\sim}Fy)$

16. $(\forall x)((Fx \vee Gx) \supset (Hx \mathbin{\&} Ix)), (\exists x){\sim}(Hx \mathbin{\&} Ix) \vdash {\sim}(\forall x)Gx$

17. $(\forall x)(Fx \supset Gx) \vdash (\forall x)((\forall y)(Gy \supset Hxy) \supset (\forall z)(Fz \supset Hxz))$

18. $(\forall x)(\forall y)((\exists z)Tyz \supset Txy) \vdash (\forall x)(\exists y)Txy \supset (\forall x)(\forall y)Txy$

19. $(\exists x)(\forall y)Ryx, (\forall x)(\forall y)(Rxy \supset {\sim}Txy), (\forall x)(Sx \supset (\exists y)Tyx) \vdash {\sim}(\forall y)Sy$

20. $(\forall x)(Gx \supset (\forall y)(Hxy \supset Dy)), (\exists x)(Gx \mathbin{\&} (\forall y)(Fy \supset Hxy)) \vdash (\forall x)(Fx \supset Dx)$

III: *Proofs of Tautologies*   Give natural deduction proofs for the following tautologies in predicate logic; for extra practice, verify by truth tree method that each proposition is a tautology before proceeding to its proof:

1. $\vdash (\forall x)(Fx \supset Fx)$

2. $\vdash (\forall x)(Fx \vee {\sim}Fx)$

3. $\vdash (\forall x){\sim}(Fx \mathbin{\&} {\sim}Fx)$

4. ⊢ (∀y)((∀x)Fx ⊃ Fy)

5. ⊢ (∃x)((∃y)Fy ⊃ Fx)

6. ⊢ (∃y)(Fy ⊃ (∃x)Fx)

7. ⊢ (∀x)(∀y)Rxy ⊃ (∃x)Rxx

8. ⊢ ~(∀x)(Fx ≡ Gx) ∨ ((∃x)Fx ≡ (∃x)Gx)

9. ⊢ (∃x)(Fx ≡ ~Gx) ∨ ((∃x)~Fx ≡ (∃x)~Gx)

10. ⊢ (∃x)(∀y)(Fy ⊃ Gxy) ⊃ (∀x)(Fx ⊃ (∃y)Gyx))

11. ⊢ (∀x)(∀y)(Fxy ≡ (∀z)(Gxz ≡ Gyz)) ⊃ (∀x)Fxx

12. ⊢ (∀x)(Fx ⊃ Gx) ⊃ (∀x)~(Fx & ~Gx)

13. ⊢ (∀x)Fx ⊃ ~(∃y)(∀x)(Gxy ≡ (Fx & ~Gxx))

14. ⊢ ~(∃x)(Fx & (Ga ⊃ Ha)) ≡ ((~Ga ∨ Ha) ⊃ ~(∃x)Fx)

15. ⊢ (∃x)((Fx & ~Gx) ∨ ~Gx) ⊃ (∃y)((Fy ∨ ~Gy) & ~Gy)

16. ⊢ (∀x)(Fx ⊃ Gx) ⊃ (∀y)((∃z)(Fz & Hyz) ⊃ (∃z)(Gz & Hyz))

17. ⊢ ~(∀z)((∃y)(Fy & Hzy) ⊃ (∃y)(Gy & Hzy)) ⊃ ~(∀x)(Fx ⊃ Gx)

18. ⊢ (∀x)(∀y)(Fxy ≡ (∀z)(Gxz ≡ Gyz)) ⊃ (∀x)(∀y)(∀z)((Fxz & Fyz) ⊃ Fxz)

19. ⊢ ((∀x)(∀y)(Rxy ⊃ Ryx) & (∀x)(∀y)(∀z)((Rxy & Ryz) ⊃ Rxz)) ⊃ (∀x)(∀y)(Rxy ⊃ Rxx)

20. ⊢ (((∃x)Fx ⊃ (∃x)(Fx & Gx)) & (~(∃x)(Fx & Gx) ⊃ (∃x)Fx)) ⊃ (∃x)(Fx & Gx)

IV: Proofs of Valid Argument Sequents from Ordinary Language   Symbolize each of the following valid arguments in predicate logic, verify by truth tree method the validity of your translation (adjusting if necessary to make the symbolization valid), and then give a natural deduction proof of the sequent:

1. All poets are dreamers. Some poets are romantics. Thus, some romantics are dreamers. (P, D, R)

2. Some Cretans are liars. But all Scythians are non-Cretans. Hence, some liars are not Scythians. (C, L, S)

3. Some friends are loyal to the bitter end. All friends are reliable when the chips are down. Therefore, some who are loyal to the bitter end are reliable when the chips are down. (F, L, R, C, D)

4. Every honcho is a both a honcho and a bigwig. Some nonbigwigs are movers and shakers. So, it follows immediately that some movers and shakers are nonhonchos. (H, B, M, S)

5. Everything is either an unconscious or immaterial entity. All sentient beings, if they are physically embodied, are material entities. Hence, no sentient physically embodied beings are conscious. (C, M, E, S, B, P)

6. Something is rotten in the state of Denmark only if all 3-day-old herrings are putrifying. There are at least some 3-day-old herrings if there are at least some 3-day-old mackerels. Thus, we may conclude that something rotten in the state of Denmark is a 3-day-old mackerel only if something is putrefying. (R, T, H, P, M, d)

7. No Buicks are Cadillacs. All Jeep Cherokees are non-Cadillacs. So, all Jeep Cherokees or Buicks are non-Cadillacs. (B, J, C)

8. All and only bachelors are unmarried male adults. From this it follows that everything is a bachelor if and only if everything is an unmarried male adult. (B, U, M, A)

9. There are sure to be some camellias or some flowers in the garden. All camellias are themselves flowers. Therefore, there are sure to be some flowers in the garden. (C, F)

10. All greengrocers are turdmerchants. Some lackadaisical greengrocers are couch potatoes. Necessarily, then, some among the lackadaisical are couch potato turdmerchants. (G, T, L, C)

11. Not everyone has the good fortune to come from Corinth. There are metaphysicians or there are epistemologists only if all have the good fortune to come from Corinth. Thus, there are no metaphysicians. (C, M, E)

12. Everything depends on something. All things that depend on everything are sustained by them. Everything that sustains all things depends on them. Therefore, there is something that sustains and is sustained by something. (D, S)

13. All treaties with the Lakota nation are to be honored. Thus, whatever is not to be honored is not a treaty with the Lakota nation, and everything is either not a treaty with the Lakota nation or it is to be honored. (T, H, l)

14. There are ghosts if and only if all ghosts or spectres are just figments of the imagination. Something is just a figment of the imagination. But not everything fails to be a ghost. Therefore, some ghosts are just figments of the imagination. (G, S, F, I)

15. Something is costly and something is free. Something is prohibitively expensive only if nothing is free. As a result, nothing is prohibitively expensive. (C, F, P)

16. All schnauzers are prize dogs and champion hunters if they are properly trained. Ralph is a schnauzer. Therefore, there is something that if properly trained is a champion hunter. (S, P, D, C, H, T, r)

17. If Annie is elected, then everything we worked to achieve in the last 4 years will be destroyed. Either Annie or Sara will be elected. But it's definitely not going to be Sara. Whatever is destroyed must be rebuilt from scratch. Hence, everything we worked to achieve in the last 4 years must be rebuilt from scratch. (E, W, D, R, a, s)

18. All giraffes are long-necked mammals of the African plains. Therefore, the tonsils of a giraffe are the tonsils of a long-necked mammal of the African plains. (G, L, M, P, T, a)

19. Either no multimillionaires are truly happy and satisfied with their lives, or some persons are dissatisfied with their lives. But everyone, at some level, is satisfied with his or her life. Therefore, all multimillionaires are dissatisfied with their lives. (M, H, S, L, P)

20. Some friends of Andy are acquaintances of Barbara and Andy. All acquaintances of some neighbors of Andy and of Andy are not mathematicians. Hence, if all friends of Andy are mathematicians, then Barbara is a neighbor of Andy. (F, A, N, M, a, b)

V: Proofs of Valid Argument Sequents and Tautologies from Previous Exercises
Give natural deduction proofs of all the propositions and argument sequents from Chapter 7's final exercises that were determined by truth tree method to be tautologies or logically valid inferences in predicate logic.

VI: Short Answer Questions for Philosophical Reflection

1. Are properties also objects? Why or why not?

2. What is a relation? Can all n-ary relations be understood as unary relational qualities, or are there fundamentally irreducible relations that hold between many objects?

3. Is identity a logical or extralogical relation? Does it belong more properly to logic and mathematics or to metaphysics?

4. Can abstract logic be used to prove the nonexistence of a particular kind of barber (one who shaves all and only those persons who do not shave themselves)? Why or why not? What are the metaphysical implications of existence proofs or disproofs in formal symbolic logic?

5. Can an expressively complete first-order predicate logic manage without referring and truly predicating properties to definitely described nonexistent objects?

6. Is it possible for definitely described objects such as the winged horse to be unique despite being nonexistent? What are the identity conditions for nonexistent objects in an ontically neutral theory of definite description?

Advanced Topics in Symbolic Logic

Where Do We Go from Here?

If you have enjoyed this introduction to symbolic logic, you may be ready to consider working on advanced topics. There are many interesting possibilities, and the following list is meant only to suggest some of the directions you might pursue.

The skills you have mastered in symbolic logic have prepared you for several types of continuing study. If you decide to investigate the higher reaches of symbolic logic, you can choose from a variety of established areas, according to your preferences. To proceed, you may want to consult other course offerings in the philosophy and mathematics departments at your college or university. You can also read and think about logic on your own, and you may be able to arrange independent study with logicians on special topics that are not included as part of the ordinary curriculum. The following ideas for further inquiry are intended to help you take the next step toward more challenging topics in symbolic logic.

Metatheory

The *metatheory* of symbolic logic describes its *metalogical properties*. The task in beginning metatheory is to define and rigorously demonstrate the scope and limits of symbolic logic. The properties investigated in metatheory include the *syntactical consistency* of propositional and predicate logic, the *semantic soundness,* including *semantic consistency* and *semantic completeness* of propositional and predicate logic, and the *decidability* and *deductive completeness* of propositional logic. Since these properties of propositional and predicate logic are directly connected with the current study, I shall devote more attention to metatheory than to the preview of other advanced topics.

The metatheory of standard symbolic logic features many historically important discoveries. There are proofs to demonstrate the strengths and weaknesses of propositional and predicate logic and metatheorems about the properties of logical deduction and about the size or *cardinality* and other properties of the logic's semantic domain. Logical metatheory not only provides a precise sense of what standard symbolic logic can and cannot do but also introduces powerful new proof methods, such as *mathematical induction* and the *arithmetization of logical syntax,* that are useful in higher level logical inquiry. Mathematical induction is indispensable in metatheory as a way of showing that if a basis of logical constructions has a certain property and, if, where one element in a series of such constructions has the property, then the next element in the series also has the property, then every element in the series has the property. The arithmetization of syntax is a way of coding expressions in a logic's symbolism as numbers so that wffs and sequents can enter proofs of metatheorems more conveniently for certain purposes as numerical values.

There are several categories of metalogical properties. In the history of metatheory, logicians have sometimes reached surprisingly different assessments of the power and limitations of the same logical systems. In recent metatheory, logicians have come to accept a cluster of important metatheoretical results about the metalogical properties of propositional and predicate logic. We cannot explain all these interesting findings here, nor shall we attempt to prove any of them in the rigorous way they are demonstrated in formal metatheory. Instead, we offer an informal description of some of the metalogical properties of propositional and predicate logics, with an emphasis on their implications especially for understanding the limitations of predicate truth trees and predicate natural deduction proofs.

We begin with some basic definitions. A system of logic is syntactically consistent if and only if it does not deductively imply any syntactically inconsistent wffs of the form $\mathbb{P}$ & $\sim\mathbb{P}$. The syntactical inconsistency of a logical system would be an undesirable metalogical property because it would make all the logic's inferences logically unsound, despite being, to their further discredit, trivially deductively valid. This is why syntactical inconsistency is to be avoided and why logicians are interested in testing logical systems for syntactical consistency or inconsistency. Syntactical consistency is not the only important metalogical property because the mere absence of contradictions in a syntactically consistent logic by itself does not prevent the logic from consistently implying contingent falsehoods along with tautologies and deductively valid sequents. Ideally, a system of logic should imply all and only the logical truths the logic is capable of expressing. That is, we also want the logic to be semantically sound.

To be semantically sound, a logic must be semantically consistent and semantically complete. To be semantically consistent, a logic must imply only tautologies and deductively valid sequents, with no inconsistencies, contingent falsehoods, or invalidities whereas to be semantically complete, a logic must imply all tautologies and deductively valid sequents. If a logic is semantically consistent, it does not follow that it is necessarily semantically complete. If a logic is semantically inconsistent, it will be semantically complete only in the trivial sense that it implies all tautologies and deductively valid sequents because it implies all wffs and all sequents. We could prove that a logic is semantically sound if we could prove that it is syntactically consistent, and that within the logic it is possible to prove all and only the logic's tautologies and valid sequents. Then we would know that the logic implies all and only logical truths, and all and only deductively valid inferences, so that the logic satisfies the definition for being semantically sound.

The question is how to prove that a logic implies all and only tautologies and valid sequents. Unfortunately, we cannot do this by applying truth trees or any other decision method to every wff and sequent. We have no complete checklist of the tautologies and valid sequents that a decision method is supposed to determine so that we can judge whether or not a particular logic proves all and only the tautologies and valid sequents on the list. The tautologies and valid sequents may timelessly belong to an abstract list, but the logician trying to prove a metatheorem about a system of logic has no access to the category's complete inventory. In a sense, whether a wff is or is not a tautology, and whether a sequent is or is not deductively valid, is decided in practice by whether or not the wff or sequent receives that evaluation from a correct application of a correct decision method. Applying decision methods to try to prove even large numbers of individual tautologies and valid sequents would be an overwhelming real-time task, and the procedure at any point in time would carry no guarantee that an inconsistency or deductively invalid sequent might not also eventually be proved. If we are uncertain about whether a logic is semantically sound, then we are equally uncertain about whether the logic's decision methods are correct. We cannot rely on truth trees or other decision methods to prove the soundness of a logical system because by raising the issue of the logic's soundness, we are also raising doubts about the system's decision methods. Logicians instead try to demonstrate the semantic consistency of a system of logic by proving that the logic has an interpretation whereby all wffs capable of being recognized as tautologies by the logic's decision methods are logically true. A logic is shown to be semantically complete by demonstrating that on such an interpretation no wff capable of being recognized as a tautology by the logic's decision methods is false.

A system of symbolic logic is also judged according to whether or not it is mechanically decidable. A mechanically decidable logic is one in which every wff and sequent can be tested by applying a decision method to correctly determine in a finite number of precisely defined syntactical operations whether or not the wff is a tautology and whether or not the sequent is deductively valid.

To know that a logic is syntactically consistent is not yet to know whether it is semantically sound (hence, semantically consistent and semantically complete), and to know that a logic is semantically sound is not yet to know whether it is mechanically decidable. In lieu of a convincing metatheorem to the contrary, we might suppose that a logic could imply tautologies and valid sequents that escape detection by any decision method. The proof of a logic's decidability is a proof that the logic's decision methods are sufficiently powerful to identify all the logic's tautologies and deductively valid sequents and to distinguish them from any wff that is not a tautology or sequent that is not deductively valid. An effective decision method is a decision method that determines of any wff of a logic whether or not it is a tautology and of any sequent of the logic whether or not it is deductively valid. A system of symbolic logic is mechanically decidable if and only if there exists an effective decision method for all its wffs and sequents. The question of whether a logic is mechanically decidable or whether an effective decision method is possible for a system of logic is known as the *decision problem*.

The metatheory of propositional and predicate logic is also developed to determine whether a system of logic is deductively complete. To know that a logic is syntactically consistent, semantically sound (hence, semantically consistent and semantically complete) and mechanically decidable is not yet to know whether its tautologies and valid sequents can all be proven by a particular system of inference rules such as those for natural deduction proofs. A logic is deductively complete if and only if for every tautology or inconsistency, $\mathbb{P}$, of the logic, either $\mathbb{P}$ is deductively provable or $\sim\mathbb{P}$ is deductively provable. A logic is deductively incomplete if and only if, from a semantic standpoint, there is at least one logically true or logically false wff, $\mathbb{P}$, of the logic such that neither $\mathbb{P}$ nor $\sim\mathbb{P}$ are deductively provable, according to the logic's syntactical inference rules.

Standard symbolic propositional logic, of the sort presented in this book, is syntactically consistent, semantically sound (hence, semantically consistent and semantically complete), and mechanically decidable. Standard symbolic predicate logic, in contrast, has been shown to be syntactically consistent, semantically sound (hence, semantically consistent and semantically complete), but mechanically undecidable and deductively incomplete. As a consequence of its greater expressive complexity, predicate logic does not satisfy all the same positive metalogical criteria as does propositional logic. The metatheoretical limitations of predicate logic are due to the possibility of defining predicate wffs that deny their own decidability as tautologies or nontautologies by mechanical methods and deny their own deductive provability. The existence of such wffs entails that predicate logic contains sentences that, if logically true, cannot be identified as true by any logically consistent mechanical decision method or proved by any logically consistent inference rules. We shall briefly discuss the implications of these important metatheoretical results—Kurt Gödel's proof of the deductive incompleteness of an application of standard first-order logic in formalizing the axioms of arithmetic and Alonzo Church's proof of the mechanical undecidability of pure standard first-order predicate logic.

At the turn of the 20th century, many logicians hoped to reduce mathematics, beginning with infinitary arithmetic, to a specialized system of applied predicate logic. The program to reduce mathematics to logic is known as *logicism*. It was most thoroughly developed by Gottlob Frege in *Begriffsschrift* (1879), and *Grundgesetze der Arithmetik* (1893–1903) and by Alfred North Whitehead and Bertrand Russell in *Principia Mathematica* (1910, 1925–1927). Gödel, in his 1931 essay "Über formal unentscheidbare Sätze der *Principia mathematica* und verwandter Systeme I" ("On Formally Undecidable Sentences of *Principia Mathematica* and Related Systems [Part] I"), refuted Whitehead and Russell's effort to carry out the logicist program. Gödel proved that when predicate logic is used to symbolize the axioms of infinitary arithmetic (including those that define addition and multiplication for an infinite semantic domain of whole numbers, together with an identity relation), then it is possible to construct wffs, which have since come to be known as *Gödel sentences,* that assert their own unprovability. The existence of Gödel sentences forces us to choose between recognizing axiomatizations of infinitary arithmetic in standard predicate logic as syntactically inconsistent or deductively incomplete.

If a Gödel sentence is true, then any logic in which the Gödel sentence can be formulated is deductively incomplete since in that case the logic contains wffs that are logically true from a semantic standpoint but formally unprovable. If a Gödel sentence is false, then it must after all be provable since it asserts of itself that it is not provable. A logically false proposition can only be deductively validly proved in a syntactically inconsistent logic. If a Gödel sentence is false, therefore, then any logic in which the Gödel sentence is a wff is syntactically inconsistent and hence semantically inconsistent. Gödel, in his first of two metatheorems, thereby proves that when predicate logic is used to symbolize infinitary arithmetic the resulting applied logic is either syntactically inconsistent or deductively incomplete. In other words, Gödel demonstrates that in any syntactically consistent system of predicate logic used to symbolize infinitary arithmetic, there exists at least one logically true wff G, such that G is deductively unprovable. To preserve the syntactical consistency of predicate logic, most logicians regard it as better to admit that any such system of logic is deductively incomplete than to say that it is syntactically and semantically inconsistent. In a second metatheorem, Gödel proves that no syntactically consistent application of a logic that symbolizes the axioms of arithmetic is powerful enough to prove its own syntactical consistency.

Gödel's proofs have been influential in understanding the limitations of the logical foundations of mathematics. As we have described Gödel's first metatheorem, it appears to concern only applied predicate logic, in which the nonlogical axioms of infinitary arithmetic are symbolized. Gödel's proof does not identify any limitation in the deductive completeness of pure predicate logic or of applied predicate logic that is not used to symbolize the axioms of infinitary arithmetic. Gödel, in his 1930 dissertation at the University of Vienna and in a published paper in the same year, "Die Vollständigkeit der Axiome des logischen Funktionenkalküls" ("The Completeness of the Axioms of the Functional Calculus of Logic"), proved that pure predicate logic is syntactically consistent and semantically sound, both semantically consistent and semantically complete. Let Σ be any set of pure predicate wffs and $\mathbb{P}$ any particular pure predicate wff, and let $\Sigma \models \mathbb{P}$ mean that if all the wffs in Γ are true, according to a particular semantic interpretation, then wff $\mathbb{P}$ is true. In contrast, as before, let $\Sigma \vdash \mathbb{P}$ mean that wff $\mathbb{P}$ is formally derivable from a set of wffs according to a logic's inference rules. Then Gödel's consistency proof of 1930 shows that $\Sigma \vdash \mathbb{P}$ if and only if $\Sigma \models \mathbb{P}$. Gödel's first incompleteness theorem shows that there is a sentence G such that, for any syntactically consistent set of applied predicate wffs Σ^a in which the axioms of infinitary arithmetic are formalized, $\Sigma^a \nvdash$ G and $\Sigma^a \nvdash {\sim}$G. This is an exciting result. But whether pure predicate logic outside of its applications to infinitary arithmetic is also mechanically decidable and deductively complete for the time being remained an open question.

It was not until 1936 that Church, in his essay "A Note on the Entscheidungsproblem [Decision Problem]," proved that even pure predicate logic is mechanically undecidable and deductively incomplete. Church's metatheorem shows that no pure predicate logic has an effective decision method. Church's metatheorem defines the *finite extension* of a logic as the nonlogical axioms definable in the logic's symbolism. Church proves that if the finite extension of a logic is undecidable, then so is the logic. The undecidable finite extension of predicate logic is its symbolization of the nonlogical axioms of arithmetic. When Gödel sentences are constructed to disprove the decidability of the predicate symbolization of arithmetic, the undecidability of arithmetic reflects back on the undecidability of the pure predicate logic of which the symbolization is a finite extension. The truth tree method, as we now know from Church's theorem, is not an effective decision method for pure predicate logic. The undecidability of pure predicate logic further implies its deductive incompleteness. The wffs of pure predicate logic that cannot be judged as tautologies or nontautologies by any decision method enter into sequents that cannot be validly proved or disproved in any logically consistent deductive proof system. Predicate truth trees give correct classifications of many but not all predicate wffs and sequents. There are wffs and sequents, as Gödel and Church formally proved in the metatheory of predicate logic, that escape even the most powerful decision methods and proof rules.

As a further implication of Church's metatheorem, note that the proof implies the irreducibility of predicate logic to propositional logic. If predicate logic could be reduced to propositional logic, then predicate logic would be a finite extension of propositional logic, in which $(\forall x)Fx$ is reduced to the conjunction $Fa\ \&\ Fb\ \&\ \dots\ \&\ Fn$ and $(\exists x)Fx$ is reduced to the disjunction $Fa \vee Fb \vee \dots \vee Fn$. Church, in proving that pure predicate logic is undecidable, proved that if a logic is mechanically decidable, then so are its finite extensions. If predicate logic could be reduced to propositional logic, then propositional logic would also be undecidable. However, since there is a rigorous proof that propositional logic is decidable, if we assume for the sake of argument that predicate logic could be reduced to propositional logic, we face the contradiction that propositional logic is decidable and undecidable. The contradiction disproves the assumption, whereby it follows that predicate logic cannot be reduced to propositional logic.

The limitations of predicate truth trees, their inability to provide an effective decision method for any arbitrary wff or sequent of predicate logic, must not be overlooked. Yet neither should they be exaggerated. The metatheorem proves that no decision method can effectively determine of every wff whether it is or is not a tautology or of every sequent whether or not it is deductively valid. However, many wffs and sequents are correctly classified by the method, despite its limitations. A predicate truth tree that closes after a finite number of steps, including a finite number of choices of constants to replace an indefinitely decomposable universally quantified wff, always gives a correct evaluation of logical inconsistency. A predicate truth tree of a stack of wffs that does not close after a finite number of steps, in which the possibilities of closure are exhausted, also always gives the correct evaluation of logical consistency. Predicate truth trees that either close or do not close when all the possibilities of closure are exhausted are *terminating* trees. In contrast, a predicate truth tree applied to a Gödel sentence is *nonterminating* in that it neither closes nor fails to close because the possibilities for closure in the tree are never either satisfied or exhausted. However, these special constructions are far removed from the ordinary applications of predicate logic that we are likely to encounter. The mechanical undecidability and deductive incompleteness of pure predicate logic are more a theoretical than practical limitation. We must be aware that predicate logic is technically limited by Gödel's and Church's metatheorems. But the limitations on decision methods need not cause undue concern about the reliability of predicate truth trees in the vast majority of instances in which we need to determine the logical properties of wffs and sequents. Despite the logic's metatheoretical limitations, all tautologies and deductively valid sequents in predicate logic are correctly identifiable by predicate truth trees and provable by predicate natural deduction rules.

There are many other important and useful results to be studied in metatheory. The arguments and formal techniques by which these conclusions are established generally represent valuable logical discoveries in their own right. The field of metatheory offers opportunities to learn new logical methods and to consider the formal properties of symbolic logic from a perspective that affords a commanding overview of its exact capabilities.

Foundations of Mathematics

Although logicism is believed by most logicians today to have failed in its attempt to reduce mathematics to logic, logic remains a useful tool in studying the *foundations of mathematics*. *Set theory* and *number theory* are the primary focus of logicians interested in using logic to understand basic concepts, inference, and proof methods of arithmetic, geometry, algebra, and higher mathematics.

The formal symbolic devices and proof methods developed in the metatheory of logic also appear in foundational studies in mathematics. The challenge of foundational analysis in mathematical logic is to define the minimally necessary logical concepts required for mathematics and to understand exactly how each part of classical mathematics can be built out of simpler concepts and operations as a system of logical relations. There are important proofs about *infinity,* the *power set* or set of all subsets of infinite sets, the existence of *transfinite sets* or *higher orders of infinity,* and the properties of and relations among *transfinite numbers*.

To get a sense of the issues, it may be helpful to begin by considering the *Dedekind–Peano axioms* for defining the whole numbers, which logicism took as part of its task to formalize in symbolic logic:

1. 0 is a number.

2. The successor of any number is a number.

3. No two numbers have the same successor.

4. 0 is not the successor of any number.

These conditions jointly define the succession of whole numbers beginning 0, 1, 2, 3, . . . , and so on indefinitely. We need only assume that the numbers after 0 are conventionally named, as noted previously, as convenient abbreviations. Thus, '1' names 'the successor of 0', '2' names 'the successor of the successor of 0' or 'the successor of 1', and so on. With the whole numbers defined, it then becomes possible to define rational numbers—as well as irrational real numbers, negative, imaginary, and transcendental numbers, and the like—by applying special functions and operations to the sequence of whole numbers as a basis. In this way, a large portion if not the entirety of classical mathematics is reducible in principle to the successor relation, taking 0 as an ultimate foundation. The exact formulation of the axioms by which these definitions of numbers and mathematical operators are best undertaken and explained is another active field for advanced research in symbolic logic.

If we consider standard *Zermelo–Fraenkel set theory* as an example, we can see how logic is used to formalize basic set theoretical concepts, useful generally in mathematics and in the formal semantics of predicate and modal logics as well as in other logical and philosophical applications. It should suffice here to introduce the axioms in logicized English to demonstrate how the principles might be symbolized in predicate logic. The concept of a set, and the relation of membership in a set, is standardly primitive or undefined. A *subset* is any member or set of members in a set, including the set itself; a *proper subset* of a set is any subset of a set, except for the set itself. Then we define the first six, most basic and easily formalized, of the nine axioms of Zermelo–Fraenkel set theory as follows:

0. The null set $\varnothing$ is a set (thus, there exists at least one set).

1. For any sets x and y, x = y if and only if for all x, x is a member of a if and only if z is a member of x.

2. For any set x, there exists a set y, such that for any z, z is a member of y if and only if z is a member of x, and z has (some) property or satisfies (some) condition, $\mathscr{F}$.

3. For any sets x and y, there exists a set z, such that x is a member of z and y is a member of z.

4. For any set x, there exists a set y, such that, for some member z of x, if any w is a member of z, then w is a member of y.

5. For any set x, there exists a set y, such that, for all z, if z is a subset of x, then z is a member of y.

6. There exists a set x, such that $\varnothing$ is a member of x, and, if any y is a member of x, then the union of y and the set consisting of y is a member of x.

As a final topic, we shall consider a consequence of axiom 5, also known as the *power set axiom*. The axiom implies that the power set, consisting of all the subsets of a set including itself and the null set, $\varnothing$, is always of greater *cardinality*, or has a greater number of members, than the set itself. This is obvious in the case of ordinary sets of finite cardinality. The set {0, 1, 2}, for example, has cardinality 3. However, its power set is the set {$\varnothing$, {0}, {1}, {2}, {0, 1}, {1, 2}, {0, 2}, {0, 1, 2}}, which has cardinality 8. Does the power set axiom also hold for infinite sets? Here, the answer is not immediately obvious because we know that we can add or subtract any, even an infinite, number from an infinite number and still have an infinite number left over. For example, there is at least an infinite number of Euclidean geometrical points in a line segment exactly 1 in. long and the same infinite number of Euclidean points in a line segment exactly 0.5 in. long. If we subtract a 0.5-in.-long line segment from the 1-in. line segment (or add infinitely many more line segments to it), we will still have infinitely many Euclidean points in the remaining segment. Therefore, it is reasonable to ask, what happens to the power set axiom in the infinite case?

We briefly mention an important result proved by Georg Cantor in 1890 that is known as *Cantor's diagonalization* or the *diagonalization argument.* Cantor assumes, for purposes of *reductio ad absurdum,* that all the infinitely many irrational real numbers (numbers whose decimal expressions are nonterminating and nonrepeating) are listed in one–one correspondence with the natural numbers (1, 2, 3, . . .). Then he defines an irrational real number that cannot possibly occur anywhere on the list. He specifies that the new number is to consist, in its nth decimal place, of a different digit than appears in the nth decimal place of the irrational real number that appears in the list at any row number n. We can simplify Cantor's diagonalization argument by considering irrationals to be written out as infinitely expanding binary expansions of the two digits 0 and 1. Then, Cantor's procedure literally cuts a diagonal path down the list by taking whatever digit, 0 or 1, that occurs in the nth binary expansion place of whatever irrational real number occurs in row number n in the list and changing it from 0 to 1 or from 1 to 0:

$$.00100101 \ldots$$
$$.11010110 \ldots$$
$$.11010101 \ldots$$
$$.01001100 \ldots$$
$$.00111010 \ldots$$
$$.10111101 \ldots$$
$$.01101110 \ldots$$
$$.10001110 \ldots$$

In this case, the method produces the irrational real number .10110001. . . . Surprisingly, this number cannot occur anywhere on the list. If it occurs on the list, it must occur at some definite row number, n. However, the number is so defined that, in its nth binary expansion place, it must have a different digit (0 rather than 1 or 1 rather than 0) than whatever number occurs in row n. This is a contradiction in the sense that the number must include both 0 and 1 in its nth binary expansion place. The original assumption was that all the irrational real numbers could be put in one–one correspondence with the natural numbers in the list. If by diagonalization we can define an irrational number that cannot appear anywhere in the list, then we have shown that there is no one–one correspondence between the infinitely many natural numbers and the irrational real numbers. It follows, among other things, that there are more irrational real numbers than natural numbers, that there are more than infinitely many irrational real numbers, and that there must be higher orders of infinity than the *denumerably* infinite number of natural numbers 1, 2, 3, ...

Cantor proves that the generalized power set axiom holds true, even when applied to infinite sets. He refers to such higher order sets as *transfinite* and is credited as a result with discovering a hierarchy of *transfinite cardinals,* each with a greater cardinality than the basis set from which it can be derived by diagonalization. The power set axiom, as the example involving {0, 1, 2} indicates, has as a further consequence that the cardinality of the power set of any set with cardinality c is always 2^c. Cantor proves that the cardinality of the set of Euclidean geometrical points in any line segment is exactly 2^c, where c is the cardinality of the denumerably infinite natural numbers, and that in the infinite case also $2^c > c$. Cantor, despite early optimism during the course of his work, was never able to prove the *continuum hypothesis,* that 2^c is the smallest nondenumerable cardinal, or the *generalized continuum hypothesis,* that there are no cardinal numbers between c and 2^c, between 2^c and 2^{2^c}, etc. Later logicians and set theoreticians, notably Paul Cohen and Gödel, proved that the continuum hypothesis is consistent with, but also independent of, the axioms of standard set theory, which means that it can neither be proved nor disproved from within the usual set theoretical framework. Thus, Cantor left a tantalizing unsolved problem in symbolic logic and the foundations of mathematics for future logicians to investigate.

A related topic that dovetails problems in the foundations of mathematics with the metatheory of predicate logic concerns interpretations of predicate wffs and the size of their semantic domains. A predicate wff, as previously discussed, can be interpreted in several equivalent ways by means of relational predicate transforms or n-tuples of objects in a semantic domain. Some predicate wffs can only be interpreted as true on certain assignments of objects to constants and quantifier bound object variables from a semantic domain containing infinitely many objects. An obvious example is the wff $(\forall x)(Nx \supset (\exists y)(Ny \& Gyx))$ as a formalization of the sentence that 'For any x, if x is a number, then there is a number that is greater than x' or, simply, 'There is no greatest number'.

In considering whether Cantor's proof of transfinite cardinals establishes orders of infinity greater than that of the positive integers 1, 2, 3, . . . , it is a topic of logical metatheory whether or not it is necessary for the truth of some predicate wffs to postulate a semantic domain consisting of more objects than are contained in the first order of infinity corresponding to the cardinality of the integers and of the rational numbers. The *Löwenheim theorem,* proved by Leopold Löwenheim in a 1915 paper titled "Über Möglichkeiten im Relativkalkül" ("On Possibilities in the Calculus of Relatives"), demonstrates that if a wff in a logically consistent set of predicate wffs in a predicate logic without the identity relation is true on at least one interpretation, then it is true on some interpretation that has the set of positive integers only as its semantic domain. If the logic is supplemented by an identity predicate, then the semantic domain of the interpretation with the set of positive integers only as its semantic domain can further be shown to be only a proper subset of the set of positive integers. Thoraf Skolem, in a 1920 paper titled "Logisch-kombinatorische Untersuchungen über die Erfüllbarkeit oder Beweisbarkeit mathematischer Sätze nebst einem Theoreme über dichte Mengen" ("Logico-Combinatorial Investigations in the Satisfiability or Provability of Mathematical Propositions"), generalized and simplified the Löwenheim theorem, whereby the proof has come to be known as the Löwenheim–Skolem theorem. This is a surprising result, sometimes referred to as *Skolem's paradox,* because the Löwenheim–Skolem theorem entails that all but the lowest order of infinity of objects in the semantic domain can be discounted in interpreting any predicate wff as true, including wffs about Cantor's higher orders of infinity, and initially interpreted for semantic domains containing more objects than can be numbered by the set of positive integers.

The Löwenheim–Skolem theorem, in addition to the "downward" direction by which the semantic domain for an interpretation of predicate wffs can be reduced to the lowest order of infinity, also has an "upward" direction. The upward direction of the theorem, less surprising than the downward direction, states that a logically consistent set of wffs interpreted by means of a semantic domain containing a lower order of infinity of objects can also be interpreted in a semantic domain with a larger cardinality, which Cantor proved must exist.

Computers, Artificial Intelligence, and Machine Theory

The decision methods of symbolic logic are mechanical procedures. They can be implemented by computers. Computers have been programmed to perform many of the logical operations associated with particular systems of formal logic. In a deeper sense, both computer circuitry hardware and the software instructions by which computers execute their tasks are physical embodiments of logical principles.

Logicians contribute to many concrete design and engineering aspects of the computer industry and to theoretical study of the capabilities and limitations of computers. Computer applications of symbolic logic include constructing and testing logic switching circuits, using formal symbolic methods to simplify electronic circuitry and software, and developing software to assist in translating propositions and arguments into symbolic logic and for automated proof discovery. Programming computers to perform logical operations and solve proofs in a formal system is sometimes part of a larger project, the prospects of which remain philosophically controversial, to build *artificial intelligence* machines to simulate human thought or even to think for themselves.

The *automation of inference* in the form of symbolic logic proof machines is of interest to cognitive psychology in formally modeling the natural processes by which the mind engages in reasoning and problem solving. There are interesting theoretical problems about the concept of a calculating machine that can be approached by way of symbolic logic. The metatheorems of predicate logic also apply to real-time computing systems so that logical metatheory provides practical insight into the logical limitations of machines. If the mind is a kind of living machine, then the abilities and limitations of machines as determined by the abilities and limitations of formal systems of symbolic logic may in turn have implications for human psychology, cognitive science, and the philosophy of mind.

An interesting development in artificial intelligence research is the use of *fuzzy logic* to simulate certain cognitive processes. Fuzzy logic is a nonstandard formal system in which objects do not simply either belong or fail to belong to the extension of a predicate but can do so to any real-numbered degree of probability between the values 0 and 1. The advantage of a fuzzy logic for modeling psychological phenomena is its greater flexibility in describing continuous gradients and real-time processes that are not naturally represented as exclusively true or false values as in conventional logics.

Modal Logic

The symbolic logic we have developed concerns categorical statements of fact. A proposition of logic states that 'It is raining' or 'All men are mortal'. We can also consider what medieval logicians referred to as the *modes* of propositions, such as 'It is possible that it is raining' or 'It is necessary that all men are mortal'. Modes qualify the truth of propositions, or ways or senses in which propositions can be true, as necessarily true, possibly true, and other ways.

We recognize the need to introduce predicate logic in order to express logical truths and deductively valid arguments that cannot be adequately formalized within the resources of propositional logic. It is similarly necessary eventually to go beyond predicate logic in order to symbolize logical truths and deductive validities about the modes or truth qualifications of propositions.

Modal logic is the formal logical theory of these modes. There are several different types of modes and many corresponding types of modal logics. *Alethic* modal logic formalizes a proposition's logical necessity or possibility. To symbolize relations of causal necessity and possibility in the laws of science or practical reasoning requires a *causal* modal logic. There are also *deontic* modal logics of moral obligation and permission, *doxastic* modal logics of belief and doubt, *epistemic* logics of knowledge and skepticism about the truth of propositions, and *temporal* modal logics that qualify the times at which propositions may be true.

Within the field of alethic modal logic alone there are many different logical systems with different logical implications and different metalogical characteristics. The formalisms of modal logics are worth studying because their interpretation involves a *model set theoretical semantics* with a variety of formal logical structures and set theoretical relations on logically complete and consistent sets of propositions that are sometimes called *possible worlds*. Semantic structures of this sort are useful in potentially unlimitedly many kinds of logical investigations. Modal logics raise interesting questions about the proper theory of semantic domains, the concept of a logically possible world, and the identity of objects from one model set or logically possible world to another. We shall briefly describe how some of the most useful alethic modal systems are defined and interpreted. We also mention a few of the philosophical issues that occur in connection with the formalization of alethic modal logic.

A weak but plausible system of modal logic is obtained by interdefining two special operators for necessity and possibility. We may want to say that for any wff $\mathbb{P}$, if $\mathbb{P}$ is necessarily true, then $\mathbb{P}$ is true. If we introduce the box symbol, '$\Box$', as a modal operator for logical necessity, then we can express this axiom of modal logic as $\Box \mathbb{P} \supset \mathbb{P}$. If it is logically necessarily true, for example, that either it is raining or it is not raining, then it is true without qualification that either it is raining or it is not raining. This is logically equivalent by contraposition to saying that if $\mathbb{P}$ is true, then it is logically possible that $\mathbb{P}$, which, defining the diamond symbol '$\Diamond$' as logical possibility, can be written as $\mathbb{P} \supset \Diamond \mathbb{P}$. If it is true that it is raining, then it logically possible that it is raining. The box and diamond operators are interdefined by a modal duality relation, which we can write as $\Box \mathbb{P} \equiv \sim\Diamond\sim\mathbb{P}$ and $\Diamond \mathbb{P} \equiv \sim\Box\sim\mathbb{P}$. These axioms state, respectively, that it is logically necessarily true that $\mathbb{P}$ if and only if it is not logically possible that $\mathbb{P}$ is false or logically impossible for $\mathbb{P}$ to be false, and that it is logically possible that $\mathbb{P}$ is true if and only if it is not logically necessary that $\mathbb{P}$ is false. As with duality relations in propositional and predicate logic, there are many useful variations of these most basic forms. We may also want to maintain that all tautologies of logic are logically necessary, which we can indicate by the axiom $\vdash \mathbb{P} \supset \vdash \Box\mathbb{P}$. Finally, we may find it intuitively true to suppose that a distribution principle holds with respect to the necessity operator over the conditional in the axiom $\Box(\mathbb{P} \supset \mathbb{Q}) \supset (\Box\mathbb{P} \supset \Box\mathbb{Q})$. This states that if it is logically necessary that if $\mathbb{P}$, then $\mathbb{Q}$, then, if it is logically necessary that $\mathbb{P}$, then it is logically necessary that $\mathbb{Q}$.

The modal principles we have considered are extremely basic. They are nevertheless helpful in formalizing some of our discourse about logical necessity and possibility, as when we say that a deductively valid argument is such that if its assumptions are true, then its conclusions must be true or are logically necessarily true, or such that it is logically impossible for the assumptions to be true and the conclusions false. There are many other applications, even for such a simple system of modal logic. Modal logic becomes more interesting when we consider the rules for predicate or quantified modal logic, when we advance to more complicated axioms for different systems involving relations between iterated modal operators, and when we try to work out a satisfactory formal semantics for different systems of elementary and predicate or quantified modal logics. Again, we cannot explore all the possibilities here. It is worth considering, however, whether $\Diamond\,(\exists x)Fx \equiv (\exists x)\,\Diamond\,Fx$, the so-called *Barcan formula* and *converse Barcan formula* (named after its discoverer, Ruth Barcan Marcus), is or should be a theorem of quantified modal logic. Although the Barcan formula, $(\exists x)\,\Diamond\,Fx \supset \Diamond\,(\exists x)Fx$, is a theorem of even very weak systems of modal logic, the converse Barcan formula, $\Diamond\,(\exists x)Fx \supset (\exists x)\,\Diamond\,Fx$, is a theorem only of stronger systems of quantified modal logic that justify inferences involving certain iterated modalities. The converse Barcan formula states that if it is logically possible that there exists an object with property F, then there definitely exists an object for which it is logically possible that it have property F. The converse Barcan formula thereby makes a commitment to the existence of an object in the logic's semantic domain which possibly has a property from the mere possible existence of such an object. In some modal logics, this relation holds true, but in others it does not.

We can foresee that there will be some kinds of iterated modalities, even in the simple system of alethic modal logic we have already sketched. For example, if where $\mathbb{P}$ is true, it follows that $\Diamond\,\mathbb{P}$ is true, then, equally, from $\Diamond\,\mathbb{P}$ it follows that $\Diamond\,\Diamond\,\mathbb{P}$. If it is logically possible that $\mathbb{P}$, then it is logically possible that it is logically possible that $\mathbb{P}$, and so on, indefinitely, for any number of iterated possibility operators. By the same principle, from $\Box\mathbb{P}$, it also follows that $\Diamond\,\Box\mathbb{P}$. If it is logically necessary that $\mathbb{P}$, then it is logically possible that it is logically necessary that $\mathbb{P}$. But what about the inference, $\Box\mathbb{P} \supset \Box\Box\mathbb{P}$—that, if it is logically necessary that $\mathbb{P}$, then it is logically necessary that it is logically necessary that $\mathbb{P}$? Or, what by modal duality amounts to the same thing, the inference $\Diamond\,\Diamond\,\mathbb{P} \supset \Diamond\,\mathbb{P}$—that, if it is logically possible that it is logically possible that $\mathbb{P}$, then it is logically possible that $\mathbb{P}$? We might be able to imagine applications in which such relations obtain. But how exactly are they to be formally interpreted? What are we saying by means of such modal iterations? What about the combined iteration $\Diamond\,\mathbb{P} \supset \Box\,\Diamond\,\mathbb{P}$? This seems to say something like if it is logically possible that $\mathbb{P}$, then it is logically necessary that it is logically possible that $\mathbb{P}$. Consider the even more daring iteration $\mathbb{P} \supset \Box \Diamond \mathbb{P}$. This says intuitively that if $\mathbb{P}$ is true, then it is logically necessary that it is logically possible that $\mathbb{P}$. What, exactly, do these expressions mean?

The latter iterations are the characteristic axioms of more complicated systems of modal logic than the basic system we first outlined. The formal semantics for modal logic involve a model set theoretical interpretation of the concept of a logically possible world. A logically possible world can be thought of as a universe that is as similar or as distinct from our own in any way that does not involve a logical contradiction. Some modal logicians do not accept the idea of a logically possible world but offer an alternative account of models consisting of or described by complete and consistent sets of wffs. Other modal logicians simply interpret the concept of a logically possible world as a complete and consistent set of wffs, where to be complete and consistent means that, for any wff, $\mathbb{P}$, either $\mathbb{P}$ or $\sim\mathbb{P}$ belongs to the set (this is what makes the set complete or, indeed, enables it to provide a description of a world) and not both $\mathbb{P}$ and $\sim\mathbb{P}$ belong to the set (this is what makes the set consistent or qualifies the description as logically possible).

When all worlds or sets of complete and consistent wffs are fully characterized in set theoretical terms, then special relations are defined over the sets of worlds. It is by means of such relations that a modal semantics interprets propositional and quantificational modal wffs for modal logics of different kinds with different characteristic axioms. These principles are sometimes described as *modal accessibility relations* because they interpret modal wffs as true at certain subsets of the set of all logically possible worlds that are said to be accessible from the world at which the wff is true. A wff that is true in all logically possible worlds is necessarily true, $\Box\mathbb{P}$, and a wff that is true in at least one logically possible world is possibly true, $\Diamond\mathbb{P}$. To say that if it is logically possible that $\mathbb{P}$, then it is logically necessary that it is logically possible that $\mathbb{P}$, for example, $\Diamond\mathbb{P} \supset \Box\Diamond\mathbb{P}$, will be true or false, depending on how the modal accessibility relations are defined for a particular system of modal logic.

In order for the modal wff, $\Diamond\mathbb{P} \supset \Box\Diamond\mathbb{P}$, to be true, a modal accessibility relation must be defined in such a way that all logically possible worlds are accessible from any particular logically possible world, in the sense that there are at least some true wffs about the same objects in every world as in any logically possible world. This is equivalent to requiring that every logically possible world have an identical semantic domain consisting of all and only the same objects. The requisite modal accessibility relation that guarantees this free accessibility of truths about all objects across all logically possible worlds must be reflexive, transitive, and symmetric. Such a modal system is known for historical reasons as quantified S5 or QS5. It should be obvious that the converse Barcan formula is true in it but not necessarily in weaker modal systems whose semantic accessibility relations do not guarantee that the same semantic domain obtains in every logically possible world. There are many possibilities for specific model set theoretical characterizations of modal semantics, for defining different specific systems of alethic modal logic, some of which are more appropriate than others for specific logical purposes.

Nonalethic modal systems can be advanced to analyze other types of modality. These include, but are not limited to, causal necessity and possibility, metaphysical necessity and possibility, belief, knowledge, moral obligation and permission. Nonalethic modal logics require much the same effort to define a special set of modal operators, establish wffs rules, provide a formal semantics, devise decision methods and inference rules, and prove the logic's metatheoretical properties as a foundation for scientific and philosophical applications. Often, it is the semantics for each system that is most philosophically interesting. These are generally given by singling out a special subset of logically possible worlds, such as those in which a given set of natural laws obtain, or in which a particular choice of moral principles are satisfied, in order to interpret wffs, for example, as causally, metaphysically, or morally necessary (obligatory) and as causally, metaphysically, or morally possible (permissible). The merits of alethic and nonalethic modal logics are determined by their ability to plausibly describe corresponding informal concepts, clarify and solve problems, and suggest fruitful lines of further inquiry.

Nonstandard Logics

In addition to the standard symbolic logic presented in this book, there are many *nonstandard logics*. Nonstandard logics are important because they formalize aspects of our reasoning that in various ways do not lend themselves to formalization in ordinary propositional and predicate logics.

If we believe that some propositions are neither true nor false, then we may wish to consider the semantic possibilities afforded by *many-valued logics,* offering more than the two standard truth values true and false, or with *truth value gaps* for propositions that fail to have any truth value. There are various possibilities for defining nonstandard truth functional connectives, and there are ongoing disputes about which systems may be intuitively more correct or better suited to particular logical tasks.

To convey a sense of how different propositional logic could look with a many-valued truth value semantics, the following truth tables for negation and the conditional are presented that were adapted from a 1930 essay published by the logician Jan Łukasiewicz. We consider 'T' and 'F' to represent the standard truth values true and false and 'U' as indicating that the truth value is undetermined. Then we have:

$\mathbb{P}$	$\sim\mathbb{P}$
T	F
F	T
U	U

$\mathbb{P}$	$\mathbb{Q}$	$\mathbb{P} \supset \mathbb{Q}$
T	T	T
T	F	F
T	U	U
F	T	T
F	F	T
F	U	T
U	T	T
U	F	U
U	U	T

We shall not try to justify Łukasiewicz's choice of values in this three-valued system. Consider only how such an altered semantic foundation has repercussions for other aspects of the resulting nonstandard propositional logic. It precludes, for example, the *principle of excluded middle,* in the usual form of the tautology, $\mathbb{P} \vee \sim\mathbb{P}$. Moreover, Łukasiewicz's logic is only one among virtually endlessly inventive ways in which nonstandard truth value semantics for symbolic logics can be devised for particular purposes in logical analysis.

Intuitionistic logics formalize a theory of truth and logical inference, whereby only propositions for which a proof actually exists are interpreted as logically true. This constraint has, among other implications, the result that double negation as an equivalence is not a logical theorem. If a proposition is proven, then it is not the case that the proposition is disproven. However, it does not follow from the fact that it is not the case that a proposition is disproven that therefore the proposition is proven. Thus, it is a theorem of intuitionistic logic that $\mathbb{P} \vdash \sim\sim\mathbb{P}$ but not $\sim\sim\mathbb{P} \vdash \mathbb{P}$. Another peculiarity of intuitionistic logic is that the law of excluded middle, as explained previously, does not hold. The reason is clear when considering the intuitionistic position that we can only assert the truth of a proposition if we have actually proved it. If $\mathbb{P}$ is a proposition that has neither been proved nor disproved, then, according to the intuitionistic scruples, we are not entitled to suppose that either $\mathbb{P}$ or its negation is true. Neither proposition is true, for the intuitionist, until it has been definitely proved or definitely disproved. There are, of course, numerous such propositions that are such that neither they nor their negations have actually been proved. A famous example is *Goldbach's conjecture* that every even number greater than 2 is the sum of two primes. An intuitionistic logic, as a result of these differences in its fundamental philosophical orientation about the nature of logical truth, is highly nonstandard in terms of its tautologies, inference rules, and semantics when compared with the propositional logic we have developed.

Relevance logics in different ways modify the standard definitions of propositional connectives so that conditionals with false antecedents or true consequents are not true by default regardless of whether or not there is any connection between their contents. Similar relevance considerations provide nonstandard logics whereby sequents are not deductively valid merely by virtue of having necessarily true conclusions or jointly necessarily false assumptions, where there is no relevant conceptual connection between the content of the argument's assumptions and conclusions. There are many ingenious proposals for achieving relevance in the concept of logical entailment. We shall remark only that in one way or another, a relevance logic is committed to avoiding the so-called *paradoxes of material implication* in standard propositional logic, whereby it follows that $\mathbb{P} \vdash \sim\mathbb{P} \supset \mathbb{Q}$ and $\mathbb{P} \vdash \mathbb{Q} \supset \mathbb{P}$.

Paraconsistent logics go beyond relevance logics by tolerating syntactical contradictions while limiting the *inferential explosion* of validly deducing any and every logical consequence. Inferential explosion standardly occurs from any logically inconsistent set of assumptions because of the standard definition of deductive validity in $\mathbb{P}$, $\sim\mathbb{P} \vdash \mathbb{Q}$. Paraconsistent logics try to control this unlimited deducibility of any and every proposition, which threatens to trivialize valid inference from contradictions. There are many applications of paraconsistent logic. We might begin by thinking of the fact that many persons knowingly or unknowingly accept beliefs that are logically inconsistent without thereby necessarily being prepared to deduce any and every proposition from their logically inconsistent belief set. If we want to be able to model their beliefs and reasoning in a system of symbolic logic, then a standard logic will not be adequate, and a paraconsistent logic might be more appropriate. The three main types of paraconsistent inference systems are (i) *nonadjunctive,* (ii) *positive-plus,* and (iii) *relevance*.

1. Nonadjunctive paraconsistent logics have been developed primarily for modeling contradictory discourse between distinct subjects, such as inconsistent testimony given by different witnesses in a single inferential context, and certain psychological episodes and dispositions of individual subjects, such as beliefs and other propositional attitudes, in which inconsistencies over time or at some level of description sometimes occur.

The forbidden inference from which nonadjunctive paraconsistent systems take their name, and by means of which they avoid the triviality of validly implying any proposition, despite inconsistency, is $\mathbb{P}$, $\mathbb{Q} \vdash \mathbb{P} \,\&\, \mathbb{Q}$. If adjunction were available in an otherwise standard paraconsistent system, then it would be possible validly to infer $\mathbb{P} \,\&\, \sim\mathbb{P}$ from $\mathbb{P}$, $\sim\mathbb{P}$, as in the standard natural deduction intelim rule, &I. From wffs, $\mathbb{P} \,\&\, \sim\mathbb{P}$, $\mathbb{Q} \,\&\, \sim\mathbb{Q}$ can be deduced for any $\mathbb{Q}$, from which $\mathbb{Q}$ follows in turn by &E, resulting in a trivializing nonparaconsistency. If two witnesses give inconsistent testimony, or if a person perhaps at different times accepts both a proposition and its negation, as opposed to accepting their conjunction, the contradiction enters the logic only in the form $\mathbb{P}$, $\sim\mathbb{P}$, which, in lieu of adjunction, does not imply $\mathbb{P}$ & $\sim\mathbb{P}$. The inconsistency is tolerated in this way without trivializing implication by being harmlessly contained in nonadjunctive form in what is otherwise a standard propositional logic.

2. Positive-plus paraconsistent logics, somewhat surprisingly, admit true contradictions. Yet they are adjunctive and bivalent and otherwise standard, except in their treatment of negation. At least some contradictions are regarded as true in a positive-plus paraconsistent logic, in accord with particular philosophical intuitions about the semantics of paradoxical constructions. The famous Liar paradox, in which a sentence declares its own falsehood, 'This sentence is false', is self-contradictory so that in one sense it is (logically) false. But since this is what the sentence says in asserting its own falsehood, it also seems in some sense to be true. It may then appear to follow that there can be true contradictions.

True contradictions do not trivialize inference in positive-plus paraconsistent logics because negation is limited by the condition that $\sim\mathbb{P}$ is true if (but *not* if and only if) $\mathbb{P}$ is false and that $\mathbb{P}$ is true if (but, again, *not* if and only if) $\sim\sim\mathbb{P}$ is true. These restrictions require that (inclusively) either $\mathbb{P}$ or $\sim\mathbb{P}$ (and possibly both) is (are) true, which makes the logic bivalent. Inference is standard in that, for any set of propositions Σ and any proposition $\mathbb{P}$, Σ entails $\mathbb{P}$, $\Sigma \vdash \mathbb{P}$, if and only if either $\mathbb{P}$ is true, or there is some proposition, $\mathbb{Q}$, which is a member of set Σ, such that $\mathbb{Q}$ is false. The tautologies of the logic are those propositions true under every truth value interpretation. This avoids triviality while preserving many features of standard inference semantics by allowing that in $\mathbb{P}$, $\sim\mathbb{P}$, and $\mathbb{P}$ & $\sim\mathbb{P}$, $\mathbb{P}$ and $\sim\mathbb{P}$ can both be true. The second standard validity clause thereby remains unsatisfied so that inconsistency in either form does not entail any and every arbitrary $\mathbb{P}$ but upholds the inference only when $\mathbb{P}$ is a tautology.

3. Relevance paraconsistent logics are more widely accepted than nonadjunctive or positive-plus systems. This family of logics avoids triviality by blocking inference even from adjoined inconsistency in the conjunction of a proposition and its negation, not (as in positive-plus systems) by requiring such propositions to be true but by allowing them paradoxically to be both true and false. Validity is so interpreted that $\mathbb{P}$ follows relevantly from a set of wffs, Σ, $\Sigma \vdash \mathbb{P}$, if and only if, on every truth value assignment, $\mathbb{P}$ is true, or there is some proposition, $\mathbb{Q}$, which is a member of set Σ, such that $\mathbb{Q}$ is false, and never either true or paradoxically true and false. The definition thereby avoids the triviality of implying any and every proposition while maintaining all the standard tautologies. A contradiction of the form, $\mathbb{P}$ & $\sim\mathbb{P}$, is paradoxically both true and false in relevance paraconsistent logic so that neither condition of the logic's

validity semantics is satisfied for arbitrary $\mathbb{P}$, but the inference is supported only when $\mathbb{P}$ is a tautology.

The philosophical interest in paraconsistent logics is partly that certain paraconsistent systems are *nonmonotonic* rather than, like standard logic, *monotonic*. A logic is monotonic if and only if, where for any set of wffs, Σ, and any wff, $\mathbb{P}$, if $\Sigma \vdash \mathbb{P}$, then, for any wff, $\mathbb{Q}$, $\Sigma, \mathbb{Q} \vdash \mathbb{P}$. *Inductive logics* and certain logics used to model changes in belief states, including those intended for artificial intelligence programming and research in the logic of cognitive psychology, are often nonmonotonic. An example in inductive reasoning is that, if the king swallowed poison, then the king will probably die. Now, if we add the additional assumption that the king also swallowed an antidote to the poison, then it need no longer follow that the king will probably die. An example in the study of belief state change is that Alice believes that all classical composers except Mozart were German (Mozart was Austrian) and believes that Wolfgang was a classical composer, on the basis of which she also believes that Wolfgang was German. Later, when she learns that Wolfgang is Mozart (whose full name was Wolfgang Amadeus Mozart), she undergoes a change of belief, and, in adding this new information to her store of beliefs, is no longer willing to conclude that Wolfgang is German. Since belief is nonmonotonic, some logicians maintain that the logic of belief should also be nonmonotonic. Nonmonotonic logics are also inferentially very different from standard logics, and some, although not all, paraconsistent systems offer one type of approach to modeling the logic of nonmonotonic reasoning.

Finally, standard predicate logic is *ontically presuppositional* in that an existentially quantified object is supposed to exist. There are nonstandard *free logics* in which these existence presuppositions are relaxed, and in which it is presupposed that the names in true predicate-constant propositions must refer to existent objects. Some logics go one step further than free logics by offering a formal theory in which it is possible to refer to and truly predicate properties of *nonexistent objects*.

Philosophical Applications

In addition to the use of symbolic logic to express philosophical concepts and answer philosophical questions, logic can be a source of philosophical problems. Logic gives rise to a family of *paradoxes* that appear to imply contradictions about truth, validity, the naming of objects, membership in sets of objects, and other logical and semantic concepts.

We have seen an example of such a paradox in the case of the Liar sentence:

(L)   Sentence (L) is false.

There are many other logical paradoxes and many philosophical approaches to their solution. The following are examples involving the concepts of validity and soundness:

(V)   Argument (V) is valid.
———————————————
Argument (V) is invalid.

(S)   Argument (S) is unsound.
———————————————
Argument (S) is unsound.

Logical paradoxes of this type usually involve the definition of a paradoxical sentence or inference, followed by an appropriate dilemma. For sentence (L), it is natural to ask whether (L) is true or false and to conclude that (L) appears to be true if and only if it is false. What happens when we ask whether argument (V) is deductively valid or invalid? What happens when we ask whether argument (S) is sound or unsound? If genuine paradoxes arise in these cases, what can and what, if anything, should we try to do about them? Can we live with such paradoxes, or must we find some way, even if it means revising standard logic, to prevent them from occurring?

The precision with which ideas can be formulated in symbolic logic makes it possible to use logical formalisms to clarify, restate, and sometimes resolve philosophical problems. Symbolic logic is used to formalize classical philosophical arguments to clarify their meaning and evaluate their logical structures. Logical symbolisms are also used as an adjunct in comtemporary constructive and critical analysis in philosophical inquiry. The applications of logic to philosophical problems are an important source of innovations in logical symbolisms, as logicians struggle to fit symbolic logic to a particular type of discourse and in some instances find it necessary to modify the syntax, semantics, or inference rules of logic in order to make sense of the problems that interest philosophers.

We have already seen symbolic logic put to good use in analyzing several philosophical arguments in examples throughout the text. The following is another illustration of how logic can help to clarify philosophical concepts and reconstruct philosophical reasoning. The problem is the medieval theologian Saint Anselm's so-called *ontological argument for the existence of God* in Chapter III of his work, the *Proslogion*. Anselm writes:

> For there can be thought to exist something whose nonexistence is inconceivable; and this thing is greater than anything whose nonexistence is conceivable. Therefore, if that than which a greater cannot be thought could be thought not to exist, then that than which a greater cannot be

thought would not be that than which a greater cannot be thought—a contradiction. Hence, something than which a greater cannot be thought exists so truly that it cannot even be thought not to exist. And You are this being, O Lord our God. Therefore, Lord my God, You exist so truly that You cannot even be thought not to exist.

(Anselm, *Anselm of Canterbury,* translated by Jasper Hopkins and Herbert Richardson, p. 94, Edwin Mellen Press, Toronto, 1974)

The argument is that God must exist because God by definition is that than which none greater is conceivable. If God did not exist, then there would be a greater conceivable being—namely, a being with all of God's properties but who existed rather than failed to exist. This, to say the least, has been a controversial proof for the existence of God in the history of philosophy. What is its logical structure?

If we wish to use symbolic logic to critically evaluate the argument, we can adopt the following conventions. We use the inverted Greek iota '$\imath$' as before as a definite descriptor. The predicate 'C' is a kind of modal operator whereby in $C(\mathbb{P})$ we qualify the content of a sentence by saying, in effect, 'It is conceivable that $\mathbb{P}$'. The predicate 'G' represents the relation of being greater than, not in the usual arithmetical sense but with whatever meaning Anselm intends when he speaks of God being that than which no greater being is conceivable. Without following our standard natural deduction format in all respects, we can then symbolize the entire argument as follows:

1. $g = (\imath x)\sim(\exists y)C(Gyx)$	Definition g
2. $(\forall x)(((\imath y)Fy = x) \supset Fx)$	Properties for $\imath$
3. $\sim(\exists x)(Fx \supset (\exists y)C(Gyx)$	Conceivable greatness
4. $\sim(\exists x)(x = g)$	Assumption for *reductio*
5. $\sim(\exists x)(x = g) \supset (\exists y)C(Gyg)$	(3 instantiation)
6. $(\exists y)C(Gyg)$	(4, 5 detachment)
7. $\sim(\exists y)C(Gyg)$	(1, 2 instantiation)
8. $(\exists x)(x = g)$	(4, 6, 7 *reductio ad absurdum*)

This is not the only way to formalize Anselm's argument. Symbolic logic makes it possible to compare the advantages and disadvantages of interpreting the logical structure of an argument such as Anselm's in several different styles. The reconstruction we have offered already shows that the argument so construed can be understood as deductively valid. Whether the assumptions are correct is another matter altogether that requires philosophical ingenuity on our part to decide. Symbolic logic does not solve such problems by itself. It is nevertheless a useful tool to help us clarify the meanings of concepts and evaluate the logical structures of arguments.

History of Logic

The symbolic logic we have studied did not appear overnight with all its notations and methods complete. It has been the result of groundbreaking discoveries and a slow accretion of minor additions and corrections that began with Aristotle, continued through the time of later Greek thought to the medieval period, with a sudden increase in dramatic improvements, especially in the 19th and 20th centuries to the present day. The history of logic is as fascinating a chapter in the progress of human endeavor as scientific discovery and the development of mathematics and scientific method, the history of medicine, technology, art and culture, or the annals of war and conquest. Accurately interpreting large-scale movements and particular episodes in the development of logic remains an active and rewarding area of research. The history of logic is thus another specialized topic toward which you may find yourself led by the study of symbolic logic.

Reference List of Demonstration Problems

Sources and Selected Readings

Anderson, Alan, and Belnap, Nuel (1975). *Entailment*. Princeton, NJ: Princeton University Press.

Barwise, Jon, and Etchemendy, John (1992). *The Language of First-Order Logic*, 3rd ed. Stanford, CA: Center for the Study of Language and Information.

Bergmann, Merrie, Moor, James, and Nelson, Jack (1998). *The Logic Book*, 3rd ed. New York: McGraw-Hill.

Berkeley, George (1957 [1710]). *A Treatise on the Principles of Human Knowledge*. Indianapolis, IN: Bobbs–Merrill.

Beth, E. W. (1959). *The Foundations of Mathematics*. Amsterdam: North-Holland.

Bocheński, Joseph (I. M.) (1961). *A History of Formal Logic* (Ivo Thomas, Trans.). Notre Dame, IN: Notre Dame University Press.

Boolos, George (1979). *The Unprovability of Consistency: An Essay in Modal Logic*. Cambridge, UK: Cambridge University Press.

Church, Alonzo (1936). A note on the Entscheidungsproblem. *Journal of Symbolic Logic,* **1,** 40–41 (Correction, 101–102).

Copi, Irving M., and Gould, James A. (Eds.) (1967). *Contemporary Readings in Logical Theory*. New York: Macmillan.

Copi, Irving M., and Gould, James A. (Eds.) (1972). *Readings on Logic*. 2nd ed. New York: Macmillan.

Curry, Hasell B. (1977). *Foundations of Mathematical Logic*, 2nd ed. New York: Dover.

Euler, Leonhard (1952 [1802]). *Elements of Algebra* (John Hewlett, Trans.). New York: Springer-Verlag.

Feynman, Richard (1965). *The Character of Physical Law* (The Messenger Lectures). Cambridge: MIT Press.

Fitch, Frederick B. (1952). *Symbolic Logic.* New York: Ronald Press.

Forbes, Graeme (1994). *Modern Logic: A Text in Elementary Symbolic Logic.* New York: Oxford University Press.

Frege, Gottlob (1893). *Grundgesetze der Arithmetik, begriffsschriftlich abgeleitet.* Jena: H. Pohle.

Frege, Gottlob (1964 [1879]). *Begriffsschrift, Eine der arithmetischen nachgebildete Formelsprache des reinen Denkens.* In *Begriffsschrift und andere Aufsätze* (Ignacio Angelelli, Ed.), 2nd ed. Hildesheim: Georg Olms Verlagsbuchhandlung.

Frege, Gottlob (1964). *The Basic Laws of Arithmetic: Exposition of the System* (partial translation of *Grundgesetze der Arithmetik,* 1893) (Montgomery Furth, Trans.). Berkeley: University of California Press.

Frege, Gottlob (1972 [1879]). *Conceptual Notation and Related Articles* (translation of *Begriffsschrift*) (Terrell Ward Bynum, Trans.). Oxford, UK: Clarendon.

Gödel, Kurt (1930). Die Vollständigkeit der Axiome des logischen Funktionenkalküls." *Monatshefte für Mathematik und Physik* **37,** 349–360.

Gödel, Kurt (1931). Über formal unentscheidbare Sätze der Principia mathematica und verwandter Systeme I." *Monatshefte für Mathematik und Physik,* **38,** 173–198.

Gödel, Kurt (1967a). On formally undecidable propositions of *Principia mathematica* and related systems I (translation of Über formal unentscheidbare Sätze der Principia mathematica und verwandter Systeme I, 1931) (J. van Heijenoort, Trans.). In van Heijenoort (1967), pp. 592–617.

Gödel, Kurt (1967b). The completeness of the axioms of the functional calculus of logic (translation of Die vollständigkeit der axiome des logischen funktionenkalküls, 1930) (J. van Heijenoort, Trans.). In van Heijenoort (1967), pp. 582–591.

Grayling, A. C. (1982). *An Introduction to Philosophical Logic.* Sussex, UK: Harvester Press.

Haack, Susan (1974). *Deviant Logic: Some Philosophical Issues.* Cambridge, UK: Cambridge University Press.

Heil, John (1995). *First-Order Logic.* Boston: Jones & Bartlett.

Hughes, G. E., and Cresswell, M. J. (1968). *An Introduction to Modal Logic.* London: Methuen.

Hume, David (1978 [1739–1740]). *A Treatise of Human Nature* (L. A. Selby-Bigge, Ed.), 2nd ed. (revised by P. H. Nidditch). Oxford, UK: Clarendon.

Hunter, Geoffrey (1971). *Metalogic: An Introduction to the Metatheory of First-Order Logic.* Berkeley: University of California Press.

Jeffrey, Richard C. (1991). *Formal Logic: Its Scope and Limits,* 3rd ed. New York: McGraw-Hill.

Kalish, Donald, Montague, Richard, and Mar, Gary (1980). *Logic: Techniques of Formal Reasoning,* 2nd ed. San Diego: Harcourt Brace Jovanovich.

Kleene, Stephen C. (1952). *Introduction to Metamathematics.* Princeton, NJ: Princeton University Press.

Kneale, William, and Kneale, Martha (1984). *The Development of Logic.* Oxford, UK: Clarendon.

Lactantius (1982). *La colère de Dieu (The Wrath of God)* (Christiane Ingremeau, Ed.). Paris: Editions du Cerf.

Leblanc, Hugues, and Wisdom, William A. (1976). *Deductive Logic,* 2nd ed. Boston: Allyn & Bacon.

Lemmon, E. J. (1978 [1965]). *Beginning Logic.* Indianapolis, IN: Hackett.

Löwenheim, Leopold (1915). Über möglichkeiten im relativkalkül. *Mathematische Annalen* **76,** 447–470.

Löwenheim, Leopold (1967). On possibilities in the calculus of relatives (translation of Über möglichkeiten im relativkalkül, 1915) (J. van Heijenoort, Trans.). In van Heijenoort (1967), pp. 228–251.

Łukasiewicz, Jan (1930). Philosophische bemerkungen zu mehrwertigen systemen des aussagenkalküls. *Comtes Rendus des Seances de la Société des Sciences et des Lettres de Varsovie* **23** (3), 51–77.

Marcus, Ruth Barcan (1946). A functional calculus of first order based on strict implication. *Journal of Symbolic Logic* **11,** 1–16.

Marcus, Ruth Barcan (1993). *Modalities: Philosophical Essays.* Oxford, UK: Oxford University Press.

Mates, Benson (1972). *Elementary Logic,* 2nd ed. New York: Oxford University Press.

Mendelson, Elliott (1964). *Introduction to Mathematical Logic.* New York: Van Nostrand.

Nagel, Ernest, and Newman, James R. (1974). *Gödel's Proof.* New York: New York University Press.

Nicod, Jean (1917). A reduction in the number of the primitive propositions of logic. *Proceedings of the Cambridge Philosophical Society* **19,** 32–41.

Nute, Donald C. (1981). *Essential Formal Semantics.* Totowa, NJ: Rowman & Littlefield.

Quine, W. V. O. (1976). *The Ways of Paradox and Other Essays* (revised and enlarged edition). Cambridge: MIT Press.

Quine, W. V. O. (1982). *Methods of Logic,* 4th ed. New York: Holt, Rinehart & Winston.

Priest, Graham, Routley, Richard, and Jean, Norman (Eds.) (1989). *Paraconsistent Logic: Essays on the Inconsistent.* Munich: Philosophia Verlag.

Ramsey, Frank (1931). *The Foundations of Mathematics and Other Essays.* London: Routledge & Kegan Paul.

Read, Stephen (1988). *Relevant Logic: A Philosophical Examination of Inference.* Oxford, UK: Basil Blackwell.

Rescher, Nicholas (1969). *Many-Valued Logic.* New York: McGraw-Hill.

Rosser, J. B. (1936). Extensions of some theorems of Gödel and Church. *Journal of Symbolic Logic* **1,** 87–91.

Rosser, J. B. (1939). An informal exposition of proofs of Gödel's theorems and Church's theorem. *Journal of Symbolic Logic* **4,** 53–60.

Rosser, J. B., and Turquette, A. R. (1952). *Many-Valued Logics.* Amsterdam: North-Holland.

Russell, Bertrand (1905). "On denoting." *Mind* **14,** 479–493; reprinted in Russell (1956), 41–56.

Russell, Bertrand (1938). *The Principles of Mathematics,* 2nd ed. New York: Norton.

Russell, Bertrand (1956). *Logic and Knowledge: Essays 1901–1950* (Robert C. Marsh, Ed.). New York: Putnam.

Russell, Bertrand (1971). *Introduction to Mathematical Philosophy.* New York: Simon & Schuster.

Schagrin, Morton L. (1979). *The Language of Logic: A Self-Instruction Text,* 2nd ed. New York: Random House.

Schopenhauer, Arthur (1966 [1819]). *The World as Will and Representation* (E. F. J. Payne, Trans.). New York: Dover.

Shanker, S. G. (Ed.) (1988). *Gödel's Theorem in Focus.* London: Routledge.

Shoenfield, Joseph R. (1967). *Mathematical Logic.* Reading, MA: Addison-Wesley.

Skolem, Thoralf (1920). Logisch-kombinatorischer Untersuchungen über die Erfüllbarkeit oder Beweisbarkeit mathematischer Sätze nebst einem Theoreme über dichte Mengen. *Videnskapsselskapets skrifter, I. Matematisk-naturvidenskabelig klasse,* No. 4.

Skolem, Thoralf (1967). Logico-combinatorial investigations in the satisfiability or provability of mathematical propositions: A simplified proof of a theorem by L. Löwenheim and generalizations of the theorem (translation of Logisch-kombinatorischer Untersuchungen über die Erfüllbarkeit oder Beweisbarkeit mathematischer Sätze nebst einem Theoreme über dichte Mengen. 1920) (J. van Heijenoort, Trans.). In van Heijenoort (1967), pp. 252–263.

Smullyan, Raymond M. (1968). *First-Order Logic.* New York: Springer-Verlag.

Stoll, Robert R. (1963). *Set Theory and Logic.* New York: Dover.

Strawson, P. F. (1952). *Introduction to Logical Theory.* London: Methuen.

Tennant, Neil (1989). *Natural Deduction.* Edinburgh, UK: University of Edinburgh Press.

van Heijenoort, Jean (1967). *From Frege to Gödel: A Source Book in Mathematical Logic, 1879–1931.* Cambridge, MA: Harvard University Press.

Venn, John (1971 [1894]). *Symbolic Logic,* 2nd ed. New York: Franklin Philosophy Monographs.

Wang, Hao (1981). *Popular Lectures on Mathematical Logic.* New York: Dover.

Whitehead, Alfred North, and Russell, Bertrand (1963 [1925–1927]). *Principia Mathematica,* 2nd ed. Cambridge, UK: Cambridge University Press.

Wittgenstein, Ludwig (1922). *Tractatus Logico-Philosophicus* (C. K. Ogden, Ed.). London: Routledge & Kegan Paul.

Glossary-Index

Deductive completeness: metalogical property of a system of logic whereby any wff that is interpreted semantically as true and any sequent that is interpreted semantically as deductively valid is provable in a finite number of steps by the logic's rules of inference, 437, 442; deductive incompleteness, 430–432, 441–443

Deductive validity: logical property of an argument (sequent) whereby if the argument's assumptions are true, then the argument's conclusions logically must also be true; alternatively and equivalently, such that it is logically impossible for the argument's assumptions to be true and its conclusions false, 1, 3, 8–10, 17, 20–25, 28, 33, 35, 38, 41–43, 46–48, 57, 138–139, 141, 149–150, 154, 161, 166, 182–184, 190, 220, 239, 260, 308, 326, 336, 360, 375, 410, 414, 420, 455; deductively valid argument, 3, 8–9, 11–14, 24–26, 29, 32, 41–42, 45–48, 55, 57, 183, 194, 253, 257, 317, 449, 451; deductive invalidity, 3, 8–10, 13, 17, 19–21, 25–27, 29–31, 33, 38–39, 42–48, 54, 109, 138–140, 142, 144, 146, 182–184, 211, 227, 239, 336, 339, 366, 369–371, 375–377, 439; deductively invalid sequent, 139, 150, 183, 239, 336, 370, 439; deductively invalid conditional inferences, 29, 31

Definite description operator, descriptor ('ı'): logical operator representing the grammatical definite article 'the', 429, 432, 459

DeMorgan, Augustus (DeMorgan duality relations in propositional logic): family of logical relations between propositions (wffs) typified by the equivalence $(P \& Q) \equiv \sim(\sim P \lor \sim Q)$, associated with the nineteenth century logician, mathematician and statistician for whom it is named, 82–83, 98, 270

Denying the antecedent, fallacy of: deductively innvalid argument form in which the negation of the consequent of a conditional proposition (wff) is incorrectly concluded from the assumption of the conditional and the negation of its antecedent; If P, then Q, not-P, therefore, not-Q, 29, 47, 52

Denying the consequent: deductively valid argument form in which the negation of the antecedent of a conditional proposition (wff) is correctly derived from the assumption of the conditional and the negation of its consequent; If P, then Q, not-Q, therefore, not-P, 27–28, 47. *See also Modus tollendo tollens*

Deontic logics: modal logics of moral obligation and permission, 450

Derived rule of natural deduction: any deductively valid natural deduction rule that can be validly proved by the twelve basic rules of natural deduction in propositional logic and four basic rules of natural deduction in predicate logic, 201, 229–233, 236, 250–251. *See also* Reiteration (R); Double negation (DN)

Descriptive discipline, psychology as, xix

Diagonalization argument: argument by *reductio ad absurdum* to prove that the rational numbers (or natural number or positive integers) cannot be put into one-one correspondence with the irrational real numbers, from which it follows that the cardinality of the irrational reals is greater than and belongs to a higher order of infinity than the cardinality of the infinitely many rational numbers, 446–447. *See also* Cantor, Georg; Transfinite numbers, sets, cardinalities

Proof and subproof spines: graphic method of distinguishing assumptions and conclusions derived from assumptions within a natural deduction proof, 197–198, 374; proof line, 195–197, 205, 209, 213, 239, 250; proof spine, 197–198, 204, 210, 212, 369, 386, 388, 390; proof step, 195–199, 204, 208, 212, 217–218, 223, 227, 250, 402

Property: whatever can be predicated of or attributed to an object or set of objects, including 1-ary qualities and n-ary relations, xx, xxii, 1, 6, 43, 55, 57, 108–109, 114, 116, 117, 142–144, 147, 149, 152, 154, 162, 164, 172, 188–189, 193–194, 257, 259–262, 264–265, 267, 270–277, 279, 281–283, 287, 289, 294, 296, 300–301, 304–307, 309–315, 317–319, 324–325, 332, 342, 345, 354–355, 357, 365, 367, 369–371, 373, 376, 409, 412, 426–430, 436–438, 443–445, 451, 453, 457, 459; property-object relation, 261–262, 265, 276, 318–319. *See also* Predicate-constant expression

Proposition: true or false sentence, xx–xxii, 1, 3–9, 13–16, 21, 26–27, 31, 33, 35–36, 38, 43, 46–48, and *passim;* series of propositions, 6–7, 15, 46–47, 195, 303, 336. *See also* Well-formed formula (wff)

Propositional connective: logical term or symbol that builds more complex propositions (wffs) out of simpler ones by joining or connecting them together in such a way that the truth value of the resulting complex wff is a truth function of its component wffs, xxii, 58–68, 70–71, 73–77, 79, 81, 83–85, 87, 89, 91–99, 109–114, 117–119, and *passim;* propositional duality, 82–83, 98; propositional semantic concepts, 116–117. *See also* Negation; Conjunction; Disjunction; Conditional; Biconditional; Main propositional connective

Propositional symbol: logical symbol (wff) that represents any colloquial language proposition or other wff, 5–6, 47, 58–60, 65, 98–99, 107, 113–115, 118, 121–123, 125, 132, 144, 159, 164, 166, 261, 268–269; propositional variable, 59–61, 74, 98–99, 266, 330–331, 386

Psychology, xix, 449, 457

Quadrivium, xxi. *See also Trivium;* Seven liberal arts

Quality: 1-ary property, as contrasted with n-ary (n > 1) relation, 262–264, 266, 270, 273, 276, 280, 282, 287, 290, 292, 300–301, 304–307, 309, 319–320, 408, 436

Quantifier: predicate logic term designating a general quantity of objects ('all' or 'some, i.e., at least one'), 265–270, 272, 274–277, 281, 283–284, 286–288, 290–297, 299–301, 304, 307, 318–319, 324, 326–331, 337–338, 341, 360–361, 365, 368–369, 371–372, 377–382, 384–386, 388, 390, 392, 395, 397, 401, 403, 422, 429; quantifier duality, 269–270, 297, 319, 331, 338, 360–361, 388; quantifier scope, 290, 292–293, 319; quantifying, 264, 301–302, 319, 381; quantity of objects, in predicate logic, xxii, 257, 261, 264–265, 275, 281, 284, 286, 294, 319; specific numbers of objects, 427–429

Ramsey, F. P., 37–38

Reconstructed argument: inference in colloquial language rewritten as numbered set of propositions in which assumptions are explicitly distinguished from conclusions by a symbolic inference indicator, 11–13, 22, 44–45, 47